CROWELL'S HANDBOOK
OF WORLD OPERA

CROWELL'S
HANDBOOK OF
WORLD OPERA

COMPILED BY

FRANK LEDLIE MOORE

INTRODUCTION BY DARIUS MILHAUD

GREENWOOD PRESS, PUBLISHERS
WESTPORT, CONNECTICUT

Library of Congress Cataloging in Publication Data

Moore, Frank Ledlie.
   Crowell's handbook of world opera.

   Reprint of the 1961 ed. published by Crowell, New
York, in series: A Crowell reference book.
   "Recordings of complete operas": p.
   1. Opera--Dictionaries. 2. Operas--Stories, plots,
etc. 3. Operas--Discography. I. Title.
[ML102.06M6 1974]   782.1'03   73-3025
ISBN 0-8371-6822-8

Designed by Laurel Wagner

Originally published in 1961 by Thomas Y. Crowell Company,
New York

Reprinted with the permission of Thomas Y. Crowell Company, Inc.

Reprinted by Greenwood Press,
a division of Williamhouse-Regency Inc.

First Greenwood reprinting 1974
Second Greenwood reprinting 1976

Library of Congress Catalog Card Number 73-3025

ISBN 0-8371-6822-8

Printed in the United States of America

INTRODUCTION

This book on opera is absolutely the source of information that we need. The general public as well as the musicologist will be able to use it, because everything concerning opera is mentioned. It is like a series of dictionaries, one for the operas—their background, their story, their cast; another for the composers, with a list of their theatrical works; another for the characters in operas. Even first lines and titles of famous numbers, a glossary of technical expressions, and a list of complete operas recorded are to be found; also an index of famous musical themes, the chronology of operas with references to general history, to opera history, and to first performances year by year from the thirteenth century to the present day.

Here everybody can find everything about opera through its long and glorious history. This book not only will be treasured by musicians, but will enrich every school, college, or university library.

I wish the fruits of Frank Moore's indefatigable research the great success it deserves.

DARIUS MILHAUD

PREFACE

Crowell's Handbook of World Opera has been designed to give you as much information as possible about all the operas that have importance of one kind or another for our time. Within these pages it will be possible for you to track down nearly any reference that may cross your mind in the course of reading about or listening to opera. Whether you begin with the first line or the nickname of an aria, or the name of some character recalled from a performance, the reference you find here will lead you on to more knowledge about the opera concerned and the people who may have been involved in it. If you are a singer, there are special indexes of vocal numbers arranged according to voice to help you build your repertoire. If you want to know about composers, conductors, and others, the biographical section will help you. For history see the chronology, and for technical facts or some practical definitions of different styles, the glossary.

In the sixty pages of musical themes two objectives governed the choice of material. I wanted first to give as full an illustration of the musical texture of certain great works as was practical, and second to introduce to those who have not heard them certain melodies of matchless beauty from the lesser-known works. Hence you will find *Boris Godunov* and *Carmen* well represented, plus samples such as the Lamento d'Arianna, which is all that remains to us of one of Monteverdi's greatest works.

As I gathered facts for this volume I received help from many. I listened as opera fans of earlier days recalled anecdotes that brought light for me into shadowy places. I hope the book itself will repay them for their contributions. Publicly I want to thank Nicolas Slonimsky, who went over the manuscript in detail and made many corrections, and Gorton Carruth who quietly whittled my concepts of the book into proper shape to present to you.

F. L. M.

CONTENTS

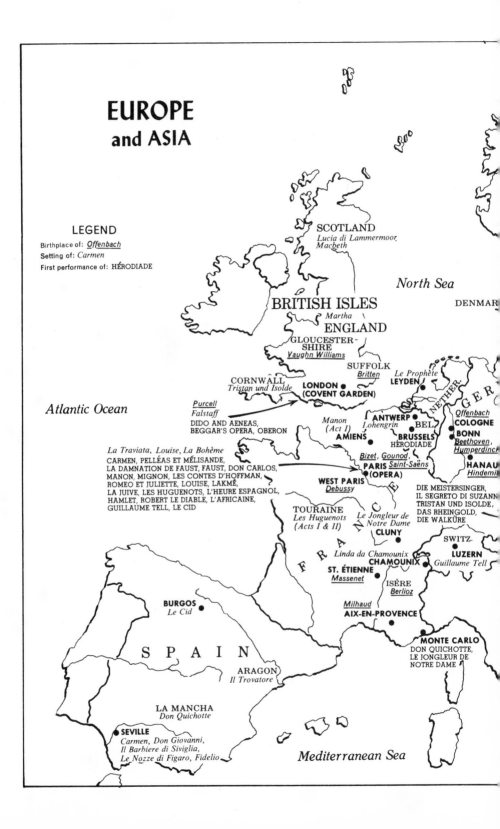

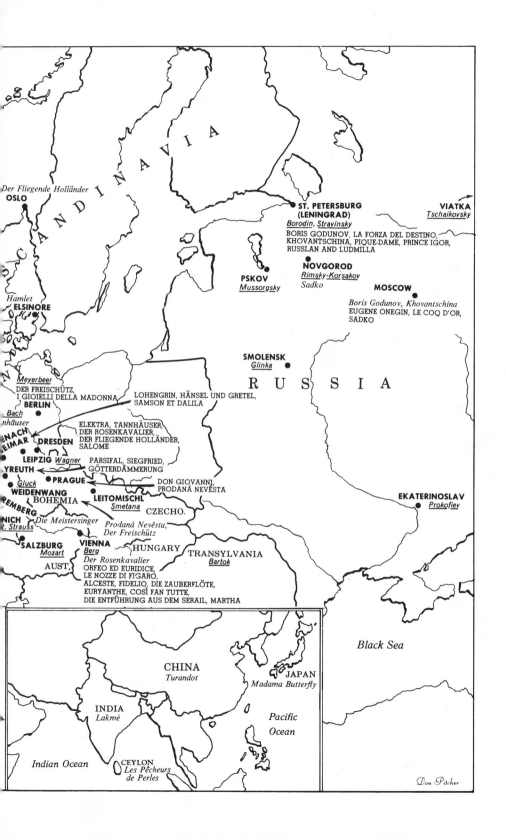

Der Fliegende Holländer
OSLO

ST. PETERSBURG
(LENINGRAD)
Borodin, Stravinsky
BORIS GODUNOV, LA FORZA DEL DESTINO,
KHOVANTSCHINA, PIQUE-DAME, PRINCE IGOR,
RUSSLAN AND LUDMILLA

VIATKA
Tschaikovsky

NOVGOROD
Rimsky-Korsakov
Sadko

PSKOV
Mussorgsky

MOSCOW
Boris Godunov, Khovantschina
EUGENE ONEGIN, LE COQ D'OR,
SADKO

Hamlet
ELSINORE

SMOLENSK
Glinka

R U S S I A

Meyerbeer
DER FREISCHÜTZ,
I GIOIELLI DELLA MADONNA
BERLIN

LOHENGRIN, HÄNSEL UND GRETEL,
SAMSON ET DALILA

Bach
nhäuser

ELEKTRA, TANNHÄUSER,
DER ROSENKAVALIER,
DER FLIEGENDE HOLLÄNDER,
SALOME

ENACH
EIMAR   **DRESDEN**

LEIPZIG *Wagner*   PARSIFAL, SIEGFRIED,
GÖTTERDÄMMERUNG
YREUTH

Gluck   **PRAGUE**   DON GIOVANNI,
PRODANÁ NEVĚSTA
WEIDENWANG
BOHEMIA   **LEITOMISCHL**
REMBERG   *Smetana*   CZECHO.

EKATERINOSLAV
Prokofiev

NICH   *Die Meistersinger*   *Prodaná Nevěsta,*
. Strauss   *Der Freischütz*

SALZBURG   **VIENNA**
Mozart   *Berg*
AUST.   *Der Rosenkavalier*
ORFEO ED EURIDICE,
LE NOZZE DI FIGARO,
ALCESTE, FIDELIO, DIE ZAUBERFLÖTE,
EURYANTHE, COSÌ FAN TUTTE,
DIE ENTFÜHRUNG AUS DEM SERAIL, MARTHA

HUNGARY   **TRANSYLVANIA**
Bartok

Black Sea

CHINA
Turandot

JAPAN
Madama Butterfly

INDIA
Lakmé

Pacific
Ocean

Indian Ocean   **CEYLON**
Les Pêcheurs
de Perles

Don Pitcher

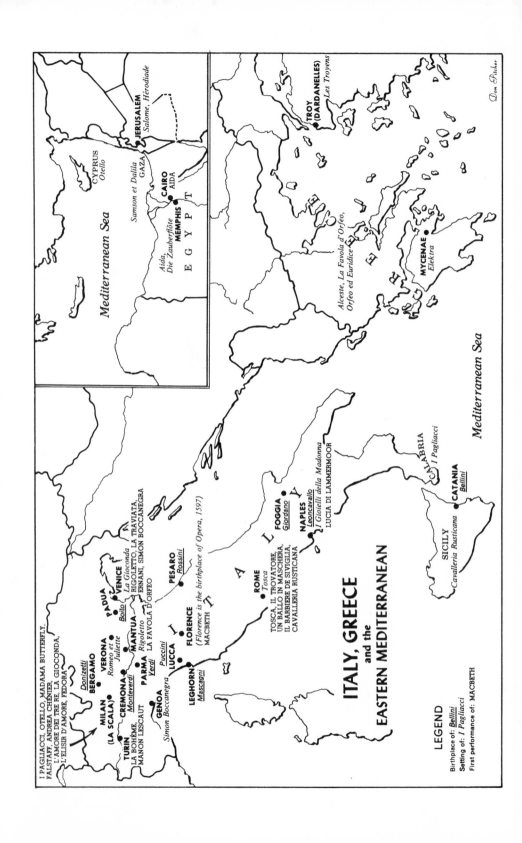

Don Pitcher

TROY
(DARDANELLES)
Les Troyens

JERUSALEM
Salome, Hérodiade

CYPRUS
Otello

Mediterranean Sea

Samson et Dalila
GAZA

CAIRO
AIDA
MEMPHIS
EGYPT

*Aida,
Die Zauberflöte*

*Alceste, La Favola d'Orfeo,
Orfeo ed Euridice,*

MYCENAE
Elektra

I PAGLIACCI, OTELLO, MADAMA BUTTERFLY,
FALSTAFF, ANDREA CHÉNIER,
L'AMORE DEI TRE RE, LA GIOCONDA,
L'ELISIR D'AMORE, FEDORA

Donizetti
BERGAMO

VERONA
*Romeo et
Juliette*

PADUA
Boito
VENICE
La Gioconda
RIGOLETTO, LA TRAVIATA,
ERNANI, SIMON BOCCANEGRA

MANTUA
Rigoletto
MILAN
(LA SCALA)
CREMONA
Monteverdi
PARMA
Verdi LA FAVOLA D'ORFEO
TURIN
LA BOHÈME,
MANON LESCAUT
Puccini
LUCCA
GENOA
Simon Boccanegra
LEGHORN
Mascagni

PESARO
Rossini

FLORENCE
(*Florence is the birthplace of Opera, 1597*)
MACBETH

I T A L Y

ROME
Tosca

TOSCA, IL TROVATORE,
UN BALLO IN MASCHERA,
IL BARBIERE DE SIVIGLIA,
CAVALLERIA RUSTICANA

FOGGIA
Giordano
NAPLES
Leoncavallo
I Gioielli della Madonna
LUCIA DI LAMMERMOOR

CALABRIA
I Pagliacci

CATANIA
Bellini

SICILY
Cavalleria Rusticana

Mediterranean Sea

ITALY, GREECE
and the
EASTERN MEDITERRANEAN

LEGEND

Birthplace of: *Bellini*
Setting of: *I Pagliacci*
First performance of: MACBETH

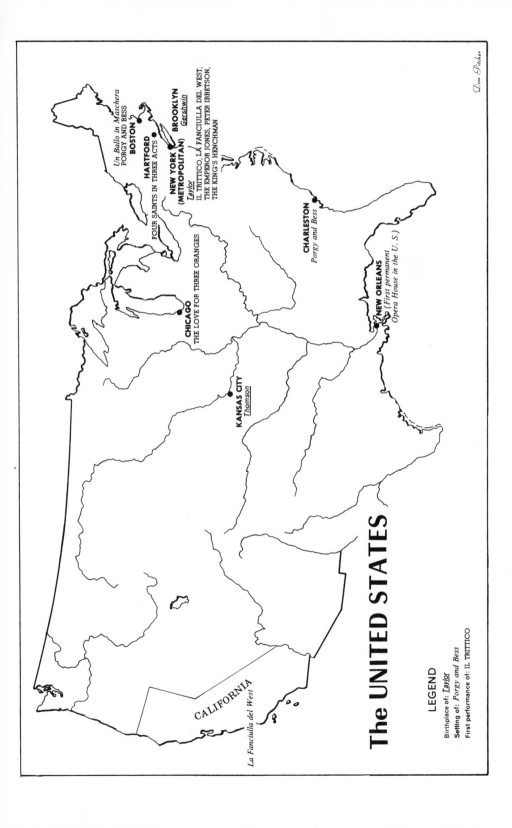

The UNITED STATES

Un Ballo in Maschera
PORGY AND BESS
BOSTON

HARTFORD
FOUR SAINTS IN THREE ACTS

BROOKLYN *Gershwin*

NEW YORK
(METROPOLITAN)
Taylor
IL TRITTICO, LA FANCIULLA DEL WEST,
THE EMPEROR JONES, PETER IBBETSON,
THE KING'S HENCHMAN

CHARLESTON
Porgy and Bess

NEW ORLEANS
(First permanent
Opera House in the U. S.)

CHICAGO
THE LOVE FOR THREE ORANGES

KANSAS CITY
Thomson

CALIFORNIA

La Fanciulla del West

LEGEND

Birthplace of: *Taylor*

Setting of: *Porgy and Bess*

First performance of: IL TRITTICO

Don Pitcher

CROWELL'S HANDBOOK
OF WORLD OPERA

THE OPERAS

The operas in this section are listed in alphabetical order according to title. Information about each one is arranged as follows:

Name of the Opera
   Its composer
   Its librettist(s)
   The source of the story

Number of acts and scenes
   Place and date of first performance
   Other significant first performances

For the more important operas there follow, then, the cast of characters, a synopsis, and, where pertinent, notes. In the listing of first performances, six theaters appear as names only. These are:

   Comique—L'Opéra Comique, Paris, France
   Covent Garden—London, England
   Drury Lane—London, England
   La Scala—Milan, Italy
   Metropolitan—New York City
   Opéra—L'Académie Royale de Musique, Paris, France

The abbreviation (*rev.*) indicates a revised version. Other abbreviations are as follows:

   S—Soprano
   MS—Mezzo-soprano
   MC—Mezzo-contralto
   A—Alto
   C—Contralto

   T—Tenor
   Bar—Baritone
   BBar—Bass-baritone
   B—Bass

Abduction from the Seraglio, The
   See *Entführung aus dem Serail, Die*

Acis and Galatea
   COMP.: G. F. Handel
   LIBR.: J. Gay

3 acts
   London, 28 May 1732
   Stockholm, 1734
   New York (Concert), 1839
   New York (Stage), 1842

Written as a masque in 1719, it may have been performed in that manner in 1721.

Acis et Galathée
   COMP.: J. B. Lully
   LIBR.: J. G. de Campistron
   Lully's last opera.

Prologue & 3 acts
   Anet, France, 6 September 1686
   Hamburg, 1689
   Amsterdam, 1933

THE OPERAS

Adam and Eve
COMP.: Everett Helm Wiesbaden, 28 October 1951
Adapted from a pre-Shakespearian English mystery play.

Adone, L'
Prologue & 5 acts
COMP.: C. Monteverdi Venice, 21 December 1639
LIBR.: P. Vendramin
From a poem by Marini
    This was the first opera Monteverdi wrote for the public stage; he was then 72 years old. His previous stage works were performed within the private houses of the nobility.

Adventures of King Pausole, The
See *Aventures du Roi Pausole, Les*

Adriana Lecouvreur
Tragedy in 4 acts
COMP.: F. Cilèa Milan, 26 November 1902
LIBR.: A. Colautti Covent Garden, 1904
From a play by Scribe and Legouvé Metropolitan, 1907

CAST

Maurizio, *Count of Saxony*	T	Adriana Lecouvreur	S
Prince de Bouillon	B	Princess de Bouillon	MS
L'Abate de Chazeuil	T	Mlle. Jouvenot, *of the Comédie Française*	S
Michonnet, *stage director*	Bar	Mlle. Dangeville, *of the Comédie*	
Quincault, *of the Comédie Française*	B	*Française*	MS
Poisson, *of the Comédie Française*	T	Chamber Maid	
Major Domo	T	Ladies, Gentlemen, Servants	

SYNOPSIS

I. The Green-room of the Comédie Française. Preparations for a performance are in progress; all is hustle and bustle as the actors and actresses compliment Adriana and go on stage. The Prince, in a quiet moment during the performance, reads a letter he has intercepted in which someone plans a tryst for that night. He thinks it is from the actress Duclos, his mistress, and prepares to expose her. But it is really from his own wife the Princess, and intended for Maurizio.

II. At the appointed place and time, the Prince and L'Abate find not the Princess, but Maurizio, who has just hidden her away. Maurizio soon realizes that they do not know who the real woman is, and plays along with their mistake. But then Adriana, who has come in answer to an anonymous note of love, makes the double discovery of her lover's true identity as the Count of Saxony and of his insincerity as a lover who already has an unknown mistress.

III. Adriana wonders who the other woman may be. There is a grand ball at the Prince's house at which she is an honored guest. All during the ball she plies the Princess with veiled questions to confirm her suspicions.

IV. In the Green-room. It is her birthday, and among the happier gifts she opens one not so happy—a box of poisoned violets, the remains of the ones she had given Maurizio before. When he presents himself, she pleads with him to tell her the truth. Suddenly she feels faint, she becomes delirious and cries that the flowers have affected her. To the horror of Maurizio she dies in his arms, thus satisfying the revenge of the Princess.

Aegyptische Helena, Die

COMP.: Richard Strauss
LIBR.: H. von Hofmannsthal

2 *acts*

Dresden, 6 June 1928
Vienna, 1928
Metropolitan, 1928

CAST

Helena, *wife of King Menelaus*	S	Da-Ud, *Altair's son*	T
Menelaus, *Greek general*	T	Servants of Aithra (2)	S, MS
Hermione, *their daughter*	S	Elves (3)	S, S, C
Aithra, *a sorceress*	S	The Omniscient Mussel	C
Altair, *desert chieftain*	Bar		

SYNOPSIS

I. Aithra's magic palace. Aithra wishes to protect those of her own sex from harm, particularly harm from men. In this case, after the Trojan War, she causes a shipwreck and has Menelaus and Helena brought before her before he has a chance to slay his wife (remorsefully) for the ill her beauty had caused Greece. Aithra bewilders Menelaus by nearly convincing him that his suspicions are groundless, that Helena spent all the ten years of the Trojan war in an enchanted sleep right here with the sorceress. Secretly she gives Helena a drink to make them forget their past danger and sends both of them to an enchanted place.

II. In a palmgrove near the desert they live in bliss. Altair visits them. He has a son, Da-Ud, who becomes infatuated with Helena but she pays him no attention. Menelaus pursues him into the desert and kills him. When he returns from the foray, Helena gives him a drink of the antidote for forgetfulness (which Aithra did not intend her to have). Menelaus remembers then that he planned to murder his wife for her sins. In desperation Aithra makes her appearance between them, protecting them from the revenge of the bereaved Altair, and at the same time re-uniting them with Hermione in the hope that their daughter's love will quell their fiercer hate—and this is perfectly successful.

Africaine, L'

COMP.: G. Meyerbeer
LIBR.: E. Scribe

Tragedy in 5 acts

Opéra, 28 April 1865
London, 1865
New York, 1865

CAST

Vasco da Gama, *seafarer and discoverer*	T	Sélika, *captured African queen*	S
Don Pedro, *councillor to the king*	B	Nélusko, *captured African nobleman*	Bar
Don Diego, *councillor to the king*	B	Grand Inquisitor	B
Don Alvar, *councillor to the king*	T	High Priest of Brahma	Bar
Inès, *Don Diego's daughter*	S	Councillors, Priests, Sailors, Soldiers,	
Anna, *her attendant*	C	Ladies, Gentlemen, Attendants, Captives,	
		Inquisitors	

SYNOPSIS

I. Vasco, having seen the New World, asks backing for an expedition. Because of Don Pedro's intrigues against him, he is turned down. He becomes furious, uttering accusations which land him in prison.

II. Sélika, his captive, takes care of him there. She loves him. But so does Inès. Inès arranges Vasco's freedom by sacrificing herself in marriage to Don Pedro, who has won the right to make the expedition originally proposed by Vasco.

III. Nélusko, taken on as pilot, steers the expedition into dangerous waters. Vasco has found a ship and followed his rival. When he sees the danger he tries to save his countrymen but Pedro has him again put in irons. The ship breaks up on the rocks of Africa's shore, leaving most of the Europeans prey to Nélusko's revenge.

IV. Sélika again saves Vasco. She is Queen in this strange land, and could demand her captive's love. But he cannot forget Inès.

V. Sélika finally relinquishes her claim upon that which she cannot win. Vasco returns to his country on a ship she provides him, taking Inès home. Standing on the shore, watching the ship grow ever smaller on the horizon, Sélika poisons herself.

NOTES

The opera is no longer very popular, chiefly because of its libretto. Sélika, as has been pointed out by others, is supposed to be an African queen, but has Hindu faith. Meyerbeer died during the final preparations of the opening performance.

Agamemnon
COMP.: D. Milhaud
LIBR.: P. Claudel (*Translator*)
From Aeschylus

Tragedy in 1 act
Paris, 14 April 1927

CAST

| Clytemnestra | S | Chorus |

This is the first part of the *Orestie* Trilogy.

Agnes von Hohenstaufen
COMP.: G. Spontini
LIBR.: E. Raupach

3 acts
Berlin, 12 June 1829

Agrippina
COMP.: G. F. Handel
LIBR.: V. Grimani

3 acts
Venice, 26 December 1709
Hamburg, 1718
Vienna, 1719

Aida
COMP.: G. Verdi
LIBR.: Verdi and Ghislanzoni
From a Scenario by du Locle after
a plot by Mariette Bey

Tragedy in 4 acts (7 scenes)
Cairo, 24 December 1871
La Scala, 1872
New York, 1873

CAST

Aida, *Ethiopian princess, slave of Amneris*	S	Amonasro, *king of Ethiopia, Aida's father*	Bar
King of Egypt	B	Ramfis, *High Priest*	B
Amneris, *his daughter*	C	Messenger	T
Radames, *captain of the guard*	T	Priests, Priestesses, Ministers, Captains, Soldiers, Officials, Ethiopian Slaves, Prisoners, Egyptians	

MUSICAL HIGHLIGHTS

ACT I. Aria *Celesta Aida* (Heavenly Aida), Radames
Aria *Ritorna vincitor* (Return victorious), Aida
Temple Scene *Nume, custode e vindici* (God, guardian and avenger), Radames, Ramfis, Chorus

ACT II. Triumphal Scene *Gloria all'Egitto* (Glory to Egypt), containing the *Grand March*
ACT III. Aria *O patria mia* (My native land) (*O cieli azzurri*), Aida
ACT IV. Duet *La fatal pietra* (The fatal stone), Aida, Radames
Death Scene, Duet *O terra addio* (O earth farewell), Aida, Radames

SYNOPSIS

I. The Palace at Memphis. A messenger from Thebes brings the unwelcome news that that city is critically threatened by Amonasro and his armies. The Egyptians need a leader. Radames, who hopes thus to be named, also hopes by victory to win the captive Aida, whom he loves. He does not know that her father is that same Amonasro he must defeat. He is chosen, thus tearing Aida's heart two ways as she cheers with the crowd for victory over her own people. Amneris, seeing the glances between her slave and Radames, suspects the reason for her own lack of success with the general. At the Temple of Vulcan, the Priests consecrate his armor before the battle.

II. When the news of victory reaches the palace Amneris, in order to discover if her suspicions of love between her slave and the general were true, tells Aida that Radames has been slain in battle. Seeing Aida's reaction, she exults in her successful deception and taunts the poor girl with the bitterness of her enslavement. Satisfied that she has no fear of rivalry from her slave, she prepares to welcome Radames.

At the Gate of Thebes the king reviews his victorious armies with his daughter, the court and the slaves gathered around. In highest honor, the king offers Radames anything he wishes. Radames utters no wish at that moment, but has the prisoners brought before the king. Aida sees her father among them, but Amonasro warns her not to give away his identity. In a powerful speech, Amonasro then tells the king that the enemy king was killed in battle. The speech ends with a plea for clemency for the prisoners, in which Radames joins. The king grants it, but the priests demand Amonasro and Aida as hostages. At the end of the act the king, in a burst of gratitude for the victory, promises Radames the hand of his daughter, Amneris.

III. On the moonlit banks of the Nile Aida hides, waiting to meet her lover. But Amonasro appears instead. In words of patriotism he implores her to tell him which way Radames plans next to march, so that Amonasro can effect an ambush against him. In despair of love against the rivalry of Amneris, she waits for Radames. When he comes they speak of their impossible love, their deep emotion. They plan to escape altogether by the road through Napata—and Amonasro hears these words. Radames discovers him but Amneris discovers them all and descends from the temple to prevent their escape. Radames delivers himself as hostage to the High Priest while Amonasro and Aida disappear in the darkness.

IV. While Amneris waits above, torn by love for the man she has betrayed as a traitor, the Priests convict Radames and entomb him alive under the temple. The final scene takes place on two levels—the Temple above and the tomb below. Radames gradually realizes that someone is with him in the tomb. It is Aida who has hidden herself there to die with him while Amneris above prays to her gods for his comfort.

NOTES

Aida was commissioned by the Khedive of Egypt to celebrate the opening of the new Suez Canal in 1869. It was immediately successful, but Verdi refused to allow the Paris Opéra to mount a performance of the work until 1880 because of the ill treatment he had suffered there with *I Vespri Siciliani* and *Don Carlos*. In the end amends were made all around, and France awarded the composer the Legion d'Honneur for *Aida*. As a matter of fact, the first performance of the work anywhere after its European opening at La Scala occurred in Buenos Aires, in October, 1873.

Aiglon, L'　　　　　　　　　　　　5 *acts*
COMP.: A. Honegger & J. Ibert　　　Monte Carlo, 11 March 1937
LIBR.: H. Cain　　　　　　　　　　Opéra, 1937
After Rostand　　　　　　　　　　Brussels, 1938

Albert Herring　　　　　　　　　*Comedy in 3 acts*
COMP.: B. Britten　　　　　　　　Glyndebourne, 20 June 1947
LIBR.: E. Crozier　　　　　　　　Hanover, 1950
From a story by Maupassant　　　New York, 1952

CAST

Lady Billows, *elderly autocrat*	S	Sid, *butcher's assistant*	Bar
Florence Pike, *her housekeeper*	C	Albert Herring, *from the greengrocer's*	T
Miss Wordsworth, *church school*		Nancy, *from the bakery*	MS
teacher	S	Mrs. Herring, *Albert's mother*	MS
Mr. Gedge, *vicar*	Bar	Emmie, *a child*	S
Mr. Upfold, *mayor*	T	Cis, *a child*	S
Superintendent Budd	B	Harry, *a child*	Treble

SYNOPSIS

I. On Mayday there must be a May Queen, to be chosen by a committee and approved by Lady Billows. Since there seem to be no more virgins left in town the committee is at a loss to choose one. Supt. Budd makes the excellent suggestion that there be a May King instead. There is only one boy innocent enough to be named—Albert Herring. Albert at that very time has been thinking hard while watching Sid make time with Nancy. Sick of his own innocence, when the committee comes to award him the prize he refuses it.

II. But to no avail. The coronation must take place, willy nilly. Sid pours rum into Albert's glass to help him withstand the ordeal. The new King of the May, Albert the Good, gets drunker and drunker. As soon as he can escape, he decides to let himself go altogether.

III. The town misses its May King; he is nowhere to be found. But little traces turn up here and there, enough to indicate possible foul play. At the height of their grief at their loss he returns to his townspeople, sorry to have caused them worry, but determined to be a man of his own decision from then on.

Alceste　　　　　　　　　　　　3 *acts*
COMP.: C. W. von Gluck　　　　　Vienna, 26 December 1767
LIBR.: R. da Calzabigi　　　　　Paris, (*rev.*) 23 April 1776
From Euripides　　　　　　　　　London, 1795
　　　　　　　　　　　　　　　　Metropolitan, 1941

CAST

Admetus, *king*	T	Thanatos, *Death*	Bar
Alceste, *his wife*	S	Voice of Apollo	Bar
High Priest of Apollo	Bar	Herald	Bar
Hercules	Bar	Children of Alceste, Spirits of the Under-	
Evander	T	world, People, Priests, Priestesses	

SYNOPSIS

I. In Ancient Greece. The king is mortally ill. The queen Alceste herself leads the prayers for his recovery. Her prayers so move the gods that a cure is granted provided someone else will willingly die in his place. Alceste resolves to sacrifice herself to save her husband.

II. During the celebration of his recovery, the happy king asks how it came about that he was cured. Nobody will tell him who vowed to take his place; therefore he refuses to accept the substitution. Suddenly the sight of his wife's face gives him the secret. But he cannot alter things now; the gods' will is unchangeable.

III. Alceste has died and gone to the underworld. Admetus follows her, leaving his palace desolate. Hercules, their old friend, arrives at their home to find nothing to greet him but sadness. He resolves to save them both. Down he goes to the shadows of Hades and battles Thanatos himself for the lives of his friends. This arouses the admiration of Apollo who intervenes, setting the husband and wife free again and making Hercules himself a god. They return to the upper world amid rejoicing.

NOTES

The score of this opera contains a famous preface written by Gluck in which he explains his concept of the dignity and simplicity of opera, the beauty of drama in music. This preface added fury to the frantic opposition of the "Piccinists"—the defenders of the old style Italian opera who gathered around the name of the quiet and retiring Piccini. The feud had little to do with the composers themselves, but raged in the ranks of the audience and dilettantes like a small civil war.

Du Rollet made changes in the libretto for the French production. Modern performances generally make use of some of these changes, particularly in the lyric of the aria *Divinités du Styx*.

Alceste ou Le Triomphe d'Alcide
COMP.: J. B. Lully
LIBR.: P. Quinault
From Euripides

Prologue & 5 acts
Paris, 19 January 1674

This was the first work of Lully's to be presented at the Palais Royal.

Alceste
See also *Alkestis*

Aleko
COMP.: S. Rachmaninov
LIBR.: V. I. Nemirovitch-Danchenko
From a poem by Pushkin

1 *Act*
Moscow, 9 May 1893
London, 1915

Alessandro
COMP.: G. F. Handel
LIBR.: P. A. Rolli

3 *acts*
London, 16 May 1726
Hamburg, 1726

Alessandro Stradella
COMP.: F. von Flotow
LIBR.: W. Friedrich

3 *acts*
Paris, 1837
Hamburg (*rev.*), 30 December 1844

Based on the legend of the life of Stradella (q.v.)

Stradella the singer elopes with Leonora, Bassi's mistress. Bassi hires assassins to kill his rival. But when they find him, they are so moved by the beauty of his music they fail to do the job. Bassi takes charge personally, but even he is dissuaded.

NOTE
The story is not in accord with the facts. Stradella did not die of old age, as in the opera, but was murdered.

Alfonso und Estrella
COMP.: F. Schubert
LIBR.: F. von Schober

3 *acts*
Weimar, 24 June 1854
Vienna, 1882

Composed 1821-22. The opera was first performed under the direction of Franz Liszt.

Alkestis
COMP.: R. Boughton
Arranged from Murray's translation
of the play of Euripides

2 *acts*
Glastonbury, 26 August 1922
Covent Garden, 1924

Almira
COMP.: G. F. Handel
LIBR.: F. C. Feustking
From a libretto by Pancieri
Handel's first opera.

3 *acts*
Hamburg, 8 January 1705

Amahl and the Night Visitors
COMP.: G.-C. Menotti
LIBR.: by the composer

Christmas Play in 1 *act*
NBC/TV 24 December 1951

CAST

Amahl, *a crippled boy*	Treble	King Balthazar	B
His mother	MS	Page	B
King Kaspar, *slightly deaf*	T	Shepherds, Villagers, Dancers	
King Melchior	Bar		

SYNOPSIS
This is a version of the Christmas story of the Three Kings. The kings, following their star, stop to rest one night at the house of Amahl's mother. All the neighboring shepherds come to see the royal sight. During the evening the kings tell Amahl about the Christ child, and the gifts they have for Him. Amahl piously adds his crutch to the lot—and discovers that he can walk without it. In the morning he goes along with them, on his own two feet, to Bethlehem.

Amelia Goes to the Ball
COMP.: G.-C. Menotti
LIBR.: by the composer

Comedy in 1 *act*
Philadelphia, 1 April 1937

CAST

Amelia	S	Police Commissioner	B
Her Husband	Bar	The Maid	MS
Her Lover	T	Semda, *the second maid*	MS
Her Friend	C	Police, Passersby	

THE OPERAS

Amelia, unable to get her husband to take her to the ball, has arranged with her lover to do so. But the husband discovers the lover and engages him in a fight during which he (the husband) is knocked out—by Amelia herself, wielding a vase. Amelia tells the crowd that has gathered that the fight was really an attempted robbery, her lover being the robber. The police chief has the robber carted away, the husband taken care of, and arranges to take Amelia to the ball himself, to her perfect satisfaction.

Amfiparnaso, L'　　　　　　　　　*Comedy*
COMP.: O. Vecchi　　　　　　　　　Modena, 1594
　　　　　　　　　　　　　　　　Published in 1597

This work immediately preceded the first operas. It is not itself an opera, but consists of 14 madrigals to illustrate a comedy of masks not intended to be acted. Nowadays, however, it is frequently acted in pantomime with a chorus.

Amico Fritz, L'　　　　　　　　*Comedy in 3 acts*
COMP.: P. Mascagni　　　　　　　Rome, 1 November 1891
LIBR.: P. Suardon (N. Daspuro)　　Covent Garden, 1892
From a novel by Erckmann-Chatrian　Philadelphia, 1892
　　　　　　　　　　　　　　　Metropolitan, 1893

CAST

Fritz Kobus, *a rich bachelor*	T	Hanezò, *Fritz's friend*	T
Suzel, *a farmer's daughter*	S	Federico, *another friend*	B
Beppe, *gypsy*	MS	Caterina, *Fritz's housekeeper*	S
David, *rabbi*	Bar		

SYNOPSIS

I. Fritz and David, old friends, make a bet (to celebrate his fortieth birthday) that Fritz will soon marry. David has been mentioning no names, but Suzel has been in and out during the scene.

II. Fritz begins to be conscious of Suzel's existence, but without result until David drops a hint that Suzel, being young and pretty, has a husband available at her beck. Suddenly Fritz decides he is in love, but that he must restrain himself.

III. David carries on the subtle warfare until Fritz, in distraction, lets slip to Suzel that he loves her. Quite to his surprise, Suzel accepts him, thus allowing David to win the bet.

Amore dei Tre Re, L'　　　　　*Tragedy in 3 acts*
(*The Love of Three Kings*)　　　　La Scala, 10 April 1913
COMP.: I. Montemezzi　　　　　　Metropolitan, 1914
LIBR.: S. Benelli　　　　　　　　Covent Garden, 1914
From a play by Benelli

CAST

Archibaldo, *king of Altura, Blind*	B	Fiora, *Manfredo's wife*	S
Manfredo, *his son*	Bar	Youth, Boy's voice, another voice, Hand-	
Avito, *son of the former king*	T	maiden, Young girl, Old woman,	
Flaminio, *castle guard*	T	People	

SYNOPSIS

I. Archibaldo suspects that Fiora, who was married to his son for political reasons, may be seeing her former fiancé Avito. Flaminio, who serves the king for eyes but also protects the intriguers, keeps Archibaldo uninformed. The king very nearly catches

9

Avito in the castle, but his searchings are interrupted by the tumult of Manfredo's return from war.

II. When war again demands Manfredo, Avito returns to see Fiora. Again Archibaldo nearly traps him, but fails. He questions Fiora, accuses her of infidelity to his son. His fury so overcomes the old king that when Manfredo returns, he finds Fiora strangled by the strong hands of blind Archibaldo.

III. Avito attends the funeral and kisses the corpse. Manfredo confronts him and challenges him, but Avito weakens and dies before his eyes, the victim of poison spread on the lips of the dead princess by Archibaldo. Manfredo, realizing the truth, also kisses her. At the last, the old king feels his way toward the bier to discover the identity of the lover he has been chasing, only to find two bodies, one of which is his son's.

NOTES

Sem Benelli created this story, full of the fury of living people but also symbolic of the political changes in Italy during its unification. Fiora therefore represents not only a woman, but also Italy the nation, loved by two young ideas and one old tradition—and finally strangled by the past.

Anacréon chez Polycrate

COMP.: A. Grétry
LIBR.: J. H. Guy

3 *acts*
Opéra, 17 January 1797
Stockholm, 1803

CAST

Anacréon, *Greek poet*
Olphide, *Anaïs' husband*
Anaïs, *Polycrate's daughter*

Lysandre, *her child*
Polycrate, *ruler of Samos*
Soldiers

Andrea Chénier

COMP.: U. Giordano
LIBR.: L. Illica

Tragedy in 4 *acts*
La Scala, 28 March 1896
New York, 1896
Manchester, 1903
Metropolitan, 1921

CAST

Major-domo	Bar	Incredible, *spy*	T
Charles Gérard	Bar	Roucher, *Chénier's friend*	Bar
Madeleine de Coigny	S	Madelon, *an old woman*	MS
Countess de Coigny, *her mother*	MS	Dumas, *presiding judge*	B
Bersi, *Madeleine's maid*	MS	Fouquier-Tinville, *attorney general*	B
Fléville, *cavalier*	Bar	Schmidt, *jailer*	B
Abbé, *poet*	T	Ladies, Gentlemen, Citizens, Soldiers,	
Andrea Chénier, *poet*	T	Servants, Peasants, Prisoners, Members	
Mathieu, *waiter* ("Populus")	Bar	of the Tribunal, Musicians, Shepherds, etc.	

SYNOPSIS

I. During the French Revolution, Andrea Chénier, a revolutionary poet, abuses the sensitivities of those who invited him to an aristocratic ball by singing one of his own inflammatory poems against the selfishness of class. The guests are cool. Significantly, a horde of beggars press at the door, but the Major-domo manages to get rid of them.

II. The revolution has come. Chénier should be careful now, but his love for Madeleine overrides caution. The revolutionaries are hunting for her. Trying to protect her, Charles

Gérard himself is wounded. His former friend Gérard warns Chénier that he is being watched.

III. Finally Gérard faces Madeleine, tells her that he loves her and that Chénier is now in prison by his order. She offers herself to him in exchange for Andrea's freedom but the revolutionary tribunal does not listen to Gérard's pleading on the captive's behalf. Andrea Chénier is condemned to die.

IV. At the last, Madeleine changes places with another prisoner so that she may die with her beloved.

Anna Bolena

COMP.: G. Donizetti
LIBR.: F. Romani

2 *acts*
Milan, 26 December 1830
London, 1831
New Orleans, 1839
New York, 1843

Antar

COMP.: G. Dupont
LIBR.: C. Ganem

4 *acts*
Opéra, 14 March 1921

Rehearsals were in progress in 1914 when the first World War intervened.

Antigonae

COMP.: C. Orff
LIBR.: F. Hölderlin
From Sophocles

Mourning play in 1 act
Salzburg, 9 August 1949

CAST

Antigonae	S	Hämon	T
Ismene, *her sister*	MS	Tiresias, *blind seer*	T
Kreon, *their uncle, king*	Bar	Messenger	Bar
Watchman	T		

NOTES

This is a choral drama with instruments. Orff, never one to make easy use of the accepted forms, has scored his *Antigonae* for six grand pianos (to be played with hands, sticks, etc.), and four harps, nine double basses, six flutes, six oboes, six trumpets with mutes, seven or eight timpani, and ten to fifteen percussion instruments. The effect is of an intense, somewhat primitive, or rather elemental, Greek tragedy. Although it has only one act, it lasts nearly three hours in performance and is intended to be played without interruption.

Antigone

COMP.: A. Honegger
LIBR.: J. Cocteau
From Sophocles

3 *acts*
Brussels, 28 December 1927
Essen, 1928
New York, 1930

Antigone

COMP.: J. Joubert

BBC, 21 July 1954

Aphrodite

COMP.: C. Erlanger
LIBR.: L. de Gramont
From a novel by Loüys

5 *acts*
Paris, 27 March 1906
New York, 1920

Arabella

COMP.: R. Strauss
LIBR.: H. von Hofmannsthal

3 *acts*

Dresden, 1 July 1933
Covent Garden, 1934
Salzburg, 1942

CAST

Graf Waldner	B	Graf Lamoral, *still another suitor*	B
Adelaide, *his wife*	MS	Fiakermilli	S
Arabella, *his daughter*	S	Fortune Teller	S
Zdenka, *his daughter*	S	Welko, *Mandryka's servant*	
Mandryka	Bar	Djura, *Mandryka's servant*	
Matteo, *officer*	T	Jankel, *Mandryka's servant*	
Graf Elemer, *Arabella's suitor*	T	Servant, Duenna, Three Cardplayers,	
Graf Dominick, *another suitor*	Bar	Doctor, Groom	

SYNOPSIS

I. Having lost practically everything in gambling, Waldner sees as his only hope to marry off his daughter to some rich man. One daughter, Zdenka, has been brought up completely as a boy because it is too expensive to maintain two daughters throughout a season in Vienna. This poor girl is in love with Matteo, but Matteo is in love with Arabella who refuses even to speak to him. There is a stranger, however, who occupies her every thought. She has seen him outside her window. Graf Waldner's troubles seem likely to be solved when the suitor calls on Arabella offering money on the side to Waldner to win the father's good will. This is Mandryka.

II. At the Fiaker ball, Arabella falls in love with Mandryka and accepts his proposal of marriage. But Zdenka has plans of her own, beginning with a note she hands to Matteo telling him to come secretly to meet Arabella at night. Coincidently Arabella disappears from the ball, leaving everyone with his private suspicions.

III. People come to the foot of the hotel stairs, led by their search for Arabella. There they find Matteo descending. Mandryka challenges Matteo on the spot. Then Zdenka, with her hair down, dressed in a very feminine negligee, appears at the head of the stairs ready to die for her desperate sin. Graf Waldner repents what he has caused, and gives Zdenka to Matteo. Arabella and Mandryka are both deeply moved by the realization of what has happened.

Archers, The

COMP.: B. Carr
LIBR.: W. Dunlap
From the tale of William Tell

Ballad Opera in 3 acts
New York, 18 April 1796
Boston, 1797

The first American opera of which parts still exist.

Ariadne auf Naxos

COMP.: R. Strauss
LIBR.: H. von Hofmannsthal

Prologue & 1 act
Stuttgart, 25 October 1912
Vienna (*rev.*), 4 October 1916
Covent Garden, 1925
Philadelphia, 1928

CAST

Of the Prologue

Major-domo	Spkr	Composer	S
Music Master	Bar	Tenor (*plays Bacchus in the Opera*)	T

Officer	T	Lackey	B
Dancing Master	T	Zerbinetta	S
Wigmaker	B	Prima Donna (*plays Ariadne*	
		in the Opera)	S

Of the Opera

Ariadne (*plays Prima Donna*		Naiade, *a nymph*	S
in the prologue)	S	Dryade, *another nymph*	C
Bacchus (*plays Tenor in the*		Echo, *another nymph*	S
prologue)	T		

Of the Intermezzo

Zerbinetta	S	Truffaldino	B
Harlequin	Bar	Brighella	T
Scaramuccio	T		

SYNOPSIS

Prologue: Preparations are under way for a private performance of the opera *Ariadne*. To the composer's horror, the Major-domo suddenly announces that his master has decided that there shall be a Harlequinade played intermittently between the scenes of the opera. Nothing can be done about it, the opera begins.

Opera: Ariadne languishes, wishing she were dead. Not even the bright Harlequinade can cheer her. Stepping out of the intermezzo, Zerbinetta pleads with her, even tries reasoning. But nothing will rouse her will. Bacchus arrives. She mistakes him for Death, but with him poor Ariadne finds comfort.

NOTES

The original intention was that the opera would be a *divertissement* during the performance of the play *Le Bourgeois Gentilhomme*, by Molière. The prologue was attached for the Vienna performance, in 1916. There was an amateur performance in New York in 1934. The first professional performance there, however, took place in the City Center in 1946.

Ariane et Barbe-Bleue
(*Ariadne and Blue-Beard*)
COMP.: P. Dukas
LIBR.: M. Maeterlinck

3 *acts*
Comique, 10 May 1907
Metropolitan, 1911
Covent Garden, 1937

CAST

Barbe-Bleue, *Bluebeard*	B	Bellangère, *a fourth*	S
Ariane, *Ariadne*	MS	Alladine, *a fifth*	Mime
Nourrice, *nurse*	C	Peasant	B
Sélysette, *a previous wife*		Second Peasant	T
of Bluebeard's	MS	Third Peasant	B
Ygraine, *another*	S	Peasants, Crowd	
Mélisande, *a third*	S		

SYNOPSIS

1. Ariane, about to be the sixth wife of the notorious Bluebeard, the others presumably murdered, insists on knowing what did happen to them. She opens a secret door and hears their voices. Bluebeard catches her in the act but a violent crowd rushes in to prevent another tragedy.

II. At last alone again, she finds her way into the hidden vault and helps the others get free.

III. The peasants have trapped Bluebeard. They bring their trussed-up prize to the women as a present for their revenge. But his five wives loosen his bonds and wash his wounds. Ariane leaves them at peace.

Arianna, L'
COMP.: C. Monteverdi
LIBR.: O. Rinuccini

Prologue & 8 scenes
Mantua, 28 May 1608
Florence, 1614
Venice, 1639

Composed to celebrate the wedding of Francesco Gonzaga.

Most of the music is lost. But one melody of great beauty remains both as an aria, and arranged by Monteverdi as a choral piece. This is the famous *Lasciatemi Morire* (O let me die), the *Lamento d'Arianna*. A reconstruction of the opera was presented at Karlsruhe in 1926 and again in Paris in 1931.

Ariodant
COMP.: E. Méhul
LIBR.: F. B. Hoffman

3 acts
Comique, 11 October 1799
Moscow, 1803
Stockholm, 1808

Arlecchino
COMP.: F. Busoni
LIBR.: by the composer

Comedy in 1 act
Zurich, 11 May 1917
London BBC, 1939
Venice, 1940

CAST

Ser Matteo del Sarto, *tailor*	Bar	Leandro	T
Abbate Cospicuo	Bar	Annunziata, *Matteo's wife*	Mute
Dr. Bombasto	B	Columbina, *Arlecchino's wife*	MS
Arlecchino	Spkr		

SYNOPSIS

Arlecchino, almost caught in the act of making love to Annunziata, leaps out the window shouting that the town is invaded by barbarians. Matteo, frightened, runs into his house. The Doctor and the Abbate hide. Arlecchino reappears as a soldier, knocks on the door, drafts Matteo into the army and sends him far, far away. He is about to recommence his amours when Columbina (exempt from any draft) catches him. Gallant Leandro swears to avenge Columbina by duelling Arlecchino. But Arlecchino outduels him with a wooden sword. Columbina, Abbate, and the Doctor find the body. But they are too drunk to do anything about it. Meanwhile, Arlecchino has fetched Matteo's wife and gone off with her.

Arlesiana, L'
COMP.: F. Cilèa
LIBR.: L. Marenco
From the story by Daudet

Tragedy in 3 acts
Milan, 27 November 1897
Naples, 1912

CAST

Rosa Mamai	MS	Metifio, *horse tender*	Bar
Federico, *her son*	T	Marco, *Rosa's brother*	B
Vivetta, *her god-daughter*	S	L'Innocente, *her second son*	MS
Baldassare, *an old shepherd*	Bar		

14

SYNOPSIS

I. Federico wishes to marry a girl from Arles, but Metifio tells Rosa the girl is a strumpet. For proof he shows her a letter.

II. Vivetta, a home-town girl, loves Federico. Rosa urges her to tell him that she does, to help him get through the loneliness of losing the girl from Arles. Federico proves unwilling, but eventually accepts the girl's affection in order to soothe his mother's misery.

III. Metifio has been having an affair with a girl—the girl from Arles. When Federico hears it, he attacks Metifio and nearly kills him. Unavenged and furious, forgetting Vivetta, Federico goes mad and kills himself.

NOTES

The opera was originally in four acts, but was reduced to three in 1898.

Armide

	5 acts
COMP.: C. W. Gluck	Opéra, 23 September 1777
LIBR.: P. Quinault	London, 1906
From Tasso	New York, 1910

Armide

COMP.: J. B. Lully	Opéra, 5 February 1686
LIBR.: P. Quinault	Rome, 1690
From Tasso	Florence, 1911

Ascanio in Alba

	2 acts
COMP.: W. A. Mozart	Milan, 17 October 1771
LIBR.: G. Parini	

Performed as half of a double bill for the wedding of the Archduke Ferdinand, with *Ruggiero*, by Hasse. This event has been pointed out as the end of the old style opera and the beginning of the new in a single performance.

Asrael

	4 acts
COMP.: A. Franchetti	Reggio Emilia, 11 February 1888
LIBR.: F. Fontana	New York, 1890
	Buenos Aires, 1901

Assassinio nel Cattedrale, L'

(*Murder in the Cathedral*)	*Tragedy in 2 acts and an interlude*
COMP.: I. Pizzeti	La Scala, 1 March 1958
LIBR.: Msgr. A. Castelli	New York, 1958
From T. S. Eliot's play	

CAST

Tomasso Becket	B	Four Knights
Three Priests		Two Leaders of the Chorus
Four Tempters		Chorus

NOTES

The first American performance had begun at Ellenville, New York, during the summer of 1958, when the tent above collapsed in torrential rain and wind, forcing a halt in the production. Thus the first complete performance occurred in Carnegie Hall in the fall of 1958.

At the Boar's Head
    COMP.: G. Holst
    From Shakespeare's King Henry IV

1 *act*
Manchester, 3 April 1925
London, 1925
New York, 1935

Atalanta
    COMP.: G. F. Handel
    LIBR.: Unknown
      First performed in celebration of the wedding of the Prince of Wales to Princess Auguste of Saxe-Gotha.

3 *acts*
Covent Garden, 23 May 1736

Attaque du Moulin, L'
    COMP.: A. Bruneau.
    LIBR.: L. Gallet
    From a story by Zola

4 *acts*
Comique, 23 November 1893
London, 1894
New York, 1910

Attila
    COMP.: G. Verdi
    LIBR.: T. Solera

Prologue & 3 acts
Venice, 17 March 1846
London, 1848
New York, 1850

Aus einem Totenhaus
    See *Z Mrtveho Domu*

Aventures du Roi Pausole, Les
    COMP.: A. Honegger
    LIBR.: A. Willemetz
    From a novel by Louÿs

3 *acts*
Paris, 12 December 1930
Geneva, 1932

Azora, the Daughter of Montezuma
    COMP.: H. Hadley
    LIBR.: D. Stevens

3 *acts*
Chicago, 26 December 1917
New York, 1918

Ballad of Baby Doe, The
    COMP.: D. Moore
    LIBR.: J. Latouche

2 *acts*
Central City, Colo., 7 July, 1956
New York, 1958

CAST

Baby Doe, *miner's wife*	S	Old Miner	T
Augusta Tabor	MS	Priest	T
Horace Tabor, *mining magnate*	Bar	Hotel Clerk	T
William Jennings Bryan, *candidate*		President Chester A. Arthur	T
for president	B	Mayor, doorman, bouncer, bellboy, foot-	
Mama McCourt, *Baby Doe's mother*	C	man, politician, friends, children	

SYNOPSIS

    Baby Doe, having left her husband, enters the life of the respectable Horace Tabor, thirty years her senior. It means ruin for him in the society of the early West, but her love for him becomes deep and true.

    The story is based on the lives of actual people in Leadville, Colorado, in the 1880's.

Ballad Singer, The
    See *Gioconda, La*

Ballo in Maschera, Un
(*The Masked Ball*)
COMP.: G. Verdi
LIBR.: Somma
From Scribe's libretto for Auber's
Gustave III

Tragedy in 3 acts
Rome, 17 February 1859
New York, 1861
London, 1861
Metropolitan, 1889

CAST

Riccardo, *Count of Warwick, Governor*
(*Gustavus III*)   T
Amelia, *Renato's wife*   S
Renato, *the governor's secretary*
(*Anckarstroem*)   Bar
Samuele, *Count Ribbing,*
the governor's enemy   B

Tomaso, *Count Horn, the governor's*
enemy   B
Silvano, *a sailor* (*Cristian*)   Bar
Oscar, *a page*   S
Ulrica, *a fortune teller* (*Arvidson*)   C
Judge, Servant, Populace, Guards,
Courtiers

SYNOPSIS

I. Riccardo is delighted to learn that there will be a masked ball at which he will have an opportunity of seeing the fair Amelia, whom he loves. He conceals his identity and pays a visit to Ulrica the fortune teller to find out what the outcome of this romance may be. There he watches Amelia, and overhears her telling Ulrica that she is in love with Riccardo. Ulrica directs her to go to a gallows at midnight to gather a certain herb. When Amelia has gone, Riccardo asks his questions. Ulrica predicts that he will be murdered by a friend.

II. He goes to the gallows to protect Amelia, who is there in veils gathering the herb. Renato follows him to warn him of conspirators who have set up an ambush. Riccardo sends the veiled woman with Renato but takes a different route himself. The conspirators capture Renato and unveil his companion. When Renato sees that the governor's beloved is his own wife, he is enraged.

III. He wants to kill her—but he loves her and cannot. Instead he decides that the governor must die. He and the conspirators draw lots from Amelia's unwilling hand to choose an assassin. It falls to Renato himself. That evening, at the masked ball, Renato ferrets out the governor and stabs him to death.

NOTES

The story is based upon the actual assassination of Gustave III of Sweden, which did take place at a masked ball. The story, however, was uncomfortable for the ruling powers in Italy in the 1850's, so that it became necessary, if there were to be a production, for Verdi to change the names and the locale to some safe place. Of all the available settings, he chose one of the most absurd—Boston. When the opera was about to open in Naples, there was an attempt on the life of Napoleon III. Crowds rioted, using "Viva Verdi" as their slogan. This was only incidentally a public comment on the composer, it was primarily a way of cheering in an acrostic for *Vittorio Emanuele, Re d'Italia* without precisely saying so.

Barbe-Bleue
(*Bluebeard*)
COMP.: J. Ibert

Lausanne Radio, 10 October 1943

Barber of Seville, The
See *Barbiere di Siviglia, Il*
See also *Nozze di Figaro, Le*

Barbiere di Siviglia, Il

COMP.: G. Paisiello
LIBR.: G. Petrosellini
From Beaumarchais' play

Comedy in 4 acts
St. Petersburg, 26 September 1782
New Orleans, 1810
Paris (rev.), 1868

This opera was at first supplanted by the much more popular work of Rossini. Lately, however, in American opera workshops, the Paisiello is again finding audiences.

Barbiere di Siviglia, Il

(*The Barber of Seville*)
COMP.: G. Rossini
LIBR.: Sterbini
From the play by Beaumarchais

Comedy in 2 acts
Rome, 5 February 1816
Covent Garden, 1818
New York, 1819
Metropolitan, 1883

CAST

Count Almaviva	T	Ambrogio, *the Doctor's servant*	B
Doctor Bartolo	B	Rosina, *the Doctor's ward*	S
Don Basilio, *a singing teacher*	B	Berta, (*Marcellina*), *Rosina's governess*	S
Figaro, *a barber*	Bar	Notary, Constable, Musicians, Soldiers	
Fiorello, *the Count's servant*	Bar		

MUSICAL HIGHLIGHTS

ACT I. Serenade *Ecco ridente in cielo* (See in the sky now smiling), Almaviva
Aria *Largo al factotum* (Room for the factotum), Figaro
Serenade *Se il mio nome saper* (Shall I then tell you my name?), Almaviva
Cavatina *Una voce poco fa* (Once a little voice I heard), Rosina
Aria *La calunnia* (Slander's power), Don Basilio
Duet *Dunque io son* (Can it therefore be?), Rosina, Figaro

SYNOPSIS

I. Figaro discovers the Count in the act of serenading Rosina. Being prepared to propose anything, he suggests a way for the Count to meet her. Her guardian, the Doctor, is very watchful, however, so that it becomes necessary for Figaro, who can accomplish anything, to act as a go-between, giving Rosina the notion that the secret lover is his own cousin. This he does, but the Doctor is aware that something is going on. When Almaviva, ridiculously disguised as a soldier, tries to force his way into her presence, the real soldiers unmask him and nearly throw him into prison. Only when he shows them his credentials as a Grandee of the Empire do they let him go.

II. He tries again, this time disguised as her music teacher. Everything seems to be getting along swimmingly, with little love notes tossed in between the others in the music lesson, when the real teacher arrives. He has to be bribed to leave without betraying them. All this takes place while the good Doctor writhes in suspicion, trapped by being shaved by the dexterous barber. Finally he can stand it no longer, and rushes into the lesson room to confront his ward with her lover. Almaviva he denounces as a rake with a mistress. He rushes out to find a notary, but when he returns *sans* that functionary it is too late— Almaviva and Rosina are man and wife, wedded before a notary hastened to the occasion by the fascinating barber of Seville.

NOTES

Paisiello's opera on the same play was very popular when Rossini introduced his own. Public feeling was against him, for people were loyal to their favorite work. Rossini had to resort to advertising a letter from the older composer granting him permission to produce his version. At the first performance this strategy was worthless. The audience was hostile; the actors hardly less so. The production was full of ludicrous errors, the audience howled it down. The next night, however, opened in better circumstances, with many changes in the score. From that time on the Rossini outshone the Paisiello.

On the 29th November, 1825, *The Barber of Seville* opened in New York, the first opera performed in Italian in that city.

Barbier von Bagdad, Der
(*The Barber from Bagdad*)
COMP.: P. Cornelius
LIBR.: By the composer
From the Arabian Nights

Comedy in 2 acts
Weimar, 15 December 1858
Metropolitan, 1890

CAST

The Caliph	Bar	Nureddin	T
Baba Mustapha, *a Cadi (magistrate)*	T	Abul Hassan Ali Ebn Bekar, *a barber*	B
Margiana, *the Cadi's daughter*	S	Servants, Friends, People, Wailing	
Bostana, *his servant*	MS	Women, The Caliph's Entourage	

SYNOPSIS

I. Nureddin, hopelessly dying of love for Margiana, revives slightly when Bostana announces an arrangement for him to go to her. With all due pomp, he prepares for his assignation, but the Barber, who is the most loquacious man in Bagdad, takes so interminably long in the process of shaving him that Nureddin fears all may be lost. To prevent the barber from following him, which indeed the Barber seems prepared to do, he has his servants forcefully restrain the man.

II. Safely beneath her windows, the lover woos his love with song. But backstage another serenade destroys the tenuous beauty of the moment. It is the Barber. Then, from somewhere else, come the pitiful cries of some poor slave being beaten. The Barber rushes in, thinking Nureddin has cried for help from an assassin. He calls a crowd. But they find nobody there—Nureddin has hidden in a chest. The Barber has the people carry out this chest, thinking his patron is dead inside. At this moment the Cadi enters to see the mob in the act of carrying away his possessions. All is utter turmoil until the Caliph enters. In the abject silence of his presence, the people open the chest to find the living Nureddin. Everything becomes clear, and all the tangles untangle.

NOTES

This work had had no performance until Liszt took interest. At that time he was carrying on a difference of opinion with the management at Weimar. When *The Barber of Bagdad* opened, there was an organized demonstration that completely wrecked the performance. At this Liszt walked out of Weimar altogether. Finally in 1885, re-orchestrated by Felix Mottl, the opera began to find success. Not until 1904 was it performed in its original shape.

Bartered Bride, The
See *Prodaná Nevěsta*

Basoche, La
COMP.: A. Messager
LIBR.: A. Carré

3 acts
Comique, 30 May 1890
London, 1891
New York, 1893

Bastien und Bastienne
COMP.: W. A. Mozart
LIBR.: F. A. Weiskern
From Favart's parody on *Le Devin du Village*

Comedy-Pastoral in 1 act
Vienna, September 1768
Berlin, 1890
London, 1894
New York, 1916

CAST

Colas, *a would-be sorcerer*	B
Bastien, *a lover*	S (or T)
Bastienne, *his beloved a shepherdess*	S

NOTES

Mozart was twelve when he wrote this. It was first performed in the garden of the famous hypnotist Mesmer.

Bat, The
See *Fledermaus, Die*

Béatrice et Bénédict
COMP.: H. Berlioz
LIBR.: By the composer
From Shakespeare's *Much Ado about Nothing*

Comedy in 2 acts
Baden-Baden, 9 August 1862
Comique, 1890
Glasgow, 1936
New York (concert), 1960

CAST

Don Pedro, *a general*	B	Claudio, *an officer*	T
Leonato, *the governor*	B	Ursula, *Hero's friend*	C
Héro, *the governor's daughter*	S	Bénédict, *an officer*	T
Béatrice, *his niece*	MS	Somarona, *orchestral conductor*	B

SYNOPSIS

I. Bénédict wishes to remain ever a bachelor. But Béatrice, whom he meets on return from battle, is too much for him.

II. Béatrice, on the other hand, used to despise amorous advances until Bénédict turned out to be too much for her. Both try to hide these unfortunate betrayals of weakness. But nothing suffices; they must admit their love and marry.

Beaucaire, Monsieur
See *Monsieur Beaucaire*

Beautiful Galatea, The
See *Schöne Galathee, Die*

Beggar Student, The
See *Bettelstudent, Der*

Beggar's Opera, The
COMP.: J. Pepusch (*Selected the music*)
LIBR.: J. Gay

Ballad Opera in 3 acts
London, 9 February 1728
New York, 1750
Hammersmith, England, 1920
(*it ran 1463 nights*)

CAST

The Beggar	Spkr	Polly Peachum, *their available daughter*	S
Mrs. Peachum	MS	Capt. MacHeath, *highwayman*	T
Mr. Peachum, *"a fence"*	B	Filch, *Peachum's man, pickpocket*	T

Lockit, *jailer, in league with Peachum*	Bar	Mat of the Mint, *and the* Gentlemen	
Lucy Lockit, *the jailer's daughter*	S	of the Road	
Diana Trapes, *the tally woman*	MS	Jenny Diver, Sukey Tawdry, *and the*	
		Ladies of the Town	

SYNOPSIS

I. Filch lets drop that dear Polly seems to be carrying on with the notorious MacHeath. The Peachums are not sure whether that would imply a rise in station for their family or not, but at least they can turn affairs to their own advantage.

II. MacHeath is indeed involved with dear Polly, but he has other entanglements with the Ladies of the Town. Peachum uses them to trap his quarry in a tavern. To jail the unfortunate hero must go, but this is all in the business. Even Lucy, the jailer's daughter is with child by MacHeath. She lets him out.

III. Again, to save face and fortune, the jailer and the fence join forces to recapture their man. They prepare to hang him to prevent more embarrassments. The two girls vie for recognition as his wife, but four more wives turn up, just as eager to see the slaughter. At the last the beggar intervenes. He thinks all operas should end happily; and this one, being his, does, with a gay chorus of "Lumps of Pudding."

NOTES

They say that Dean Swift once suggested that "A Newgate Pastoral might be made a pretty thing." Pepusch and Gay took up the idea; Rich produced it. The ballad opera was so remarkably successful that it caused Handel considerable annoyance. It has run intermittently up to the present day. The satire of the corruptions of courtiers and Italian opera carries even to the point of using, for the grand march of the highwaymen to their job, a famous march from *Rinaldo*. There are sixty-nine musical numbers, one of the most beautiful being a variant of "Over the Hills and Far Away."

Beggar's Opera, The
See also *Dreigroschenoper, Die*

Belle Hélène, La
COMP.: J. Offenbach
LIBR.: Meilhac & Halevy

3 *acts*
Paris, 17 December 1864
London, 1866
New York, 1867

Belmont und Constanze
COMP.: J. André
LIBR.: C. F. Bretzner

Berlin, 25 May 1781

To Bretzner's unavailing protest, the text of this opera was somewhat altered for use as a libretto for Mozart—*Die Entführung aus dem Serail*.

Benvenuto Cellini
COMP.: H. Berlioz
LIBR.: du Wailly & Barbier

3 *acts*
Opera, 10 September 1838
Covent Garden, 1853
Glasgow, 1939

CAST

Cardinal Salviati	B	Francesco, *an artisan*	T
Balducci, *the papal treasurer*	B	Bernadino, *another artisan*	B
Teresa, *Balducci's daughter*	S	Fieramosca, *the papal sculptor*	Bar
Benvenuto Cellini, *famous goldsmith*	T	Pompeo	Bar
Ascanio, *his apprentice*	MS		

SYNOPSIS

I. In sixteenth century Rome, the romantic sculptor, Benvenuto Cellini, barely concerned with his work, plans to elope with Teresa during the carnival. This fact is well known to his rival, Fieramosca. But when the suspicious father surprises his daughter in her room, he catches not the right man but Fieramosca.

II. Cellini, as do all artists, needs money. He manages to squeeze a little out of the treasury by promising to finish his *Perseus* by morning. The carnival takes precedence, however. Fieramosca attends in the same disguise that he knows Cellini will wear in order to confuse Teresa and prevent the elopement. There is a fight. One of the disguised ones kills Pompeo. In the confusion again the wrong man is caught—Fieramosca.

III. The *Perseus* is still unfinished. The cardinal threatens to have someone else complete the work. Finally remembering his call to art, Benvenuto rushes to finish the casting. When the moment of his arrest for murder is ripe, he unveils the new statue. Its beauty saves his life.

NOTE

The same subject was used by Franz Lachner, whose opera opened in Munich in 1849, and many others.

Bettelstudent, Der
(*The Beggar Student*)
COMP.: K. Millöcker
LIBR.: Zell & Genée

3 *acts*
Vienna, 6 December 1882
New York, 1883
London, 1884

CAST

Palmatica, *the Countess Nowalska*	MS	Col. Ollendorf, *governor of Cracow*	B
Countess Laura, *her daughter*	S	Enterich, *prison governor*	Bar
Countess Bronislava, *Laura's sister*	S	Richtofen, *Saxon officer*	
Simon, *the Beggar Student*	T	Wangenheim, *another*	
Jan Janitsky, *his friend*	T	Henrici, *a third*	

SYNOPSIS

I. In order to avenge his feelings on Palmatica, Ollendorf arranges for two prisoners, one a beggar, to be disguised as nobles and win the hand of her daughters Laura and Bronislava.

II. These two are no ordinary men; they are revolutionists who want to get money to help the Polish insurgents now at the gates of Cracow. Simon tries to tell Laura who he really is, but Ollendorf intercepts the note. When the wedding has been performed, Ollendorf lets his secret out.

III. But Laura is not dismayed, she loves Simon. In another attempt to help the insurrection, Simon has spread the rumor that he is the general of its army. For this he is about to be beheaded when the army breaks in and saves him.

Billy Budd
COMP.: B. Britten
LIBR.: Forster & Crozier
From Herman Melville's novel

4 *acts*
Covent Garden, 1 December 1951
Wiesbaden, 1952
Paris, 1952

CAST

Capt. Vere, *in command*	T	Mr. Redburn, *First Lieutenant*	Bar
Billy Budd	Bar	Mr. Flint, *Sailing Master*	Bar
Claggert, *Master at Arms*	B	Lt. Ratcliffe	B

Red Whiskers, *an impressed seaman*	T	Maintop	T
Donald, *seaman*	Bar	Novice's Friend	Bar
Dansker, *an old seaman*	B	Arthur Jones, *an impressed seaman*	Bar
Novice	T	Four Midshipmen	Boys
Squeak, *ship's corporal*	T	Cabin Boy	Spkr
Bosun	Bar	Officers, Sailors, Powder Monkeys,	
First *and* Second Mates	Bar (2)	Drummers, Marines	

SYNOPSIS

I. (*Prologue*) Captain Vere recalls his life:

Once three seamen were thrown aboard, captured from another ship and brought to swell the crew. One of them was the stammerer, Billy Budd. There was hardly time to introduce them to the ship's tasks before the first battle came up.

II. Claggert intends to entrap Billy, his enemy, and embroil him in a framed-up plot for mutiny. Dansker warns the victim, but Billy is a happy-go-lucky sort who pays little attention.

III. Claggert has begun to drop hints to the Captain when the watch aloft sights an enemy sail. The battle lasts but one shot—there is no wind to manoeuvre with. In the doldrums Claggert reinforces his accusations. Being a good sailor, the captain insists that Claggert make the charge to Billy's face. Poor Billy, stifled by stammering, swings at Claggert and accidentally kills the man. By the articles of war he is condemned to be hanged.

IV. Dansker comforts him in the last moments. The yardarm is prepared, the prisoner taken to it. Then the crew boils into mutiny which is quelled—and (*Epilogue*) we see Capt. Vere again alone, contemplating this distant memory.

Billy Budd
COMP.: G. F. Ghedini   Venice, 7 September 1949

This work appeared before the Britten version, but has not been as successful.

Blind King, The
See *Roi Aveugle, Le*
See also *Amore dei Tre Re, L'*

Blue Forest, The
See *Forêt Bleue, La*
See also *Wald, Der*

Bluebeard
See *Ritter Blaubart*
See also *Duke Bluebeard's Castle*
See also *Ariane et Barbe-Bleu*
See also *Barbe-Bleu*

Boar's Head, The
See *At the Boar's Head*

Boatswain's Mate, The
COMP.: E. Smyth
LIBR.: By the composer
From a story by W. W. Jacobs

Comedy in 1 act, 2 parts
London, 14 January 1916
Old Vic, 1922

THE OPERAS

CAST

Harry Benn, *former boatswain*	T	Policeman	B
Ned Travers, *former soldier*	Bar	Farm laborers, Two cats behind	
Mrs. Waters, *an eligible landlady*	S	the scenes.	
Mary Ann, *her servant*	Spkr		

SYNOPSIS

Benn, to impress Mrs. Waters, conspires with Travers to perform a fake hold-up in which Benn may capture Travers, thus saving the lady from imminent danger.

The plan goes awry when Mrs. Waters catches the "thief" herself, pretends to kill him, and scares the wits out of Benn. To top it all, she is so impressed not with Benn but with Travers, she chooses to set her cap for that landsman instead.

NOTE

Dame Ethel Smyth was England's foremost woman composer.

Bohème, La — *Tragedy in 4 acts*
COMP.: R. Leoncavallo — Venice, 6 May 1897
LIBR.: By the composer — Hamburg, 1897
From a novel by Murger — Paris, 1899

The fact that Puccini's opera on the same subject came out before Leoncavallo's doomed the work.

Bohème, La — *Tragedy in 4 acts*
COMP.: G. Puccini — Turin, 1 February 1896
LIBR.: Giacosa & Illica — Covent Garden, 1897
From a novel by Murger — New York, 1898
— Metropolitan, 1900

CAST

Rodolfo, *a poet*	T	Parpignol, *a peddler*	T
Marcello, *a painter*	Bar	Customs Official	B
Colline, *self-styled philosopher*	B	Musetta	S
Schaunard, *musician*	Bar	Mimi, *an embroiderer*	S
Benoit, *their landlord*	B	Students, Girls, Citizens, Shopkeepers,	
Alcindoro, *State Councillor*	B	Vendors, Soldiers, Waiters, Boys	

MUSICAL HIGHLIGHTS

ACT I. Narrative *Che gelida manina* (Your tiny hand is frozen), Rodolfo
Aria *Mi chiamano Mimi* (My name is Mimi), Mimi
Duet *O soave fanciulla* (O beautiful maiden), Rodolfo, Mimi
ACT II. Waltz *Quando me'n vo, soletta per la via* (When I go alone along the street), Musetta
ACT III. Duet *Donde lieta usci* (Let us leave here happy) Rodolfo, Mimi
Quartet *Addio dolce svegliare* (Farewell until sweet morning), Mimi, Rodolfo, Musetta, Marcello
ACT IV. Duet *Mimi tu più* (Mimi, you false one), Rodolfo, Marcello
Death Scene *Sono andati* (Have they gone?), Mimi, Rodolfo

SYNOPSIS

I. Christmas Eve. The four artists share a garret on the left bank. There Rodolfo, who is alone for the moment, meets Mimi, who lives across the hall. She is visibly wasting away with "consumption." He falls in love with her immediately.

II. Into the crowded street they go for happiness. They find his room-mates and

Musetta, Marcello's former flame. She quickly drops her latest companion, Alcindoro, and follows her old friends into the evening of pleasures.

III. Later, in February, we find them at the edge of the city, quarreling and tense. Mimi and Rodolfo bitterly decide to separate. Musetta likewise fights with Marcello. But they do not part.

IV. Back to the attic, Musetta brings the now dying Mimi. Too late Rodolfo tries to help, too late they regret their bitterness. She dies in his arms.

Bolivar

COMP.: D. Milhaud
LIBR.: M. Milhaud
From Jules Supervielle

Paris, 12 May 1950

Boris Godunov

COMP.: M. Mussorgsky
LIBR.: By the composer
From the play by Pushkin

Tragedy in Prologue & 4 acts
St. Petersburg, 8 February 1874
Paris, 1908
Drury Lane, & Metropolitan, 1913

CAST

Boris Godunov, *Tsar of Russia*	Bar	Rangoni, *a Jesuit in disguise*	B
Feodor, *his son*	MS	Varlaam, *a vagrant*	B
Xenia, *his daughter*	S	Missail, *another vagrant*	T
The Nurse	C	The Innkeeper	MS
Prince Shuisky	T	Nikititch, *the constable*	B
Shchelkalov, *secretary of the Douma*		The Simpleton	T
(*Parliament*)	Bar	Two Jesuits	B (2)
Pimen, *a monk, chronicler*	B	Peasants and Serfs, Members of the
Grigori, *later the pretender* Dmitri	T	Douma, Polish Ladies, Monks,
Marina Mnishek, *Polish princess*	S	Guards, Soldiers, etc.

MUSICAL HIGHLIGHTS

PROLOGUE. *Coronation Scene*, Boris, Chorus
ACT I. Pimen's Chronicle *Still one more page*, Pimen, Grigori
  Song of the duck, Innkeeper
  The Siege of Kazan, Varlaam
ACT II. *Song of the gnat*, Nurse
  The clapping game, Feodor, Nurse
  Aria *I have attained the power*, Boris
ACT III. *Chorus of the girls of Sandomir*, Chorus
  Mazurka *Life is dreary*, Marina
  Polacca *No, milord, I scarce believe you*, Marina, Chorus
ACT IV. Pimen's Tale *A peaceful monk*, Pimen
  Death of Boris *Farewell my son*, Boris, Feodor, Chorus
  Simpleton's song *Flow, ah flow my bitter tears*, Simpleton

SYNOPSIS

PROLOGUE: The people, oppressed and weary of oppression, submit to the whips of the Boyards and chant for Boris to accept the crown and be their Tsar. Boris, having committed murder to accomplish this, accepts the office but already his heart is heavy with foreboding.

I. For five years plague rules the land. The peasants are as badly off as ever. Boris must take all the blame. In his quiet cell in the monastery Pimen puts the last words to his chronicle of the history of Russia. He pauses to tell his disciple, Grigori, how the former Tsar and all his family were murdered, the bodies left in the open for the world to see. There is a slight possibility that the Tsarevitch, Dmitri, may have lived. Grigori decides to exploit that possibility. He escapes to Poland to get support for a revolution.

II. Boris, in agony of guilt, hearing of intrigues in Poland, calls Shuisky before him. Shuisky tells him more of the bad news, and insinuates more evil for the Tsar. Alone, Boris becomes hysterical, seeing hostile images even in the mechanical clock in the corner.

III. In Poland, in the color and beauty of the court, Grigori, now called Dmitri, becomes the target of the ambitions of Marina who sees herself as Tsarevna, and of Rangoni, the ecclesiastical enemy of Russia. Rangoni uses Marina to worm his way into Dmitri's future and goads the pretender to return as Tsar.

IV. Boris speaks to the assembled parliament, but in a state of madness. Shuisky has Pimen brought in. Pimen tells all the tale of the murders and the possibility of the survival of Dmitri. Boris collapses. They take the Tsar to privacy, and while he speaks there with his son he hears the funeral chanting of the monks. In terror he dies.

Dmitri, the tool of the Jesuits, marches into Russia. But to the peasants he offers no change, they live like wolves. After all have passed by only the Simpleton is left, weeping in his own way for Russia.

NOTES

The synopsis follows the original order of scenes. Rimsky-Korsakov, as he did for many musical works that fell into his hands, re-orchestrated and revised the original. The opera was generally performed in that revised form until recently. It is still a matter of hot debate whether the so-called crudities of Mussorgsky's harmony and orchestration may reveal more of the real beauty of the work than the smoothing out of his friend's.

The Imperial Theatre rejected the manuscript in 1869. It was revised and again rejected in 1872. In February of that year a concert performance of the *Coronation Scene* took place, and in April of the *Polonaise* from the Polish scenes. In 1873 three scenes, including that at the inn, were most successful. The first complete performance exhibited the poor vision of the professional critics—they all objected to the work, making it a critical failure in spite of its tremendous popular success.

Boris Godunov is without doubt the masterpiece of Russian opera. Its importance is not only in its beauty and its magnificence however; it represents, like the work of Gluck, a great change of style particularly in that it is almost (again like Gluck) a choral drama.

Brief Life, The
See *Vida Breve, La*

Bronwen
See *Cauldron of Anwyn, The*

Bronze Horse, The
See *Cheval de Bronze, Le*

Brother in Love, The
See *Frate 'Nnamorato, Lo*

Butterfly, Madame
See *Madama Butterfly*

Caïd, Le
COMP.: A. Thomas
LIBR.: T. Sauvage

2 *acts*
Comique, 3 January 1849
New Orleans, 1850
London, 1850
New York, 1852

Camacho's Wedding
See *Hochzeit des Camacho, Die*

Campana Sommersa, La
(*The Sunken Bell*)
COMP.: O. Respighi
LIBR.: C. Guastalla
From a play by G. Hauptmann

4 *acts*
Hamburg, 18 November 1927
New York, 1928

Cantarina, La
(*The Songstress*)
COMP.: J. Haydn
LIBR.: Unknown

2 *acts*
Esterhaz, Austria, 1767
Bielefeld, Germany, 1939

Canterbury Pilgrims, The
COMP.: R. de Koven
LIBR.: P. W. MacKaye
From Chaucer

Metropolitan, 8 March 1917
Philadelphia, 1917

Capriccio
COMP.: R. Strauss
LIBR.: C. Krauss

1 *act*
Munich, 28 October 1942
Vienna, 1951
Covent Garden, 1953

CAST

Countess	S	M. Taupe	T
Clarion, *an actress*	C	Two Italian Singers	S, T
Flamand, *a musician*	T	Dancer	Dancer
Olivier, *a poet*	Bar	Major-domo	B
Count, *the Countess' brother*	Bar	Eight Servants	4T, 4B
La Roche, *a theatrical director*	Bar	Three Musicians	Violin, Cello, Cembalo

SYNOPSIS

At the time of the war of the Gluckists and Piccinists, the Countess' friends have gathered in her salon. Flamand and Olivier are rivals for her affection. They take up the subject of opera and use it as a means each to win over the other. The opera becomes therefore a discussion of music, words and theater, with each character taking the side of that art with which he is most closely allied—and all for love.

Capuletti ed i Montecchi, I
COMP.: V. Bellini
LIBR.: F. Romani
From Shakespeare's *Romeo and Juliet*

Tragedy in 4 parts
Venice, 11 March 1830
London, 1833
Boston, 1847

Cardillac

COMP.: P. Hindemith
LIBR.: F. Lion
From a novel by Hoffman

4 *acts*
Dresden, 9 November 1926
Zurich (*rev.*), 1952
London (Concert), 1936

CAST

Cardillac, *a famous goldsmith*	Bar	Klymene, *the Alto of Lully's Opera*	A
His Daughter	S	Phaeton, *The Tenor of Lully's Opera*	T
His Friend	T	Apollo, *The Bass of Lully's Opera*	B
First Singer of the Opera	S	Chorus and Dancers *for Lully's Opera*	
Officer	B	Marquis	Mute
Cavalier	T	People, Theater Personnel, Night Watch	

SYNOPSIS

Cardillac the goldsmith has such a fanatic love for the products of his own art that he contrives to murder anyone who manages to buy a piece for himself. The town hates him and fears him, but not until his fiendish revenge misses its mark in an attempt on his own daughter's lover do they become sufficiently aroused to tear him to pieces.

Carmelites, The

See *Dialogues des Carmélites, Les*

Carmen

COMP.: G. Bizet
LIBR.: Meilhac and Halévy
From a novel by Mérimée

Tragedy in 4 acts
Comique, 1 March 1875
London, 1878
New York, 1879

CAST

Don José, *corporal of the guard*	T	Frasquita, *gypsy friend of Carmen*	S
Escamillo, *famous Toreador*	Bar	Mercédès, *gypsy friend of Carmen*	S, MS
El Dancairo, *smuggler*	Bar	Carmen, *a gypsy*	S, MS
El Remondado, *smuggler*	T	Innkeeper, Guide	
Zuniga, *captain of the guard*	B	Officers, Dragoons, Boys, Cigarette Girls,	
Morales, *officer of the guard*	B	Gypsies, Smugglers	
Micaela, *peasant girl in love with Don José*	S		

MUSICAL HIGHLIGHTS

ACT I. March *Avec la garde montant* (Marching with the changing guard), Children and Soldiers
Habañera *L'amour est un oiseau rebelle* (Love is a dangerous bird), Carmen
Seguidilla *Près des ramparts de Séville* (Near the ramparts of Seville), Carmen

ACT II. Aria *Les Tringles des sistres tintaient* (The tingling music of guitars), Carmen
Toreador's Song *Votre toast je peux le rendre* (To your toast I'll give another), Escamillo, chorus
Flower Song *La Fleur que tu m'avais jetée* (The flower that you tossed to me), Don José

ACT III. Aria *Je dis que rien ne m'épouvante* (I say I will not be dismayed), Micaela
Procession of the Toreadors

SYNOPSIS

I. A square in Seville with a cigarette factory on one side. Micaela threads her way through the city crowd. She is looking for someone. Morales offers that he himself is willing to be found, but Micaela wants to see Don José. She is frightened. She runs away, intending to come back when the guard changes and Don José becomes free. Amid the soldiering of little boys, the guard changes. People tell José his girl was looking for him; he decides to wait for her there. Since he loves her sincerely he pays no attention at all to the cigarette girls as they come out for a break in the sun. Suddenly Carmen is there, the center of all eyes, singing her love-maddening Habañera, tossing her beauty tantalizingly before the unwilling eyes of Don José. At the end of it, leaving her brand upon his heart she tosses a flower to his feet and leaves. The man hardly thinks of the trap as he picks it up, puts it in his tunic and looks up to see Micaela returning.

Carmen gives them no time for love. She causes a fight inside the factory, stabbing another girl. Zuniga orders her arrest, sending Don José in to do the job. But the insulting, attractive girl mocks the soldier so that Zuniga orders her hands to be tied. Don José stands alone with her, guarding the prisoner. She talks to him but he orders her not to talk. She sings to him. He cannot stop her. She sings of love and how to find her later at Lillas Pastia's. This Seguidilla tortures the corporal's soul so much he loosens her hands. When the other guards return to take her away, she frees herself and escapes with a taunting reminder of love lingering behind.

II. At Lillas Pastia's tavern Carmen lives in a kaleidoscope of men and gypsy girls, making love with Captain Zuniga. Escamillo enters her life, the famous Torero, the thrilling image of new possibility of romance. But, work before play; the smugglers call the girls together to plan their next job. Carmen should bring José into their ring, they could use a brave man. She agrees with delight to seduce him. He comes, she caresses him, she tempts him with dance. But he hears the distant bugle calling him to duty. Duty? She hurls the insult back at him, making him plead with her that he loves her. She has his love, but his loyalty to the guard will not waver. Just then Zuniga surprises them, Carmen's latest lover and José's captain. Rank should prevail, Zuniga orders the corporal out. But this straw breaks the back of duty. José draws his sword against his captain, thus committing himself to a criminal life in one gesture.

III. Now the military man has become a smuggler. He has become, also, unhappy. He has learned how brief may be the passion of such a girl as Carmen. Carmen is morose too, and cuts cards with her friends to predict her fate. Spades; death drops its hint. Business stirs them into action. All the smugglers take to the trail leaving Don José alone to guard their camp. When all have gone, a guide brings Micaela to the place. She doesn't find José, although he is nearby in his hiding place as she sings of her forlorn and faithful love. There is another sound in the night—Escamillo climbs to the hideout looking for Carmen. Don José stops him and challenges him on the spot. The fight is fierce until the gypsies return and separate the combatants. Escamillo, the proud bullfighter, invites all of them to see his next fight. Now, in the quiet after his departure, somebody finds Micaela. Don José is blind to her love and deaf to her pleas. Only when she tells him his mother is dying does he decide to go with her.

IV. Crowds gather outside the arena, waiting for the bullfight to begin. The procession enters; bandilleros, picadors, toreros, and finally Escamillo himself, with Carmen on his arm. Everyone goes in to see the fight except Carmen. Just before they leave her, one of her gypsy friends warns that Don José is nearby, with a knife. The glorious noise of the bullfight grows and grows while the two come together again in the square. José begs her once more to come with him. She haughtily refuses. A shout in the arena echos in her own shout for Escamillo's victory in love and fighting. José stabs her. Suddenly it is over, the people pour out of the arena onto the empty stage to find José standing over her body, ready to give himself up as her murderer.

NOTES

This French work symbolizes Spain to every opera audience except, for some reason, the Spanish. Carmen is certainly a masterpiece of the art of welding dramatic event into musical event. The most active moments in the play happen in set pieces of musical form —the Seguidilla in which Carmen effects her escape, the Toast of Escamillo, the contrapuntal mixing of bullfight music and aria in which the sacrificial bull inside the arena and the beautiful woman outside are both stabbed. Perhaps this achievement was one of the reasons the opening night audience seemed to receive the work coldly—the critics again made sure to point out all that was wrong with the work. It was months before people began to realize what a brilliant drama had been brought to them. After the opening performance, Bizet wandered about the city with his friend Guirard, perhaps unhappy at the reception of his greatest work. He died three months later.

There are several innovations of importance. In Carmen, the chorus must not stand still but is required to move and act while singing. They must also smoke cigarettes. These changes of tradition were difficult for singers and provoked a good deal of opposition to the production. The work was cut out of new cloth even to the point of the style of staging and the manner of orchestration. Audiences hardly ever take such changes with goodwill.

One song, the Habañera, was transcribed from an earlier work of Yradier. Bizet was unaware of its authorship while writing the opera.

Carmina Burana
COMP.: C. Orff   Frankfurt, 8 June 1937
LIBR.: Arranged by the composer from medieval texts

Although this work has been staged in various ways ranging from stylized motion of a chorus to ballet against a choral background it is not so much an opera as it is a collection of choral songs based upon thirteenth century texts in Latin and German vernacular by men who had taken their leave of the monasteries.

Carriera d'un Libertino
See *Rake's Progress, The*

Castor et Pollux
COMP.: J. P. Rameau
LIBR.: P. J. Bernard

Prologue & 5 acts
Opéra, 24 October 1737
Glasgow (by amateurs), 1927

Cauldron of Anwyn
COMP.. J. C. Holbrooke
LIBR.. T. E. Ellis

Trilogy

This trilogy consists of the following operas, each first performed as shown:
Children of Don London, 15 June 1912
Dylan   London, 4 July 1913
Bronwen   Huddersfield, 1 February 1929

Cavalier of the Rose
See *Rosenkavalier, Der*

THE OPERAS

Cavalleria Rusticana
(Rustic Chivalry)
COMP.: P. Mascagni
LIBR.: Menasci and Targioni-Tozzetti
From a play by Verga

1 *act*
Rome, 17 May 1890
Philadelphia, 1891
Metropolitan, 1891

CAST

Turiddu, *young soldier*	T	Mamma Lucia, *Turiddu's mother*	C
Alfio, *village teamster*	Bar	Santuzza	S
Lola, *Alfio's wife*	MS	Villagers, Peasants, Boys	

SYNOPSIS

Turiddu loved and betrayed Santuzza. He has left her and returned to his old love, Lola, now Alfio's wife. Santuzza pleads with him to come back to her but he pays no attention. Seeing Lola he follows her into the church. Alfio comes along. Santuzza tells him about his wife and her lover. When Turiddu comes out of church, Alfio challenges him to fight with knives. Turiddu calls across the stage to tell his mother he is going away for a moment. The next thing Santuzza hears is the moan of the women outside saying Turiddu has been murdered.

Cellini
See *Benvenuto Cellini*

Cenerentola, La
(Cinderella)
COMP.: G. Rossini
LIBR.: J. Ferretti
From a libretto for Isouard's
  opera *Cendrillon*

2 *acts*
Rome, 25 January 1817
London, 1820
New York, 1826
Covent Garden, 1830

CAST

Don Ramiro, *Prince of Salerno*	T	Thisbe, *another daughter*	MS
Dandini, *his valet*	B	Angelina, *his step-daughter,*	
Don Magnifico, *Baron Mountflagon*	B	*called Cinderella*	C
Clorinda, *his daughter*	S	Alidoro, *a philosopher*	B

SYNOPSIS

I. The prince, disguising himself as his own valet, pays a personal visit to the baron's house in order to see the available daughters with his own eyes. Quickly he falls in love with Cinderella. Her sisters have planned to attend the prince's ball, but they will not permit Cinderella, who is little more than a servant to them, to go with them. Alidoro, who represents the fairy godmother, comes to her aid. She prepares to attend as an unknown lady.

II. Dandini, dressed up as the prince, falls in love with Cinderella but she politely refuses him saying she loves his servant, who is really the disguised prince. She identifies herself to him by giving him one of a pair of bracelets.

At home later, the sisters voice their suspicions. Alidoro conjures a storm to drive the unsuspecting prince into their house. During this uncomfortable visit, the prince notices the matching bracelet on Cinderella's arm. They recognize each other. Much to the amazement of the haughty sisters, their underling goes off to the palace with the prince to be married.

Céphale et Procris
COMP.: A. Grétry
LIBR.: J. Marmontel

3 *acts*
Versailles, 30 December 1773
Brussels, 1930

Chalet, Le
COMP.: A. Adam
LIBR.: Scribe and Mélesville

1 *act*
Comique, 25 September 1834
New York, 1836
London, 1845

Charles the Fifth
See *Karl V*

Cheval de Bronze, Le
COMP.: F. Auber
LIBR.: A. Scribe

3 *acts*
Comique, 23 March 1835
Covent Garden, 1835
New York, 1837

Children of Don
See *Cauldron of Anwyn*

Choëphores
COMP.: D. Milhaud
LIBR.: P. Claudel
Translated from Aeschylus

Tragedy in 1 *act*
Paris (Concert), 15 June 1919
Brussels (Stage), 27 March 1935

CAST

Electre, *daughter of Clytemnestre*	S	Solo Leaders *from the chorus*	S, C
Oreste, *her brother*	Bar	Chorus	

NOTE

This is the second part of the *Orestie* Trilogy. The first part is *Agamemnon*, the third is *Eumenides*.

Christophe Colomb
COMP.: D. Milhaud
LIBR.: P. Claudel

2 *parts*, 27 *scenes*
Berlin, 5 May 1930
London (Concert), 1937
New York (Concert), 1952

CAST

Isabella, *queen of Spain*	S	Master of Ceremonies	T
Christopher Columbus I,		Cook	T
as an old man	Bar	King of Spain	B
Christopher Columbus II,		Commandant	B
as a young man	Bar	Messenger	Bar
Narrator	Spkr	Sultan Miramolin	T
Counsel for the Prosecution	Spkr	Officer, Counsel, Creditors, People, and	
Representative of the Sailors	Spkr	Cinematic Effects	
Major-domo	T		

SYNOPSIS

1. This is the book of the life of Columbus. The Narrator explains this, and shows us in cinema the position of the earth, spinning in space, and a dove. He summons the old man to consider his past life and allow the judgment of posterity upon it.

The young queen was given a dove in a cage by the Sultan Miramolin. She let it go free, and it flew over the seas. (Colombe, in French, is Dove).

Columbus conquers the sea. But his creditors dog him, making his life miserable. He goes to the court for help. The queen arranges to support an expedition for him, urged by the vision (in cinema) of the glories of Spain and of the New World. Columbus fits out three ships, and in spite of the crowd of the evil demons of discovery, sets sail on his voyage.

II. The king listens to hostile advice about his navigator and the new troubles that come with the gold of the New World. Columbus is put in chains aboard ship. The Cook tries to comfort him, but he remembers all the misfortunes he has allowed to happen.

The queen is dead. Columbus is alone now, defenseless against creditors. Suddenly we are in Paradise with the queen and all her past life present. She waits for Columbus to join her, but he cannot. She prays for Columbus.

Le Cid   4 *acts*
COMP.: J. Massenet   Opéra, 30 November 1885
LIBR.: d'Ennery, Gallet, Blau   New Orleans, 1890
From Corneille's play

Cinderella
See *Cenerentola, La*

Clandestine Marriage, The
See *Matrimonio Segreto, Il*

Clemenza di Tito, La   2 *acts*
(*The Clemency of Titus*)   Prague, 6 September 1791
COMP.: W. A. Mozart   London, 27 March 1806
LIBR.: C. Mazzolà   Falmouth, England, 1930
From a play by Metastasio

CAST

Titus, *emperor of Rome*	T	Annius, *young patrician*	MS
Vitellia, *daughter of the deposed emperor*	S	Servilia, *Sextus' sister*	S
Sextus, *young patrician*	C	Publius, *captain of the guard*	B

SYNOPSIS

I. To prevent Titus from marrying her rival Berenice, Vitellia conspires with Sextus against him. Titus, however, changes his mind and plans to marry Servilia instead. But she is in love with Annius. The good Titus dislikes breaking up other people's pleasures; he therefore again changes his mind and decides to marry Vitellia. This chain of events prevents the treacherous murder Vitellia had arranged.

II. For his part in the plotting, Sextus has been condemned to death. At the last possible moment Vitellia tells all. Titus, the example of imperial clemency, pardons both.

NOTES

This opera was commissioned for the coronation of Leopold II, as King of Bohemia. It was composed and performed within eighteen days of the commission. The 1806 performance in London was the first production of any Mozart opera in England.

Cleopatra's Night   2 *acts*
COMP.: H. Hadley   Metropolitan, 31 June 1920
LIBR.: A. Pollock
From a story by Th. Gautier

Cloak, The
See *Tabarro, Il*

Coachman of Longjumeau, The
See *Postillion de Longjumeau. Le*

Cock of Gold, The
See *Coq d'Or, Le*

Columbus
See *Christophe Colomb*
See also *Cristoforo Columbo*

Combattimento di Tancredi e Clorinda, Il

	Dramatic Cantata
COMP.: C. Monteverdi	Venice, 1624
From Tasso's *Gerusalemme Liberata*	Published, 1638

NOTES

This work was written for pantomime by actors on the stage while singers sang the roles at one side. For orchestra Monteverdi used a string quartet, double bass and harpsichord.

Consul, The   3 *acts*

COMP.: G.-C. Menotti	Philadelphia, 1 March 1950
LIBR.: By the composer	London, 1951
	La Scala, 1951

CAST

John Sorel	Bar	Foreign Woman	S
Magda Sorel, *his wife*	S	Anna Gomez	S
Mother	C	Vera Boronel	C
Secret Police Agent	B	Nika Magadoff, *magician*	T
Plainclothes Men (2)	Mute	Assan, *Sorel's friend*	Bar
Secretary	MS	Voice on the Record	S
Mr. Kofner	BBar		

SYNOPSIS

I. Sorel has been wounded while working for the underground. The police find nothing to incriminate him in his house. Magda tries to see the consul for help but an endless chain of bureaucratic delays prevents this.

II. A month later she gets word from her husband that she must get out of the country. At the consulate the wall of bureaucratic delays has cracked enough so that she is just about to see the consul. But the person who has been seeing him just before her is the Secret Police Agent.

III. Back at the apartment, she sends another message to her husband via Assan. She is there but a moment when John bursts in, pursued by the secret police. She leaves for a moment. When she returns, no one is there. The phone is ringing but she does not answer. She turns on the gas and waits for death.

Contes d'Hoffmann, Les   *Prologue, 3 acts, Epilogue*
(*The Tales of Hoffmann*)   Comique, 10 February 1881
COMP.: J. Offenbach   New York, 1882
LIBR.: Barbier   London, 1907
From a play by Barbier and Carré   Metropolitan, 1913

THE OPERAS

Lindorf, *Councillor of Nurnberg**	B	Giulietta, *courtesan*	S
Andrès, *Stella's servant*	T	Schlemil, *her lover*	B
Hermann, *a student*	Bar	Dapertutto, *a sorcerer**	Bar
Nathanael, *a student*	T	Pittichinaccio, *Giulietta's admirer*	T
Luther, *innkeeper*	Bar	Antonia, *singer*	S
Hoffmann, *poet*	T	Crespel, *her father,*	
Nicklausse, *his muse in disguise*	MS	*Councillor of Munich*	Bar
Spalanzani, *inventor of*		Frantz, *his servant*	T
strange machines	T	Dr. Miracle, *doctor**	Bar
Cochenille, *his servant*	T	Antonia's Mother's Voice	MS
Coppelius, *scientist,*		Stella, *opera singer*	S
*Spalanzani's rival**	Bar	Muse of Poetry	S
Olympia, *a mechanical doll*	S		

* Played by the same man

MUSICAL HIGHLIGHTS

ACT I. Doll's Song *Les Oiseaux dans la Charmille* (The birds in the bushes), Olympia

ACT II. Barcarolle *Belle nuit, O nuit d'amour* (Beauteous night, O night of love), Giulietta and Nicklausse

Aria *Scintille, Diamant* (Sparkle, Diamond), Dapertutto

SYNOPSIS

PROLOGUE. Hoffmann has been going through an affair with Stella. Lindorf has been discussing it with the others when the poet enters the tavern. At their insistence, he agrees to tell the stories of his three great loves.

I. *Olympia.* Hoffmann made the mistake of falling in love with a mechanical doll. She nearly danced him to death, and sang his ears off. Only the fury of her creator's rival, Coppelius, smashing the machine to bits, released Hoffmann from his trance.

II. *Giulietta.* Hoffmann was determined not to fall in love, but Dapertutto provided the girl with a magic diamond with which to trap him. She stole his shadow from him with a magic mirror and left him to fight with one Schlemil, who had been likewise bewitched. Hoffmann won, but Giulietta had disappeared.

III. *Antonia.* He loved the consumptive Antonia. He discovered that a Doctor Miracle was treating her for her disease by making her sing, which would most certainly contribute to her death. Hoffmann finds her dead from frantic singing. He wants to call a doctor, but Dr. Miracle answers the call.

EPILOGUE. Hoffmann finishes his story and his wine. He is in love with Stella, but when she comes in he is dead drunk, face on the table. She tosses a flower toward him and leaves with Lindorf.

NOTES

Offenbach died only four months before the opening. The orchestration was completed by Ernest Guiraud.

Coq d'Or, Le
(*The Golden Cockerel*)
COMP.: N. Rimsky-Korsakov
LIBR.: V. Bielsky
From Pushkin

3 *acts*
Moscow, 7 October 1907
Drury Lane, 1914
Metropolitan, 1918

CAST

King Dodon	B	Amelfa, *royal housekeeper*	C
Prince Guidon	T	Astrologer	T
Prince Afron	Bar	Queen of Shemakha	S
General Polkan	B	The Golden Cockerel	S

SYNOPSIS

I. To protect the kingdom, the royal astrologer provides his king with a Golden Cockerel which will warn of any danger. With such a safety, the king and all his entourage fall asleep. When the cock crows, the king wakes enough to send out an army, then falls asleep again. It crows again. This time the king wearily puts on his rusty armor.

II. He finds his sons dead. He finds the Queen of Shemakha. The cock crows and crows but the king falls in love with her. Heedless of warning he takes her back to his kingdom.

III. The astrologer demands the Queen of Shemakha as payment for the Golden Cockerel. The king strikes him dead. At this the cock flies through the air and kills the king. Everything goes black. When light returns the queen and the cock have disappeared.

Corregidor, Der

(*The Magistrate*)
COMP.: H. Wolf
LIBR.: Rosa Mayreder-Obermeyer
From a story by de Alarcon

4 *acts*
Mannheim, 7 June 1896
London, 1934
New York (Concert), 1959

CAST

Don Eugenio de Zuniga, *Magistrate*	T	Pedro, *his secretary*	T
Doña Mercedes, *his wife*	S	Manuela, *maid*	MS
Repela, *his valet*	B	Tonuelo, *court messenger*	B
Tio Lucas, *a miller*	Bar	A Neighbour	T
Frasquita, *his wife*	MS	Duenna, *to Doña Mercedes*	MS
Juan Lopez, *mayor*	B		

SYNOPSIS

I. Frasquita, to win favor for her nephew, dances with the magistrate. To his misfortune he falls in love with her. This embarrassment causes him to swear revenge on her husband, Tio Lucas.

II. Tio is arrested. The magistrate appears at Frasquita's door all wet, as if he had fallen in the river. She lets him stay in the house while she goes to find out what happened to her husband. The magistrate hangs up his wet clothes and crawls into bed.

III. Tio escapes his guards and comes home to find the strange clothes hanging there and the magistrate, seen through the keyhole, in his own bed. In revenge he dresses in the now dry clothes and goes after Doña Mercedes. Unaware of this, the magistrate puts on Tio's clothes.

IV. All is soon explained. The miller and the magistrate both receive accidental but significant beatings, and the marriages remain firm as rocks.

Cosa Rara, Una

COMP.: V. Martin Y Soler
LIBR.: L. da Ponte

2 *acts*
Vienna, 17 November 1786
Halle, 1921
Barcelona, 1936

Mozart quotes from this opera in his own *Don Giovanni*. The work was very popular in its time and is showing some signs of life even now.

Così fan Tutte
COMP.: W. A. Mozart
LIBR.: L. da Ponte

Comedy in 2 acts
Vienna, 26 January 1790
London, 1811
Metropolitan, 1922

CAST

Fiordiligi	S	Guglielmo, *Fiordiligi's fiancé*	B
Dorabella, *her sister*	S	Don Alfonso	Bar
Ferrando, *Dorabella's fiancé*	T	Despina, *the sisters' maid*	S

SYNOPSIS

I. The two swains make a bet with Don Alfonso that their fiancées are trustworthy even to the point that they could not be swayed by their own lovers disguised as strangers. To test it, Alfonso announces to the girls that the boys must go off to war. The parting, though full of sentiment, fails to disturb Alfonso in his certainty.

He introduces them to the two "strangers." Wooing begins, but the girls are not moved. The strangers try poison as a demonstration of their devotion. But Despina, disguised as a doctor, brings them back to life with mesmerism. Still the girls remain constant to their departed lovers.

II. Despina, a bit bored perhaps, convinces the girls there's no harm in giving in just a little. The serenading is therefore more successful, and Guglielmo manages to exchange a locket with Dorabella for a medallion containing Ferrando's picture. This astounds Ferrando. They carry their masquerade to the point that the girls finally agree to marry the two strangers. At the last moment, the strangers disclose their real identities. But love has short memory, and all forgive each other the divergences.

Cricket on the Hearth, The
See *Heimchen am Herd, Das*

Cristoforo Columbo
COMP.: A. Franchetti
LIBR.: L. Illica

4 acts and Epilogue
Genoa, 6 October 1892
Buenos Aires, 1902
Philadelphia, 1913

This opera was written to celebrate the 400th anniversary of the discovery of America.

Cyrano de Bergerac
COMP.: W. Damrosch
LIBR.: W. J. Henderson
From Rostand's play

4 acts
Metropolitan, 27 February 1913

Czar and Carpenter
See *Zar und Zimmerman*

Czar's Bride
See *Tsar's Bride, The*

Dafne
COMP.: M. da Gagliano
LIBR.: O. Rinuccini

Mantua, January 1608
Florence, 1610
Moscow, 1911

Dafne

COMP.: J. Peri
LIBR.: O. Rinuccini

Prologue & 6 scenes
Florence, 1597

The first opera. The production may have been a cooperative affair. Caccini and Jacopo Corsi also wrote music for certain parts of the libretto; in fact the only remaining fragments are by Corsi, in whose house this work was first performed.

Dafne

COMP.: H. Schütz
LIBR.: Translated by Opitz
From Rinuccini's libretto

Torgau, 23 April 1627

This was the first German opera, written to celebrate the wedding of Princess Sophie of Saxony to George, Landgrave of Hesse. The music has been lost.

Dalibor

COMP.: B. Smetana
LIBR.: J. Wenzig

Tragedy in 3 acts
Prague, 16 May 1868
Vienna, 1892
Berlin, 1940

CAST

Vladislav, *king of Bohemia*	Bar	Milada	S
Dalibor, *knight*	T	Jitka	S
Budivoj, *captain of the guard*	Bar	Zdenek's Ghost	
Benes, *jailer*	B	Nobles, Soldiers, Men and Women	
Vitek, *Dalibor's squire*	T		

SYNOPSIS

I. In revenge for the death of his friend Zdenek, Dalibor killed Milada's brother. His own words of defense impress the bereaved lady, but the king condemns him to life imprisonment.

II. Milada finds her way into the jail, disguised as a boy. She searches for Dalibor and asks his pardon for her accusation which got him into prison.

III. There is an attempt to free Dalibor, but it fails. To prevent further attacks the prisoner is condemned to die. Milada joins the warriors to help in storming the castle, but in the second successful attempt she is wounded. Dalibor himself carries her out, but stabs himself when the king's troops surround him.

Dame Blanche, La

COMP.: F. Boieldieu
LIBR.: E. Scribe
From Scott's *Guy Mannering* and
The Monastery

3 acts
Comique, 10 December 1825
Drury Lane, 1826
New York, 1827
Metropolitan, 1904

CAST

Gaveston	B	Jenny, *his wife*	S
Anna, *his ward*	S	Marguerite, *old servant*	S
Georges Brown, *an English officer*	T	Gabriel, *Dickson's man*	B
Dickson, *tenant*	T	MacIrton, *Justice of the Peace*	B

SYNOPSIS

I. Poor Dickson has been summoned to appear for judgment before the ghost of the White Lady, who protects innocent females from false-hearted suitors. Georges offers to go in his place.

II. The castle is up for auction. Anna has been acting the part of the White Lady's ghost in order to keep the place out of Gaveston's hands. When Georges appears instead of Dickson she recognizes him as a soldier whose life she once saved. When the auction takes place, Georges bids for the castle, and with Anna's spurring, wins it with a tremendously high bid.

III. It turns out that he is heir of the castle anyway. But to pay the large sum he bid for it, the White Lady conveniently finds a chest full of money.

Damnation de Faust, La

COMP.: H. Berlioz
LIBR.: Berlioz, Girard, Gandonnière

Dramatic Legend in 4 parts
Opéra (Concert), 6 December 1846
Drury Lane (in part), 1847
Manchester (Complete), 1880
New York, 1880

CAST

Marguerite	S	Brander	B
Faust	T	Students, Soldiers, Citizens,	
Méphistophélès	B	Men and Women, Fairies	

SYNOPSIS

I. Faust contemplates nature and the solitude of intelligence.

II. Faust laments his existence. He considers the church, but Mephisto tempts him to a life of pleasure. Together they visit a beer hall and sing with the students and soldiers, then the banks of the Elbe where all is peace and the air is as perfume.

III. Faust woos Marguerite.

IV. Marguerite has been condemned to death. Faust sees her as in a vision, carried into hell. He gives his own soul to Mephisto for her salvation. In an Epilogue, the spirits of hell seize him while the spirits of heaven gently take her up among the seraphim.

NOTE

The work was first adapted for stage by Raoul Gunsbourg, for a production at Monte Carlo, 18 February 1893. The first production at the Metropolitan was in 1906.

Danae

See *Liebe der Danae, Die*

Dantons Tod

(*Danton's Death*)
COMP.: Gottfried von Einem
LIBR.: B. Blacher
From the play by Büchner

2 acts, 6 scenes
Salzburg, 6 August 1947

CAST

Georg Danton	Bar	Young Man	T
Camille Desmoulins	T	Two Hangmen	T
Hérault de Séchelles	T	Julie, *Danton's wife*	MS
Robespierre	T	Lucile, *Desmoulins' wife*	S
St. Just	B	Lady	S
Herrmann	Bar	A Wife	C
Simon	B		

The story of the death of Georges Danton, French revolutionist, and the intrigues of Robespierre.

Daphne
See *Dafne*

Daphne   1 *act*
COMP.: R. Strauss   Dresden, 15 October 1938
LIBR.: J. Gregor   La Scala, 1942
                                           Buenos Aires, 1948

CAST

Peneios, *fisherman*	B	Apollo	T
Gaea, *his wife*	C	Four Shepherds	T, Bar, B, B
Daphne, *their daughter*	S	Two maids	S
Leukippos, *shepherd*	T		

SYNOPSIS

Leukippos loves Daphne, but she loves nature, not Leukippos. Peneios has long been convinced that the gods will once again walk the earth. One day one does; Apollo comes to him dressed as a shepherd.

The people ridicule Peneios for thinking this young man is a god. He calls his daughter to see. She falls in love with Apollo, but tears herself away because she does not want love.

There is a feast at which Leukippos makes advances toward Daphne. Apollo, powerful and jealous, lets fly with a thunderclap, then identifies himself to her. She will have neither of them. Apollo kills Leukippos, but in remorse transforms the girl into a tree—the laurel.

Dardanus   *Prologue and 5 acts*
COMP.: J. P. Rameau   Opéra, 19 November 1739
LIBR.: C. L. de la Bruère   Staged in Algiers, 1934

Dark Waters
COMP.: E. Krenek   University of So. California, 1951

Daughter of the Regiment, The
See *Figlia del Reggimento, La*

David   5 *acts*, 12 *scenes*
COMP.: D. Milhaud   Jerusalem, 1 June 1954
LIBR.: A. Lunel

NOTES

This huge work was commissioned by the Koussevitzky Foundation and composed for the three thousandth anniversary of Israel.

Dead City, The
See *Tote Stadt, Die*

Debora e Jaele   *Tragedy in 3 acts*
COMP.: I. Pizzetti   La Scala, 16 December 1922
LIBR.: By the composer   Buenos Aires, 1923

CAST

Debora, *prophetess*	MS	Navi, *prince of Nephthali*	Bar
Jaele, *Hever's wife*	S	Barak, *Jewish commander*	B
Mara	MS	Azriel	T
Hever, *the Kenite, spy*	Bar	Shillem	T

Jesser	Bar	Piram	Bar
King Sisera	T	Jafia	T
Adonisedek	BBar	Enan, *the blind*	B

SYNOPSIS

I. The people clamor to Debora that Sisera has demolished Israel. They curse Jaele as his consort. Debora satisfies them with a promise of victory over the King through a woman.

II. Jaele goes to Sisera at Debora's bidding to betray the King and to save her own reputation with her people. But Sisera is a man worthy of love rather than hate. She cannot bring herself to stab him.

III. The Jews open the battle and are victorious. Sisera, in flight, goes to Jaele for safety. The Jews follow him there but when they enter her tent they find only his corpse. He has been slain by Jaele to protect him from their vengeance.

Déserteur, Le

3 *acts*

COMP.: P. Monsigny — Paris, 6 March 1769
LIBR.: J. M. Sedaine — London, 1773
New York, 1787

Deux Journées, Les

3 *acts*

(*The Two Days* or *The Water Carrier*) — Paris, 16 January 1800
COMP.: L. Cherubini — Covent Garden, 1801
LIBR.: J. N. Bouilly — New Orleans, 1811
New York, 1827

A favorite of Beethoven, Mendelssohn, and Spohr.

Devin du Village, Le

1 *act*

(*The Village Soothsayer*) — Fontainebleau, 18 October 1752
COMP.: J. J. Rousseau — Drury Lane, 1766
LIBR.: By the composer — New York, 1790

One of the first operas with spoken dialogue. It uses the same story as *Bastien und Bastienne*.

Dialogues des Carmélites, Les

3 *acts*, 12 *scenes*

COMP.: F. Poulenc — La Scala, 26 January 1957
LIBR.: G. Bernanos — San Francisco, 1957

CAST

Blanche	S	S. Mathilde	MS
Marquis de la Force, *her father*	Bar	Father Confessor	T
Le Chevalier, *his son*	T	First Officer	T
Mme. de Croissy,		Second Officer	Bar
prioress of the Convent	C	Jailer	Bar
Mme. Lidione, *the new prioress*	S	Thierry, *valet*	Bar
Mother Marie of the Incarnation	MS	M. Javelinot, *physician*	Bar
S. Constance of St. Denis	S	Nuns, Officials, Officers, Police,	
Mother Jeanne	C	Prisoners, Guards, Townspeople	

NOTE

The story recalls the martyrdom of the Carmelite Nuns.

Dido and Aeneas

COMP.: H. Purcell
LIBR.: N. Tate

Prologue and 3 acts
Chelsea, London, ca. Christmas, 1689
New York, 1924
Florence, 1940

CAST

Dido, *queen of Carthage*	MS	Two witches	S
Aeneas	T	Spirit	S
Belinda, *Dido's lady in waiting*	S	Greek Sailor	T
Sorceress	MS	Courtiers, People, Witches, Sailors	
Two Women	S, MS		

SYNOPSIS

I. Dido laments her grief which she admits is caused by the offer of the love of Aeneas, the Trojan hero. Belinda and the chorus urge her to put away her troubles and accept his love. But there is a sorceress elsewhere in Carthage, plotting the destruction of the city.
II. Dido and Aeneas are enjoying a hunt together when a violent storm sends all but the warrior to shelter. When he is alone, he sees the image of Mercury who warns him to leave Carthage and to go found a great city.
III. The fleet prepares to leave, at which the sorceress rejoices. But the man weakened by love changes his mind and swears he will stay with Dido and risk the vengeance of the gods. This show of indecision is abhorrent to her—if he could have left her before, his promise to remain can be of little worth. He must leave. She turns away from him and prepares to die with the famous lament *When I am Laid in Earth.*

Dimitri

See *Dmitrij*
See also *Boris Godunov*

Dinorah

COMP.: G. Meyerbeer
LIBR.: Barbier and Carré

3 acts
Comique, 4 April 1859
Covent Garden, 1859
New York, 1862
Metropolitan, 1892

CAST

Dinorah, *peasant girl*	S	Huntsman	B
Hoël, *goatherd*	Bar	Harvester	T
Corentino, *bagpiper*	T	Goatherds (*two*)	S, C

Djamileh

COMP.: G. Bizet
LIBR.: L. Gallet
From *Namouna*, by de Musset

I act
Comique, 22 May 1872
Covent Garden, 1893
Boston, 1913

CAST

Djamileh, *a slave*	MS	Splendiano, *his secretary*	T
Haroun, *prince*	T	A Slave Merchant	

SYNOPSIS

Djamileh has fallen in love with her master, but he has become tired of her and shows signs of wanting to shop around for another. She arranges with Splendiano to win the prince back or to marry Splendiano instead.

The slave merchant shows the prince his wares. One of them is Djamileh, who in disguise dances and enthralls the prince. He buys her. When he discovers her trick his love is again renewed.

Dmitrij

COMP.: A. Dvořák
LIBR.: M. Červinková-Riegrová

4 *acts*

Prague, 8 October 1882
Vienna, 1892

CAST

Dmitrij, *pretender to the throne*	T	Xenia, *daughter of Tsar Boris*	S
Marfa, *Tsar Ivan's widow*		Shuisky, *prince*	
Marina	S		

NOTE

This is the story of the brief appearance of Dimitri who rode into power at the death of Boris Godunov, and was himself deposed by the accession of Shuisky. The more famous treatment is the opera *Boris Godunov*. Another opera on the same subject (called *Dimitri*) was produced by V. de Joncières in Paris in 1876.

Doctor Faust

See *Doktor Faust*

Docteur Miracle, Le

Offenbach offered a prize for an opera to be written to this libretto. Both Georges Bizet and Alexandre Lecocq submitted works in 1857 and shared the prize.

Doktor Faust

COMP.: F. Busoni
LIBR.: By the Composer
From the ancient puppet play

6 *Tableaux*

Dresden, 21 May 1925
London (Concert), 1937
Florence, 1942

CAST

Doctor Faust	Bar	Jurist	B
Wagner, *his attendant*	Bar	Doctor of Natural History	Bar
Mephistopheles	T	Four Students from Wittenberg	T(4)
Duke of Parma	T	Gravis, *spirit voice*	B
Duchess of Parma	S	Levis, *spirit voice*	B
Master of Ceremonies	B	Asmodus, *spirit voice*	Bar
Brother of the Girl, *a soldier*	Bar	Beelzebub, *spirit voice*	T
Lieutenant	T	Megärus, *spirit voice*	T
Three students from Krakov	T, B, B	Church goers, Soldiers, Courtiers,	
Theologian	B	Hunters, Students, Countrypeople	

NOTES

This opera was taken not from Goethe but from the more ancient puppet play. Mephisto appears as a Man in Black, Monk, Herald, Chaplain, Courier, Watchman, and a voice. The work was completed by Jarnach.

Doktor Faust

COMP.: I. Walter
LIBR.: H. Schmieder
From Goethe

Tragedy in 4 *acts*

Bremen, 28 December 1797
Regensburg (*rev.*), 1819

This is the earliest opera on the subject of Faust.

Doktor und Apotheker
(Doctor and Apothecary)
COMP.: K. von Dittersdorf
LIBR.: G. Stephanie

2 *acts*
Vienna, 11 July 1786
London, 1788
Boston, 1795

Don Carlos
COMP.: G. Verdi
LIBR.: Méry and du Locle
From Schiller

Tragedy in 5 acts
Opéra, 11 March 1867
Covent Garden, 1867
New York, 1877

CAST

Elisabeth de Valois, *queen of Spain*	S	Monk	B
Princess Eboli, *her lady-in-waiting*	MS	Tebaldo, *Elisabeth's page*	S
Don Carlos, *heir to the throne*	T	Count Lerma	T
Rodrigo, *marquis of Poia*	Bar	Royal Herald	T
Filippo II, *king of Spain*	B	Heavenly Voice	S
Grand Inquisitor	B		

SYNOPSIS

I. Don Carlos, betrothed as a condition of peace to Elisabeth of France, falls in love with her. He cannot have her, however, since the king of Spain himself asks her hand to end the war with France.

II. Carlos arranges an interview with her when she has become his new stepmother, but she can no longer accept his vehement love. At this time in the policies of the nation, Rodrigo advises the king it would be wise to ease his repressions in Flanders lest he become infamous. In turn the king warns Rodrigo of his personal liabilities with the Inquisition.

III. Eboli makes an attempt to win Don Carlos' love. When she fails she threatens trouble for him. But he courts trouble himself when at a ceremony of the death of Flemish heretics he openly opposes the king, drawing his sword. Only Rodrigo's intervention prevents serious trouble.

IV. The Grand Inquisitor demands punishment for Rodrigo. The king, at Eboli's suggestion, has searched for and found a picture of Don Carlos in the Queen's possession. Carlos is sent to prison for this. He speaks there with Rodrigo, but an assassin puts an end to Rodrigo's life. Eboli stirs the people to riot to free Carlos.

V. Carlos meets Elisabeth for a short moment in secret before the emperor's tomb. There the king and the Inquisition capture them, but a voice from the tomb stops them and ushers Carlos into the sanctuary.

NOTES

The five act structure of the opera was required by the conditions of its production at the Opéra. Verdi had such differences with the management in Paris that it affected the rest of his relations with that house (see *Aida*).

Don César de Bazan
COMP.: J. Massenet
LIBR.: d'Ennery and Chantepie
Massenet's second opera.

3 *acts*
Comique, 30 November 1872
Vienna, 1874

Don Giovanni
COMP.: W. A. Mozart
LIBR.: L. da Ponte
From a libretto by Bertati.

Comedy in 2 acts
Prague, 29 October 1787
London, 1817
Philadelphia, 1818

THE OPERAS

CAST

Leporello, *Don Giovanni's servant*	B	Donna Elvira, *a lady of Burgos*		S
Donna Anna, *Don Ottavio's fiancée*	S	Zerlina, *Masetto's fiancée, peasant*		S
Don Giovanni, *a noble libertine*	Bar	Masetto, *a peasant*		B
Commendatore, *Donna Anna's father*	B	Peasants and Invisible Demons		
Don Ottavio, *Donna Anna's betrothed*	T			

MUSICAL HIGHLIGHTS

ACT I. Aria *Notte e giorno faticar* (That's a servant's life indeed), Leporello

The Catalog *Madamina*, Leporello

Aria *Ho capito, signor si* (Don't mistake me, signor, don't), Masetto

Duet *Là ci darem la mano* (Do put your hand in my hand), Don Giovanni and Zerlina

Aria *Fuggi il traditore* (Beware that traitor), Donna Elvira

Quartet *Non ti fidar o misera* (Do not trust yourself to him), Donna Elvira, Donna Anna, Don Giovanni, Don Ottavio

Aria *Or sai chi l'onore* (I will have vengeance), Donna Anna

Aria *Dalla sua pace* (She is the measure), Ottavio

Aria *Finch' han dal vino* (Song, women, wine), Don Giovanni

Aria *Batti, batti O bel Masetto* (Scold me, scold me, dear Masetto), Zerlina

The *Menuet*

Trio of the Masks *Protegga il giusto cielo* (Protect us, in the shadows), Elvira, Anna, Don Ottavio

ACT II. Trio *Ah taci, ingiusto core* (Ah, silence, unworthy heart) Donna Elvira, Don Giovanni, Leporello

Serenade *Deh vieni alla finestra* (Look down from your window), Don Giovanni

Aria *Vedrai, carino* (I'm here, my dearest), Zerlina

Aria *Il mio tesoro intanto* (Here is my treasure beloved), Don Ottavio

Aria *Mi tradì quel alma ingrata* (He betrayed me with his attentions), Donna Elvira

Duet *O statua gentilissima* (O Gentlest statue), Leporello and Don Giovanni

Aria *Non mi dir* (Don't tell me), Donna Anna

SYNOPSIS

I. Don Giovanni, who according to Leporello's catalog of affairs has scandalously betrayed some two thousand innocent women, is still busy knocking at the heart of Donna Anna when her father surprises them, challenges the interloper, and is unfortunately killed. Don Ottavio swears to avenge the death of his fiancée's father.

Again on the prowl, Don Giovanni comes upon a band of peasants celebrating a betrothal. He interjects himself here, too, making overtures for the girl's love himself. Masetto threatens revenge but it is Donna Elvira, bitter from her own experience, who comes upon the scene with warning for the innocent Zerlina. Donna Anna, in turn, hearing the noble libertine's voice recognizes her father's murderer.

But Zerlina was not really so completely innocent. She spends a little time in the garden with her lover Masetto, explaining that she loves him and so forth. Then she goes to the ball as she had intended. There three masked ones dance with the others. They are Elvira, Anna, and Ottavio looking for an opportunity for revenge. Don Giovanni manages to remain safe, however, and to woo Zerlina in the bargain.

II. While Don Giovanni, dressed as his own servant, sings a serenade below Zerlina's window, Masetto and his friends come to murder the man. Since they don't recognize him, he sends them off various ways and drubs Masetto privately himself. Leporello, in his master's clothes, very nearly gets the hanging. He escapes, however, and meets Don Giovanni in a convenient churchyard. There they are startled to see the statue of the murdered Commendatore who speaks to them in sepulchral tones. The Don makes Leporello issue the stone image an invitation to visit him. To his horror, during preparations for a supper before Donna Anna's marriage, the statue does appear. Pits of flames open under his feet and Don Giovanni is carried off to hell.

NOTES

This masterpiece was commissioned by the Prague Opera. They say Mozart was enjoying a party the night before the opening when someone reminded him that there was no overture yet. He thereupon excused himself and wrote, with his wife's company to keep him at it, the whole curtain piece. There is also a fairly probable story that he was unsatisfied with the way the Zerlina screamed during rehearsals. He is said to have sneaked back to the wings and to have pinched her at just the right time, getting precisely the effect he wanted. But this has been told of many others.

The opera first appeared in the United States under the title *The Libertine*.

Don Juan

Mozart's opera was certainly not the only successful work on the subject. There were plays such as: *El Burlador de Seville* (Tirso de Molina, 1571–1641), *Le Festin de Pierre* (Molière, 1665, introducing Donna Elvira as a character), *The Libertine* (Shadwell, 1676), *Don Giovanni Tenorio* (Goldoni, 1736), and an opera by Gazzanigo with libretto by Bertati, which was the actual source of Mozart's and da Ponte's libretto.

Don Juan de Mañara

	4 *acts*
COMP.: E. Goossens, III	Covent Garden, 24 June 1937
LIBR.: A. Bennett	
(See also *Ombra di Don Giovanni*)	

Don Pasquale

	Comedy in 3 acts
COMP.: G. Donizetti	Paris, 3 January 1843
LIBR.: G. Ruffini	London, 1843
From Anelli's *Ser Marcantonio*	New York, 1846

CAST

Don Pasquale, *an old bachelor*	B	Norina, *a young widow*	S
Doctor Malatesta, *his friend*	Bar	Notary	Bar
Ernesto, *his nephew*	T		

SYNOPSIS

I. Don Pasquale has forbidden Ernesto's love for Norina on pain of losing his inheritance. But he himself wishes to be married. His friend, Malatesta, engineers a plan by which a marriage is arranged for him with none other than Norina. Somehow this was to help relieve the bad situation with Ernesto, but Norina doesn't enjoy the idea at all.

II. Playing the shy bride, she does win over the old bachelor. But the moment the false contract has been signed, she changes her colors and suddenly appears as a veritable spitfire to Don Pasquale, demanding every conceivable change in his ways.

III. Finally Pasquale begs for Malatesta to get him off the hook by any possible means. By arranging for Ernesto to take over the difficult bride, everything works out to everyone's complete satisfaction.

Don Procopio 2 *acts*
  COMP.: G. Bizet Monte Carlo, 10 March 1906
  LIBR.: C. Cambiaggio Rome, 1908
    This work, very much in the style of Rossini, was not produced until well after Bizet's death. It was written in 1858.

Don Quichotte 5 *acts*
  (*Don Quixote*) Monte Carlo, 19 February 1910
  COMP.: J. Massenet London, 1912
  LIBR.: H. Cain New Orleans, 1912
  From Cervantes' novel Philadelphia, 1913

CAST

La Belle Dulcinée	C	Rodriguez, *a third*	T
Don Quichotte	B	Juan, *a fourth*	T
Sancho Panza, *his squire*	Bar	Two Servants	Bar
Pedro, *an admirer of Dulcinée*	S	Tenebrun, the Chief Bandit, Other	
Garcias, *another*	S	Bandits, Friends	

SYNOPSIS

    I. The insane Don serenades his paramour. She agrees to accept him if he will first recover a stolen necklace.

    II. He hunts the bandits. On the way to their hideout he fights the windmills thinking they are giants.

    III. He fights the bandits. They are about to kill him when his politeness wins them over. They give him the necklace he came for.

    IV. He returns victorious, claiming his bride. But she refuses to go along with it.

    V. Now an old man, he dies among his affectionate friends.

Don Rodrigue 5 *acts*
  COMP.: G. Bizet
  LIBR.: Gallet and Blau
    Never performed. Only vocal parts and a few sketches remain.

Don Sebastiano 5 *acts*
  COMP.: G. Donizetti Opéra, 13 November 1843
  LIBR.: A. E. Scribe New York, 1864

Double Trouble
  COMP.: R. Mohaupt Louisville, Ky., 4 December 1954
  LIBR.: Maren
  From Plautus' *Menaechmi*

Dragons du Villars, Les 3 *acts*
  (*Villar's Dragoons*) Paris, 19 September 1856
  COMP.: L. Maillart New Orleans, 1859
  LIBR.: Lockroy and Corman London, 1875

Dream, The
  See *Rêve, Le*

Dreigroschenoper, Die
(*The Threepenny Opera*)
COMP.: K. Weill
LIBR.: B. Brecht
From *The Beggar's Opera*, with added
poems by François Villon

Ballad Opera
Berlin, 31 August 1928
New York, 1933

This work is not merely a revision of the old *Beggar's Opera*, but a more bitter kind of parody of the same subjects. In an arrangement by Marc Blitzstein it has had a nearly continuous run in New York for several years.

Due Litiganti
See *Fra I Due Litiganti*

Duke Bluebeard's Castle
COMP.: B. Bartok
LIBR.: B. Balázs

1 *act*
Budapest, 24 May 1918
New York, 1952
London, 1953

CAST

Duke Bluebeard	B	Bard, *narrator*	Spkr
Judith, *his latest wife*	MS	Three former wives	Mute

SYNOPSIS

Judith has heard the stories. She wants to know what lies behind the row of closed doors in her husband's castle. She unlocks each one and sees various glorious treasures of his kingdom, all spattered with blood. Behind the sixth door she finds his former wives and lets them free. When they have gone she goes out through the last door, leaving him alone.

Dumb Girl of Portici, The
See *Masaniello*

Dylan
See *Cauldron of Anwyn*

Edgar
COMP.: G. Puccini
LIBR.: F. Fontana
From a story by de Musset

3 *acts*
La Scala, 21 April 1889
Ferrara (*rev.*), 1892
Buenos Aires, 1905

Originally in 4 acts, the opera was reduced to three for the performance in Ferrara.

Egyptian Helen, The
See *Aegyptische Helene, Die*

Elektra
COMP.: R. Strauss
LIBR.: H. von Hofmannsthal
From Sophocles

Tragedy in 1 *act*
Dresden, 25 January 1909
New York, 1910
Covent Garden, 1910
Metropolitan, 1932

CAST

Klytemnestra, *Agamemnon's widow*	MS	Aegisth, *Klytemnestra's lover*	T
Elektra, *her daughter*	S	Orest, *her son by Agamemnon*	Bar
Chrysothemis, *another daughter*	S	Tutor of Orest	B

48

Klytemnestra's Confidante	S	Old Servant	B
Klytemnestra's Trainbearer	S	Overseer	S
Young Servant	T	Five Maidservants	C, MS, MS, S, S

SYNOPSIS

Elektra lives for only one purpose, to join with their brother in killing their mother and Aegisth for the murder of their father Agamemnon. Chrysothemis fears this as Elektra tells her precisely what she intends to do.

Klytemnestra has heard that her son Orest is dead. But one day while Elektra digs like an animal in the yard a stranger bothers her with many questions. When he is sure of her he identifies himself as her living brother ready to avenge Agamemnon.

Orest goes inside and kills his mother. When Aegisth arrives, Elektra graciously ushers him in to see the corpse. He, too, is murdered. Chrysothemis is bewildered as Elektra, in frenzy, drops dead.

NOTE

Madame Schumann-Heink laboriously worked her way through the part of Klytemnestra, but after the production had taken place she objected that this wild music was too much for any singer.

Elisir d'Amore, L'
(*The Elixir of Love*)
COMP.: G. Donizetti
LIBR.: F. Romani

Comedy in 2 acts
Milan, 12 May 1832
London, 1836
New York, 1838
Metropolitan, 1904

CAST

Nemorino, *young peasant*	T	Dulcamara, *purveyor of magic potions*	B
Adina, *wealthy young landowner*	S	Gianetta, *peasant girl*	S
Belcore, *sergeant*	Bar		

SYNOPSIS

I. Nemorino has been courting Adina in such a shy way for so long that she complains there is no elixir of love. In desperation she accepts the proposal of Sergeant Belcore, who at least acts in a military way. One day Dulcamara arrives in town advertising, of all things, an elixir which is really nothing but cheap wine. Nemorino buys some and drinks himself to inebriation, thus making it possible to forget his difficulties in love. The Sergeant has been ordered to move to his next post. He wants an immediate marriage. Poor Nemorino is far too drunk to be able to prevent the preparations.

II. He has enlisted with Belcore to get money. He buys a second bottle of elixir and proceeds to break up the wedding ceremony with loud protestations of his prowess in war. Adina realizes the real cause of all this bombast. Secretly she buys back Nemorino's enlistment papers and then contrives to faint right into his arms. This turns the tables completely. Nemorino comes to his senses. Dulcamara unloads his entire cargo of elixir, and Sergeant Belcore goes off, like a true soldier, to war.

Emperor Jones, The
COMP.: L. Gruenberg
LIBR.: K. de Jaffa
From Eugene O'Neill's play

Prologue and 2 acts
Metropolitan, 7 January 1933
Amsterdam, 1934

THE OPERAS

CAST

Brutus Jones, *emperor*	Bar	Soldiers, Formless Fears, Jeff, Negro
Henry Smithers, *cockney trader*	T	Convicts, Prison Guard, Planters,
An old native woman	S	Auctioneer, Slaves
The Congo witch-doctor	dancer	

SYNOPSIS

The Negroes suffer under the harsh rule of their self-styled emperor. He has told them that nothing but a silver bullet can kill him. They plan his murder. Only Smithers, the cynical trader who profits from their misery, protects Jones. The boastful emperor professes not to be afraid of the plot, but very gradually, succumbing to the unrecognizable sounds and shadows of the jungle he disintegrates into a frantic animal. He remembers when he was a convict, he recalls slave auctions before the Civil War. Finally, in a paroxysm of fear intensified by the witch doctor, he kills himself with his own, prized, silver bullet.

Enfant et les Sortilèges, L'
(*The Child and Witchcraft*)
COMP.: M. Ravel
LIBR.: Colette

2 parts
Monte Carlo, 21 March 1925
San Francisco, 1930
Buenos Aires, 1944

CAST

Child	MS	Pâtre, *shepherd*	C
Mother	C	La Fauteuil, *armchair*	B
La Bergère, *Louis XV chair*	S	L'Horloge Comtoise,	
Chinese Cup	MC	*grandfather clock*	Bar
Fire*	S	La Théière, *tea pot*	T
Princess*	S	Arithmetic†, *a little old man*	T
Cat	MS	Tom Cat	Bar
La Libellule, *dragonfly*	MS	Tree	B
La Rossignol, *nightingale**	S	La Rainette†, *frog*	T
La Chauve-Souris, *bat*	S	Bench, Sofa, Ottoman, Wicker Chair,	
La Chouette, *little owl*	S	Numbers, Shepherds, Frogs, Animals,	
L'Écureuil, *squirrel*	MS	Trees	
Pastourelle, *shepherdess*	S		

* By the same soprano   † By the same tenor

SYNOPSIS

The child, in order that he may do his lessons for school, has been locked in his room. He hates it. Suddenly he gets up and proceeds to tear everything apart. When he has done with it, he sulks.

Then everything becomes alive. First the chairs, then the clock, the fire and so on. Each speaks of the hostility of the child, and its desire for revenge for what he has done. They drive the child to tears.

The tomcat, meanwhile, has met a sleek white cat. They sing a weird cat duet, then leap out the window into the wide outside world. Suddenly the child is out there, in the garden which he tore to shreds the day before. The animals berate him for their past wounds and frights. Finally, when he helps a little squirrel by binding up a wound, they relent and cease the torture.

NOTE

Colette originally intended this to be a ballet. Productions have been mounted in which the cast consists mainly of dancers.

THE OPERAS

Enfant Prodigue
See *Prodigal Son, The*

Engelbrekt   *4 acts*
COMP.: N. Berg   Stockholm, 21 September 1929
LIBR.: By the composer   Brunswick, Germany, 1933

Enrico Clifford   *3 acts*
COMP.: I. Albéniz   Barcelona, 8 May 1895
LIBR.: Arteaga y Pereira
Translated from an English libretto by Money-Coutts

Entführung aus dem Serail, Die   *Singspiel in 3 acts*
(*The Abduction from the Seraglio*)   Vienna, 16 July 1782
COMP.: W. A. Mozart   Brooklyn, New York, 1860
LIBR.: G. Stephanie   Covent Garden, 1827
C. F. Bretzner's libretto for Johann   Metropolitan, 1946
   André's opera *Belmonte et Constance*

CAST

Constance, *a Spanish lady*	S	Pasha Selim	Spkr
Blonde, *her English maid*	S	Osmin, *overseer of the harem*	B
Belmonte, *a Spanish nobleman*	T	Turkish Soldiers, Guards, Women	
Pedrillo, *his servant*	T		

MUSICAL HIGHLIGHTS

ACT I. Aria *Wer ein Liebchen hat gefunden* (When a maiden takes your fancy), Osmin
Aria *O wie ängstlich* (O such anguish). Belmonte
Trio *Marsch, Marsch, Marsch* (March, March, March), Pedrillo, Belmonte, Osmin
ACT II. Aria *Durch Zärtlichkeit* (With tenderness), Blonde
Duet *Traurigkeit ward mir zum Lose* (Sadness will e'er be my fate), Blonde and Constance
Aria *Martern aller Arten* (Tortures unabating), Constance
Aria *Welche Wonne, welche Lust* (O what happiness, what joy), Blonde
Duet *Vivat Bacchus* (Long live Bacchus), Osmin, Pedrillo
Serenade *Im Mohrenland* (In Moorish lands), Pedrillo

SYNOPSIS

I. Belmonte comes to the Pasha's house to rescue Constance, Blonde, and Pedrillo. Constance has managed, during her captivity, to remain faithful to Belmonte. In order to gain admittance, Belmonte has himself introduced to the Pasha as a famous architect.

II. The Pasha presses his love toward Constance, but she remains adamant. Meanwhile Pedrillo persuades Osmin, the Pasha's chief watchdog, to drink himself into a blind stupor so that they may escape.

III. They are on their way out when a wakeful guard catches them and the sobered Osmin confronts them with evident anticipation of revenge. When all are dragged before the Pasha for his judgement he turns out to be a kindly sort, willing to release them all. Before they leave they all join in a chorus in his praise.

NOTE

In 1779 Mozart worked on a Singspiel, *Zaïde*, which was very much like *Die Entführung aus dem Serail*, but was not finished.

51

Ernani   *Tragedy in 4 acts*
  COMP.: G. Verdi   Venice, 9 March 1844
  LIBR.: F. Piave   London, 1845
From a play by Victor Hugo   New York, 1847
                     Metropolitan, 1903

CAST

Don Carlos, *king of Castile*	Bar	Iago, *di Silva's squire*	B
Don Ruy Gomez di Silva, *grandee*	B	Elvira, *related to di Silva*	S
Ernani, *or John of Aragon,*		Giovanna, *her servant*	S
bandit chief	T	Bandits, Mountaineers, Ladies, Electors,	
Don Riccardo, *the king's squire*	T	Pages, Followers of Silva and of Carlos	

SYNOPSIS

I. Ernani and his men plan to carry off Elvira whom he loves. She is preparing, against her will, to marry the old di Silva. While Ernani is with her, Don Carlos comes to woo her. Silva discovers them all in this situation, but lets them go free when the king reveals who he is.

II. Ernani tries again, disguised as a monk. But when he sees Elvira this time in her bridal gown he throws off his disguise and offers his life to di Silva, since it is now worthless to himself. At this moment the king approaches to capture Ernani. Silva swears that though Ernani is his enemy he is also his guest, and that he must therefore protect him from the king's attack. The king takes Elvira as hostage to force di Silva to give up Ernani. Ernani then swears to give his life to di Silva whenever di Silva shall blow his hunting horn, but that first they should join forces to save the girl.

III. Hidden in the tomb of Charlemagne, the king listens while his enemies formulate their plot against him. The scene is interrupted by the entrance of a procession in the cathedral to proclaim Don Carlos emperor. As his very first imperial act, urged by Elvira, the new monarch pardons the conspirators and allows her marriage to Ernani.

IV. Di Silva gives Ernani brief happiness. As the man and wife stand on a parapet enjoying their peace together they hear the hunting horn. Ernani, remembering his promise, stabs himself to death.

Esther de Carpentras   *Comedy in 2 acts*
  COMP.: D. Milhaud   Comique, 1 February 1938
  LIBR.: A. Lunel

CAST

Hadassa (Esther)	MS	Vaucluse, *his valet*	T
Artaban, *financier*	T	Mask Seller	S
Barbacan, *concierge of the synagogue*	B	Jewish Doctor	Bar
Cacan, *a theater-lover*	Bar	Disguised Jews, Esther's Friends,	
Cardinal, *bishop of Carpentras*	T	Prelates, Children, Guards.	

Étoile du Nord, L'   3 *acts*
  COMP.: G. Meyerbeer   Comique, 16 February 1854
  LIBR.: E. Scribe   New Orleans, 1855
                     Covent Garden, 1855

In this opera Meyerbeer made use of six pieces of music from an earlier opera *Ein Feldlager in Schlesien*.

Eugene Onegin

3 *acts*

COMP.: P. Tchaikovsky
LIBR.: Tchaikovsky and Shilovsky
From Pushkin's poem

Moscow, 29 March 1879
London, 1892
Metropolitan, 1920

CAST

Madame Larina, *landowner*	MS	Prince Gremin, *a General*	B
Tatyana, *her daughter*	S	Captain	B
Olga, *another daughter*	C	Zaretsky	B
Filipievna, *Tatyana's nurse*	MS	M. Triquet	T
Lensky, *Olga's fiancé*	T	Reapers	
Eugene Onegin, *his friend*	Bar		

SYNOPSIS

I. Tatyana, who thinks it's a secret, is in love with Onegin. She writes him a long letter of love. But he discourages her; he would be a brother to her, not a lover.

II. At a ball he dances with Olga. At this, Lensky becomes jealous enough to challenge his friend. They duel in the dawn and Lensky dies.

III. Years later, Onegin sees Tatyana as the wife of Prince Gremin. He is in love with her at last. She weeps for him, but she leaves him and returns to her husband.

Eumenides

Tragedy

COMP.: D. Milhaud
LIBR.: P. Claudel
Translated from Aeschylus

Antwerp, 27 November 1927

CAST

Apollon	Bar	Ghost of Clytemnestra	MS
Oreste, *son of Agamemnon*	Bar	Statue of Athena, *triple voice*	S, MS, C
La Pythie	S	Erinnyes and People	

Euridice

Prologue and 6 Scenes

COMP.: J. Peri
LIBR.: O. Rinuccini

Florence, 6 October 1600
Milan, 1916
Munich, 1934

Not the first opera (see *Dafne*) but the earliest of which significant parts still exist. It was composed for the wedding festivities of Henry IV and Maria de Medici at the Pitti Palace in Florence. Peri sang Orpheus, and Corsi played harpsichord. Caccini wrote music for the same libretto at the same time, but his work was not produced until two years later (5 December 1602).

Euridice

See also *Orfeo*
See also *Orpheus*

Euryanthe

3 *acts*

COMP.: C. M. von Weber
LIBR.: H. von Chézy
From a story of de Nevers

Vienna, 25 October 1823
Covent Garden, 1833
Metropolitan, 1887

CAST

Euryanthe of Savoy	S	Count Lysiart of Forêt	Bar
Eglantine of Puiset	MS	Count Adolar of Nevers	T

Louis VI	B	Berthe	S
Rudolph, *knight*	T		

SYNOPSIS

I. Lysiart and Adolar have made a bet on Euryanthe's constancy. Meanwhile Eglantine, rival for Adolar's love, has discovered that Euryanthe has knowledge of the murder of Adolar's sister.

II. Lysiart, to win his bet, betrays this secret. Adolar sadly takes her into the forest where he intends to kill her and commit suicide.

III. The murder is prevented by a serpent, with whom Adolar fights. The king, hunting, finds Euryanthe there and hears her story. Adolar goes to watch the wedding of Lysiart and Eglantine. Suddenly the bride shouts to all who can hear of her treachery in fathoming Euryanthe's secret and thus causing her death. At this Adolar challenges Lysiart, but the king intervenes. Lysiart kills Eglantine, and is led off as Euryanthe returns to the repentant Adolar.

Evangeline
COMP.: O. Luening   New York, 5 May 1948

Fair at Sorotchinsk, The
	3 acts
COMP.: M. Mussorgsky	St. Petersburg (Concert), 1911
LIBR.: By the composer	St. Petersburg (Stage), 27 October 1917
From Gogol's *Evenings on a Farm*	Metropolitan, 1930

CAST

Tcherevik, *old country man*	B	Tcherevik's friend	B
Parassia, *his daughter*	S	Gypsy	B
Khivria, *his wife*	MS	Young Men and Women, Gypsies,	
Gritzko, *young country man*	T	Merchants, Cossacks, Jews	
Son of the Priest	T		

SYNOPSIS

I. Parassia, on her first visit to the fair, meets Gritzko who immediately asks for her hand in marriage. An old gypsy offers to help them win over her old parents.

II. The priest's son visits Khivria as her lover and hides while Tcherevik and his friends carouse. Suddenly they have hallucinations, thinking they see the devil disguised as a pig. In their confusion they discover the lover and burst into laughter.

III. Because of the discovery of the priest's son, Tcherevik now has a scandal to hold over his wife. Thus he can now freely give his approval to their daughter's marriage to Gritzko, without the wife's interference.

Fair Maid of Perth, The
See *Jolie Fille de Perth, La*

Fairy Queen, The
	Prologue and 5 acts
COMP.: H. Purcell	London, April 1692
LIBR.: E. Settle	Drury Lane, 1703
Adapted from Shakespeare's	Cambridge, 1920
Midsummer Night's Dream	

The score of this opera was lost in 1700, causing the famous advertisement to be published in the London *Gazette* offering a reward of twenty guineas. Evidence that advertising sometimes works may be read from the data of the Drury Lane performance. The first modern stage performance was in Cambridge, England, in 1920.

Falstaff

		Comedy in 3 acts	
COMP.: G. Verdi		La Scala, 9 February 1893	
LIBR.: A. Boito		Covent Garden, 1894	
From Shakespeare		New York, 1895	

CAST

Sir John Falstaff	Bar	Alice Ford, *Ford's wife*	S
Fenton, *young gentleman*	T	Nanetta, *her daughter Anne*	S
Ford, *wealthy burgher*	Bar	Mistress Page, *Meg*	MS
Doctor Caius	T	Dame Quickly	C
Bardolph, *Falstaff's friend*	T	Burghers, Streetfolk, Servants	
Pistol, *Falstaff's friend*	B		

SYNOPSIS

I. Falstaff is interested in both Mrs. Page and Mrs. Ford. He intends to woo them simultaneously. He sends, therefore, identical letters. Unfortunately the ladies read them to each other and plan to play a trick on him. Also his friends, Bardolph and Pistol, betray his plans to Mr. Ford so that Falstaff's secret is secret no more.

II. Dame Quickly delivers a message to the effect that Falstaff should visit Alice between two and three o'clock. Ford, in disguise, also arranges with Falstaff to have Falstaff woo Alice for him, her "suitor." Then, while the wooing is in progress, Ford comes with friends to surprise the interloper. The women hide Falstaff in a basket so that Ford catches only Nanetta and Fenton kissing behind a screen. When Ford has left the room, the good ladies empty the basket into the Thames.

III. Dame Quickly invites Falstaff to meet Alice a second time, this time disguised as a ghost in the forest. When he makes his appearance in that condition, they surround him with sprites, fairies, and phantasies until the trick finally dawns upon his mind. In a final burst of trickery and disguises, Fenton and Nanetta are blessed in betrothal by Ford who had intended not to do it, and all join in a fugue of the relish of jest.

NOTE

Verdi worked on this opera in privacy, telling his friends that he was not writing for a performance, but for himself. The same subject has been used by Salieri (Vienna, 1798), Balfe (London, 1838), Nicolai (see *Lustigen Weiber von Windsor*), Adam (Paris, 1856, in one act), and Vaughan Williams (see *Sir John in Love*).

Fanciulla del West, La

(*The Girl of the West*)		3 acts	
COMP.: G. Puccini		Metropolitan, 10 December 1910	
LIBR.: Civinini and Zangarini		Covent Garden, 1911	
From Belasco's play		La Scala, 1912	
The Girl of the Golden West			

CAST

Minnie, *saloon keeper*	S	Sonora, *miner*	Bar
Jack Rance, *sheriff*	Bar	Trim, *miner*	T
Dick Johnson, *the bandit Ramerrez*	T	Sid, *miner*	Bar
Nick, *bartender*	T	Handsome, *miner*	Bar
Ashby, *the Wells Fargo man*	B	Harry, *miner*	T

Joe, *miner*	T	Wowkle, *his squaw*	MS
Happy, *miner*	Bar	Jake Wallace, *minstrel*	Bar
Larkens, *miner*	B	José Castro, *bandit*	B
Billy Jackrabbit, *Indian*	B	Courier	T

SYNOPSIS

I. Rance, on the prowl for Ramerrez, is one of the crowd at the bar when Johnson drops in. Minnie, who used to know Johnson, dances with him. They plan to see each other in private later.

II. While he is with her in her cabin, the sheriff and his men pay her a visit to say that they know quite a bit about Ramerrez now that they have a photograph of the bandit. Unbeknownst to them, their quarry is hiding directly overhead in her loft. They leave. After a suitable time Johnson attempts to leave but a shot from Rance hits him. Johnson hides again in the loft, but Rance, searching, sees drops of blood which lead him to the hiding place. Minnie makes Rance an offer: whoever shall win two of three hands of poker shall have the bandit. In order to win, she cheats.

III. Later, outside, Ramerrez has been caught again and is about to be hanged by the nearest tree when Minnie arrives. With a great speech she convinces the posse that Johnson has sworn to her he will go straight from then on. They are won over and let the man go free.

Faust

	Tragedy in 5 acts
COMP.: C. Gounod	Paris, 19 March 1859
LIBR.: Barbier and Carré	London, 1863
From part of Goethe's play	New York, 1863
	Metropolitan's Opening, 1863

CAST

Faust, *learned doctor*	T	Martha Schwerlein, *Marguérite's*	
Méphistophélès	B	*neighbor*	MS
Marguérite	S	Students, Soldiers, Villagers, Angels,	
Valentin, *soldier, Marguérite's*		Demons	
brother	Bar	Cleopatra, Laïs, Helen of Troy,	
Siebel, *her lover*	MS	Phryne	Mutes
Wagner, *student*	Bar		

MUSICAL HIGHLIGHTS

ACT I. Duet *A moi les plaisirs* (All pleasures for me), Faust and Méphistophélès

ACT II. Aria *Avant de quitter ces lieux* (Now before I leave this place), Valentin
Aria *Le veau d'or* (The golden calf), Méphistophélès
Waltz, The *Kermesse*

ACT III. Serenade *Faites-lui mes aveux* (Bear her my confession), Siebel
Cavatina *Salut, demeure chaste et pure* (Hail to the house so chaste and pure), Faust
Ballad *Il était un roi de Thulé* (There was a king of Thule), Marguérite
Jewel Song *Ah, je ris* (Ah I laugh), Marguérite

ACT IV. Soldiers' Chorus *Gloire immortelle* (Immortal glory), Chorus
Serenade *Vous qui faites l'endormie* (You who seem to be sleeping), Méphistophélès

ACT V. Ballet of Walpurgis Night
Trio *Anges purs, anges radieux* (Angels pure, Angels radiant), Marguérite, Faust, Méphistophélès

SYNOPSIS

I. Faust has failed to solve the riddle of life. He curses life and calls for Satan. Up comes Méphistophélès at his invitation to convert him to a life of pleasures.

II. In a beer hall Méphistophélès taunts the students with more brilliant wit and better wine made magically than they can get by legitimate means. Especially he tortures Valentin. Then he takes Faust to meet Marguérite. Faust falls in love with her beauty while Méphistophélès shudders with laughter by himself.

III. Faust leaves jewels at her door. Then he walks with her in the garden while Méphistophélès escorts her friend Martha conveniently out of the way.

IV. Faust, driven by the devil, deserts Marguérite. Valentin challenges him but the duel is fixed by Méphistophélès and ends with Valentin dead. As he dies he curses his sister.

V. Méphistophélès tries to divert Faust with an exhibition of the famous beauties of antiquity, but Faust sees a vision of Marguérite and insists on seeing her. She is in prison, condemned for killing her child. Delirious with her insanity, she dies in the presence of the man who wronged her. Méphistophélès does not triumph. He gets Faust's soul, but angels come to take Marguérite's to heaven.

NOTE

In Germany, since it uses only the story of Marguérite and Faust, the opera is entitled *Margarethe*.

Faust
COMP.: L. Spohr
LIBR.: J. K. Bernard

Tragedy in 2 acts
Prague, 1 September 1816
London, 1840

Faust
See also *Doktor Faust*
See also *Damnation of Faust*
See also *Mefistofele*

Favola d'Orfeo, La
(*The Fable of Orpheus*)
COMP.: C. Monteverdi
LIBR.: A. Striggio

Tragedy in Prologue and 5 acts
Mantua, February Carnival, 1607
Breslau, 1913
Smith College, Mass., 1929

SYNOPSIS

I. Shepherds and Nymphs rejoice in the marriage of Orpheus and Euridice.

II. During a tableau of a contest in singing, a messenger brings Orpheus the news that Euridice is dead. Orpheus is transfixed by grief.

III. Orpheus descends into Hades to find her. He wins safe passage with the great beauty of a song.

IV. Pluto releases Euridice to her husband, but on condition that he must not look upon her face until they have reached the outer world. She cannot withstand this avoidance. She makes him look back to be sure she is coming. Immediately she returns to the abode of the dead.

V. Orpheus, alone, laments his lost love until Apollo appoints him to live among the stars whence he can again behold her.

NOTE

This extraordinarily beautiful work has been revived in modern instrumentation by various composers, Malipiero, d'Indy and Orff among them. The performance at Smith was in Malipiero's version with Charles Kullman as Orpheus and Werner Josten conducting.

Favorita, La   4 *acts*
COMP.: G. Donizetti   Opéra, 2 December 1840
LIBR.: Royer and Vaëz   Drury Lane, 1843
From a play by d'Arnaud   New York, 1843
                                         Metropolitan, 1895

CAST

Alfonso XI, *king of Castile*	Bar	Leonora de Gusman, *the king's*	
Ferdinand, *novice (Fernando)*	T	*mistress*	S
Don Gaspar, *the king's minister*	T	Inez, *her confidante*	S
Balthasar, *monastery superior*		Courtiers, Guards, Monks, Ladies,	
(*Baldassare*)	B	Attendants	

SYNOPSIS

I. Ferdinand renounces his novitiate in order to go again to his beloved. She keeps from him the fact of her relationship to the king, and arranges an army commission to keep him busy.

II. He becomes a national hero and the secret of his love is almost out when a Papal Bull is read ordering the king to restore his legitimate wife to the throne and put away his mistress.

III. Alfonso tells the hero to name his own prize for victory. He asks for Leonora's hand, which the king is forced by publicity to grant. Leonora tries to tell Ferdinand about her past by sending a note via Inez, but the note never reaches him. He learns the truth harshly in remarks made in open court. In disgust he renounces his honors and returns to the monastery.

IV. Leonora seeks him out and tells him the whole story. He relents but it is too late; she dies.

Fedora   *Tragedy in 3 acts*
COMP.: U. Giordano   Milan, 17 November 1898
LIBR.: A. Colautti   Covent Garden, 1906
From a play by Sardou   Metropolitan, 1906

CAST

Princess Fedora Romanov	S	Désiré, *valet*	T
Count Loris Ipanov	T	Baron Rouvel	T
De Serieux, *diplomat*	Bar	Lorek, *surgeon*	Bar
Countess Olga Sukarev	S	Borov, *doctor*	Bar
Grech, *policeman*	B	Nicola, *footman*	T
Cirillo, *coachman*	Bar	Sergio, *footman*	Bar
Dmitri, *groom*	C	Boleslav Lazinski, *pianist*	Mime
Savoyard	MS		

SYNOPSIS

I. Count Andreievich has been murdered. Grech gathers all the suspects together and narrows the case down to Ipanov, who has escaped.

II. Fedora herself also hunts for the murderer of her fiancé and manages to have him attend her reception in Paris. Loris proves to her that it was a justified murder, that the count had betrayed Loris' wife and caused her death.

III. They live in hiding in Switzerland, but the police search goes on. When Loris hears that it was Fedora who first put the police on his trail, he tries to kill her, but she foils him by taking poison. His sudden rage melts, but it is too late to save her.

Fedra
COMP.: I. Pizzetti
LIBR.: G. d'Annunzio

Tragedy in 3 acts
La Scala, 20 March 1915
Buenos Aires, 1920
Opéra, 1923

Femme Nue, La
COMP.: H. Février
LIBR.: L. Payen
From a play by Bataille

4 acts
Monte Carlo, 23 March 1929
Comique, 1932

Fennimore und Gerda
COMP.: F. Delius
LIBR.: By the composer in German

Frankfurt, 21 October 1919

Fernando Cortez
COMP.: G. Spontini
LIBR.: Esménard and Jouy
From a play by Piron

Tragedy in 3 acts
Opéra, 28 November 1809
New York, 1888
Naples (rev.), 1951

Fête Galante
COMP.: E. Smyth
LIBR.: E. Shanks
From a story by Baring

Dance Dream in 1 act
Birmingham, 4 June 1923
Covent Garden, 1923

CAST

King	BBar	Columbine	S
Lover	T	Four Puppets	S, A, T, B
Pierrot	Bar	Pantaloon, Courtiers, Guests, Satyrs,	
Harlequin	T	Bacchantes, Guards	
Queen	MS		

SYNOPSIS

A gala evening in the palace garden. Columbine and the king mistake Pierrot and the queen's lover for each other, causing obvious complications and embarrassments which are finally ironed out only by military force.

Fêtes de l'Amour et de Bacchus, Les
(*Festival of Love and of Bacchus*)
COMP.: J. B. Lully
LIBR.: P. Quinault

Prologue and 3 acts
Opéra, 15 November 1672

Lully's first opera, using parts of previously successful ballets.

Feuersnot
(*Fire Famine*)
COMP.: R. Strauss
LIBR.: E. von Wolzogen

1 act
Dresden, 21 November 1901
London, 1910
Philadelphia, 1927

Fidelio

COMP.: L. van Beethoven	*Tragedy in 2 acts*
LIBR.: Joseph and Georg Sonnleithner	Vienna, 20 November 1805
From a drama by Bouilly	Covent Garden, 1835
	New York, 1839
	Metropolitan, 1884

CAST

Florestan, *Spanish nobleman*	T	Rocco, *chief jailer*		B
Leonora, *his wife, later Fidelio*	S	Marcellina, *Rocco's daughter*		S
Don Fernando, *king's minister*	B	Jacquino, *Rocco's assistant*		T
Don Pizarro, *prison governor*	B	Soldiers, Prisoners, People		

MUSICAL HIGHLIGHTS

Overture: Of four composed, one called the *Fidelio Overture* is generally used to open the opera. Another, called the *Leonora Overture, Number* 3, is generally played between the scenes of the second act.

ACT I. Quartet in form of canon *Mir ist so wunderbar* (It seems so wonderful), Leonora, Marcellina, Jacquino, Rocco

Aria *Ha! welch ein Augenblick!* (Ha! in a twinkling!), Pizarro

Scena *Abscheulicher!* (Accursed one!) Leonora

Chorus of Prisoners *O welche Lust* (O such a joy!), chorus

ACT II. Aria *In des Lebens Frühlingstagen* (In my younger spring-like days), Florestan

Duet *O namenlose Freude* (Inexpressible joy), Florestan and Leonora

SYNOPSIS

I. Leonora has disguised herself as a man called Fidelio in order to gain access as a workman to the prison where she believes her husband may be still alive. With some complication by the fact that the jailer's daughter has taken a mistaken fancy toward Fidelio, she finally learns that her suspicions were true, that Florestan is indeed in this place.

At the same time Pizarro has learned that the king's minister is nearby and intends to make an inspection of the prison. It is urgent that Pizarro get rid of Florestan, who is his personal enemy, without the king's minister's knowledge. Pizarro therefore gives orders to dig the prisoner's grave while he prepares to kill him himself.

II. The job falls to Rocco and Fidelio. By this means she actually sees the prisoner and learns that it is her husband. She gives him food and drink. When Pizaro comes with a dagger to do the deed she draws a pistol from her garments and holds him off. At that moment a distant trumpet indicates the minister is at hand. He comes to the dungeon, recognizes Florestan as the king's friend and releases him. Pizarro becomes prisoner in his place.

NOTES

Fidelio was originally in three acts, but it lasted only three performances before failing. It was reduced to two acts for 1806. There was to be a new overture for this performance, but it was not ready. Hence the *Ruins of Athens* overture was used in its place. The libretto was then re-written by Treitschke and produced in what is now its final form in 1814. Of the four overtures, the so-called *Leonora Overture number two* was used at the premiere. Number one was intended for Prague, but the production never took place. When the opera was performed at the Park Theater, for the first time in New York, someone must have thought the work insufficient to stand by itself. It was therefore followed by a solo dance, then an extravaganza on the *Deep Deep Sea* in which the Leonora appeared as The Great Sea Monster (Kobbé).

Fierrebras   3 *acts*
COMP.: F. Schubert   Karlsruhe, Germany, 9 February 1897
LIBR.: J. Kupelwieser   Brussels, 1926
From a play by Calderón
The opera was written in 1823.

Fiesta
COMP:. D. Milhaud   Berlin, 1958
LIBR:. B. Vian   Los Angeles, 1959

Figlia del Reggimento, La   2 *acts*
(*The Daughter of the Regiment*)   Comique, 11 February 1840
COMP.: G. Donizetti   New York, 1843
LIBR.: St. Georges and Bayard   London, 1847
                                       Metropolitan, 1902

CAST

Marie, *the "daughter" of the regiment*	S	Corporal	B
Sulpice, *sergeant of grenadiers*	B	Peasant	T
Tonio, *Tyrolean peasant, Marie's lover*	T	Duchesse de Krakenthorp	S
Marquise de Birkenfeld	S	Soldiers, Peasants, Friends of the Marquise	
Hortensio, *her steward*	B		

SYNOPSIS

I. Tonio, caught sneaking around the grenadiers' camp during a battle, is pardoned when Marie, the foundling brought up with the regiment, tells them that he is her rescuer and lover. Tonio decides to join up so that the grenadiers, who want their girl to marry one of their own, will permit him that honor. There is, however, a refugee, the Marquise de Birkenfeld, whose name is soon recognized as one mentioned on papers that were found in Marie's possession when the regiment found her. It turns out that Marie is her niece, and may not therefore marry as planned.

II. The Marquise arranges a fine marriage with a Krakenthorp. To avoid it, Marie and Tonio plan to elope. But when Marie by chance sings a song of her own childhood with the soldiers, the Marquise is deeply touched and allows them to marry.

Fille de Madame Angot, La   3 *acts*
(*Madame Angot's Daughter*)   Brussels, 4 December 1872
COMP.: A. Ch. Lecocq   London, 1873
LIBR.: Clairville, Siraudin and Koning New York, 1873
From a vaudeville by Maillot

Finta Giardiniera, La   3 *acts*
COMP.: W. A. Mozart   Munich, 13 January 1775
LIBR.: R. Calzabigi   New York, 1927
                                       London, 1930

Finta Semplice, La   3 *acts*
COMP.: W. A. Mozart   Salzburg, 1 May 1769
LIBR.: M. Coltellini   Karlsruhe, 1921
From a libretto by Goldoni   Vienna, 1925

Fire Famine
See *Feuersnot*

61

Flauto Magico, Il
See *Zauberflöte, Die*

Fledermaus, Die
(*The Bat*)
COMP.: J. Strauss
LIBR.: Haffner and Genée
From a vaudeville by Meilhac
and Halévy

Comedy in 3 acts
Vienna, 5 April 1874
London, 1876
New York, 1879
Metropolitan, 1905

CAST

Gabriel von Eisenstein	T	Doctor Falke, *Eisenstein's friend*	Bar
Rosalinda, *his wife*	S	Doctor Blind, *attorney*	T
Frank, *prison governor*	Bar	Adele, *Eisenstein's maid*	S
Prince Orlovsky, *a rich Russian*	MS	Frosche, *jailer*	Spkr
Alfred, *singer*	T		

SYNOPSIS

I. Eisenstein is about to serve eight days in prison. In celebration his wife plans first to send him off with a delicious dinner and second to attend a masquerade ball at Orlovsky's that night. But Eisenstein has decided to celebrate himself, and goes off to the costume ball before the dreary business of going to jail. Thus when the prison governor comes for Eisenstein at the appointed time, he finds Alfred at the house. To prevent gossip, Alfred has to go to jail in his place.

II. At the magnificent Straussian ball Eisenstein makes every attempt to conquer the strange Hungarian Lady who is really his own wife. But promptly at six a.m. he remembers his appointment and goes off to jail.

III. He can't get in; there is someone already there, an impostor, masquerading as Eisenstein. Eisenstein disguises himself therefore as his own attorney and proceeds to cross-examine the prisoner Alfred and his visitor Rosalinda until their liaison is revealed.

At the last, Falke appears and confesses that he has engineered the whole mix-up as revenge for the time when, at another masquerade ball, Eisenstein forced Falke to appear in the streets in daylight in costume as a bat.

Fliegende Holländer, Der
(*The Flying Dutchman*)
COMP.: R. Wagner
LIBR.: By the composer
From Heine's *Memoires of Herr von Schnabelewopski*

Tragedy in 3 acts
Dresden, 2 January 1843
Drury Lane, 1870
Philadelphia, 1876
Metropolitan, 1889

CAST

Daland, *Norwegian sea captain*	B	Steersman	T
Senta, *his daughter*	S	The Dutchman	Bar
Eric, *huntsman*	T	Sailors, Maidens, Hunters	
Mary, *Senta's nurse*	C		

SYNOPSIS

Unless the Dutchman can find someone who will love him faithfully, he remains condemned to sail the seas forever. Each seventh year he may come to shore to search for love. On one of these sabbaticals he dropped anchor in Daland's harbor to woo the Norwegian's daughter Senta. She recognized him from the legend which she had always known, but she did not tell him. She swore to love him forever, but once he overheard her former lover, Eric, pleading with her to return to him. The Dutchman misunderstood. Thinking her unfaithful he set sail again. Seeing his ship depart, she cast herself into the seas for his love. In a storm of waves they sailed off to peace and oblivion together.

NOTE

Wagner intended that the work should be played without division into acts. It is said that he was reminded of Heine's poem while tossed and tormented by a tremendous storm on a voyage from Riga to Paris. He set about the writing soon after.

Forest, The
See *Wald, Der*

Forêt Bleue, La	3 *acts*
(*The Blue Forest*)	Geneva, 7 January 1913
COMP.: L. Aubert	Boston, 1913
LIBR.: J. Chenevière	Comique, 1924
From a story by Perrault	London, 1928

Forza del Destino, La	*Tragedy in 4 acts*
(*The Power of Destiny*)	St. Petersburg, 10 November 1862
COMP.: G. Verdi	New York, 1865
LIBR.: F. M. Piave	London, 1867
From a tragedy by The Duke of Rivas	Metropolitan, 1918

CAST

Donna Leonora di Vargas	S	Fra Melitone, *Franciscan*	Bar
Preziosilla, *gypsy*	MS	Curra, *Leonora's maid*	MS
Don Alvaro, *Leonora's lover*	T	Mayor of Hornachuelos	B
Don Carlo di Vargas, *her brother*	Bar	Trabucco, *muleteer*	T
Padre Guardiano, *Franciscan*	B	Surgeon	T
Marchese di Calatrava, *Leonora's father*	B		

MUSICAL HIGHLIGHTS

ACT I. Aria *Me pellegrina* (As a wanderer), Leonora
ACT II. Prayer *Madre, pietosa vergine* (Mother, pious virgin), Leonora
ACT III. Duet *Solenne in quest' ora* (In this solemn hour), Don Alvaro, Don Carlo
ACT IV. Prayer, *Pace, pace, mio Dio* (Peace, peace O God), Leonora
    Trio *Non imprecare* (Do not curse me), Leonora, Alvaro, Padre Guardiano

SYNOPSIS

I. Leonora and Don Alvaro delay so much during their elopement that the Marchese discovers them in the act. In the ensuing argument, Don Alvaro's pistol accidentally discharges, killing the old man.

II. They separate and flee. Leonora sees Don Carlo in disguise. He had been searching for her and for her lover to avenge his father's death. She seeks sanctuary and penance in a cave in a monastery where she intends to live her life in solitude.

III. Both disguised, and unknown to each other, Don Carlo and Don Alvaro meet elsewhere during a severe battle and swear eternal friendship. Don Alvaro, badly wounded, extracts his friend's promise, in case he should die, to burn, unopened, a letter he has in his possession. Don Carlo does not need to read the letter to recognize the portrait of his sister that accompanies it. Don Alvaro revives. Don Carlo tries then to provoke a duel with him, but without success.

IV. Alvaro joins the Franciscans and seeks personal peace as a monk. But Carlo seeks him out and goads him into a duel. They fight near the cell of the hermit, who is really Leonora. There the monk kills his rival. He calls the hermit to administer to the dying man. Leonora rushes out to find her brother dying and her former lover standing over him. Carlo, not willing to forget her part in his father's death, stabs her as he dies.

Four Saints in Three Acts

COMP.: V. Thomson
LIBR.: G. Stein

4 *acts*

Hartford, Conn., 8 February 1934
New York, 1934
Paris, 1952

CAST

Compère	B	St. Chavez	T
Commère	MS	St. Settlement	S
St. Therese I	S	Other Saints in a double choir	
St. Therese II	C	Dancers	
St. Ignatius Loyola	Bar		

SYNOPSIS

Since a saint may be both inside and outside at the same time, there must be two Saints Therese. We participate in visions of the life of St. Therese. We consider the problems of saints, such as how to fly and how to count the windows and doors in the Heavenly Mansion. We think next of the religious thoughts of St. Ignatius. And then; there *should* be four acts. We see the saints in Heaven, at peace and amid glory.

Fra Diavolo

COMP.: D. Auber
LIBR.: E. Scribe

Tragedy in 3 acts

Comique, 28 January 1830
Drury Lane, 1831
New York, 1831

CAST

Fra Diavolo, *bandit chief*	T	Matteo, *innkeeper*	B
Lord Cockburn, *tourist*	T	Zerlina, *his daughter*	S
Lady Pamela, *wife to the tourist*	MS	Giacomo, *bandit*	B
Lorenzo, *officer*	T	Beppo, *bandit*	T

SYNOPSIS

I. Cockburn has been waylaid and robbed near Matteo's tavern. He offers a reward to catch the thieves. While he expostulates, Fra Diavolo draws near in disguise and commiserates with the poor fellow. He also, however, passes his time most efficiently by paying compliments to Pamela and extracting from her information of the whereabouts of Cockburn's money.

II. The bandit and his assistants hide in Zerlina's room in order to be near Cockburn's and finish their job. Beppo makes a noise. But Fra Diavolo reveals himself to Cockburn and then to Matteo, telling each he has a rendezvous with the other's feminine relation. This explains everything satisfactorily, except to Lorenzo who challenges him.

III. Lorenzo discovers, before the duel is to take place, who Beppo and Giacomo really are. With this knowledge he entraps Fra Diavolo. The opera then may end either happily or sadly, depending upon whether the producer has Fra Diavolo go free or be shot in ambush.

Francesca da Rimini

COMP.: R. Zandonai
LIBR.: T. Ricordi
From d'Annunzio's play

Tragedy in 4 acts
Turin, 19 February 1914
Covent Garden, 1914
Metropolitan, 1916

CAST

Francesca	S	Garsenda, *Francesca's woman*	S
Samaritana, *her sister*	S	Altichiara, *Francesca's woman*	MS
Ostasio, *her brother*	Bar	Donella, *Francesca's woman*	MS
Giovanni lo Sciancato,		Slave, *Francesca's slave*	C
Malatesta's lame son	Bar	Ser Toldo Berardengo, *lawyer*	T
Paolo il Bello,		Jester	B
Malatesta's handsome son	T	Archer	T
Malatestino dall-occhio,		Torchbearer	Bar
Malatesta's one-eyed son	T	Archers, Torchbearers, Musicians	
Biancofiore, *Francesca's woman*	S		

SYNOPSIS

I. For political reasons, Francesca is betrothed to Giovanni. To trick her into it she is introduced to Paolo instead and falls in love with him as he does with her.

II. During a battle between the Guelphs and Ghibellines, Francesca, now married, and Paolo each try to be exposed to death but neither succeeds. The Malatestas win the battle. Paolo is rewarded by becoming a captain and being given a post in Florence.

III. Paolo and Francesca meet again much later. Their love renews.

IV. Again he visits her. But his brothers have been watching. They find him. In the vicious fighting Giovanni makes a thrust at Paolo which kills Francesca instead. With double fury he cuts Paolo down and then breaks his bloody sword over his knee.

Fra i Due Litiganti il Terzo Gode

(*Between Two Litigants, a Third Succeeds*)
COMP.: G. Sarti
From Goldoni's *Le Nozze*

3 acts
Milan, 14 September 1782
London, 1784

Mozart used an air from this popular work in his own *Don Giovanni*.

Françoise de Rimini

COMP.: A. Thomas
LIBR.: Barbier and Carré
See also *Francesca da Rimini*.

Prologue, 4 acts and Epilogue
Opéra, 14 April 1882
Antwerp, 1883

Frate 'nnamorato, Lo

(*The Brother in Love*)
COMP.: G. Pergolesi
LIBR.: G. A. Federico

Comedy in 3 acts
Naples, 23 September 1732

Frau ohne Schatten, Die

(*The Woman Without a Shadow*)
COMP.: R. Strauss
LIBR.: H. von Hofmannsthal

3 acts
Vienna, 10 October 1919
La Scala, 1940
Buenos Aires, 1949
San Francisco 1959

CAST

Emperor	T	Barak, *dyer*	BBar
Empress	S	His wife	S
Nurse, *die Amme*	MS	One-eye, *his brother*	B
Spirit, *messenger*	Bar	One-arm, *his brother*	B
Temple Gatekeeper	S or T	Hunchback, *his brother*	T
Apparition of a Youth	T	Children's voices	3S, 3C
Voice of the Falcon	S	Nightwatchmen's voices	3B
Voice from Above	C	Servants, Strange Children, Spirits	

SYNOPSIS

The Empress is a magic person, sprung from a gazelle. She is barren and hence throws no shadow.

I. A messenger tells the nurse that if the Empress cannot find a shadow for herself within three days, she must return to her magic state. In that case the Emperor, likewise, will die. She and the nurse descend to Earth. There they find Barak's wife whom they persuade to give up her shadow, thus remaining childless.

II. When the third day comes, Barak's wife has lost her shadow but the Empress still has none. Barak is about to kill his wife for the loss but the Empress stops him, saying that killing is too high a price to pay. The earth swallows up Barak.

III. In a dark vault the Empress hears the cries of Barak and his wife calling to each other without answer. The Empress stands before her father in judgement. She steadfastly refuses to take the woman's shadow from her at the price they will have to pay. Even the sight of the Emperor slowly turning to stone does not shake her.

Suddenly she has a shadow. The Emperor is saved. As they embrace in their new-found love they see Barak and his wife also restored to each other.

Freischütz, Der

(*The Freeshooter*)	3 *acts*
COMP.: C. M. von Weber	Berlin, 18 June 1821
LIBR.: J. F. Kind	London, 1824
	New York, 1825
	Metropolitan, 1884

CAST

Prince Ottokar	Bar	Hermit	B
Cuno, *head ranger*	B	Samiel, *the wild huntsman*	Spkr
Max, *forester*	T	Agathe, *Cuno's daughter*	S
Caspar, *forester*	B	Aennchen, *her cousin*	S
Kilian, *rich peasant*	T		

SYNOPSIS

I. To win Agathe, Max must prove he is the best shot in the district. Unfortunately he is a very bad shot. But Caspar shows him the power of magic bullets. Max agrees to meet Caspar at midnight in the Wolf's Glen to make some of them.

II. Agathe sees Max for a moment. He depresses her by his impatience to leave to go to the Wolf's Glen. She and Aennchen do their best to dissuade him from going to that haunted place.

Caspar shows him the way there and introduces him to the Wild Huntsman who shows him how to make magic bullets. Six will go straight to the mark, the seventh will hit where Samiel directs it. Even the ghost of Max's mother, appearing to him there, cannot change his determination to avail himself of the help of the Devil.

III. Agathe and Aennchen dress for the competition. The shooters arrive. Max has already used up his six predictable bullets in a fabulous hunt beforehand. As Max prepares to shoot his final shot in the competition, Agathe shouts to prevent it. She is too late, Caspar falls dead. Max would have been banished for this accidental murder, but the Hermit wins his reprieve.

Fremde Erde
(Strange Land)
COMP.: K. Rathaus
LIBR.: K. Palffy-Wanieck

5 acts
Berlin, 10 December 1930

Friedenstag
(Peace Day)
COMP.: R. Strauss
LIBR.: J. Gregor

1 act
Munich, 24 July 1938
Berlin, 1939
Venice, 1940

CAST

Commander of the Town	Bar	Front Line Officer	Bar
Maria, *his wife*	S	Piedmontese	T
Sergeant	B	Holsteiner, *commander of the enemy*	B
Corporal	Bar	Burgomaster	T
Private	T	Bishop	Bar
Musketeer	B	Woman	S
Bugler	B	Soldiers, Elders, Women,	
Officer	Bar	Townspeople	

SYNOPSIS

The Commander will not allow the town to save itself by surrendering to the besiegers. But under pressure from the townspeople he finally agrees to allow it, on condition that it will not happen until noon and that he will give the signal himself. He plans to signal by blowing up his own garrison.

When the final moment is near, just before the fuse is to be lit, the enemy ceases firing. The Holsteiner comes up to offer peace. This the Commander refuses until again the townspeople and his wife urge him to accept. To the sound of a great hymn to peace the opera ends.

From a House of the Dead
See *Z Mrtvého Domu*

Galatea
See *Schöne Galatee*
See also *Acis and Galatea*

Gazza Ladra, La
COMP.: G. Rossini
LIBR.: G. Gherardini
From a drama by d'Aubigny and
Caigniez

2 acts
La Scala, 31 May 1817
London, 1821
Philadelphia, 1827
New York, 1830

Genoveva
COMP.: R. Schumann
LIBR.: R. Reineck altered by Schumann
From plays by Ticek and Habbel

4 acts
Leipzig, 25 June 1850
Drury Lane, 1893
Paris (Concert), 1894

Gianni Schicchi

COMP.: G. Puccini
LIBR.: G. Forzano

Comedy in 1 *act*
Metropolitan, 14 December 1918
Buenos Aires, 1919
Covent Garden, 1920

CAST

Gianni Schicchi, 50	Bar	Simone, *Buoso's cousin*, 70, *heir*	B
Lauretta, *his daughter*, 21	S	Marco, *his son*, 45, *heir*	Bar
Zita, *Buoso's cousin*, 60, *heir*	C	La Ciesca, *Marco's wife*, 38, *heir*	MS
Rinuccio, *her nephew*, 24, *heir*	T	Maestro Spinellocchio, *doctor*	B
Gherardo, *Buoso's nephew*, 40, *heir*	T	Ser Amantio di Nicolao, *lawyer*	Bar
Nella, *his wife*, 34, *heir*	S	Pinellino, *cobbler*	B
Gherardino, *their son*, 7, *heir*	C	Guccio, *painter*	B
Betto di Segna, *Buoso's brother-in-law, heir*	B		

SYNOPSIS

Buoso has just died. His heirs have gathered around his deathbed to pray for his soul and to reap their inheritances. When the will is read, however, they find that all his money went to a monastery. In desperation they turn one and all to Gianni Schicchi in the hope that he can do something about it. He hits upon a plan.

He jumps into the deathbed and draws the curtains. When the doctor comes, Gianni Schicchi mimics the dead man's voice and says he's much better, thank you. That gets rid of the doctor. Gianni then calls for a lawyer.

To the lawyer he dictates a new will, giving little tokens to each relative. But when he comes to a big prize he assigns it—to himself! Not one of those present can utter the slightest protest, since all agreed to the fraud in the first place and witnesses are present. Gianni therefore gives himself the great house, throws all the relatives out and makes his daughter very happy with Rinuccio, whom she loves.

NOTES

This is the third of three one-act operas written for the Metropolitan. The first was *Il Tabarro*, the second *Suor Angelica*. Puccini called the three *Il Trittico*. The subject of the ghoulish Gianni Schicchi is mentioned in a line of the thirteenth canto of Dante's *Inferno* as one who suffers for having counterfeited another's shape.

Ginevra

COMP.: M. Delannoy

Comique, 1942

Gioconda, La

(*The Ballad Singer*)
COMP.: A. Ponchielli
LIBR.: A. Boito

Tragedy in 4 *acts*
La Scala, 8 April 1876
Covent Garden, 1883
Metropolitan, 1883

CAST

La Gioconda, *ballad singer*	S	Zuane, *boatman*	B
La Cieca, *her blind mother*	C	Isèpo, *public scribe*	T
Alvise Badoero, *inquisitor*	B	Pilot	B
Laura, *his wife*	MS	Monks, Senators, Sailors, Shipwrights,	
Enzo Grimaldo, *Genoese nobleman*	T	Ladies, Gentlemen, Populace,	
Barnaba, *spy for the inquisition*	Bar	Masquers, Guards	

SYNOPSIS

I. *The Lion's Mouth.* Barnaba loves Gioconda, but she is in love with Enzo, an enemy to the city, who is in disguise. To win her in spite of this obstacle, Barnaba spreads the rumor that La Cieca is a witch. A riot ensues during which Enzo's men act to protect her. Alvise puts a stop to the uproar and pardons La Cieca at Laura's intercession. Enzo recognizes the inquisitor's wife as the Laura to whom he was once betrothed. Barnaba therefore arranges to have Alvise discover his wife in the act of escaping with Enzo. Gioconda overhears the plot.

II. *The Rosary.* Gioconda goes to the boat to confront Laura, but instead of making trouble, she saves her rival by sending her away when Barnaba appears. Enzo sees her there, and sees the Venetians, his enemies, coming also. He sets fire to his ship.

III. *The House of Gold.* Alvise, made aware of her infidelity, forces his wife to drink poison. But Gioconda has substituted a drug in its place. The inquisitor exhibits her, thinking she is dead, to his guests, among whom is Enzo. Enzo, taken by surprise, reveals himself and is seized by the guards.

IV. *The Orfano Canal.* Gioconda helps Enzo and the revived Laura to escape. Barnaba comes for her, but she thwarts his revenge by stabbing herself before his eyes.

Gioielli della Madonna, I	*Tragedy in 3 acts*
(*The Jewels of the Madonna*)	Berlin, 2 December 1911
COMP.: E. Wolf-Ferrari	Chicago and New York, 1912
LIBR.: Golisciani and Zangarini	Covent Garden, 1912
	Metropolitan, 1925

CAST

Gennaro, *blacksmith*	T	Stella	S
Maliella, *Carmela's adopted daughter*	S	Concetta	S
Rafaele, *Camorrist leader*	Bar	Serena	C
Carmela, *Gennaro's mother*	MS	Rocco, *Camorrist*	B
Biaso, *scribe*	T	Grazia	Dancer
Ciccillo, *Camorrist*	T	Vendors, Monks, People	

SYNOPSIS

I. Gennaro is finishing a candelabra for the Festival of the Madonna which has already begun. The Camorrists, a band of extortionists, arrive in town. Rafaele seizes Maliella, kisses her laughingly and gives her a flower. He pleads passionate love, and says he would steal even the jewels from the image of the Madonna for her. Gennaro warns her against this man.

II. Gennaro is desperate to protect her from the flamboyant Rafaele. He himself goes off in the night and steals the jewels to foil Rafaele at his own game. Maliella melts with rapture into his arms.

III. For her change of affections Rafaele rejects the girl. The Camorrists shrink from her when they see her wearing the sacred jewels. Finally she is so full of remorse she drowns herself in the sea while Gennaro, full of guilt, stabs himself.

Giorno di Regno, Un	*Comedy in 2 acts*
COMP.: G. Verdi	La Scala, 5 September 1840
LIBR.: F. Romani	Venice, 1845
Verdi's second opera.	

Gli Equivoci nel Sembiante

COMP.: A. Scarlatti
LIBR.: D. F. Contini
Scarlatti's first opera.

3 *acts*
Rome, February 1679
Vienna, 1681

Girl of the Golden West, The

See *Fanciulla del West, La*

Gloriana

COMP.: B. Britten
LIBR.: W. Plomer

3 *acts*
Covent Garden, 8 June 1953

CAST

Queen Elizabeth the First	S	Henry Cuffe, *Essex's satellite*	Bar
Robert Devereux, *earl of Essex*	T	Lady-in-Waiting	S
Frances, *countess of Essex*	MS	Blind Ballad Singer	B
Charles Blount, *Lord Mountjoy*	Bar	Recorder of Norwich	B
Penelope, *Lady Rich, sister of Essex*	S	Housewife	MS
Sir Robert Cecil,		Spirit of the Masque	T
secretary of the Council	Bar	Master of Ceremonies	T
Sir Walter Raleigh,		City Crier	Bar
captain of the guard	B	Chorus, Dancers, Actors, Musicians	

SYNOPSIS

I. Essex, jealous of Mountjoy's popularity, provides occasion for a fight and comes away slightly wounded. The queen upbraids them both. She feels herself married to her people, but when Essex sings to her at least it eases her moods. Essex looks upon Raleigh as his rival.

II. The queen witnesses a masque in her honor at Norwich (set for *a capella* voices). She has been delaying the award to Essex of an appointment as Lord Deputy in Ireland. At a ball the queen, rendered ridiculously jealous by the attractiveness of Lady Essex, arranges to steal that unfortunate lady's dress and stalk about in it, badly fitted upon herself. After this demonstration of her feelings, she allows the appointment to go through.

III. Essex is a failure in Ireland. He returns precipitously to England and compounds his ill favor by bursting in upon the queen while she is not yet made-up for the day. After he leaves her she has him put under watch.

Essex is tried and condemned.

In the final scene we see a panorama of the rest of her life, the affairs of England, prayers for the queen and finally her death.

NOTE

Gloriana was written to celebrate the coronation of Elizabeth the Second.

Golden Cockerel, The

See *Coq d'Or, Le*

Goldene Kreuz, Das

(*The Golden Cross*)
COMP.: I. Brüll
LIBR.: S. Mosenthal
From a play by Mélesville and Brazier

2 *acts*
Berlin, 22 December 1875
London, 1878
New York, 1879
Metropolitan, 1886

THE OPERAS

Götterdämmerung
(*The Twilight of the Gods*)
COMP.: R. Wagner
LIBR.: By the Composer

Music Drama in Prologue and 3 acts
Bayreuth, 17 August 1876
London, 1882
Metropolitan, 1888

CAST

Siegfried	T	First Norn	C
Gunther	Bar	Second Norn	MS
Alberich	BBar	Third Norn	S
Hagen	B	Woglinde	S
Brünnhilde	S	Wellgunde	S
Gutrune	S	Flosshilde	MS
Waltraute	MS	Vassals and Women	

MUSICAL HIGHLIGHTS

PROLOGUE. Siegfried's Rhine Journey
ACT I. Waltraute's Narrative
ACT III. Siegfried's Narrative

SYNOPSIS

PROLOGUE. The three Norns weave the thread of life. The skein breaks and the doom of the gods is foretold.

Siegfried takes leave of Brünnhilde and sets out on a journey down the Rhine.

I. Hagen, of the tribe of Alberich, greets Siegfried, welcomes him to his home, and gives him a potion that makes him forget Brünnhilde and fall in love with Gutrune. Siegfried quickly agrees to bring Brünnhilde to be Gunther's wife; she means nothing to him any more. Therefore he goes back, disguised by the magic Tarnhelm as Gunther, seizes the Ring of the Nibelungs from Brünnhilde's finger and brings her to Hagen's hall.

II. Hagen summons his vassals for the double wedding. But Brünnhilde recognizes the ring on Siegfried's finger and shouts for all to hear that she is already married, to Siegfried. Hagen and Gunther plan to murder the warrior.

III. While Siegfried is resting on a hunt next day, Hagen kills him with a spear in the back. The men carry his body upon his shield to the hall where Brünnhilde directs the construction of a funeral pyre. When the blaze is at its height she rides into it with the ring. At this the Rhine overflows its banks, the Rhinemaidens snatch the ring which was once stolen from them, and Valhalla itself, the abode of the gods, is consumed by the flames.

NOTES

This is the final part of *Der Ring des Nibelungen*. Originally called *Siegfrieds Tod*, it was written in 1848 and orchestrated in 1874.

Goyescas
COMP.: E. Granados
LIBR.: F. Periquet
From Goya

3 scenes
Metropolitan, 28 January 1916
Buenos Aires, 1929
London, 1951

CAST

Rosario, *high born young lady*	S	Pepa, *Paquiro's sweetheart*	MS
Fernando, *her lover, an officer*	T	Majas, Majos	
Paquiro, *toreador*	Bar		

71

SYNOPSIS

I. During a holiday Paquiro sees Rosario and invites her to a candlelight ball. Her lover, Fernando, becomes jealous and formally states that he will escort the lady. Pepa also becomes jealous. She vows to win satisfaction from Rosario.

II. At the ball Fernando's airs amaze everybody. Paquiro challenges him to a duel.

III. While the lady waits, the duel goes on in her garden. She hears Fernando scream. She rushes to him and holds him in her arms as he dies.

NOTE

The composer was on his way home after the opening in New York when his ship was torpedoed at sea by a German submarine and sank with him aboard.

Grande Duchesse de Gérolstein, La
COMP.: J. Offenbach
LIBR.: Meilhac and Halévy

3 *acts*
Paris, 12 April 1867
New York, 1867
Covent Garden, 1867

Guarany, Il
COMP.: A. Gomez
LIBR.: A. Scalvini
From a novel by Alencar

4 *acts*
La Scala, 19 March 1870
Covent Garden, 1872
New York, 1884

Guillaume Tell
(*William Tell*)
COMP.: G. Rossini
LIBR.: de Jouy, Bis,
From Schiller

3 *acts* (*Originally* 4)
Opéra, 3 August 1829
Drury Lane, 1830
New York, 1831
Metropolitan, 1884

CAST

Guillaume Tell, *Swiss patriot*	Bar	Rudolph, *captain of the guards*	T
Hedwige, *his wife*	S	Walter Furst, *Swiss patriot*	B
Jemmy, *his son*	S	Leuthold, *shepherd*	B
Arnold, *Mathilde's suitor*	T	Ruedi, *fisherman*	T
Melcthal, *his father*	B	Peasants, Knights, Pages, Ladies, Hunters,
Gessler, *tyrant governor*	B	Soldiers, Guards, Three Bridal Couples
Mathilde, *his sister*	S		

SYNOPSIS

I. Tell risks his life to help Leuthold escape the tyrant's guards. In revenge, the guards seize old Melcthal in his place.

II. Arnold, who is in love with Mathilde, learns from Tell that Melcthal has been killed under Gessler's orders. He joins with Tell and Walter to help rid Switzerland of the hated foreign rulers.

III. At the hundredth anniversary of Austrian rule over Switzerland, Gessler has set up his hat on a pole and ordered that all the Swiss bow to it. Tell refuses. Gessler has him seized and commands him to show his prowess by shooting an arrow off his own son's head. Tell takes aim and does this with his first arrow. With his second he kills Gessler as the Swiss, united, arise to throw off the tyrants.

Gunlöd   3 *acts*
COMP.: P. Cornelius   Weimar, 6 May 1891
LIBR.: By the composer   Cologne (*rev.*), 1906
    Halle, 1918
This work was completed by C. Hoffbauer.

Gwendoline   2 *acts*
COMP.: E. Chabrier   Brussels, 10 April 1886
LIBR.: C. Mendés   Dresden, 1890
    Opéra, 1893

Gypsy Baron, The
See *Zigeunerbaron*

Habanera, La   3 *acts*
COMP.: R. Laparra   Comique, 26 February 1908
LIBR.: By the composer   Covent Garden, 1910
    Boston, 1910

Halka   4 *acts*
COMP.: S. Moniuszko   Vilna, Lithuania, 16 February 1854
LIBR.: W. Wolski   New York, 1903
From a story by Wójcicki   Milwaukee, Wisc., 1923
This opera was originally performed in two acts. There was an amateur production at Vilna in 1847.

Hamlet   *Tragedy in 5 acts*
COMP.: A. Thomas   Opéra, 9 March 1868
LIBR.: Barbier and Carré   Covent Garden, 1870
From Shakespeare   New York, 1872
Perhaps this is the earliest opera to use a saxophone in the orchestra.

Hans Heiling   *Prologue and 3 acts*
COMP.: H. Marschner   Berlin, 24 May 1833
LIBR.: E. Devrient   Vienna, 1846

Hänsel und Gretel   3 *acts*
COMP.: E. Humperdinck   Weimar, 23 December 1893
LIBR.: A. Wette (his sister)   London, 1894
    New York, 1895

CAST

Hänsel, *a little boy*	MS	Peter, *their father, a broom maker*	Bar
Gretel, *his sister*	S	Sandman	S
Witch	MS	Dew Fairy	S
Gertrude, *the children's mother*	S, MS		

SYNOPSIS

1. Gertrude, in despair to see her children playing when poverty demands labor, sends them out to the woods to look for berries. When Peter comes home quite drunk, carrying a load of sausages and things for supper, she tells him where they have gone. He has heard that there is a wicked witch living in those woods. Both the parents rush off to save their children.

II. Hänsel and Gretel have been eating up their berries as soon as they collect them. Night finds them in the woods. They feel very sleepy. After saying their prayers, they fall asleep together and the Sandman comes to seal their eyes.

III. In the morning they are very hungry. But what do they find? It is a house all made of candy. They break off bits and eat away in joy until the witch catches them at it. She sticks Hänsel into a kennel to fatten him up, and makes Gretel help her with the work. But Gretel is a smart little girl. She manages to free her brother and together they trick the witch into her own oven. When their distracted parents find them the old witch has been baked into a honey cake and all the other little boys and girls who had been caught by the witch have resumed their natural shapes by Gretel's dexterity with the witch's wand.

Harlequin
See *Arlecchino*

Harmonie der Welt, Die
(*The Harmony of the World*)
COMP.: Paul Hindemith
LIBR.: By the composer

5 acts
Munich, 11 August 1957

CAST

Kaiser Rudolf II/Kaiser Ferdinand II (*The Sun*)	B	Tansur (*Saturn*)	B
Johannes Kepler, *astronomer* (*The Earth*)	Bar	Baron Starbemberg	Bar
		Christoph, *Kepler's brother*	T
		Susanna, *later Kepler's wife* (*Venus*)	S
Wallenstein, *Commander in Chief* (*Jupiter*)	T	Katharina, *Kepler's mother* (*The Moon*)	C
Ulrich Grüsser, *Kepler's assistant, later a soldier* (*Mars*)	T	Little Susanna, *Kepler's daughter by his first wife*	S
Daniel Hizler, *Vicar, later vicar of Regensburg* (*Mercury*)	B	Magistrate, Lawyer, People, Soldiers, Stars	

Háry János
COMP.: Z. Kodály
LIBR.: Paulini and Harsányi

Fable in 3 acts
Budapest, 16 October 1926
Cologne, 1931
New York (Juilliard), 1960

CAST

Háry János	Bar	Kaiser Franz of Austria, Countess Melusine and Countess Estrella, Hungarian Sentry, Russian Sentry, General Blood and Thunder, General Dufla, Two Hussars, Two Artillerymen, Village Elder, Student, Abraham the Innkeeper, Two peasants	Spkrs
Ilka, *his fiancée*	S		
The Empress of Austria	S		
Emperor Napoleon	Bar		
Marie-Louise, *his wife*	MS		
Old Marzci, *her coachman*	Bar		
Ritter von Ebelasztin, *her chamberlain*	T	Generals, Soldiers, Peasants, Court Servants	

SYNOPSIS

Háry János is a great teller of tall tales.

First he helps the empress get across the Russian frontier, which is utterly impassable to others. Then he causes the French to declare war on Austria. He takes Napoleon prisoner, turns down Marie-Louise as a wife but takes Ilka instead. And, since she is dead and gone now, who can contradict him?

Häusliche Krieg, Der
(*The Domestic War*)
COMP.: F. Schubert
LIBR.: I. F. Castelli
From *Lysistrata* by Aristophanes
  Schubert completed this opera in 1823.

1 *act*
Frankfort, 29 August 1861
New York, 1877
London (Concert), 1872

He Who Gets Slapped
COMP.: R. Ward
LIBR.: B. Stambler
From Andreyev's play

New York, 17 May 1956
(*Columbia University*)
New York (N.Y. City Opera), 1959

CAST

Count Mancini	T	Bezano	T
Zinida	S	Baron Regnard	Bar
Pantaloon	Bar	Tilly	Silent
Consuelo	S	Polly	Silent

NOTE
  In its first production, by Columbia University, the opera was called *Pantaloon*.

Heimchen am Herd, Das
(*The Cricket on the Hearth*)
COMP.: K. Goldmark
LIBR.: M. Willner
From the story by Charles Dickens

3 *acts*
Vienna, 21 March 1896

CAST

John	Bar	Edward Plummer	T
Dot, *his wife*	S	Tackleton	B
May	S	Cricket	S

Helen
See *Belle Hélène, La*

Helen in Egypt
See *Aegyptische Helene, Die*

Helen Retires
COMP.: G. Antheil
LIBR.: J. Erskine

3 *acts*
New York (Juilliard), 28 February 1934

Henry VIII
COMP.: C. Saint-Säens
LIBR.: Détroyat and Silvestre

4 *acts*
Opéra, 5 March 1883
Covent Garden, 1898

Her Foster Daughter
See *Její Pastorkyňa*

Hérodiade
COMP.: J. Massenet
LIBR.: Milliet and Hartmann
From a story by Flaubert

Tragedy in 4 *acts*
Brussels, 19 December 1881
New Orleans, 1884
Covent Garden, 1904
New York, 1909

Herodias
See also *Salome*

Heure Espagnole, L'
(*The Spanish Hour*)
COMP.: M. Ravel
LIBR.: F. Nohain

Comedy in 1 act
Comique, 19 May 1911
Covent Garden, 1919
Chicago and New York, 1920
Metropolitan, 1925

CAST

Concepcion, *Torquemada's wife*	S	Ramiro, *muleteer*	Bar
Gonsalve, *poet*	T	Don Inigo Gomez, *banker*	B
Torquemada, *a clockmaker*	T		

SYNOPSIS

Torquemada is about to spend the day away from home fixing the clocks in town when Ramiro drops in to have his watch fixed. Torquemada asks him to wait until he returns.

This is the day Concepcion receives her lovers. They are hiding in the clocks, unwilling to be discovered by Ramiro. Concepcion asks the visitor if he'd mind moving some of the heavy clocks for her. Obligingly he carries this one up to her bedroom, that one back downstairs, and so on. Pretty soon he realizes what is going on. He himself is quite taken with Concepcion's beauty. Gradually he woos and wins her.

When Torquemada returns he finds the lovers hidden, each in a clock. He sells each one a clock and sends them away. But he is very glad to have Ramiro stay. Ramiro is such a handy fellow to have around.

Hin und Zurück
COMP.: P. Hindemith
LIBR.: M. Schiffer

1 act
Baden-Baden, 17 July 1927
Basle, 1928

Hippolyte et Aricie
COMP.: J. P. Rameau
LIBR.: L'Abbé Pellegrin

Prologue and 5 acts
Opéra, 1 October 1733
Paris, 1908

Hochzeit des Camacho, Die
(*Camacho's Wedding*)
COMP.: F. Mendelssohn
LIBR.: C. von Lichtenstein
From *Don Quixote* by Cervantes
Camacho's Wedding has been staged only once.

2 acts
Berlin, 29 April 1827
Boston (Concert), 1885
Berlin (Concert), 1886

Hoffmann
See *Contes d'Hoffmann, Les*

Holy Devil, The
COMP.: N. Nabokov

Louisville, Ky., 18 April 1958

In Europe this opera is performed as *Rasputin*.

Hubička
(*The Kiss*)
COMP.: B. Smetana
LIBR.: E. Krasnohorska

Comedy in 2 acts
Prague, 7 November 1876
Liverpool, 1948

CAST

Paloucky, *peasant*	BBar	Martinka, *Vendulka's aunt*	C
Vendulka, *his daughter*	S	Matous, *smuggler*	B
Lukas, *young widower*	T	Barce, *servant*	S
Tomes, *his brother-in-law*	Bar	Guard at the Frontier	T

SYNOPSIS

I. Vendulka is engaged to Lukas. He comes to woo her. He wants to kiss her but no—she refuses. Again and again he makes the attempt but always she refuses. In the end both are furious as he marches away. Outside her window, and in plain sight of everyone in her house including her father who objected to their betrothal anyway, Lukas makes a show of dancing with and kissing every pretty girl he can find.

II. She goes away to escape the humiliation. Their friends arrange for them to meet again. Lukas most formally begs her pardon. Then he kisses her.

Hugh the Drover

COMP.: R. Vaughan Williams
LIBR.: H. Child

2 acts
London, 4 July 1924
Toronto, 1932
New York, 1952

CAST

Showman	Bar	Susan	S
Mary, *the constable's daughter*	S	Nancy	C
Aunt Jane, *the constable's sister*	C	William	T
Turnkey	T	Robert	B
Constable	B	Fool	B
John the Butcher	BBar	Innkeeper	B
Hugh the Drover	T	Sergeant	Bar
Cheap Jack	Bar	Stallkeeper, Juggler, Dancing Girl,	
Shellfish Seller	B	Trumpeter	
Primrose Seller	C	Townspeople, Toysellers, Boys, Soldiers	
Ballad Seller	T		

SYNOPSIS

I. When Hugh saw Mary at the fair it was love at first sight. But she had already agreed to marry John on the morrow. What to do? John fought Hugh but Hugh won. John accused him of being a French spy and Hugh was arrested.

II. Mary stole her father's keys to let Hugh out of the stocks, but people came by at the wrong time. She changed her strategy and took the place next to him in the stocks. For this John insulted her and her father disowned her. But when the soldiers came to take Hugh away they discovered that he was certainly not a spy but a famous patriot well known to them. In place of Hugh, therefore, they took John, leaving the lovers free to do as they pleased.

Huguenots, Les

COMP.: G. Meyerbeer
LIBR.: A. E. Scribe
From Deschamps

Tragedy in 5 acts
Opéra, 29 February 1836
Covent Garden, 1842
New York, 1845
Metropolitan, 1883

Valentine, *betrothed to de Nevers*	S	Tavannes, *Catholic gentleman*	T
Marguerite de Valois, *betrothed*		de Retz	Bar
to Henry IV	S	Raoul de Nangis, *Huguenot*	
Urbain, *her page*	MS	*nobleman*	T
Count de St. Bris, *Catholic*		Marcel, *Huguenot soldier*	B
nobleman	Bar	Bois-Rosé, *Huguenot soldier*	T
Count de Nevers, *Catholic*		Maurevert, *Catholic nobleman*	B
nobleman	Bar	Catholic Ladies and Gentlemen, Huguenot
Cossé	T	Ladies and Gentlemen, Soldiers, Pages,
Méru, *Catholic gentleman*	Bar	Citizens, Populace, Night Watch,
Thoré, *Catholic gentleman*	Bar	Monks, Students

SYNOPSIS

I. Raoul and Marcel attend a banquet at the house of de Nevers. There Marcel defies the other guests by singing Huguenot hymns. Raoul falls in love with an unknown lady who is there, but she is the count's guest.

II. Marguerite sends for Raoul to bring him and Valentine (the unknown lady) together. She hopes to avert war by uniting a Catholic with a Huguenot. But Raoul thinks Valentine is de Nevers' mistress and refuses her.

III. Valentine then is betrothed to de Nevers. Raoul sends St. Bris his challenge. Valentine hears of a plot to kill Raoul of which she warns him. Not until then does Raoul finally learn that Valentine did love him.

IV. Raoul visits her, even though she is married, and listens as the nobles plan their massacre of the Huguenots. De Nevers refuses to take part in the plot. For that he is imprisoned.

V. During the massacre, de Nevers is killed. Valentine pleads with Raoul to become a Catholic and marry her but he refuses. While they speak St. Bris mounts his attack and kills them without realizing that one of the shadowy figures is his own daughter.

Idomeneo

		3 *acts*
COMP.: W. A. Mozart		Munich, 29 January 1781
LIBR.: Abbé Varesco		Glasgow, 1934
From an opera by Campra		Tanglewood, Mass., 1947
and Danchet		

CAST

Idomeneo, *king of Crete*	T	High Priest of Neptune	T
Idamante, *his son*	S	Voice of Neptune	B
Ilia, *Trojan princess*	S	People of Crete, Trojan Prisoners, Sailors,
Elektra, *Greek princess*	S	Soldiers, Priests of Neptune, Dancers
Arbace, *the king's confidant*	T	

SYNOPSIS

I. Ilia, a prisoner sent to Crete from the Trojan war, has fallen in love with Idamante. The prisoners are to be set free in celebration of Idomeneo's return but a storm nearly puts a stop to it. As guarantee of his safety Idomeneo has promised to sacrifice the first person he sees after landing. This person turns out to be Idamante.

II. Arbace advises the king to send his son away to avoid the vow. To Ilia's loss, he is to go away with Elektra to Greece. Again, however, Neptune intervenes to prevent the deception.

III. Idamante goes to fight a monster Neptune has sent against Crete. Idomeneo prepares to go ahead with a sacrifice. Ilia pleads to be substituted for Idamante. Finally Neptune relents on condition that Idomeneo relinquish his throne in favor of his son. Thus the tragic opera ends happily.

Iernin

3 acts

COMP.: G. Lloyd — Penzance, England, 6 November 1934
LIBR.: W. Lloyd — London, 1935

Ilsebill

5 scenes

COMP.: F. Klose — Karlsruhe, 7 June 1903
LIBR.: H. Hoffman — Munich, 1905
From a fairy tale by the brothers Grimm. — Basle, 1923

Immortal Hour, The

2 acts

COMP.:, R. Boughton — Glastonbury, England, 26 August 1914
LIBR.: By the composer — London, 1922
From a poem by Fiona MacLeod — New York, 1926

Impresario, The

See *Schauspieldirektor, Der*

In the Pasha's Garden

1 act

COMP.: J. L. Seymour — Metropolitan, 24 January 1935
LIBR.: H. Tracy
From a story by Dwight

Incoronazione di Poppea, L'

Prologue and 3 acts

COMP.: C. Monteverdi — Venice, Autumn, 1642
LIBR.: G. F. Busenello — Naples, 1651

This is Monteverdi's last opera. It was staged in Paris in 1913 and at Smith College, Massachusetts, in 1926. It is perhaps the earliest opera on a historical subject.

Intermezzo

2 acts

COMP.: R. Strauss — Dresden, 4 November 1924
LIBR.: By the composer — Berlin, 1925
Zurich, 1951

CAST

Christine	S	His wife	S
Little Franz, *her son*		Kapellmeister Stroh, *Storch's*	
Hofkapellmeister Robert Storch,		*partner*	T
her husband	Bar	Commercial Councillor, *a partner*	Bar
Anna, *chambermaid*	S	Justizrat, *a partner*	Bar
Baron Lummer	T	Kammersänger, *a partner*	B
Notary	Bar		

SYNOPSIS

I. Storch and his wife bicker constantly. He is packing to leave; Christine prepares to go skating. There she meets Lummer and tries to impress him about her husband the composer. Later the young Baron approaches her for money. Still later she intercepts a letter from an unknown woman to her husband. At last everything adds up; she decides to leave Storch immediately.

II. Storch, her telegram in his hand, is bewildered, wondering why his wife should want a divorce. Stroh suggests perhaps the mysterious letter was intended for him, the spelling of their names being similar. Stroh goes to Christine to explain, Storch himself finally arrives home and the reconciliation is complete.

NOTE

Strauss gave detailed descriptions of his own house as directions to the designer of the sets. The opera is partly autobiographical.

Iphigénie en Aulide

3 *acts*

COMP.: C. von Gluck

Opéra, 19 April 1774

LIBR.: Calzabigi

Oxford, 1933

From the tragedy by Racine

Philadelphia, 1935

CAST

Agamemnon, *king*	Bar	Achilles, *warrior and general*	T
Kalchas, *priest*	B	Patroclus, *his friend*	Bar
Clytemnestra, *queen*	MS	Arkas, *messenger*	B
Iphigénie, *princess, daughter of*		Greeks	
Agamemnon	S		

SYNOPSIS

I. The Gods have demanded that Agamemnon sacrifice his daughter in exchange for a favorable wind to Troy. He cannot worm out of it; she arrives at Aulis ready to marry Achilles in spite of her father's attempt to keep her away by spreading a rumor that Achilles is not worthy of her.

II. Unaware of the sacrifice, Achilles and Iphigénie approach the altar to be wedded. Achilles, hearing of the danger, swears to defend her and defies his general. Agamemnon, torn three ways by this fate, again tries to escape it by sending Iphigénie to Mycenae.

III. The Greeks, whose success in the war depends upon proper observance of the sacrifices required by the gods, force Agamemnon to fulfill his oath. Achilles again defies him, this time with an army. At this the gods declare the sacrifice no longer necessary since Agamemnon has fully demonstrated his intention to comply with it. Thus all is reconciled and the armies depart to make war upon Troy.

Iphigénie en Tauride

Tragedy in 4 *acts*

COMP.: C. W. Gluck

Opéra, 18 May 1779

LIBR.: F. Guillard

London, 1796

From Euripides

Metropolitan, 1916

CAST

Iphigénie, *Priestess of Diana*	S	Thoas, *King of Scythia*	B
Oreste, *her brother*	Bar	Diana, *Goddess*	S
Pylade, *his friend*	T	Scythians, Greeks, Priestesses	

MUSICAL HIGHLIGHTS

ACT I. Aria *De noirs pressentiments* (Such dark presentiments), Thoas

ACT II. The *Mad Scene* of Oreste

Aria *Unis dès la plus tendre enfance* (Together from the tenderest childhood), Pylade

ACT III. Aria *O malheureuse Iphigénie* (O unhappy Iphigénie), Iphigénie

Aria *Je t'implore et je tremble* (I implore you, I tremble), Iphigénie

SYNOPSIS

I. Iphigénie, now the Priestess of Diana, has dreamed that misfortune has befallen her family, whom she has not seen for many years. King Thoas has likewise heard of possible threats to his own safety. He calls for human sacrifice to prevent danger. Two captives are brought to the temple to be victims; they are Oreste and Pylade.

II. Oreste has been driven to the edge of madness by the Furies, his punishment for murdering his own mother. Iphigénie questions him. He tells her that King Agamemnon was murdered by Clytemnestra, and that Oreste slew her. But he does not reveal to Iphigénie that he is Oreste.

III. Iphigénie resolves to send him to Mycenae with a message. This would save him from the sacrifice. But he refuses to leave his friend. Pylade is therefore forced to go in his place.

IV. At the moment of the sacrifice, Iphigénie recognizes Oreste as her own brother. She pleads, but Thoas will not permit him to be relieved of the sacrifice. Pylades arrives at that time with help and saves them.

NOTES

According to Kobbé, Gluck's conducting was interrupted during a rehearsal when some of the orchestra objected that the accompaniment to *Le calme rentre dans mon coeur* (Calm returns to my heart) was too agitated to express the thought. Gluck replied "Go on all the same; he lies, he has killed his mother!"

Iphigénie en Tauride

	Tragedy in 4 acts
COMP.: N. Piccini	Opéra, 23 January 1781
LIBR.: A. Dubreuil	Copenhagen, 1787

This work was written at the instigation of the anti-Gluck faction in the war of the Gluckists and Piccinists. At the opening the prima donna was drunk. The opening was so complete a failure that the Piccinists could no longer carry on their side of the battle, thus letting the war end in favor of the Gluckists. It should be remembered that Gluck and Piccini themselves had very little to do with this partisanship. Piccini's *Iphigénie en Tauride* has been revived several times since.

Iphigénie en Tauride

The subject was used by Campra in 1704 and Galuppi in 1768.

Iris

	3 *acts*
COMP.: P. Mascagni	Rome, 27 November 1898
LIBR.: L. Illica	Philadelphia, 1902
	New York, 1902

CAST

Il Cieco, *blind man*	B	Ragpicker, Shopkeepers, Geishas,
Iris, *his daughter*	S	Laundry Girls, Samurai, Citizens,
Osaka, *rich young man*	T	Strolling Players, Beauty, Death, and a
Kyoto	Bar	Vampire

THE OPERAS

SYNOPSIS

The story concerns the kidnapping of Iris from her father by people in the pay of Osaka. Her father repudiates her because he thinks she freely chose to become a geisha.

Isis
COMP.: J. B. Lully
LIBR.: P. Quinault

Prologue and 5 acts
Paris, 5 January 1677

Quinault was banished for a time for suspected allusions in this libretto to a court scandal revolving around the king's mistress.

Italiana in Algeri, L'
(*The Italian Girl in Algiers*)
COMP.: G. Rossini
LIBR.: A. Anelli

2 acts
Venice, 22 May 1813
London, 1819
New York, 1832

CAST

Mustafa, *Bey of Algiers*	B	Lindoro, *Isabella's Italian lover*	T
Elvira, *his wife*	S	Isabella	C
Zulma, *her confidante*	C	Taddeo, *an old Italian*	Bar
Haly, *the Bey's captain*	B	Eunuchs of the Harem	

SYNOPSIS

I. The Bey of Algiers, tired of the same old harem, sends Haly to fetch for him an Italian wife. He has heard that Italian girls are much more interesting. Isabella, who was shipwrecked while hunting for her lost Lindoro, fits the bill perfectly. Haly brings her to the palace. Lindoro, as a matter of fact, is a captive and therefore a slave in the palace. The Bey has been unsuccessful in getting him to marry Elvira, of whom the Bey would gladly wash his hands.

II. Isabella organizes all the Italian captives and they connive to escape by a trick. She announces to the Bey that for him to be a model Italian husband he must be insensitive to all infidelities and must most certainly fall asleep after dinner. They test him. Isabella embraces Lindoro right before his eyes. Finally, in the supreme test of the Bey's after-dinner belief, they all climb into a boat and set sail for home.

NOTE

Rossini wrote this opera, in the style of *Commedia dell'Arte*, in less than a month.

Ivan Susanin
COMP.: M. Glinka
LIBR.: G. F. Rozen

Tragedy in 4 acts and Epilogue
St. Petersburg, 9 December 1836
La Scala, 1874
Covent Garden, 1887

CAST

Antonida, *Susanin's daughter*	S	Polish Commander	Bar
Ivan Susanin, *peasant*	B	Soldiers, Polish soldiers, People,	
Sobinin, *Antonida's bridegroom*	T	Procession of the Tsar	
Vanya, *orphan adopted by Ivan*	C		

SYNOPSIS

I. The Polish raiders have been repulsed. Sobinin returns from war to claim his bride. But Ivan delays the preparations until he learns that a Tsar has been proclaimed for Russia.

II. The Poles have learned this also and make plans to kidnap him.

III. Sweeping into the town again they capture Susanin and demand from him directions for reaching the Tsar's home. Ivan plays along with them, but sends Vanya ahead to warn the Tsar.

IV. While Sobinin and his army search for the raiders, Susanin leads the suspicious Poles deep into a forest, far away from the Tsar. When they discover his trick they kill him.

Epilogue. The Tsar's procession enters the capital amid rejoicing, thanks to the peasant Ivan Susanin.

NOTE

Before the communist revolution of 1917 the opera was known as *A Life for the Tsar*. With the revolution came not only a change in title, but certain changes of the text so that what was the personified glory of Russia, its Tsar, became less a reminder of the old days.

Ivan le Terrible
COMP.: G. Bizet   Bordeaux, 12 October 1951
LIBR.: Leroy and Trianon

Ivan the Terrible
See also *Pskovityanka*

Jeanie Deans
COMP.: H. Maccunn
LIBR.: J. Bennett
From Sir Walter Scott's novel
The Heart of Midlothian

4 *acts*
Edinburgh, 15 November 1894
London, 1896

Její Pastorkyňa (Jenufa)
(*Her Foster-Daughter (Jenufa)*)
COMP.: L. Janáček
LIBR.: By the composer
From a story by Preissová

3 *acts*
Brno, Czechoslovakia, 21 January 1904
Metropolitan, 1924
Venice, 1941

CAST

Grandmother Buryja, *mill owner*	C	His wife	MS
Laca Klemen, *her grandson*	T	Karolka, *their daughter*	MS
Steva Buryja, *her grandson*	T	Maid	MS
Kostelnicka Buryjovka,		Barena, *mill servant*	S
her widowed daughter-in-law	S	Jano, *shepherd boy*	S
Jenufa, *her foster daughter*	S	Aunt	C
Foreman at the Mill	Bar	Villagers, Musicians, Recruits	
Mayor	B		

SYNOPSIS

I. Jenufa waits for Steva, by whom she is pregnant. Laca, bitter because Steva is the favored grandson, quarrels with her. In comes the favored one, drunk, rejoicing to be out of the army. But his joy is harshly broken up when Kostelnicka tells him he may not marry Jenufa until he has managed to stay sober for one year. Later Laca, more bitter than ever to hear Jenufa given as prize to the favored brother, slashes her cheek with his knife.

II. The child is born. Kostelnicka confronts Steva with his responsibility, but he tells her he has arranged to marry Karolka. This gives Laca his opportunity. He comes to Kostelnicka to tell her of his love for Jenufa. But when he hears of the baby he draws back. Kostelnicka tells him not to worry, the baby is dead. Then, secretly, she takes it out and kills it.

III. Laca and Jenufa prepare for their wedding. They are interrupted by the shout of someone who has discovered the baby's body. The people accuse Jenufa of the murder, until Kostelnicka confesses publicly to her crime. Jenufa forgives her.

Jenufa withdraws from Laca, but his love for her is sincere. To her his gentleness is a new discovery. They come together now with new devotion.

Jenufa
See *Její Pastorkyňa*

Jeu de l'Amour et du Hasard, Le
(*The Game of Love and Chance*)   Monte Carlo, 1954
COMP.: H. Rabaud

Jewels of the Madonna
See *Gioielli della Madonna, I*

Jewess, The
See *Juive, La*

Jocelyn   4 *acts*
COMP.: B. Godard   Brussels, 25 February 1888
LIBR.: Silvestre and Capoul   Paris, 1888
From a poem by Lamartine
  This work contains the famous *Berceuse*.

Johnny Plays On
See *Jonny Spielt Auf*

Jolie Fille de Perth, La   4 *acts*
(*The Fair Maid of Perth*)   Paris, 26 December 1867
COMP.: G. Bizet
LIBR.: St. Georges and Adenis
From Sir Walter Scott

Jonny Spielt Auf   2 *parts*, 11 *scenes*
(*Johnny Plays On*)   Leipzig, 10 February 1927
COMP.: E. Krenek   Metropolitan, 1929
LIBR.: By the composer   Copenhagen, 1930
  A European attempt at jazz opera.

Jongleur de Notre Dame, Le   *Tragedy in* 3 *acts*
(*The Juggler of Notre Dame*)   Monte Carlo, 18 February 1902
COMP.: J. Massenet   Covent Garden, 1906
LIBR.: M. Lena   New York, 1908

CAST

Jean, *a tumbler*	T or S	Painter Monk	Bar
Boniface, *cook at the monastery*	Bar	Musician Monk	Bar
Prior	B	Sculptor Monk	B
Poet Monk	T	Two Angels	S, MS

SYNOPSIS

1. The prior caught Jean singing blasphemous songs outside the monastery. In the course of remonstrating with him he persuaded him to join the monks and dedicate himself to the church.

II. Jean was the only member of the group who had no art. The prior reminded him, however, that even the humblest art can serve religion.

III. All alone before the statue of the virgin, Jean performed his feats of juggling. The monks were scandalized and advanced to stop him, but stopped in wonder as the statue's arm rose to bless the boy. Then the prior and the others went forward to him as he collapsed in death.

Joseph   3 *acts*
COMP.: E. Méhul   Comique, 17 February 1807
LIBR.: A. Duval   Birmingham, England (Concert), 1826
                         New York, 1857

Jota, La   2 *acts*
COMP.: R. Laparra   Comique, 26 April 1911
LIBR.: By the composer

Juan, Don
See *Don Juan*
See also *Don Giovanni*
See also *Ombra di Don Giovanni, L'*

Judith   1 *act*
COMP.: E. Goossens, III   Covent Garden, 25 June 1929
LIBR.: A. Bennett   Philadelphia, 1929

Judith   3 *acts*
COMP.: A. Honegger   Monte Carlo, 13 February 1926
LIBR.: R. Morax   Boston, 1927

Judith   5 *acts*
COMP.: A. Serov   St. Petersburg, 28 May 1863
LIBR.: Serov and Maikov   Paris, 1909
From a play by Giacometti

Juggler of our Lady, The
See *Jongleur de Notre Dame, Le*

Juif Polonais, Le   3 *acts*
(*The Polish Jew*)   Comique, 11 April 1900
Comp.: C. Erlanger   St. Petersburg, 1904
LIBR.: Cain and Gheusi   Vienna, 1906
From a novel by Erckmann-Chatrain

Juive, La   *Tragedy in 5 acts*
(*The Jewess*)   Opéra, 23 February 1835
COMP.: J. Halévy   New York, 1845
LIBR.: A. E. Scribe   Drury Lane, 1846

CAST

Princess Eudoxia, *the emperor's niece*	S	Ruggiero, *provost*	Bar
Rachel, *Eléazer's daughter*	S	Albert, *sergeant*	B
Eléazer, *Jewish goldsmith*	T	Cardinal de Brogni	B
Leopold, *prince employed by Eléazer*		Soldiers, Populace	
as Samuel	T		

SYNOPSIS

I. During a great Christian festival the Jew Eléazer is dragged up before Ruggiero for working in his shop when everything else is closed. Ruggiero is harsh, but the Cardinal, recognizing Eléazer, pardons him. Later his apprentice Samuel, really the prince Leopold, serenades Rachel whom he loves.

II. During the Passover ceremony at the shop Rachel notices that Leopold does not take part. Her thoughts are interrupted however by the entrance of the princess Eudoxia who wants to buy a gold chain for her husband. Leopold is very careful not to be discovered. Later Eléazer finds out that although Samuel is in love with his daughter he cannot marry her. This enrages the father.

III. At the palace Rachel has traced prince Leopold to find that he is rumored to be in love with a Jewess, herself.

IV. The Cardinal tries to make Eléazer become a Christian in order to save Leopold. This the Jew refuses to do.

V. The Jewish father and daughter are thereupon executed. As Rachel is thrown into the flames ahead of her father, Eléazer turns to the Cardinal whom he has known all his life and informs him, "Your daughter dies there."

Julien	*Prologue and 4 acts*
COMP.: G. Charpentier	Comique, 4 June 1913
LIBR.: By the composer	Metropolitan, 1914
A sequel to *Louise*.	Prague, 1914
Jürg Jenatsch	*6 scenes*
COMP.: H. Kaminski	Dresden, 27 April 1929
LIBR.: By the composer	Nuremburg, 1937
From a novel by Meyer	
Kamyenny Gost	*3 acts*
(*The Stone Guest*)	St. Petersburg, 28 February 1872
COMP.: A. Dargomizhsky	Salzburg, 1928
LIBR.: Pushkin	Prague, 1935
On the subject of Don Juan. Score completed by Cui and Rimsky-Korsakov.	
Karl V	*2 parts*
COMP.: E. Krenek	Barcelona (in part), 18 April 1936
LIBR.: By the composer	Prague, 15 June 1938
Kata Kabanova	*Tragedy in 3 acts*
COMP.: L. Janáček	Brno, Czechoslovakia, 23 October 1921
LIBR.: Cervinka	Sadlers Wells, 1951
From Ostrovsky's *The Storm*	New York, 1960

CAST

Vanya Kudrjas, *Dikoy's clerk*	T	Tichon Ivanovitch Kabanov, *her son*		T
Glashka, *servant*	MS	Barbara, *foster child*		MS
Dikoy, *merchant*	B	Katerina Kabanova (Káta),		
Boris Grigorievitch, *his nephew*	T	Tichon's wife		S
Feklusha, *servant*	MS	Kuligin, *Vanya's friend*		Bar
Marfa Kabanova, *widow, Kabanička*	C			

SYNOPSIS

I. Boris is in love with the married Káta. The lovers live under the constant oppression of Dikoy and Kabanička. Only the confidence of Barbara helps Káta through the ordeal. To protect herself from temptation she tries to make her husband order her to remain faithful to him while he is away. He cannot understand why he should do such a thing.

II. He is gone. The lovers meet at night. Resistance to each other becomes impossible.

III. There is a terrible storm. The people are driven all into the same shelter by the rain. There, for all to hear, Káta screams to her returned husband of the terrible sin she has committed. She runs away. In the forest she meets Boris for a moment, then leaves him in sadness. She throws herself into the river and drowns.

Kenilworth Prologue and 3 acts
COMP.: B. O. Klein Hamburg, 13 February 1895
LIBR.: W. Müller
From Scott's novel

Khovantschina 5 acts
COMP.: M. Mussorgsky St. Petersburg, 21 February 1886
LIBR.: Mussorgsky and Stassov Drury Lane, 1913
Philadelphia, 1928

CAST

Prince Ivan Khovansky	B	Varsonofiev, *Vassily's attendant*	Bar
Prince Andrey Khovansky, *his son*	T	Kuzka, *archer*	Bar
Prince Vassily Galitsin	T	Three Archers	T, B, B
The Boyar Shaklovity	Bar	Streshniev, *an Old Believer*	T
Dositheus, *leader of the Old Believers*	B	Susanna, *an Old Believer*	S
Martha, *widow, an Old Believer*	MS	Archers, Old Believers, Maids in Waiting,
Scrivener	T	Slaves, Bodyguards, Populace
Emma, *young girl*	S	

SYNOPSIS

I. Shaklovity sends a message, via the Scrivener, to the Tsar to warn him against the Khovanskys. The Princes have allied themselves with the Old Believers to capture the throne. Meanwhile the young Prince, Andrey, has ceased his affair with Martha in order to woo Emma. Martha meets him in public and upbraids him for this. The prince would have killed her had not his father arrived on the scene and had Emma arrested for his own whimsical pleasure.

II. Dositheus wields subtle power among the various intrigues in the city. He repairs the torn relations between the old prince and Galitsin in time to protect their revolutionary interest before the Tsar suddenly arrives to suppress them.

III. The people are disturbed by the ravages of the Tsar's troops near the city. The archers range here and there in anarchic uncertainty. The people would rise against the Tsar but prince Khovansky counsels them to submit.

IV. As the old prince relaxes amid his pleasures Varsonofiev tries to warn him of his impending murder. He pays no attention. Shaklovity stabs him and kills him there. The murderer is banished and the archers are condemned for their opposition to the Tsar.

v. The Old Believers have lost their case; now they live under official persecution. With Martha and Andrey, who has followed her into this exile, the remaining ones mount a huge pyre on which they have decided to perish rather than to submit to the troops sent to capture them.

NOTE

The official premiere of *Khovantschina* took place in St. Petersburg, 7 November 1911. It opened in the Metropolitan in 1950. Like other magnificent works of Mussorgsky, it was completed and re-orchestrated by Nicolai Rimsky-Korsakov.

King Arthur, or The British Worthy   *Prologue, 5 acts, Epilogue*
COMP.: H. Purcell   London, May or June 1691
LIBR.: J. Dryden   New York, 1800
                                                                Cambridge, England, 1928

King in Spite of Himself
See *Roi Malgré Lui, Le*

King's Henchman, The   *3 acts*
COMP.: D. Taylor   Metropolitan, 17 February 1927
LIBR.: E. St. Vincent Millay

King of Lahore, The
See *Roi de Lahore, Le*

Kiss, The
See *Hubička*
See also *Poisoned Kiss, The*

Kitezh   *4 acts*
COMP.: N. Rimsky-Korsakov   St. Petersburg, 20 February 1907
LIBR.: V. Bielsky   Covent Garden, 1926
                                                          Ann Arbor, Mich. (Concert), 1932
Full title: *The Legend of the Invisible City of Kitezh and the Maiden Fevronia.*

Kluge, Die
(*The Wise Maiden*)   Frankfurt, 20 February 1943
COMP.: C. Orff
LIBR.: By the composer

CAST

King	Bar	Man with a Donkey	T
Farmer	B	Man with a Mule	Bar
Farmer's Daughter	S	Three Tramps	T, Bar, B
Jailer	B		

NOTE

Called *The Story of the King and the Wise Maiden*, the opera takes place in a simultaneous staging, with little stages in front of and above the main acting area. The costumes and masks, Orff stipulates, must be fantastic in their coloring and expression. *Die Kluge* provided an excellent show for the Marionette Theater in Munich.

Knight Bluebeard
See *Ritter Blaubart*

Knight of the Rose, The
See *Rosenkavalier, Der*

Koanga
COMP.: F. Delius
LIBR.: C. F. Keary
From a novel by Cable

3 *acts and Epilogue*
Elberfeld, Germany, 30 March 1904
Covent Garden, 1935

König Manfred
COMP.: C. Reinecke
LIBR.: F. Roeber

5 *acts*
Wiesbaden, 26 July 1867
Leipzig, 1868

Königin von Saba, Die
(*The Queen of Sheba*)
COMP.: K. Goldmark
LIBR.: H. von Mosenthal

Tragedy in 4 *acts*
Vienna, 10 March 1875
Metropolitan, 1885
Manchester, England, 1910

CAST

King Solomon	Bar	Sulamith, *his daughter*	S
Baal Hanan, *palace overseer*	Bar	Queen of Sheba	MS
Assad	T	Astaroth, *her slave*	S
High Priest	B	Voice of the Temple Watchman	B

SYNOPSIS

I. Assad, who was sent by the king to bring back the queen of Sheba, returns confused and in love because of the sight of a beautiful woman in a grove of the cedars of Lebanon. When the queen arrives Assad recognizes her as that woman, but she shows no recognition of him.

II. Assad marries Sulamith. At the wedding ceremony the queen interrupts, feigning to bring a wedding gift for the bride. But Assad throws his ring upon the floor thus desecrating the temple. For this he is condemned to death.

III. The queen intercedes with Solomon to win a reprieve for Assad. This the king will not grant. Instead, he allows the condemned man to be banished into the desert.

IV. There, banished, Assad formally refuses the queen's love, the cause of his losing Sulamith. Sulamith finds him, repentant, dying of exposure. She forgives him.

Königskinder, Die
(*The King's Children*)
COMP.: E. Humperdinck
LIBR.: E. Rosmer

3 *acts*
Metropolitan, 28 December 1910
Covent Garden, 1911
Boston, 1912

This was originally no more than music for a play, produced in Munich in 1897. Humperdinck expanded and developed it later.

Kovantchina
See *Khovantschina*

Lady Macbeth of Minsk
COMP.: D. Shostakovitch
LIBR.: Shostakovitch and Preis
From a novel by Lyeskov

4 *acts*
Leningrad, 22 January 1922
Cleveland, 1935
New York, 1935

Lakmé
COMP.: L. Délibes
LIBR.: Gondinet and Gille
From *Le Mariage de Loti*

Tragedy in 3 *acts*
Comique, 14 April 1883
London, 1885
New York, 1886

CAST

Lakmé, *Nilakantha's daughter*	S	Gérald, *English officer*	T
Mallika, *her slave*	MS	Nilakantha, *Brahmin priest*	BBar
Ellen, *English lady*	S	Frédéric, *English officer*	Bar
Rose, *English lady*	S	Hadji, *Nilakantha's servant*	T
Mistress Bentson, *their governess*	MS	Soldiers, Sailors, Tourists	

MUSICAL HIGHLIGHTS

ACT I. Invocation *Blanche Dourga Pâle Silva* (Fair Durga, Pale Silva), Lakmé
Barcarole *Dôme épais* (O Jasmine), Lakmé and Mallika
ACT II. Bell Song *Où va la jeune Hindoue?* (Where goes the Hindu maiden?), Lakmé

SYNOPSIS

I. Brahminism has been forbidden by the British governor, but Nilakantha keeps up his religion undismayed. Some English tourists have broken into his temple garden to see the sights. When they leave, one of their escorts, Gérald, stays behind to sketch some jewels. There Lakmé discovers him. It is love at first sight for Gérald. Lakmé makes him leave just before her father comes to kill the intruder.

II. Nilakantha does not know who it was that desecrated his temple. He sets Lakmé as bait for a trap. She is to sing a song in the crowd at the bazaar until Nilakantha spots the passerby who notices her. She sings the famous Bell Song. Suddenly, at the sight of Gérald, she faints and Nilakantha has the information he wants. During a procession that night Gérald falls from a stab wound, but Lakmé manages to spirit him away where she can nurse him back to health.

III. Gérald and Lakmé pledge eternal love for each other. In a while Frédéric finds them and reminds Gérald of his duty as a soldier. Lakmé, realizing that Gérald will now leave her, eats a poisonous plant that grows nearby and dies in his arms in the sight of Nilakantha who has come to kill the Englishman.

Lalla Roukh
COMP.: F. David
LIBR.: Lucas and Carré
From the poem by Thomas Moore

2 *acts*
Comique, 12 May 1862
Vienna, 1863
Budapest, 1863

This almost forgotten work won the State Prize of twenty thousand francs.

Leap Over the Shadow, The
See *Sprung über den Schatten*

Leonora
COMP.: W. H. Fry
LIBR.: J. R. Fry (his brother)
From Bulwer-Lytton's novel

3 *acts*
Philadelphia, 4 June 1845
New York, 1857
New York (in part), 1929

Probably the first "grand" opera by an American.

Leonora
See also *Fidelio*

Leonore 40/45
COMP.: R. Liebermann
LIBR.: H. Strobel

Basel, 25 March 1952
Berlin, 1953

Let's Make an Opera

COMP.: B. Britten
LIBR.: E. Crozier

Entertainment for Young People in 2 parts,
3 acts
Aldeburgh, England, 14 June 1949

CAST

Gladys Parworthy, *later* Miss Baggot, *housekeeper*	C	Anne Dougall, *later* Juliet Brook, 14	S
Norman Chaffinch, *later* Black Bob, *sweepmaster, and later* Tom, *the coachman*	B	Mr. Harper, *later* conductor	
		John, *later* Sam, *sweep boy*, 8	Treble
		Bruce, *later* Gay Brook, 13	Treble
Max Westleton, *later* Clem, *Bob's assistant, and later* Alfred, *gardener*	T	Monica, *later* Sophie Brook, 10	S
		Peter, *later* John Crome, 15	Treble
Pamela Wilton, *later* Rowan, *maid*	S	Mavis, *later* Tina Crome, 8	S
		Ralph, *later* Hugh Crome, 8	Treble

SYNOPSIS

I. Miss Parworthy tells everybody a story. The children decide to make an opera of it.
II. They rehearse, with the help of the audience.
III. This is the opera: A little chimneysweep named Sam is saved from the horrible Black Bob and Clem by the children and Rowan who hide him until it is safe for him to leave.

Libuša

COMP.: B. Smetana
LIBR.: J. Wenzig (Translated by Spindler)

3 acts
Prague, 11 June 1881
Vienna, 1924
Zagreb, 1933

Liebe der Danae, Die

(*The Love of Danae*)
COMP.: R. Strauss
LIBR.: J. Gregor

Comedy in 3 acts
Salzburg, 14 August 1952
La Scala, 1953
Covent Garden, 1953

CAST

Jupiter	Bar	Semele, *Queen*	S
Mercury	T	Europa, *Queen*	S
Pollux, *King of Eos*	T	Alcmene, *Queen*	MS
Danae, *his daughter*	S	Leda, *Queen*	C
Xanthe, *her servant*	S	Four Watchmen	4B
Midas, *King of Lydia*	T	Creditors, Servants, Followers, People	
Four Kings, *nephews to Pollux*	2T, 2B		

SYNOPSIS

I. Poor Pollux has seen bad times. His creditors hound him; everything seems awry. In a last effort to stave them off he tells them that rich King Midas is on his way to marry Danae. At this the girl dreams of a rain of gold and pearls. Midas does come, but in disguise. Then Jupiter, seizing the opportunity to woo a mortal beauty, comes made up as Midas, making a grand entrance.

II. The four queens recognize the absurd god. They are very jealous. But Jupiter prevents Midas from giving him away by threatening to withdraw the gift of the touch of gold. Midas then, dressed as himself, approaches Danae. She does not quite understand just who he is, but when she allows his embrace she turns immediately to gold. Jupiter and Midas defy each other, but the voice of Danae chooses the mortal king.

III. Midas renounces gold and returns to comfortable poverty. Quite willingly Danae goes along. Jupiter causes a rain of gold to get Pollux out of his financial mess and once again tries for Danae but to no avail; she will not betray her husband.

NOTE

The opera was in the final stages of rehearsal in 1944 when Hitler ordered all theaters closed. The production was held up eight years. Actually the work was written in 1940.

Life for the Tsar, A
See *Ivan Susanin*

Life of Orestes
COMP.: E. Krenek

Life of Orestes
See *Orestie*

Linda di Chamounix
COMP.: G. Donizetti
LIBR.: G. Rossi

3 *acts*
Vienna, 19 May 1842
London, 1843
New York, 1847

CAST

Marquis de Boisfleury	Bar	Antonio	Bar
Charles, *Vicomte de Sirval*	T	Maddalena	S
Prefect	B	Intendant	T
Pierrotto	C	Peasants, Savoyards	
Linda	S		

Lobetanz, Der
COMP.: L. Thuille
LIBR.: O. Bierbaum

3 *acts*
Karlsruhe, 6 February 1898
Vienna, 1901
New York, 1911

Lodoiska
COMP.: L. Cherubini
LIBR.: C. F. Loraux

3 *acts*
Paris, 18 July 1791
Berlin, 1797
New York, 1826

Lodoletta
COMP.: P. Mascagni
LIBR.: G. Forzano
From Ovida—*Two Little Wooden Shoes*

3 *acts*
Rome, 30 April 1917
Metropolitan, 1918
Vienna, 1920

Lohengrin
COMP.: R. Wagner
LIBR.: By the composer

3 *acts*
Weimar, 28 August 1850
Covent Garden, 1875
New York, 1871
Metropolitan, 1885

CAST

Henry the Fowler, *king of Germany*	B	Elsa of Brabant	S
Lohengrin, *knight of the Grail*	T	Duke Godfrey, *her brother*	Bar

Frederick of Telramund, *count of*		King's Herald	B
Brabant	Bar	Counts, Nobles, Ladies of Honor,	
Ortrud, *his wife*	MS	Pages, Attendants	

MUSICAL HIGHLIGHTS

ACT I. Elsa's Dream
ACT II. Aria *Euch Lüften* (Fair Breezes), Elsa
ACT III. Prelude
Bridal Chorus
Narrative *Im fernen Land* (In distant lands), Lohengrin
Lohengrin's Farewell (The Swan Song).

SYNOPSIS

I. Before the king, Frederick accuses Elsa of having murdered her brother Godfrey. For that reason, he explains, he married Ortrud instead of Elsa. The king demands a trial by battle between Frederick and Elsa's champion. Elsa says a knight of her dream will be her champion. The king commands trumpets to sound to the four directions, and Lohengrin appears in a boat drawn by a white swan. He exacts one promise from Elsa, that she will never ask his name. When she has agreed, he challenges Frederick and wins.

II. Ortrud conspires with her banished Frederick to sow the seed of curiosity in Elsa's mind and thus to regain their position. At the wedding of the strange knight and Elsa, Ortrud shouts that the bride does not know who her bridegroom may be.

III. After the wedding, in the privacy of night, Elsa asks the forbidden question. There is a moment of danger when Frederick breaks in to murder Lohengrin, but the White Knight kills the intruder.

Lohengrin takes her to the spot where he first appeared, where the knights have gathered. There he tells her that he is the son of Parsifal. His swan reappears. He is about to depart when Ortrud shouts that the swan is really the bewitched brother Godfrey, changed by Ortrud's evil magic. Silently Lohengrin prays and the swan changes to a man, Godfrey brought back to life. With this act Lohengrin departs in his boat, drawn by a dove.

NOTES

Wagner wrote *Lohengrin* backwards—first the last act, then the second, finally the first. It was finished in 1847 but the composer's complicity in the revolt of 1849 prevented its production until the mighty Liszt used his influence to mount it at Weimar. Wagner did not hear the opera until he was allowed to return to Germany in 1861.

Lombardi, I
	4 *acts*
COMP.: G. Verdi	La Scala, 11 February 1843
LIBR.: T. Solera	London, 1846
From a poem by Crossi	New York, 1847

I Lombardi was the first of Verdi's operas to be heard in New York.

Louise
	Romance in 4 *acts*
COMP.: G. Charpentier	Comique, 2 February 1900
LIBR.: By the composer	New York, 1908
	Covent Garden, 1909
	Metropolitan, 1921

CAST

Louise	S	Julien, *artist*	T
Her Mother	C	Louise's father	B
Irma	S	Noctambulist	T
Camille	S	Ragman	B
Gertrude	C	Bohemian	Bar
Errand Girl	S	Song Writer	Bar
Elise	S	Junkman	B
Blanche	S	Painter	B
Suzanne	C	Two Philosophers	T, B
Street sweeper	MS	Poet	Bar
Ragpicker	MS	Student	T
Forewoman	MS	Two Policemen	2Bar
Milk Woman	S	Street Arab	S
Newspaper Girl	S	Sculptor	Bar
Coalgatherer	MS	Old Clothes Man	T
Marguérite	S	Apprentice	Bar
Madeleine	C	King of Fools	T
Dancer		Pedlars, Workmen, People	

SYNOPSIS

I. Louise insists that Julien go through the formality of writing to her parents to ask for her hand in marriage. Her tyrannical mother hates Julien, but at least her father seems more considerate.

II. She is at work in a dressmaking factory when Julien serenades her outside the factory window, driving her to tears. She has to go to him.

III. They run off to live together in raptures of bohemian joy until her mother intervenes to tell her that her father has become seriously ill and needs his daughter.

IV. When her father has recovered, the parents refuse to let Louise return to the former life of love she led with Julien. Finally, however, she defies them and runs away.

NOTE

In act III occurs the celebrated romance *Depuis le Jour* (E'er since the day), which concert audiences still enjoy although the opera is losing its popularity.

Love for Three Oranges, The

Prologue and 4 acts

COMP.: S. Prokofiev   Chicago, 30 December 1921
LIBR.: By the composer   New York, 1922
From a comedy by Gozzi   La Scala, 1947

CAST

King of Clubs, *ruler*	B	Lineta, *princess in an orange*	C
Prince, *his son*	T	Nicoletta, *princess in an orange*	MS
Princess Clarissa, *his niece*	C	Ninetta, *princess in an orange*	S
Leandro, *the Prime Minister and King of Spades*	Bar	Cook	B
		Farfarello, *devil*	B
Truffaldino, *the king's jester*	T	Smeraldina, *Fata Morgana's servant*	MS
Pantaloon, *the king's adviser*	Bar	Master of Ceremonies	T
Celio, *magician, the king's protector*	B	Herald	B
Fata Morgana, *witch, Leandro's protector*	S	Trumpeter	Bass Trombone
		Ten Reasonable Spectators	5T, 5B

94

Monsters, Drunkards, Gluttons, Guards,
Servants, Soldiers, Jokers, Highbrows,

Wits, Romantics, Lowbrows, Little
Devils, Doctors, Courtiers

SYNOPSIS

I. The prince, unfortunately, is a hypochondriac. Only if he laughs may he be cured. Pantaloon and the king make a valiant attempt, but Leandro intends to prevent their success. With Clarissa ready to marry him, he plans to fill the prince with gloomy poetry, thus enhancing his own chances to win the throne.

II. Truffaldino puts on his funniest shows, but the prince will not laugh. Only when Fata Morgana accidentally trips over something does he burst into paroxysms. The embarrassed and enraged witch curses him saying he will fall in love with three oranges.

III. The prince and Truffaldino are wafted away to a castle guarded by the Cook. They snatch three oranges from this worthy and run away into the desert. Truffaldino slits one open. Out steps a princess, dying of thirst. There being no water handy she does die. Another orange, another princess. Again a death of thirst. The prince opens the third, and this princess would die also but for the Ten Reasonable Spectators who quickly provide her with a bucket of water. This is only a temporary triumph. Fata Morgana turns the girl into a rat and substitutes Smeraldina.

IV. The princess being very ugly as a rat, Celio works to restore her original appearance. When he has succeeded the king condemns all the prince's enemies, filling the stage with a great rout.

Love in a Village
COMP.: T. Arne
LIBR.: I. Bickerstaffe

3 acts
Covent Garden, 8 December 1762
Philadelphia, 1767
New York, 1768

This opera was partly written by Arne and partly selected by him from pieces by fifteen composers. It was performed in Kingston, Jamaica, in 1779, Calcutta in 1791, and in modern times in London, 1923.

Love of Danae
See *Liebe der Danae*

Love of Three Kings
See *Amore dei tre Re, L'*

Lowlands
See *Tiefland*

Lucia di Lammermoor
COMP.: G. Donizetti
LIBR.: S. Cammarano
From Scott's novel

Tragedy in 3 acts
Naples, 26 September 1835
London, 1838
New York, 1843
Metropolitan, 1883

CAST

Lord Henry Ashton of
Lammermoor (*Enrico*) — Bar
Lucy, *his sister* (*Lucia*) — S
Edgar, *master of Ravenswood*
(*Edgardo*) — T
Lord Arthur Bucklaw (*Arturo*) — B

Raymond, *chaplain of Lammermoor*
(*Raimondo*) — B
Alice, *Lucy's companion* (*Alisa*) — MS
Norman, *follower of Ashton*
(*Normando*) — T
Relatives, Retainers, Friends

95

THE OPERAS

MUSICAL HIGHLIGHTS

ACT I. Legend *Regnava nel silenzio* (The night was all in silence), Lucia
Aria *Quando rapita* (With such speed), Lucia
Duet *Verranno a te sull'aure* (My sighs will reach you), Lucia, Edgardo
ACT II. Sextet *Chi mi fena* (What restrains me?), Lucia, Alisa, Edgardo, Enrico, Arturo, Raimondo
ACT III. Mad Scene, Lucia
Aria *Tu che a Doi* (You who to heaven), Edgardo

SYNOPSIS

I. The last of his hereditary enemies remains a trouble to Henry when he learns that Edgar and Lucy have been seeing each other. He swears to kill Edgar. But Lucy loves him, and sees him before he leaves for France.

II. Henry arranges for her to marry Bucklaw and at the same time contrives to undermine her faith in Edgar by means of a forged letter hinting that he has betrayed her. But at the moment of signing the marriage compact, Edgar reappears.

III. Henry challenges Edgar to a duel. Meanwhile Lucy has become insane and has killed her new husband. When the time for the duel arrives, Edgar sees not his antagonist but a funeral procession for Lucy, who has died. Full of remorse, realizing that her madness must have been caused by his misunderstanding of her marriage, he stabs himself to death.

Lucio Silla　　　　　　　　　　　3 *acts*
COMP.: W. A. Mozart　　　　　　　Milan, 26 December 1772
LIBR.: G. de Gamerra (altered by　　Prague, 1929
Metastasio)

Lucretia
See *Rape of Lucretia, The*

Lucrezia Borgia　　　　　　　　*Prologue and 2 acts*
COMP.: G. Donizetti　　　　　　　La Scala, 26 December 1833
LIBR.: F. Romani　　　　　　　　London, 1839
From Victor Hugo　　　　　　　　New York, 1844

CAST

Alfonso d'Este, *duke of Ferrara*	Bar	Rustighello, *follower of Don Alfonso*	T
Lucrezia Borgia	S	Gubetta, *Lucrezia's servant*	B
Maffio Orsini	C	Astolfo	B
Gennaro, *Venetian nobleman*	T	Gentlemen-at-Arms, Officers, Nobles of	
Liverotto, *Venetian nobleman*	T	the Venetian Republic, Ladies-in-Wait-	
Vitellozzo, *Venetian nobleman*	B	ing, Capuchin Monks, etc.	
Gazello	B		

SYNOPSIS

PROLOGUE. At a festival Lucrezia, in disguise, discovers Gennaro asleep on a bench. He wakes and they speak together until his friends arrive. Among them is Maffio Orsini who tears off Lucrezia's mask and reveals to Gennaro that she is a murderess.

I. Alfonso has condemned Gennaro to death for having insulted him. The duke insists that Lucrezia poison him, since he believes that Gennaro is her secret lover. She gives Gennaro an antidote, however, and helps him to escape.

II. At a banquet in Ferrara Lucrezia poisons all the guests, thinking they are all her enemies. But one of them is Gennaro. In horror she tells him that he is her own illegitimate son. She tries to give him an antidote which he refuses; he would rather die with his friends.

NOTE

This opera, unfortunately, perpetuates the myth that Lucrezia Borgia was a ruthless murdress. In reality, she was one of the great women of a violent era, whose biography (by Bellonci) is well worth reading. The famous poisonings and other murders were accomplished by men, some of them by Lucrezia's brother Cesare.

Luisa Miller   *Tragedy in 3 acts*
COMP.: G. Verdi   Naples, 8 December 1849
LIBR.: S. Cammarano   New York, 1852
From Schiller's play *Kabale und*   London, 1858
   Liebe

CAST

Count Walter	B	Laura, *peasant girl*	C
Rodolfo, *his son*	T	Wurm	B
Miller, *old soldier*	Bar	Ladies, Pages, Servants, Archers,	
Luisa, *his daughter*	S	Villagers	
Federica, *Duchess of Ostheim,*			
Walter's niece	C		

SYNOPSIS

I. Wurm, rival for Luisa's love, tells Miller that her suitor is really Rodolfo, his master's son. But the count has promised a marriage between Rodolfo and the widow Federica. Rodolfo prevents the imprisonment of the Millers by threatening to reveal how Walter gained his title by means of murder.

II. Miller is put in prison anyway. To save him, Luisa agrees to write a letter saying her love for Rodolfo was faked. When Rodolfo is confronted with this evidence, he agrees to the arranged marriage, but swears also to kill Luisa and himself.

III. He seeks her out and hears her admit that she wrote the letter. He produces poison which they both drink. Only then does she tell him how Wurm compelled her to do it, though it was a lie. Just before their deaths, Rodolfo avenges them both by killing their traitor.

Lulu   *Tragedy in 3 acts*
COMP.: A. Berg   Zürich (in part), 2 June 1937
LIBR.: By the composer   Venice (Complete), 1949
From Wedekind   Essen, 1953

CAST

Lulu	S	Alwa, *his son, writer*	T
Gräfin Geschwitz	MS	Animal Tamer (*in Prologue*)	B
Wardrobe Mistress	C	Rodrig, *athlete* (*Act* II)	
Schoolboy, *gymnasiast* (*the same*		(*same singer as above*)	
singer as above)		Schigolch, *old man*	B
Doctor	Spkr	Prince, *traveller in Africa*	T
Painter	T	Theater Director	B
Dr. Schön, *editor*	Bar		

97

In the Prologue we are introduced to the Animal Trainer's troupe, which includes, significantly, Lulu. I. Lulu is a dangerously attractive girl. The painter cannot paint for lust for her. While he is struggling to win a kiss from her, her husband breaks in and sees the event. The shock of it kills him. When the painter has become her husband, the whole sequence occurs again, this time involving Dr. Schön. She forces Schön to break off his engagement to another in favor of herself.

II. Now Schön is the husband. But the new suitor is the Gräfin Geschwitz, which gives a different sort of bitter twist to Lulu's progress. Schön discovers that there are several other lovers including even Alwa. Schön loses his reserve, drives the others away and tries to get Lulu to shoot herself. In this he fails; she takes the revolver and shoots him instead. In a filmed interlude she is brought to trial and condemned, but makes her escape with the help of the Gräfin.

III. Her past chases her to Paris, and from there to London. Finally she reaches the depths of walking the streets. Her last pickup is Jack the Ripper who murders her.

NOTE
Unlike *Wozzeck*, which was written in an extension of ordinary tonality, *Lulu* entirely conforms to the dodecaphonic system of harmony. The entire opera, like *Wozzeck*, is composed in formal periods so that parts are in sonata form, parts in rondo. Berg had not completed the last act before he died, but the remainder was fully sketched.

Lurline	3 *acts*
COMP.: W. Wallace	Covent Garden, 23 February 1860
LIBR.: E. Fitzball	Cambridge, Mass., 1863
	New York, 1869

Lustigen Weiber von Windsor, Die	*Comedy in 3 acts*
COMP.: O. Nicolai	Berlin, 9 March 1849
LIBR.: H. von Mosenthal	Philadelphia, 1863
From Shakespeare's *The Merry Wives*	London, 1864
of Windsor	Metropolitan, 1900

CAST

Sir John Falstaff	B	Dr. Caius	B
Herr Fluth (*Mr. Ford*)	Bar	Frau Fluth (*Mistress Ford*)	S
Herr Reich (*Mr. Page*)	B	Frau Reich (*Mistress Page*)	MS
Fenton	T	Jungfer Anna Reich (*Anne Page*)	S
Junker Spärlich (*Slender*)	T	Erster Burger (*First Citizen*)	T

SYNOPSIS
I. We listen as Mrs. Ford and Mrs. Page compare love letters they have each received from Falstaff. Then we listen to Mr. Page telling his daughter's suitors that he wishes her to marry Slender. He does not like either Caius or Fenton.

Falstaff comes to court Mrs. Ford but must hide in a laundry basket when the husband surprises them, as the women had secretly planned.

II. Ford, calling himself Bach, seeks out Falstaff in his favorite tavern and extracts what he can of the knight's affair with his wife. Meanwhile all three young suitors serenade Anne in her garden. Home again, Ford hunts for traces of Falstaff's presence but the culprit, dressed as an old, deaf woman escapes handily.

III. In Windsor Forest poor Falstaff is surrounded by strange beings disguised as sprites and phantoms, completing the ladies' plan for his chastisement.

Lustigen Weiber von Windsor, Die
See also *Falstaff*
See also *Sir John in Love*

Macbeth	*Tragedy in Prologue and 3 acts*
COMP.: E. Bloch	Comique, 30 November 1910
LIBR.: E. Fleg	Naples, 1938
From Shakespeare	

Macbeth	*Tragedy in 3 acts*
COMP.: L. Collingwood	Sadler's Wells, 12 April 1934
LIBR.: By the composer	
From Shakespeare	

Macbeth	*Tragedy in 4 acts*
COMP.: G. Verdi	Florence, 14 March 1847
LIBR.: F. M. Piave	New York, 1850
From Shakespeare	Dublin, 1859
	Metropolitan, 1959

CAST

Lady Macbeth	S	Malcolm, *Duncan's son*	T
Macbeth, *a general*	Bar	Fleance, *Banquo's son*	Mute
Banquo, *a general*	B	Doctor	B
Macduff, *Scottish noble*	T	Three Witches	
Duncan, *King of Scotland*	Mute	Hecate, *witch*	
Lady in Waiting, to Lady Macbeth	S		

SYNOPSIS

I. Three witches tell Macbeth he will become powerful. But the king lives, occupying the ultimate power Macbeth could aspire to. Therefore, goaded by his wife, he plans to murder the king while the royal entourage stay as guests at his house. The deed is done while the king sleeps. Banquo and Macduff discover the body.

II. To insure the final steps toward power, Banquo must be murdered too. Macbeth has this done by hired assassins. But they fail to complete their work. Fleance escapes them. That evening Macbeth holds a festive banquet. It turns sour when Banquo's ghost attends, visible only to Macbeth's tortured mind.

III. Again the witches prophesy for Macbeth. This time they foretell his death at Dunsinane, and of the future kings who will spring from Banquo's line. Lady Macbeth urges him, being now so powerful, to overlook these grim forebodings.

IV. There is a battle at Dunsinane, between Malcolm's army and Macbeth's. During the height of it, news reaches Macbeth that his wife is dead. He fights with renewed vigor. But Macduff finds him alone and in single combat slays him.

NOTES

This opera was a favorite of Verdi's. He began with a scenario and worked from it. When time came for rehearsals he become most particular that each detail should be perfect. This made it necessary to rehearse the duet after the murder more than one hundred and fifty times, and to go over the sleepwalking scene constantly for a period of three months. Nevertheless the work has its difficulties with audiences, not the least of which is a certain ludicrous quality about the witches.

Macbeth
See also *Lady Macbeth*

Madama Butterfly
COMP.: G. Puccini
LIBR.: Giacosa and Illica
From Belasco's play

Tragedy in 2 acts
La Scala, 17 February 1904
Covent Garden, 1905
New York, 1906

CAST

Cio-Cio San, *Madame Butterfly*	S	Prince Yamadori	Bar
Suzuki, *her servant*	MS	The Bonze, *priest, Cio-Cio San's uncle*	B
Kate Pinkerton, *Pinkerton's*		Imperial Commissioner	B
American wife	MS	Official Registrar	Bar
Lieutenant B. F. Pinkerton, *USN*	T	Trouble, *Cio-Cio San's child*	
Sharpless, *U.S. Consul at Nagasaki*	Bar	Relatives of Cio-Cio San, Friends,	
Goro, *marriage broker*	T	Servants	

MUSICAL HIGHLIGHTS

ACT I. Love duet *Viene la sera* (Evening is falling), Cio-Cio San and Pinkerton
ACT II. Aria *Un bel dì vedremo* (One fine day he'll come home), Cio-Cio San
Aria *Sai cos'ebbe cuore* (Do you hear what he's saying?), Cio-Cio San

SYNOPSIS

I. Pinkerton, far from home, had arranged to entertain himself by having a Japanese wife and home while he was there. Sharpless tried to dissuade him, especially after he met the bride and found out that she was seriously in love with the American. She had even renounced her religion. When The Bonze heard about this, he called down the curses of her family and her ancestors upon her.

II. The marriage lasted not at all. Pinkerton was called away from Japan and stayed three years. During all that time Cio-Cio San kept herself faithful to him in spite of every attempt Sharpless could make to tell her that Pinkerton was married in America. Sharpless tried to get her to understand a letter from Pinkerton explaining that he was about to arrive with his American wife, but Cio-Cio San was too thrilled to see his ship coming to understand the facts.

When Pinkerton came to the house, Suzuki had managed to put Cio-Cio San to sleep upstairs. Pinkerton could not stand the thought of telling her the truth; he left abruptly so that when Cio-Cio San descended she found Sharpless and Kate waiting for her. Quietly she sent them with a message asking Pinkerton to come for his son in half an hour. Then she stabbed herself with a ceremonial sword.

NOTES

Puccini went from Italy to London to see the play, of which he could not have understood very much, his English being not remarkable. He was moved by it, however, and set to work on the opera, taking three years for the job. The first performance was a notorious fiasco, but with a few revisions it was successfully revived two months later at Brescia.

Madame Angot's Daughter
See *Fille de Madame Angot, La*

Madame Chrysanthème
COMP.: A. Messager
LIBR.: Hartmann and Alexandre
From a novel by Loti

Prologue, 4 acts and Epilogue
Paris, 30 January 1893
Montreal, 1912
New York, 1920

Madame Sans-gêne
COMP.: U. Giordano
LIBR.: R. Simoni
From a play by Sardou and Moreau

3 *acts*
Metropolitan, 25 January 1915
Turin, 1915
Comique, 1916
Breslau, 1931

Madonna Imperia
COMP.: F. Alfano
LIBR.: A. Rossato
From a story by Balzac

1 *act*
Turin, 5 May 1927
Metropolitan, 1928
Vienna, 1928

Madrisa
COMP.: H. Haug
LIBR.: J. Jegerlehner

3 *acts*
Basel, 15 January 1934

Maestro di Musica, Il
COMP.: *Unknown*

2 *acts*
1731

Although this work is commonly attributed to Pergolesi, its author is unknown.

Magic Flute
See *Zauberflöte, Die*

Magistrate, The
See *Corregidor, Der*

Maid Marian
See *Robin Hood*

Maid Mistress
See *Serva Padrona, La*

Maid of Arles, The
See *L'Arlesiana*

Maid of Pskov, The
See *Pskovityanka*

Mala Vita
COMP.: U. Giordano
LIBR.: N. Daspuro

3 *parts*
Rome, 21 February 1892
Berlin, 1892

Malheurs d'Orphée, Les
(*The Griefs of Orpheus*)
COMP.: D. Milhaud
LIBR.: A. Lunel

3 *scenes*
Brussels, 7 May 1926
Paris, 1927
Buenos Aires, 1927

CAST

Orphée	Bar	Four Animals	S, C, T, B
Euridice	S	Three Bohemians	S, MS, C

THE OPERAS

Man Without a Country, The
COMP.: W. Damrosch
LIBR.: A. Guiterman
From the story by Hale

2 *acts*
Metropolitan, 12 May 1937

Manfred
See *König Manfred*

Manon
COMP.: J. Massenet
LIBR.: Meilhac and Gille
From the novel by Prévost

Tragedy in 5 acts
Comique, 19 January 1884
Liverpool, 1885
New York, 1885

CAST

Chevalier des Grieux	T	Javotte, *actress*	S
Count des Grieux, *his father*	B	Rosette, *actress*	S
Lescaut, *Manon's cousin*	Bar	Innkeeper, Sergeant, Soldier, Students,	
Guillot de Morfontaine, *old roué*	T	Gamblers, Merchants, Wives, Croup-	
de Bretigny, *nobleman*	Bar	iers, Sharpers, Guards, Travellers,	
Manon Lescaut	S	Ladies, Gentlemen, Porters, Postillions,	
Pousette, *actress*	S	People	

MUSICAL HIGHLIGHTS

ACT II. Aria *Adieu, notre petite table* (Goodby, our little table), Manon
The Dream *En fermant les yeux* (On closing my eyes), des Grieux
ACT III. Gavotte *Obéissons quand leur voix appelle* (O listen when the voice of youth), Manon
Aria *Ah! Fuyez douce image* (Ah! leave me, sweetest dream), des Grieux

SYNOPSIS

I. At very first sight, des Grieux and Manon fall in love. Commandeering a carriage reserved for Guillot they fly to Paris.

II. There her cynical cousin Lescaut, with de Bretigny, finds them living together but unmarried. They arrange to have des Grieux taken away from her, leaving her free to take up with de Bretigny.

III. She does, and leads a life of richness and pleasure. But one day she hears that des Grieux has decided to enter a monastery. She goes there to see him. The interview weakens his determination to take the orders.

IV. Together again they go gambling at the casino. Luck is with the indecisive des Grieux. He wins so much so quickly that Guillot calls the police to arrest him as a cheat and her as a prostitute.

V. Des Grieux goes free but Manon is condemned to be deported to the new colony of Louisiana. Des Grieux intercepts the march of the prisoners to the harbor and bribes the guard to let Manon go free. She is so weakened that she sees visions of brilliant jewels as she dies in his arms.

Manon
See also *Portrait de Manon*

Manon Lescaut
COMP.: F. Auber
LIBR.: A. E. Scribe
From the novel by Prévost

Comique, 23 February 1856
Liège, 1875

102

THE OPERAS

Manon Lescaut
COMP.: G. Puccini
LIBR.: Praga, Oliva and Illica
From the novel by Prévost

Tragedy in 4 acts
Turin, 1 February 1893
Covent Garden, 1894
Philadelphia, 1894
Metropolitan, 1907

CAST

Manon Lescaut	S	Music Master	T
Lescaut, *her brother*	Bar	Musician	MS
Chevalier des Grieux	T	Lamplighter	T
Geronte de Ravoir, *Treasurer General*	B	Naval Captain	B
Edmondo, *student*	T	Wig maker	Mime
Innkeeper	B	Sergeant of Archers	B

SYNOPSIS

I. Manon and des Grieux fall in love at first sight and elope to Paris.

II. Geronte, whom she jilted for des Grieux, manages to retrieve her and keep her amid magnificence. Des Grieux sees her once but she will not run away with him and give up her new jewels. This delay in their second elopement causes them to be caught. As an abandoned woman she is tried and condemned to be sent to Louisiana.

III. Des Grieux pleads to be allowed to go with her. The captain of the ship warns him against it, but takes him along.

IV. In the harshness of the new world she dies.

Maria di Rudenz
COMP.: G. Donizetti
LIBR.: S. Cammarano

3 acts
Venice, 30 January 1838
Rio de Janeiro, 1851

Maria Golovin
COMP.: G.-C. Menotti
LIBR.: By the composer

Brussels, 20 August 1958
New York, 1958

Marie Galante
COMP.: K. Weill

Maritana
COMP.: V. Wallace
LIBR.: E. Fitzball
From the play *Don César de Bazan*

3 acts
Drury Lane, 15 November 1845
Philadelphia, 1846
New York, 1848

CAST

Maritana, *gypsy*	S	Captain of the guard	Bar
Don César de Bazan	T	Marquis of Montefiore	B
Don José de Santarem, *courtier*	Bar	King	B
Lazarillo, *poor boy*	MS	Alcade	B
Marchioness of Montefiore	MS	Soldiers, Gypsies, Populace	

Marouf
COMP.: H. Rabaud
LIBR.: L. Népoty

5 acts
Comique, 15 May 1914
Metropolitan, 1917

CAST

Princess Saamcheddine	S	Two Merchants	T, B
Fatimah, *Marouf's wife*	S	Chief Sailor	T
Marouf, *cobbler*	T or Bar	Two Muezzins	T
Sultan of Khaitan	B	Ahmad, *pastry cook*	B
Vizier	Bar	Cadi	B
Ali	Bar	Two Mamaliks	B
Fellah	T		

SYNOPSIS

I. Marouf is unhappy. His wife is a bad one. She runs to the Cadi to complain that Marouf beats her. For this the Cadi has him whipped. All in all there is only one thing to do; he goes away with the sailors.

II. He is shipwrecked but found by Ali. Ali sets him up in style as a rich merchant. His reputation becomes such that even the Sultan wishes to see him.

III. The Sultan offers Marouf a princess for a bride. Of course he accepts.

IV. When the princess discovers that her husband is really not rich at all she shows how intelligent she is by disguising herself as a boy and getting him to fly with her away from the city.

V. Just before the Sultan's army catches up with them they discover a magic ring. By proper manipulation of this object they produce a genie who produces riches, thus giving body to their deception and saving their lives.

Marriage, The
See *Zhenitba*

Marriage of Figaro, The
See *Nozze di Figaro, Le*

Martha   5 *acts*
COMP.: F. von Flotow   Vienna, 25 November 1847
LIBR.: W. Friedrich   Drury Lane, 1849
From a Ballet-Pantomime   New York, 1852

CAST

Lady Harriet Durham, *Maid of*		Nancy, *Lady Harriet's waiting maid*	C
Honor to the Queen	S	Sheriff	B
Lord Tristan de Mikleford,		Three Man Servants	T, B, B
her cousin	B	Three Maid Servants	S, S, MS
Plunkett, *young farmer*	B	Courtiers, Pages, Ladies, Hunters,	
Lionel, *his foster brother*	T	Huntresses, Farmers, Servants	

Masaniello   *Tragedy in 5 acts*
COMP.: F. Auber   Opéra, 29 February 1828
LIBR.: Scribe and Delavigne   Drury Lane, 1829
                                                         New York, 1831

CAST

Alfonso d'Arcos, *son of the Viceroy*	T	Fenella, *Masaniello's sister*	Dancer
Lorenzo, *his confidant*	T	Borella, *fisherman*	B
Selva, *officer in the guard*	B	Moreno, *fisherman*	B
Masaniello, *fisherman*	T	Elvira, *Princess*	S
Pietro, *his friend*	Bar	Maid of Honor to the Princess	MS

THE OPERAS

SYNOPSIS

I. Alfonso has cast off the mute Fenella in order to marry the Princess. The Princess, however, hears of the dumb girl's plight and is able to learn from her in pantomime that Alfonso has betrayed her.

II. By the same means, Fenella tells Masaniello and Pietro of her trouble. The men swear to depose the tyrants who oppress them.

III. Alfonso sends soldiers to find Fenella. This is enough provocation for Masaniello to call his revolt into being.

IV. Having won, Masaniello is now the strong man. To him come Alfonso and Elvira, begging protection from the mobs. For his seeming change of heart Pietro swears revenge against the revolutionary leader.

V. He poisons Masaniello, but the poisoned man is still able to go out with his soldiers once more. Masaniello dies protecting Elvira and Fenella kills herself in remorse.

NOTES

Masaniello is a milestone in operatic history, being one of the earliest realistic tragedies. It had its effect on history also, when at Brussels, 25 August 1830, its performance triggered the outbreak of the Belgian revolution.

Masked Ball, The
See *Ballo in Maschera, Un*

Massimilla Doni
COMP.: O. Schoeck
LIBR.: A. Rueger
From a novel by Balzac

3 *acts*
Dresden, 2 March 1937
Zürich, 1937

Master Peter's Puppet Show
See *Retablo de Maese Pietro, El*

Mastersingers, The
See *Meistersinger, Die*

Mathis der Maler
(*Mathias the Painter*)
COMP.: P. Hindemith
LIBR.: By the composer

7 *scenes*
Zürich, 28 May 1938
London (Concert), 1939
Edinburgh, 1952

CAST

Albrecht von Brandenburg, *Archbishop of Mainz*	T	Truchsess von Waldburg, *confederate leader*	B
Mathis (Grünewald), *Painter*	Bar	Sylvester von Schaumberg, *his officer*	T
Lorenz von Pommersfelden, *dean of Mainz*	B	Graf von Helfenstein	Mute
Wolfgang Capito, *Cardinal's councillor*	T	Gräfin von Helfenstein, *his wife*	C
Riedinger, *rich Lutheran*	B	Ursula, *Riedinger's daughter*	S
Hans Schwalb, *peasant leader*	T	Regina, *Schwalb's daughter*	S

SYNOPSIS

I. Mathis, at work on a fresco, interrupts himself to help the rebel Schwalb and his daughter to escape pursuit.

II. Before the Cardinal von Brandenburg the painter defends the peasants' rebellion. The Cardinal cannot disobey his church and help them. He gives Mathis permission, however, to withdraw from his service.

III. For a year he is gone. When he returns he meets Ursula, whom he loves. She is unaware that there is a political plan to marry her to the Cardinal as a means of helping the cause of Lutheranism.

III. There is a battle between peasants and soldiers. It teaches one fact of importance to Mathis—he is no warrior. He does help to save the life of Regina, after her father is killed, however.

V. The Cardinal refuses to break his vow of celibacy, but he grants the Lutherans permission to meet publicly.

VI. Mathis and Regina make their escape together. During the course of it they rest for a while. He dreams of his temptations: wealth, luxury, and so forth. The vision tortures him. He seems to see the Cardinal, as St. Paul, advising and comforting him.

VII. Regina dies. At the end, Ursula and Mathis are with her. Feeling his own mortality, Mathis slowly puts away his tools and his various works.

NOTES

This is Hindemith's fifth opera, famous enough in performance but made more famous by the orchestral suite he made from it. The sixth scene is based upon Grünewald's great painting over the altar at Isenheim.

Matrimonio Segreto, Il
(The Secret Marriage)
COMP.: D. Cimarosa
LIBR.: G. Bertati
From Colman *The Clandestine Marriage*

Comedy in 2 acts
Vienna, 7 February 1792
La Scala, 1793
London, 1794
Metropolitan, 1934

CAST

Geronimo	B	Fidalma, *his sister*	MS
Elisetta, *his daughter*	S	Count Robinson, *English nobleman*	B
Carolina, *his daughter*	S	Paolino	T

SYNOPSIS

I. Paolino and Carolina have become secretly wed. She wants to reveal it. She pleads with him to let the secret out. Meanwhile the Count has sent overtures to her father mentioning his interest in Elisetta but Elisetta is in love with Paolino. When this becomes clear to the Count, he graciously changes his affections to favor her sister Carolina. Poor Geronimo cannot fathom it all.

II. Geronimo and the Count finally agree it shall be Carolina. Desperately Paolino works to prevent a terrible situation, but Elisetta and Fidalma make matters worse by intriguing to have Carolina sent to a convent.

Finally Elisetta hears love-making going on behind Carolina's door. Thinking to catch the Count, she rouses the whole house. Fortunately it was not the Count, but the properly though secretly married Paolino and Carolina. Geronimo forgives them, the Count marries Elisetta after all and everybody is happy.

NOTE

Leopold II so enjoyed hearing this comedy that he invited the entire company to a late supper after opening night, then requested they repeat the opera, which they did with gusto.

THE OPERAS

Mavra
COMP.: I. Stravinsky
LIBR.: By the composer
From a folktale

1 *act*
Opéra, 2 June 1922
New York, 1923
BBC, 1935

Mavra was privately performed at the house of Princess Polignac in Paris, 1922.

Maximilien
COMP.: D. Milhaud
LIBR.: A. Lunel

3 *acts*
Opéra, 4 January 1932

From a German libretto by Hoffman and Franz Werfel's *Juarez and Maximilian*.

Maximilien
See also *Massimilla*

Medée
COMP.: D. Milhaud
LIBR.: M. Milhaud (his wife)
From Euripides, Seneca, and Corneille.
Commissioned by the Government of France.

1 *act*, 3 *scenes*
Antwerp, 7 October 1939
Opéra, 1940

Medea
The subject has been used also by Marc Antoine Charpentier (1693), Luigi Cherubini (1797), Giovanni Pacini (1843), and Lehman Engel (1935).

Medium, The
COMP.: G.-C. Menotti
LIBR.: By the composer

2 *acts*
New York, 8 May 1946
London, 1948

CAST

Monica, *Flora's daughter*	S	Mrs. Gobineau, *her client*	S
Toby, *mute*	Dancer	Mr. Gobineau, *her husband, client*	Bar
Madame Flora (*Baba*), *the Medium*	C	Mrs. Nolan, *their friend, client*	MS

SYNOPSIS

I. While in the process of deceiving her clients with the sepulchral imitations of her accomplices, Madame Flora feels something touch her. She sends the clients away and tries to discover who has played a trick on her. She is terribly frightened.

II. When the clients return she tries to tell them that she has been a fraud, but they refuse to believe it. She throws them all out. Later, intoxicated, she takes a gun and shoots wildly about the room at what she thinks is a ghost. Blood appears on the floor as Toby falls dead behind a curtain.

Mefistofele
COMP.: A. Boito
LIBR.: By the composer

Prologue, 4 acts, Epilogue
La Scala, 5 March 1868
London, 1880
New York, 1880
Metropolitan, 1883

CAST

Mefistofele	B	Wagner	T
Faust	T	Elena	S
Margherita	S	Pantalis	C
Martha	C	Nereo	T

Mystic Choir, Celestial Phalanxes, Cherubs, Penitents, Wayfarers, Men at arms, Huntsmen, Students, Citizens, Populace, Townsmen, Witches, Wizards, Greek Chorus, Sirens, Naiads, Dancers, Warriors

SYNOPSIS

PROLOGUE. Mefistofele wagers that he can turn the good Faust to evil.

I. He reveals himself to Faust and agrees to provide him with one hour of untroubled peace in exchange for his soul.

II. Mefistofele takes Faust and Margherita to a witches' sabbath. Faust sees there a vision of Margherita in chains. But she has fallen in love with him and he with her.

III. Bereft of her lover, Margherita languishes in prison, insane. Faust returns to help her, but she dies.

IV. In the Vale of Tempe Faust meets Helen of Troy and again falls in love.

EPILOGUE. The old Faust rejects all transient pleasures, finding salvation only in the Scriptures. Mefistofele fails to ensnare him. Faust dies in salvation.

Meistersinger von Nürnberg, Die	3 acts
(*The Mastersingers of Nürnberg*)	Munich, 21 June 1868
COMP.: R. Wagner	Drury Lane, 1882
LIBR.: By the composer	Metropolitan, 1886

CAST

Hans Sachs, *cobbler*	Bar	Hans Schwarz, *stocking weaver*	B
Veit Pogner, *goldsmith*	B	Hans Foltz, *coppersmith*	B
Kunz Vogelgesang, *furrier*	T	Walther von Stolzing,	
Conrad Nachtigall, *buckle maker*	B	*Franconian knight*	T
Sixtus Beckmesser, *town clerk*	B	David, *Sachs' apprentice*	T
Fritz Kothner, *baker*	Bar	Night Watchman	B
Balthazar Zorn, *pewterer*	T	Eva, *Pogner's daughter*	S
Ulrich Eisslinger, *grocer*	T	Magdalena, *her nurse*	MS
Augustin Moser, *tailor*	T	Burghers, Journeymen, Apprentices,	
Hermann Ortel, *soap boiler*	B	Girls	

MUSICAL HIGHLIGHTS

The Overture

ACT I. Pogner's Address

Aria *Am stillen Herd* (By silent hearth), Walther

ACT II. Sach's Monologue *Wie duftet doch der Flieder* (How sweet the scent of Elder), Sachs
Cobbler's Song, Sachs

ACT III. Monologue, *Wahn, Wahn, überall, Wahn!* (Mad, mad, everyone's mad!), Sachs
Dance of the Apprentices
Prize Song, Walther

SYNOPSIS

I. In church Walther and Eva exchange silent signallings and messages of love during the end of the service. The congregation is hustled out in order to make room for the contest of the Mastersingers which is to take place there later. Pogner speaks with his daughter to propose that he announce that her hand will be the prize this year. She agrees to it and Walther immediately becomes a candidate. The trials come. Beckmesser, who is, as Sachs points out, a rival for the girl's hand, marks every error of accepted style that Walther makes in his song, thus winning the first round.

II. In the evening Sachs learns of Eva's love for Walther. The good man decides to help. When Beckmesser comes to serenade her, Sachs turns the tables on him by marking each of his mistakes with a resounding bang of the hammer on his last. The constant interruptions, the constant crescendo required of Beckmesser, everything combines to raise the whole neighborhood screaming for silence in the night time.

III. Walther shows Sachs the words of a song he has composed for the contest. Sachs allows the manuscript to fall into Beckmesser's hands on the correct assumption that Beckmesser will make an ass of himself trying to reproduce someone else's inspiration. When the contest opens this succeeds magnificently. Sachs proposes that Walther sing his own song and all the town rejoices in its beauty. All honor goes to Sachs after congratulations to Walther and his new fiancée.

Mephistopheles
See *Faust*
See also *Mefistofele*
See also *Doktor Faust*

Mermaid, The
See *Russalka*

Merrie England
COMP.: E. German
LIBR.: B. Hood

2 acts
London, 2 April 1902

Merry Mount
COMP.: H. Hanson
LIBR.: R. Stokes
From a story by Hawthorne
Merry Mount was first performed in concert in Ann Arbor, Michigan, 1933.

3 acts
Metropolitan, 10 February 1934

Merry Wives of Windsor, The
See *Lustigen Weiber von Windsor, Die*
See also *Falstaff*
See also *Sir John in Love*

Midsummer Night's Dream
See *Songe d'une Nuit d'Été, Le*

Mignon
COMP.: A Thomas
LIBR.: Barbier and Carré
From Goethe's *Wilhelm Meister*

3 acts
Comique, 17 November 1866
Drury Lane, 1870
New York, 1871
Metropolitan, 1883

CAST

Mignon, *kidnapped in childhood*	MS	Lothario, *wandering minstrel*	B
Philine, *actress*	S	Giarno, *gypsy*	B
Frédéric, *nobleman*	T or C	Antonio, *servant*	B
Wilhelm Meister, *travelling student*	T	Townspeople, Gypsies, Actors, Actresses,	
Laertes, *actor*	T	Servants	

MUSICAL HIGHLIGHTS

ACT I. Aria *Connais-tu le pays?* (Knowest thou the land?), Mignon
Entr'acte *Gavotte*

ACT II. Aria *Adieu Mignon* (Goodby, Mignon), Wilhelm
Duet *As-tu souffert?* (Have you suffered?), Mignon, Lothario
Polonaise *Je suis Titania* (I am Titania), Philine

ACT III. Aria *Elle ne croyait pas* (Ah, don't believe it), Wilhelm

SYNOPSIS

I. Seeing her about to be beaten by the gypsy, Wilhelm saves Mignon by buying her from him. She falls in love with him.

II. But Philine loves him too, which makes Mignon jealous. Wilhelm finally decides Mignon must go and bids her farewell. Distracted by this she wanders near the conservatory while Philine is inside acting in Shakespeare. There she meets Lothario who, in his cloudiness of mind, thinks to do her a favor by setting fire to the place. By accident, Mignon is the only one inside at the time. Wilhelm saves her from the flames.

III. Wilhelm buys an old derelict castle for the girl. They all go to see it, including Lothario. Strange memories stir in the old minstrel's heart as he begins to recognize it as his former home, left when his daughter was kidnapped long ago. Certain tokens they both remember bring out the identity of Mignon as the missing daughter.

Mireille   3 acts *(Originally 5)*
COMP.: C. Gounod   Paris, 19 March 1864
LIBR.: Carré   London, 1864
From Mistral's poem *Mireio*   Metropolitan, 1919

CAST

Mireille	S	Taven, *old woman*	MS
Vincent, *her lover*	T	Andreloux, *shepherd*	MS
Ourrias, *bull tender*	Bar	Maître Ambroise, *Vincent's father*	B
Maître Ramon, *Mireille's father*	B	Clémence	S

SYNOPSIS

I. Against the approval of her parents, Mireille has fallen in love with Vincent.

II. Ourrias asks for her hand, but is refused. Ambroise asks for it for his son but he is likewise turned down.

III. Ourrias makes an attempt on the life of Vincent. The lovers meet in the sanctuary. There her father finds them and relents, blessing her union with the man she loves.

Mitridate re di Ponto   3 acts
(*Mithridates, King of Ponto*)   Milan, 26 December 1770
COMP.: W. A. Mozart
LIBR.: V. Cigna-Santi
From the tragedy by Racine

Mona   3 acts
COMP.: H. Parker   Metropolitan, 14 March 1912
LIBR.: B. Hooker
This work won the ten thousand dollar Metropolitan prize.

Mond, Der
(*The Moon*)   Munich, 5 February 1939
COMP.: C. Orff
LIBR.: By the composer

CAST

Narrator	Another Mayor
Four youths, *who steal the moon*	Three groups of people
Farmer	Old man
Village Mayor	Little Child
Landlord	

Monna Vanna   *4 acts*
 COMP.: H. Février   Opéra, 13 January 1909
 LIBR.: M. Maeterlinck   Boston, 1913
 From Maeterlinck's play   New York, 1914

Monsieur Beaucaire   *Prologue and 3 acts*
 COMP.: A. Messager   Birmingham, England, 7 April 1919
 LIBR.: Rivoire and Veber   London, 1919
 From the story by Tarkington New York, 1919

Montezuma's Daughter
 See *Azora*

Mörder, Hoffnung der Frauen
 COMP.: P. Hindemith   Stuttgart, 4 June 1921
 LIBR.: O. Kokoschka   Prague, 1923

Mother, The
 COMP.: S. Hollingworth   1954

Mother of Us All, The   *Pageant in 2 acts, 8 scenes*
 COMP.: V. Thomson   New York, 7 May 1947
 LIBR.: G. Stein

CAST

Susan B. Anthony	S	Constance Fletcher	S
Anne	S	Gloster Heming	MS
Gertrude S.	MS	Isabel Wentworth	MS
Virgil T.	Bar	Anna Hope	MS
Daniel Webster	Bar	Lillian Russell	S
Jo the Loiterer	T	Jenny Reefer	S
Chris the Citizen	Bar	Ulysses S. Grant	Bar
Indiana Elliott	MS	Herman Atlan	Bar
Angel More	S	Donald Gallup	T
Henrietta M.	S	A.A. and T.T.	
Henry B.	T	Andrew J.	T
Anthony Comstock		Negro Man and Woman	
John Adams	T	Indiana Elliott's Brother	
Thaddeus Stevens	T		

THE OPERAS

NOTE

The authors call *The Mother of Us All* a Pageant. Its theme is the winning in the United States of political rights for women. People enter the pageant from all periods in history to remark upon the event.

Muette de Portici, La
(*The Dumb Girl of Portici*)
See *Masaniello*

Murder in the Cathedral
See *Assassinio nel Cattedrale, L'*

Mute Wife, The
See *Schweigsame, Frau, die*

Mutter, Die
COMP.: A. Hába
LIBR.: By the composer

10 *scenes*

Munich, 17 May 1931

Die Mutter won the Czech State Prize in 1931. It is one of the foremost examples of opera written with microtones.

Nabucco
COMP.: G. Verdi
LIBR.: T. Solera

4 *acts*

La Scala, 9 March 1842
London, 1846
New York, 1848

CAST

Abigaille, *slave,*		Nabucco, *king of Babylon*	
supposed daughter of Nabucco	S	(*Nebuchadnezzer*)	Bar
Fenena, *Nabucco's daughter*	S	Zaccaria, *high priest of Jerusalem*	B
Ismaele, *nephew of the*		High Priest of Babylon	B
King of Jerusalem	T	Abdallo, *Nabucco's officer*	T
		Anna, *Zaccaria's sister*	S

SYNOPSIS

I. Nabucco's army advances toward Jerusalem where Fenena is being held hostage in the temple by Ismaele who loves her. Abigaille, leading some of the troops, invades the temple and threatens Ismaele with death unless he will renounce Fenena for her. In a moment, however, Nabucco himself arrives. Zaccaria attempts to kill the hostage, but Ismaele stops him while Nabucco ravages the place.

II. Back in Babylon, Fenena, who rules during her father's absence, grants a general amnesty to the captive Hebrews. Abigaille lays claim to the crown, but Nabucco returns and puts a stop to all pretensions by proclaiming that he is not only king, but god. In a clap of thunder the crown is wrested from him and the king is reduced to madness.

III. Abigaille becomes regent. Her first act is to arrange to wipe out the Jews. Zaccaria prophesies the fall of Babylon, but the Jews have nearly given up hope.

IV. With the help of Abdallo, Nabucco breaks out of his imprisonment in time to save Fenena from the trumped-up execution ordered by Abigaille. He has prayed to Jehovah for pardon, causing the idols to be destroyed as if by magic, a triumph for Zaccaria. There is general rejoicing but for Abigaille who poisons herself and dies.

Nadeshda
COMP.: A. Thomas
LIBR.: J. R. Sturgis

4 *acts*
Drury Lane, 16 April 1885
Dublin, 1885·

Naïla
COMP.: P. Gaubert
LIBR.: M. Léna

3 *acts*
Opéra, 7 April 1927

Natoma
COMP.: V. Herbert
LIBR.: J. Redding

3 *acts*
Philadelphia, 25 February 1911
New York, 1911

Navarraise, La
COMP.: J. Massenet
LIBR.: Claretie and Cain

2 *acts*
Covent Garden, 20 June 1894
Metropolitan, 1895
Saigon, 1900

Nebuchadnezzer
See *Nabucco*

Nerone
COMP.: P. Mascagni
LIBR.: Targioni-Tozzetti
From a comedy by Cossa

Comedy in 3 acts
La Scala, 16 January 1935
Zürich, 1937

Nerone
COMP.: A. Boito
LIBR.: By the composer

Tragedy in 4 acts
La Scala, 1 May 1924
Rome, 1928
Buenos Aires, 1926

CAST

Nerone, *emperor of Rome (Nero)*	T	Tigellino, *follower of Nerone*		B
Simon Mago, *sorcerer*	Bar	Gobrias, *follower of Mago*		T
Fanuèl, *Christian*	Bar	Dositeo, *Roman*		Bar
Asteria	S	Perside, *Christian*		S
Rubria, *Vestal Virgin,*		Cerinto		C
secretly a Christian	MS			

SYNOPSIS

I. Nero, full of guilt for murdering his mother, buries her ashes. Suddenly a figure seems to rise from the grave and threaten him. Nero flies from it. Simon Mago stays to find that it is Asteria, whom he can use in his future evil workings. Two Christians meet nearby to speak of love together. They are Rubria and Fanuèl. In Mago they see their worst enemy.

II. Simon produces a prodigious but wholly false ritual including oracles, visions of goddesses, and so forth, with which to charm Nero. Nero recognizes Asteria playing goddess and destroys the illusion. He condemns Simon to be thrown from a tower and fly—if he can.

III. Simon manages to escape and hunt out the Christians in their secret meeting. He betrays them to the guards. Meekly but with fortitude the Christians submit to capture.

IV. Nero orders magnificent games to amuse himself and the people of Rome. Rubria, as Vestal Virgin, pleads to him to save the Christians but the thought is so abhorrent to him that he has her thrown in with them as another victim. He settles back with the audience to watch the sport as flames rise in the background, burning Rome in a fire set by Simon Mago for revenge. In the pit where the torn bodies of victims are heaped together, Rubria and Fanuèl confess to each other their love and their resignation.

NOTE

Boito spent most of his mature life working on this opera, which was produced posthumously.

Neues vom Tage
(News of the Day)
COMP.: P. Hindemith
LIBR.: M. Schiffer

3 *parts*
Berlin, 8 June 1929

Nibelungenlied
See *Ring des Nibelungen, Der*

Nightdancers
COMP.: E. Loder
LIBR.: G. Soane

2 *acts*
London, 28 October 1846
New York, 1847

Night Flight
See *Volo di Notte*

Nightingale, The
See *Rossignol, Le*

Noël
COMP.: F. d'Erlanger
LIBR.: J. and P. Ferrier

3 *acts*
Comique, 28 December 1910
Chicago, 1913

Norma
COMP.: V. Bellini
LIBR.: F. Romani
From a tragedy by Soumet

Tragedy in 2 acts
La Scala, 26 December 1831
London, 1833
New York, 1841

CAST

Pollione, *roman pro-consul in Gaul*	T	Clotilda, *Norma's friend*	S
Oroveso, *archdruid, Norma's father*	B	Flavio, *centurion*	T
Norma, *druid high priestess*	S	Priests, Gauls, Priestesses, Temple Virgins,	
Adalgisa, *temple virgin*	S	Norma's children	

MUSICAL HIGHLIGHTS

ACT I. Aria *Casta diva* (Chaste goddess), Norma
ACT II. Duet *Mira, O Norma* (Hear me, O Norma), Adalgisa, Norma
    Duet *Qual cor tradisti* (How you have betrayed), Norma, Pollione

SYNOPSIS

I. Once long ago, while Pollione and Norma were in love, she bore him a child. But the love is past now, and Pollione is interested rather in Adalgisa whom he asks to go with him to Rome. Adalgisa is a faithful friend to the forlorn Norma. She tells her of her love and Norma finds out who the man is.

II. It would be better if Adalgisa would go with him; it would free Norma of a dangerous entanglement with a national enemy. Since she will not go, however, Norma incites the Gauls to war against the Romans. Meanwhile Pollione, who has been looking for Adalgisa, breaks into the temple and is caught there by the Gauls. To save him Norma tells them there is a worse traitor present, herself. They build a pyre upon which the traitor must be sacrificed. When it is in flames, Pollione leaps upon it to join her in death.

North Star, The
See *Étoile du Nord, L'*

Notre Dame de Paris
COMP.: W. Fry   Philadelphia, 3 May 1864

Nozze di Figaro, Le   *Comedy in 4 acts*
(*The Marriage of Figaro*)   Vienna, 1 May 1786
COMP.: W. A. Mozart   London, 1812
LIBR.: L. da Ponte   Covent Garden, 1819
From Beaumarchais *La Folle Journée ou*   New York, 1824
Le Mariage de Figaro

CAST

Figaro, *valet to the count*	Bar	Don Basilio, *music master*	T
Susanna, *maid to the countess*	S	Countess Almaviva	S
Dr. Bartolo	B	Antonio, *gardener, Susanna's uncle*	B
Marcellina, *duenna*	S	Don Curzio, *lawyer*	T
Cherubino, *former page to the countess*	S	Barbarina, *Antonio's niece*	S
Count Almaviva	Bar	Chorus of Villagers	

MUSICAL HIGHLIGHTS

The Overture

ACT I. Aria *Se a caso Madama* (If my lady should call you), Figaro
Aria *Se vuol ballare* (If you'd go dancing), Figaro
Aria *La vendetta* (Now comes vengeance), Dr. Bartolo
Aria *Non so più cosa son, cosa faccio* (I don't know if it's pain or pleasure), Cherubino
Aria *Non più andrai* (No more play), Figaro

ACT II. Aria *Porgi Amor* (God of love), Countess
Cavatina *Voi che sapete* (You who have seen him), Cherubino
Aria *Cognoscete, signor Figaro* (You must tell me, Mr. Figaro), Almaviva

ACT III. Duet *Crudel, perchè finora* (O why are you so cruel), Susanna and the Count
Aria *Vedrò mentr'io sospiro* (Must I withhold my breathing), Count
Aria *Dove sono?* (O where are they?), Countess
Letter Duet *Che soave zeffiretto* (How soft the evening breezes), Susanna and the Countess

ACT IV. Aria *Aprite un po' quegli occhi* (Open your eyes just a little), Figaro
Cavatina *Deh vieni non tardar* (O come and don't delay), Susanna

SYNOPSIS

I. Figaro and Susanna are about to be married. There are complications, however. The count is interested in her; Cherubino cannot be trusted in that respect; and Marcellina intends to blackmail the groom into marrying her instead.

II. Too, the countess has long languished for attention and love from her own husband. She agrees quite easily to an intrigue by which Cherubino will dress as Susanna and keep a rendezvous with the count. While they dress the boy for the part, the count surprises them, nearly catching the young page. The count is completely bewildered but he suspects the plot, even though each person manages to cover up for the other.

III. The plot takes shape as Susanna delivers the treacherous letter, asking for the assignation with the count during the preparations for the marriage.

IV. At the appointed time and place Figaro happens to see the countess dressed as Susanna and vice versa and believes the worst as he sees first Cherubino and then the count have their supposedly secret meetings with what he thinks is his own bride. When Figaro sees the supposed countess, however, he recognizes who is who and woos Susanna so that the count, who is obviously watching, believes his wife unfaithful. As the unfortunate count approaches the height of his fury the real countess reveals herself and intercedes for the servants. All ends happily and all marriages become sublime.

NOTES

This fascinating masterpiece was not so well received at its opening in Vienna. Not until a subsequent production at Prague did it meet with the success we take now for granted. It is said that Mozart wrote the music very quickly, perhaps in less than a month. He had a good libretto to work with, shaped by da Ponte from the complex and funny play by Beaumarchais.

Nusch-Nuschi

COMP.: P. Hindemith	1 act
LIBR.: F. Blei	Stuttgart, 4 June 1921
	Prague, 1923

Oberon

COMP.: C. M. von Weber	3 acts
LIBR.: J. R. Planché	Covent Garden, 12 April 1826
From the poem *Oberon* by Wieland	New York, 1828
from the story *Huon de Bordeaux*	Metropolitan, 1918

CAST

Sir Huon of Bordeaux	T	A Sea Nymph	S
Sherasmin, *his squire*	Bar	Charlemagne, Haroun al Rashid,	
Oberon, *king of the fairies*	T	Babekan, Almanzor, Abdullah,	
Puck	S	Titania, Roshana, Namouna,	
Reiza, *daughter of Haroun al Rashid*	S	Nadina	Spkrs
Fatima, *her attendant*	MS		

SYNOPSIS

I. Oberon in a fury vows never to be reconciled with Titania until he shall find two lovers who remain faithful throughout every trouble. His trusty Puck tells him of Huon who has been sentenced, for an affront to Charlemagne, to go alone into Bagdad to kill the Caliph's right-hand man and marry his daughter. Oberon has the knight and his squire brought before him in a charmed sleep, and presents Huon with a vision of Reiza, thus adding fire to the warrior's duty. Off go Huon and Sherasmin to Bagdad. On the way they come across Babekan whom they rescue, but who in turn betrays them since he claims priority to Reiza's hand.

II. Using the magic horn given to him by Oberon, Huon invades the very court of Haroun al Rashid and carries off Reiza and Fatima. Now begins the trial of love that Oberon requires. Puck causes the returning knight to be shipwrecked and attacked by pirates. The pirates carry off Reiza, leaving Huon a castaway on the barren shore.

III. Rumors whisper to Huon that Reiza is captive of the kindly Emir of Tunis. When he goes to rescue her he finds that the Emir's wife Roshana wishes to have help in killing her husband to assuage her jealousy over Reiza. Huon will not help her. She tries to do it herself but fails. The Emir has them captured and condemns Huon to be put to death for complicity. A blast on the magic horn, however, brings Oberon to the rescue. All are transported back to the court of Charlemagne with a chorus of thanksgiving.

NOTES

The libretto for this very influential opera was written in English. In the original work there were extensive scenes without musical accompaniment for which Mahler later composed musical connections and a few accompaniments which were to go with a new German translation by Brecher.

Oberto, Conte di S. Bonifacio
(*Oberto, Count of St. Boniface*)
COMP.: G. Verdi
LIBR.: A. Piazza (altered by Morelli and Solera)
Verdi's first opera.

2 acts
La Scala, 17 November 1839
Barcelona, 1842
Chicago (Concert), 1903

Oedipus
COMP.: G. Enesco
LIBR.: E. Fleg
This work made some use of microtones.

Tragedy in 4 acts
Opéra, 10 March 1936

Oedipus Rex
COMP.: I. Stravinsky
LIBR.: J. Cocteau (Translated into Latin by Danielou)
From Sophocles

Opera-Oratorio in 2 acts
Paris (Oratorio), 30 May 1927
Vienna (Opera), 1928
New York (Opera), 1931
London (Oratorio), 1936

CAST

Narrator		Tiresias, *soothsayer*	B
Oedipus, *King of Thebes*	T	Shepherd	T
Jocasta, *his wife*	MS	Messenger	BBar
Creon, *her brother*	BBar	Chorus of the Old Men of Thebes	

SYNOPSIS

I. There has been a terrible plague in the city of Thebes. Creon, returning from a visit to the oracle, announces to the king and to the people that the cause of the plague is the presence within the city of the murderer of the former king. Oedipus curses the unknown murderer and orders that he be found. To him, under duress, comes the blind Tiresias who tells him only one fact: the king's murderer is himself a king.

II. Jocasta, deriding the oracle, accidentally reveals that the old king, her former husband, was killed at a certain meeting of three roads. On such a morning Oedipus, travelling from his home, had once killed a man. Suspicions are still dim in his mind when a Shepherd comes to tell him that his father, Polybus, is dead. This is a shock to the king, for long ago the oracle had declared that he would slay his own father. That indeed was his reason for travelling away from home. Thus Polybus could not have been his father, but the circumstances incriminate Oedipus as the murderer of the former king of Thebes who must have been his father. The truth is exposed. At the news that Jocasta has hanged herself, Oedipus goes and tears out his own eyes.

Oedipus Tyrannus
COMP.: C. Orff

Stuttgart, 1959

Oca del Cairo, L'
COMP.: W. A. Mozart
LIBR.: G. Varesco

2 acts
Paris, 6 June 1867
London, 1870
Salzburg, 1936

Actually the opera Mozart wrote under this name was not finished. The performances at Paris and elsewhere were made up of the unfinished work plus additions from *Lo Sposo Deluso* and others.

Old Maid and the Thief, The
COMP.: G.-C. Menotti
LIBR.: By the composer

1 act, 14 scenes
NBC radio, 22 April 1939
Philadelphia, 11 February 1941

CAST

Laetitia	S	Miss Pinkerton	S
Miss Todd	C	Bob, *a tramp*	Bar

SYNOPSIS

The two sweet old maids are busy having tea together when there is a knock at the door. They open it to find a poor tramp, Bob, who asks them for a little food. Delighted with his handsomeness they take him in and feed him. Further delighted at the presence of a man in the house, they prevail upon him to stay over for a while.

News reaches them that there has been a jailbreak nearby. Thinking Bob may be the escapee, they keep him hidden away while they resort to sneaking and even stealing in order to keep him both happy and safe.

When he finally explains that he is not an escapee at all, they are horrorstricken at what they have done. Miss Todd, in a grand huff, goes off to call the police. But while she is away Laetitia invites the young man to run off with her, in Miss Todd's car and with Miss Todd's little trinkets to sell. This he reluctantly accepts.

Olympia
COMP.: G. Spontini
LIBR.: Dieulafoy and Brifaut
From a tragedy of Voltaire

Tragedy in 3 acts
Opéra, 22 December 1819
Berlin, 1821
Rome, 1885

Ombra di Don Giovanni, L'
(*The Shade of Don Juan*)
COMP.: F. Alfano
LIBR.: E. Moschino

3 acts
La Scala, 2 April 1914
Florence, 1941

The performance at Florence was billed under the title: *Don Giovanni di Manara*.

Operas-Minutes
COMP.: D. Milhaud
LIBR.: H. Hoppenot
L'Enlèvement d'Europe
L'Abandon d'Ariane
La Délivrance de Thésée

Wiesbaden, 20 April 1928

8 scenes
1 Act
1 Act

The first of these tiny works was produced separately at Baden-Baden on 17 July 1927.

Oracolo, L'
COMP.: F. Leoni
LIBR.: C. Zanoni
From a story by Fernald

1 act
Covent Garden, 28 June 1905
New York, 1915
Metropolitan, 1926

THE OPERAS

Orestes
See *Orestie*
See also *Life of Orestes*
See also *Elektra*

Orestes *Trilogy*
COMP.: S. Taneief

Orestes *Tragedy, in 3 parts*
COMP.: F. Weingartner — Leipzig, 15 February 1902
LIBR.: By the composer — Berlin, 1902
From Aeschylus — Prague, 1909

Orestie *Trilogy*
This consists of three operas by Milhaud:
  Agamemnon
  Choëphores
  Eumenides

Orfeo
Composer unknown — Mantua, 1472
LIBR.: A. Poliziano
This play with musical numbers is known to have been produced with sets by Raphael.

Orfeo
See *Favola d'Orfeo*
See also *Euridice*
See also *Orpheus*

Orfeo ed Euridice *Tragedy in 3 acts*
COMP.: C. W. Gluck — Vienna, 5 October 1762
LIBR.: R. da Calzabigi — London, 1770
New York, 1863
Metropolitan, 1891

CAST

Orfeo	C	Shepherds and Shepherdesses, Furies
Euridice	S	and Demons
Amor, *god of love*	S	Heroes and Heroines in Hades
A Happy Shade	S	

MUSICAL HIGHLIGHTS

ACT I. Aria *Chiamo il mio ben* (Hear me, O my love), Orfeo and chorus
ACT II. Scene *Chi mai dell'Erebo* (Who dares to enter hell), Orfeo and Chorus
  Aria *È quest' asilo ameno e grato* (In this tranquil and lovely abode), Euridice and chorus
  Aria *Che puro ciel* (What heavenly light), Orfeo
ACT III. Duet, *Su, e con me vieni, o cara* (Trust me and come with me O dear one), Orfeo and Euridice
  Duet *Che fiero momento* (How proud the moment), Orfeo and Euridice
  Aria *Che farò senza Euridice* (I have lost my Euridice), Orfeo.

THE OPERAS

SYNOPSIS

I. Orfeo weeps for the death of his wife. Called by the lamentation, the god of love appears and tells Orfeo that he may go if he wishes into Hades and bring her back, provided that he avoids looking upon her until they shall have reached the outside world. After the easy promise, Orfeo goes to find her.

II. Confronted by the furies of hell who bar his way, Orfeo sings. Their ferocity abates and they let him enter the abode of the dead. There, in the valley of the blest, the shades bring Euridice to him. Without looking at her he takes her hand and leads her back toward the living world.

III. She cannot understand his avoidance. She pleads with him to look upon her face. She weeps for his love. Unable to resist at last, he clasps her in his arms. Hardly has the thought taken action before she is snatched from him and taken back into death. Forlorn he sings again of his lost love, again so beautifully that Amor restores her to him without conditions.

NOTES

This is the earliest of the classic operas to remain steadily in repertory in modern times. Gluck makes remarkable use of the chorus both musically and dramatically throughout the work. In this respect, together with a few modern operas, it stands as one of the great achievements in the search for a dramatic and musical successor to the classic Greek drama as sought by the Florentine group in 1600 (See *Euridice* by Peri). Gluck wrote the part of Orfeo for the male contralto Guadagni. In French productions he added tenor arias for Legros, who played that role. Berlioz, however, restored the original voice distribution.

Orphée aux Enfers
(*Orpheus in Hades*)
COMP.: J. Offenbach
LIBR.: Halévy and Crémieux

Comedy in 2 acts
Paris, 21 October 1858
New York, 1861
London, 1865

CAST

Pluton, *god of the underworld,*		Morphée, *god of sleep*	T
called *Aristée*	T	Euridice, *Orphée's wife*	S
Jupiter, *king of the gods*	Bar	Diane, *goddess of the hunt*	S
Orphée, *violinist*	T	L'Opinion Publique, *public opinion*	MS
John Styx, *fool*	Bar	Vénus, *goddess of love*	C
Mercure, *messenger of the gods*	T	Cupidon, *Cupid*	S
Bacchus, *god of wine*	Spkr	Junon, *goddess, Jupiter's wife*	MS
Mars, *god of war*	B	Minerve	S

SYNOPSIS

I. Orpheus and his wife do not get along with any notable harmony. She is heartily sick of him and his violin playing. When an opportunity for love presents itself to her in the person of Aristée she is quick to snap it up. Since Aristée is Pluton, however, he requires her to go to the underworld with him. What an adventure! Leaving Orphée a little note saying she is dead, off she goes. Orpheus is delighted to be free, but Public Opinion insists that he go to Hades and fetch her up again. The fact that he is unwilling makes the deed even more heroic in Opinion's eyes. Orpheus, thus goaded, makes his half-hearted appeal to Jupiter on Olympus and is granted permission to retrieve the errant wife. All the gods and goddesses decide to go down with him to take a look for themselves.

II. Jupiter finds her first. He does his reputation as a lover no damage by assuming the form of a fly and buzzing a little love-duet with her, wooing her for himself. The gods love Euridice and she loves them. Everyone is marvelously happy. They all break into a can-can to celebrate the initiation of such a lively girl into their midst.

Then Orpheus with his prim companion arrives. Jupiter lays down a condition to the bargain: Orpheus must take her out without looking back at her. That agreed, the reluctant husband begins his journey. Everything is going well, much too well to satisfy Jupiter who sees his latest amour being led away by her husband. To prevent such an irreparable loss the god hurls a thunderbolt at Orpheé's heels. The poor man, startled for a moment, glances back, sees his wife and loses his bargain. With joy she trips back into the circle of deliriously happy gods and her relieved spouse goes back where he would rather be.

Not once was he able to sing his famous song to open the gates of Hades. The gods had known the tune all along and sang it to him before he had a chance to clear his throat.

NOTES

Offenbach was trying to make ends meet at his theater *Les Bouffes Parisiennes* when he brought out his Orpheus. It was an astounding success.

Orpheus und Euridike   3 *acts*
  COMP.: E. Krenek   Kassel, Germany, 27 November 1926
  LIBR.: O. Kokoschka

Orpheus and Euridice
  See also *Orfeo ed Euridice*
  See also *Favola d'Orfeo*

Orpheus in Hades
  See *Orphée aux Enfers*

Otello   *Tragedy in 3 acts*
  COMP.: O. Rossini   Naples, 4 December 1816
  LIBR.: B. di Salsa   London, 1822
  From Shakespeare   New York, 1826

Otello   *Tragedy in 4 acts*
  COMP.: G. Verdi   La Scala, 5 February 1887
  LIBR.: A. Boito   New York, 1888
  From Shakespeare   London, 1889
                                Metropolitan, 1891

CAST

Otello, *a moor, Venetian governor of*		Montano, *Otello's predecessor*	B
Cyprus	T	Herald	B
Iago, *his ensign*	Bar	Desdemona, *Otello's wife*	S
Cassio, *his lieutenant*	T	Emilia, *her lady, Iago's wife*	MS
Roderigo, *Venetian gentleman*	T	Soldiers, Sailors, Ladies and Gentlemen,	
Lodovico, *Venetian ambassador*	B	Cypriotes	

MUSICAL HIGHLIGHTS

ACT I. Scena *Esultate!* (Rejoice!), Otello and Chorus
    Duet *Già nella notte* (Here in the night), Otello and Desdemona
ACT II. Aria *Credo in un dio crudel* (I believe in a cruel god), Iago
    Aria *Ora e per sempre addio* (Now and forever, goodbye), Otello

ACT IV. Willow Song *Piangea cantando* (With weeping and in song), Desdemona
Ave Maria, Desdemona

SYNOPSIS

I. Triumphant after defeating the enemies of Cyprus, Otello returns to the island. His ensign in his absence has conceived a deep hatred for him because Cassio was made lieutenant instead of himself. Therefore Iago plans to use Cassio in an intrigue to destroy Otello.

II. He sends Cassio to Desdemona to plead for her intercession with the governor to restore Cassio to the favor which was lost through Iago's machinations. Advertising their meeting in the most cunning way, Iago makes sure that the Moor interprets it as a tryst behind his back. At the height of Otello's jealousy Iago speaks openly to him of Desdemona's "faithlessness" saying that Cassio has even her handkerchief, given to her by Otello.

III. Otello demands the handkerchief from her, but she cannot find it. Iago arranges for Otello to see it in Cassio's hand. At this the Moor swears to kill his wife. The last straw breaks when Venetian ambassadors arrive to inform the governor that he has been recalled to Venice and that Cassio has been appointed governor in his place.

IV. At night Desdemona sings a little song to herself as she prepares for bed. When Emilia is about to leave her, Desdemona suddenly cries farewell to her, in tears. Then Otello comes. She cannot admit any crime against him; she knows of none. But he cannot believe her against such mounting, visible evidence. He strangles her with his bare hands. Emilia discovers them; then Cassio rushes in to tell him that he has discovered Iago's plot. In remorse Otello kills himself in their presence, beside his murdered wife.

Our Lady's Juggler
See *Jongleur de Notre Dame, Le*

Pagliacci, I
(*The Players*)
COMP.: R. Leoncavallo
LIBR.: By the composer

Tragedy in Prologue and 2 acts
Milan, 17 May 1892
New York, 1893
Metropolitan, 1893
Covent Garden, 1893

CAST

Canio, *chief player*, "*Pagliaccio*"	T	Beppe, *a player*, "*Harlequin*"	T
Nedda, *his wife* "*Columbine*"	S	Silvio, *villager*	Bar
Tonio, *clown* "*Taddeo*"	Bar	Villagers	

MUSICAL HIGHLIGHTS

PROLOGUE. *Si può? signore, signori* (By your leave, ladies and gentlemen), Tonio
ACT I. Balatella *O, che volo d'augelli* (O how beautifully birds sing), Nedda
Aria *Vesti la giubba* (On with the play), Canio
ACT II. Serenade *O Colombina*, Harlequin
Scena *No!, Pagliaccio non son* (No, I'm no longer playing), Canio

SYNOPSIS

Tonio steps before the curtain and sings the prologue, introducing the play.

I. To the delight of everybody, the players arrive in a new village amid shouting and drumming, marching down the street. Soon the citizens notice a rivalry between Tonio and Canio, and someone suggests perhaps Tonio intends to make a play for Canio's wife, just as he does in character in the Harlequinade. Canio darkly refuses to believe it. But the clown does love Nedda, and tries to win her. With disgust she drives him away with a whip, stirring a thirst in his heart for revenge. He overhears her planning an elopement with a villager, Silvio. This information he takes immediately to Canio who comes to witness the betrayal with his own eyes. Canio tries to catch him, but Silvio gets away clean, In vain Canio tries to beat the name of her lover from Nedda.

II. The play begins. It is the old story in which Harlequin and Columbine plan to elope, leaving her husband forlorn. Pagliaccio suspects them, but Harlequin escapes. Pagliaccio tries to frighten Columbine into telling him who the lover is—but at this point Canio can no longer contain his personal feelings. He demands to know the name of Nedda's lover. The villagers in the audience at first think he is a marvelously gifted actor. But soon they begin to realize that something serious is going on as he takes out a dagger and chases the frightened actress off the stage. As he stabs her to death Silvio rushes upon him, only to be stabbed by her side. Thus the comedy is finished.

NOTES

Leoncavallo was sued for plagiarism by another author. Although there have been many plays on similar subjects, he defended himself by pointing out that he had heard of a real case of such a murder in a travelling theatrical troupe, his own father being judge at the trial. He had used his memory of the event for his source. The suit was withdrawn.

Palestrina

		3 acts
COMP.: H. Pfitzner		Munich, 12 June 1917
LIBR.: By the composer		Vienna, 1919

CAST

Pope Pius IV	B	Silla, *his pupil*	MS
Giovanni Morone, *papal legate*	Bar	Bishop Ercole Severolus	BBar
Bernardo Novagerio	T	Five singers of Santa Maria	
Cardinal Christoph Madruscht	B	Maggiore	2T, 3B
Carlo Borromeo, *Cardinal*	Bar	Two Papal Nuncios, Jesuits, Massarelli	
Cardinal of Lorraine	B	the Bishop of Thelesia, Secretary of	
Abdisu, *patriarch of Assyria*	T	the Council, Giuseppe, an old	
Anton Brus von Müglitz,		Servant	Mutes
archbishop of Prague	B	Lucretia, *Palestrina's dead wife*	C
Count Luna, *envoy from Spain*	Bar	Nine dead composers	3T, 3Bar, 3B
Bishop of Budoja, *Italian bishop*	T	Three Angelic Voices	S
Theophilis of Imola, *Italian bishop*	T	Singers of the Papal Chapel,	
Avosmediano, *bishop of Cadiz*	BBar	Archbishops, Bishops, Abbots,	
Giovanni Pierluigi da Palestrina	T	Ambassadors, Envoys, Theologians,	
Ighino, *his son*	S	Servants, Soldiers, People, Angels	

SYNOPSIS

The story concerns the composition of the *Missa Papae Marcelli* and its companion works which Palestrina wrote in demonstration of the worth of polyphonic music in the church. By the great beauty of this music the Pope was convinced that polyphony would not destroy the ritual continuity and texture of the service, and that it would be unnecessary for him to issue his orders requiring the church to revert to the ancient Gregorian plainsong.

Paolo and Francesca

See *Francesca da Rimini*

THE OPERAS

Pantaloon
See *He Who Gets Slapped*
Pardon de Ploërmel, Le
See *Dinorah*
Parsifal   *Stage Dedication Festival Play in 3 acts*
COMP.: Richard Wagner   Bayreuth, 26 July 1882
LIBR.: By the composer   Metropolitan, 1903
From traditional legends   Covent Garden, 1914

CAST

Amfortas, *ruler of the kingdom*		Kundry	S
of the Grail	BBar	Two Knights	T, B
Titurel, *his father*	B	Four Esquires	2S, 2T
Gurnemanz, *knight of the Grail*	B	Six Flower Maidens	S
Klingsor, *magician*	B	Knights of the Grail, Youths, Boys, Two
Parsifal	T	choirs of Flower Maidens

SYNOPSIS

Amfortas, contesting against Klingsor, lost to him the sacred spear with which Klingsor thereupon dealt him an unhealing wound. Only a guileless innocent may retrieve the spear from Klingsor and heal Amfortas.

I. Gurnemanz waits in the forest while the king tries to salve his wound in the lake. Speaking with youths, he tells them of the wound and the spear that made it. Kundry comes to him, bringing an Arabian ointment to soothe the king. Suddenly the knights bring in a stranger who has shot a sacred swan. He is so unconscious of any guilt and so guileless that he seems to be the proper candidate for saving the spear. His name is Parsifal. Gurnemanz takes him to see the unveiling of the Holy Grail in the castle, but the fool understands nothing of the ceremony and is thrown out.

II. The bewitched Kundry lures Parsifal into Klingsor's magic garden and there kisses him. But rather than enslaving him, the kiss reveals to him his mission. Kundry shouts to warn Klingsor, who hurls the sacred spear at Parsifal. But instead of killing him it comes to rest in his unharmed hand. Parsifal makes the sign of the cross and the magic castle is destroyed.

III. After many wanderings Parsifal returns on Good Friday to the forest of the Grail. Here the aged Gurnemanz opposes him. But when Parsifal shows him the sacred spear Gurnemanz greets him as the new King of the Grail. As king, Parsifal's first act is to baptize Kundry, thus freeing her from her ancient curse. They enter the castle where Parsifal heals Amfortas with the touch of the spear that wounded him. Then he leads the knights in their sacrament.

NOTES

At the opening of *Parsifal* there were three casts, alternating from night to night. The story was based upon legends of the Grail; *Percival le Galois*, or *Contes de Grail*, Chrétien de Troyes (1190), *Parsifal*, by Wolfram von Eschenbach, and the so-called *Mabinogion manuscript* of the 14th century. One of the most memorable motives from the opera is taken from the Dresden Fourfold Amen.

Partenope   *3 acts*
COMP.: G. F. Handel   London, 7 March 1730
LIBR.: S. Stampiglia   Covent Garden, 1737
                                                         Göttingen, 1935

THE OPERAS

Pastor Fido, Il
(*The Faithful Shepherd*)
COMP.: G. F. Handel
LIBR.: G. Rossi
From a play by Guarini
  Handel composed two versions of the opera, the first performed in London on 3 December 1712, the second on 29 May 1734.

Paul Bunyan
COMP.: B. Britten

New York, 5 May 1941

Paul et Virginie
COMP.: V. Massé
LIBR.: Barbier and Carré
From a story by St. Pierre

3 *acts*
Paris, 15 November 1876
Covent Garden, 1878
New Orleans, 1879

Pauvre Matelot, Le
(*The Poor Sailor*)
COMP.: D. Milhaud
LIBR.: J. Cocteau

Tragedy in 3 acts
Comique, 16 December 1927
Philadelphia, 1937
London, 1950

CAST

Wife	S	Father in law	B
Sailor	T	Friend	Bar

SYNOPSIS

I. After years of absence, during which his good wife remains faithful and sure that he will return to her, the sailor returns unrecognized. Instead of going directly home he proposes to spend the night at his friend's house.

II. Next morning he knocks at his wife's door and tells her he has news of her husband. Unrecognizing, she hears that her husband will return in a couple of weeks, but that he is now very, very poor. He even suggests that she should debase herself to earn money to get her poor husband out of debt. She rejects this, she loves her husband whether he be rich or poor. Saying that he needs a safe place to spend the night with his gold on his person, the sailor requests permission to sleep that night at her house. This she grants. As he drops off to sleep she remarks on how this rich man resembles her own poor husband.

III. That night, desperate to get money to get her husband out of debt, the wife takes a hammer and kills the poor sailor, really her husband, as he sleeps unrecognized in his own house.

Peace Day
See *Friedenstag*

Pearl Fishers, The
See *Pêcheurs de Perles, Les*

Pearl of Brazil, The
See *Perle du Brésil, La*

Pêcheurs de Perles, Les
(*The Pearl Fishers*)
COMP.: G. Bizet
LIBR.: Cormon and Carré

Tragedy in 3 acts
Paris, 30 September 1863
Covent Garden, 1887
Philadelphia, 1893
Metropolitan (2 acts only), 1896

THE OPERAS

CAST

| Leïla, *priestess of Brahma* | S | Zurga, *king of the fishermen* | Bar |
| Nadir, *fisherman* | T | Nourabad, *high priest of Brahma* | B |

SYNOPSIS

I. Nadir and Zurga, who once had been rivals for the hand of Leïla, have sworn eternal friendship. There is an invisible goddess who has been protecting the fishermen at sea. It turns out that Leïla is this person. Nadir recognizes her and tells her privately of his continuing love.

II. As they had sworn their friendship, she has vowed to remain alone as protectress of the fishermen. Love, however, overwhelms her reservation so that Nourabad is able to surprise and trap her together with Nadir. Thus the fishermen are imperilled without their protectress. Zurga swears vengeance for all and for himself.

III. At the last moment, however, Zurga saves them from the death Nourabad had intended for them. While they escape, Nourabad makes sure that Zurga is stabbed to death.

Peer Gynt
COMP.: W. Egk   Berlin, 24 November 1938
LIBR.: By the composer
From Ibsen's play

Pelléas et Mélisande
COMP.: C. Debussy
LIBR.: M. Maeterlinck
From Maeterlinck's play

Tragedy in 5 acts
Comique, 30 April 1902
New York, 1908
Covent Garden, 1909
Metropolitan, 1925

CAST

Arkel, *king of Allemonde*	B	Golaud, *Arkel's grandson*	Bar
Geneviève, *mother of Pelléas and Golaud*		Mélisande	S
	C	Yniold, *Golaud's son*	S
Pelléas, *Arkel's grandson*	T	Physician	B

SYNOPSIS

I. Golaud brings to his grandfather's castle a strange, mysterious and beautiful girl, Mélisande. In this gloomy place she meets Pelléas.

II. They walk together secretly in the groves, slowly falling in love. In a fountain near a pool she lost her ring. Golaud sends her back there to find it.

III. Pelléas must leave. Tender with love is their leave-taking until Golaud interrupts. Full of suspicion he searches for some hint of intrigue in their glances.

IV. He is tormented by his suspicions. Finding them together saying goodbye, he slays Pelléas.

V. Later Mélisande dies with Golaud weeping beside her, haunted without any proof of his suspicions.

Pénélope
COMP.: G. Fauré
LIBR.: R. Fauchois

3 acts
Monte Carlo, 4 March 1913
Antwerp, 1924

Pepita Jiménez
COMP.: I. Albéniz
LIBR.: F. Money-Coutts
From a story by Valera

1 act, 2 scenes
Barcelona, 5 January 1896
Prague, 1897
Comique, 1923

Pepys, Samuel
See *Samuel Pepys*

Perfect Fool, The
COMP.: G. Holst
LIBR.: By the composer

1 *act*
Covent Garden, 14 May 1923

Périchole, La
COMP.: J. Offenbach
LIBR.: Meilhac and Halévy

2 *acts*
Paris, 6 October 1868
New York, 1869
London, 1870

There was a production of *Périchole* in New York, 1887, in Yiddish.

Perle du Brésil, La
(*The Pearl of Brazil*)
COMP.: F. David
LIBR.: Gabriel and St. Étienne

3 *acts*
Paris, 22 November 1851
Brussels, 1852
Rouen, 1889

Peter Grimes
COMP.: B. Britten
LIBR.: M. Slater
From the poem *The Borough* by
George Crabbe

Tragedy in Prologue, 3 acts, and Epilogue
Sadlers Wells, 7 June 1945
Berkshire Festival, Mass., 1946
Metropolitan, 1948

CAST

Peter Grimes, *fisherman*	T	Swallow, *lawyer*	B
John, *his apprentice*	Mute	Mrs. Sedley	MS
Ellen Orford, *widow, schoolmistress*	S	Rev. Horace Adams, *rector*	T
Captain Balstrode, *retired skipper*	Bar	Ned Keene, *apothecary and quack*	Bar
Auntie, *tavernkeeper*	C	Dr. Thorp	Mute
Two Nieces, *main attractions*		Hobson, *carrier*	B
at the tavern	S	Townspeople, Fisherfolk	
Bob Boles, *fisherman, Methodist*	T		

SYNOPSIS

There is an inquest into the cause of the death at sea of Peter Grimes' apprentice. Although the townspeople are convinced that Peter Grimes is guilty, the court acquits him.

I. Now the fisherman needs a new apprentice. With the reputation so vividly described in the prologue, he seems hard put to keep one, but Ellen Orford offers to help by taking care of the new boy. A storm is raging as the new boy is brought to Peter, who takes him home.

II. On Sunday, for others a day of rest, Grimes puts his new apprentice to his first day's work. The congregation at church, stirred to action by the inflammatory speeches of Bob Boles, go in a body to Peter's hut to see for themselves what is going on there. Grimes tells the boy to hide, but in hiding the lad falls off the cliff upon the rocks and dies.

III. The enraged people, extremely suspicious at finding neither the boy nor his harsh master there, find the boy's shirt in the water. Captain Balstrode and Ellen, his only defenders, finally convince Peter to quiet the town by sinking his boat in the sea. Next morning someone sights the overturned craft drifting in the waves, but nobody cares much about it any more.

Peter Ibbetson
COMP.: D. Taylor
LIBR.: Taylor and Collins
From the novel by du Maurier

3 *acts*
Metropolitan, 7 February 1931

Peter the Shipwright
See *Zar und Zimmerman*

Phèdre
See *Fedra*

Philémon et Baucis
COMP.: C. Gounod
LIBR.: Barbier and Carré

3 *acts*
Paris, 18 February 1860
Liverpool (Amateurs), 1888
Metropolitan, 1893

Pickwick
COMP.: A. Coates
LIBR.: By the composer
From Dickens

3 *acts*
Covent Garden, 20 November 1936

Pierrot and Pierette
COMP.: J. Holbrooke
LIBR.: W. Grogan

2 *scenes*
London, 11 November 1909

Pilgrim's Progress, The
COMP.: R. Vaughan Williams
LIBR.: By the composer
From Bunyan's allegory

Morality in Prologue, 4 acts and Epilogue
Covent Garden, 26 April 1951

CAST

John Bunyan, *writer*	BBar	Madam Wanton	S
Pilgrim	Bar	Madam Bubble	MS
Evangelist	B	Pontius Pilate	B
Pliable, *neighbor*	T	Usher	T
Obstinate, *neighbor*	B	Lord Hate-Good	B
Mistrust, *neighbor*	Bar	Malice	S
Timorous, *neighbor*	T	Pickthank	C
Three Shining Ones	S, MS, C	Superstition	T
Interpreter	T	Envy	B
Watchful, *porter*	Bar	Woodcutter's boy	S
Herald	Bar	Mr. By-Ends	T
Apollyon	B	Madam By-Ends	C
Two Heavenly Beings	S, C	Three Shepherds	T, Bar, B
Lord Lechery	T	Voice of a bird	S
Jester	dancer	Celestial Messenger	T
Demas	Bar	Men, Women, Certain Persons clothed
Simon Magus	B	in gold, Doleful Creatures, Traders,
Worldly Glory	Bar	Angels

SYNOPSIS

Bunyan reads his story to us:

1. Pilgrim sets out to discover the secret of eternal life. Reaching the House Beautiful he lays his burden aside.

II. Traveling by way of the straight road through the Valley of Humiliation he conquers Apollyon.

III. By dint of much struggle he threads his way through Vanity Fair and resists its temptations. But Lord Hate-Good imprisons him. Using the Key of Promise he effects his escape.

IV. He approaches the Delectable Mountains. There, crossing the River of Death he finally enters the Celestial City.

Thus Bunyan has finished his tale.

Pipe of Desire, The

	1 *act*
COMP.: F. Converse	Boston, 31 January 1906
LIBR.: G. Barton	Metropolitan, 1910

The first American opera performed at the Metropolitan.

Pique-Dame

(*The Queen of Spades*)	*Tragedy in 3 acts*
	St. Petersburg, 19 December 1890
COMP.: P. Tchaikovsky	La Scala, 1906
LIBR.: M. Tchaikovsky (his brother)	Metropolitan, 1910
From Pushkin	London, 1915

CAST

Tchekalinsky, *officer*	T	Governess	MS
Sourin, *officer*	B	Mascha, *Lisa's maid*	S
Herman, *young officer*	T	Master of Ceremonies	T
Count Tomsky (Plutus)	Bar	Tchaplitsky, *gambler*	T
Prince Yeletsky	Bar	Narumoff, *gambler*	B
Countess	MS	Chloë	S
Lisa, *her granddaughter*	S	Servants, Guests, Gamblers, Children,	
Pauline, *Lisa's friend* (Daphnis)	C	Nurses, Governesses	

SYNOPSIS

I. Herman has fallen in love with Lisa; prince Yeletsky has become engaged to Lisa. The countess was once a very successful gambler, said to have had a magic combination. Herman, aware of this rumor, sets out to discover its secret. Also secretly he visits Lisa to declare his love.

II. At a ball, after a masque of Daphnis and Chloë, Lisa gives her lover a key with which he may visit her. On the way there he hides in the countess' room and surprises her with a pistol, threatening to shoot her if she will not tell him her gambling secret. The countess faints away and dies.

III. Her ghost pays Herman a visit and tells him the secret, naming three cards by which he may win, on condition that he marry Lisa.

He goes to Lisa, but his desire to gamble is too strong to be delayed. When she hears of his complicity in the death of the countess, and sees his thirst to gamble, Lisa throws herself in despair into the canal and drowns. Herman gambles everything on the three fateful cards. By accident he turns up the Queen of Spades and sees in it the face of the ghost. At the sight he stabs himself to death.

Pirata, Il

(*The Pirate*)	2 *acts*
	La Scala, 27 October 1827
COMP.: V. Bellini	London, 1830
LIBR.: F. Romani	New York, 1832

Poacher, The
See *Wildschütz, Der*

Poia
COMP.: E. Nevin
LIBR.: R. Hartley
From legend

3 *acts*
Pittsburgh, Pa. (Concert), January 1907
Berlin, 23 April 1910

Poirier de Misère, Le
COMP.: M. Delannoy
LIBR.: Limozin and de la Tourrasse

3 *acts*
Comique, 21 February 1927

Poisoned Kiss, The
COMP.: R. Vaughan Williams
LIBR.: E. Sharpe
From stories by Garnett and
  Hawthorne

Romantic Extravaganza in 3 acts
Cambridge, 12 May 1936
Sadlers Wells, 1936
New York, 1937

CAST

Dipsacus, *magician*	B	Three Mediums, *assistants to the*	
Tormentilla, *his daughter*	S	empress	
Angelica, *her maid*	S	Empress Persicaria	C
Amaryllus, *the Empress' son*	T	Hob, *assistant to Dipsacus*	
Gallanthus, *his jester*	Bar	Gob, *assistant to Dipsacus*	
		Lob, *assistant to Dipsacus*	

SYNOPSIS

I. Tormentilla, who has been reared from birth on various poisons, does not understand when her new acquaintance Amaryllus kills a snake, her pet, in the woods. She was brought up in this virulent manner by Dipsacus to win revenge for him by poisoning with a kiss the son of the Empress, who had once refused Dipsacus. Tormentilla abhors the idea of being a murder-tool. Her father therefore banishes her.

II. The empress, on the other hand, protects herself from the loss of her son's affections by poisoning any girls who get too near. Of course, Tormentilla is immune to this. But the assistants of Dipsacus, Hob, Gob, and Lob, have more success. They bring the two young people together and the poisoned lips seem to do their job well.

III. But he isn't dead, the Empress has stuffed him with antidotes since birth. Nor is he completely cured, however, until Tormentilla can be present to cheer him. When Dipsacus comes to boast to the empress that he has won revenge, his boasting dwindles and they, the parents, fall in love all over again. Marriages are subsequently arranged for all.

Polish Jew, The
See *Juif Polonais, Le*

Polly
COMP.: J. Pepusch and Arnold
LIBR.: J. Gay

Ballad Opera in 3 acts
London, 19 June 1777
New York, 1925

Called *An Opera, being the Second Part of the Beggar's Opera*, this second product of the collaboration of Pepusch and Gay was composed in 1729 but forbidden performance until certain alterations had been made in 1777. Even then, being less a spontaneous creation than an attempt to ride the ragged coattails of the *Beggar*, it did not have notable success.

THE OPERAS

Pomone
COMP.: R. Cambert
LIBR.: P. Perrin

Prologue and 5 acts
Opéra, 3 March 1671
London, 1674

This, the first French opera, was the first presented at the Académie Royal de Musique.

Poor Sailor, The
See *Pauvre Matelot, Le*

Porgy and Bess
COMP.: G. Gershwin
LIBR.: I. Gershwin and DuBose Heyward
From a play by DuBose Heyward

Tragedy in 3 acts
Boston, 30 September 1935
Zürich, 1945
Copenhagen, 1946

CAST

Porgy, *cripple*	BBar	Annie	MS
Bess, *Crown's girl*	S	Lily, *strawberry woman*	MS
Crown, *stevedore*	Bar	Jim, *cottonpicker*	Bar
Serena, *Robbins' wife*	S	Undertaker	Bar
Clara, *Jake's wife*	S	Nelson	T
Maria, *cookshopkeeper*	C	Crab Man	T
Jake, *fisherman*	Bar	Mr. Archdale, *white man*	Spkr
Sportin' Life, *dope peddler*	T	Detective, *white man*	Spkr
Mingo	T	Policeman, *white man*	Spkr
Robbins	T	Coroner, *white man*	Spkr
Peter, *the honeyman*	T	Scipio, *small boy*	Spkr
Frazier, *"lawyer"*	Bar		

MUSICAL HIGHLIGHTS

ACT I. Lullaby *Summertime*, Clara and Chorus
Burial Scene *My man's gone now*, Serena and Chorus
ACT II. Song *O I got plenty o' nuttin*, Porgy
Duet *Bess, you is my woman now*, Porgy and Bess
Sermon *It ain't necessarily so*, Sportin' Life and Chorus
Song *A red headed woman*, Crown
ACT III. Song *There's a boat that's leaving soon for New York*, Sportin' Life
Finale *O Lord, I'm on my way*, Porgy and Chorus

SYNOPSIS

I. Catfish row, Charleston, South Carolina. Porgy gets around by means of a little cart, a lonely man. He likes Bess, but she's Crown's girl. During a crap game one night there is an altercation in which Crown kills Robbins with his bale hook. Crown has to leave. He tells Bess to take care of herself, but to remember he'll be back to renew his claim on her when the search dies down. But nobody will take her in after he goes, except Porgy. At the burial, during which everybody puts what coins he can spare into a plate to help pay the cost of the service, the police interrupt to find out who the murderer may be. Since no one says a word, the police haul away Peter as an example of their intentions.

II. Porgy is happy now; Bess stays with him. Sportin' Life can't entice her away—not from Porgy, who is the first person who ever treated her with tenderness. Everybody's going to a picnic on Kittiwah Island. Bess wants to go, but of course she hates to leave Porgy behind. Porgy makes her go along, however, rather than let her feel left out of things.

THE OPERAS

At the picnic Crown appears, snatches Bess away from the returning people and forces her to stay with him in hiding. Two days later she returns to Porgy, sick and broken-hearted. She's afraid of Crown, but she loves Porgy and he loves her.

There is a terrible hurricane sweeping in from the sea. Jake and his men are out fishing when it hits. Crown comes out of hiding, boasting that he is the only one there man enough to go out and fight the Lord to save Jake.

III. That night, in the quiet after the storm, Crown struggles back to Catfish row, weary and nearly drowned. As he passes by Porgy's door, the crippled man's strong arm reaches out and stabs the stevedore to death. Again the police come; this time everybody swears that Crown was the murderer they were after before, but nobody knows who murdered him. In the turmoil Sportin' Life has finally won Bess over to the temptations of New York, and of dope. She has left her man. Porgy, unconcerned that New York is a great distance away, starts pushing his little cart to follow her and bring her back home.

NOTES

There are many American operas, written and not yet written, that may claim a deeper musical conception, but Porgy and Bess remains the most brilliant and deeply moving operatic work in its field. The music is not really Negro, but it sounds Negro. The songs are not really folk music, but they have that same quality of unquestionable accuracy that folk music is supposed to have. The rhythmic texture throughout the work is commonly called jazz, and yet actually it is Gershwin rhythm, Gershwin texture which has influenced jazz composition so strongly that the two are hard to distinguish. Although the two works are hardly comparable in other ways, both Porgy and Boris Godunov celebrate the people in magnificent choral scenes which make action move in the play.

There are one or two interesting stories about productions of Porgy which are worth retelling here. One concerns the opening in Boston. There was, the story goes, a res-taurateur whose business near the theater where rehearsals were in progress was about to fold up for lack of trade. When Porgy opened, business picked up. Porgy stayed so long that business mounted to the point where the man could open a branch restaurant, then another, and another, and so on. Porgy later moved, but the restaurateur was able with such a boost to develop a nationwide chain of roadside restaurants with business in the millions of dollars.

The second story was heard by this author in conversation with some of the cast who had recently returned from a triumphal tour of Europe and Asia (which began, incidentally, against the judgment of the State Department which thought the play might harm foreign relations). The troupe had found it difficult to work with the musicians who made up the various orchestras in Europe. The musicians did not seem to feel free with the jazz rhythms, and the improvisatory quality of the score. Someone thought of the ideal remedy. Some members of the cast could play instruments. It was decided that during certain scenes, notably the picnic, these actors would produce their horns from under their jackets and improvise in jazz fashion while the orchestra and chorus went through the scene. However, the effect, at least to one well versed in jazz, was not entirely desirable.

Portrait de Manon, Le   1 act
COMP.: J. Massenet   Comique, 8 May 1894
LIBR.: G. Boyer   New York, 1897

A sequel to Manon in which des Grieux, now old, sees a girl in New Orleans who bears a remarkable resemblance to the portrait of Manon, who was the girl's mother.

Postillon de Longjumeau, Le

COMP.: A. Adam
LIBR.: Brunswick and de Leuven

Comedy in 3 acts
Comique, 13 October 1836
London, 1837
New York, 1840

CAST

Madeleine, *Chappelou's wife*	S	Marquis de Corcy, *chief of the Opéra*	T
Rose	S	Bijou, *Chappelou's friend*	Bar
Chappelou, *postillion*	T	Bourdon	B

SYNOPSIS

I. Unfortunately Chappelou made the mistake of singing at his own wedding. His voice was heard by the Marquis, who happened to be passing by at that moment, causing this impresario to hire Chappelou on the spot and demand that he leave his new wife immediately and join the Opéra.

II. Ten years later the faithful Madeleine, who has inherited a fortune, travels to Paris to find her husband. As a rich but unknown lady, she entraps him into a love affair and marriage without his once catching on.

III. The Marquis, who also has conceived a passion for the rich lady, has Chappelou arrested as a bigamist. But at that juncture Madeleine reveals her identity and saves the day.

Power of Evil, The

COMP.: A. Serov

5 acts
St. Petersburg, 1 May 1871

Serov died before finishing this opera. It was completed by N. T. Solovyev.

Pré aux Clercs, Le

COMP.: L. Hérold
LIBR.: F. de Planard

3 acts
Comique, 15 December 1832
London, 1833
New York, 1843

Prigioniero, Il

COMP.: L. Dallapiccola

Florence, 20 May 1950
New York (Juilliard), 1951
New York City Opera, 1960

Prince Igor

COMP.: A. Borodin
LIBR.: By the composer
From a medieval Russian chronicle,
Arranged by Stassov.

Tragedy in Prologue and 4 acts
St. Petersburg, 4 November 1890
Drury Lane, 1914
Metropolitan, 1915

CAST

Igor Sviatoslavovitch, *Prince*	Bar	Skoula, *gudok player*	B
Yaroslavna, *his wife*	S	Eroshka, *gudok player*	T
Vladimir Igorevitch, *his son*	T	Yaroslavna's Nurse	S
Vladimir Galitsky,		Maiden, *Polovtsian*	S
Yaroslavna's brother	B	Princes and Princesses, Boyars and	
Kontchak, *Polovtsian Khan*	B	their wives, Old Men, Warriors,	
Gzak, *Polovtsian Khan*	B	Young Women, People, Polovtsian	
Kontchakovna, *Kontchak's daughter*	MS	Chiefs, Slaves, Prisoners, Soldiers.	
Ovlour, *Polovtsian*	T		

THE OPERAS

SYNOPSIS

PROLOGUE. In medieval Russia, Prince Igor departs with his army to pursue the Polovtsi (Mongols).

I. Galitsky has been left in charge of things at home, but Yaroslavna keeps him under control, thus winning the goodwill of the people. News comes that the prince has been defeated and is taken prisoner.

II. The Khan promises Igor his freedom if the prince will give his word not to make war on the Polovtsi again. This Igor refuses, knowing it is impossible.

III. The other prisoners urge Igor to escape, even though it is against his pledge. Vladimir tries to go with him, but because his love for Kontchakovna delays him he is caught.

IV. Igor returns to his home and to Yaroslavna, giving Russia again the hope of winning against the Mongols.

Prodaná Nevěsta
(*The Bartered Bride*)
COMP.: B. Smetana
LIBR.: K. Sabina

Comedy in 3 acts
Prague, 30 May 1866
Chicago, 1893
Drury Lane, 1895
Metropolitan, 1909

CAST

Kruschina, *peasant*	Bar	Jenik, *Micha's first wife's son*	T
Katinka, *his wife*	S	Kecal, *marriage broker*	B
Marenka, *his daughter*	S	Springer, *manager of actors*	T
Micha, *landlord*	B	Esmeralda, *dancer*	S
Agnes, *his wife*	MS	Muff, *comedian*	T
Vasek, *his son*	T	Clowns, Dancers	

SYNOPSIS

I. Marenka loves Jenik, but her parents have promised her instead to Micha's son. To prevent their going through with the formalities, she tells them that she and Jenik are engaged.

II. The timid Vasek goes to woo Marenka under his parents' orders, but she shunts him off to another girl. Kecal tries to bargain with Jenik to get him to relinquish his claim, which Jenik finally does but only in favor of Micha's eldest son. Only he knows that the eldest son is himself.

III. Marenka, of course, is hurt and furious to discover that her affections have been sold for money. But when the strangely worded contract is publicly announced Micha recognizes Jenik and acknowledges him as the eldest.

Prodigal Son, The
Three works have appeared under this name as follows:
    by A. Ponchielli, Milan, 1880
    by F. Jacobi, (1944)
    by G. Malipiero, Florence, 1957

Prométhée
(*Prometheus*)
COMP.: G. Fauré
LIBR.: Lorrain and Hérold

Lyric Tragedy in 3 acts
Béziers, France, 27 August 1900
Paris, 1907

THE OPERAS

Prophète, Le
COMP.: G. Meyerbeer
LIBR.: A. E. Scribe

Tragedy in 5 acts
Opéra, 16 April, 1849
Covent Garden, 1849
New Orleans, 1850
Metropolitan, 1884

CAST

John of Leyden	T	Zacharias, *Anabaptist*	B
Fides, *his mother*	MS	Count Oberthal	Bar
Bertha, *his bride*	S	Nobles, Citizens, Anabaptists, Peasants,	
Jonas, *Anabaptist*	T	Soldiers, Prisoners, Children	
Matthisen, *Anabaptist*	B		

SYNOPSIS

I. Oberthal, coming across three Anabaptists, orders them beaten by his soldiers. Seeing Bertha, who is betrothed to John, the count has her sent to his castle for his own pleasure.

II. She escapes, but John, in order to save his mother's life, turns Bertha back to Oberthal. With mounting hatred, the Anabaptists urge John to join their cause and to fight this oppressor.

III. John is proclaimed prophet. Leading a siege of Münster he captures the Count.

IV. To prevent his identification, the Anabaptists have spread the rumor that John of Leyden was killed by the prophet, but when his coronation as emperor takes place, Fides cries out that he is her son. By a ruse he makes her deny the fact.

V. Bertha, unaware of the masquerade, plots to blow up the castle he now occupies. The Anabaptists have revolted from him; thus she learns that the prophet is indeed John. Powerless to prevent the explosion she herself planted, she kills herself. John, so that they may all die at once, gathers all his enemies together in the banquet room in time for the catastrophe.

NOTES

Meyerbeer worked thirteen years on this megalithic tragedy. For his story he used the true history of Jan Beukelszoon.

Protagonist, Der
COMP.: K. Weill
LIBR.: G. Kaiser

1 act
Dresden, 27 March 1926
Berlin, 1928

Prozess, Der
(*The Trial*)
Comp.: G. von Einem
Libr.: Blacher and von Cramer
From Kafka's novel

2 acts, 9 scenes
17 August 1953

CAST

Josef K.	T	Franz	B
Student	T	Thrasher	B
Lawyer	Bar	Court Attendant	B
Titorelli	T	Manufacturer	Bar
Examining Judge	Bar	Director/Representative	B
Overseer	Bar	Government Director	B
Albert K.	B	Passer-by	Bar
Willem	Bar	Youth	T

Three Young People	T, Bar, B	Frau Grubach	MS
Fräulein Bürstner	S	An Obsequious Girl	S
Wife of the Court Attendant	S	Mute Crowds, Soldiers, Maidens.	
Leni	S		

Pskovityanka

Tragedy in 4 acts

(*The Maid of Pskov*)
COMP.: N. Rimsky-Korsakov
LIBR.: By the composer
From a play by Mei

St. Petersburg, 13 January 1873
Paris, 1909
Drury Lane, 1913

CAST

Tsar Ivan the Terrible	B	Princess Olga Yourievna Tokmakova	S
Prince Youry Ivanovitch Tokmakov, *mayor of Pskov*	B	Boyardin Stepanida Matuta, *her friend*	S
Boyard Nikita Matuta	T	Vlassievna, *nurse*	C
Prince Afanasy Viazemsky	T	Perfilievna, *nurse*	MS
Bomely	B	Sentry	T
Michael Andreievitch Tutcha	T	Officers, Judges, Boyars, Burgher's Sons	
Youshko Velebin, *messenger*	B	Bodyguards, Pages, Archers, Maidens, Boys, People, Huntsmen	

SYNOPSIS

I. Ivan the Terrible approaches Pskov to deal punishment to the town. Tokmakov argues that the people should meet him humbly, but Michael goes out to offer a fight.

II. Ivan arrives. Meeting Olga he inquires her identity and learns that she is of an unknown father. This news moves him so deeply that he grants Pskov a reprieve from punishment, because he is her father.

III. Matuta brings Olga to the Tsar as a kind of offering. The Tsar throws him out, but keeps Olga there to tell her that he, Ivan, is her real father. At that moment Michael makes his attack. As her lover approaches the tent to kill Ivan, Olga rushes out to stop him. The bullet meant for Michael kills her instead.

Puritani, I

3 acts

(*The Puritans*)
COMP.: V. Bellini
LIBR.: Count Pepoli
From a play by Ancelot and Saintine

Paris, 25 January 1835
London, 1835
Philadelphia, 1843
Metropolitan, 1883

CAST

Lord Gaultiers Walton, *Puritan*	B	Sir Benno Robertson, *Puritan*	T
Sir George Walton, his brother, *Puritan* (Giorgio)	B	Henrietta, *widow of Charles I of France* (Enrichetta)	S
Lord Arthur Talbot, *Cavalier* (Arturo)	T	Elvira, *Lord Walton's daughter*	S
Sir Richard Forth, *Puritan* (Riccardo)	Bar	Puritans, Soldiers of the Commonwealth, Men-at-Arms, Women, Pages	

SYNOPSIS

I. Elvira prepares for her marriage to Arthur with, in spite of the partisan warfare between Puritans and Cavaliers, her father's permission. Arthur, in an attempt to save

Henrietta, who has been sentenced to death, conducts her away in Elvira's bridal gown. When this deed is discovered, Elvira goes mad, thinking her lover unfaithful.

II. To avenge her madness, Richard and George prepare to meet Arthur in battle.

III. Arthur pays Elvira a visit in secret, but this fails to relieve her insanity. The Puritans capture him and are about to kill him when news comes that the war has been settled. Elvira revives and happily accepts her lover again.

Quattro Rusteghi, I
(*The Four Rustics*)
COMP.: E. Wolf-Ferrari
LIBR.: G. Pizzola
From a comedy by Goldoni

Comedy in 3 acts
Munich, 19 March 1906
Milan, 1914
London, 1946
New York, 1951

CAST

Lunardo, *Mr. Crusty, Venetian merchant*	B	Simon, *Mr. Gruff, her husband*	BBar
Margarita, *Margery, his second wife*	MS	Canciano, *Sir James Pinchbeck, wealthy merchant*	B
Lucieta, *Lucinda, his daughter by his first wife*	S	Felice, *Felicia, his wife*	S
Maurizio, *Mr. Hardstone, merchant*	BBar	Count Riccardo Arcolai, *visitor to Venice*	T
Filipeto, *Peter, his son*	T	Young Maid	
Marina, *Maria, his aunt*	S		

SYNOPSIS

I. Without a thought of consulting the pair who have not even met, the two fathers arrange a marriage between Lucieta and Filipeto, paying great attention to detail.

II. The bridegroom, who insists upon seeing his bride before he becomes attached for life, disguises himself as a girl to effect, with Riccardo's help, a meeting. When this insubordination comes to the attention of Canciano and Lunardo, their anger puts a stop to the wedding preparations.

III. The indomitable Felice upbraids the fathers for such high-handed conduct and proves to them that it can be a good thing if the young couple take a liking to each other, as they have. Thus all ends happily.

Queen of Cornwall, The
COMP.: R. Boughton
LIBR.: T. Hardy
From a play by Hardy

2 acts
Glastonbury, 21 August 1924
Liverpool, 1927

Queen of Sheba, The
See *Königin von Saba, Die*
See also *Reine de Saba, La*

Queen of Spades, The
See *Pique-Dame*

Rake's Progress, The
COMP.: I. Stravinsky
LIBR.: W. H. Auden and C. Kallman

Tragedy in 3 acts and Epilogue
Venice, 11 September 1951
Edinburgh, 1953
Metropolitan, 1953

CAST

Truelove	B	Baba the Turk, *a bearded lady*	MS
Anne, *his daughter*	S	Sellem, *auctioneer*	T
Tom Rakewell	T	Keeper of the madhouse	B
Nick Shadow	Bar	Whores and Roaring Boys, Servants,	
Mother Goose, *proprietress of a*		Citizens, Madmen	
brothel	MS		

SYNOPSIS

I. Nick, appearing just after the good Tom has professed his love for (1) Anne, and (2) idleness, takes the innocent in hand and leads him into the hell of London. There he is snatched up into the whirl of the world of Mother Goose. Anne, left lamenting at home, decides to go find him.

II. Tom, in spite of all the pleasures of vice, becomes unhappy. Nick prescribes marriage as a cure, suggesting the bearded Baba. Tom agrees. After the wedding Tom catches a brief glimpse of Anne who urges him to return to her; London is no place for him. But, being married, he is no longer free. Soon the marriage begins to pall on him. Baba's incessant chatter having ground away his patience, he wishes for release. Nick, ever resourceful, provides him with a machine which will make bread from stones, or so he convinces Tom.

III. Tom, still unhappy, challenges Nick to a game of cards to win back his soul. He wins, but Nick curses him with insanity. The next we see of poor Tom he is an idiot in Bedlam. There Anne goes to find him. Taking his sick head in her arms she sings him to soothing sleep and leaves him dying.

Rape of Lucretia, The
COMP.: B. Britten
LIBR.: R. Duncan
From the play by Obey

Tragedy in 2 acts
Glyndebourne, 12 July 1946
Basle, 1947
New York, 1949

CAST

Male Chorus	T	Lucia, *her attendant*	S
Female Chorus	S	Bianca, *her nurse*	C
Lucretia	C	Tarquinius, *prince of Rome*	Bar
Collatinus, *her husband*	B	Junius, *general*	Bar

SYNOPSIS

I. Tarquinius the arrogant rules Rome. One evening during a lull in battle away from the city the soldiers wonder what their wives may be doing at home. Each is unsure whether his own wife is more trustworthy than any other's, but Collatinus has faith in his Lucretia's chastity. By this Tarquinius' lust is aroused. He resolves, secretly, to make Collatinus a cuckold with the rest.

At home all is quiet as Lucretia and her girls prepare for the night's sleep. In the streets one may hear the approaching hoofbeats of the horse bearing her betrayer.

II. Tarquinius attacks Lucretia in her bed. Next morning she sends urgently for Collatinus. When he arrives she greets her husband in robes of mourning. Unable to bear her guilt she stabs herself and falls into his arms.

Rappresentazione dell' Anima e del Corpo, Il.
COMP.: E. de'Cavalieri   Rome, 1600
A morality play set to simple music, with hymns between the episodes and stage

directions in the score. This work, not quite an opera, immediately preceded the first actual operas.

Raymond   3 *acts*
    COMP.: A. Thomas   Comique, 5 June 1851
    LIBR.: de Leuven and Rosier   Vienna, 1857
                                       Prague, 1862

Regina   *Prologue and* 3 *acts*
    COMP.: M. Blitzstein   New York, 31 October 1949
    LIBR.: By the composer
From the play *The Little Foxes*, by Lillian Hellman

Reine de Saba, La   4 *acts*
    COMP.: C. Gounod   Opéra, 28 February 1862
    LIBR.: Barbier and Carré   New Orleans, 1889
                                       London, 1865

Reine de Saba, La
See also *Königin von Saba, Die*

Resurrection
See *Risurrezione*

Retablo de Maese Pedro, El   1 *act*
(*Master Peter's Puppet Show*)   Sevilla, 23 March 1923
    COMP.: M. de Falla   New York, 1925
    LIBR.: By the composer   London, 1928
From an episode in *Don Quixote* by Cervantes

Return of Ulysses, The
See *Ritorno d'Ulisse in Patria, Il*

Rêve, Le   4 *acts*
(*The Dream*)   Comique, 18 June 1891
    COMP.: A. Bruneau   Covent Garden, 1891
    LIBR.: L. Gallet   Königsberg, 1892
From Emile Zola

Rheingold, Das   *Prologue to Der Ring des Nibelungen*, 4 *scenes*
    COMP.: R. Wagner   Munich, 22 September 1869
    LIBR.: By the composer   London, 1882
                                       Metropolitan, 1889

CAST

Wotan, *chief of the gods*	BBar	Mime, *Nibelung dwarf*	T
Donner	BBar	Fricka, *goddess*	MS
Froh	T	Freia, *goddess of youth*	S
Loge	T	Erda, *goddess*	MS
Fasolt, *a giant*	BBar	Woglinde, *daughter of the Rhine*	S
Fafner, *a giant*	B	Wellgunde, *daughter of the Rhine*	S
Alberich, *Nibelung dwarf*	BBar	Flosshilde, *daughter of the Rhine*	MS

I. Alberich watches bitterly as the beautiful Rhine Maidens swim. Suddenly he sees their hidden gold that cannot be stolen except by him who renounces love. Quickly making his decision, Alberich makes the renunciation and rushes off with his prize.

II. The giants have built Valhalla for the abode of the gods. In payment they demand Freia from Wotan, but the god is unwilling to keep his promise. Loge describes to them the ring that he knows Alberich has made from the Rhine gold. They propose that Wotan should get them that magic ring as ransom for the goddess.

III. Alberich has made more than the ring, however. He has also fashioned a magic helmet, the Tarnhelm, which will render its wearer invisible to others, or provide him another shape. Loge, who came with Wotan to negotiate with the dwarf, tricks him into assuming the shape of a toad. While Alberich is in that small condition, Loge snatches away the Tarnhelm, binds up the toad and takes him up to the outside world.

IV. There they carry on their negotiations with more with which to bargain. Alberich agrees to give them the Rhine gold and the ring he made from it to win his freedom. With the ransom, however, goes his curse. With the gold, the Tarnhelm and finally the ring, Wotan saves Freia from the giants. But the giants, heir now to the curse of Alberich, fall to fighting immediately, and Fasolt is slain. In vain do the Rhine Maidens cry to have their ring as Wotan and the gods ascend a rainbow bridge toward Valhalla.

Richard Coeur de Lion
(Richard the Lion-Hearted)
COMP.: A. Grétry
LIBR.: J. Sedaine

3 *acts*
Paris, 21 October 1784
London, 1786
Boston, 1797

Riders to the Sea
COMP.: R. Vaughan Williams
LIBR.: J. M. Synge
From the play by Synge

1 *act*
London, 1 December 1937
Cambridge, Mass. 1938

Rienzi
COMP.: R. Wagner
LIBR.: By the composer
From the novel by Bulwer-Lytton

5 *acts*
Dresden, 20 October 1842
New York, 1878
London, 1879
Metropolitan, 1886

CAST

Cola Rienzi, *Roman tribune*	T	Baroncelli, *Roman citizen*	T
Irene, *his sister*	S	Cecco del Vecchia, *Roman citizen*	B
Steffano Colonna	B	Messenger of Peace	S
Adriano, *his son*	MS	Ambassadors, Nobles, Priests, Monks,	
Paolo Orsini	B	Soldiers, Messengers, People	
Raimondo, *Papal Legate*	B		

SYNOPSIS

Colonna fights to protect Irene from abduction by Orsini. In the battle Rienzi becomes enraged and urges the people to revolt against the nobles. His revolution succeeds, but the nobles lay a plot to kill him.

When the people hear that their new leader plans to enter a league with Germany they turn against him. The church excommunicates him, and finally he is burned to death in the flames of the capitol.

THE OPERAS

Rigoletto

COMP.: G. Verdi
LIBR.: F. Piave
From Victor Hugo's play
Le Roi s'Amuse

Tragedy in 3 acts
Venice, 11 March 1851
Covent Garden, 1853
New York, 1857

CAST

Duke of Mantua	T	Cavaliere Marullo, *courtier*		Bar
Rigoletto, *his jester*	Bar	Countess Ceprano		MS
Count Ceprano	Bar	Gilda, *Rigoletto's daughter*		S
Count Monterone	B	Giovanna, *her duenna*		MS
Sparafucile, *an assassin by profession*	B	Maddalena, *Sparafucile's sister*		C
Matteo Borsa, *courtier*	T	Courtiers, Nobles, Pages, Servants		

MUSICAL HIGHLIGHTS

ACT I. Aria *Questa o quella* (This or that one), Duke
Soliloquy *Pari siamo* (How alike we are), Rigoletto
Aria *Caro nome* (Dearest name), Gilda
ACT II. Duet *Piangi, fanciulla* (Weep my dearest), Rigoletto and Gilda
ACT III. Aria *La donna è mobile* (A woman is changeable), Duke
Quartet *Bella figlia dell'amore* (Fairest daughter of the graces), Maddalena, Gilda, Duke, Rigoletto

SYNOPSIS

I. The Duke is intrigued by the memory of an unknown girl he has seen. But meanwhile, making hay while the sun shines, he woos the Countess Ceprano who is among the guests at his ball. Rigoletto tortures the Count about his wife's infidelity. At this the Count decides to be repaid for such damage by means of the girl he believes is the jester's mistress. Suddenly old Count Monterone breaks into the party to denounce the Duke for dishonoring his daughter. Rigoletto mocks the old man. Monterone curses the jester with a father's curse, leaving Rigoletto visibly shaken.

In disguise, the Duke meets Gilda in her garden and pledges his love. Then Ceprano and his friends, using Rigoletto as their unsuspecting dupe, kidnap the girl who is really the jester's daughter although they think she is his mistress. When they are gone Rigoletto realizes the validity of Monterone's curse.

II. Rigoletto finds Gilda in the Duke's palace, where she was taken. Together they weep.

III. He hires Sparafucile to kill the Duke. Maddalena will be bait for the trap. She lures him, but she begins to fall in love with him herself. At the assassin's place she urges Sparafucile to murder someone else, to let the Duke go free. Finally it is agreed that the next man who enters the door will be the victim. It is Gilda who enters, in man's clothes in order to escape from Mantua in secret. The murderers kill her and stuff her body into a sack which they give to Rigoletto as evidence of having done what he paid them for. While the fool hauls the sack toward the river to get rid of it, he hears the Duke singing in the night. Tearing open the sack he finds his own daughter, still breathing, but dying in fulfillment of the old count's curse.

NOTES

Rigoletto is said to have been written in forty days. The censors made it necessary for the locale to be shifted from France to avoid political complications. The play itself had been banned in 1832 as immoral.

THE OPERAS

Rinaldo
COMP.: G. F. Handel
LIBR.: G. Rossi
From Tasso

3 *acts*
London, 7 March 1711
Dublin, 1711
Naples, 1718

The celebrated *March* from *Rinaldo* was brilliantly satirized as the march of the thieves in the *Beggar's Opera. Rinaldo* was the first opera Handel wrote for London.

Ring des Nibelungen, Der
(*The Ring of the Nibelungs*)
A Stage Festival play for Three Days and an Evening.

The first performance of the entire tetralogy was mounted in Bayreuth, in August 1876, twenty-eight years after Wagner had begun the work. The first complete performances in London and at the Metropolitan were in May 1882 and March 1889 respectively. Wagner wrote the libretti of the four parts in reverse order. For casts and individual synopses see the individual parts:

Rheingold, Das
Walküre, Die
Siegfried
Götterdämmerung

SYNOPSIS OF THE CYCLE

Alberich lusts for wealth and power. To rob the Rhine Maidens of the gold he renounces love. From the gold he forges a magic ring, but Wotan tricks him out of it and gives it to the giants Fafner and Fasolt as ransom for Freia, the goddess of youth and beauty. But a curse goes with the ring, first destroying Fasolt.

To restore the ring to the Rhine Maidens and thus avoid the curse is the burden of the three remaining operas. This cannot be accomplished except by one whose motives are unselfish. Wotan fathers Siegmund and Sieglinde, human beings, to do it. Their illicit child, Siegfried, slays Fafner with Siegmund's sword and gives the magic ring to Brünnhilde, whom he has saved from a ring of fire put around her by Wotan in punishment for having shielded Siegmund from his wrath.

Siegfried is treacherously slain by Hagen, Alberich's son. Brünnhilde, taking the ring with her, plunges into his funeral pyre. Now the Rhine Maidens can retrieve their gold, because of Brünnhilde's unselfish act. But Valhalla, the abode of the gods, is destroyed in the flames.

Rip van Winkle
COMP.: R. de Koven
LIBR.: P. MacKaye
From the story by Washington Irving

3 *acts*
Chicago, 2 January 1920
New York, 1920

Risurrezione
(*Resurrection*)
COMP.: F. Alfano
LIBR.: C. Hanau
From the novel by Tolstoi

4 *acts*
Turin, 30 November 1904
Chicago, 1925
Santiago, Chile, 1928

Ritorno d'Ulisse in Patria, Il
COMP.: C. Monteverdi
LIBR.: G. Badoaro

Prologue and 5 acts
Venice, February 1641
Paris, 1925
Florence, 1942

CAST

Giove (*Jove, Jupiter*)	T	Pisandro, *Penelope's suitor*	T
Nettuno (*Neptune*)	B	Anfinomo, *Penelope's suitor*	T
Minerva	S	Eurimaco	T
Ulisse (*Ulysses, Odysseus*) *Greek hero*	T	Melanto	MS
Penelope, *his wife*	C	Eumete	T
Telemaco, *his son*	MS	Iro, *jester*	T
Antinoo, *Penelope's suitor*	B	Ericlea, *old nurse*	MS

(*Note: Voicing according to Dallapiccola's arrangement*)

SYNOPSIS

I. Penelope laments for Ulysses, absent for twenty years now, ten in the Trojan war, and ten on the way home. Giove and Nettuno discuss the sins of men as Minerva finds Ulysses cast up on a foreign shore.

II. Ulysses, with the help of that goddess, arrives home in disguise. Telemaco, who has been searching for his father, returns also and discovers him outside their palace. Inside, Penelope, who has been plagued for years with suitors she does not want, puts them off yet a little longer in the hope that her husband may actually be returning.

III. As a beggar, Ulysses, the hero, takes part in an arrow-shooting contest among the suitors. After his astoundingly accurate display he turns on the suitors themselves and kills them all. But Penelope will not believe even yet that it is really her husband until Ericlea identifies him by marks she remembered from his boyhood.

NOTES

Today *Ulysses* is performed in modern arrangements of the ancient score by Dallapiccola and by d'Indy. The original version was not published until nearly three hundred years after its composition, when it was printed in Vienna in 1923.

Ritter Blaubart   3 *acts*
(*Knight Bluebeard*)   Darmstadt, 29 January 1920
COMP.: E. von Reznicek   Berlin, 1920
LIBR.: H. Eulenberg   Prague, 1922

Robert le Diable   5 *acts*
(*Robert the Devil*)   Paris, 22 November 1831
COMP.: G. Meyerbeer   Drury Lane, 1832
LIBR.: Scribe and Delavigne   New York, 1834
          Metropolitan, 1883

CAST

Alice, *Robert's foster sister*	S	Robert, *duke of Normandy*	T
Isabella, *princess of Sicily*	S	Bertram, *the unknown*	B
Abbess	Dancer	Raimbaut, *minstrel*	T

SYNOPSIS

In reality Bertram is the Devil and Robert's father. He attempts by every means within his power to drive Robert to evil but Alice fights and succeeds in preserving the good in him. In the end Robert marries Isabella.

Robin Hood   3 *acts*
COMP.: R. de Koven   Chicago, 9 June 1890
LIBR.: H. Smith   Boston, 1890
          London, 1890

Rognyeda
COMP.: A. Serov
LIBR.: D. Averkiev

5 acts
St. Petersburg, 8 November 1865
Moscow, 1868

Roi de Lahore, Le
(*The King of Lahore*)
COMP.: J. Massenet
LIBR.: L. Gallet

5 acts
Opéra, 27 April 1877
Covent Garden, 1879
New Orleans, 1883

Roi d'Ys, Le
(*The King of Ys*)
COMP.: E. Lalo
LIBR.: Lalo and Blau
From a Breton legend

Tragedy in 3 acts
Comique, 7 May 1888
Covent Garden, 1901
Metropolitan, 1922

CAST

The King of Ys	B	Karnac	Bar
Margared, *his daughter*	S	St. Corentin	B
Rozenn, *his daughter*	S	Jahel	Bar
Mylio	T	Nobles, Warriors, Soldiers, People	

SYNOPSIS

I. Margared is in love with Mylio, but unfortunately she is engaged for political reasons to Karnac. Rozenn also loves Mylio although she is unaware that he is the same man whom Margared loves. Mylio pays Rozenn a secret visit. When the king comes to take Margared to meet her future husband, Rozenn tells her that she has reason to believe that Margared's lover is nearby. Therefore Margared bravely refuses to marry Karnac, and the war which might have come to an end continues.

II. There is to be a battle. The lines are drawn, all is ready for the blood to be shed when Margared, realizing that Rozenn meant that same Mylio that she loves, curses his name. Mylio is victorious, but Margared finds Karnac and betrays the city by revealing to him how he can let loose a flood of waters upon it.

III. Rozenn marries Mylio. The floods come. The people climb to the highest point in the city to avoid drowning. There Margared thinks it over and regrets her thirst for revenge at such a cost. Knowing that nothing will save the city until the waters have claimed a victim for her curse, she leaps to her death.

Roi d'Yvetot, Le
(*The King of Yvetot*)
COMP.: C. Adam
LIBR.: de Leuven and Brunswick
From a poem by Béranger

3 acts
Comique, 13 October 1842
Leipzig, 1843
London, 1850

Roi d'Yvetot, Le
(*The King of Yvetot*)
COMP.: J. Ibert
LIBR.: Limozin and de la Tourasse

4 acts
Comique, 15 June 1930
Düsseldorf, 1936
Prague, 1937

Roi l'a Dit, Le
(*The King Said So*)
COMP.: L. Delibes
LIBR.: E. Gondinet

3 acts
Comique, 24 May 1873
Prague, 1874
London, 1894

Roi Malgré Lui, Le
(*King in Spite of Himself*)
COMP.: E. Chabrier
LIBR.: Burani and de Najac
From a comedy by Ancelot

Comedy in 3 acts
Comique, 18 May 1887
Karlsruhe, 1890
Prague, 1931

Roi Pausole, Le
See *Aventures du Roi Pausole, Les*

Romeo and Juliet
See also *Village Romeo and Juliet, The*
and *Capuletti ed I Montecchi, I*

Roméo et Juliette
COMP.: C. Gounod
LIBR.. Barbier and Carré
From Shakespeare

Tragedy in 5 acts
Paris, 27 April 1867
Covent Garden, 1867
New York, 1867
Metropolitan, 1891

CAST

Duke of Verona	B	Stephano, *Romeo's page*	S
Count Paris	Bar	Gregory, *Capulet's retainer*	Bar
Count Capulet	B	Friar Lawrence	B
Juliette, *his daughter*	S	Benvolio, *Montagues' retainer*	T
Gertrude, *her nurse*	MS	Friar Jean	B
Tybalt, *Capulet's nephew*	T	Nobles, Ladies, Citizens, Soldiers,	
Romeo, *a Montague*	T	Monks, Pages	
Mercutio	Bar		

SYNOPSIS

I. Romeo, hidden behind a mask at his enemy's ball, falls in love with Juliette at first sight, as does she with him. Tybalt hears of it, but old Capulet will not allow his party to be broken up by murder.

II. Romeo visits her at night by climbing to her balcony.

III. In secret they marry in Friar Lawrence's cell. Near the Capulet House, Stephano sings an insulting song and sparks a street battle during which Mercutio and Tybalt are killed. For this Romeo is banished from Verona.

IV. Again the lovers meet by night. When Romeo has gone, Capulet comes with Friar Lawrence to arrange Juliette's marriage with Paris. But the good Friar provides the girl with a drink with which she may escape this fate by seeming to be dead.

V. Hearing that Juliette has died, Romeo breaks into her tomb and kills himself there. She awakes from the potion only to find her husband dying at her side. Rather than live without him, she stabs herself and dies with him.

Rondine, La
(*The Swallow*)
COMP.: G. Puccini
LIBR.: G. Adami
From a libretto by Willner and Reichert

Comedy in 3 acts
Monte Carlo, 27 March 1917
Bologna, 1917
Rome, 1918
Metropolitan, 1928

CAST

Magda, *Rambaldo's mistress*	S	Crébillon, *his friend*	BBar
Lisette, *her maid*	S	Yvette, *Magda's friend*	S
Ruggero, *young man*	T	Bianca, *Magda's friend*	S
Prunier, *poet*	T	Suzy, *Magda's friend*	MS
Rambaldo, *wealthy Parisian*	Bar	Steward	B
Périchaud,	BBar	Ladies and Gentlemen, Citizens, Students,	
Gobin, *his friend*	T	Artists, Demi-mondaines, Dancers	

SYNOPSIS

I. Magda wishes she could relive the good old days on the left bank. Ruggero helpfully suggests that the best Bohemian place to go, in Paris, is Boullier's.

II. There they all meet. Magda, dressed as in the old days, enters into a little affair with Ruggero. Rambaldo finds her in this condition.

III. She and Ruggero, having gone off together, find they cannot live happily. She feels out of place in the innocence of his life. She therefore leaves him, and ceases the attempt to recapture her past, to return to Rambaldo.

Rosamond
COMP.: T. Arne
LIBR.: J. Addison

3 acts
London, 18 March 1733
Dublin, 1743

Only six songs and a duet remain of this opera.

Rose et Colas
COMP.: P. Monsigny
LIBR.: J. Sedaine
From a tale of La Fontaine

1 act
Paris, 8 March 1764
Warsaw, 1765
Vienna, 1776

Rosenkavalier, Der
(*The Knight of the Rose*)
COMP.: R. Strauss
LIBR.: H. von Hofmannsthal

Comedy in 3 acts
Dresden, 26 January 1911
Covent Garden, 1913
Metropolitan, 1913

CAST

Princess von Werdenberg,		Notary	B
the Marschallin	S	Innkeeper	T
Baron Ochs von Lerchenau	B	Singer	T
Octavian	MS	Three Orphans	S, MS, C
Herr von Faninal, *wealthy parvenu*	Bar	Dressmaker	S
Sophie, *his daughter*	S	Animal Tamer	T
Marianne, *her duenna*	S	Four Servants of the Marschallin	2T, 2B
Valzacchi, *scandalmonger*	T	Four Waiters	T, 3B
Annina, *his partner*	C	Flute Player, Hairdresser, Scholar,	
Police Commissioner	B	Widow	Mutes
Major-Domo to the Marschallin	T	Mahomet and other pages	Mutes
Major-Domo to von Faninal	T		

MUSICAL HIGHLIGHTS

ACT I. Italian Aria *Di rigori armato il seno*, Singer
ACT II. Waltzes
ACT III. Trio *Hab' mir's gelobt* (This is my vow), Marschallin, Sophie, Octavian
Duet *Ist ein Traum* (It's a dream), Octavian and Sophie

I. Ochs interrupts a very romantic moment between Octavian and the Princess to ask her to appoint an intermediary, a knight of the Rose, to take a symbolic rose to Sophie as token of his proposal of an engagement to that girl. He leaves; the Marschallin dallies about it but then sends Octavian away. Suddenly making up her mind she sends the rose after him.

II. In pomp and with gracious ritual Octavian completes his mission. Seeing Sophie, he falls in love with her. When the famous Baron Ochs comes to stake his claim after sending his token, Sophie is repelled by him and knows that she loves Octavian. This is a godsend for the evil Valzacchi and his accomplice. They tell the baron; the baron challenges Octavian to a duel and in a very delicate fight receives a very slight wound. Lying alone, reduced to utter pain, he receives a note by the hand of Annina who has been hired for the occasion by Octavian. The note invites Ochs to an assignation.

III. Dressed as a girl, his young rival receives Baron Ochs in a special room at an inn. There he is subjected to all the tortures and tricks of Valzacchi and Octavian until somebody calls for the police. But he can hardly explain the situation without getting his own name muddy. The Marschallin, hearing of the whole affair, arrives in time to set everything straight with the Commissioner, to subdue Ochs, and to forgive Octavian, for whom she was certainly not young enough anyway. With magnaminity the Princess gives the boy to Sophie for a lover.

Rosiera, La

	3 *acts*
COMP.: V. Gnecchi	Gera, Germany, 12 February 1927
LIBR.: Gnecchi and Zangarini	Vienna, 1928
From a story by de Musset	Pilsen, 1927

This opera is one of the few which makes use of microtones.

Rossignol, Le

	3 *acts*
(*The Nightingale*)	Opéra, 26 May 1914
COMP.: I. Stravinsky	London, 1914
LIBR.: Stravinsky and Mitousoff	Metropolitan, 1926
From a fairy tale by Andersen	Buenos Aires, 1927

CAST

Fisherman	T	Three Japanese Envoys	2T, Bar
Nightingale	S	Emperor of China	Bar
Cook	MS	Death	C
Chamberlain	B	Courtiers, Ghosts	
Bonze	B		

SYNOPSIS

I. The nightingale is formally invited to sing before the emperor.

II. The envoys of Japan offer the emperor a mechanical bird which they claim is superior to the natural variety. In shame and grief the real nightingale flies away. This insubordination is insulting to the emperor who banishes it forever from his empire.

III. When the emperor lies dying, the nightingale returns. So beautiful is her song that the emperor does not die but becomes well again, proving that live music is always better than the canned substitute.

NOTES

This delicious work lasts only fifty minutes. It is best known to American audiences through recordings of a suite made from it.

Royal Palace, The
COMP.: K. Weill
LIBR.: I. Goll

1 *act*
Berlin, 2 March 1927

Rusalka
(*The Mermaid*)
COMP.: A. Dargomizhsky
LIBR.: By the composer
From a poem by Pushkin

4 *acts*
St. Petersburg, 16 May 1856
New York, 1922
London, 1931

Rusalka
COMP.: A. Dvořák
LIBR.: J. Kvapil

3 *acts*
Prague, 31 March 1901
Vienna, 1910
Stuttgart, 1929

Russlan and Ludmilla
COMP.: M. Glinka
LIBR.: Composer, Shirkov, Bakhturin, and others
From Pushkin

5 *acts*
St. Petersburg, 9 December 1842
London, 1931
Berlin, 1951

CAST

Svictosar, *prince of Kiev*	B	Gorislava, *Ratmir's slave*	S
Ludmilla, *his daughter*	S	Finn, *benevolent wizard*	T
Russlan, *a knight, suitor*	Bar	Naina, *malevolent witch*	MS
Ratmir, *oriental prince, suitor*	C	Bayan, *bard*	T
Farlaf, *warrior, suitor*	B	Tchernomor, *evil dwarf*	

SYNOPSIS

I. In the midst of festivities, Ludmilla disappears. Svietosar offers her hand in marriage to him who can rescue her.

II. Russlan, one who could win her, finds a lance, a sword, and a shield all with magic properties, and learns where to find the girl's captor.

III. He passes through an enchanted palace.

IV. He finds Tchernomor and fights him. But having won, he is unable to waken Ludmilla from her enchanted sleep.

V. Finn gives him a magic ring with which he breaks the spell; Ludmilla awakens and becomes his prize. NOTE

Because of Pushkin's death in a duel, Shirkov and Bakhturin were called in to complete the libretto.

Rustic Chivalry
See *Cavalleria Rusticana*

Sacrifice, The
COMP.: F. Converse
LIBR.: Converse and Macy

3 *acts*
Boston, 3 March 1911

Sadko
COMP.: N. Rimsky-Korsakov
LIBR.: Rimsky-Korsakov and Bielsky

7 *scenes*
Moscow, 7 January 1898
Metropolitan, 1930
London, 1931

THE OPERAS

CAST

King of the Ocean	B	Viking Merchant	B
Volkhova, *his daughter*	S	Hindu Merchant	T
Sadko, *singer*	T	Venetian Merchant	Bar
Lubava, *his wife*	MS	Four Buffoons	2MS, T, B
Nezhata, *musician*	MS	Two Elders of Novgorod	T, B

SYNOPSIS

I. The people of Novgorod listen as Sadko sings. He sings wistfully that if only Novgorod were at the sea, everyone would become rich.

II. The sea princess Volkhova falls in love with Sadko.

III. Lubava grieves to have lost him.

IV. Sadko catches three golden fish and becomes rich. He decides to go to Venice.

V. After twelve years Sadko is becalmed on the way home. He frees his ship only by disembarking from it himself.

VI. At the bottom of the sea Sadko marries Volkhova in a fury of celebration.

VII. Volkhova takes her temporary husband back in his sleep to Novgorod. Leaving him there she transforms herself into a great river connecting the city with the sea.

NOTE

Sadko contains one of the most famous of Rimsky-Korsakov's songs, the *Song of India*, sung by the Hindu Merchant.

Safié
COMP.: H. Hadley
LIBR.: E. Oxenford

1 *act*
Mainz, 4 April 1909

Saint of Bleecker Street, The
COMP.: G.-C. Menotti
LIBR.: By the composer

3 *acts, 5 scenes*
New York, 27 December 1954
La Scala, 1955

Sakuntala
This subject was used for operas by Ignace Paderewski, Louis Coerne (1904), and Franco Alfano (1922).

Salammbô
COMP.: L. Reyer
LIBR.: C. du Locle
From a novel by Flaubert

5 *acts*
Brussels, 10 February 1890
New Orleans, 1900
New York, 1901

Salome
COMP.: R. Strauss
LIBR.: H. Lachmann
From Oscar Wilde

1 *act*
Dresden, 9 December 1905
Metropolitan, 1907 once only, revived 1933
Covent Garden, 1910

CAST

Herod Antipas	T	Five Jews	4T, B
Herodias, *his wife*	MS	Two Nazarenes	T, B
Salome, *her daughter*	S	Two Soldiers	B
Jokanaan, *John the Baptist*	Bar	Cappadocian	B
Narraboth, *Syrian captain of the guard*	T	Slave	
Page	C		

THE OPERAS

The Dance of the seven veils
Finale—*Scene of Salome with the head of John the Baptist*

SYNOPSIS

For a moment the powerful voice of the captive Jokanaan casts fear into the hearts of the soldiers of Herod's guard. But Salome, hearing it, is filled with a voracious lust for the man. When he stands before her she is consumed with hot desire. She bends to him, tempts him, but he will not listen. Herod covets her, himself thirsting with lust but she has no eyes but for the prisoner. Herod asks her to dance for him, he promises to give her anything she wants.

Salome dances before Herod, wearing seven veils, one of which she removes, then another and another. In payment she demands the head of Jokanaan who would not kiss her alive, but who cannot withhold his lips when dead. Herod offers her anything else, but she wants only the head.

It is brought to her, bleeding, upon a silver tray. Seizing it in her claws she kisses its mouth. Herod, utterly sickened by the sight of her depravity, orders the soldiers to crush her to death.

NOTE

Sometimes the *Dance of the Seven Veils* is performed by a dancer in substitution for the singer. Once a prima donna tried to do the dance herself, but they say Strauss was taken so aback by the gyrations she produced that he insisted she desist.

The board of directors of the Metropolitan had the opera taken off after a dress rehearsal and one performance. It has since, nevertheless, become a standard exhibition piece for great singing actresses in the more seriously progressive companies, not excluding the Metropolitan.

Salome
See also *Herodiade*

Samson et Dalila
COMP.: C. Saint-Saëns
LIBR.: F. Lemaire

Tragedy in 3 acts
Weimar, 2 December 1877
Covent Garden (concert), 1893
Metropolitan, 1895

CAST

Dalila, *a Philistine*	MS	Old Hebrew	B
Samson, *warrior*	T	Messenger of the Philistines	T
High Priest of Dagon	Bar	Hebrews, Philistines	
Abimelech, *satrap of Gaza*	B		

MUSICAL HIGHLIGHTS

ACT I. Scena *Je viens célébrer la victoire* (I come to celebrate your victory), Dalila and chorus
ACT II. Aria *Amour, viens aider ma faiblesse* (O love, come aid me in my weakness), Dalila
Aria *Mon Coeur s'ouvre à ta voix* (My heart opens at thy voice), Dalila
ACT III. *Baccanale*

SYNOPSIS

I. Samson, in a desperate effort to provide the weary Hebrews with some deed of encouragement, slays their enemy Abimelech with his own sword. In the flush of such a victory he is unaware of the sinister undertones of the suppliant ovation of the Philistine maidens with Dalila at their head.

II. She is determined, he is uncertain. She worms from Samson the secret of his tremendous strength, his hair. While he relaxes his vigil against treachery she cuts it off so that he is easily defeated by the resurgent Philistine host.

III. Blinded and imprisoned Samson is the toy of his enemies. They drag him out to be exhibited at the dedication of a new temple to Dagon. There, in chains, the hero prays to Jehovah for strength. Seizing the pillars of the temple he brings it down on all their heads, sacrificing himself.

Samuel Pepys   1 *act*
  COMP.: A. Coates   Munich, 21 December 1929
  LIBR.: Drury and Pryce
From the diary of Samuel Pepys

Sancta Susanna   1 *act*
  COMP.: P. Hindemith   Frankfurt, 26 March 1922
  LIBR.: A. Stramm   Prague, 1923

Sapho   3 *acts*
  COMP.: C. Gounod   Opéra, 16 April 1851
  LIBR.: E. Augier   Covent Garden, 1851
                                        Antwerp, 1894

  Gounod's first opera.

Sapho   5 *acts*
  COMP.: J. Massenet   Comique, 27 November 1897
  LIBR.: Cain and Bernède   New York, 1909
From the novel by Daudet   New Orleans, 1913

Šarka   3 *acts*
  COMP.: Z. Fibich   Prague, 28 December 1897
  LIBR.: A. Schulzová

Šarka   3 *acts*
  COMP.: L. Janácek   Brno, 11 November 1925
  LIBR.: J. Zeyer
Janáček's first opera. The date of the first performance is uncertain.

Savitri   1 *act*
  COMP.: G. Holst   London, 5 December 1916
  LIBR.: By the composer   Cincinnati, 1939
From the *Maha Bharata*   Covent Garden, 1923

CAST

| Satyavan, *woodman* | T | Death | B |
| Savitri, *his wife* | S | Hidden Female Chorus | |

SYNOPSIS

Death comes for Satyavan. Savitri pleads with Death and wins his life back.

NOTE

Savitri is intended for performance in the open air.

Scala di Seta, La
(*The Silken Ladder*)
COMP.: G. Rossini
LIBR.: G. Rossi
From a French libretto by Planard

1 *act*
Venice, 9 May 1812
Barcelona, 1823
Lisbon, 1825

Scarecrow, The
COMP.: N. Lockwood

New York, 19 May 1945

Scarlet Letter, The
COMP.: W. Damrosch
LIBR.: G. Lathrop
From the story by Hawthorne, who
was Lathrop's father-in-law

3 *acts*
Boston, 10 February 1896
New York, 1896

Scarlet Letter, The
COMP.: V. Giannini

Hamburg, 2 June 1938

Schauspieldirektor, Der
(*The Impresario*)
COMP.: W. A. Mozart
LIBR.: G. Stephanie

Comedy in 1 *act*
Vienna, 7 February 1786
London, 1857
New York, 1870

This parody of the opera business was written for a garden party at Schönbrunn. It consists of an overture, 2 airs, trio and finale, plus dialogue. The story deals with the troubles of an unfortunate impresario with his prima donna, or the story of Mozart, Schikaneder and Madame Hofer.

Schöne Galathea, Die
(*The Beautiful Galatea*)
COMP.: F. von Suppé
LIBR.: L. von Kohlenegg

1 *act*
Berlin, 30 June 1865
New York, 1867
London, 1872

School for Fathers, The
See *Quattro Rusteghi, I*

Schwanda the Bagpiper
See *Švanda Dudák*

Schweigsame Frau, Die
(*The Silent Woman*)
COMP.: R. Strauss
LIBR.: S. Zweig
From the play *Epicoene* by Ben Jonson

Comedy in 3 *acts*
Dresden, 24 June 1935
La Scala, 1936
Zurich, 1936
New York, 1958

CAST

Sir Morosus Blunt	B	Carlotta, *actress*	MS
Housekeeper	C	Morbio, *actor*	Bar
Schneidebart, *barber*	Bar	Vanuzzi, *actor*	B
Henry Morosus Blunt, *actor*	T	Farfallo, *actor*	B
Aminta, *his wife, actress*	S	Actors, Neighbors	
Isotta, *actress*	S		

THE OPERAS

I. His housekeeper is very interested in Sir Morosus. She engages the barber in a plot to get him to marry her. The old man hates any kind of noise in the house and until now has managed to keep the place in a state somewhat akin to that of a mausoleum. Back, as if from the dead, comes his nephew Henry with a wife and a troupe of actors. This is too much for Sir Morosus. He begs the barber to find him a wife, a silent wife. Thus the housekeeper's pot begins to boil.

II. From three candidates whisked before the old man, Sir Morosus chooses to marry Aminta. She plays her part very silently; the other actors conspire as priests and notary to perform the mock ceremony in the most delicate quiet. When all is said and done Aminta suddenly breaks into a veritable torrent of words at the top of her voice, nagging and noisy, calculated to make Sir Morosus wish he had never been married to such a woman.

III. The hoax goes on. Aminta orders carpenters to make all kinds of alterations in the house, which the actors seem about to carry out. Finally another actor arrives, in the character of chief justice. Sir Morosus pleads with him for a divorce, but it is refused. The old man is nearly mad when finally the actors reveal themselves to him and tell him of their hoax. With relief he relaxes, and there seems to be hope for an easier future in the house.

Secret Marriage, The
See *Matrimonio Segreto, Il*

Segreto di Susanna, Il
(*The Secret of Susanna*)
COMP.: E. Wolf-Ferrari
LIBR.: E. Golisciani

Comedy in 1 act
Munich, 4 December 1909
New York, 1911
Covent Garden, 1911
Metropolitan, 1912

CAST

| Count Gil, 30 | Bar | Santi, *their servant*, 50 | Mute |
| Countess Susanna, 20 | S | | |

SYNOPSIS

In the house where smoking is forbidden, Gil smells the tell-tale odor of cigarettes. He meets, he greets, he kisses his wife and smells tobacco. In the depths of his dark suspicion he begins to wonder who may be the lover with whom she has taken up secret meetings, a lover who smokes. In fury and grief he separates from her.

Santi picks things up around the room.

Gil storms out. Susanna, alone at last, lights a forlorn but comforting cigarette. Gil returns, she hides it. But he smells it again and believes the secret lover must be present. His jealousy knows no bounds. While he shouts at her he wonders what secret she is hiding from him behind her back. He snatches at it, then jumps back, slightly burned. It was not a lover at all, but his own wife who smoked. With relief he forgives her.

Selva Incantata, La
(*The Enchanted Forest*)
COMP.: V. Righini
LIBR.: A. da Caramondani
From Tasso's *Gerusalemme Liberata*

Berlin, 17 January 1803
Stockholm, 1831

THE OPERAS

Semiramide
COMP.: G. Rossini
LIBR.: G. Rossi
From Voltaire

2 acts
Venice, 3 February 1823
London, 1824
New York, 1845
Metropolitan, 1893

CAST

Semiramide, *queen of Babylon*	S	Azema, *princess*	S
Arsace, *general of the Assyrians*	C	Idreno, *Indian prince*	T
Ghost of Nino	B	Mitrane, *captain of the guard*	T
Oroe, *high priest of the Magi*	B	Magi, Guards, Satraps, Slaves	
Assur, *prince*	Bar		

SYNOPSIS

Semiramide, who with the help of Assur, murdered her husband Nino, has conceived a love for Arsace. Arsace, however, is her own unrecognized son. The ghost of Nino rises to name Arsace as the rightful king of Babylon, and orders him to visit the tomb of his father to learn of the assassination. Assur goes there also, to kill Arsace. But in the fighting Semiramide intervenes and loses her life. Arsace is victorious.

NOTE

Semiramide, a most Italian sounding piece which was once censured as being too "German," was written in three weeks.

Semiramide Riconosciuta
(*Semiramide Rewarded*)
COMP.: C. von Gluck
LIBR.: Metastasio
Composed in honor of the birthday of Maria Theresa.

3 acts
Vienna, 14 May 1748
Hamburg, 1936

Serse
(*Xerxes*)
COMP.: G. F. Handel
LIBR.: N. Minato (with alterations)

2 acts
London, 26 April 1738
Northampton, Mass., 1928
London, 1935

This most serious work is based upon a comic plot. It contains the celebrated "Largo from Xerxes," *Ombra mai fu*.

Serva Padrona, La
(*The Servant-Mistress*)
COMP.: G. Pergolesi
LIBR.: G. Federico

Intermezzo in 2 parts
Naples, 28 August 1733
London, 1750
New York, 1858

CAST

Uberto	B	Vespone, *another servant*	Mute
Serpina, *his servant*	S		

SYNOPSIS

I. Uberto, tyrannized by his servant Serpina, complains that he has to wait three hours for his chocolate. But Serpina so overwhelms him with words that he pleads with Vespone to go find him a wife for his protection. Serpina jumps at the chance to fight for that coveted position.

II. To win him she plots a complex trick with Vespone as her ferocious lover. Her sweet demeanor and sad pleas evoke pity from her master, thus trapping him into uncertainty whether he may perhaps be in love with his own servant. When Vespone plays his part, Uberto falls straight into the trap, but he cannot escape even when he sees how it was sprung.

NOTES

This famous work first appeared between the acts of *Il Prigioniero Superbo*. The subject was also used by Giovanni Paisiello.

Servante Maîtresse, La
See *Serva Padrona, La*

Shade of Don Juan, The
See *Ombra di Don Giovanni, L'*

Shàmus O'Brien
COMP.: C. Stanford
LIBR.: G. Jessop
From a poem by Le Fanu

2 *acts*
London, 2 March 1896
New York, 1897
Dublin, 1924

Shanewis
COMP.: C. W. Cadman
LIBR.: N. Eberhardt

2 *acts*
Metropolitan, 23 March 1918
Denver, 1924

CAST

Shanewis
Lionel
Amy

Philippe Harjo
Mrs. Everton

Siberia
COMP.: U. Giordano
LIBR.: L. Illica

3 *acts*
La Scala, 19 December 1903
New Orleans, 1906
New York, 1908

Sicilian Vespers, The
See *Vespri Siciliani, I*

Siege of Rhodes, The
COMP.: M. Locke (in part)
LIBR.: W. d'Avenant

Opera in 5 entries
London, September 1656

The music of this first opera in English is lost. The vocal parts were by Matthew Locke (4th entry), Henry Lawes (1st and 5th entries), and Henry Cook (2nd and 3rd entries). The instrumental sections were by Charles Coleman and George Hudson.

Siegfried
COMP.: R. Wagner
LIBR.: By the composer

Music Drama in 3 acts
Bayreuth, 16 August 1876
London, 1882
Metropolitan, 1887

CAST

Siegfried, *son of Siegmund*		Fafner, *giant*	B
and Sieglinde	T	Erda	C
Mime, *Nibelung dwarf*	T	Forest Bird	S
Wotan, *disguised as The Wanderer*	BBar	Brünnhilde	S
Alberich	BBar		

THE OPERAS

I. The foundling Siegfried has been reared by Mime in the hope that he may be useful in retrieving the Ring of the Nibelungs from Fafner. Mime has been trying to weld the broken sword of Siegmund into useful shape, but he has had no success. Wotan, who also wants the ring back, comes in disguise to Mime and drops the hint that only Siegfried can repair the sword. Siegfried seizes the fragments of his father's sword and welds them together masterfully. To test it he splits the anvil in two.

II. Mime conducts his foundling to the mouth of Fafner's cave. There the giant, in the shape of a dragon, faces him. But Siegfried soon slays him with the invincible sword. When the victor touches the blood of the giant to his lips suddenly he understands the songs of birds. One of them tells him of the magic ring, the Tarnhelm and the Rhine Gold. These he takes for himself, killing Mime when he comes to claim them. The bird speaks to Siegfried and leads him away.

III. As the Wanderer, Wotan bars the way but Siegfried shatters the god's spear and goes on into the circle of fire. Within it he finds Brünnhilde. The goddess awakens to see the handsome man standing over her and they immediately fall in love with each other. As the curtains close Siegfried seals their marriage with the ring of the Nibelungs.

Sigurd
COMP.: L. Reyer
LIBR.: Blau and du Locle

4 *acts*
Brussels, 7 January 1884
New Orleans, 1891
Covent Garden, 1884

Silent Woman, The
See *Schweigsame Frau, Die*

Silken Ladder, The
See *Scala di Seta, La*

Simon Boccanegra
COMP.: G. Verdi
LIBR.: F. M. Piave
From a play by Gutierrez

Prologue and 3 acts
Venice, 12 March 1857
La Scala, 1881
New York, 1932

CAST

Amelia Boccanegra, *alias Maria, and*		Jacopo Fiesco, *patrician,*	
in *Act I called Amelia Grimaldi*	S	*former Doge (Duke)*	B
Gabriele Adorno, *patrician*	T	Paolo Albiani, *plebian*	B
Simon Boccanegra, *plebian,*		Captain	T
the Doge (Duke)	Bar	Pietro, *plebian*	B

SYNOPSIS

Simon Boccanegra becomes Doge (Duke) by favor of the plebian majority. But an old scandal in his life comes to plague him to add to the difficulties of the patrician's plots against him. His natural daughter Amelia is in love with his enemy Gabriele. Adorno would have killed the Doge, but the news that Amelia is his daughter dissuades him. His older enemy, Paolo, has poisoned the Doge with a slow poison. When the revolt has been crushed, Fiesco is to be hanged for his part in it. The two ancient enemies face each other at the last instant and make atonement. Adorno is appointed successor to Boccanegra as the Doge dies.

THE OPERAS

NOTE
The opera was unsuccessful at first, but after extensive revisions by Boito and Verdi, principally in the finale of Act I, it became more popular.

Simon Bolivar
See *Bolivar*

Simplicius Simplicississimus Jugend, Der
COMP.: K. Hartmann   Cologne, 23 October 1948

Sir John in Love   4 *acts*
COMP.: R. Vaughan Williams   London, 21 March 1929
LIBR.: From Shakespeare's *Merry*   London, 1939
Wives of Windsor

Sister Angelica
See *Suor Angelica*

Sleepwalker, The
See *Sonnambula, La*

Snow Maiden, The
See *Snyegurotchka*

Snyegurotchka   *Prologue and 4 acts*
(*Snow-Maiden*)   St. Petersburg, 10 February 1882
COMP.: N. Rimsky-Korsakov   New York, 1922
LIBR.: By the composer   Sadlers Wells, 1933
From a play by Ostrovsky

CAST

Snyegurotchka, *the Snow Maiden*	S	Page	MS
Shepherd Lehl	C	Tsar Berendey	T
Koupava	S	Mizgir	Bar
Fairy Spring	MS	King Frost	B
Bobilicka	MS	Bobil	T
Spirit of the Forest	T	Bermiata	

SYNOPSIS

PROLOGUE. Spring entrusts her daughter, the Snow Maiden, to the Spirit of the Forest for safe keeping. She is immediately adopted by Bobil and Bobilicka.

I. Mizgir falls in love with her, but she will not have him.

II. Koupava claims damages for the loss of Mizgir's love. In court, when the Snow Maiden pleads her case and states that she has no lover, the Tsar orders her to go get one.

III. Lehl offers, but she is shy. Mizgir tries, but she will not have him.

IV. Her mother helps her; then she falls in love with Mizgir after all. But because of love there is sunshine in the Snow Maiden's heart, and she must die.

Socrate   3 *parts*
COMP.: E. Satie   Paris, (Concert), 14 February 1920
LIBR.: V. Cousins
Translated from the *Dialogues of Plato*

THE OPERAS

Satie, never willing to fit his works into stereotype molds, called this a *Drame Symphonique avec Voix*.

Songe d'une Nuit d'Été, Le   3 acts
(*The Midsummer Night's Dream*)   Comique, 20 April 1850
COMP.: A. Thomas   New Orleans, 1851
LIBR.: Rosier and de Leuven   New York, 1852
This is *not* the play by Shakespeare, but a play *about* Shakespeare.

Songstress, The
See *Cantarina, La*

Sonnambula, La   2 acts
COMP.: V. Bellini   Milan, 6 March 1831
LIBR.: F. Romani   London, 1831
    New York, 1835

CAST

Count Rodolpho, *Lord of the Castle*	B	Elvino, *farmer*	T
Teresa, *miller*	S	Alessio, *villager*	B
Amina, *her foster daughter*	S	Notary, Villagers	
Lisa, *innkeeper*	S		

MUSICAL HIGHLIGHTS

ACT I. Aria *Vi ravviso o luogho ameni* (As I view the scenes of childhood), Rodolpho
Duet *D'un pensiero* (Not a single thought), Amina and Elvino
ACT II. Sleepwalking scene *Ah, non credea* (Ah, do not believe), Amina
Aria, *Ah, non giunge*, Amina

SYNOPSIS

I. In spite of the jealousy of Lisa, Amina and Elvino have mutually pledged their troth. A stranger, really Rodolpho in disguise, has come to town to recall his carefree childhood and is in his room at the inn when Amina, walking in her sleep, climbs into his window and into bed. Lisa takes Elvino to witness what looks like his bride's infidelity.

II. Elvino takes back the ring he had given her, and promises to marry Lisa instead. He cannot understand what Rodolpho is talking about in his explanation of Amina's somnambulism. But finally the unnerving exhibition of the frail girl, again sound asleep, walking over a dangerous bridge above the millwheel and then singing a sleepy narration of her difficulty with Elvino brings the man back to his senses and makes him again her bridegroom.

NOTE

The role of Amina was long a favorite for sopranos who wished to make striking debuts. The most famous of these was Malibran, who first appeared in the role in the first performance of it in English at Drury Lane in 1833.

Sophie Arnould
COMP.: G. Pierné   Comique, 21 February 1927

Spanish Hour, The
See *Heure Espagnole, L'*

Sposo Deluso, Lo
COMP.: W. A. Mozart
For details of the use of this unfinished work, see *Oca del Cairo*.

Sprung über den Schatten, Der 3 *acts*
(*The Leap over the Shadow*) Frankfurt, 9 June 1924
COMP.: E. Krenek Leningrad, 1927
LIBR.: By the composer

Star of the North, The
See *Étoile du Nord, L'*

Statue, The 3 *acts*
COMP.: L. Reyer Paris, 11 April 1861
LIBR.: Barbier and Carré Weimar, 1864

Stone Guest, The
See *Kamyenny Gost*
See also *Don Juan*

Stradella
See *Alessandro Stradella*

Strange World
See *Fremde Erde*

Street Scene 2 *acts*
COMP.: K. Weill New York, 9 January 1947
LIBR.: E. Rice, L. Hughes
From the play by Elmer Rice
"An American Opera," according to the heading on the score. The work consists in part of songs in the popular tradition, and yet it has so much orchestral music that it cannot be called a ballad opera.

Sunken Bell, The
See *Campana Sommersa, La*

Suor Angelica 1 *act*
(*Sister Angelica*) Metropolitan, 14 December 1918
COMP.: G. Puccini Rome, 1919
LIBR.: G. Forzano Covent Garden, 1920

CAST

Suor Angelica	S	Suor Osmina	S
Princess, *her aunt*	C	Suor Dulcina	MS
Abbess	MS	Aspirant Sisters	MS
Alms Collector	S	Nursing Sister	S
Mistress of Novices	MS	Novices, Sisters	
Suor Genoveva	S		

SYNOPSIS

Angelica, repenting for illegitimate motherhood, has been in the convent for seven long years. When her aunt visits on other business Angelica asks about her child only to learn that it has been dead for two years. From flowers the nun concocts a poison and drinks it, begging forgiveness for this suicide.

NOTE

This short work is one of a trilogy containing *Il Tabarro* and *Gianni Schicchi*. The first performance listed above included, as *Il Trittico*, all three.

Susannah
COMP.: C. Floyd
LIBR.: By the composer

2 *acts*
Tallahassee, Florida, 24 February 1955
New York, 1956

Susanna's Secret
See *Segreto di Susanna, Il*

Susanna
See also *Sancta Susanna*

Švanda Dudák
(*Schwanda the Bagpiper*)
COMP.: J. Weinberger
LIBR.: M. Kares

2 *acts*
Prague, 27 April 1927
Metropolitan, 1931
Covent Garden, 1934

CAST

Švanda the Bagpiper	Bar	Executioner	T
Dorotka, *his wife*	S	Devil	B
Babinsky, *romantic bandit*	T	Devil's Familiar Spirit	T
Queen Iceheart	MS	Captain of Hell's Guard	T
Magician	B	Two Forest Rangers	T, B
Judge	T		

SYNOPSIS

I. Hiding from the pursuit of the rangers, Babinsky meets Švanda and his wife. His talk of the world entrances the poor bagpiper until he decides to leave home behind and go travelling with the romantic wanderer.

First he meets the queen, who falls in love with him. They marry and share the throne. Dorotka sweeps him off that seat, however, and the queen condemns both of them to death. Babinsky gets them away from the guards, and Švanda's energetic bagpiping keeps everyone dancing until they effect their escape. At Dorotka's insistence, Švanda swears by the devil that he never kissed the queen. For this boldfaced lie the devil takes him.

II. The devil makes Švanda play. He has the musician's soul, but only for a moment; Babinsky wins it back for Švanda in a game of cards. Back goes the Bagpiper to the arms of his dear wife, never again to venture forth.

Swallow, The
See *Rondine, La*

Tabarro, Il
(*The Cloak*)
COMP.: G. Puccini
LIBR.: G. Adami
From a play by Didier Gold

Tragedy in 1 act
Metropolitan, 14 December 1918
Buenos Aires, 1919
Covent Garden, 1920
La Scala, 1922

CAST

Michele, *bargeman*, 50	Bar	Talpa, *stevedore*, 55	B
Luigi, *stevedore*, 20	T	Giorgetta, *Michele's wife*, 25	S
Tinca, *stevedore*, 35	T	Frugola, *Talpa's wife*, 50	MS

SYNOPSIS

Luigi and Giorgetta are lovers. Giorgetta's husband Michele suspects the fact. He is on deck one evening quietly smoking when Luigi sees the flick of his match and mistakes it for a signal from Giorgetta for their midnight meeting. When Luigi appears, Michele springs on him and strangles him to death. Giorgetta discovers the body hidden under a cloak when she rushes on deck to see what is the matter.

NOTES

This melodrama is the first part of *Il Trittico*, a trilogy containing also *Suor Angelica* and *Gianni Schicchi*. The first performance listed above was actually the first performance of the entire series.

Tableau Parlant, Le　　　　　　1 *act*
(*The Talking Table*)　　　　　　　Paris, 20 September 1769
COMP.: A. Grétry　　　　　　　　Charleston, S.C., 1794
LIBR.: L. Anseaume　　　　　　　Philadelphia, 1796

Tale of the Invisible City of Kitezh, The
See *Kitezh*

Tales of Hoffmann, The
See *Contes d'Hoffmann, Les*

Taming of the Shrew, The
COMP.: V. Giannini　　　　　　Cincinnati (Concert), 31 January 1953
From Shakespeare　　　　　　　New York (TV), 1954

Taming of the Shrew, The
See also *Widerspenstigen Zähmung, Der*

Tammany　　　　　　　　　　3 *acts*
COMP.: J. Hewitt　　　　　　　New York, 3 March 1794
LIBR.: A. J. Hatton　　　　　　Philadelphia, 1794
　　　　　　　　　　　　　　　Boston, 1796

This opera, also called *America Rediscovered*, was sponsored by the Tammany Society of New York. The music has been lost.

Tancred
See *Combattimento di Tancredi e Clorinda, Il*

Tancredi　　　　　　　　　　2 *acts*
COMP.: G. Rossini　　　　　　　Venice, 6 February 1813
LIBR.: G. Rossi　　　　　　　　London, 1820
From Tasso's *Gerusalemme Liberata*　New York, 1825

This was the first Italian opera to be presented at Boston, where it was produced in 1829.

Tannhäuser und der Sängerkrieg
auf dem Wartburg　　　　　　3 *acts*
(*Tannhäuser, and the Singing Contest*　Dresden, 19 October 1845
at the Wartburg)　　　　　　　New York, 1859
COMP.: R. Wagner　　　　　　　Covent Garden, 1876
LIBR.: By the composer

CAST

Hermann, *Landgrave of Thuringia*	B	Walter von der Vogelweide,	
Tannhäuser, *knight and minnesinger*	T	*minnesinger*	T
Wolfram von Eschenbach,		Biterolf, *minnesinger*	B
knight and minnesinger	Bar	Heinrich der Schreiber, *minnesinger*	T

Reinmar von Zweter, *minnesinger*	B	Four Noble Pages	2S, 2A
Elisabeth, *Herman's niece*	S	Nobles, Knights, Ladies, Pilgrims, Sirens,	
Venus	S	Naiads, Nymphs, Bacchantes	
Young Shepherd	S		

MUSICAL HIGHLIGHTS

ACT I. *Venusberg Music*
  Dich Teure Halle (Hail hall of song), Elisabeth
ACT II. Hymn to Venus, *Dir Göttin der Liebe* (Thou goddess of love), Tannhäuser
ACT III. Song to the Evening Star, *O du mein holder Abendstern* (O thou bright shining Evening Star), Wolfram
  Pilgrims' Chorus

SYNOPSIS

I. Trapped by the soporific beauties of the enchanted palace of Venus, Tannhäuser longs to return to the outside world. Uttering a Christian prayer, he suddenly finds himself alone on a mountainside, listening to a band of pilgrims on their way to Rome. He starts to go with them, but the sight of a troop of minnesingers and the recognition of his friend Wolfram who tells him of Elisabeth's continuing love for him leads Tannhäuser back to the Wartburg.

II. There he takes part in a singing contest for which the prize is to be Elisabeth's hand in marriage. The Landgrave is sure of Tannhäuser's victory as is everyone else present. But after all the others have had their songs, Tannhäuser bursts unwillingly into such a praise of pagan Venus that all draw their swords against him. Only Elisabeth's intervention prevents his death. The Landgrave sends him out with the pilgrims to Rome, there to beg forgiveness.

III. He fails to return. Elisabeth, watching for him in vain finally gives up and goes home to die in sorrow. Wolfram stands alone, singing to himself of the beauteous evening star, when Tannhäuser stumbles up the path, worn and dejected, unforgiven. He is about to throw himself again into the oblivion of the Venusberg when a procession comes by, with the corpse of Elisabeth. Tannhäuser falls upon the bier, dying just as more pilgrims arrive from Rome bearing the Pope's staff, which has borne leaves in sign of his redemption.

NOTES

For the production at Paris in 1861 Wagner made extensive changes in the score, considerably enlarging some of the scenes and generally rendering the work more dramatic.

Tender Land, The   1 *act*
COMP.: A. Copland   New York, 1 April 1954
LIBR.: H. Everett

CAST

Laurie	S	Top, *a drifter*
Beth, *a child*	S	Splinters, *postman*
Ma Moss		Mrs. Splinters
Grandpa Moss		Mrs. Jenks
Martin, *a drifter*		Mr. Jenks

Tempest, The   3 *acts*
COMP.: N. Gatty   London, 17 April 1920
LIBR.: R. Gatty (his brother)
From Shakespeare
This subject has been used also by Frank Martin and by Alois Haba.

Templar und die Judin, Der
(*The Knight and the Jewess*)
COMP.: H. Marschner
LIBR.: W. Wohlbrück
From *Ivanhoe*, by Scott

3 *acts*
Leipzig, 22 December 1829
London, 1840
New York, 1872

Testament de la Tante Caroline, La
(*Aunt Caroline's Will*)
COMP.: A. Roussel
LIBR.: Nino

Comedy in 3 *acts*
Olomouc, Czechoslovakia, 14 November
1936
Comique, 1937

Thaïs
COMP.: J. Massenet
LIBR.: L. Gallet
From the novel by Anatole France

Tragedy in 3 *acts*
Opéra, 16 February 1894
New York, 1907
Covent Garden, 1911

CAST

Athanaël, *young monk*	Bar	Thaïs, *courtesan*	S
Nicias, *young Alexandrian*	T	Crobyle, *slave*	S
Palémon, *old Cenobite*	B	Myrtale, *slave*	MS
Servant of Nicias	Bar	Albine, *abbess*	C

SYNOPSIS

Athanaël returns to his convent scandalized at the temptings of Thaïs which he has witnessed in Alexandria. He resolves to take her out of her life of sin. Persuasion fails, but later, of her own accord, she comes to him ready to enter the novitiate. But the poor theologian is in love with her. This terrible magic works within him. At the same time the separation of convent life stifles her so that, in spite of his ardent wish to save her, she dies.

Thieving Magpie, The
See *Gazza Ladra, La*

Three Penny Opera, The
See *Dreigroschenoper, Die*
See also *Beggar's Opera*

Tiefland
(*The Lowlands*)
COMP.: E. d'Albert
LIBR.: R. Lothar
From the play *Terra Baixa*
by Guimerá

Tragedy in Prologue and 2 acts
Prague, 15 November 1903
Berlin, 1907
Vienna, 1908
Metropolitan, 1908
Covent Garden, 1910

CAST

Sebastiano, *rich landowner*	Bar	Rosalia	C
Tommaso, *village elder*	B	Nuri, *little girl*	S
Moruccio, *miller*	Bar	Pedro, *shepherd*	T
Marta, *Sebastiano's mistress*	S	Nandro, *shepherd*	T
Pepa	S	Priest	Mute
Antonia	S		

THE OPERAS

SYNOPSIS

PROLOGUE. In order to provide a shield for his affair with his mistress, Marta, Sebastiano has decided upon Pedro as a husband for her. Pedro, therefore, must leave the mountains and live in the village.

I. The marriage is performed as intended, but Pedro does not know about the relationship that exists between Marta and Sebastiano. When the bride insists upon going into her room without her legal husband, Pedro refuses to leave her side or to let her leave his. They settle down for the night on the floor.

II. Pedro is in love with the girl. She is beside herself trying to get the true facts across to him. When it finally penetrates his romantic disbelief, his fury and suspicions give way to despair at the loss of her love. But she begins to love him. They decide to go away together. As they get ready to depart Sebastiano stops them and has Pedro taken away. Later Pedro escapes, finds Sebastiano and strangles him with his bare hands.

Till Eulenspiegel

COMP.: O. Jeremiaš   Prague, 13 May 1949

Tosca   *Tragedy in 3 acts*
COMP.: G. Puccini   Rome, 14 January 1900
LIBR.: Giacosa and Illica   Covent Garden, 1900
From a play by Sardou   Metropolitan, 1901

CAST

Floria Tosca, *celebrated singer*	S	Jailer	B
Mario Cavaradossi, *painter, her lover*	T	Shepherd Boy	C
Baron Scarpia, *chief of police*	Bar	Roberti, *executioner*	
Cesare Angelotti, *political prisoner*	B	Cardinal, Judge, Scribe, Officer, Sergeant	
Sacristan	Bar	Soldiers, Police, Ladies, Nobles, Citizens,	
Spoletta, *police agent*	T	Artisans	
Sciarrone, *gendarme*	B		

MUSICAL HIGHLIGHTS

ACT I. Aria *Recondita armonia* (Strange harmony), Mario
  Duet *Non la sospiri la nostra casa* (Not the sweet hope of our home), Tosca and Mario

ACT II. Cantabile *Già mi dicon venal* (Some may call me venal), Scarpia
  Aria *Vissi d'arte, vissi d'amore* (I have lived for art and love), Tosca

ACT III. Aria *È lucevan le stelle* (The stars were brightly shining), Mario

SYNOPSIS

I. Cavaradossi is painting in the chapel when the prisoner Angelotti escapes jail and asks his help in hiding. The fugitive is out of sight when Tosca comes to see her lover. She suspects him of being unfaithful because of his preoccupation and what she sees in the portrait he has begun. She leaves in time for Mario to help Angelotti get away just before the police come. Scarpia searches the chapel and voices his suspicions of Cavaradossi. Then he sees Tosca to tell her, as a goad to further his own ends, that Mario has another lover.

II. Scarpia captures Cavaradossi and has him tortured in the next room while he questions Tosca for information. Finally, when the prisoner's cries become too unbearable to her, she reveals Angelotti's hiding place.

Scarpia bargains with her for her love, saying he can save Mario from execution if she will give in to him. She agrees, but while he is writing out her safe-conduct she steals a knife from the table and stabs him. In terrible formality she puts candles near his body and a crucifix upon his breast before leaving.

III. Believing Scarpia's promise, that the execution by firing squad of her lover Cavaradossi, upon the high roof of the fortress tomb of Hadrian in Rome, is to be only a mock for the sake of appearances, she goes to watch it. But Scarpia's tricks outlive the man. As the rifles crack, Mario falls dead. Tosca leaps over the edge of the roof to her own death.

NOTE

Sardou's play was a favorite of Sarah Bernhardt.

Tote Stadt, Die
(The Dead City)
COMP.: E. Korngold
LIBR.: P. Schott
From a play by Rodenbach

3 *acts*
Hamburg and Cologne, 4 December 1920
Metropolitan, 1921
Prague, 1922

Transatlantic
COMP.: G. Antheil
LIBR.: By the composer
This was originally called *The People's Choice*

3 *acts*
Frankfurt, 25 May 1930

Traviata, La
(The Frail One)
COMP.: G. Verdi
LIBR.: F. M. Piave
From *La Dame aux Camélias*, by
    A. Dumas

Tragedy in 3 acts
Venice, 6 March 1853
London, 1856
New York, 1856
Metropolitan, 1883

CAST

Alfredo Germont, *Violetta's lover*	T	Giuseppe, *Violetta's servant*	T
Giorgio Germont, *his father*	Bar	Violetta Valery, *courtesan*	S
Gastone de Letorières	T	Flora Bervoix, *her friend*	MS
Baron Douphol, *Alfredo's rival*	Bar	Annina, *her confidante*	S
Marchese d'Obigny	B	Ladies and Gentlemen, Servants, Masks,
Doctor Grenvil	B	Dancers, Guests

MUSICAL HIGHLIGHTS

ACT I. Brindisi *Libiamo, libiamo* (Let's drink, let's drink), Alfredo, Violetta and chorus
    Duet *Un dì felice* (Some fine day), Alfredo and Violetta
    Aria *Ah! fors' è lui* (Ah, but for love), Violetta
    Aria *Sempre libera* (Always freely), Violetta
ACT II. Aria *De' miei bollenti spiriti* (So wild my dream of ecstasy), Alfredo
    Aria *Dite alla giovine* (Tell it to me, young as I am), Violetta
    Aria *Imponete* (You command me), Violetta
    Aria *Di provenza il mar* (In our home land by the sea), Giorgio
ACT III. *Prelude*
    Aria *Addio del passato* (Goodbye to my happiness), Violetta
    Duet *Parigi, o cara* (We must leave Paris), Alfredo and Violetta
SYNOPSIS

I. The courtesan, Violetta, already aware that she is increasingly sick, is deeply touched that Alfredo professes his undying love for her. On the surface, however, she seems to brush it off quite lightly.

II. They take up a new life together, in poverty in Paris. Their happiness is complete until Alfredo's father visits her to plead with her to leave his son because of her past. She does, and returns to her former life. Believing that she left him out of unfaithfulness, Alfredo follows her and publicly insults her.

III. Later, alone and forlorn, Violetta lies dying in her room. The elder Germont has told his son the true cause of her separation from him. Alfredo returns to her to hold her in his arms during her last moments. NOTES

It was the misfortune of *La Traviata* to have one of the most ill-fated debuts of any famous and successful opera. The tenor had a cold; the baritone in a fit of pique walked most languidly through the entire role. It was a failure, a poor beginning for one of the most melodious and most famous works of the Italian stage. It is said that Verdi wrote the entire score in four weeks, immediately after the opening of *Il Trovatore*.

Trial of Lucullus
COMP.: R. Sessions   Berkeley, Calif., 18 April 1947
LIBR.: B. Brecht

Triomphe de l'Amour sur Bergers   1 act
et Bergères, La   The Louvre, 22 January 1655
*The Triumph of love over Shepherds
and Shepherdesses)*
COMP.: M. la Guerre
LIBR.: C. de Beys
Perhaps the first French opera. The music is lost.

Tristan und Isolde   *Tragedy in 3 acts*
COMP.: R. Wagner   Munich, 10 June 1865
LIBR.: By the composer   Drury Lane, 1882
From legends   Metropolitan, 1886
                                CAST

Tristan, *knight of Cornwall*	T	Brangäne, *Isolde's maid*	MS
King Marke of Cornwall,		Shepherd	T
Tristan's uncle	B	Sailor	T
Isolde, *Irish princess*	S	Helmsman	Bar
Kurwenal, *Tristan's retainer*	Bar	Sailors, Knights, Men at Arms, Esquires	
Melot, *courtier*	Bar		

MUSICAL HIGHLIGHTS

ACT II. Duet (The Love Duet) *Isolde, Tristan geliebter* (Isolde, Tristan my lover), Tristan and Isolde
ACT III. Liebestod (The Love Death) *Mild und leise* (Mildly, softly), Isolde
SYNOPSIS

I. Tristan, deeply in love with Isolde who also loves him, brings her from Ireland to be the king's bride. Full of the idea, however, that her knight does not love her and that she is to be wedded to someone else, she intends to kill herself and him by poison. Brangäne thwarts her wish by substituting a magic love-potion for the poison so that Tristan and Isolde embrace in raptures of love before the ship reaches Cornwall.

II. In darkness they meet while the king is away hunting. High in a tower, Brangäne watches for his return. Suddenly hunters appear and Brangäne warns them in time for

Tristan to make sure Isolde is hidden for the moment. But Melot, his enemy, draws his sword and wounds Tristan.

III. Near death in his own home, Tristan waits for Isolde's coming. She arrives and he dies in her arms. King Marke and his knights have followed her but Kurnewal battles with them, slaying Melot but being himself slain. The king had come, however, not as an enemy but with forgiveness. He was too late: Isolde has cast herself upon the corpse of her lover and dies before his arrival.

NOTES

Wagner made note of the story of Tristan and Isolde in *Die Meistersinger von Nürnberg* wherein Hans Sachs says that he will have no such fate for himself as a lover as did Tristan. The opera *L'Elisir d'Amore* also makes oblique reference to the story, this opera being a satire on the subject of love potions.

Trittico, Il
See *Suor Angelica; Tabarro, Il; Gianni Schicchi.*

Triumph of St. Joan, The
COMP.: N. Dello Joio   Bronxville, N.Y., 9 May 1950
LIBR.: Dello Joio and Machlis

Troilus and Cressida
COMP.: W. Walton
LIBR.: Chr. Hassall
From Chaucer

3 *acts*
Covent Garden, 3 December 1954
San Francisco, 1955

CAST

Calkas, *High Priet of Pallas*	B	Evadne, *her servant*	MS
Antenor, *Captain of Trojan Spears*	Bar	Horaste, *a friend of Pandarus*	Bar
Troilus, *Prince of Troy*	T	Diomede, *Prince of Argos*	Bar
Pandarus, *Brother of Calkas*	T	Priests, Priestesses of Pallas, Trojans,	
Cressida, *Daughter of Calkas, a widow*	S	Greeks	

Commissioned originally for a BBC broadcast, the opera was actually first performed, with BBC permission, on the stage.

Trojans, The
See *Troyens, Les*

Trompeter von Säkkingen, Der
(*The Trumpeter from Säkkingen*)
COMP.: V. Nessler
LIBR.: R. Bunge
From a poem by von Scheffel

4 *acts*
Leipzig, 4 May 1884
Metropolitan, 1887
London, 1892

Troubadour, The
See *Trovatore, Il*

Trovatore, Il
(*The Troubadour*)
COMP.: G. Verdi
LIBR.: S. Cammarano
From a play by Gutierrez

Tragedy in 4 acts
Rome, 19 January 1853
New York, 1855
Covent Garden, 1855
Metropolitan, 1883

THE OPERAS

CAST

Count di Luna, *of Aragon*	Bar	Duchess Leonora	S
Ferrando, *his captain of guard*	B	Inez, *her confidante*	S
Manrico, *troubadour,*		Azucena, *gypsy woman of Biscay*	MS
supposed son of Azucena	T	Followers of di Luna and Manrico,	
Ruiz, *one of his soldiers*	T	Messengers, Jailers, Soldiers, Nuns,	
Old Gypsy	Bar	Gypsies	

MUSICAL HIGHLIGHTS

ACT I. Aria *Tacea la notte* (Calmly the evening), Leonora
Romance, *Deserto sulla terra* (In this deserted land), Manrico
ACT II. *The Anvil Chorus,* Gypsies
Aria *Stride la vampa* (Upward the flames roll), Azucena
Aria *Mal reggendo all'aspiro assalto* (At my mercy I hold my enemy), Manrico
Aria *Il balen del suo sorriso* (How glowingly her smile), Count
Aria *Per me ora fatale* (For me the fatal hour), Count
Chorus of Nuns *Ah se l'error t'ingombra* (Ah, in the shadow of error)
ACT III. Aria *Ah si, ben mio coll'essere* (Ah yes, beloved, I'm here with you), Manrico
Scena *Di quella pira* (The fatal fire), Manrico and Chorus
ACT IV. Miserere *Ah! che la morta ognora* (Ah, how death delays me), Manrico
Duet *Ai nostri monti* (Back to our mountains), Manrico and Azucena

SYNOPSIS

In revenge for the death of her mother, Azucena the gypsy stole one of two babies from the castle years ago. This child she brought up as Manrico, the troubadour.

I. *Il Duello* (The Duel). Ferrando, hoping to capture the unknown troubadour who serenades Leonora, waits for him one evening and narrates the story of the kidnapping to pass the time. When the troubadour makes his appearance, he finds not only Leonora but the count ready for him. The count challenges him to a duel.

II. *La Zingara* (The Gypsy). Having spared the count, Manrico, back at the camp of the gypsies, ponders his reasons. Ruiz interrupts his introspection to urge him to the defense of Biscay, telling him incidentally that Leonora has planned to enter a convent. Manrico goes to the convent to prevent her, but finds the count there for the same purpose. Manrico takes her away.

III. *Il Figlio della Zingara* (The son of the gypsy). The count and his men lay siege to Manrico, capturing Azucena whom he recognizes and throws into prison. The news of the gypsy woman's impending death reaches Manrico just as he and Leonora are about to be married. He rushes to her aid.

IV. *Il Supplizio* (The torture). He fails in his mission and is imprisoned with her. Leonora visits him and then wins his freedom by promising to marry the count. But she takes poison instead, and dies in Manrico's arms. The count orders Manrico to be killed, making Azucena witness the execution. But as she watches, she turns and informs the count that Manrico was his own brother, kidnapped by her when he was a baby.

Troyens, Les
(*The Trojans*)
COMP.: H. Berlioz
LIBR.: By the composer
From the *Aeneid* of Virgil

In two parts 5 acts
First complete performance,
Karlsruhe, 5 and 6 December 1890

THE OPERAS

SYNOPSIS

I. Cassandre has been cursed by Apollo. She can foresee the truth, but no one will believe her. All the Trojans rush off to see the fabulous wooden horse left by the Greeks on the shore as they seemingly beat a retreat. Aeneas has seen a terrifying vision. He suggests that they bring the horse within the city to placate the goddess it represents. The people comply with his request, tearing a breach in their own walls to bring the huge object in.

II. Hector's ghost warns Aeneas to take his son and leave the city, to sail westward and found a new empire on the Italian peninsula. Meanwhile the Greek warriors, hidden by the wily Odysseus within the huge wooden horse, burst out of it and sack the city from inside.

Aeneas leaves his doomed homeland. The Greek forces enter and find Cassandre who stabs herself as an example to the other Trojan women.

SYNOPSIS

III. The Trojan fleet, headed by Aeneas, lands at Carthage to find the city threatened by invasion by its enemies. The Trojan general offers his help, and leading the Carthaginian army he beats off the hostile forces.

In a dream of magic in an enchanted forest, Dido and Aeneas realize their love for each other.

IV. After the battle Aeneas returns to Carthage and to Dido. Having experienced the same delicious dream, they approach each other with love. But over the Trojan warrior hovers the remembrance of the voice of Hector's ghost which sent him westward to found a city.

v. Aeneas decides to leave. Dido begs him to stay but he will not. After he has left she causes a ceremonial pyre to be raised. When the flames are high enough she kills herself.

NOTES

This huge double opera has been performed most frequently in separate parts. Part One was first shown in Nice (1891), and Paris (1899). Part Two appeared in Paris, 4 November 1863, then in Liverpool (1897), and so on. The two parts together were performed as noted above, with Part One being heard then for the first time. There was another complete performance in Glasgow in 1935.

Trumpeter of Säkkingen, The

See *Trompeter von Säkkingen, Der*

Tsar's Bride

See *Tsarskaya Nyevesta*

Tsarskaya Nyevesta

(*The Tsar's Bride*)
COMP.: N. Rimsky-Korsakov
LIBR.: L. Mey

3 *acts*
Moscow, 3 November 1899
Seattle, Wash., 1922
London, 1931

Turandot

COMP.: F. Busoni
LIBR.: By the composer
From a play by Gozzi

Chinese Fable in 2 acts
Zürich, 11 May 1917
Frankfurt, 1918
Venice, 1940

CAST

Emperor Altoum	B	Tartaglia, *minister*	B
Turandot, *his daughter*	S	Pantaleone *minister*	B
Adelma, *her confidante*	MS	Eight Doctors	T, B
Calaf, *young unknown prince*	T	Singer	MS
Barak, *his servant*	Bar	Slaves, Weeping Women, Eunuchs,	
Queen Mother of Samarkand, *Negress*	S	Soldiers, Dancers, a Priest	
Truffaldino, *chief eunuch*	T		

SYNOPSIS

I. In spite of the evident risk of losing his life as had all the contestants before him, Calaf answers the riddles propounded by the royal mind and wins the hand of Turandot.

II. The tables are turned. Turandot must guess the name of her betrothed in order to get herself out of the bargain of marriage. This is not so difficult, however, when Adelma, who knew Calaf before, gives him away. The princess, in a triumph of virginal revenge, reveals her ill-gotten knowledge to the prince, but then she relents and marries him anyway.

NOTE

The opera was developed from incidental music written for the play, produced by Max Reinhardt.

Turandot

COMP.: G. Puccini
LIBR.: Adami and Simoni
From a fable by Gozzi

Romance in 3 acts
La Scala, 25 April 1926
Metropolitan, 1926
Covent Garden, 1927

THE OPERAS

CAST

Princess Turandot	S	Ping, *Grand Chancellor of China*	Bar
Emperor Altoum, *her father*	T	Pang, *Supreme Lord of Provisions*	T
Timur, *exiled Tartar King, blind*	B	Pong, *Supreme Lord of the*	
Calaf, *his son*	T	*Imperial Kitchen*	T
Liù, *slave*	S	Mandarin	Bar

SYNOPSIS

I. Turandot's beauty inspires love in the hearts of all young men who see her, but to win her hand one must answer three difficult riddles. To fail is death. Calaf sees her, falls in love, and in spite of his father's objections makes the proper arrangements for the test.

II. He answers the riddles perfectly. But the princess does not want to keep her part of the bargain. He agrees that if she can discover who he is, he will submit to death.

III. No torture can extract his name. Turandot tries with Timur, but Liù cries that only she can reveal it. She refuses to do so, however, because of her own love for Calaf. To prevent being tortured, Liù stabs herself to death.

Calaf forcibly kisses Turandot, and suddenly she melts into a real woman. In the court she announces that she has discovered his name: it is Love.

NOTE

Act III was completed by Franco Alfano.

Turco in Italia, Il
(*The Turk in Italy*)
COMP.: G. Rossini
LIBR.: F. Romani

2 *acts*, 7 *scenes*
La Scala, 14 August 1814
London, 1821
New York, 1826

Turn of the Screw, The
COMP.: B. Britten
LIBR.: M. Piper
From the story by Henry James

2 *acts and Epilogue*
Venice, 14 September 1954
Sadlers Wells, 1954
Stratford, Conn., 1958
New York, 1958

CAST

Governess		Mrs. Grose	S
Miles, *a boy*		Miss Jessel	MS
Quint's Ghost	T	Flora	S

Twelfth Night
COMP.: C. A. Gibbs
From Shakespeare

1947

Twilight of the Gods, The
See *Götterdämmerung*

Un Ballo in Maschera
See *Ballo in Maschera, Un*

Un Giorno di Regno
See *Giorno di Regno, Un*

Undine
COMP.: E. Hoffmann
LIBR.: F. Fouqué

3 *acts*
Berlin, 3 August 1816
Aachen, 1922

Undine
COMP.: A. Lortzing
LIBR.: By the Composer
From the story by Fouqué

4 acts
Magdeburg, 21 April 1845
New York, 1856
Brussels, 1867

Valkyr, The
See *Walküre, Die*

Vampyr, Der
(*The Vampire*)
COMP.: H. Marschner
LIBR.: W. Wohlbrück

2 acts
Leipzig, 29 March 1828
London, 1829
Liège, 1845

Vanessa
COMP.: S. Barber
LIBR.: G–C. Menotti

4 acts
Metropolitan, 15 January 1958
Salzburg, 1958

CAST

Vanessa	S	Anatol	T
Erika, *her niece*	MS	Baroness	C
Doctor	B	Major-Domo	B

SYNOPSIS

Vanessa was once, long ago, in love with a man named Anatol, and has kept herself and her house shut off from the world ever since losing him. A guest arrives, named Anatol, who is actually the son of her lover. In his first night he seduces Erika, but later he takes up with Vanessa, giving that older woman a new breath of youth. Erika is pregnant and tries to kill herself, but fails in the attempt. As Vanessa and her lover go off gaily to their honeymoon, Erika orders the house closed up again, in token of her having lost her lover as her aunt had before.

Venus
COMP.: O. Schoeck
LIBR.: A. Rüeger
From a story by Mérimée

3 acts
Zürich, 10 May 1922
Berne, 1934

Veronique
COMP.: A. Messager
LIBR.: Vanloo and Duval

3 acts
Paris, 10 December 1898
London, 1903
New York, 1905

Vespri Siciliani, I
(*The Sicilian Vespers*)
COMP.: G. Verdi
LIBR.: Scribe and Duveyier

Tragedy in 5 acts
Opéra, 13 January 1855
La Scala, 1856
Drury Lane, 1859
New York, 1859

CAST

Duchess Elena	S	Count Vaudermont, *French officer*	B
Arrigo, *young Sicilian*	T	Ninetta, *Elena's attendant*	S
Guido di Monforte, *governor of Sicily*	Bar	Danieli, *young Sicilian*	T
Giovanni da Procida, *Sicilian doctor*	B	Tebaldo, *French soldier*	T
di Béthune, *French officer*	B	Roberto, *French soldier*	B
		Manfredo, *Sicilian*	T

THE OPERAS

I. There is a good deal of friction in Sicily, known always for the quick passions of its people, because of the occupation by French troops. Elena makes her contribution to unrest by publicly singing an inflammatory song of patriotism. Only the appearance of Manfredo prevents the incipient riot.

II. Procida returns from exile to rouse the Sicilians against the oppressive French. In order to stir the people to overt action, he effects what appears to be a mass kidnapping of Sicilian girls by the soldiers.

III. The revolutionary leader arranges for his partisans to attend a masked ball to be given at Monforte's palace. But there Arrigo, who has discovered that he is the long lost son of Monforte, notices the conspirators in the crowd. He is torn between his revolutionary sentiments and love for his newly discovered father. But at the last moment, when the assassination is about to take place, Arrigo steps in to betray his friends,

IV. The assassins are tried and condemned. Arrigo demands that he be executed along with them, since he was fully in accord with their aims. Monforte offers them pardon if he will acknowledge him as father. At last he does, and the prisoners are freed. Elena and Arrigo thereupon become publicly betrothed.

V. The wedding bells were to be a signal for a new insurrection against the French. Elena tries to prevent this, but Monforte, unaware of the plans, causes the bells to ring and the havoc to commence.

NOTES

I Vespri Siciliani was commissioned for the Great Exposition of 1855. Verdi disliked the libretto. But that was not all that made the production difficult: Cruvelli, who was was assigned the part of Elena, disappeared during the preparations without explanation. One month later she returned, also without explanation, but quite evidently she had spent the time most romantically with a man she later married.

Vestale, La
COMP.: G. Spontini
LIBR.: Étienne de Jouy

3 *acts*
Opéra, 16 December 1807
Philadelphia, 1828
London, 1826

Vida Breve, La
(*The Brief Life*)
COMP.: M. da Falla
LIBR.: C. F. Shaw

Tragedy in 2 acts
Nice, 1 April 1913
Buenos Aires, 1923
Metropolitan, 1926

CAST

Salud, *gypsy*	S	Singer	Bar
Grandmother	MS	Manuel, *Carmela's brother*	Bar
Carmela	MS	Voice in the Forge, Voice of a	
Paco	T	Street-Seller, Distant Voice	T
Uncle Sarvaor	B		

SYNOPSIS

I. Uncle Sarvaor knows that Paco plans to wed someone, not Salud, the next day. He would have revenge, for Salud loves Paco very much.

II. Salud interrupts the festivities of the announcement of Paco's betrothal to Carmela. She tells him of her love, then drops dead at his feet.

NOTE

This famous Spanish work was composed in 1904–05.

Village Romeo and Juliet, A
COMP.: F. Delius
LIBR.: By the composer
From a story by Keller

Prologue and 3 acts
Berlin, 21 February 1907
Covent Garden, 1910

CAST

Manz, *rich farmer*	Bar		
Marti, *rich farmer*	Bar	Wheel of Fortune Woman	S
Sali, *son of Manz, as a child*	S	Cheap Jewelry Woman	MS
as a man	T	Showman	T
Vreli, *Marti's daughter*	S	Merry-go-round Man	Bar
Dark Fiddler	Bar	Slim Girl	S
Two Peasants	Bar	Wild Girl	MS
Three Women	S, MS	Poor Hornplayer	T
Gingerbread Woman	S	Hunchbacked Bass Fiddler	B

SYNOPSIS

A feud develops between Marti and Manz over the boundaries between their lands. But their children are in love. This love tears them from their unyielding parents. They go off together to join a band of vagabonds, never to return.

Villar's Dragoons
See *Dragons de Villars, Les*

Villi, Le
COMP.: G. Puccini
LIBR.: F. Fontana

4 acts
Milan, 31 May 1884
Manchester, England 1897
New York, 1908

Puccini's first opera.

Vintage, The
COMP.: M. Pelissier
LIBR.: Dunlap

New York, 1799

According to Ritter, this is one of the earliest operas to be composed in New York.

Volo di Notte
COMP.: L. Dallapiccola
From *Night Flight*, by St. Exupéry

Florence, 18 May 1940

Wald, Der
(*The Forest*)
COMP.: E. Smyth
LIBR.: By the composer

Prologue, 1 act and Epilogue
Berlin, 9 April 1902
Covent Garden, 1902
Metropolitan, 1903

Walküre, Die
(*The Valkyr*)
COMP.: R. Wagner
LIBR.: By the composer

Music Drama in 3 acts
Munich, 26 June 1870
New York, 1877
Covent Garden, 1892

CAST

Siegmund, *the Wälsung*	T	Fricka	MS
Hunding	B	Gerhilde, Orlinde, Waltraute,	
Wotan	BBar	Schwertleite, Helmwige, Siegrune,	
Sieglinde	S	Grimgerde, Rossweisse, *Valkyrs*	S, MS
Brünnhilde	S		

174

THE OPERAS

I. Siegmund staggers, wounded, into the hall of Hunding who is away from home. Sieglinde, Siegmund's sister and Hunding's unwilling wife, without recognizing the warrior, gives him water. They fall in love. When Hunding returns, Siegmund relates the story of his fight to protect his sister. By this Hunding recognizes him as his enemy and determines to kill him the next day. Buried in the ash tree which grows through the center of the hall is a sword which none but Siegmund may wield. When Sieglinde tells him of its story he understands who she is and takes the sword.

II. Fricka demands of Wotan that the two humans be punished for their incestuous love for each other, an insult to her as the goddess of marriage. Wotan sends Brünnhilde to see that Hunding succeeds in killing Siegmund, but Brünnhilde tries to save the warrior instead. It is necessary for Wotan himself to intervene, helping Hunding while the disobedient Valkyr takes up Sieglinde and rides out of reach of the god's wrath.

III. Safely hidden in Fafner's forest, Brünnhilde tells Siegmund that she will bear a son, Siegfried, by him. Their escape is short-lived. Wotan finds her and places her in isolation, circled by magic fire which none but a hero may penetrate. Wotan had attempted to end the curse of the Nibelungs by the destruction of Siegmund, but the birth of Siegfried carries the battle onward.

Wallenstein　　　　　　　　　　*6 scenes*
COMP.: J. Weinberger　　　　　　Vienna, 18 November 1937
LIBR.: M. Kares
From Schiller

Wally, La　　　　　　　　　　*Tragedy in 4 acts*
COMP.: A. Catalani　　　　　　　La Scala, 20 January 1892
LIBR.: L. Illica　　　　　　　　Metropolitan, 1909
　　　　　　　　　　　　　　　Manchester, England, 1919

CAST

Wally	S	Giuseppe Hagenbach, *of Sölden*	T
Stromminger, *her father*	B	Vincenzo Gellner, *of Hochstoff*	Bar
Afra, *landlady*	C	Messenger, *of Schnals*	T
Walter, *strolling minstrel*	S		

SYNOPSIS

I. Stromminger hopes that his daughter will marry Gellner, but she wishes otherwise. She is in love with Hagenbach. She threatens to leave her father if he insists she marry Gellner, but she keeps secret the fact of her love.

II. When her father dies, Wally inherits his fortune. But still she cannot get rid of Gellner. Gellner tries intrigue, telling her that Hagenbach is engaged to Afra. At this news Wally is infuriated and insults her rival. Hagenbach swears to avenge the insult. They dance together, and Hagenbach is so entranced as to fall in love with Wally. But she does not know his change of heart; she promises herself in despair to Gellner.

III. Gellner tries to murder Hagenbach by pushing him off a precipice. He fails; the man is brought up alive and given over, to Wally's mortification, to Afra to be nursed back to health.

IV. Wally has made up her mind to commit suicide when Hagenbach comes to her to confess that he does love her. They are fully reconciled. He leaves her, and after a moment she calls out to him. Hearing no response she rushes out the door to die with him in an avalanche.

Warrior, The
COMP.: B. Rogers
LIBR.: N. Corwin

1 *act, 4 scenes*
Metropolitan, 11 January 1947

CAST

Samson	Bar	Three Captains	2T, Bar
Delilah	S or MS	Officer	Bar
Four Lords	2T, Bar, B	Boy	S or MS

Water Nymph, The
See *Rusalka*

War and Peace
COMP.: S. Prokofiev
From Tolstoy's novel

Leningrad, 12 June 1946

Werther
COMP.: J. Massenet
LIBR.: Blau, Milliet and Hartmann
From the novel by Goethe

Tragedy in 4 acts
Vienna, 16 February 1892
Metropolitan, 1894
Covent Garden, 1894

CAST

Werther, *poet*, 23	T	Johann, *Le Bailli's friend*	B
Albert, *young man*, 25	Bar	Charlotte, *Le Bailli's daughter*, 20	MS
Le Bailli, 50	B	Sophie, *her sister*, 15	S
Schmidt, *Le Bailli's friend*	T	Children, Neighbors	

SYNOPSIS

I. Charlotte loves Werther, and he loves her. But her father is intent on marrying her to Albert.

II. After her marriage, the unsuccessful Werther cannot keep himself away from her.

III. She still loves him; they see each other again and again and sing of their passion. Then, dejected, he leaves her. A moment after that he sends Albert a message asking to to borrow some pistols.

IV. Realizing the significance of his message, Charlotte rushes to his room but finds him dying. He will not let her leave him to get help, but dies confident in her love.

White Lady, The
See *Dame Blanche, La*

Widerspenstigen Zähmung, Der
(*The Taming of the Shrew*)
COMP.: H. Goetz
LIBR.: J. Widman
From Shakespeare

Comedy in 4 acts
Mannheim, 11 October 1874
Drury Lane, 1878
New York, 1886

Wife of Martin Guerre, The
COMP.: W. Bergsma
LIBR.: Janet Lewis

New York, 15 February 1956

Wildschütz, Der
(*The Poacher*)
COMP.: A. Lortzing
LIBR.: By the composer
From a play by Kotzebue

3 *acts*
Leipzig, 31 December 1842
Drury Lane, 1895

CAST

Count of Eberbach	Bar	Baculus, *schoolmaster*	B
Countess, *his wife*	C	Gretchen, *his fiancée*	S
Baron Kronthal, *her brother*	T	Pancratius, *major-domo to the count*	Spkr
Baroness Freimann, *the count's*		Servants, Huntsmen, Peasants,	
widowed sister	S	Schoolboys	
Nanette, *her maid*	S		

SYNOPSIS

I. Quite accidentally Baculus shot a buck on the grounds of the count's estate. He is summoned to defend himself against the charge of poaching. The good baroness arranges with Gretchen to exchange clothes with her and make an appearance before the count in behalf of the poor schoolmaster. Thus she may surreptitiously see her betrothed, Kronthal.

II. At the castle everybody falls in love with the intercessor. The baron offers the schoolmaster a fortune, instead of a lawsuit, if he will give up his claim to his "betrothed".

III. Baculus does his best, trying to persuade her who he thinks is Gretchen to transfer her affections from him to the count. But in this embarrassing act he discovers that the girl is not Gretchen at all. This leads to obvious complications on all sides until the false Gretchen's identity is finally revealed. Then everyone is happy again, and the schoolmaster, who never intended to hit anything anyway, is pardoned for his accidental shot.

William Tell
See *Guillaume Tell*

Wir Bauen eine Stadt
(*We Build a City*)
COMP.: P. Hindemith

Children's Opera
Berlin, 21 June 1930

Wise Maiden, The
See *Kluge, Die*

Witch of Salem, A
COMP.: C. W. Cadman
LIBR.: N. R. Eberhadt

2 *acts*
Chicago, 8 December 1926

Woman Without a Shadow, The
See *Frau ohne Schatten, Die*

Wozzeck
COMP.: A. Berg
LIBR.: By the composer
From the play by Büchner

Tragedy in 3 acts, 15 scenes
Berlin, 14 December 1925
Philadelphia and New York, 1931
London (Concert), 1931
N.Y. City Opera, 1952

THE OPERAS

CAST

Wozzeck, *a soldier*	Bar	Fool	T
Drum Major	T	Marie	S
Andres	T	Margret	C
Captain	T	Marie's Child	Treble
Doctor	B	Soldiers, Maids, Servants, Children	
Two Workmen	Bar, B		

MUSICAL ANALYSIS (Berg)

ACT I. *Five Character Pieces*
Scene 1. *Suite* (Wozzeck and the Captain)
    2. *Rhapsody* (Wozzeck and Andres)
    3. *Military March and Lullaby* (Marie and Wozzeck)
    4. *Passacaglia* (Wozzeck and the Doctor)
    5. *Andante Affetuoso* (*quasi Rondo*)(Marie and the Drum Major)
ACT II. *Symphony in five movements*
Scene 1. *Sonata* (Marie, the Child, Wozzeck)
    2. *Fantasy and Fugue* (Captain, Doctor, Wozzeck)
    3. *Largo* (Marie and Wozzeck)
    4. *Scherzo* (In the Beer Garden)
    5. *Rondo con introduzione* (In the Barracks)
ACT III. *Six Inventions*
Scene 1. *Invention on a theme* (Marie and the Child)
    2. *Invention on one note* (Marie and Wozzeck)
    3. *Invention on a rhythm* (At the Inn)
    4. *Invention on a chord of six notes* (Wozzeck's death)
       Interlude, Invention on a key
    5. *Invention on a quaver figure* (Children at play)

SYNOPSIS

I. The lowly Wozzeck shaves the captain while the latter enjoys himself by interfering in the underling's life with unwanted advice. Later, while Wozzeck and Andres are cutting wood, Wozzeck worries about ghosts and sorcerers. For a moment, before going back to the barracks, he sees Marie. But she is frightened by his weird vagaries. The doctor uses Wozzeck as a sort of inexpensive guinea pig for his experiments, and indulges, as did the captain, in lofty hints. Marie, in the meanwhile, takes in the drum major.

II. Wozzeck gives all his money to Marie as a matter of course. But the captain and the doctor continue to torment him about supporting a prostitute. When Wozzeck sees Marie, he can hardly talk. His anger mounts as he watches her dancing with the drum major. In the barracks his rival roughs him up a little.

III. Marie weeps over the Bible. Then Wozzeck takes her out in the soft night air, into the woods, and stabs her to death. Back at the dance hall he dances with Margret until Margret sees blood on him. He returns to the woods to hide the knife and drowns himself in a pond. The children stop their play to run to see the body of the dead woman, while Marie's son, unknowing, hops and hops in his little game.

NOTES

This remarkable work was completed in 1921. It has never entered the repertory of any company without a good deal of controversy. Its music, as may be guessed from the above analysis, is extremely tightly composed in tenuous tonalities. The vocal lines are mostly in what one usually calls *Sprechstimme*—speechlike but musical intonation. The work might be called atonal in that it is based upon the most ephemeral relations of tonalities rather than, as for instance in classic music, upon simple relationships of keys. The relationships between the parts of *Wozzeck* are more differentiated by their form than by their tonal levels. The composer did not, however, make use of the dodecaphonic system (based upon the twelve equally-tuned notes of the piano keyboard) as he did in his later work, *Lulu*. Whereas *Der Rosenkavalier* once held the spotlight for having a very large orchestra of 112, *Wozzeck* has edged into it by having, at the performance in 1959 at the Metropolitan, 113.

Berg found it necessary, after making the musical analysis of the work and after many explanations of the complexity of its melodic structure, to remind listeners that it is a work of music, not of mathematics. And indeed when one listens to a performance, the beautiful experience of the harsh story and its musical expression should never be disturbed by an awareness of the technicalities.

Wreckers, The
COMP.: E. Smyth
LIBR.: H. Brewster

Tragedy in 1 act
Leipzig, 11 November 1906
Prague (Concert), 1906
London (Concert), 1906

CAST

Pascoe, *headman and preacher*, 55	BBar	Mark, *fisherman*	T
Lawrence, *lighthouse keeper*	Bar	Thirza, *Pascoe's wife*, 22	MS
Harvey, *his brother in law*	B	Avis, *Lawrence's daughter*, 17	S
Tallan	T	Fishermen, Shepherds, Miners, Women,	
Jack, *his son*, 15	MS	Wreckers, Pietists	

SYNOPSIS

The wreckers make their living by looting the cargoes of ships wrecked on their coasts. The ships are directed to doom by the placement of false signals in the night. But Thirza has been setting a beacon to counteract the false ones. The people search for the traitor and capture her. They condemn her, along with her lover Mark, to be locked in a tidal cave while the tide rises.

Wuthering Heights
COMP.: C. Floyd
LIBR.: By the composer
From the novel by Brontë

Prologue and 3 acts
Santa Fe, N.M., 16 July 1958
New York, 1959

Xerxes
See *Serse*

Z Mrtvého Domu
(*From the House of the Dead*)
COMP.: L. Janáček
LIBR.: By the composer
From Dostoyevsky

Tragedy in 3 acts
Brno, 12 April 1930
Prague, 1931
Mannheim, 1930

The text was completed by O. Zitek, the music by B. Bakala.

Zaïda
COMP.: W. A. Mozart
LIBR.: J. Schachter (rewritten by Gollmick)

Singspiel in 2 acts
Frankfort, 27 January 1866
Vienna, 1902
Monte Carlo, 1930

THE OPERAS

Mozart left this work unfinished. It is very similar, in some respects, to *Die Entführung aus dem Serail.*

Zagmuk
COMP.: A. Krein

Moscow, 29 May 1930

Zampa
COMP.: L. Hérold
LIBR.: A. Mélesville

3 *acts*
Comique, 3 May 1831
London, 1833
New York, 1833

Zar und Zimmermann
(*Tsar and Carpenter*)
COMP.: A. Lortzing
LIBR.: By the composer
From the French play by Merle

Comedy in 3 acts
Leipzig, 22 December 1837
New York, 1857
London, 1871

CAST

Peter I, *Tsar of Russia*	Bar	Lord Sydenham, *English ambassador*		B
Peter Ivanov, *runaway soldier*	T	Marquis de Chateauneuf,		
van Bett, *burgomaster*	B	*French ambassador*		T
Marie, *his niece*	S	Witwe Browe		C
Admiral Lefort, *Russian ambassador*	B			

SYNOPSIS

I. The Tsar, incognito, works as a shipwright in Holland in order to learn Dutch techniques. The ambassadors of England and France have some slight suspicion of this, and hire van Bett to locate him for them. Van Bett, quite mistakenly, introduces them to Ivanov. But the French ambassador, without telling anyone, recognizes the real Tsar.

II. Van Bett, much impressed with the importance of his position, entertains the ambassadors and the others at dinner. But when he feels the fire of the drinks within him, he incautiously demands to know who the various worthies may be. This leads to an open altercation between the parties who do not wish to be known to each other. The real Tsar defends himself in the mêlée with a sword.

III. Van Bett, still happy in his mistake, prepares a gallant send-off for Ivanov. But in the midst of the speeches, the salutes of cannon announce the departure of the real Tsar elsewhere, in all pomp and festivity.

NOTE

The English title of the work is usually *Peter the Shipwright.*

Zauberflöte, Die
(*The Magic Flute*)
COMP.: W. A. Mozart
LIBR.: E. Schikaneder

Comedy in 2 acts
Vienna, 30 September 1791
London, 1811
New York, 1833

CAST

Tamino, *Egyptian prince*	T	Monostatos, *Sarastro's*	
Three Ladies, *attendants to the*		*brutish servant*	T
Queen of the Night	2S, MS	Pamina, *daughter of the*	
Papageno, *a bird catcher*	Bar	*Queen of the Night*	S
Queen of the Night	S	Three Genii	2S, MS

Orator	B	Papagena	S
Sarastro, *high priest of Isis*		Two men in armor	T, B
and Osiris	B	Slaves, Priests, People	
Two Priests	T, B		

MUSICAL HIGHLIGHTS

ACT I. Aria *Der Vogelfänger bin ich ja* (I am a happy bird catcher), Papageno

Aria *Dies Bildnis ist bezaubernd schön* (This picture has a beauteous look), Tamino

Scena *O zittre nicht* (O do not fear), Queen of the Night

Recitative *O ew'ge Nacht* (O endless night), Tamino and Chorus

ACT II. Prayer *O Isis und Osiris*, Sarastro

Aria *Alles fühlt der Liebe* (Now in the heat of love), Monostatos

Aria *Der Hölle Rache* (To my revenge), Queen of the Night

Aria *In diesen heil'gen Hallen* (In this most holy temple), Sarastro

Aria *Ach, ich fühl's* (Ah, 'tis gone), Pamina

SYNOPSIS

I. Tamino, in battle with a serpent, stumbles into the magic realm of the Queen of the Night. Three ladies with magic swords kill the serpent, saving the handsome prince, and then disappear in the shadows. Along comes Papageno, a birdcatcher singing his song. Tamino mistakes him for the one who saved him. Papageno graciously accepts the prince's praise until the three ladies seal his lips to cut off such lying. They tell Tamino that he is in the realm of the Queen of the Night, and that he may be the one to save the princess, who is ensnared by danger in the palace of Sarastro. To clinch his determination the three ladies show him a picture of the girl, who is ravishingly beautiful. Thereupon the queen herself appears to plead with him to make the attempt to save her daughter. Fired with love and duty he undertakes the task, fore-armed with a magic flute and with the help of Papageno who carries magic bells to add to his birdcatcher's pan-pipes. Papageno is the first to find Pamina, trapped by the lustful Monostatos who runs away mistaking Papageno for some devil. Papageno takes her with him back to Tamino. Tamino, meanwhile, has heard that Sarastro is no evil person, but a magnanimous priest of Isis and Osiris. The reason behind the kidnapping is withheld from him. When Papageno brings Pamina to him Monostatos comes in pursuit to capture all three. But the prompt appearance of his master Sarastro protects all.

II. In a grand and mystic ceremony the priests decide to permit Tamino to undergo the ordeal of the search for truth. He and Papageno are commanded to keep silence, then sent on their way. They pass the first tests fairly easily. Monostatos has meanwhile recaptured Pamina, whom he found sleeping. He is about to attack her when the Queen of the Night stops him with her magic and a warning. She wakes Pamina and gives her a dagger, ordering her to kill Sarastro. The priest, when he hears of it, promises Pamina he will not harm her mother. Papageno's particular torture is an old woman who bothers him by saying she'll be his wife. Tamino's is Pamina, who cannot understand why he keeps silent in her presence. When Papageno finally agrees to his marriage, the old woman becomes the delightful Papagena. For Tamino, however, the ordeal goes almost to the point of Pamina's suicide before they have safely passed all the trials and arrived at the temple of success. Now the light of day triumphs over darkness, the Queen of the Night and all her shadowy cohorts dissolve in the golden flood of sunlight and Sarastro blesses the lovers with his benediction.

NOTES

Freemasonry was outlawed in Austria when Schikeneder (of *Schauspieldirektor* fame) and Mozart took up the subject of *The Magic Flute*. They were both Masons, and saw in the circumstances a chance to use some of the ritual in opera. Originally Schikeneder had been working on a puppet show, but another producer anticipated him. He therefore made extensive alterations in the story (*Lulu*, by Liebeskind), turning it into the libretto for *Zauberflöte*. The aria of the Queen of the Night *Der Hölle Rache* is one of the most brilliant showpieces in the soprano repertory, written, some say, to provide a challenge to the first Queen of the Night who was the composer's sister in law.

Zazà

		4 acts	
COMP.: R. Leoncavallo		Milan, 10 November 1900	
LIBR.: By the composer		London, 1909	
		Metropolitan, 1920	

CAST

Zazà, *music hall singer*	S	Lartigon, *monologist*	B
Anaide, *her mother*	C	Duclou, *stage manager*	Bar
Floriana, *music hall singer*	S	Michelin, *journalist*	Bar
Natalia, *Zazà's maid*	MS	Courtois	B
Mme. Dufresne	MS	Mario, *Dufresne's butler*	T
Milio Dufresne, *man about town*	T	Toto, *Dufresne's child*	S
Cascart, *music hall performer*	Bar	Auguste	T
Bussy, *journalist*	Bar	Claretta	S
Marlardot, *proprietor of the music hall*	T	Simona	S

SYNOPSIS

I. Zazà boasts that she'll win the love of Milio. When Bussy goes to see Milio she finds that the boast has already come true.

II. Everything goes along nicely until Cascart hints that Milio is untrue to her.

III. Zazà discovers that the rival is really Milio's legal wife.

IV. Lying, she tells Milio she has revealed the scandal to his wife. For this treachery he beats her, ends the affair and goes home.

Zémire et Azor

	Comedy in 4 acts
COMP.: A. Grétry	Fontainebleau, 9 November 1771
LIBR.: J. Marmontel	London, 1776
From a comedy by La Chaussée	New York, 1787

Zenobia

	3 acts
COMP.: L. Coerne	Bremen, 1 December 1907
LIBR.: O. Stein	

The first American opera to be performed in Europe.

Zhenitba

(*The Marriage*)	St. Petersburg, 1 April 1909 (with piano
COMP.: M. Mussorgsky	accompaniment)
LIBR.: By the composer	Paris, 1923
From a comedy by Gogol	Essen, 1937

This opera was composed in 1868. It was edited for the Paris performance by Ravel, and for Essen by Alexander Tcherepnin.

Zigeunerbaron   *Operetta in 3 acts*
 (*The Gypsy Baron*)   Vienna, 24 October 1885
 COMP.: J. Strauss   New York, 1886
 LIBR.: J. Schnitzer   London, 1935
 From a libretto by Jokai

CAST

Graf Peter Homonay	Bar	Mirabella, *her governess*	C
Conte Carnero	Bar	Ottokar	T
Sandor Barinkay	T	Czipra, *gypsy leader*	MS
Kalman Zsupan, *pig farmer*	Bar	Saffi, *her foster daughter*	S
Arsena, *his daughter*	S	Pali, *gypsy*	B

MUSICAL HIGHLIGHTS

The Overture

ACT I. Waltz *Als flotter Geist*, Barinkay

ACT II. Trio *Mein Aug'bewacht* (My eyes are wide), Saffi, Barinkay, Czipra
Treasure Waltz *Ha, seht es winkt'* (Ha, see it beckon), Saffi, Barinkay, Czipra
Duet *Wer uns getraut?* (Who married us?), Saffi and Barinkay

SYNOPSIS

I. Barinkay has inherited a castle in which, Czipra says, there is a treasure which he may find only through a faithful wife. At first he courts Arsena for this project, but she will not have less than a noble husband. As soon as he meets Saffi, however, he forgets the difficulty and joins the gypsies, being made their baron.

II. He, his love and Czipra find the treasure just as it was predicted. He is happy until Czipra tells him that Saffi is really a princess and is therefore higher in station than he. Dejected he goes off to the wars with his friends.

III. Barinkay and Ottokar return from war each rewarded for heroism by a grant of nobility, thus paving the way toward renewed happiness with Saffi as is indicated by the grand waltz of the finale.

THE PEOPLE IN OPERA

This section lists the best-known singers, authors, conductors, and other persons in opera. After each singer's name appears a list of some of the roles he or she has sung; after each composer, a list of some of the most significant operas he wrote.

An index to this section, arranged according to voice (soprano, contralto, etc.) or function (conductor, librettist, etc.) will be found at the end of the book.

Beneath a few of the names in this list no birth dates appear. In most cases, particularly of singers, the information is not available.

Ackté, Aïno   *Soprano*
b. Helsinki, 1876: d. there, 1944
Debut as Marguérite at Opéra, 1897; at Metropolitan, 1904.
Elisabeth, Elsa, Gilda, Juliette, Nedda, Ophélie, Salome, Sieglinde.

Adam, Adolphe Charles   *Composer*
b. Paris, 1803: d. there, 1856
Called one of the creators of opéra-comique, Adam composed fifty-three works for the stage. He was also an organist and composer of nonoperatic music such as the famous *Cantique de Noël*, and the ballet *Giselle*. In 1847 he organized and managed the Théâtre Nationale, but soon went heavily into debt. His most famous works were:

Pierre et Catherine	Opéra-Comique	1829
Le Chalet	„	1834
Le Postillon de Longjumeau	„	1836
Le Fidèle Berger	„	1838
Le Brasseur de Preston	„	1838
Régine, ou Les Deux Nuits	„	1839
La Reine d'un Jour	„	1839
Le Roi d'Yvetot	„	1842
Cagliostro	„	1844

Si j'étais Roi	Lyrique	1844
Richard en Palestine	Opéra	1854

Adam de la Halle   *Composer*
b. Arras, France circa 1230: d. Naples, 1287
A *trouvère*, he wrote the famous *Jeu de Robin et de Marion* for the court of Aragon at Naples, in 1285. The work has been re-orchestrated and edited by Darius Milhaud for modern performance.

Adamberger, Valentin   *Tenor*
b. Munich, 1743: d. Vienna, 1804
Called Adamonti in Italy. He sang the first Belmonte (*Die Entführung aus dem Serail*), the part being written for him. He played a part also in *Der Schauspieldirektor*.

Adams, Suzanne   *Soprano*
b. Cambridge, Mass., 1872: d. London, 1953
She made her debut at the Opéra in 1895 as Juliette. In 1899 she did the same role in her Metropolitan debut.
Cherubino, Elvira, Euridice, Gilda, Marguérite (trained by Gounod), Micaela, Zerlina.

Adler, Kurt   *Conductor*
b. Neuhaus, Czechoslovakia, 1907:
Pianist and conductor in Berlin, Prague

184

and Kiev before coming to the United States. Chorusmaster and conductor at the Metropolitan since 1943.

Adler, Kurt Herbert   *Conductor*
b. Vienna, 1905:
Conductor at Salzburg, then at Chicago. In 1943 he became conductor, then artistic director at San Francisco.

Adler, Peter Herman   *Conductor*
b. Jablonec, Czechoslovakia, 1899:
Conductor at Bremen, Kiev and New York. Music Director of NBC Opera Theater since 1949.

Agthé, Rosa   *Soprano*
b. Weimar, 1827: d. there, 1906
First Elsa in *Lohengrin*. Married the baritone von Milde.

Albanese, Licia   *Soprano*
b. Bari, Italy, 1913:
Debut at Parma in 1935, at Metropolitan, 1940, as Cio-cio San.
Concepcion, Giorgetta, Inez, Lauretta, Liù, Margherita (*Mefistofele*), Mimi, Tosca, Violetta.

Albani, Emma   *Soprano*
(*Really* Marie Louise Cécilie Emma Lajeunesse)
b. Chambly, Montreal, 1847: d. London, 1930
Having made her professional beginning singing in church in Albany, N.Y., she took her stage name from the name of the city. She made her operatic debut as Aminta at Messina in 1870, then Covent Garden, 1872, and the New York Academy of Music in 1874. She married Ernest Gye in 1878, 'retired from the stage to sing in concerts after 1896, and was made a Dame of the British Empire in 1925.
Antonida, Desdemona, Elisabeth, Elsa, Eva, Isolde, Lucia, Marguérite, Mignon, Ophélie.

Albéniz, Isaac   *Composer*
b. Camprodón, Spain, 1860: d. Cambo-Les-Bains, Pyrénées, 1909
At thirteen he ran away from home and traveled throughout Spain, making his living as a pianist. Thence he went to Puerto Rico, Cuba and the United States, living by the same means until 1875. He lived mostly in Paris after 1893.

The Magic Opal	London	1893
San Antonio de la Florida	Madrid	1894
Merlin (*part of a trilogy*)		
Enrico Clifford	Barcelona	1895
Pepita Jiménez	,,	1896

Albert, Eugene, Francis Charles d'   *Composer*
b. Glasgow, 1864: d. Riga, 1932
He led a troubled life, married and divorced six times. He was a pianist and a conductor, and studied with Franz Liszt.

Der Rubin	Karlsruhe	1893
Ghismonda	Dresden	1895
Tiefland	Prague	1903
Flauto Solo	,,	1905
Die Toten Augen	Dresden	1916
Der Golem	Frankfurt	1926
Mr. Wu	Dresden	1932

(*The last was completed by Blech.*)

Alboni, Marietta   *Contralto*
b. Cesena, Italy, 1823: d. Ville d'Avray, France, 1894
She was a pupil of Rossini in preparing roles in his works. Her debut was as Saffo (Pacini), in 1842.
1st Zerlina (*Fra Diavolo*), Fidès, Maffio Orsini, Rosina (*Il Barbiere di Siviglia*), Semiramide.

Alda, Frances   *Soprano*
(*Really* Frances Davies)
b. Christchurch, New Zealand, 1883: d. Venice, 1952
She made her debut at the Opéra-Comique in 1904 as Manon, and as Gilda in 1908 at the Metropolitan,

opposite Caruso. In 1910 she married Giulio Gatti-Casazza, and became, in 1939, a citizen of the United States.

Aida, Desdemona, Francesca, Harriet (*Martha*), Juliette, Louise, Manon Lescaut, Margherita (*Mefistofele*), Marguérite (*Faust*), Micaela, Mimi, Princess (*Marouf*), Rozenn (*Roi d'Ys*), Violetta.

Alessandro, Victor   *Conductor*
b. Waco, Tex. 1915:
Conductor at Oklahoma City, then at San Antonio.

Alfano, Franco   *Composer*
b. near Naples, 1876: d. San Remo, 1954
Besides his own works, he completed Puccini's *Turandot*.

Miranda	Leipzig	1896
La Fonte di Enscir	Breslau	1898
Risurrezione	Turin	1904
Madonna Imperia	,,	1927

Allin, Norman   *Bass*
b. Ashton-on-Lyne, England, 1885:
After establishing himself as a singer, he became director of the British National Opera Company.

Aged Hebrew (*Samson et Dalila*), Bartolo (*Le Nozze di Figaro*), Dositheus, Falstaff (*Die Lustigen Weiber von Windsor*), Gurnemanz, Parsifal, Ragman (*Louise*).

Althouse, Paul   *Tenor*
b. Reading, Penna., 1889: d. New York, 1954
Cola Rienzi, Dmitrij, Erik (*Der Fliegende Holländer*), Huon, Lohengrin, Max (*Der Freischütz*), Parsifal, Tannhäuser, Tristan, Siegfried, Siegmund, Walther.

Alvarez, Albert Raymond   *Tenor*
(*Really* Albert Gourron)
b. Bordeaux, 1860: d. Nice, 1933
He began as Faust, in Paris in 1892, then as Roméo at the Metropolitan in 1899. Eventually he built up his repertory to nearly sixty roles.

1st Nicias (*Thaïs*), Faust (*La Damnation de Faust*), Don José, Otello, John of Leyden, Tannhäuser, Walther.

Alvary, Lorenzo   *Bass*
b. Debrecen, Hungary, 20 February 1909:
Don Alfonso (*Così fan Tutte*), Angelotti, Arkel, Le Bailli (*Werther*), Bonze (*Butterfly*), Foltz, Hortensius, Masetto, Baron Ochs, Pimen, Samuele (*Un Ballo in Maschera*), Simone (*Gianni Schicchi*), Truffaldino (*Ariadne auf Naxos*), Zuniga (*Carmen*).

Alvary, Max   *Tenor*
(*Really* Max Achenbach)
b. Düsseldorf, 1856: d. Thuringia, 1898
He made his debut at the Metropolitan in 1885 as Don José. Later he made himself a specialist in Wagnerian roles.

Adolar (*Euryanthe*), Cola Rienzi, Lohengrin, Parsifal, Siegfried, Siegmund, Tannhäuser, Tristan, Walther.

Amara, Lucine   *Soprano*
b.
Antonia, Countess Almaviva, Countess Ceprano (*Rigoletto*), Helmwige, Micaela, Mimi, Nedda, Tatyana,

Amato, Pasquale   *Baritone*
b. Naples, 1878: d. New York, 1942
Amato made his debut at Naples in 1900 as Germont, and in the same role in 1918 at the Metropolitan.

1st Rance, Amfortas, Escamillo, Giovanni (*Francesca da Rimini*), Golaud, Manfredo, Napoleone (*Madame Sans-Gêne*).

Ancona, Mario   *Baritone*
b. Livorno, Italy, 1870: d. Florence, 1931
He made his debut as Scindia in *Le Roi de Lahore*. He played the first Tonio in London and in New York.

1st Silvio, Alfonso (*La Favorita*), Amonasro, Figaro (*Il Barbiere di Siviglia*), Hans Sachs, Nelusko, de Nevers, Telramund, Zurga (*Les Pêcheurs de Perles*).

Anderson, Marian   *Contralto*
b. Philadelphia, 1902:

Marian Anderson, made famous by her concert career, became the first Negro on the principal staff of the Metropolitan. In February, 1939, she was denied an appearance at the hall of the Daughters of the American Revolution in Washington, D.C., because of her race. A committee headed by the wife of the President was immediately formed and found a chance for her to sing in the open, on the steps of the Lincoln Memorial, to an immense crowd of grateful Washingtonians. She frequently has sung Ulrica at the Metropolitan.

Angeles, Victoria de los   *Soprano*
b. Barcelona, 1923:

Having made her debut in opera at Madrid in 1944, she first appeared in the United States at Carnegie Hall in 1950 and at the Metropolitan the same year.

Cio-cio San, Elisabeth (*Tannhäuser*), Eva, Manon, Marguérite, Mélisande, Micaela, Mimi, Rosina (*Il Barbiere di Siviglia*), Salud.

Angelo, Louis d'   *Bass*
b. Naples, 1888: d. Jersey City, N.J., 1958

He first sang at the Metropolitan in 1917 and stayed nearly thirty years, leaving in 1946 after having sung almost three hundred roles.

Bartolo (*Il Barbiere di Siviglia*), Uberto (*La Serva Padrona*).

Ansseau, Fernand   *Tenor*
b. near Mons, France, 1890:

Faust, des Grieux (*Manon*), Don José, Julien, Orfeo (as originally written for male voice), Romeo.

Antheil, George   *Composer*
b. Trenton, N.J., 1900: d. New York, 1959

Antheil was famous in Europe for flamboyant modernism, to accomplish which he went to extreme lengths, using even airplane engines to make new sounds. This became the subject of a most remarkable little book on the creation of music by Ezra Pound.

Transatlantic (*to his own libretto using jazz rhythms*)		1930
Helen Retires		1934

Arditi, Luigi   *Composer*
b. Crescentino, Italy, 1822: d. near Brighton, England, 1903

Famous not only as a composer, but also as a conductor. He supplied recitatives for the production of *Die Entführung aus dem Serail* in London, 1866. He is the composer of a famous vocal waltz, *Il Bacio*.

I Briganti	Milan	1841
Il Corsaro	Havana	1846
La Spia	New York	1856

Arensky, Antony Stepanovich *Composer*
b. Novgorod, 1861: d. Finland, 1906

Voyevoda (*A Dream on the Volga*)	Moscow	1891
Raphael	„	1894
Nal and Damayanti	„	1904

Ariosti, Attilio   *Composer*
b. Bologna, 1666: d. (place unknown) circa 1740

An accomplished organist and player upon the viola d'amore, Ariosti was a co-director, with Handel and Bononcini, of the Royal Academy of Music at London in 1720. For a short time he lived as a Dominican friar.

Tirsi	Venice	1686
Morte Placado	Vienna	1707
Mars und Irene	Berlin	1703
Artaserse	London	1724

Arne, Thomas Augustine   *Composer*
b. London, 1710: d. there, 1778

It is said that as a boy Arne, forbidden to study music, used to borrow servants' clothes in order to stand in the shadows of the mighty and watch operas. Later, before making the definite break with parental authority, he tried being a solicitor for a while.

Rosamund	London	1733
Tom Thumb	„	1733
Alfred (*masque, with* Rule Britannia *as its finale*)	Clivedon,	1740
The Temple of Dullness	Drury Lane,	1745
Artaxerxes (*his first in the Italian manner*)		1762
Love in a Village (*ballad opera*)	Drury Lane,	1762

Arnould, Madeleine Sophie   *Soprano*
b. Paris, 1740: d. there, 1802
Sophie Arnould commenced a most notorious career with a debut at the Opéra in 1757. She lives on as the subject of a one-act comedy by Gabriel Pierné. She sang the first Iphigénie (*Iphigénie en Aulide*), and the first Euridice.

Auber, Daniel François Esprit
Composer
b. Caen, 1782: d. Paris, 1871
Auber was director of the Paris Conservatoire from 1842 to 1871.

Le Séjour Militaire	Paris	1813
Le Testament et les Billets-Doux	Comique	1819
La Bergère Châtelaine	„	1820
Masaniello	Opéra	1828
Fra Diavolo	Comique	1830
Le Cheval de Bronze	„	1835
Les Diamants de la Couronne	Comique	1841
Manon Lescaut	„	1856

Aubert, Louis François   *Composer*
b. Paramé, Belgium, 1877:
| La Forêt Bleue | Boston | 1913 |

Audran, Edmund   *Composer*
b. Lyons, 1840: d. Tierceville, France, 1901
A writer of comic operas such as:
La Mascotte		1880
L'Oeuf rouge		1890
M. Lohengrin		1896

Austin, Frederick   *Bass*
b. London, 1872: d. there, 1952
Austin was not only a singer but a successful arranger and composer of operatic and orchestral works. He edited and arranged the production of the revived *Beggar's Opera* for Hammersmith (London).
Guglielmo (*Cosi fan Tutte*), Gunther, Peachum.

Austin, Sumner   *Baritone*
b. London, 1888:
A member of the Carl Rosa Opera Company, famous for his Gianni Schicchi.

Autori, Federico   *Bass*
b.
Archibaldo, Matteo (*Fra Diavolo*).

Baccaloni, Salvatore   *Bass*
b. Rome, 1900:
Beginning as a student of architecture, Baccaloni switched to opera and made his debut under Toscanini at La Scala in 1926. He first played at the Metropolitan as Bartolo in 1940.
Alcindoro, Bartolo (*Le Nozze di Figaro* and *Il Barbiere di Siviglia*), Benoit, Dulcamara, Falstaff (*Falstaff*), Gianni Schicchi, Leporello, Don Pasquale, Sacristan (*Tosca*), Sulpice, Uberto.

Bach, Johann Christian   *Composer*
b. Leipzig, 1735: d. London, 1782
The eleventh son of Johann Sebastian Bach and an organist like his father, Johann Christian wrote thirteen operas, much chamber music and many concertos. He is called the London Bach.

Artaserse (*Metastasio*)		1761
Catone in Utica (*Metastasio*)		1761
Orione(*first opera to use clarinets in the orchestra in England*)		1763
Alessandro nell'Indie	Naples	1762
Lucio Silla	Mannheim	1776

Baklanov, George *Baritone*
b. St. Petersburg, 1882: d. Basel, 1938
He made his debut in St. Petersburg in 1905. In 1935 he sang the first Agamemnon (*Iphigénie en Aulide*) in the United States, at Philadelphia.
Boris, Rigoletto, Scarpia.

Balaban, Emanuel *Conductor*
b. New York, 1895:
Conductor at Dresden, then in the Opera Department of the Eastman School of Music in Rochester, N.Y., 1927–1953. Afterwards he conducted in New York City. He is presently on the faculty of Juilliard School of Music.

Balfe, Michael William *Composer*
b. Dublin, 1808: d. Hertfordshire, 1870
Balfe was not only a composer but also a violinist and a baritone. He played in the orchestra at Drury Lane in 1824. He sang Figaro (*Il Barbiere di Siviglia*) for Rossini at Paris, and Papageno for the first production in England of *Die Zauberflöte*.

The Siege of Rochelle	Drury Lane	1835
The Maid of Artois	London	1836
Falstaff	,,	1838
The Bohemian Girl	Drury Lane	1843
The Rose of Castile	London	1857

Bamberger, Carl *Conductor*
b. Vienna, 1902:
After conducting opera in Danzig, Darmstadt, Russia and Egypt he came to the United States. Here he conducted for NBC and CBS, and was head of the opera department of the Mannes College of Music from 1939.

Bamboschek, Giuseppe *Conductor*
b. Trieste, 1890:
After making his conducting debut at Trieste in 1908 he became accompanist to Pasquale Amato, traveling throughout the United States in 1913. From 1916 to

1926 he was conductor at the Metropolitan. He then directed opera at Philadelphia.

Bampton, Rose *Soprano*
b. Cleveland, 1909:
Rose Bampton made her first debut as a mezzo-soprano at the Metropolitan in 1932, playing Gioconda. In 1937 she came out a second time at the same place, singing the soprano role of Leonora (*Il Trovatore*).
Aida, Amneris, Donna Anna, Daphne, Laura (*Gioconda*), Gioconda, Leonora (*Il Trovatore*), Norma, Sieglinde.

Bantock, Sir Granville *Composer*
b. London, 1868: d. there, 1946
He was known not only as composer, but as a conductor and teacher. From 1907 to 1934 he was professor of music at Birmingham. He was knighted in 1930.

Caedmar	London	1892
The Pearl of Iran		1894
The Seal Woman	Birmingham	1924

(*all on Celtic subjects*)

Barber, Samuel *Composer*
b. West Chester, Pa., 1910:
A nephew of Louise Homer and a singer himself. Not a prolific composer, but a very sure one. He is a close associate of Menotti, who wrote the libretto for Barber's only full-scale opera. In 1960 the pair brought out a tiny, nine-minute scene, *A Hand of Bridge*.

| Vanessa | New York | 1958 |

Barbier, Jules Paul *Librettist*
b. Paris, 1822: d. there, 1910
An associate of Carré, with whom he wrote libretti for *Dinorah*, *Faust*, *Roméo et Juliette*, *Mignon*, *Les Contes d'Hoffmann*. With du Wailly he turned out *Benvenuto Cellini*.

Barbieri, Fedora *Contralto*
Adalgisa, Amneris, Azucena, Carmen, Dalila, Princess Eboli, Laura (*La Gioconda*), Orfeo (*La Favola d'Orfeo*), Santuzza.

Barbot, Joseph Théodore Désiré *Tenor*
b. Toulouse, 1824: d. Paris, 1897
The first Faust. Studied with Manuel Garcia.

Bardi, Giovanni *Patron*
b. Florence, 1534: d. Rome, 1612
The Count of Vernio, a patron of music and an amateur composer. In his house, about 1600, were held the meetings that led to the invention of opera. The new art, stemming from a desire to re-create the beauty of Greek drama, was the outcome of many conversations between his friends, among whom were Vincenzo Galilei (Galileo's father), Bernardo Strozzi, Girolamo Mei, Ottavio Rinuccini, Giulio Caccini (his secretary), Jacopo Peri, Giacomo Corsi, and Emilio dei Cavalieri. These, constituted as the *Camerata*, were the inventors of modern opera. Bardi himself, besides taking part in the productions, wrote madrigals and prose works.

Barrientos, Maria *Soprano*
b. Barcelona, 1884: d. Ciboure, France, 1946
A famous Lucia, having made her debut in that role at the Metropolitan in 1916. Her first role in opera was that of Selika, in Barcelona in 1899, when she was only fifteen. She was also a pianist, violinist, and composer; she wrote a symphony when she was still a child.
Dinorah, Gilda, Lakmé, Linda di Chamounix, Martha, Philine, Mireille, Ophélie, Urbain.

Bartók, Béla *Composer*
b. Nagy-szent-miklós, Hungary, 1881: d. New York, 1945
One of the greatest composers of the twentieth century, and one whose style had very deep influence upon practically all the composers of the following generation. He is famous also as a collector of thousands of Hungarian folk songs and dances which he, in association with Kodály, analyzed in great detail. His six string quartets are generally considered to be masterworks in the form; they are also revolutionary in their rhythmic and harmonic style. Among the most popular of his larger works are such extended pieces for small groups of instruments as the *Sonata for Two Pianos and Percussion*, and his *Music for Strings, Percussion and Celesta*.
Duke Bluebeard's
Castle   Budapest   1918

Bassani, Giovanni Battista *Composer*
b. Padova, 1657: d. Bergamo, 1716
A composer of oratorios, masses, suites, sonatas and operas. He was also a violinist and organist.
Amorosa Preda di
Paride   Bologna   1683
Alarico, Re de Goti   Ferrara   1685
Falaride, Tiranno
d'Agrigento   1684

Bassi, Luigi *Baritone*
b. Pesaro, 1766: d. Dresden, 1825
He made his debut in the town of his birth in 1779, at thirteen. Mozart wrote the part of Don Giovanni for him when he was only twenty-two, and listened to the singer's advice on technical details.
1st Don Giovanni, Almaviva (*Le Nozze di Figaro*), Barnaba, Gennaro.

Baum, Kurt *Tenor*
b. Prague, Czechoslovakia, 15 March 1908:
Don Alvaro, Drum Major (*Wozzeck*), Enzo, Grigorij, Don José, Mario, Radames, Singer (*Der Rosenkavalier*), Turiddu.

Beard, John *Tenor*
b. circa 1717: d. 1791
A singer in Handel's operas in London. He was the first Captain MacHeath.

Beaumarchais, Pierre Augustin Caron de
Playwright
b. Paris, 1732: d. there, 1799

This most famous French playwright also made a name for himself as a flutist and harpist. He wrote the trilogy for which Mozart, Paisiello and Rossini composed three of the most famous operas in the history of the comic stage. The plays were:

Le Barbier de Seville
Le Mariage de Figaro
La Mère Coupable

Beck, Johann Nepomuk   Baritone
b. Budapest, 1827: d. Pressburg, 1904
Almaviva (Le Nozze di Figaro), Amonasro, Don Giovanni, Guillaume Tell, Hamlet, Hans Heiling, Nelusko, Orestes, Richard (I Puritani).

Beck, Karl   Tenor
b. Austria, 1814: d. Vienna, 1879
The first Lohengrin.

Beecham, Sir Thomas   Conductor
b. near Liverpool, 1879: d. London, 1961
Born wealthy, he made use of his money and his talent, as did Mendelssohn, to bring out great works of music, especially operas. He conducted the first performances in England of Elektra, Salomé, Der Rosenkavalier, Ariadne auf Naxos, A Village Romeo and Juliet, The Wreckers, Tiefland, Dylan and The Critic. In 1928 he toured the United States. He conducted at Seattle from 1941 through 1943, then at the Metropolitan from 1942 to 1944. He organized the Royal Philharmonic Orchestra of London in 1947. Among musicians he was noted for his acid but accurate criticisms and his uncompromising attention to obtaining the maximum effort from the players.

Beethoven, Ludvig van   Composer
b. Bonn, 1770: d. Vienna, 1827
This celebrated creator of nine symphonies was not a child prodigy as were many of his contemporaries, but was, nevertheless, a professional musician early in his life, playing the organ and other keyboard instruments in the orchestra of the Elector of Bonn, for whom his father worked. His duties included not only the usual organ playing for religious occasions, but also the accompaniment and conducting of private performances of operas. Thus, quite early, he became acquainted both with the keyboard works of Johann Sebastian Bach, and the stage works of Gluck, Paisiello and others.

In 1787 he is said to have visited Vienna where he played before the famous Mozart and took a few lessons. The following year the new Elector established a national theater at Bonn, in the orchestra of which young Beethoven played viola and learned more about music for the stage. In 1792 Haydn visited the court, and Beethoven was able to show him some of his works. Encouraged by the great man's approval, and supported financially by the Elector, Beethoven went to study with Haydn in Vienna in his twenty-first year. Bonn, meanwhile, was taken over by the advancing French armies, and the composer was never again required to go home.

By 1803, Beethoven was famous as a composer and performer. He agreed to compose an opera to be produced by the impresario Schikaneder. It was not, however, until the idea had mulled for some time and the request had been repeated that he finally, in the early months of 1805, began to work on the piece. After very intense labor the score was finished that summer and shown to friends, the composer roaring the vocal lines as he played the piano. It was first performed in November.

At that time Vienna was occupied by the French, but Beethoven's concentration upon his music was not materially distracted. After the first production of his opera he withdrew it and began to make changes. It was brought out briefly in 1806, but withdrawn again and extensively repaired and altered. In 1814 it finally appeared in the form we know it, with a revised libretto and many changes in the score.

After *Fidelio*, Beethoven wanted to compose another opera. He read libretto after libretto but was never quite satisfied. He tried *Melusine* by Grillparzer, but ceased working when he heard of a ballet on the same subject. According to friends, he had always searched for a noble and "elevating" subject, rather than a scandalous one such as might have pleased Mozart. He never found one to his liking.

While *Fidelio* was being composed, Beethoven's deafness had just begun to bother him. By 1816 he was forced to use an ear-trumpet, and by 1820 was totally deaf.

Fidelio	Vienna	1805

Bellincioni, Gemma   *Soprano*
b. Monza, Italy, 1864: d. Naples, 1950
She made her debut in Naples in 1881; the same year she married Robert Stagno. She was the first Fedora, Santuzza and Sapho.
Carmen, Fedora, Santuzza, Sapho, Violetta.

Bellini, Vincenzo   *Composer*
b. Catania, Sicily, 1801: d. near Paris, 1835
This very famous composer of many operas lived only thirty-four years, but wrote works which are still in repertory throughout the world. Perhaps some of his success came from luck. A performance of an opera while he was still in school led to his first commission, for the San Carlo theater at Naples, in 1826. One success led to another, and his career was launched. Bellini's importance stretches beyond his own stage works. He is greatly admired by many for the simplicity of his melodic line, and this has influenced the work of composers as different from Bellini's tradition as, for instance, Stravinsky.

Il Pirata	La Scala	1827
La Straniera	„	1829
I Capuletti ed I Montecchi	Venice	1830
La Sonnambula	Milan	1831
Norma	La Scala	1831
I Puritani	Paris	1835

Bemberg, Herman   *Composer*
b. Paris, 1859: d. Bern, 1931
Bemberg won the Rossini prize in 1885. He composed operas, cantatas and songs.

Le Baiser de Suzon	Paris	1888
Elaine	Covent Garden	1892

Bender, Paul   *Bass*
b. Westerwald, Germany, 1875: d. Munich, 1947
He made his Metropolitan debut in 1922.
Amfortas, Gurnemanz, Hans Sachs, Baron Ochs, Pizarro, Sarastro, Wotan.

Bennett, Robert Russell   *Composer*
b. Kansas City, Kan., 1894:
Best known for his arrangements in the Broadway style, his largest and most successful venture was the arrangement of *Carmen Jones* in 1943.

Maria Malibran	New York	1935
The Enchanted Kiss	„	1944

Benoist, François   *Composer*
b. Nantes, 1794: d. Paris, 1878

Léonore et Félix	1821
L'Apparition	1848

Benoist, Peter   *Composer*
b. Harlebeke, Belgium, 1834: d. Antwerp, 1901
He was a composer of oratorios and cantatas. He founded a school of music which, in 1898, became the Royal Flemish Conservatory.

Het Dorp in't gebergte (*A Mountain Village*)	Brussels	1856
Roi des Aulnes	„	1859
Isa (*in Flemish*)	„	1867

Bentonelli, Joseph *Tenor*
(*Really* Benton)
b. Sayre, Okla., 1900:
The first American Achilles, in *Iphigénie en Aulide* at Philadelphia in 1935. He studied with Jean de Reszke and made his Metropolitan debut in 1936, singing des Grieux.

Berg, Alban *Composer*
b. Vienna, 1885: d. there, 1935
One of the most advanced composers of the twelve-tone school, a follower of Schönberg, whom he excels in many ways. He wrote several well-known works for orchestra and for various smaller combinations of instruments.

Wozzeck	Berlin	1925
Lulu (*unfinished*)	Zürich	1937

Berg, Natanael *Composer*
b. Stockholm, 1879:
He began as a student of medicine. He composed works for ballet and orchestra and the following operas:

Lelia	Stockholm	1912
Engelbrekt	„	1929
Judith	„	1936
Birgitta	„	1942
Genoveva	„	1947

Berger, Erna *Soprano*
b. Dresden, 1900:
Her Metropolitan debut took place in 1949.
Anne (*Rake's Progress*), Constanze, Leila, Pamina, Sophie, Zerlina (*Fra Diavolo*).

Berger, Rudolph *Baritone/Tenor*
b. Moravia, 1874: d. New York, 1915
He made his debut as a baritone in 1891 at Brünn. Changing to tenor, he came out at Berlin in 1909 as Lohengrin. In 1913 he married Marie Rappold. His repertory is said to have included ninety-six baritone and eighteen tenor roles.
Eric (*Der Fliegende Holländer*), Jokanaan (*seventy-nine times*), Lohengrin, Parsifal, Siegfried, Siegmund, Tannhäuser, Tristan, Walther.

Bergsma, William *Composer*
b. Oakland, Calif., 1921:

The Wife of Martin Guerre	New York	1956

Berkeley, Lennox *Composer*
b. near Oxford, 1903:

Nelson	London

(*Preview*, 1953; *complete*, 1954.)

A Dinner Engagement	Aldeburgh, England	1954

Berlioz, Hector *Composer*
b. La Côte Saint-André, 1803: d. Paris, 1869
A great innovator of instrumentation, and a great critic of music. From 1852 to his death he held the sinecure of librarian of the Paris Conservatory. He restored Gluck's *Orfeo* to its original shape and prepared recitatives for *Der Freischütz* for Paris in 1841. His most famous works are *The Fantastic Symphony* and *The Requieme*.

Benvenuto Cellini	Opéra	1838
Béatrice et Bénédict	Baden-Baden	1862
Les Troyens		
Part Two	Paris	1863
Entire	Karlsruhe	1890
La Damnation de Faust		
(*concert*)	Opéra-Comique	1846
(*staged*)	Monte-Carlo	1893

Bernstein, Leonard *Composer*
b. Lawrence, Mass., 1918:
Most famous as a pianist and conductor (of the New York Philharmonic), Bernstein has also written much music for the theater including the musical shows *On the Town*, *Wonderful Town*, *West Side Story* and the ballet *Fancy Free*. He was the first American to conduct a regular performance of opera at La Scala.

Trouble in Tahiti	Waltham, Mass.	1952

Berwald, Franz Adolf *Composer*
b. Stockholm, 1796: d. there, 1868
He wrote six symphonies, five cantatas, and other works.

Estrella di Soria	Stockholm	1862
Drottningen af Golconda	„	1864

Betz, Franz *Tenor, Baritone*
b. Mainz, 1835: d. Berlin, 1900
The first Siegfried, Walther and Wotan.
He made his debut as Don Carlos (*Ernani*), in Berlin in 1859.
Don Carlos, Falstaff, Hans Sachs, Siegfried, Walther, Wotan.

Bible, Frances *Mezzo-soprano*
b.
Amneris, Angelina, Cherubino, Hansel, Lola, Mrs. Nolan (*The Medium*), Octavian, Page (*Salomé*), Siebel, Smeraldina, Suzuki.

Billington, Elizabeth *Soprano*
(*Née* Weichsel)
b. London, circa 1765: d. near Venice, 1818
She made her debut in Dublin as Euridice in 1784, and as Rosetta in *Love in a Village* at Covent Garden in 1786. In 1809 she retired.

Bing, Rudolf *Manager*
b. Vienna, 1902:
Manager of the Darmstadt State Theater from 1928 to 1930, the opera at Charlottenberg, 1930–1933, at Glyndebourne, 1935–1939 and again from 1946 to 1949, and director of the Edinburgh Festival from 1947 to 1949. Since 1949 he has been general manager of the Metropolitan, making many long-overdue improvements in the house and the company.

Bishop, Henry Rowley *Composer*
b. London, 1786: d. there, 1855
He wrote nearly one hundred thirty works for the stage. He was also a conductor and became a knight in 1809.

The Circassian Bride	Drury Lane	1809
Cortez		1823
Clari, or the Maid of Milan (*containing* Home Sweet Home)	Covent Garden	1823
The Fall of Algiers		1825
Aladdin		1826
The Fortunate Isles		1841

Bispham, David Scull *Baritone*
b. Philadelphia, 1857: d. New York, 1921
He made his debut in London in 1891. In 1896 he sang for the first time at the Metropolitan, as Beckmesser. He organized a Society of American Singers to stimulate opera in English, and established the Bispham prize for it.
Alberich, Colas, (*Bastien und Bastienne*), Dutchman, Escamillo, Falstaff (*Falstaff*), Iago, Kurnewal, Masetto, Peter (*Hänsel und Gretel*), Pizarro, Schikaneder, Telramund, Wolfram, Wotan.

Bittner, Julius *Composer*
b. Vienna, 1874: d. there, 1939
Bittner practiced law until 1920. Besides operas, he wrote ballets, orchestral music, etc.

Die Rote Gret	Frankfurt	1907
Der Musikant	Vienna	1910
Der Bergsee	„	1911
Der Abenteurer	Cologne	1913
Das Höllisch Gold	Darmstadt	1920
Das Rosegärtlein	Mannheim	1923
Mondnacht	Berlin	1928
Das Vielchen	Vienna	1934

Bizet, Georges *Composer*
(*Really* Alexander César Léopold)
b. Paris, 1838: d. there, 1875
Bizet won the Prix de Rome and wrote a good deal of music to which the world paid practically no attention. With the exception of his music for *L'Arlésienne* he had no public success until the scandalous "critical failure" of *Carmen*. When Bizet

died, three months after the opening of that most famous work, he was unaware that it had begun to be recognized as a masterpiece. In 1857, he shared with Lecocq the Offenbach prize for his music to the libretto *Le Docteur Miracle*. In 1869 he married Geneviève Halévy, the daughter of his teacher. Otherwise his life was one of interminable labor on his music and unrelieved difficulties with the arbiters of taste in Paris in his time.

La Prêtresse	1854
Le Docteur Miracle	1857
Don Procopio	1906
La Guzla de l'Emir	
Les Pêcheurs de Perles	1863
La Jolie Fille de Perth	1867
Numa	1871
Djamileh	1872
Carmen	1875
Ivan le Terrible	1951

(*The above list shows the order of composition of the operas. The dates indicate the actual first performances which, in the cases of* Don Procopio *and* Ivan le Terrible *were long after Bizet's death.*)

Bjoerling, Jussi *Tenor*
b. Stora, Sweden, 1907: d. near Stockholm, 1960

Born to a singing family, Jussi Bjoerling first appeared in the United States as a member of his family's male quartet, singing Swedish folk songs at community gatherings. He made his operatic debut in Stockholm in 1930 as Don Ottavio. Again he toured the United States as a concert singer in 1937, before making his debut as Rodolfo at the Metropolitan in 1938. Bjoerling was especially remarkable as one of the few singers from the north who excelled in Italian roles.

Calaf, des Grieux, Duke (*Rigoletto*), Faust (by Gounod), Manrico, Don Ottavio, Rhadames, Riccardo (*Un Ballo in Maschera*), Rodolfo, Romeo, Turiddu.

Blacher, Boris *Composer*
b. Newchang, China, 1903:

A composer of ballets, orchestral music and opera, and also a librettist. Blacher wrote the texts of *Dantons Tod* and *Der Prozess*. In 1953 he became director of the Hochschule für Musik in West Berlin.

Fürstin Tarakanova	Dresden	1941
Die Flut	„	1947
Die Nachtschwalbe	Leipzig	1948
Das preussisches Märchen		
(*ballet opera*)	Berlin	1952
Abstract Opera No. 1	Frankfurt	1953

Blauvelt, Lillian Evans *Soprano*
b. Brooklyn, N.Y., 1874: d. Chicago, 1947

The first Xenia in the opera of that name by her husband, Savine. She made her debut in Brussels in 1893 singing Mireille.

Blech, Leo *Composer*
b. Aachen, 1871: d. Berlin, 1958

A pupil of Humperdinck. He was also a conductor at Prague, Berlin, Riga and Stockholm.

Aglaja		1893
Cherubina		1894
Das war ich	Dresden	1902
Rappelkopf	Berlin	1917
Aschenbrödel	Prague	1905
Versiegelt	Hamburg	1908

Blitzstein, Marc *Composer*
b. Philadelphia, 1905:

In 1960 he was commissioned to compose an opera on the subject of Sacco and Vanzetti for the Metropolitan.

The Harpies	New York	1931
The Cradle Will Rock	„	1937
No for an Answer	„	1941
Regina	Boston	1949

Bliss, Arthur *Composer*
(*Really* Edward Drummond)
b. London, 1891:

A composer of much ballet, orchestral music and music for films. He was knighted in 1950.

The Olympians	London	1949

Bloch, Ernst *Composer*
b. Geneva, 1880: d. Portland, Oregon, 1959

Bloch's fame rests upon his orchestral works, particularly the rhapsody *Schelomo*, and upon his liturgical music for the synagogue. He was Director of the Cleveland Conservatory of Music and the San Francisco Conservatory before joining the staff of the University of California in 1944. He then went to live in Oregon.

| Macbeth | Opéra-Comique | 1910 |
| Jézabel | (*unfinished; begun* 1918) | |

Blockx, Jan *Composer*
b. Antwerp, Belgium, 1851: d. there, 1912

Jets Vergeten	Antwerp	1877
Herbergprinses	,,	1896
Maître Martin	Brussels	1892
Thyl Eulenspiegel	,,	1900
De Bruid der Zee	Antwerp	1901
De Kapel	,,	1903
Chanson d'Amour	,,	1912

Bockelmann, Rudolf *Baritone*
b. Bodenteich, Germany, 1892:

A member of the Chicago Opera for a brief period in the thirties, he is famous for his three major Wagnerian roles: Dutchman, Hans Sachs, Wotan.

Bodansky, Artur *Conductor*
b. Vienna, 1877: d. New York, 1939

Assistant Conductor at Vienna, Berlin, Prague, Mannheim and at the Metropolitan from 1915. He also composed recitatives for the production of *Oberon* at the Metropolitan in 1918.

Böhm, Karl *Conductor*
b. Graz, Austria, 1894:

Conductor at Dresden, Vienna, Chicago, and the Metropolitan.

Bohnen, Michael *Bass*
b. Keulen, Germany, 1886:

He made his debut in Düsseldorf in 1910, and as Francesco (*Mona Lisa*), at the Metropolitan in 1923. Gurnemanz, King Marke.

Boïeldieu, François Adrien *Composer*
b. Rouen, 1775: d. Jarcy, 1834

His career began with an opera on a libretto by his father and ended with painting, which he took up late in his life. From 1803 to 1811 he tried the life of Court Composer at St. Petersburg, but returned to Paris for his greatest successes.

La Fille Coupable	Rouen	1793
La Famille Suisse	Paris	1797
Le Caliphe de Bagdad	,,	1801
La Dame Blanche	,,	1825

Boito, Arrigo *Composer*
b. Padua, 1842: d. Milan, 1918

One of the great poets of opera, Boito wrote the magnificent libretti for *Otello* and *Falstaff* and revised *Simon Boccanegra* to make it dramatically practical. He wrote words for *La Gioconda* too, and composed his own operas. To add to his trades, he conducted the opening of his own *Mefistofele*.

| Mefistofele | La Scala | 1868 |
| Nerone | Milan | 1924 |

Bonci, Alessandro *Tenor*
b. Cesena, Italy, 1870: d. near Rimini, 1940

Bonci made his debut at Parma in 1896, singing Fenton. *I Puritani* was revived for him at the Manhattan Opera in 1906 for his American debut, in which he sang the role of Arturo.

Fra Diavolo, Duke (*Rigoletto*), Faust, Riccardo (*Un Ballo in Maschera*), Rodolfo (*La Bohème*).

Bonelli, Richard *Baritone*
(*Really* Bunn)
b. Port Byron, N.Y. 1894:

Bonelli first sang as Valentin in Brooklyn, 1915. He studied with Jean de Reszke and appeared for the first time at the Metropolitan, singing Germont, in 1932.

In 1945 he retired, but was soon heard again, singing Giorgio as late as 1952. Barnaba, Giorgio, Germont, Manfredo, Tonio.

Bononcini, Giovanni   *Composer*
b. Modena, 1670: d. Vienna, 1747
Bononcini, or Buononcini, was associated with Handel in the establishment of the Royal Academy of Music in London. He also wrote his part of one of those multi-composer works for the stage that were favorite but soon forgotten devices of the time, *Muzio Scevola*, London, 1721. He returned to the Continent and invested his money in an alchemist's scheme to make gold. Having lost everything, he died in poverty.

Serse	Rome	1694
Tullio Ostilio	,,	1694
Arstarto	London	1720

Borgatti, Giuseppe   *Tenor*
b. Cento, Italy, 1871: d. Lago Maggiore, 1950
The first Andrea Chenier.
Andrea Chenier, Herod, Mario Cavaradossi, Tristan.

Borghi-Mamo, Adelaide   *Mezzo-soprano*
b. Bologna, 1829: d. there, 1901
She made her debut in 1846 at Urbino.
Leonora (*Favorita*), Marguérite (*Faust*).

Borgiolo, Dino   *Tenor*
b. Florence, 1891: d. there, 1960
Borgioli made his debut in Milan in 1918, singing in *La Favorita*. He made his name there under Toscanini at La Scala, then toured to Rome, Madrid, Portugal, Vienna, London, Paris, and Argentina. His American debut took place at the opening of the San Francisco War Memorial Opera House in 1932. He first appeared in New York as Rodolfo in *La Bohème* at the Metropolitan.
Duke (*Rigoletto*), Fritz (*L'Amico Fritz*), Mario Cavaradossi, Don Ottavio, Riccardo (*Un Ballo in Maschera*), Rodolfo.

Bori, Lucrezia   *Soprano*
(*Really* Lucrezia Borja y Gonzalez de Riancho)
b. Valencia, 1887: d. New York, 1960
She made her debut as Micaela in Rome, 1908. Four years later she appeared for the first time at the Metropolitan, singing Manon Lescaut.
She was one of the most popular members of the Metropolitan company, famous not only for her singing and acting, but also for her lack of the normal vanity and insecurity of prima donnas. She was a member of the board of directors. She left the stage, intentionally quitting while still in command of her great technique, in 1936.
Antonia (*Les Contes d'Hoffman*), Concepcion, Fiora, Iris, Juliette, Louise, Magda (*La Rondine*), Manon, Mary (*Peter Ibbetson*), Mélisande, Mignon, Mimi, Norina, Snyegurotchka, Susanna (*Il Segreto di Susanna*), Suzel, Violetta.

Borkh, Inge   *Soprano*
b. Mannheim, 1921:
She made her debut at Lucerne in 1940 singing Agathe.
Aida, Eglantine, Elektra, Freia, Lady Macbeth, Leonora (*Fidelio*), Magda (*The Consul*), Marie (*Wozzeck*), Mona Lisa, Salome, Senta, Sieglinde, Tosca, Turandot.

Borodin, Alexander   *Composer*
b. St. Petersburg, 1833: d. there, 1887
Borodin was famous as a chemist, and taught that subject at a school of medicine for women in St. Petersburg, besides writing treatises. He is one of the "Mighty Five" of nineteenth-century Russian music, and is best known for his "Polovtzian Dances" from *Prince Igor*.

| Bogatyry (*The Valiant Knights*) | Moscow | 1867 |
| Prince Igor | St. Petersburg | 1890 |

Bottesini, Giovanni   *Composer*
b. Lombardy, 1821: d. Parma, 1889

Bottesini was the first real virtuoso of the double bass. He conducted opera in Italy, New Orleans, and at Paris. It was he who conducted the première of *Aida* in Cairo.

Cristoforo Colombo	Havana	1847
L'Assedio di Firenze	Paris	1856
Ali Baba	London	1871
Il Diavolo della Notte	Milan	1858
Marion Delorme	Palermo	1862
Vinciguerra	Paris	1870
Ero e Leandro	Turin	1879
La Regina di Nepal	,,	1880

Boughton, Rutland *Composer*
b. Aylesbury, England, 1878:
An advocate of choral drama.

The Birth of Arthur		
	Glastonbury	1915
The Immortal Hour	,,	1914
Snow White		1914
The Round Table		1916
Bethlehem	,,	1915
Alkestis	,,	1922
The Queen of Cornwall		
	,,	1924
The Ever Young		1928
The Lily Maid		1934
Galahad		1944
Avalon		1946

Bouhy, Jacques Joseph André *Baritone*
b. Pepinster, Belgium, 1848: d. Paris, 1929
The first Escamillo and the first Don César de Bazan. He was director of the New York Conservatory from 1885 to 1889. He made his operatic debut at the Opera in 1871 singing Méphistophélès in *Faust*.

Boulanger, Marie Julie *Mezzo-soprano*
(*Née* Hallinger)
b. 1786: d. 1850
The first Pamela (*Fra Diavolo*). Not to be confused with Lili Boulanger, the composer, nor with Nadia, the conductor and teacher.

Bovy, Vina *Soprano*
b. Ghent, 1900:
After a debut as Violetta at the Metropolitan in 1936, she sang in various opera houses. In 1948 she became manager of the opera at Ghent. She is also a pianist.

Bouvier, Hélène *Soprano*
b.
Jocasta (*Oedipus Rex*).

Bower, Minnia *Soprano*
b.
One of the Nieces in the first production of *Peter Grimes*, in 1945.

Bowles, Paul Frederick *Composer*
b. New York, 1910:
A composer of ballet, orchestral music and little pieces for the piano. He is better known for his work in the novel.

| Denmark Vesey | 1937 |
| The Wind Remains | 1943 |

Braham, John *Tenor*
(*Really* Abraham)
b. London, 1774: d. there, 1856
The first Sir Huon. He made his debut in Covent Garden in 1787. His voice was phenomenal, having a compass of three octaves. Not only did he sing, however; he also composed his own parts in several operas.
Don Giovanni, Masaniello, Max, Guillaume Tell.

Braithwaite, Warwick *Conductor*
b. Dunedin, New Zealand., 1898:
Has conducted the National Orchestra of Wales, and at Sadlers Wells and Covent Garden.

Brand, Max *Composer*
b. Lwow, Poland, 1896:
Formerly a dodecaphonist, his one opera had a spectacular success during the early 1930's.

| Maschinist Hopkins | | |
| | Duisberg, Germany | 1929 |

Brandt, Marianne   *Soprano and Contralto*
(*Really* Marie Bischoff)
b. Vienna, 1842: d. there, 1921
   The second person to appear as Kundry, there being three to share the opening three performances. She made her debut as Rachel in *La Juive* at Graz in 1867.
   Amneris, Azucena, Brangäne, Eglantine, Elsa, Elvira, Eva, Fidès, Gerhilde, Hedwige (*Guillaume Tell*), Irene, Kundry, Leonora (*Fidelio*), Margarethe (*Genoveva*), Rachel, Selika.

Braun, Karl   *Bass*
b. Meisenheim, Prussia, 1885:
   Famous as Gurnemanz, he made his debut at the Metropolitan in 1913, retiring in 1939.
   Gurnemanz, Rocco, Thoas.

Braunfels, Walter   *Composer*
b. Frankfort, 1882: d. Cologne, 1954

Princess Bambilla	Stuttgart	1909
Till Eulenspiegel	„	1913
Die Vögel(Aristophanes' The Birds)	Munich	1920
Don Gil von den Grünen Hosen	Munich	1924
Der Gläserne Berg	Cologne	1928
Ein Traum, ein Leben	„	1929
Galathea	„	1930
Die Heilige Johanna		1942

Brema, Marie   *Mezzo-soprano*
(*Really* Minny Fehrman)
b. Liverpool, 1856: d. Manchester, 1925
   She made her debut at Oxford in 1891 as Adriana Lecouvreur.
   Adriana Lecouvreur, Amneris, Brangäne, Brünnhilde, Dalila, Fricka, Kundry, Lola Marcellina (*L'Attaque du Moulin*), Orfeo, Ortrud.

Britten, Benjamin   *Composer*
b. Lowestoft, 1913:
   The foremost opera composer of present-day England. He has also taken an active part in the establishment of grass-roots opera in that country. He arranged

Dido and Aeneas for a production at Hammersmith, and *The Beggar's Opera* for Cambridge and for film.

Paul Bunyan	New York	1941
Peter Grimes	London	1945
Rape of Lucretia	Glyndebourne	1946
Albert Herring	„	1947
Let's Make an Opera	Aldeburgh	1949
Billy Budd	London	1951
Gloriana	Covent Garden	1953
The Turn of the Screw	Venice	1954
Midsummer Night's Dream		1960

Brouwenstijn, Gré   *Soprano*
b. Holland, 1915:
   Debut at Covent Garden, 1951 as Aida.
   Aida, Amelia (*Un Ballo in Maschera*), Countess Almaviva, Desdemona, Elizabeth, Elisabeth de Valois, Iphigénie (*Iphigénie en Aulide*), Yaroslavna, Jenufa, Leonora (*Fidelio* and *Trovatore*), Rezia, Rusalka, Santuzza, Tatyana, Tosca.

Brownlee, John Donald Mackenzie
   Baritone
b. Geelong, Australia, 1900:
   Melba discovered this young singer. He went on to a debut as Rigoletto at Covent Garden in 1926 and at the Metropolitan in 1937. From 1956 he was director of the Manhattan School of Music in New York.
   Don Alfonso, Almaviva (*Le Nozze di Figaro*), Dr. Falke, Don Giovanni, Kothner, Don Ottavio, Papageno, Rigoletto, Sharpless, von Faninal.

Brüll, Ignaz   *Composer*
b. Prossnitz, Moravia, 1846: d. Vienna, 1907

Die Bettler von Samarkand		1864
Das Goldene Kreuz	Berlin	1875
Der Landfriede	Vienna	1877
Bianca	Dresden	1879
Königin Marietta	Munich	1883
Gloria	Hamburg	1886

Das Steinerne Herz	Vienna	1888
Gringoire	Munich	1892
Shach dem Könige	„	1893
Der Husar	Vienna	1898

Bruneau, Alfred Composer
b. Paris, 1857: d. there, 1934

Kerim	Opéra-Comique	1887
Le Rêve	„	1891
L'Attaque du Moulin	„	1893
Messidor	„	1897
L'Ouragan	„	1901
L'Enfant Roi	„	1905
Naïs Micoulin	Monte Carlo	1907
La Faute de L'Abbé Mouret	Opéra Comique	1907
Les Quatre Journées	„	1916
Le Roi Candaule	„	1920
Angelo, Tyran de Padove	„	1928
Virginie	„	1931

Bülow, Hans Guido von Conductor
b. Dresden, 1830: d. Cairo, 1894

An advocate of Wagner and Brahms, he gave to the former not only his best efforts as a conductor but also his wife Cosima, whom he had married in 1857; she left him and married Wagner in 1869. He conducted the first *Tristan und Isolde* and the first *Die Meistersinger von Nürnberg*.

Bunn, Alfred Librettist
b. 1796: d. Bologne, 1860

Bunn wrote the libretto for *The Bohemian Girl*, among others. He was manager and director of Drury Lane for a time.

Burgstaller, Alois Tenor
b. Holzkirchen, Germany, 1871: d. Gmund, 1945

Cosima Wagner urged him to take up singing professionally. He made his Metropolitan debut in 1903 in *Die Walküre*. He sang Siegfried and the first Parsifal in America.

Burian, Karel Tenor
(*Sometimes* Burrian)
b. Rousinow, Czechoslovakia, 1870: d. near Prague, 1924

Burian made his debut at Brno in 1891, at Bayreuth as Parsifal in 1898, and as Tannhäuser at the Metropolitan in 1906. He was also the first Herod in *Salome*. One evening after a final curtain, while removing his make-up, Burian picked up a glass of what he thought was a drink prepared for him. The disinfectant in the glass irreparably burned his throat.

Burke, Edmund Arbrickle Bass
b. Toronto, 1876:

Abimelech, Amfortas, Prince Igor, Méphistophélès, Nilakantha, Nourabad, Pogner.

Busch, Fritz Conductor
b. Westphalia, 1890: d. London, 1951

Conducted at Stuttgart, Dresden, Glyndebourne, the Metropolitan and in South America.

Busoni, Ferruccio Benvenuto Composer
b. Empoli, Italy, 1866: d. Berlin, 1924

Busoni was most famous as a pianist and a composer of music for that instrument. His *Doktor Faust* was completed by his pupil, Jarnach.

Die Brautwahl	Hamburg	1912
Turandot	Zurich	1917
Arlecchino	„	1917
Doktor Faust	Dresden	1925

Butt, Clara Contralto
b. Sussex, 1873: d. Oxford, 1936

She made her debut as Ursula in *The Golden Legend*. In 1920 she was made a Dame of the British Empire.

Caccini, Giulio Composer
b. Rome, circa 1546: d. Florence, 1618

Caccini was one of the inventors of opera. Parts of his music for *Euridice* were performed in the first production of that first opera by Peri. In 1602 his entire work on the theme came out. He was not only a composer, but a singer and lutenist as well. His wife composed, and even their daughter was both composer and singer. Caccini contributed to the understanding of the new principle of monodic music—the single voice accompanied—with the publication in 1602 of his collected songs, *Nuove Musiche*.

Il Rapimento di Cefalo
Florence 1600
Euridice   „   1602

Cadman, Charles Wakefield   *Composer*
b. Johnstown, Pa., 1881: d. Los Angeles, 1946

A founder of the Hollywood Bowl Concerts, and a fairly well known composer of songs including *At Dawning*.

Shanewis   Metropolitan 1918
The Sunset Trail   Denver   1922
The Garden of Mystery
                    New York   1925
A Witch of Salem   Chicago   1926
The Willow Tree   NBC   1933

Cahier, Madame Charles   *Contralto*
(*Née* Sara Jane Layton-Walker)
b. Nashville, Tenn., 1870: d. Manhattan Beach, Calif., 1951

A pupil of Jean de Reszke, she made her debut in Nice in 1904.

Carmen, Brangäne, Fricka, Ortrud

Caldara, Antonio   *Composer*
b. Venice, 1670: d. Vienna, 1738

Caldara wrote the first of his eighty-seven operas in 1688.

Callas, Maria Meneghini   *Soprano*
(*Née* Calogeropoulos)
b. New York, 1923:

This famous prima donna made her debut in Verona, 1947, singing Laura in *La Gioconda*. In 1956 she made her first appearance at the Metropolitan singing Norma, which she had sung in Chicago in 1954 and Covent Garden, 1952. She became a journalistic treasure in 1957 and

1958 with her pyrotechnic public relations and her vociferous battle with Rudolf Bing about the priority and privilege of her position as prima donna. Bing won, but Callas remained newsworthy. In her defense she pointed with pride to her record of having a large repertory in which were many roles not usually known by other sopranos.

Aida, Amelia, Amina, Armida, Cio-cio San, Elena, Elvira (*I Puritani*), Fiorilla (*Il Turco in Italia*), Gilda, Lady Macbeth, Laura (*La Gioconda*), Leonora (*La Forza del Destino*), Leonora (*Il Trovatore*), Medea (Cherubini), Mimi, Nedda, Norma, Rosina (*Il Barbiere di Siviglia*), Santuzza, Tosca, Turandot, Violetta.

Calvé, Emma   *Soprano*
(*Really* Emma Calvet)
b. Aveyron, France, 1858: d. Millau, 1942

The first Anita (*La Navarraise*), and the first Sapho. Calvé made her debut at Brussels in 1882 as Marguerite, and at the Metropolitan as Santuzza in 1893. When she first sang Ophélie at La Scala in 1887 her performance was roundly hissed. But later performances wrested cheers from the audience.

Carmen, Leïla, Margherita (*Mefistofele*), Marguerite (*La Damnation de Faust*), Ophélie, Santuzza.

Calzabigi, Raniero   *Librettist*
b. Livorno, Italy, 1714: d. Naples 1795

Calzabigi was creator of the famous libretti for Gluck's operas: *Alceste*, *Orfeo ed Euridice*, *Iphigénie en Aulide*, and *Paride ed Elena*. He was also a public supporter of the Gluckists in their war against the Piccinists.

Cambert, Robert   *Composer*
b. Paris, circa 1628: d. London, 1677

The first French composer of opera. In association with Perrin, Cambert brought out the first opera at the Académie Royale de Musique (L'Opéra) in 1671. Later

Lully managed to snatch away the royal patent and took over the Académie for himself.

La Pastorale en Musique *(lost)*		1659
Ariane, ou le Mariage de		
Bacchus *(lost)*		1661
Pomone *(the first*		
French Opera)	Paris	1671
Les Peines et les Plaisirs		
de l'Amour	Paris	1671

Cammarano, Salvatore   *Librettist*
b. Naples, 1801: d. there, 1852
He was a pupil of Gabriele Rossetti. He wrote the libretti of *Lucia di Lammermoor, Don Pasquale, Luisa Miller, Il Trovatore* and many others.

Campanari, Giuseppe   *Baritone*
b. Venice, 1855: d. Milan, 1927
He came to the United States not as a singer but as a cellist. He sang, however, the first performance in this country of *Pagliacci*, taking the part of Tonio. Escamillo was another of his favorite roles.

Campanini, Cleofonte   *Conductor*
b. Parma, 1860: d. Chicago, 1919
His brother, the tenor Italo Campanini, helped him to make the right acquaintances to become a conductor in the United States. Here he brought out many works never heard in this country before. These included *Thaïs, Hérodiade, Louise, Il Segreto di Susanna, Sapho, Pelléas et Mélisande*, and the first Chicago performance of *La Favola d'Orfeo*. He conducted the first American performance of Verdi's *Otello* and was principal conductor and general director at Chicago from 1910 until his death.

Campanini, Italo   *Tenor*
b. Parma, 1845: d. near there, 1896
Brother of Cleofonte Campanini. He fought for Garibaldi in the war for the unification of Italy, and was wounded in battle. In 1869 he made his debut in opera, singing the part of Manrico at Odessa. In

1872 in London, and in 1873 in New York, he appeared as Gennaro, in *Lucrezia Borgia*. One episode of his career established him as a typical Italian in his treatment of Wagner's roles, when he appeared as Lohengrin with a great blue plumed hat on his head.

Edgardo, Faust *(La Damnation de Faust)*, Faust (in the opening performance of the Metropolitan, 1883), Faust *(Mefistofele)*, Gennaro *(Lucrezia Borgia)*, Ferdinand *(La Favorita)*, Don José, Lohengrin, Manrico, Otello, Radames, Raoul.

Campenhout, François von   *Composer*
b. Brussels, 1779: d. there, 1848
Composer of six operas, many cantatas and other works. Best known for his song *La Brabançonne*, which became the Belgian national anthem.

Grotius	1808
Le Passe-partout	1815

Camporese, Violante   *Soprano*
b. Rome, 1785: d. there, 1839
Donna Anna, Desdemona, Penelope (by Cimarosa), Sesto *(La Clemenza di Tito)*, Susanna *(Le Nozze di Figaro)*.

Camprá André   *Composer*
b. Aix en Provence, 1660: d. Versailles, 1744

L'Europe Galante	Paris	1697
Le Carnival de Venise	,,	1699
Tancrède	,,	1702
Iphigénie en Tauride	,,	1704
Idoménée	,,	1712

Caniglia, Maria   *Soprano*
b.
Adriana Lecouvreur, Aida, Amelia, Desdemona, Elisabetta *(Don Carlos)*, Fedora, Francesca, Iphigénie *(Iphigénie en Tauride)*, Madeleine *(Andrea Chénier)*, Manon Lescaut, Margherita *(Mefistofele)*, Minnie, Selika, Tosca, Wally.

Capoul, Joseph Amédée Victor   *Tenor*
b. Toulouse, 1839: d. Pujaudron du Gers, 1924

In 1861 he made his debut as a singer in the role of Daniel (*Le Chalet*), at the Opéra-Comique. In 1897 he became a stage manager.

Almaviva (*Il Barbiere di Siviglia*), Daniel (*Le Chalet*), Faust, Romeo, Wilhelm (*Mignon*).

Carey, Francis Clive Savill　　*Baritone*
b. Essex, 1883:
Carey produced the operas and sang these roles:
Figaro (*Le Nozze di Figaro*), Don Giovanni, Papageno (*Die Zauberflöte*).

Carey, Henry　　*Composer*
b. Yorkshire(?), circa 1690: d. London, 1743
Henry Carey wrote nine ballad operas and the words of the song *Sally in our Alley*. His son claimed he wrote *God Save the King*, but this has been refuted. Carey died a suicide.

The Contrivances	1729
A Wonder, or the Honest Yorkshireman	1735

Carissimi, Giacomo　　*Composer*
b. near Rome, 1605: d. Rome, 1674
Carissimi wrote no operas, but his development of the techniques of recitative in his oratorios were influential to the composers who did.

Caron, Rose　　*Soprano*
b. Monerville, France, 1857: d. Paris, 1930
In 1884 at Brussels she made her debut singing Alice in *Robert le Diable*. She was the first Lorance (*Jocelyn*).

Alice (*Robert le Diable*), Desdemona, Leonore (*Fidelio*), Lorance (*Jocelyn*), Sieglinde.

Carr, Benjamin　　*Composer*
b. London, 1768: d. Philadelphia, 1831
Benjamin Carr established the first music store in America, at Philadelphia, and published the first American music,

including the forever famous *Yankee Doodle*. Only fragments of his own opera survive.

The Archers	New York and Boston 1796

Carroll, Joan　　*Soprano*
b.
The first in the United States to sing Aminta (*Die Schweigsame Frau*).

Caruso, Enrico　　*Tenor*
b. Naples, 1873: d. there, 1921
Certainly one of the greatest tenors of modern times. He was the eighteenth child in a family of twenty. The seventeen who preceded him did not survive. In 1894 he made his debut in Naples. He sang for the first time in London in 1902 and at the Metropolitan in 1903 as the Duke in *Rigoletto*, one of his most famous roles. He was at work in San Francisco when the earthquake struck that city in 1906. There was a scandal in New York when his fiancée's father refused to allow him to marry Dorothy Benjamin, which event took place anyway in 1918. There was another scandal when a New York woman haled him into court for making advances to her in Central Park. This was soon quashed. He sang for the last time in New York in 1920. One of the few failures in his singing career was with Lohengrin, which he sang only three times, in Buenos Aires. He was the first Johnson (*La Fanciulla del West*), the first Loris (*Fedora*), Federico (*L'Arlesiana*), and Maurizio (*Adriana Lecouvreur*).

Don Alvaro, Canio, The Duke (*Rigoletto*), Edgardo, Eleazar, Enzo, Faust (in *Faust* and in *Mefistofele*), Federico, Ferdinand (*La Favorita*), des Grieux (*Manon*), des Grieux (*Manon Lescaut*), John of Leyden, Johnson (*La Fanciulla del West*), Don José, Lionel, Lohengrin, Loris (*Fedora*), Manrico, Mario Cavaradossi, Maurizio, Nadir (*Les Pêcheurs de Perles*), Nemerino (*L'Elisir d'Amore*), Osaka (*Iris*),

Pinkerton, Radames, Raoul, Riccardo (*Un Ballo in Maschera*), Rodolfo, Samson.

Carvalho, Eleazar de   *Composer*
b. Iquato, Brazil, 1912:
He is not only a composer, but a conductor. He also once played tuba in the Brazilian Navy Band.

| Descoberta do Brasil | Rio da Janeiro | 1939 |
| Tiradentes | „ | 1941 |

Carvalho, Marie Caroline Félix
   Soprano
b. Marseilles, 1827: d. near Dieppe, 1895
The first Marguérite (*Faust*), the first Mireille and Juliette. She made her debut as Lucia at the Opéra-Comique in 1849. In 1885 she retired.

Cherubino, Countess Almaviva, Dinorah, Donna Elvira, Isabella (*Le Pré aux Clercs*), Juliette, Lucia, Mathilde, Marguérite, Mireille, Pamina, Oscar (*Un Ballo in Maschera*), Rosina (*Il Barbiere di Siviglia*), Zerlina (*Fra Diavolo*), Zerlina (*Don Giovanni*).

Cary, Anna Louise   *Contralto*
b. Wayne, Maine, 1841: d. Norwalk, Conn., 1921
She studied with Viardot-Garcia and made her debut in Copenhagen as Azucena. In 1874 she became the first American to sing Ortrud, at New York.

Amneris, Azucena, Elena (*Mefistofele*), Leonora (*La Favorita*), Ortrud, Urbain.

Casa, Lisa Della   *Soprano*
b. near Berne, 1919:
The first Fräulein Burstner and the first Leni. She made her debut as Cio-cio San.

Donna Anna, Antonia, Arabella, Countess (*Capriccio*), Countess Almaviva, Donna Elvira, The Marschallin, Marzellina, Mimi, Nedda, Octavian, Pamina, Sophie, Zdenka (*Arabella*), Zerlina.

Cassell, Walter   *Baritone*
b.
Almaviva, Escamillo, Ford, Giorgio Germont, Don Giovanni, Jokanaan, Ramiro (*L'Heure Espagnole*), Scarpia.

Castagna, Bruna   *Mezzo-soprano*
b. Bari, 1908:
Her debut was in Mantua, singing Marina Mnishek in 1927. In 1936 she sang for the first time at the Metropolitan, as Amneris.

Amneris, Carmen, Laura, Marina Mnishek.

Castelnuovo-Tedesco, Mario   *Composer*
b. Florence, 1895:
A composer of oratorios, orchestral and chamber music and of music for Hollywood films.

La Mandragola (*his own libretto*) 1926

Catalani, Alfredo   *Composer*
b. Lucca, 1854: d. Milan, 1893

Elda	Turin	1880
Dejanice	Milan	1883
Edmea	„	1886
La Wally	„	1892

Catalani, Angelica   *Soprano*
b. Sinigaglia, 1780: d. Paris, 1849
She made her debut as a singer at Venice, 1795, then at La Scala in 1801. But in 1814 she took over the management of the *Théâtre des Italiens* in Paris, a job she held until 1817.

Cavalieri, Emilio del   *Composer*
b. circa 1550: d. Rome, 1602
Composer of the first known oratorio, and one of the first to use the "figured bass" notation, one of the steps toward monody and opera. He was a member of the *Camerata* in Florence. His most famous work is *La Rappresentazione dell'Anima e del Corpo*, "A Morality with simple music, with hymns between the episodes; meant to be acted."

Il Satiro   1590

La Disperazione di Fileno   1595
Il Giuoco della Cieca   1595
(*These three are approaches to opera.*)
La Rappresentazione
    dell'Anima e del Corpo
            Rome   1600(?)

Cavalieri, Katharina   *Soprano*
b. Währing, near Vienna, 1760: d.
Vienna, 1801
    She was the first Constanze in *Die
Entführung aus dem Serail,* and the first
Madame Silberklang in *Der Schauspieldirektor.* Mozart wrote the aria *Mi Tradi*
for her voice. Never once did she sing
outside Vienna.

Cavalli, Pier Francesco   *Composer*
b. Crema, Italy, 1602: d. Venice, 1676
    He got his training in the new art of
monody partly by singing under Monteverdi at San Marco in Venice.

Le Nozze di Teti	Venice	1639
Giasone	,,	1649
Serse	,,	1654
and thirty nine more.		

Cavan, Marie   *Soprano*
b. New York, 1889:
    She made her debut in Chicago in 1910,
singing Irma in *Louise.* She sang Mimi
opposite Caruso.

Cebotari, Maria   *Soprano*
b. Bessarabia, 1910: d. Vienna, 1949
    The first Aminta(*Die Schweigsame Frau*),
she made her debut as Mimi in Dresden.
    Aminta, Antonida (*Ivan Susanin*), Cio-
cio San, Countess (*Capriccio*), Daphne,
Mimi, Salome.

Cehanovsky, George   *Baritone*
b.
    Betto (*Gianni Schicchi*), Corporal (*La
Figlia del Reggimento*), Dancaire, Douphol
(*La Traviata*), Fiorello (*Il Barbiere di
Siviglia*), Johann (*Werther*), Marullo,
Melot, Schaunard, Sciarrone, Silvano (*Un
Ballo in Maschera*), Silvio, Surgeon (*La

Forza del Destino*), Tchelkalov (*Boris
Godunov*), Watchman (*Die Meistersinger*),
Yamadori, Zuane (*La Gioconda*).

Cesti, Marcantonio   *Composer*
b. Arezzo, 1623: d. Florence, 1669
    A Franciscan monk who not only
composed, but sang tenor.

L'Orontea	Venice	1649
Cesare Amante	,,	1651
Argia	Innsbrück	1655
Semiramide	Vienna	1667
La Schiava Fortunata	,,	1674

Chabrier, Emanuel   *Composer*
b. Ambert, France, 1841: d. Paris, 1894
    Chabrier was a government clerk until
1862, when he was finally able to free
himself for music. He is best known
for his orchestral rhapsody *España.*

L'Étoile	Paris	1877
L'Éducation Manquée	,,	1879
Gwendoline	Brussels	1886
Le Roi Malgré Lui	Opéra-Comique	1887
Briseïs	(*unfinished*)	

Chadwick, George Whitefield   *Composer*
b. Lowell, Mass., 1854: d. Boston, 1931
    A composer for the organ, the piano,
the voice and of chamber music.

The Quiet Lodging	Boston	1894
Tabasco (*burlesque*)	,,	1894
Judith	Worcester, Mass.	1901
The Padrone		1915
Love's Sacrifice		1917

Chaliapin, Feodor Ivanovitch   *Bass*
b. Kazan, Russia, 1873: d. Paris, 1938
    One of the most famous basses of
modern times, and certainly the most
famous to sing the role of Boris Godunov.
He was the first Don Quichotte, both on
stage and on film. He made his Metropolitan debut as Mefistofele in 1907.
    Don Basilio (*Il Barbiere di Siviglia*),
Boris Godunov, Don Quichotte, Ivan
(*Pskovityanka*), Leporello, Melnik

(*Rusalka*), Mefistofele, Méphistophélès (*Faust*).

Charpentier, Gustave   *Composer*
b. Dieuze, France, 1860: d. Paris, 1956
Charpentier had an abiding interest in the alleviation of poverty around him, and especially in the plight of young girls working in factories. In 1900 he founded a society to help them out. He wrote the libretti for his own operas.

| Louise | Opéra | 1900 |
| Julien | ,, | 1913 |

Charpentier, Marc Antoine   *Composer*
b. Paris, 1634: d. there, 1704
One of Lully's many enemies, made so by Lully's successful intrigues with the Dauphin for Charpentier's job.

Medée	1693
Les Amours d'Acis et Galatée	1678
Endimion	1681
Philomèle	

Charton-Demeur, Ann Arsène
               Mezzo-soprano
b. Sanjon, France, 1824: d. Paris, 1892
The first Didon (*Les Troyens*), and the first Béatrice (*Béatrice et Bénédict*). She made her debut as Lucia.
Amina, Béatrice, Desdemona, Lucia, Madeleine (*Le Postillion de Longjumeau*).

Chausson, Ernest   *Composer*
b. Paris, 1855: d. Mentes sur Seine, 1899

Hélène		1885
Les Caprices de Marianne		1880
Le Roi Arthus (*his own*		
libretto)	Brussels	1903

Cherubini, Luigi   *Composer*
(*Full name* Maria Luigi Carlo Zenobia Salvatore Cherubini)
b. Florence, 1760: d. Paris, 1842
He wrote a mass at thirteen, and his first successful opera, *Armida*, in 1782.

| Démophon | Opéra | 1788 |
| Marguerite d'Anjou | | 1790 |

Lodoïska	Paris	1791
Elisa	,,	1794
Medée	,,	1797
L'Hotellerie Portugaise	,,	1798
La Punition	,,	1799
Les Deux Journées	,,	1800
Faniska	Vienna	1807
Ali Baba	Opéra	1833

Chollet, Jean Baptiste Marie   *Tenor*
b. Paris, 1798: d. Nemours, 1892
The first Fra Diavolo and the first Chappelou (*Le Postillion de Longjumeau*).

Christoff, Boris   *Bass*
b. Sofia, 1918:
Famous for his recording of *Boris Godunov* in France. He made his debut in Rome in 1946 and in San Francisco as Boris in 1956.
Boris, Méphistophélès (*Faust*), Mosè (*by Rossini*)

Cibber, Susanna Maria   *Soprano*
b. 1714: d. 1766
Handel composed the part of Micah in his oratorio *Samson* for her. She was famous as a great actress among singers. To Handel's chagrin she sang Polly in *The Beggar's Opera*.

Cigna, Gina   *Soprano*
b. Paris, 1904:
After her debut in La Scala in 1929 she appeared for the first time at the Metropolitan as Aida in 1937.
Alceste, Aida, Amelia, Asteria (*Nerone*), Daphné, Elisabeth (*Don Carlos*), Francesca, Gioconda, Leonora (*La Forza del Destino*), Marguerite (*La Damnation de Faust*), Tosca, Turandot, Wally.

Cilèa, Francesco   *Composer*
b. Calabria, 1866: d. Varazze, 1950

Gina	Naples	1889
La Tilda	Florence	1892
L'Arlesiana	Milan	1897
Adriana Lecouvreur	,,	1902
Gloria	La Scala	1907

Cimarosa, Domenico   *Composer*
b. near Naples, 1749: d. Venice, 1801
A most prolific composer. During the single year 1781 he brought out five new works. From 1787 to 1791 he stayed in St. Petersburg. In 1798 he was imprisoned in Naples for a short term because of his part in a revolutionary uprising. In all he turned out seventy-six operas.

La Finta Parigiana	Naples	1773
L'Italiana in Londra	Rome	1778
Il Matrimonio Segreto	Vienna	1792

Cleva, Fausto   *Conductor*
b.
Conducted at the Metropolitan and other houses.

Coates, Albert   *Composer*
b. St. Petersburg, 1882: d. near Cape Town, 1953
He made a name as a conductor at Eberfeld, Dresden, Mannheim, in Russia and in England. He taught at the Eastman School of Music, Rochester, N.Y.,

Assurbanipal		1919
Samuel Pepys	Munich	1929
Pickwick	London	1936
Tafelberg se Kleed		
(*Van Hanks and the Devil*)	Cape Town	1952

Coates, Edith   *Contralto*
b.
The first Auntie in *Peter Grimes*, 1945. She has also sung Carmen.

Cobelli, Giuseppina   *Soprano*
b.
Adriana Lecouvreur, Fiora (*L'Amore dei Tre Re*), Isolde, Marguerite (*La Damnation de Faust*), Minnie, Tosca.

Coerne, Louis Adolphe   *Composer*
b. Newark, N.J., 1870: d. Boston, 1922
Coerne received the first Ph.D. in music in America from Harvard University. His *Zenobia* was also the first opera by an American to be performed in Europe.

Sakuntala		1907
Zenobia	Bremen	1907

Cole, Blanche   *Soprano*
b. Portsmouth, England, 1851: d. London, 1888
Amina, Marie (*Zar und Zimmerman*).

Collingwood, Lawrance Arthur   *Composer*
b. London, 1887:

Macbeth	Sadlers Wells	1944
The Death of Tintagiles (*concert*)		1950

Colzani, Anselmo   *Baritone*
b.
Made his debut at the Metropolitan as Simon Boccanegra in 1960.
Barnaba, Nabucco, Simon Boccanegra

Conley, Eugene   *Tenor*
b.
Alfredo, Duke (*Rigoletto*), Don Ottavio, Mario, Pinkerton, Rinuccio (*Gianni Schicchi*), Rodolfo, Tom Rakewell, Turiddu, Werther.

Conner, Nadine   *Soprano*
b.
Mélisande, Micaela, Mimi, Sophie, Zerlina (*Le Nozze di Figaro*).

Converse, Frederick Shepherd   *Composer*
b. Newton, Mass., 1871: d. Boston, 1940
Dean of the New England Conservatory of Music from 1930 to 1938. He wrote four operas, oratorios, cantatas and other works.

The Pipe of Desire	Boston	1906
(*The first American Opera to be performed at the Metropolitan, in 1909.*)		
The Sacrifice	,,	1911

Cooper, Emil   *Conductor*
b. Kherson, Russia, 1877: d. New York, 1960
Conductor at the Metropolitan from 1940–1950.

Copland, Aaron *Composer*
b. Brooklyn, N.Y., 1900:
One of the best-known modern composers in the United States, and famous for his diatonic style, which seems to give an open-air American atmosphere to most of his orchestral works. The most renowned are *El Salon Mexico* and *Appalachian Spring*.

| The Tender Land | New York | 1954 |
| The Second Hurricane | ,, | 1961 |

Corena, Fernando *Bass*
b. Geneva, 1917:
Corena made his Metropolitan debut as Gianni Schicchi in 1954.

Dr. Bartolo (*Le Nozze di Figaro*), Fra Melitone, Gianni, Schicchi, Leporello, Don Pasquale, Sacristan (*Tosca*).

Cornelius, Peter *Composer*
b. Mainz, 1824: d. there, 1874
Cornelius began professional life as an actor, but he failed. As a composer he was much better, but political intrigues among directors cost him performances. When Liszt conducted his *Barber* at Weimar, a planned demonstration against him in the audience caused the great conductor to quit his position.

The Barber of Bagdad	Weimar	1858
Der Cid	,,	1865
Gunlöd	,,	1874

Corsi, Jacopo *Patron*
b. circa 1560: d. Florence, 1604
At his house in Florence the first opera, *Dafne*, was performed. It was by Peri, but it contained some parts written by Corsi, who also played harpsichord. Corsi was a member, with Bardi, of the famous *Camerata*, the group of Florentines who first conceived opera.

Cowell, Henry Dixon *Composer*
b. Menlo Park, Calif., 1897:
A spectacular modernist famous for using his elbows and wooden boards to make "tone-clusters" on the keyboard.

He has written more than a thousand works of all kinds.

| O'Higgins of Chile | 1949 |

Crivelli, Gaetano *Tenor*
b. Bergamo, 1774: d. Brescia, 1836
Don Ottavio, Fiorello (*Il Barbiere di Siviglia*).

Crooks, Richard Alexander *Tenor*
b. Trenton, N.J., 1900:
He made his debut in Philadelphia in 1930 as Mario Cavaradossi. In 1933 he sang des Grieux in his first appearance at the Metropolitan. He has also sung Romeo.

Cross, Joan *Soprano*
b. London, 1900:
The first Ellen Orford, the first Queen Elizabeth in *Gloriana*, the first Mrs. Billows and Mrs. Goose (*The Turn of the Screw*).

Aida, Amelia, Mrs. Billows, Carmen, Cherubino, Cio-cio San, Desdemona, Dido (*Dido and Aeneas*), Elisabeth, Ellen Orford, Elsa, Donna Elvira, Frasquita, Mrs. Goose (*The Turn of the Screw*), Lady Macbeth (*by Collingwood*), Marenka (*Prodaná Nevěsta*), The Marschallin, Mary (*Hugh the Drover*), Mercedes, Micaela, Mimi, Pamina, Queen Elisabeth (*Gloriana*), Tatyana, Violetta.

Cruvelli, Jeanne Sophie Charlotte *Soprano*
b. Westphalia, 1826: d. Monte Carlo, 1907
The first Duchess Elena in *I Vespri Siciliani*.
Countess Almaviva, Duchess Elena, Leonora (*Fidelio*), Valentine (*Les Huguenots*).

Cuenod, Hugues *Tenor*
b.
The first Sellem (*The Rake's Progress*).

Cui, César *Composer*
b. Vilna, Russia, 1835: d. Petrograd, 1918

A government worker, as were the other members of "The Mighty Five," Cui worked in a technical capacity as topographer and expert on fortification. He was tutor in military engineering to Tsar Nicholas the second. Not only did he write many operas, but he also completed *The Fair at Sorotchinsk*.

The Mandarin's Son	St. Petersburg	1859
The Captive in the		
Caucasus	St. Petersburg	1883
William Ratcliffe	,,	1869
Angelo	,,	1876
Le Flibustier	,,	1889
The Saracen	Comique	1899
The Captain's		
Daughter	,,	1911
Mam'zelle Fifi	Moscow	1903
Matteo Falcone	,,	1908
A Feast in Time		
of Plague	,,	1901

Curtin, Phyllis *Soprano*
b.
Alice Ford, Fräulein Burstner, Catherine (*Wuthering Heights*), Leni, Salomé, Susanna Polk, Wife of the Court Attendant.

Dallapiccola, Luigi *Composer*
b. Pisino, Istria, 1904:
Perhaps the foremost Italian composer of the twelve-tone school. He has written a great deal of music for ballet, orchestra and so forth. For the production in Florence in 1942 he transcribed *Il Ritorno d'Ulisse in Patria*.

Volo di Notte	Florence	1940
Il Prigioniero	,,	1950
(*Previously broadcast*, 1949.)		

Dalmorès, Charles *Tenor*
b. Nancy, 1871: d. Hollywood, 1939
A famous tenor, teacher of singing and virtuoso of the French horn, Dalmorès made his operatic debut in Rouen, 1899, and in New York, as Faust, in 1906. He was the first to sing Parsifal in Chicago.

Faust (*La Damnation de Faust*), John (*Salomé*), Don José, Julien, Lohengrin, Parsifal, Pedro (*La Habanera*), Tristan.

Damrosch, Leopold *Conductor*
b. Posen, 1832: d. New York, 1895
Damrosch was a most successful orchestral conductor in New York when the Metropolitan Opera slumped toward disaster after its first season. He offered to take over the artistic direction and supply singers and orchestra for a season provided that the management would allow him a certain freedom in the matter of repertory. His offer was accepted and the Metropolitan thereupon embarked on a season so German in its texture as to give the company a Teutonic reputation for years. He did save it from collapse, and he provided New York with brilliant productions of *Fidelio*, the first *Ring des Nibelungen*, *Die Meistersinger*, etc. He is certainly one of the fathers of music in New York, responsible for the Symphony Society which later became the New York Philharmonic Society, and for the opera itself. It is interesting to note that he won the degree of M.D. in Berlin in 1854, although his medical practice was limited, probably, to sick musical organizations.

Damrosch, Walter Johannes *Composer*
b. Breslau, 1862: d. New York, 1950
The son of Leopold Damrosch carried on in his father's tradition. He conducted the first American performances of *Samson et Dalila*, *Eugene Onegin*, and *Parsifal*. He was the first to conduct a network symphonic broadcast, in 1926. From 1894 to 1899 he led his own opera company on a nationwide tour. Most listeners who were in grammar school in the 1930's remember Walter Damrosch as the voice who told them all about Wagner, Brahms and Bach over the air.

The Scarlet Letter   Boston   1896
The Dove of Peace   „   1912
Cyrano de
   Bergerac   Metropolitan   1913
The Man Without
   a Country   „   1937
The Opera Cloak   New York   1942

Danco, Suzanne   *Soprano*
b. Brussels, 1911:
She made her American debut in 1950.
Donna Anna, Cherubino, Ellen Orford,
Fiordiligi, Jocasta, Marie (*Wozzeck*).

Dargomyzhsky,
Alexander Sergeyevitch   *Composer*
b. Tula, Russia, 1813: d. St. Petersburg,
1869
As did his younger contemporaries, the
"Mighty Five," Dargomyzhsky worked
for the government until 1835. He was a
great champion and influence for "The
Five."
   Esmeralda   Moscow   1847
   Russalka   St. Petersburg   1856
   Kamennyi Gost
   (*The Stone Guest*)
   (*Completed by*
   Cui and Rimsky-
   Korsakov.)   St. Petersburg   1872

Davenant, William   *Librettist*
b. 1606: d. 1668
Davenant was the earliest English opera
manager.

David, Félicien César   *Composer*
b. Vaucluse, France, 1810: d. St. Germaine-en-Laye, 1876
Successor to Berlioz in the sinecure of
librarian of the Conservatoire. He
composed many works for piano, voice
and orchestra. Although the Théâtre
Lyrique rejected his *Herculaneum*, it was
accepted by the Opéra and won the state
prize of twenty thousand francs.
   La Perle du Brésil   Paris   1851
   Herculaneum   Opéra   1859
   Lalla Roukh   Opéra-Comique   1862
   Le Saphir   „   1865

Davies, Tudor   *Tenor*
b.
The first Hugh (*Hugh the Drover*.)
Jenik (*Prodaná Nevěsta*), Rinuccio, Florestan, Wilhelm (*Mignon*).

Davis, John David   *Composer*
b. Birmingham, 1867: d. Portugal, 1942
   The Zaporogues
   (*The Cossacks*)   Antwerp   1903

Debussy, Achille Claude   *Composer*
b. St. Germaine-en-Laye, 1862: d. Paris,
1918
A revolutionary composer, closely
allied with the impressionist poets of his
day. Debussy wrote much for the piano
and concert orchestra including his very
famous *Clair de Lune* and his *L'Après-midi
d'un Faune*. He planned two operas
beyond *Pelléas et Mélisande*, but never
worked on them. His death, attributed
to cancer, occurred during a bombard-
ment of the city during the First World
War.
   Pelléas et Mélisande   Paris   1902

Delannoy, Marcel   *Composer*
b. Ferté Alais, France, 1898:
   Le Poirier de Misère   Paris   1927
   Arlequin Radiophile   Paris   1946
   Ginevra   Comique   1942
   Puck   Strasbourg   1949

Delibes, Clément Philibert Léo
     Composer
b. St. Germaine du Val, France, 1836: d.
Paris, 1891
Besides *Lakmé*, Delibes is best known
for his two ballet scores *Coppelia* and
Sylvia.
   La Roi l'a Dit   Opéra-Comique   1873
   Jean de Nivelle   „   1880
   Lakmé   1883
   Kassya (*completed by Massenet*)   1893

Delius, Frederick   *Composer*
b. Bradford, Engl., 1862: d. Grez-sur-
Loing, France, 1934

Delius wrote some of the calmest music imaginable. One of his best-known works is the *Walk to the Paradise Garden* which occurs in his *A Village Romeo and Juliet*. Another is his rhapsody on *Over the Hills and Far Away*. In 1922 he became paralyzed, then blind.

Irmelin (*written* 1892)	Oxford	1953
The Magic Fountain		1893
Margot la Rouge		1902
A Village Romeo and Juliet	Berlin	1907
Fennimore and Gerda	Frankfurt	1919
Koanga	Elberfeld	1904

Delmas, Jean François *Bass*
b. Lyons, 1861: d. St. Alban de Monthel, 1933
The first Athanaël (*Thaïs*). He made his debut as St. Bris at the Opéra in 1886.
Gurnemanz, Hans Sachs, King (*Lohengrin*), Méphistophélès (*Faust*), Nadir, St. Bris, Wotan.

Delna, Marie *Contralto*
(*Really* Marie Ledan)
b. Meudon, France, 1875: d. Paris, 1932
She made her debut singing Didon in *Les Troyens* at the Opéra-Comique in 1892.
Orfeo, Charlotte (*Werther*), Didon, Françoise (*L'Attaque du Moulin*).

Destinn, Emmy *Soprano*
(*Née* Kittl)
b. Prague, 1878: d. Budejovice, Czechoslovakia, 1930
This celebrated singer claimed a repertory of eighty roles. She took her stage name from her teacher's. When she sang in her native land she called herself Destinnová. Her debut occurred in Berlin in 1898 as Santuzza. In 1904 she sang for the first time at Covent Garden as Donna Anna, and in 1908 at the Metropolitan as Aida. She was the first Minnie (*La Fanciulla del West*).
Amelia, Aida, Donna Anna, Cio-cio San, Diemut (*Feuersnot*), Elsa, Gioconda, Lisa (*Pique-Dame*), Louise, Marenka (*Prodaná Nevěsta*), Marta (*Tiefland*), Nedda, Salomé, Santuzza, Senta, Tatyana, Tosca, Valentine (*Les Huguenots*), Wally.

Dickons, Maria *Soprano*
b. London, 1770: d. there, 1833
Countess Almaviva, Polly Peachum, Rosina (*Il Barbiere di Siviglia*).

Didur, Adamo *Bass*
b. Galicia, 1874: d. Katowice, Poland, 1946
This famous basso made his debut in Rio de Janeiro in 1894. His debut at the Metropolitan in 1908 was as Mefistofele. He was the first Michele (*Il Tabarro*), and the first Boris in America.
Archibaldo, Boris Godunov, Geronte, Guglielmo (*Così fan Tutte*), Gremin, Mefistofele, Oberthal, Ramfis.

Dippel, Johann Andreas *Tenor*
b. Cassell, 1866: d. Hollywood, 1932
Dippel made his debut in Bremen in 1887 and at the Metropolitan in 1890. Once in New York he was spending the evening peacefully at home. The leading tenor at that night's performance was taken sick just before curtain time. The trusty Dippel, who could always be counted upon in an emergency, was rushed to the dressing room just as the messenger found him—in his bathrobe. His career included not only singing but management. He was administrative manager of the Metropolitan from 1908 to 1910, and general manager at Chicago after that. In 1913 he founded an independent company to tour with light operas.
Fenton, Parsifal, Raoul, Steuerman, Tannhäuser, Walther.

Dittersdorf, Karl Ditters von *Composer*
b. Vienna, 1739: d. near Neuhaus, 1799
Beethoven wrote a set of variations on a theme by his friend von Dittersdorf.

His operas total twenty-eight, but he also wrote chamber music and choruses.

Doktor und Apotheker	Vienna	1786
Hieronymous Knicker		1787
Die Lustigen Weiber von Windsor		1797

Dobbs, Mattiwilda *Soprano*
b.
Gilda, Olympia (*Les Contes d'Hoffmann*), Queen of Shemakha (*Le Coq d'or*).

Dönch, Karl *Baritone*
b.
Beckmesser, Doctor (*Wozzeck*).

Donizetti, Gaetano *Composer*
b. Bergamo, 1797: d. there, 1848
Donizetti was one of the most prolific and successful of all opera composers. He lived to be only fifty-one, yet he turned out sixty-six operas, choral music and songs.

Anna Bolena	Milan	1830
L'Elisir d'Amore	,,	1832
Lucrezia Borgia	La Scala	1833
Lucia di Lammermoor	Naples	1835
La Figlia del Reggimento	Opéra-Comique	1840
La Favorita	Opéra	1840
Linda di Chamounix	Vienna	1842
Don Pasquale	Paris	1843
Don Sebastiano	,,	1843
Maria di Rohan	Vienna	1843

Dorus-Gras, Julie Aimée Josèphe
Soprano
b. Valenciennes, 1805: d. Paris, 1896
The first Alice (*Robert le Diable*), the first Marguerite (*Les Huguenots*), and the first Teresa (*Benvenuto Cellini*).

Dow, Dorothy *Soprano*
b. Houston, Texas, 1920:
She made her debut at Buffalo, N.Y., in 1946.
Danae (*Die Liebe der Danae*), Gioconda, Lady Macbeth, Marie (*Wozzeck*).

Draghi, Antonio *Composer*
b. Rimini, 1635: d. Vienna, 1700
One of the more prolific composers of the early years of opera. He wrote sixty-seven, plus many musical plays, oratorios, etc. He spent the last thirty years of his life in Vienna.
La Monarchia Latina Trionfante.

Ducloux, Walter *Conductor*
b. Kriens, Switzerland, 1913:
Assistant conductor at the Festival of Lucerne, 1938 and 1939. In New York during the Second World War; he made broadcasts for the Voice of America from 1949 to 1952, and afterwards was engaged as opera director at the University of Southern California.

Dufranne, Hector *Baritone*
b. Mons, Belgium, 1870: d. Paris, 1951
The first Golaud. He made his debut as Valentin (*Faust*) at Brussels in 1896. His first appearance in New York was at the Manhattan Opera in 1908.

Dukas, Paul *Composer*
b. Paris, 1865: d. there, 1935
Dukas is most famous for his programmatic orchestral scherzo *L'Apprenti-Sorcier* (The Sorcerer's Apprentice).

Ariane et Barbe-Bleue	Comique	1907

Duncan, Todd *Baritone*
b. Danville, Kentucky, 1903:
The first Porgy (*Porgy and Bess*).

Dupont, Gabriel *Composer*
b. Caen, France, 1878: d. Vésinet, 1914

La Cabrera	Milan	1904
La Glu	Nice	1910
La Farce du Cuvier	Brussels	1912
Antar	Opéra	1921

Duprez, Gilbert *Tenor*
b. Paris, 1806: d. Passy, 1896
The first Benvenuto Cellini, the first Edgardo. He was the thirteenth of twenty-two children (*see* Caruso). Not

only did he sing, he also composed eight operas and wrote treatises on the art of singing. He made his debut in Paris, 1825, singing Almaviva.

Duval, Denise *Soprano*
b.
Blanche (*Les Dialogues des Carmélites*)

Duval, Franca *Soprano*
b.
The first Maria Golovin in New York. Concepcion (*L'Heure Espagnole*).

Dux, Claire *Soprano*
b. Poland, 1885:
She made her debut in Cologne, 1906. Eva, Pamina, Sophie.

Dvořák, Anton *Composer*
b. Mulhausen (near Prague), 1841: d. there, 1904
Dvořák made a famous visit to the United States during which he listened and looked with great care. The outcome of this was his celebrated *New World Symphony*. His chief inspiration, however, was the folk music of his Bohemian homeland.

King and Collier	Prague	1874
Vanda	,,	1876
The Peasant and the Rogue	,,	1878
Dimitrij	,,	1882
The Jacobin	,,	1889
The Devil and Kate	,,	1899
Rusalka	,,	1901
Armida	,,	1904

Dyke, Ernest van *Tenor*
b. Antwerp, 1861: d. Berlaer-lez-Lievre, 1923
He made his debut as Lohengrin in Paris, 1887.
Lohengrin, Parsifal, Tannhäuser.

Eames, Emma *Soprano*
b. Shanghai, China, 1867: d. New York, 1952
Emma Eames was brought up in Bath,

Maine. She made her debut at the Opéra as Juliette in 1889 and at Covent Garden as Marguérite in 1891. She sang the first Colombe in *Ascanio*.
Aida, Alice Ford, Charlotte, Colombe (*Ascanio*), Countess Almaviva, Desdemona, Elisabeth, Elsa, Eva, Iris, Juliette, Margherita (*Mefistofele*), Marguérite (*Faust*), Micaela, Pamina, Santuzza, Sieglinde, Tosca.

Easton, Florence Gertrude *Soprano*
b. Middlesbrough, England, 1884: d. New York, 1955
The first Lauretta (*Gianni Schicchi*). She made her debut in Covent Garden, 1903, as Cio-cio San, and at the Metropolitan in 1917 as Santuzza. She is sometimes known by her married name; MacLennan.
Aida, Brünnhilde, Carmen, Cio-cio San, Dulcinée, Elektra, Elena (*Mefistofele*), Elsa, Lauretta (*Gianni Schicchi*), The Marschallin, Rachel, Salome, Santuzza, Serpina, Sieglinde, Turandot.

Edvina, Marie Louise Lucienne *Soprano*
(*Née* Martin)
b. Montreal, circa 1885: d. London, 1948
The first Francesca da Rimini. She made her debut as Marguérite in *Faust*.
Du Barry, Fiora (*L'Amore dei Trè Re*), Francesca da Rimini, Louise, Maliella, Manon, Marguérite, Mélisande, Thaïs, Tosca.

Egk, Werner *Composer*
b. Bavaria, 1901:

Die Zaubergeige	Frankfurt	1935
Columbus	,,	1942
(*Previously heard in radio, 1933.*)		
Peer Gynt	Berlin	1938
Circe	,,	1948
Irische Legende	Salzburg	1955
Der Revisor	Schwetzingen	1957

Einem, Gottfried von *Composer*
b. Bern, 1918:
A pupil of Boris Blacher, who wrote for him the libretti of his operas. For

four months in 1938 von Einem was imprisoned by the Gestapo.

| Dantons Tod | 1947 |
| Der Prozess | 1953 |

Elias, Rosalind   *Mezzo-soprano*
b.
Giulietta (*Les Contes d'Hoffmann*), Grimgerde, Marina Mnishek, Olga (*Eugene Onegin*).

Elmo, Cloe   *Contralto*
b. Lecce, Italy:
Azucena, Nancy (*Martha*), Penelope (*Il Ritorno d'Ulisse in Patria*), Pepa (*Goyescas*), Princess de Bouillon.

Enesco, Georges   *Composer*
b. Rumania, 1881: d. Paris, 1955
Georges Enesco, well known as a composer for his second *Rumanian Rhapsody*, was famous also as a violinist and as a conductor. His native town was renamed Enescu (the Rumanian form of Enesco) in his honor. The opera, *Oedipus*, is a grandiose opera in a modern manner using a few quarter-tones in one section.

| Oedipus | Paris | 1932 |

Engel, A. Lehman   *Composer*
b. Jackson, Miss., 1910:
He is known for his scores for stage plays, and as a conductor.

Pierrot of the Minute		
	Cincinnati	1928
Medea		1935
The Soldier	New York	1956

Erede, Alberto   *Conductor*
b. Genoa, 1908:
Conducted in England in the thirties and after the Second World War. He conducted in New York, NBC, 1939, and joined the Metropolitan in 1954.

Erlanger, Camille   *Composer*
b. Paris, 1863: d. there, 1919

St. Jean l'Hospitalier		1896
Kermaria	Paris	1897
Le Juif Polonais	,,	1900

Le Fils de L'Étoile	,,	1904
Aphrodité	,,	1906
Bacchus Triomphant	Bordeaux	1909
L'Aube Rouge	Rouen	1911
La Sorcière	Paris	1912
Le Barbier de Deauville		1917
Forfaiture	Comique	1921

Erlanger, Frederic d'   *Composer*
b. Paris, 1868: d. London, 1943
The Baron d'Erlanger frequently wrote under the pseudonym Frédéric Regnal.

Jehan de Saintré	Aix (Aachen)	1893
Inez Mendo	London	1897
Tess of the d'Urbervilles		
	Naples	1906
Noël	Paris	1910

Erskine, John   *Librettist*
b. New York, 1879: d. there, 1951
President of the Juilliard School from 1928 to 1937. A pianist and a novelist, with *The Private Life of Helen of Troy* to his credit. He wrote the libretti for *Helen Retires*, and *Jack and the Beanstalk*.

Esplá, Oscar   *Composer*
b. Alicante, 1886:
Like other late nineteenth-century Russians, Esplá was a technical man besides being a composer. He was a civil engineer.

| La Bella Dormiente | Vienna | 1909 |
| La Balteira | | 1939 |

Evans, Edith   *Mezzo-soprano*
b.
Annina, Cherubino, Flora (*La Traviata*), Frau Grubach, Lola, Margret (*Wozzeck*), Mercedes, Mrs. Nolan (*The Medium*), Octavian, Shepherd (*Tosca*), Smeraldina (*The Love for Three Oranges*), Suzuki, Tisbe (*La Cenerentola*).

Falcon, Marie Cornélie   *Soprano*
b. Paris, 1814: d. there, 1897
The list of her firsts includes: Rachel, Valentine (*Les Huguenots*), Mrs. Anckarström (*Gustave III*), Morgiana (Cherubini's

Ali Baba), and Leonora (*Alessandro Strad-ella*). She made her debut in 1832 at the Opéra singing Alice (*Robert le Diable*). In 1838 she lost her voice and in 1840 had to leave the stage altogether. She was also famous for her Donna Anna and her Julie (*La Vestale*).

Falk, Richard   *Conductor*
b. Moringen, Germany, 1879: d. New York, 1949
He conducted in the United States after 1939.

Falla, Manuel de   *Composer*
b. Cádiz, 1876: d. Córdoba, Argentina, 1946
One of the great modern Spanish composers. He is best known for his ballet music *El Amor Brujo* and *The Three-Cornered Hat.*

El Retablo de Maese
  Pedro   Paris   1923
La Vida Breve   Nice   1913

Farrar, Geraldine   *Soprano*
b. Melrose, Mass., 1882:
This almost legendary singer made her debut as Marguérite in *Faust* at Berlin, 1901. In 1906 she appeared as Juliette at the Metropolitan. She was the first Suor Angelica.

Ariane (*Ariane et Barbe-Bleue*), Carmen (*both stage and film*), Charlotte, Caterina (*Madame Sans-Gêne*), Cherubino, Cio-cio San (*first time in United States*), Desdemona, Elisabeth, Elsa, Donna Elvira, Eva, Gilda, Juliette, Manon, Marguérite (*Faust*), Marguerita (*La Damnation de Faust*), Marguerite (*Mefistofele*), Micaela, Mignon, Mimi, Suor Anglica, Susanna (*Le Nozze di Figaro*), Susanna (*Il Segreto di Susanna*), Thaïs, Tosca, Violetta, Zara, Zerlina (*Don Giovanni*).

Farrell, Eileen   *Soprano*
b. Willimantic, Conn., 1920:
Famous as a concert and radio singer, particularly in her interpretations of the

arias and cantatas of J. S. Bach. She made her operatic debut in a concert perform-ance of *Medea* (Cherubini), in 1955.

Alcestis, Ariadne (*Ariadne auf Naxos*), La Gioconda, Leonora (*Il Trovatore*), Medea (*Cherubini*).

Faull, Ellen   *Soprano*
b.
Donna Anna, Birdie (*Regina*), Chryso-themis (*Elektra*), Cio-cio San, Countess Almaviva, Fata Morgana, Helmwige, Miss Pinkerton (*The Old Maid and the Thief*).

Fauré, Gabriel Urbain   *Composer*
b. Pamiers, France, 1845: d. Paris, 1924
A pupil of Saint-Saëns, Fauré carried along the great classical tradition of France by teaching Ravel, Enesco, Nadia Boulanger and others. He was director of the Paris Conservatoire from 1905 to 1920. Most music-lovers know him best by his *Requiem.*

Promethée   Béziers   1900
Pénélope   Monte Carlo   1913

Faure, Jean Baptiste   *Baritone*
b. Moulins, 1830: d. Paris, 1914
The first Rodrigo (*Don Carlos*). He made his debut at the Opéra-Comique, 1852. He is also known as a great teacher of singing and the composer of the song *Les Rameaux.*

Alfonso (*Lucrezia Borgia*), Assur, Cacique (*Il Guarany*), Caspar, De Nevers, Fernando (*La Gazza Ladra*), Figaro, Don Giovanni, Guillaume Tell, Hamlet, Hoël, Iago (Rossini's *Otello*), Lotario (*Mignon*), Mar-quis (*Manon Lescaut*), Méphistophélès (*Faust*), Nelusko, Peter (*Zar und Zimmer-man*), Pietro (*Masaniello*), Rodrigo (*Don Carlos*), Rudolph (*La Sonnambula*), St. Bris.

Favart, Charles Simon   *Librettist*
b. Paris, 1710: d. there, 1792
He is said to have written nearly one hundred and fifty libretti. Some of them

were used by such composers as Gluck and Grétry. The first version of *Bastien and Bastienne* is Favart's. He became stage manager of the Opéra-Comique in 1758, then director.

Favero, Mafalda *Soprano*
b.

Adriana Lecouvreur, Cio-cio San, Harriet (*Martha*), Liù, Louise, Magda (*La Rondine*), Manon, Manon Lescaut, Mimi, Suzel (*L'Amico Fritz*), Thaïs, Wife (*Le Pauvre Matelot*), Zaza.

Fenn, Jean *Soprano*
b.

She made her debut in San Francisco as Elena in *Mefistofele* in 1952. Her first appearance in New York was as Musetta in 1953.

Nedda, Rosalinda (*Die Fledermaus*), Violetta.

Fenton, Lavinia *Soprano*
(*Really* Beswick)
b. London, 1708: d. Greenwich, 1760
She was the first Polly Peachum. Her fame from that brilliant, long-run masterpiece led her to a marriage by which she became Duchess of Bolton.

Ferrari, Benedetto *Composer*
b. Reggio, Italy, 1597: d. Modena, 1681
He wrote the libretto for *Andromeda*, by Manelli, the first opera ever performed for the public, 1637. He also wrote the libretti for his own works.

Armida	Venice	1639
Il Pastor Regio	,,	1640
La Ninfa Avara	,,	1641
Il Principe Giardiniero	,,	1643
Erosilde	Modena	1658

Ferrari-Fontana, Edoardo *Tenor*
b. Rome, 1878: d. Toronto, 1936
The first Avito (*L'amore dei Tre Re*).
Avito (*L'Amore dei Tre Re*), Canio, Don José, Wagner (*Faust*).

Ferrier, Kathleen *Contralto*
b. Lancashire, England, 1912: d. London, 1953
The first Lucretia (*The Rape of Lucretia*). She was famous for her singing of Orfeo at Glyndebourne and at Covent Garden. Cancer hastened her death.

Fevrier, Henri *Composer*
b. Paris, 1875: d. there, 1957
A pupil of Fauré, Massenet and others.

Le Roi Aveugle	Paris	1906
Monna Vanna	Paris	1909
Ghismonda	Chicago	1919
La Damnation de Blanche-Fleur	Monte-Carlo	1920
La Femme Nue	,,	1929

Fibich, Zdenko *Composer*
b. Všeboriče, Czechoslovakia, 1850: d. Prague, 1900
A prolific composer not only of opera but also of music for stage plays, orchestra, chorus and chamber music.

Bukovín	Prague	1871
Blaník	,,	1881
Nevěsta Messinska (*The Bride of Messina*)	,,	1884
Bouře (*The Tempest*)	,,	1895
Hédy	,,	1896
Sárka	,,	1897
Pad Arkuna (*The Fall of Arkun*)	,,	1900

Figner, Nicolay Nicolayevitch *Tenor*
b. St. Petersburg, 1857: d. Kiev, 1919
He made his debut in St. Petersburg in 1887. He took part in the first performance of *Pique-Dame*, and was famous for his Lensky.

Fischer, Emil *Bass*
b. Brunswick, 1838: d. Hamburg, 1914
This famous Wagnerian basso made his debut at Graz in 1857, and at the Metropolitan in 1885.
Daland, Hans Sachs, Henry the Fowler, King Marke, Louis VI (*Euryanthe*), Steffano Colonna.

Fischer, Ludwig   *Bass*
b. Mainz, 1745: d. Berlin, 1825
The first Osmin in *Die Entführung aus dem Serail*.

Fischer-Dieskau, Dietrich   *Baritone*
b. Berlin, 1925:
He made his debut in Berlin in 1948 and in New York, 1955.
Kurnewal, Orfeo, Papageno.

Fisher, Sylvia   *Soprano*
b. Melbourne, Australia
Agathe, Donna Anna, Brünnhilde, Elisabeth, Ellen Orford, Elsa, Isolde, Kostelnika (*Její Pastorkyňa,*) Leonore (*Fidelio*), The Marschallin, Ortrud, Sieglinde.

Flagstad, Kirsten   *Soprano*
b. Hamar, Norway, 1895:
The great Flagstad made her debut as Nuri (*Tiefland*) in 1913. She first sang at Bayreuth as Brünnhilde in 1934 and at the Metropolitan as Sieglinde in 1935. Her reputation for Wagnerian roles is unsurpassed. Her husband was accused of being a Quisling during the Second World War. After the war, she felt that the Americans were somewhat less pleased with her and retired to her homeland.
Aida, Alceste, Anne Page, Brünnhilde, Dido (*Dido and Aeneas*), Elisabeth, Elsa, Euryanthe, Gutrune, Isolde, Leonore (*Fidelio*), Kundry, Mimi, Minnie, Nuri (*Tiefland*), Ortlinde, Rezia, Senta, Sieglinde.

Fleischer, Editha   *Soprano*
b. Falkenstein, Germany, 1898:
A pupil of Lilli Lehman, she made her debut at Berlin in 1919 and at the Metropolitan in 1926.
Aithra, Lisette (*La Rondine*), Serpina, Zerlina (*Don Giovanni*).

Flem, Paul Le   *Composer*
b. Lézardieux, France, 1881:
Le Rossignol de St.
Malo   Comique   1942

La Clairière des Fées   1943
La Magicienne de la Mer   Paris   1954

Flotow, Friedrich von   *Composer*
b. Teutendorf, Germany, 1812: d. Darmstadt, 1883
La Naufrage de Méduse   Paris   1839
Alessandro Stradella   Hamburg   1844
Martha   Vienna   1847

Floyd, Carlisle   *Composer*
b. Latta, S.C., 1926:
The Fugitives   1951
Susanna   1955
Wuthering Heights
     Santa Fe, N.M.   1958

Fodor-Mainvielle, Joséphine   *Soprano*
b. Paris, 1789: d. Lyons, 1870
Desdemona (*Otello*, by Rossini). Ninetta (*Il Barbiere di Siviglia*), Rosina (*Il Barbiere di Siviglia*), Semiramide (Rossini), Zelmira, Zerlina (*Don Giovanni*).

Foerster, Joseph Bohuslav   *Composer*
b. Prague, 1859: d. Novy Vestec, 1951
Deborah   Prague   1898
Eva   ,,   1899
Jessica   ,,   1905
Nepřemozeni
  (*The Conquerors*)   ,,   1906
Srdce (*The Heart*)   ,,   1923
Bloud   ,,   1936

Foli, Allen James   *Bass*
(*Really* Foley)
b. Tipperary, 1835: d. Southport, 1899
Assur, Don Basilio, Bertram, Caspar, Commedatore, Daland, Elmiro, Hermit (*Der Freischütz*), Marcel, Méphistophélès (*Faust*), Oroe (*Semiramide*), Priest (*Die Zauberflöte*), Rodolfo (*La Sonnambula*), Sarastro, St. Bris, Sparafucile.

Formes, Karl Johann   *Bass*
b. Mulheim am Rhein, 1815: d. San Francisco, 1889
He made his debut at Cologne in 1841.
Don Basilio (*Il Barbiere di Siviglia*),

THE PEOPLE IN OPERA

Bertram, Caspar, Leporello, Marcel, Rocco, Sarastro.

Formichi, Cesare *Baritone*
b. Rome, 1887:
Amonasro, Gerard (*Andrea Chénier*), Iago, Méphistophélès (*La Damnation de Faust*), Rigoletto, Scarpia, Tonio.

Fornia-Labey, Rita *Mezzo-soprano*
(*Née* Neumann).
b. San Francisco, 1878: d. Paris, 1922
A pupil of Jean de Reszke, she began as a soprano, then changed to mezzo. She joined the Metropolitan in 1908 and stayed until 1922. Her stage name was constructed from the last letters of the name of her native state.

Amneris, Carmen, Elisabeth, Gutrune, Leonora (*Fidelio*), Nedda, Ortrud, Rosina (*Il Barbiere di Siviglia*), Sieglinde, Venus, Woglinde.

Forrest, Hamilton *Composer*
b. Chicago, 1901:
Yzdra 1925
Camille (for Mary Garden) 1930

Forsyth, Cecil *Composer*
b. Greenwich, England, 1870: d. New York, 1941
Best known as the author of a treatise on orchestration.
Westward Ho! London
Cinderella „

Forti, Anton *Baritone*
b. Vienna, 1790: d. there, 1859
Figaro (*Il Barbiere di Siviglia*), Figaro (*Le Nozze di Figaro*), Don Giovanni, Pizzaro (*Fidelio*), Telasco (*Fernando Cortez*).

Foss, Lucas *Composer*
(*Really* Fuchs)
b. Berlin, 1922:
Griffelkin NBC TV 1955

Franchetti, Alberto *Composer*
b. Turin, 1860: d. Viareggio, 1942
Asraël Reggio 1888

Cristoforo Colombo	Genoa	1892
Fior d'Alpe	Milan	1894
Il Signor di Pourceaugnac	„	1897
Germania	La Scala	1902
La Figlia di Jorio	Milan	1906
Notte di Leggenda	„	1915
Giove a Pompeii (*with Giordano*)	Rome	1921
Glauco	Naples	1922

Franci, Benvenuto *Baritone*
b.
Alfio, Barnaba, Fanuel (*Nerone*), Gerard, High Priest (*Alceste*), Marcello (*La Bohème*), Michele (*Il Tabarro*), Orfeo (*La Favola d'Orfeo*), Rance, Rigoletto, Scarpia.

Franck, César Auguste *Composer*
b. Liège, 1822: d. Paris, 1890
Famous as an organist and a teacher. He is best known for his *Symphony in D minor*.
Le Valet de Ferme 1852
Hulda Monte Carlo 1894
Ghisèle (*completed by his pupils*) „ 1896

Franke, Paul *Tenor*
b.
Dr. Blind, Borsa, Captain (*Wozzeck*), Count Lerma, David (*Die Meistersinger*), Flavio (*Norma*), Goro, Major Domo to von Faninal (*Der Rosenkavalier*), Messenger (*Aida*), Parpignol, Sellem (*The Rake's Progress*), Shepherd (*Tristan und Isolde*), Schuisky (*Boris Godunov*), Simpleton (*Boris Godunov*).

Fremstad, Olive *Soprano and Contralto*
b. Stockholm, 1871: d. Irvington on Hudson, N.Y., 1951
A pupil of Lilli Lehman, she made her debut in Cologne, 1895, as Azucena. At her Metropolitan debut, 1903, she sang Sieglinde. She was the first in Paris and the first in the United States to sing Salome. She also sang the first Iolanthe (*Der Wald*).

Armida, Azucena, Brangäne, Brünn-hilde, Carmen, Elisabeth, Elsa, Fricka, Isolde, Kundry, Salome, Santuzza, Selika, Sieglinde, Tosca, Venus.

Fricsay, Ferenc *Conductor*
b. Budapest, 1914:
Conducted at Budapest, throughout Europe and the United States, and over the Berlin radio (RIAS).

Fry, William Henry *Composer*
b. Philadelphia, 1813: d. Santa Cruz, W.I., 1864
His *Leonora* was the first opera by a native American to be performed here. He also wrote four symphonies and other orchestral music. But beyond that he ranged very far: he was a politically active professional journalist and a lecturer.

Leonora	Philadelphia	1845
Notre Dame de Paris	,,	1864
The Bride of Dunure		
Aurelia the Vestal		

Fuchs, Marta *Soprano*
b.
Brünnhilde, Isolde, Kostelnicka, Kundry.

Fursch-Madi, Emma *Soprano*
b. Bayonne, France, 1847: d. Warren-ville, N.Y., 1894
She made her debut in Paris as Mar-guérite.
Aida, Donna Anna, Laura, Lucrezia Borgia, Marguérite (*Faust*), Ortrud.

Furtwängler, Wilhelm *Conductor*
b. Berlin, 1886: d. Baden-Baden, 1954
Conductor of opera in Switzerland and Germany, Music Director of the Berlin State Opera in 1919. He was also a composer of orchestral and choral music and a writer of essays.

Gadski, Johanna *Soprano*
b. Prussia, 1873: d. Berlin, 1932

The first Hester Prynne (*The Scarlet Letter*, by Damrosch). She made her debut in Berlin in 1889 as Undine (by Lortzing). In 1895 she appeared for the first time in New York, singing Elsa. From 1898 to 1917 she sang, intermittently, at the Metropolitan.
Agathe, Aida, Anna (*La Dame Blanche*), Brünnhilde, Elisabeth, Elsa, Euridice, Eva, Isolde, Sieglinde, Undine.

Gagliano, Marco da *Composer*
b. Gagliano, Italy, 1575: d. Florence, 1642
A member of the Florentine Camerata (*see* Bardi). Gagliano wrote masses and cantatas in polyphonic form as well as operas.

Dafne	Mantua	1608
La Flora (*with* Peri)	Florence	1628

Gál, Hans *Composer*
b. Brunn, Austria, 1890:

Der Arzt der Sobeide	Breslau	1919
Die Heilige Ente	Düsseldorf	1923
Das Lied der Nacht	Breslau	1926
Der Zauberspiegel	,,	1930
Die Beiden Klaas	,,	1933

Galassi, Antonio *Baritone*
b. Lovetto, Italy, 1845: d. 1904
One of the most famous singers at the old New York Academy of Music.
Enrico (*Lucia di Lammermoor*), Escamillo, Iago, Riccardo (*I Puritani*), Rigoletto.

Galeffi, Carlo *Baritone*
The first Fanuél (*Nerone*), and the first Manfredo (*L'Amore dei Tre Re*).
Fanuél (*Nerone*), Gianni Schicchi, Man-fredo (*L'Amore dei Tre Re*), Méphisto-phélès (*La Damnation de Faust*), Michele (*Il Tabarro*), Orfeo (*La Favola d'Orfeo*), Rance, Scarpia.

Galilei, Vincenzo *Composer*
b. Florence, 1533: d. there, 1591
Father of Galileo Galilei, the astronomer and physicist. Vincenzo was one of the most influential members of the Florentine

Camerata (*see* Bardi) that conceived opera as an approach to the great Greek drama. He may have been the first to compose music in monodic form (i.e., single-voice with accompaniment). He also composed madrigals and cantilenas, some of which are published.

Galli, Amintore *Composer*
b. Talamello, Italy, 1845: d. Rimini, 1919
Il Como d'Oro   Turin   1876
David   Milan   1904

Galli, Filippo *Baritone*
b. Rome, 1783: d. there, 1853
The first Fernando (*La Gazza Ladra*), and the first Maometto (Rossini's opera). He began his career as a tenor, but later became a baritone.

Galli-Curci, Amelita *Soprano*
b. Milan, 1889:
At first this famous prima donna studied to be a pianist. She instructed herself in singing. Her debut came in 1909 in Rome where she sang Gilda.. She sang for the first time in Chicago in 1916 in the same role, and at the Metropolitan as Violetta in 1920.
Amina, Dinorah, Donna Elvira, Gilda, Juliette, Lakmé, Leila, Lucia, Rosina (*Il Barbiere di Siviglia*), Violetta.

Galli-Marie, Marie Célestine Laurence
Mezzo-soprano
b. Paris, 1840: d. near Nice, 1905
The first Carmen, the first Mignon. She made her debut in Strasbourg in 1859 and as Serpina at the Comique in 1862.

Galuppi, Baldassare *Composer*
b. Burano, Italy, 1706: d. Venice, 1785
Called the father of Opera Buffa, Galuppi wrote one hundred twelve operas, twenty oratorios, music for the harpischord, and so on.
Dorinda   1729
Didone Abbandonata   1752
Il Re Pastore   1762
Ifigenia in Tauride   1768

García, Eugénie *Soprano*
(*Née* Mayer)
b. Paris, 1818: d. there, 1880
The wife of Manuel Patricio García. She made her debut at the Opéra-Comique in 1842.

García, Gustave *Baritone*
b. Milan, 1837: d. London, 1925
The son of Manuel Patricio García. He sang Don Giovanni, among other roles.

García, Manuel del Pópolo Vicente
Tenor
b. Seville, 1775: d. Paris, 1832
The first Almaviva; one might also refer to him as the first García, in honor of the family he founded. Two of his daughters, Maria Malibran and Viardot-García became internationally famous. His son Manuel Patricio was one of the great teachers of singing. Manuel himself produced the first Italian opera in America, opening in New York with *Il Barbiere di Siviglia* on 29 November 1825. When he first sang Almaviva in that opera's Italian premiere, he appeared with a guitar to sing a Spanish song of his own suggestion. The guitar had lost a string, and thus began a chain of events that culminated with a demonstration in the audience against the whole opera. Rossini quickly replaced the Spanish song with the famous *Ecco Ridente in Cielo*, in time to save his reputation.
García also composed many an opera for his troupe.

García, Manuel Patricio Rodriguez
Bass
b. Madrid, 1805: d. London, 1906
Inventor of the laryngoscope, and a famous teacher of singing. He taught at the Royal Academy of Music in London from 1848 to 1895. Among his pupils was the celebrated Jenny Lind. He was the son of Manuel del Pópolo Vicente García and sang in his father's company for

a short while, singing Leporello and Figaro (*Il Barbiere di Siviglia*).

Garden, Mary   *Soprano*
b. Aberdeen, Scotland, 1877:
The first Camille in an opera by Hamilton Forrest commissioned by her. The first Mélisande. In the latter role her appearance caused Maeterlinck, the author of the play, to break with Debussy. Maeterlinck had expected his mistress to be the star. Mary Garden made her debut on particularly short notice as Louise at the Opéra-Comique in 1900, substituting for Rioton. She made her Manhattan debut, as Thaïs, in 1907 and in Chicago in 1910. She was manager of the Chicago Opera from 1921 to 1922.

     Camille, Carmen, Dulcinée, Jean (*Le Jongleur de Notre Dame*), Louise, Manon, Marguérite (*Faust*), Mélisande, Salome, Sapho, Thaïs.

Garrison, Mabel   *Soprano*
b. Baltimore, 1886:
She made her debut in Boston in 1912, playing Philine in *Mignon*. She joined the Metropolitan in 1914 and sang there until 1922.

Gassier, Édouard   *Baritone*
b. 1820: d. Havana, 1872
     Ambrose (*Mireille*), Assur, Figaro (*Il Barbiere di Siviglia*), Figaro (*Le Nozze di Figaro*), Don Beltrano (*L'Oca del Cairo*), Ferrando (*Il Trovatore*), Laertes (*Mignon*), Malatesta (*Don Pasquale*), Fra Melitone, Méphistophélès (*Faust*), Page (*Die Lustigen Weiber von Windsor*), Pirro (*I Lombardi*), Count Rodolpho, Thoas (*Iphigénie en Tauride*).

Gatti, Gabriele   *Soprano*
b.
     Euridice (*La Favola d'Orfeo*), Marguérite (*La Damnation de Faust*), Marie (*Wozzeck*).

Gatti-Casazza, Guilio   *Manager*
b. Udine, Italy, 1868: d. Ferrara, 1940

Director of La Scala from 1898 to 1908, General Manager of the Metropolitan from 1908 until 1935. He was instrumental in bringing out new works and operas not before heard in the United States. It was he who brought Toscanini to the Metropolitan. In 1910 he married Frances Alda, but they were divorced in 1929.

Gatty, Nicholas Comyn   *Composer*
b. Bradford, England, 1874: d. London, 1946

Greysteel	London	1906
Duke or Devil	,,	1909
Prince Ferelon	,,	1919
The Tempest	,,	1920
Macbeth		

Gaubert, Philippe   *Composer*
b. Cahors, France, 1879:
Best known for his music for the flute, of which he is an accomplished player. He has also conducted opera, notably *Alceste* at Covent Garden in 1937.

Sonia	Nantes	1913
Naïla	Paris	1927

Gavazzeni, Gianandrea   *Conductor*
b. Bergamo, 1909:
A composer of music for orchestra, chamber orchestra and so forth. He has conducted at La Scala and Chicago.

Gay, John   *Librettist*
b. Devon, England, 1685: d. London, 1732
His association with Rich, in the production of *The Beggar's Opera*, led to the famous remark that the work made "Gay rich and Rich gay." His attempt, again with the composer/editor Pepusch, to ride the crest of the wave with a sequel, *Polly*, was unsuccessful.

The Beggar's Opera	London	1728
Black Eyed Susan		
Polly	London	1777

Gay, Maria   *Contralto*
b. Barcelona, 1879: d. New York, 1943

While in prison for her part in a political demonstration, she took up the study of the violin. This led to a general study of music and finally to singing, which she learned by herself. She made her debut in Brussels in 1902 as Carmen, and at the Metropolitan in 1908 in the same role. She sang in Boston, 1910 to 1912, and in Chicago until 1927. In 1913 she married Giovanni Zenatello.

Azucena, Brangäne, Carmela (*I Gioielli della Madonna*), Carmen, Charlotte, Dalila, Geneviève (*Pelléas et Mélisande*), Maddalena (*Rigoletto*), Mother (*Louise*), Orfeo, Suzuki.

Gazzaniga, Giuseppe *Composer*
b. Verona, 1743: d. Crema, 1818
He wrote a total of fifty operas. *Il Finto Cieco* was to a libretto by Lorenzo da Ponte.

Il Finto Cieco	Vienna	1770
Il Convietato di Pietro		1787

Gedda, Nicolai *Tenor*
b.
Flamand (*Capriccio*), Hoffmann, Don Narciso (*Il Turco in Italia*), Don Ottavio, Pinkerton, Tamino.

Genée, Franz Richard *Composer*
b. Danzig, 1823: d. Vienna, 1895
A composer of operettas. Together with Haffner he wrote the libretto for *Die Fledermaus*.

Der Geiger aus Tirol	1857
Der Musikfiend	1862

German, Edward *Composer*
(*Originally* Edward German Jones)
b. Whitechurch, 1862: d. 1936

The Rival Poets	London	1886
The Emerald Isle (*with Arthur Sullivan*)	„	1901
Merrie England	„	1902
A Princess of Kensington	„	1903
Tom Jones	„	1907

Gershwin, George *Composer*
b. Brooklyn, N.Y., 1898: d. Beverly Hills, Calif., 1937
A songwriter of spectacular success, the composer of *Embraceable You, Of Thee I Sing, Rhapsody in Blue*, and so forth. He wrote a large number of Broadway shows such as *Lady Be Good, Funny Face, Girl Crazy*. His style was so thoroughly developed that it became the Broadway style. His single opera has achieved a tremendous success throughout the world, although Europeans tend to see it as a tour de force, and some Americans as too simple an imitation of Negro music.

Porgy and Bess	Boston	1935

Gerster, Etelka *Soprano*
b. Kschau, Hungary, 1855: d. near Bologna, 1920
She made her debut as Gilda in Venice, 1876. In 1877 she sang for the first time in London, as Amina, and in 1878 in New York in the same role.

Amina, Elvira (*I Puritani*), Gilda, Lucia, Ophélie.

Gerster, Ottmar *Composer*
b. Braunfels, 1897:

Liselotte	Essen	1933
Enoch Arden	Düsseldorf	1936
Die Hexe von Passau	„	1941
Das Verzauberte Ich	„	1949

Gerville-Réache, Jeanne *Contralto*
b. Orthez, France, 1882: d. New York, 1915
A pupil of Viardot-Garcia, she made her debut as Orfeo at the Comique in 1900. She was the first Geneviève (*Pelléas et Mélisande*), and the first Katherine (*Le Juif Polonais*).

Gevaert, François Auguste *Composer*
b. Huysse, Belgium, 1828: d. Brussels, 1908
Not only a composer of orchestral

music, choral music and opera, but also the author of books of history of music and of orchestration.

Georgette	1852
Le Billet de Marguerite	1854
Quentin Durward	1858
Le Diable au Moulin	1859
Les Deux Amours	1861
Le Capitaine Henriot	1861

Ghedini, Giorgio Federico　　*Composer*
b. Cuneo, Italy, 1892:

Maria d'Alessandria	Bergamo	1937
Re Hassan	Venice	1939
La Pulce d'Oro	Genoa	1940
La Baccanti	Milan	1948
Billy Budd	Venice	1949
L'Ipocrita Felice	Milan	1956

Ghislanzoni, Antonio　　*Librettist*
b. Lecco, Italy, 1824: d. Caprino, 1893
　Besides *Aida*, he wrote nearly sixty libretti. But he was also a baritone, and made his debut in Lodi, 1846.

Giannini, Dusolina　　*Soprano*
b. Philadelphia, 1902:
　The sister of Vittorio Giannini, she studied with Sembrich and made her debut at Carnegie Hall in New York in 1925. In 1927 she sang in her first opera, at Hamburg, Germany, and in 1936 at the Metropolitan as Aida.
　Aida, Carmen, Cio-cio San, Hester Prynne (*The Scarlet Letter* by her brother), Maliella (*I Gioielli della Madonna*).

Giannini, Vittorio　　*Composer*
b. Philadelphia, 1903:
　Brother of Dusolina Giannini, and a composer of much music for orchestra and for voice.

Lucedia	Munich	1934
Flora		1937
The Scarlet Letter	Hamburg	1938
Beauty and the Beast	(radio)	1938
Blennerhasset	,,	1939
The Taming of the Shrew	TV	1954

Gibbs, Cecil Armstrong　　*Composer*
b. near Chelmsford, England, 1889:

The Blue Peter	1924
Twelfth Night	1947
The Great Bell of Burley (*for children*)	1949

Gigli, Beniamino　　*Tenor*
b. Recanati, Italy, 1890: d. Rome, 1957
　Well known in the United States not only for his operatic roles on the stage, but also for his appearances in films. He made his debut at the Metropolitan as Faust in *Mefistofele* in 1920, and stayed until 1932.
　Alfredo (*La Traviata*), Don Alvaro, Andrea Chénier, Avito (*L'Amore dei Tre Re*), Canio, Duke (*Rigoletto*), des Grieux (*Manon*), des Grieux (*Manon Lescaut*), Lionel, Lohengrin, Milio (*Zaza*), Mylio (*Le Roi d'Ys*), Nemerino, Osaka (*Iris*), Riccardo (*Un Ballo in Maschera*), Rodolfo, Romeo, Ruggero (*La Rondine*), Vasco da Gama, Wilhelm (*Mignon*).

Gilardi, Gilardo　　*Composer*
b. San Fernando, Argentina, 1889:

Ilse	Buenos Aires	1923
La Legenda de Urutaú	,,	1934

Gilbert, William Schwenck　　*Librettist*
b. London, 1836: d. Middlesex, 1911
　In twenty years' association with Arthur Sullivan (*q.v.*), Sir William Gilbert produced some of the most famous operetta libretti ever played. He was knighted in 1907.

Giordano, Umberto　　*Composer*
b. Foggia, 1867: d. Milan, 1948

Mala Vita	Rome	1892
Regina Diaz	,,	1894
Andrea Chénier	La Scala	1896
Fedora	Milan	1898
Siberia	La Scala	1903
Marcella	Milan	1907
Mese Mariano	Palermo	1910
Madame Sans-Gêne	Metropolitan	1915

Giove a Pompeii	Rome	1921
La Cena delle Beffe	La Scala	1924
Il Re	La Scala	1929

Giraldoni, Eugenio *Baritone*
b. Marseilles, 1871: d. Helsinki, 1924
The first Scarpia. He made his debut
in Barcelona as Don José in 1891.

Giraudet, Alfred Auguste *Bass*
b. Étampes, Belgium, 1845: d. New
York, 1911
A teacher of opera in New York. He
made his debut as Méphistophélès (*Faust*)
at Paris in 1868.

Glanville-Hicks, Peggy *Composer*
b. Melbourne, 1912:
A pupil of Vaughan Williams.
Caedmon
The Transposed Heads
                     Louisville, Ky.   1954

Glaz, Herta *Contralto*
b. Vienna, 1914:
She made her debut at Breslau and
appeared for the first time at the Metropolitan in 1942 as Amneris.
    Annina (*Der Rosenkavalier*), Maddalena,
Magdalene (*Die Meistersinger*), Mercedes
(*Carmen*), Shepherd (*Tosca*), Siegrune.

Glazunov, Alexander Constantinovitch
                                  Composer
b. St. Petersburg, 1865: d. Paris, 1936
    Although he wrote no operas of his
own, Glazunov helped complete *Prince
Igor* after Borodin's death.

Glière, Reinhold Moritzovitch
                                  Composer
b. Kiev, 1875: d. Moscow, 1956
    He is best known in the United
States for selections, particularly the
Sailors' Dance, from his ballet *The Red
Poppy*.
    Shah Senem   Baku 1927

Glinka, Mikhail Ivanovitch *Composer*
b. Smolensk, 1803: d. Berlin, 1857

Ivan Susanin (*A Life*		
for the Tsar)	St. Petersburg	1836
Russlan and		
Ludmilla	„	1842

Gluck, Alma *Soprano*
(*Really* Reba Fiersohn)
b. Bucharest, 1886: d. New York, 1938
    Alma Gluck sang in opera from 1909,
when she made her debut at the Metropolitan as Sophie (*Werther*), until 1912
when she retired. She had also sung
Armide and Mimi.

Gluck, Christoph Willibald Ritter von
                                  Composer
b. Bavaria, 1714: d. Vienna, 1787
    One of the greatest composers of opera
and a continuing influence upon other
composers. Gluck had written for years
in the accepted Italian style before, with
Orfeo, he rebelled against it and produced
a kind of choral opera which he considered
nearer to what musical drama should be.
He outlined his ideas in the preface to his
next work, *Alceste*, and then moved to
Paris where his arrival and his ideas
stirred up a war between those who
agreed with him and those who did not.
The dissenters rallied around the name of
the unfortunate Piccini and thus the battle
of the Gluckists and Piccinists was joined.
It ended in a resounding triumph for
Gluck when Piccini was prevailed upon to
write an *Iphigénie en Tauride* to replace
Gluck's. Because of a number of ludicrous
troubles at the opening and the inebriation
of the prima donna, the replacement was
howled down. Gluck changed the face of
opera by deleting the harpsichord, adding
clarinets, trombones, harps and percussion,
throwing out so-called *secco recitatif*,
simplifying the aria and using the chorus as
characters with legitimately choral music.

Artaserse	Milan	1741
Orfeo ed Euridice	Vienna	1762
Alcestis	„	1767
Paride ed Elena	„	1770

Iphigénie en Aulide	Paris	1774
Armide	,,	1777
Iphigénie en Tauride	,,	1779

Gnecchi, Vittorio *Composer*
b. Milan, 1876: d. there, 1954

Virtù d'Amore		1896
Cassandra	Bologna	1905
La Rosiera (*written* 1910)		1927

Gobbi, Tito *Baritone*
b. Bassano del Grappo, Italy, 1915:
Gobbi made his debut at Rome in 1938, then in San Francisco in 1948 and at the Metropolitan as Scarpia in 1956.

Amonasro, Falstaff (*Falstaff*), Figaro (*Il Barbiere di Siviglia*), Giorgio Germont, Méphistophélès (*La Damnation de Faust*), Pimen, Renato (*Un Ballo in Maschera*), Rigoletto, Scarpia, Simon Boccanegra, Tonio, Wozzeck.

Godard, Benjamin Louis Paul
Composer
b. Paris, 1849: d. Cannes, 1895
Godard is chiefly remembered for the *Berceuse* from *Jocelyn*.

Les Bijoux de Jeannette		1878
Pedro de Zalamea	Antwerp	1884
Jocelyn	Brussels	1888
Dante	Comique	1890
La Vivandière	Paris	1895
Les Guelphs	Rouen	1902

Goedicke, Alexander Fedorovitch
Composer
b. Moscow, 1877: d. there, 1957

| At the Crossing | 1933 |
| Jacquerie | 1937 |

Goetz, Hermann *Composer*
b. Königsberg, 1840: d. near Zürich, 1876

Der Widerspenstigen Zähmung (*The Taming of the Shrew*)		
	Mannheim	1874
Francesca da Rimini (*Completed by Ernest Frank.*)	,,	1877

Goldberg, Theo *Composer*
b. Chemnitz, Germany, 1921:

| Minotauros | | |
| Schwere Zeiten für Engel | Berlin | 1952 |

Goldmark, Karl *Composer*
b. Készthely, Hungary, 1830: d. Vienna, 1915
Goldmark worked on his only opera that is still remembered, *The Queen of Sheba*, for ten years.

Die Königin von Saba	Vienna	1875
Merlin	,,	1886
Das Heimchen am Herd (*The Cricket on the Hearth*)	,,	1896
Die Kriegsgefangene	,,	1899
Götz von Berlichingen	Budapest	1902
Ein Wintermärchen (*A Winter's Tale*)	Vienna	1908

Goldovsky, Boris *Conductor*
b. Moscow, 1908:
Founder and director of the New England Opera Theater in 1946, and of the opera workshop at Tanglewood, Lenox, Massachusetts.

Goltz, Christel *Soprano*
b. Dortmund, Germany:
The first Penelope in Liebermann's opera in Salzburg, 1954.

Agathe, Aida, Amelia, Antigonae (*Antigonae*, by Carl Orff), Ariadne (*Ariadne auf Naxos*), Desdemona, Elisabeth, Eva, Fiordiligi, Jenufa, Leonora (*Fidelio*), Marie (*Wozzeck*), Musetta, Octavian, Penelope (Liebermann), Rezia, Salome, Santuzza, Tosca.

Gomez, Antonio Carlos *Composer*
b. Compinas, Brazil, 1836: d. Parà, Belém, 1896

Noite do Castillo	Rio de Janeiro	1861
Joanna de Flandres	,,	1863
Il Guarany	La Scala	1870

Salvator Rosa	Genoa	1874
Maria Tudor	La Scala	1879
Lo Schiavo	Rio de Janeiro	1889
Condor	La Scala	1891

Goossens, Eugene III *Composer*
b. London, 1893:
Conducted the Rochester Philharmonic Orchestra from 1923 to 1930, the Cincinnati Symphony from 1931 to 1946 and in Sydney, Australia, 1947–1956.

Judith	Covent Garden	1929
Don Juan	„	1937

Gorin, Igor *Baritone*
b. Ukraine, 1908:
Not only a singer, but a composer of songs.

Goritz, Otto *Baritone*
b. Berlin, 1873: d. Hamburg, 1929
He made his debut as Matteo in Neustrelitz, 1895, and at the Metropolitan as Klingsor in 1903.

Gotovac, Jakov *Composer*
b. Split, Yugoslavia, 1895:

Morana	Brno	1930
Ero s onoga Svijeta	Zagreb	1935
Kámenik	„	1946
Mila Gojsalica	„	1952

Gounod, Charles François *Composer*
b. Paris, 1818: d. there, 1893
One of his most widely known works is the vocal line he added to the first Prelude of Bach's *Well-Tempered Clavichord*, making an *Ave Maria*.

Sapho	Opéra	1851
Faust	Paris	1859
Mireille	„	1864
Philémon et Baucis	„	1860
La Reine de Saba	„	1862
Roméo et Juliette	„	1867

Grad, Gabriel *Composer*
b. near Kovno, Lithuania, 1890:
Living in Tel Aviv since 1924.
Judith and Holofernes

Graener, Paul *Composer*
b. Berlin, 1872: d. Salzburg, 1944
Don Juans Letztes

Abenteuer	Leipzig	1914
Theophano	Munich	1918
Schirrin und Gertaude	Dresden	1920
Hanneles Himmelfahrt	„	1927
Friedemann Bach	Schwerin	1931
Der Prinz von Hamburg		
	Berlin	1935
Schwanhild	Cologne	1941

Graf, Herbert *Stage Director*
b. Vienna, 1904:
Directed at the Philadelphia Grand Opera from 1934 to 1935, then at the Metropolitan. In 1949 he became head of the opera department of the Curtis Institute in Philadelphia.

Granados, Enrique *Composer*
b. Lérida, Catalonia, 1867: d. at sea, 1916
Granados had attended the opening of his *Goyescas* at the Metropolitan and was en route to Europe when his ship was torpedoed by a German submarine in the English Channel.

María del Carmen	Madrid	1898
Picarol	Barcelona	1901
Follet	„	1903
Gaziel	„	1906
Liliana	„	1911
Goyescas	Metropolitan	1916

Grandi, Margherita *Soprano*
b.
Elisabeth (*Don Carlos*), Lady Macbeth, Maria (*Friedenstag*), Oscar, Tosca.

Grau, Maurice *Manager*
b. Brünn, Austria, 1849: d. Paris, 1907
Manager at the Metropolitan from 1883 to 1884, then 1891 to 1903 (intermittently).

Graziani, Lodovico *Tenor*
b. Fermo, Italy, 1823: d. there, 1855
The first Alfredo (*Traviata*); it is worth noting that he was hoarse at the opening. Don Carlos, Radames.

Grétry, André Ernest Modeste
Composer
b. Liège, 1741: d. Montmorency, 1813
One of the great composers of opera and religious music. Even his daughter Lucille composed two operas.

Zémire et Azor	Fontainebleau	1771
Céphale et Procris	Versailles	1773
Richard Coeur de Lion	Paris	1784
Anacréon chez Polycrate	,,	1793
La Rosière Républicaine	,,	1794

Grisi, Giuditta
Mezzo-soprano
b. Milan, 1805: d. near Cremona, 1840
The first Romeo (*I Capuletti ed I Montecchi*). She made her debut in Vienna in 1823.

Grisi, Giulia
Soprano
b. Milan, 1811: d. Berlin, 1869
The first Elvira (*I Puritani*), the first Norina (*Don Pasquale*), Adalgisa (*Norma*) and Juliette (*I Capuletti ed I Montecchi*). She made her debut as Emma in Rossini's *Zelmira* in 1828. In 1832 she appeared as Semiramide in Paris, and in 1834 as Ninetta (*La Gazza Ladra*) in London. She married the tenor Mario in 1844.

Griswold, Putnam
Bass
b. Minneapolis, 1875: d. New York, 1914
He made his debut in Berlin in 1904 and at the Metropolitan, singing Hagen, in 1911.
Beckmesser, Daland, Gurnemanz, Hagan, Hans Sachs, Henry the Fowler, Hermann (*Tannhäuser*), Hunding, King Marke, Paolo Orsini, Pogner, Wotan.

Grob-Prandl, Gertrude
Soprano
b.
Amelia, Brünnhilde, Isolde, Turandot.

Gruenberg, Louis
Composer
b. near Brest-Litovsk, Poland, 1884:
A pupil of Busoni, he also wrote orchestral and vocal music.

The Witch of Brocken	1912
The Bride of the Gods	1913

The Mute Wife		1921
Jack and the Beanstalk		
	New York	1931
The Emperor Jones	,,	1933
Queen Helena		1936
Green Mansions	CBS radio	1937
Volpone		1937

Gruhn, Nora
Soprano
b. London, 1908:
She made her debut at Covent Garden in 1931 and at Sadlers Wells, 1946.

Guadagni, Gaetano
(Male) Contralto
b. Lodi, 1725: d. 1785 (?)
The first Orfeo, and a very famous singer. Gluck wrote the part for him, as did Handel in writing Samson. Guadagni also composed arias.

Guarnieri, Carmago
Conductor
b. São Paulo, Brazil, 1907:
A conductor of opera and a composer of songs, piano music and music for the orchestra.

Guarrera, Frank
Baritone
b.
Escamillo, Figaro (*Il Barbiere di Siviglia*), Guglielmo (*Così fan Tutte*), Lescaut (*Manon Lescaut*), Manfredo (*L'Amore dei Tre Re*), Marcello, Tonio.

Gudehus, Heinrich
Tenor
b. Hanover, 1845: d. Dresden, 1909
The second person to sing Parsifal, there being three who alternated in the opening performances. He made his debut in Berlin in 1871.
Parsifal, Tamino, Tristan, Walther.

Gueden, Hilde
Soprano
b. Vienna, 1917:
She made her debut in Munich as Zerlina (*Don Giovanni*), in 1939, and at the Metropolitan as Gilda in 1951.
Amor, Anne Trulove, Cherubino, Despina, Fiordiligi, Gilda, Ilia (*Idomeneo*), Lucretia (*The Rape of Lucretia*), Micaela, Mimi, Musetta, Norina (*Don Pasquale*),

227

Rosalinda (*Die Fledermaus*), Sophie (*Der Rosenkavalier*), Susanna (*Le Nozze di Figaro*), Zerlina (*Don Giovanni*).

Guerre, Michel La *Composer*
b. Paris, 1605: d. there 1679
Composer of what is probably the earliest French opera.

| Le Triomphe de l'Amour sur Bergers et Bergères | The Louvre | 1655 |

Guerrini, Guido *Composer*
b. Faenza, 1890:

Zalebi		1915
Nemici	Bologna	1921
La Vigna	Rome	1935
Enea	,,	1953

Gui, Vittorio *Conductor*
b. Rome, 1885:
He conducted memorable performances at Florence and Edinburgh. He is also a composer.

| Fata Malerba | Turin | 1927 |

Guiraud, Ernst *Composer*
b. New Orleans, 1837: d. Paris, 1892
A friend of Bizet, he composed the recitatives for *Carmen*'s performances outside the Opéra-Comique. He also completed the orchestration of *Les Contes d'Hoffmann*. Saint-Saëns completed Guiraud's *Frédégonde*.

En Prison	Paris	1869
Le Kobold	,,	1870
Madame Turlepin	,,	1872
Piccolino	,,	1876
Galante Aventure	,,	1882
Frédégonde	,,	1895

Gulbranson, Ellen *Soprano*
(*Née* Norgren)
b. Stockholm, 1863: d. Oslo, 1947
She made her debut at Stockholm in 1889. She was famous in the following roles:
Amneris, Brünnhilde, Kundry.

Gundry, Inglis *Composer*
b. London, 1905:
A pupil of Ralph Vaughan Williams.

Naaman	1938
The Return of Odysseus	1941
The Partisans	1946
Aron	1949

Gura, Eugen *Bass-baritone*
b. Bohemia, 1842: d. Bavaria, 1906
He made his debut in Munich in 1865.
Amfortas, Barber (*Der Barbier von Bagdad*), Donnor, Gunther, Hans Sachs, King Marke, Lysiart (*Euryanthe*), Minister (*Fidelio*).

Guridi, Jesús *Composer*
b. Vittoria, Spain, 1886:

Mirentxu		
Amaya	Bilbao	1920
La Meiga	Madrid	1928

Gurlitt, Manfred *Composer*
b. Berlin, 1890:
A pupil of Humperdinck, a composer of opera, orchestral and chamber music and a conductor.

Die Heilige	Bremen	1920
Wozzeck (*see also* Berg, Alban)	,,	1926
Soldaten		1929
Nana		1933
Seguidilla Bolero		1937

Gutheil-Schoder, Marie *Mezzo-soprano*
b. Weimar, 1874: d. there, 1935
She made her debut at Weimar in 1891. In 1926 she was appointed stage manager at Vienna.
Carmen, Elektra, Louise, Octavian, Salome.

Gyrowetz, Adalbert *Composer*
b. Bohemia, 1763: d. Vienna, 1850
He wrote about thirty operas.

Agnes Sorel	1806
Der Augenarzt	1811
Helene	1816

Haas, Joseph *Composer*
b. Maihingen, Germany, 1879:
Tobias Wunderlich   Kassel   1937
Die Hochzeit des Jobs   Dresden   1944

Hába, Alois *Composer*
b. Moravia, 1893:
Hába is one of the foremost proponents of microtones, and all his operas have been written in that system, as have his works for special pianos and chamber groups.
Die Mutter   Munich   1931
Nová Země   1935
Thy Kingdom Come   1940

Hába, Karel *Composer*
b. Moravia, 1898:
Brother of Alois Hába, but although interested in microtones, he has written his major works in conventional scales.
Janošík   Prague   1934

Hackett, Charles *Tenor*
b. Worcester, Mass., 1889: d. New York, 1942
He made his debut in Genoa, then appeared in 1919 as the Count in *Il Barbiere di Siviglia* at the Metropolitan.

Hadley, Henry Kimball *Composer*
b. Somerville, Mass., 1871: d. New York, 1937
A pupil of G. W. Chadwick. He was also a conductor at Seattle in 1909, in San Francisco from 1911 to 1915, with the New York Philharmonic until 1922, and with the Manhattan Symphony from 1929 to 1932.
Safie   Mainz   1909
The Atonement
of Pan   San Francisco   1912
Azora   Chicago   1917
Nancy Brown
Bianca   New York   1918
Cleopatra's Night   Metropolitan   1918
A Night in Old Paris   1925

Hageman, Richard *Composer*
b. Leeuwarden, Netherlands, 1882:

A writer of songs and conductor at the Metropolitan from 1908 to 1926.
Caponsacchi   Freiburg   1932
The Crucible   Los Angeles   1943

Hahn, Reynaldo *Composer*
b. Caracas, 1875: d. Paris, 1947
A pupil of Massenet.
L'île du Rêve   Comique   1898
La Carmelite   ,,   1902
Fête Triomphante   Opéra   1919
Nausicaa   Monte Carlo   1919
La Colombe de Buddha   Cannes   1921
Ciboulette   Paris   1923
Le Marchand de Venise   Opéra   1935
Malvina   Paris   1935

Halász, László *Conductor*
b. Debrecen, Hungary, 1905:
Conductor at Budapest, Prague, Vienna, and beginning in 1939 at St. Louis. From 1943 to 1951 he conducted the New York City Opera Company.

Halévy, Jacques François Fromental Elie *Composer*
(*Originally* Lévy)
b. Paris, 1799: d. Nice, 1862
Gounod was his pupil. Bizet was his pupil also, and became his son-in-law.
La Juive   Opéra   1835
L'Éclair   Opéra   1835

Halévy, Ludovic *Librettist*
b. Paris, 1834: d. there, 1908
With Meilhac he wrote the libretti of *Carmen*, *La Belle Hélène*, *La Vie Parisienne*, and *La Grande Duchesse de Gérolstein*. With Crémieux he wrote *Les Contes d'Hoffmann*.

Hamerik, Asger *Composer*
b. Copenhagen, 1843: d. Fredericksborg, 1923
A pupil of Berlioz and himself a teacher. From 1872 to 1898 he was director of the Peabody Conservatory in Baltimore.
Tovelille   Paris   1865
Hjalmar und Ingeborg

| La Vendetta | Milan | 1870 |
| Der Reisende | | |

Hamerik, Ebbe   *Composer*
b. Copenhagen, 1898:
Son of Asger Hamerik. A writer of
orchestral and piano music and songs.

Stepan	Mainz	1924
Leonardo da Vinci	Antwerp	1939
Marie Grubbe	Copenhagen	1940
Rejsekammeraten	,,	1946

Hamlin, George   *Tenor*
b. Elgin, Ill., 1868: d. New York, 1923
He made his debut in Philadelphia in
1911.
Don José, Mario.

Hammerstein, Oscar   *Manager*
b. Stettin, Germany, 1846: d. New York,
1919
Hammerstein made his money in the
cigar-making business. He invented a
machine for the process in 1868. In 1906
he established the Manhattan Opera
House, which became a very serious rival
of the Metropolitan. In 1908 he did the
same thing in Philadelphia. In 1910 the
Metropolitan got rid of the threat by
buying him out.

Handel, Georg Friedrich   *Composer*
b. Halle, Germany, 1685: d. London,
1759
The great German composer of oratorios and operas, a contemporary of
J. S. Bach. He studied in Italy and settled
in England, becoming famous there in the
reign of George the First, who had been
his patron as the Elector of Hannover in
Germany. Handel wrote in all forms.
Oratorio was his favorite. Perhaps it
eventually served him as a substitute for
opera. His style was uproariously satirized in *The Beggar's Opera* by the un-
authorized use of a march from *Rinaldo*
as the March of the Thieves.

| Almira (*his first*) | Hamburg | 1705 |
| Agrippina | ,, | 1709 |

Rinaldo	London	1711
Il Pastor Fido (*first version*)	,,	1712
Scipione	,,	1726
Partenope	,,	1730
Il Pastor Fido (*second version*)	,,	1734
Serse	,,	1738
Deidamia (*his last*)	,,	1741

Hanson, Howard Harold   *Composer*
b. Wahoo, Nebr., 1896:
An advocate of American music,
founder of the National Association of
American Composers and Conductors.
He was director of the Eastman School of
Music from 1924.

| Merry Mount | Metropolitan | 1934 |

(*Commissioned by the Metropolitan*)

Harling, William Franke   *Composer*
b. London, 1887: d. Sierra Madre, Calif.,
1958

A Light from St. Agnes		
	Chicago	1925
Deep River	New York	1926

Harman, Carter   *Composer*
b. Brooklyn, 1918:
Charms for the Savage

Harrell, Mack   *Baritone*
b. Celeste, Tex., 1909: d. Dallas, Tex.,
1960
He made his debut at the Metropolitan
in 1939 but later became a teacher at
Southern Methodist University. He also
taught at the Juilliard School of Music.
Nick Shadow, Kothner, Samson

Harrison, Lou   *Composer*
b. Portland, Oregon, 1917:
A pupil of Henry Cowell and Arnold
Schönberg.

| Rapunzel | New York | 1959 |

Harsányi, Tibor   *Composer*
b. Magyarkanizsa, Hungary, 1898: d.
Paris, 1954

| Illusion | Paris (Radio) | 1949 |
| Les Invités | Gera, Ger. | 1930 |

Harshaw, Margaret *Contralto, then Soprano*
b. Narbeth, Penna, 1912:
At first a contralto, she made her debut at the Metropolitan in 1942. In 1950 she came out as a soprano.
Amneris, Donna Anna, Azucena, Brünnhilde, Elisabeth, Isolde, Kundry, Ortrud.

Hart, Frederick Patton *Composer*
b. Aberdeen, Wash. 1898:

The Wheel of Fortune	1934
The Romance of the Robot	1937

Hartmann, Carl *Tenor*
b. Solingen, 1895:
He made his debut as Tannhäuser at Elberfeld in 1928. His first appearance at the Metropolitan was in 1937, as Siegfried. He has also sung Tristan.

Hartmann, John Peder Emilius *Composer*
b. Copenhagen, 1805: d. there, 1900

The Raven	Copenhagen	1832
The Corsairs	„	1835
Little Christina	„	1846

Hartmann, Karl Amadeus *Composer*
b. Munich, 1905:

Des Simplicius Simplicissimus Jugend	Cologne	1949

Hastreiter, Helene *Contralto*
b. Louisville, Ky. 1858: d. Varese, Italy, 1922
Dalila, Euridice, Orfeo, Ortrud, Senta

Hauer, Josef Matthias *Composer*
b. Vienna, 1883: d. there, 1959
A theorist of the dodecaphonic school.

Salammbo	1930
Die Schwarze Spinne	1931

Haug, Hans *Composer*
b. Basel, 1900:
A pupil of Ernst Lévy.

Don Juan in der Freunde	Basel	1930

Madrisa	Basel	1934
Tartuffe	„	1937
Der Spiegel del Agrippina		1944
Le Malade Imaginaire	Zürich	1947

Hauk, Minnie *Mezzo-soprano*
(*Née* Hauck)
b. New York, 1852: d. near Lucerne, Switzerland, 1929
Said to have had a repertory of one hundred roles, she made her debut as Amina in Brooklyn in 1866. It was she who produced the first *Cavalleria Rusticana* in Chicago.
Aida, Amina, Carmen, Inez (*L'Africaine*), Juliette, Lucia, Manon, Marguérite (*Faust*), Norma, Zerlina.

Haydn, Franz Joseph *Composer*
b. Rohrau, Austria, 1732: d. Vienna, 1809.
The "father of the symphony," Haydn was one of the most prolific of the great composers. He wrote about one hundred fifty symphonies, some of which his wife chose to burn up, leaving one hundred four. He also, however, turned out one singspiel, four Italian comedies, fourteen buffe, five musical plays for marionettes, pieces for mechanical clocks (one of which machines he is known to have built himself), and many, many more. Haydn had the benefit of a complete musical and theatrical establishment under his direction at the magnificient court of Esterház. This included even a marionette theater, of which he was especially fond. Some of his operas were:

L'Infedeltà Delusa	Esterház	1773
Philémon et Baucis	„	1773
La Vera Costanza	„	1776
La Fedeltà Premiata	„	1780
Ritter Roland	„	1782
Armida	„	1783
L'Isola Disabitata	„	1785
Orfeo	„	1791

Heger, Robert   *Composer*
b. Strasbourg, 1886:
He composed in many forms. He also conducted at Strasbourg, Nuremberg, Vienna, Berlin, and Munich.

Ein Fest auf Haderslev		
	Nuremberg	1919
Der Bettler Namelos	Munich	1932
Der Verlorene Sohn	Dresden	1936
Lady Hamilton	Nuremberg	1951

Helm, Everett   *Composer*
b. Minneapolis, 1913:
A pupil of Malipiero and Vaughan Williams.

Adam and Eve	Wiesbaden	1951
The Siege of Tottenburg		
	Radio (Germany)	1956

Hempel, Frieda   *Soprano*
b. Leipzig, 1885: d. Berlin, 1955
She made her debut in Berlin in 1905 and appeared at the Metropolitan for the first time in 1912 as the Queen in *Les Huguenots*.

Amelia, Antonia, Constanze, Countess Almaviva, Euryanthe, Eva, Fiordiligi, Gilda, Giulietta (*Les Contes d'Hoffmann*), Leila, Lucia, Martha, Mimi, Olympia, Pamina, Queen (*Les Huguenots*) Rosina, Violetta.

Henneberg, Albert   .   *Composer*
b. Stockholm, 1901:
Inka
Bolla och Badin
I Madonnas Skugga

Henriques, Fini Valdemar   *Composer*
b. Copenhagen, 1867: d. there, 1940
A violinist and composer of ballets, orchestral and chamber music.

Staerstikkeren	Copenhagen	1922

Hensel, Heinrich   *Tenor*
b. Neustadt, 1874: d. Hamburg, 1935
He made his debut at the Metropolitan in 1911 singing Lohengrin.

Henze, Hans Werner   *Composer*
b. Güttersloh, Germany, 1926:

Das Wundertheater		
	Heidelberg	1949
Boulevard Solitude	Hanover	1952
König Hirsch	Berlin	1956

Herbert, Victor   *Composer*
b. Dublin, 1859: d. New York, 1924
Composer of many famous shows and operettas, such as *The Red Mill, Babes in Toyland*.

Natoma	Philadelphia	1911
Madeleine	Metropolitan	1913

Hérold, Louis Joseph Ferdinand
     Composer
b. Paris, 1791: d. Les Ternes, 1833

Zampa	Comique	1831
Le Pré aux Clercs	,,	1832

Herrmann, Josef   *Baritone*
b.
Wozzeck

Herrmann, Bernard   *Composer*
b. New York, 1911:

Wuthering Heights		1950

Herrmann, Hugo   *Composer*
b. Ravensburg, Germany, 1896:
Gazellenhorn
Picknick
Vasantasena
Das Wunder
Paracelsus
Der Rekord
Der Überfall
Die Heinzelmännchen

Hertog, Johannes Den   *Conductor*
b. Amsterdam, 1904:
Assistant conductor at the Concertgebouw, 1938 to 1941. Conductor of the Flemish Opera since 1948.

Hertz, Alfred   *Conductor*
b. Frankfort, 1872: d. San Francisco, 1942
He conducted the first American performance of *Parsifal*. From 1915 to

1930 he was in San Francisco. It was he who organized the summer concerts at the Hollywood Bowl.

Hertzog, Emilie *Soprano*
b. Diessenhofen, Germany, 1859: d. Aarburg, Switzerland, 1923:
She made her debut in Munich in 1880.

Hess, Ludwig *Composer*
b. Marburg, Germany, 1877: d. Berlin, 1944

Abu und Nu	Danzig	1919
Vor Edens Pforte		
Kranion	Erfurt	1933

Hewitt, James *Composer*
b. Dartmoor, England, 1770: d. Boston, 1827

Tammany	New York	1794
The Patriot	,,	1794
Columbus	,,	1799

Hidalgo, Huan *Composer*
b. circa 1600, d. Madrid, 1685
The earliest known Spanish opera composer.

Celos aún del Aire Matan		
	Madrid	1660
La Púrpura de la Rosa	,,	1660

Hillis, Margaret *Conductor*
b. Kokomo, Ind., 1921:
Although she specializes in choral conducting, she has made a point of helping to bring out the more ancient operas.

Hinckley, Allen Carter *Bass*
b. Gloucester, Mass., 1877: d. Yonkers, N.Y., 1954
He made his debut as Henry the Fowler at Hamburg, 1903.

Hindemith, Paul *Composer*
b. Hanau, 1895:
Certainly one of the great modernists and a very prolific composer of music in every conceivable form.

Mörder, Hoffnung		
der Frauen	Stuttgart	1921
Das Nusch-Nuschi	,,	1921

Sancta Susanna	Frankfurt	1922
Cardillac	Dresden,	1926
Hin und Zurück	Baden Baden	1927
Neues vom Tage	Berlin	1929
Wir Bauen eine Stadt	,,	1930
Mathis der Maler	Zürich	1938
Die Harmonie der Welt		
	Munich	1957

Hines, Jerome *Bass*
b.
His Metropolitan debut took place in 1947.
Arkel, Banquo, Don Basilio (*Il Barbiere di Siviglia*), Grand Inquisitor, Padre Guardiano, Gurnemanz, Hermann, Nick Shadow, Philip the Second, Pimen, Sparafucile.

Hinshaw, William *Baritone*
b. Union, Iowa, 1867: d. Washington, D.C., 1947
Famous as a teacher. He made his debut at St. Louis in 1899 singing Méphistophélès (*Faust*). In 1910 he appeared at the Metropolitan. He founded a school of opera in Chicago which merged with the Chicago Conservatory with Hinshaw as its president. From 1920 to 1926 he managed his own opera company.

Hislop, Joseph *Tenor*
b. Edinburg, 1887:
Alfredo, Duke (*Rigoletto*), Faust (*Faust*), Rodolfo, Romeo.

Höffding, Finn *Composer*
b. Copenhagen, 1899:

Kejserens nye Klaeder		
(*The Emperor's New Clothes*)	Copenhagen	1928
Kilderejsen	,,	1942

Höffer, Paul *Composer*
b. Barmen, Germany, 1895: d. Berlin, 1949

| Borgia | | 1931 |
| Der Falsche Waldemar | | 1934 |

Hofman, Ludwig   *Baritone*
b. Frankfurt, 1895:
He made his debut at the Metropolitan in 1932, singing Hagen.

Hofmannsthal, Hugo von   *Librettist*
b. 1874: d. 1929
One of the great librettists. *Elektra, Ariadne auf Naxos, Die Aegyptische Helene, Arabella, Der Rosenkavalier,* all were his products.

Holbrooke, Joseph Charles   *Composer*
b. London, 1878: d. London, 1958

Pierrot and Pierrette	London	1909
The Cauldron of Anwyn, *consisting of*		
The Children of Don	London	1912
Dylan	„	1913
Bronwen	Huddersfield	1929
The Wizard		1915
The Stranger		1924
The Enchanter	Chicago	1915

Hollingsworth, Stanley   *Composer*
b. Berkeley, Calif., 1924:
A pupil of Milhaud.

The Mother		1954
La Grande Bretèche	NBC	1957

Holoubek, Ladislav   *Composer*
b. Prague, 1913:

Stella	Bratislava	1939
Svitanie	„	1941
Túžba (*Desire*)	„	1944

Holst, Gustav Theodore   *Composer*
(*Originally* von Holst)
b. Cheltenham, England, 1874: d. London, 1934

Savitri	London	1916
The Perfect Fool	Covent Garden	1923
At the Boar's Head	Manchester	1925
The Wandering Scholar		1929

Homer, Louise Beatty   *Mezzo-soprano*
b. Pittsburg, 1871: d. Winter Park, Fla., 1947

She made her debut at Vichy in 1898 singing Leonora (*La Favorita*). She first appeared with the Metropolitan on tour in San Francisco in 1900 as Amneris.
Amneris, Azucena, Brangäne, Dalila, Dame Quickly, Erda, Fidés, Fricka, Laura, Leonora (*La Favorita*), Lola, Magdalene (*Die Meistersinger*), Orfeo, Ortrud, Suzuki, Waltraute, The Witch (*Hänsel und Gretel*).

Honegger, Arthur   *Composer*
b. Le Havre, 1892: d. Paris, 1955
One of "*Les Six*" known for his realistic orchestral movement, *Pacific 231.*

Judith	Monte Carlo	1926
Antigone	Brussels	1927
Les Aventures du Roi Pausole	Paris	1930
Amphion	Paris	1931
L'Aiglon (*with Ibert*)	Monte Carlo	1937
Charles le Téméraire	Mezières	1944

Hoose, Ellison van   *Tenor*
b. Murfreesboro, Tenn., 1868: d. Houston, Texas, 1936
A pupil of Jean de Reszke. He made his debut as Tannhäuser in Philadelphia in 1897.

Hopf, Hans   *Tenor*
b.
Lohengrin, Walther.

Hotter, Hans   *Baritone*
b. Offenbach, Germany, 1909:
The first Commandant (*Friedenstag*), the first Jupiter (*Liebe der Danae*). He made his debut in Prague in 1922.
Altair, Commandant, Dutchman, Hans Sachs, Jupiter, King Henry (*Lohengrin*), Hunding, Jokanaan, Kurnewal, King Marke, Pogner, La Roche (*Capriccio*), Wotan.

Howard, Kathleen   *Contralto*
b. Clifton, Ontario, 1884: d. Hollywood, 1936

A pupil of Jean de Reszke. For the period from 1928 to 1933 she was fashion editor of *Harper's Bazaar*. She made her debut at Metz in 1907 and in New York in 1914. She joined the Metropolitan in 1916 and stayed twelve years. She is said to have known eighty roles.

Hubay, Jenö (Eugen)   *Composer*
b. Budapest, 1858: d. there, 1937
Luthier de Crémone
                                    Budapest   1894

Huber, Hans   *Composer*
b. Eppenberg, Switzerland, 1852: d.
Locarno, 1921
Weltfrühling   Basel   1894
Die Schöne Bellinda   Bern   1916

Huehn, Julius   *Baritone*
b. Revere, Mass., 1910:
He made his debut at the Metropolitan in 1935 singing the Herald in *Lohengrin*.

Hugo, John Alden   *Composer*
b. Bridgeport, Conn., 1873: d. there, 1945
The Temple Dancer
                            Metropolitan   1919
The Hero of Byzanz

Humperdinck, Engelbert   *Composer*
b. near Bonn, 1854: d. Neustrelitz, 1921
Wagner's assistant and close friend. Humperdinck's sister wrote the libretto of *Hänsel und Gretel*.
Hänsel und Gretel   Weimar   1893
Dornröschen   Frankfurt 1902
Die Heirath wider willen
                              Berlin   1905
Königskinder   Metropolitan 1910
Die Marketenderin   Cologne   1914
Gaudeamus   Darmstadt 1919

Hurley, Laurel   *Soprano*
b. Allentown, Penn., 1927:
She made her debut in New York in 1952 as Zerlina at the City Center of Music and Drama. In 1955 she sang for the first time at the Metropolitan.

Clorinda (*La Cenerentola*), Gretel, Laetitia (*The Old Maid and the Thief*), Micaela, Princess Ninetta (*The Love for Three Oranges*), Oscar, Rosalinda (*Die Fledermaus*), Susanna (*Le Nozze di Figaro*), Zerlina.

Hyde, Walter   *Tenor*
b. Birmingham, 1875: d. London, 1957
He studied with Gustave Garcia.
Parsifal, Pinkerton, Siegmund, Walther.

Ibert, Jacques   *Composer*
b. Paris, 1890:
Ibert was a pupil of Fauré. He became director of the French Academy at Rome in 1937, and director of the Paris Opéra and of the Opéra-Comique in 1955. He has written much for the ballet, for voice, orchestra and small groups.
Angélique   Paris   1927
Persée et Andromède   Paris   1929
Le Roi d'Yvetot   „   1930
Gonzague   Monte Carlo   1935
L'Aiglon
(*with Honegger*)   „   1937
Les Petites Cardinal
(*with Honegger*)   Paris   1938
Barbe-Bleue   Lausanne (radio) 1943

Ilitsch, Daniza   *Soprano*
b. Belgrade, 1919:
She made her debut as Nedda at Berlin in 1936. Her first appearance at the Metropolitan was in 1947, as Desdemona. In 1944 she was imprisoned by the Nazi regime in Vienna for four months.

Illica, Luigi   *Librettist*
b. near Piacenza, 1857: d. there, 1919
This most prolific librettist was responsible for *La Wally*, *Andrea Chénier*, *Iris*, and (with Giacosa) *La Bohème*, *Tosca*, *Madama Butterfly*. With Praga and Oliva he wrote *Manon Lescaut*.

Incledon, Charles Benjamin   *Tenor*
b. Cornwall, England, 1763: d. London, 1826

One of the famous portrayers of Captain MacHeath, and a very famous tenor in many roles in England.

Indy, d', Paul Marie Theodore Vincent
Composer
b. Paris, 1851: d. there, 1931

One of the great composers of romantic symphonic works of nineteenth-century France, D'Indy made a very significant contribution to opera not only with his own works but with his practical re-orchestrations and arrangements of *La Favola d'Orfeo* and *Il Ritorno d'Ulisse in Patria* by Monteverdi, making these stage masterpieces again available for performance in modern times. He was a pupil of César Franck and carried on the traditions of French style by teaching many modern French composers himself.

Fervaal	Brussels	1897
L'Étranger	,,	1903
La Legende de St.		
Christophe	Opéra	1920
Le Rêve de Cynias	Paris	1927

Inghelbrecht, Désiré Émile *Composer*
b. Paris, 1880:

This composer was also a conductor and director of the Opéra-Comique from 1924 to 1933. He conducted at the Opéra after 1945.

La Nuit Vénitienne	1908

Inghilleri, Giovanni *Baritone*
b.

Barnaba, Father (*Le Pauvre Matelot*), Gerard, Iago, Manfredo (*L'Amore dei Tre Re*).

Ippolitov-Ivanov, Michael Mikhailo-vitch *Composer*
b. Gatchina, Russia, 1859: d. Moscow, 1935

It was he who completed Mussorgsky's unfinished opera *Zhenitba* (The Marriage).

Ruth	Tiflis	1887
Asra	,,	1890
Asva	Moscow	1900

Treason		1909
The Spy		1912
Ole from Nordland	Moscow	1916
The Last Barricade		1934

Ivogün, Maria *Soprano*
(*Really* Inge von Gunther)
b. Budapest, 1891:

The first Ighino (*Palestrina*), and the first Laura (*Der Ring des Polycrates*). She made her debut in Munich, 1913.

Gilda, Ighino, Laura, Zerbinetta.

Jachino, Carlo *Composer*
b. San Remo, 1889:

Giocondo e il suo Re	Milan	1924

Jackson, William *Composer*
b. Exeter, England, 1730: d. there, 1803

Jackson's claim to historic fame rests partly on the fact that his opera *The Lord of the Manor* had a libretto by General Burgoyne, who had previously led the British redcoats into the unfortunate (for him) Battle of Bennington in the American Revolution.

The Lord of the Manor		
	London	1780
The Metamorphosis	,,	1783

Jacobi, Frederick *Composer*
b. San Francisco, 1891: d. New York, 1952

The Prodigal Son	1944

Jadlowker, Herrmann *Tenor*
b. Riga, Lithuania, 1878: d. Tel Aviv, 1953

He made his debut at Cologne in 1889, and sang Faust in his first appearance at the Metropolitan in 1910.

Jagel, Frederick *Tenor*
b. Brooklyn, N.Y., 1897:

He made his debut as Rodolfo in 1924 at Leghorn, Italy. In 1927 he sang for the first time at the Metropolitan, as Radames.

Avito, Gennaro, Gérald (*Lakmé*), Luigi (*Il Tabarro*), Rodolfo, Radames.

Janáček, Leoš   *Composer*
b. Moravia, 1854: d. there, 1928
One of the great Czech composers, mostly known for his opera, *Její Pastorkyňa* (performed often under the title *Jenufa*).

Počátek Románu	Brno	1894
Její Pastorkyňa	„	1904
Káta Kabanová (*in*		
German, Katia Kabanowa)	„	1921
Šarka (*written* 1887)	„	1925
Věc Makropulos	„	1926
Příhody Lišky Bystroušky	„	1928
Z mrtvého Domu (*From*		
a House of the Dead)	„	1930
Osud (*written* 1904)		
	Brno (radio)	1934

Janssen, Herbert   *Baritone*
b. Cologne, 1895:
Famous as Amfortas, he made his debut with the Metropolitan as Wotan while on tour in Philadelphia, 1934.
Amfortas, Dutchman, Orest (*Elektra*), Wotan.

Jaques-Dalcroze, Émile   *Pedagogue*
b. Vienna, 1865: d. Geneva, 1950
The founder of the Dalcroze Schools of Eurythmics, of particular value to opera singers and composers. He composed in all forms, and has written many French songs that are sometimes mistaken for folk songs.

Le Violon Maudit	Geneva	1893
Sancho Panza	„	1897
Fête de la Jeunesse et		
de la Joie	„	1932

Jarno, Georg   *Composer*
b. Budapest, 1868: d. Breslau, 1920

Die Schwarze Kaschka	Breslau	1895
Der Richter von Zalamea	„	1899
Der Goldfisch	„	1907
Die Förster-Christel	Vienna	1907
Das Musikantenmädel	„	1910
Die Marine-Gustel	„	1912
Das Farmermädchen	Berlin	1913

Jenkins, David   *Composer*
b. Trecastle, Wales, 1848: d. Aberstwyth, 1915
The Enchanted Island

Jensen, Ludwig Irgens   *Composer*
b. Oslo, 1894:
Heimferd   Oslo   1947

Jepson, Helen   *Soprano*
b. Titusville, Pa., 1905:
A pupil of Mary Garden's. She made her debut at the Metropolitan in 1935.
Fiora (*L'Amore dei Tre Re*), Mélisande, Thaïs.

Jeremiáš, Jaroslav   *Composer*
b. Pisek, Czechoslovakia, 1889: d. Budějovice, 1919
Starý Král (*The Old King*)   Prague   1919

Jeremiáš, Otakar   *Composer*
b. Pisek, Czechoslovakia, 1892:
Brother of Jaroslav Jeremiáš. Director of the Prague Opera since 1945, and a composer of orchestral and chamber music for concert and for film.

The Brothers Karamazov		
	Prague	1928
Till Eulenspiegel	„	1949

Jeritza, Maria   *Soprano*
(*Really* Jedlitzka)
b. Brünn, Austria, 1887:
The first Ariadne (*Ariadne auf Naxos*), and the first Nurse in *Die Frau ohne Schatten*. She made her debut as Elsa in 1910 at Olmütz, and appeared for the first time at the Metropolitan in 1921 singing Mariette in *Die Tote Stadt*.
Ariadne, Carmen, Elisabeth, Elsa, Fedora, Helena (*Aegyptische Helene*), Jenufa, Maliella (*I Gioielli della Madonna*), Marguérite, Mariette (*Die Tote Stadt*), Minnie, Salome, Santuzza, Sieglinde, Thaïs, Tosca, Turandot, Violetta.

Jirák, Karel Boleslav   *Composer*
b. Prague, 1891:

Apollonius of Tyana
Woman and the God   Brno   1928

Jochum, Eugen   *Conductor*
b. Babenhausen, Germany, 1902:
Beginning at Munich, in 1927, he has conducted opera at Mannheim, Duisberg, Berlin (*radio*), Hamburg and Munich (*radio*).

Jochum, Georg Ludwig   *Conductor*
b. Babenhausen, Germany, 1909:
Like his older brother, he conducted opera at Frankfurt, beginning in 1937, and in Linz.

Johnson, Edward   *Tenor*
b. Guelph, Ontario, 1878: d. there, 1959
Called "di Giovanni" in Italy, he made his debut at the Metropolitan in 1922. But his reputation rests chiefly on his general management of that organization from 1935 to 1950.
Luigi (*Il Tabarro*), Peter Ibbetson, Rinuccio (*Gianni Schicchi*).

Joio, Norman Dello   *Composer*
b. New York, 1913:
A very successful composer in New York.

The Triumph of St. Joan	1950
The Ruby	1955
The Trial at Rouen	1956

Jolivet, André   *Composer*
b. Paris, 1905:

Dolores	Paris (radio)	1947

Joncières, Victorin de   *Composer*
(*Originally* Félix Ludger Rossignol)
b. Paris, 1839: d. there, 1903
He was a painter at first.

Sardanapale	Paris	1867
Le Dernier Jour de		
Pompeii	„	1869
Dimitri	„	1876
La Reine Berthe	„	1878
Le Chevalier Jean	„	1885
Lancelot du Lac	„	1900

Jones, Rowland   *Tenor*
b.
Boris (*Kata Kabanova*), Lensky (*Eugene Onegin*), Werther.

Jones, Sidney   *Composer*
b. London, 1861: d. there, 1946
He wrote thirteen operas in all.

Geisha	London	1896

Josten, Werner   *Conductor*
b. Elberfeld, Germany, 1885:
He composed orchestral and chamber music. In the 1920's he went to the United States and taught at Smith College for many years. It was there that he conducted the first American stage performance of *La Favola d'Orfeo*, in 1929.

Joubert, John   *Composer*
b. Capetown, S. Africa, 1927:

Antigone	BBC	1954

Journet, Marcel   *Bass*
b. Grasse, France, 1867: d. Vittel, 1933
The first Simon Mago. He made his debut at Montpellier in 1893, and sang for the first time at the Metropolitan in 1908.
Escamillo, Langrave (*Tannhäuser*), Méphistophélès (*Faust*), Simon Mago(*Nerone*)

Juch, Emma   *Soprano*
b. Vienna, 1863: d. New York, 1939
She made her debut in London in 1883. In 1888 she toured Mexico and the United States with her own company, which managed to last for three years.
Aida, Elisabeth, Elsa, Isabella (*Robert le Diable*), Marguérite (*Faust*), Martha, Mignon, Queen (*Les Huguenots*), Queen of the Night, Senta, Sieglinde, Valentine (*Les Huguenots*), Violetta.

Jurinac, Sena   *Soprano*
b. Yugoslavia, 1921:
Antonia (*Les Contes d'Hoffmann*), Ariadne(*Ariadne auf Naxos*), Cherubino, Composer (*Ariadne auf Naxos*), Countess Almaviva (*Le Nozze di Figaro*), Dorabella,

Donna Elvira, Eva, Fiordiligi, Freia, Giulietta (*Les Contes d'Hoffmann*), Ighino, Ilia (*Idomeneo*), Lisa (*Pique-Dame*), Manon, Marenka, Marguérite (*Faust*), Mimi, Octavian, Pamina.

Kabalevsky, Dmitri Borisovitch
Composer
b. St. Petersburg, 1904:

Colas Breugnon	Leningrad	1938
Before Moscow	,,	1942
The Family of Taras	Moscow	1947
Nikita Vershinin	,,	1955

Kadosa, Paul
Composer
b. Leva, Hungary, 1903:
A pupil of Kodály.

Adventure at Hoszt	1950

Kalisch, Paul
Tenor
b. Berlin, 1855: d. St. Lorenz, Austria, 1946
A famous Tristan, he made his debut in *Der Fliegende Holländer* at the Metropolitan in 1889. He had married Lilli Lehmann the year before.

Kalnins, Alfred
Composer
b. Zehsis, Latvia, 1879: d. Riga, 1951
A composer in all forms, he is especially noted for his works for chorus.

Banuta	Riga	1920
Salinieki (*The Islanders*)	,,	1925
Dzimtenes Atmoda		
(*The Nations Awakening*)	,,	1933

Kalnins, Janis
Composer
b. Riga, 1904:
Son of Alfred Kalnins. He settled in Canada in 1944, and was engaged as conductor of the conservatory orchestra at Fredericton, New Brunswick, in 1952.

Hamlet	Riga	1936

Kalomiris, Manolis
Composer
b. Smyrna, 1883:
Founder of the National Conservatory of Athens.

Protomastoras	Athens	1916
L'Anneau de la Mère	,,	1917

Kamienski, Lucian
Composer
b. Gniezno, Poland, 1885:

Tabu	Königsberg	1917
Dami i Huzary	Poznan	1938

Kaminski, Heinrich
Composer
b. Baden, 1886: d. Bavaria, 1946

Jürg Jenatsch	Dresden	1929

Kapp, Ergen
Composer
b. Astrakhan, 1908:
Twice a winner of the Stalin Prize.

Flames of Vengeance	Tallinn	1945
Freedom's Singer	,,	1950

Kappel, Gertrude
Soprano
b. Halle, 1884:
A famous Isolde, she made her debut at Hannover in 1903 and at San Francisco in 1933.
Brünnhilde, Isolde, Elektra.

Karajan, Herbert von
Conductor
b. Salzburg, 1908:
Conductor of the opera at Berlin from 1938 to 1945, and in Vienna since 1956.

Karel, Rudolf
Composer
b. Pilsen, Czechoslovakia, 1880: d. Teresin, 1945
His death occurred in a concentration camp at the end of the Second World War.

Ilseino Srdce		
(*Ilsea's Heart*)	Prague	1924
Smrt Kmotřička		
(*Godmother Death*)	,,	1933

Karyotakis, Theodore
Composer
b. Argos, Greece, 1903:

Moon's Flower	1953

Kassern, Tadeusz Zygfried
Composer
b. Lvov, Poland, 1904: d. New York, 1957

The Anointed	1951
Sun Up	1952

Kastalsky, Alexander
Composer
b. Moscow, 1856: d. there, 1926

A pupil of Tchaikovsky, and a composer of orchestral, choral and piano music.

Clara Milich   Moscow 1916

Kastle, Leonard   *Composer*
b. New York, 1929:
The Swing   NBC-TV   1956
Deseret   NBC-TV   1961

Kauffman, Leo Justinus   *Composer*
b. Alsace, 1901: d. Strasbourg, 1944:
Kauffman died during an air raid near the end of the Second World War.
Die Geschichte vom
  Schönen Annerl Strasbourg 1942

Kaufmann, Walter   *Composer*
b. Karlsbad, 1907:
Der Himmel Bringt es
  an den Tag   1934
Anasuya   Bombay Radio 1938
Parfait for Irène   1952
Bashmashkin   1952

Kaun, Hugo   *Composer*
b. Berlin, 1863: d. there, 1932
Sappho   Leipzig   1917
Der Fremde   Dresden   1920
Menandra   Kiel   1925

Keilberth, Joseph   *Conductor*
b. Karlsruhe, 1908:
Conductor of the opera at his birthplace from 1935 to 1940, at Dresden from 1945 to 1951, and subsequently at Bayreuth.

Keldorfer, Robert   *Composer*
b. Vienna, 1901:
Verena   Klagenfurt 1951

Kellogg, Clara Louise   *Soprano*
b. Sumpterville, S.C., 1842: d. New Hartford, Conn., 1916
A pupil of E. Muzio, she made her debut at New York in 1861, and later as Marguérite at London in 1867. From 1873 to 1875 she managed her own "English Opera Company."

Aida, Gilda, Linda, Lucia, Marguérite (*Faust*), Martha, Philine, Violetta, Zerlina (*Don Giovanni*).

Kelly, Michael   *Tenor*
b. Dublin, 1762: d. Margate, 1826
Michael Kelly is famous for his reminiscences of Mozart and his times. He sang the first Don Basilio and the first Don Curzio in *Le Nozze di Figaro*. Beside all that, he was a composer himself, and wrote music to accompany the performances of sixty-two plays.

Kelley, Norman   *Tenor*
b.
The first to sing Doctor Zuckertanz in Menotti's *Maria Golovin*.
Eugenio (*Der Corregidor*), Gonsalve (*L'Heure Espagnole*), Nika Magadoff, Doctor Zuckertanz.

Kemp, Barbara   *Soprano*
b. Kochenn, Germany, 1886: d. Berlin, 1959
She was famous as Kundry. In 1923 she married Max Schillings, the composer of *Mona Lisa*.
Arline (*The Bohemian Girl*), Empress (*Die Frau ohne Schatten*), Kundry, Mona (*Mona Lisa*, by Schillings).

Kempe, Rudolf   *Conductor*
b. near Dresden, 1910:
Conductor of the Munich Opera from 1952 to 1954.

Kenessy, Jenö   *Composer*
b. Budapest, 1906:
Gold and the Woman
                      Budapest 1943

Kerll, Johann Caspar   *Composer*
b. Saxony, 1627: d. Munich, 1693
Famous as composer and as organist.
Oronte   1657
Erinto   1661

Kienzl, Wilhelm   *Composer*
b. Austria, 1857: d. Vienna, 1941
A pupil of Franz Liszt.

Heilmar, der Narr	Munich	1892
Der Evangelimann		
(*The Apostle*)	Berlin	1895
Don Quixote	„	1898
Der Kuhreigen	Vienna	1911
Das Testament	„	1916
Hassan, der Schwärmer		
	Chemnitz	1925
Sanctissimum	Vienna	1925

Kiepura, Jan *Tenor*
b. Sosnowiec, Poland, 1902:
Kiepura made his debut in Warsaw in 1923, and sang Rodolfo (*La Boheme*) in his first appearance at the Metropolitan in 1938.

Kind, Johann Friedrich *Librettist*
b. Leipzig, 1768: d. Dresden, 1843
Among his many libretti, *Der Freischütz* is the most famous.

Kindermann, August *Baritone*
b. Berlin, 1817: d. Munich, 1891
The first Wotan
Figaro, Titurel, Wotan.

Kipnis, Alexander *Bass*
b. Zhitomir, Russia, 1891:
One of the most famous bassos. He made his debut at Wiesbaden in 1917. In 1923 he sang Pogner for his first appearance in the United States. He came out at the Metropolitan in 1940 as Gurnemanz.
Boris Godunov, Gurnemanz, King Marke, Baron Ochs, Pogner, Rocco (*Fidelio*), Sarastro.

Kirkby-Lunn, Louise *Mezzo-soprano*
b. Manchester, England, 1873: d. London, 1930
She made her Metropolitan debut in 1902.
Amneris, Brangäne, Dalila, Kundry, Laura, Ortrud.

Kirsten, Dorothy *Soprano*
b. Montclair, N.J., 1917:
Her debut was in Chicago in 1940. In 1942 she appeared for the first time in New York City, singing Mimi. Her Metropolitan debut, in 1945, was in the same role.
Blanche (*Dialogues des Carmélites*), Ciocio San, Fiora (*L'Amore dei Tre Re*), Louise, Manon Lescaut, Mimi, Tosca, Violetta.

Klafsky, Katharina *Soprano*
b. Hungary, 1855: d. Hamburg, 1896
She made her debut in Salzburg in 1875. In 1895 she married Otto Lohse.
Brünnhilde, Sieglinde.

Klebe, Giselher *Composer*
b. Mannheim, 1925:
| Die Räuber | Düsseldorf | 1957 |

Kleiber, Erich *Conductor*
b. Vienna, 1890: d. Zürich, 1956
Beginning at Darmstadt in 1912, he conducted at Elberfeld, Mannheim and elsewhere in Germany before becoming Musical Director of the Berlin Opera from 1923 to 1935. From 1936 to 1949 he directed the opera at Buenos Aires, and afterwards conducted the State Opera in Vienna.

Klein, Bruno Oscar *Composer*
b. Osnabrück, 1858: d. New York, 1911
| Kenilworth | Hamburg | 1895 |

Klemperer, Otto *Conductor*
b. Breslau, 1885:
Conductor of the Berlin Opera from 1927 to 1933, and in Budapest from 1947 to 1950.

Klenau, Paul August von *Composer*
b. Copenhagen, 1883: d. there, 1946
Kjarten und Gudrun	Mannheim	1918
Die Lästerschule	Frankfurt	1926
Michael Kohlhaas	Stuttgart	1933
Rembrandt von Rijn	Berlin	1937
Elisabeth von England	Kassel	1939

Klose, Friedrich *Composer*
b. Karlsruhe, 1862: d. Lugano, 1942
| Ilsebill | Munich | 1905 |

Klose, Margarete *Mezzo-soprano*
b.
Brangäne, Fricka, Klytemnestra (*Elektra*), Ulrica (*Un Ballo in Maschera*).

Knappertsbusch, Hans *Conductor*
b. Elberfeld, Germany, 1888:
Conductor of the Munich Opera from 1922 to 1938, and since then at Vienna.

Knoch, Ernst *Conductor*
b. Karlsruhe, 1875: d. New York, 1959
Conductor at Strasbourg in 1901, then Bayreuth, Essen and Cologne, etc.

Knote, Heinrich *Tenor*
b. Munich, 1870: d. Garmisch, 1953
He made his debut at Munich in 1892 and at the Metropolitan ten years later.

Kobart, Ruth *Contralto*
b.
The first Agata in Menotti's *Maria Golovin*, and the first to sing the Housekeeper (*Die Schweigsame Frau*) in New York.

Koch, Erland von *Composer*
b. Stockholm, 1910:
Lasse Lucidor 1943

Kodály, Zoltán *Composer*
b. Kecskemét, Hungary, 1882:
An associate of Bartók in a far-reaching study of Hungarian folk music.
Háry János Budapest 1926
Czinka Panna „ 1948

Kondracki, Michal *Composer*
b. Ukraine, 1902:
Popieliny Warsaw 1934

Konetzni, Anni *Soprano*
b.
Elektra, Duchess Elena (*I Vespri Siciliani*) Marschallin, Reiza (*Oberon*), Selika.

Konetzni, Hilde *Soprano*
b.
Chrysothemis (*Elektra*), Empress (*Die Frau ohne Schatten*), Lisa, Marenka, Milada (*Dalibor*)

Konjović, Petar *Composer*
b. Poland, 1882:
Vilin Vee (*The Wedding of Milos*) Zagreb 1917
Koštana „ 1931
Knez od Zete (*The Duke of Zeta*) Belgrade 1939
Sel Jaci (*The Peasants*) „ 1952

Korngold, Erich Wolfgang *Composer*
b. Brno, Czechoslovakia, 1897: d. Hollywood, 1957
Der Ring des Polycrates Munich 1916
Violanta „ 1916
Die Tote Stadt Hamburg 1920
Die Wunder der Heliane „ 1927
Kathrin Stockholm 1937
Die Stumme Serenade Dortmund 1954

Kósa, Gyorgy *Composer*
b. Budapest, 1897:
A pupil of Bartók.
The King's Robe 1927
The Two Knights Budapest 1936
Cenodoxus 1942
Anselmus 1945
The Bees 1946

Koussevitzky, Sergey *Conductor*
b. Russia, 1874: d. Boston, 1951
Celebrated conductor and virtuoso of the double bass. He left Russia in 1920 after a successful career in both fields, conducted in Paris for a while, then became the conductor of the Boston Symphony Orchestra at which post he stayed until 1950. He established a foundation in memory of his wife with the principal object of stimulating the composition of new works, including operas, by commissioning them.

Koven, Reginald de *Composer*
b. Middletown, Conn., 1859: d. Chicago, 1920

Robin Hood		1890
The Canterbury		
Pilgrims	Metropolitan	1917
Rip van Winkle		
	Chicago and New York	1920
Rob Roy		1894

Krasa, Hans   *Composer*
b. Prague, 1899: d. Oswiecim, 1944

Betrothed in a Dream	1933
Brundibar	1940

Krauss, Ernst   *Tenor*
b. Erlangen, Germany, 1863: d. Wörthsee, 1941
He made his debut as Tamino at Mannheim in 1893.

Kraus, Felix von   *Bass*
b. Vienna, 1870: d. Munich, 1937
This famous Gurnemanz made his debut as Hagen at Bayreuth in 1899. In the same year he married Adrienne Osborne.

Kraus, Otakar   *Baritone*
b.
The first Nick Shadow (*The Rake's Progress*).

Krauss, Clemens   *Conductor*
b. Vienna, 1893: d. Mexico City, 1954
Strauss dedicated his *Friedenstag* to Krauss and Ursuleac. Krauss conducted its premiere. He was conductor at Frankfurt, Berlin, Munich, Salzburg and Vienna.

Krauss, Marie Gabrielle   *Soprano*
b. Vienna, 1842: d. Paris, 1906
In 1860 she made her debut in Vienna singing Mathilde in *Guillaume Tell*.
Aida, Anna (*La Dame Blanche*), Donna Anna, Elsa, Gilda, Katherine (*Henry VIII*), Leonore (*Fidelio*), Leonora (*Trovatore*), Lucia, Lucrezia Borgia, Mathilde (*Guillaume Tell*), Norma, Rachel, Sapho, Semiramide, Valentine (*Les Huguenots*).

Krein, Alexander   *Composer*
b. Nizhni-Novgorod, 1883: d. Moscow, 1951

Zagmuk	Moscow	1930
Daughter of the People		1949

Krejčí, Iša   *Composer*
b. Prague, 1904:

The Revolt of		
Ephesus	Prague	1946

Krejči, Miroslav   *Composer*
b. Czechoslovakia, 1891:

Léto (*Summer*)	Prague	1940
Posledni Hejtman (*The*		
Last Captain)	,,	1948

Krenek, Ernst   *Composer*
b. Vienna, 1900:

Zwingburg	Berlin	1924
Der Sprung über den		
Schatten	Frankfurt	1924
Orpheus und Eurydike	Kassel	1926
Jonny Spielt Auf	Leipzig	1927
Leben des Orest	,,	1930
Charles V	Prague	1938
Tarquin	Poughkeepsie, N.Y.	1941

Kreutzer, Rodolphe   *Composer*
b. Versailles, 1766: d. Geneva, 1831
This is the famous violinist to whom Beethoven dedicated his *Kreutzer Sonata*. He wrote forty operas.

Jeanne d'Arc	Paris	1790
Paul et Virginie	,,	1791
Lodoïska	,,	1791

Křička, Jaroslav   *Composer*
b. Moravia, 1882:

Hipolyta	Prague	1917
Ogaři		1919
Bilý Pán (*White Ghost*)	Brno	1929
Král Lávra (*King*		
Lawrence)	Prague	1940
Jachym a Juliana		1948

Krips, Joseph   *Conductor*
b. Vienna, 1902:
Conductor at Vienna and at Salzburg.

Kronold, Selma   *Soprano*
b. Krakov, 1866: d. New York, 1920
In 1882 she came out as Agatha (*Der Freischütz*), in Leipzig. Her Metropolitan debut was in 1896. In 1904 she retired.
Agatha, Nedda, Santuzza.

Krueger, Karl   *Conductor*
b. Atchison, Kansas, 1894:
Assistant conductor at Vienna from 1919 to 1924. Conductor of the Detroit Symphony from 1943 to 1949.

Kubelík, Rafael   *Conductor*
b. Near Kolín, Czechoslovakia, 1914:
Although best known as a conductor on both sides of the Atlantic, he also composed an opera:
Veronika   Brno   1947

Kullman, Charles   *Tenor*
b. New Haven, Conn., 1903:
He made his debut as Pinkerton in Berlin, 1931. In 1935 he sang for the first time at the Metropolitan, as Faust.
Avito (*L'Amore dei Tre Re*), Belmonte, Eisenstein (*Die Fledermaus*), Faust, Sir Huon, Jenik (*Prodaná Nevĕsta*), Orfeo (in the first American stage performance of *La Favola d'Orfeo*), Pinkerton, Schuisky (*Boris Godunov*), Tannhäuser.

Kunz, Eric   *Bass*
b.
Beckmesser, Figaro (*Le Nozze di Figaro*), Leporello, Papageno.

Kurka, Robert   *Composer*
b. 1922: d. New York, 1957
The Good Soldier
Schweik (*posthumous*)
          New York   1957

Kurt, Melanie   *Soprano*
b. Vienna, 1880: d. New York, 1941
She was not only an opera singer, but also a pianist, winning the Liszt Prize. Her opera debut came in Lübeck, in 1902, when she sang Elisabeth. She sang

Isolde in her first appearance at the Metropolitan in 1915.
Elisabeth, Iphigénie (*Iphigénie en Tauride*), Isolde, Kundry.

Kurz, Selma   *Soprano*
b. Silesia, 1875: d. Vienna, 1933
She made her debut at Covent Garden in 1904 singing Gilda.
Gilda, Oscar, Violetta, Zerbinetta (*Ariadne auf Naxos*).

Labia, Maria   *Soprano*
b. Verona, Italy, 1880:
She made her debut in Stockholm, in 1905, singing Mimi. Her first appearance at New York occurred in 1908, when she sang Tosca.
Carmen, Giorgetta (*Il Tabarro*), Mimi, Nedda, Tosca, Violetta.

Lablache, Luigi   *Bass*
b. Naples, 1794: d. there, 1858
Lablache has been called the greatest of all Leporellos. He made his debut at Naples in 1812. He sang the first Giorgio (*I Puritani*) and the first Don Pasquale.
Assur (*Semiramide*), Dandini (*Cenerentola*), Geronimo (*Il Matrimonio Segreto*), Giorgio (*I Puritani*), Don Giovanni, Henry VIII (*Anna Bolena*), Leporello, Méphistophélès (*Faust*), Oroveso, Don Pasquale, Podestà (*La Gazza Ladra*).

Labroca, Mario   *Composer*
b. Rome, 1896:
A pupil of Malipiero, and a composer of orchestral and chamber music.
La Principessa di Perepepè
          Rome   1927
Le Tre Figliuole di
Pinco Pallino   „   1928

Lachner, Franz   *Composer*
b. Rain am Lech, Germany, 1803: d. Munich, 1890
Brother of Ignaz Lachner.
Die Bürgschaft   Pest   1828
Alidia   Munich   1839

| Catarina Cornaro | „ | 1841 |
| Benvenuto Cellini | „ | 1849 |

Lachner, Ignaz   *Composer*
b. Rain am Lech, Germany, 1807: d. Hanover, 1895
Brother of Franz Lachner.

Der Geisterturm	Stuttgart	1837
Die Regenbrüder	„	1839
Loreley	Munich	1846

Lacombe, Louis Brouillon   *Composer*
b. Bourges, 1818: d. St-Vaast-la-Hougue, 1884

L'Amour	Paris	1859
La Madone	„	1861
Winkelried	Geneva	1892
Le Tonnelier	Coblenz	1897

Lail, Lorri   *Mezzo-soprano*
b. Oslo, 1904:

Lajtha, László   *Composer*
b. Budapest, 1891:
A composer of music for ballet, for orchestra, and for chorus.

| Chapeau Bleu | | 1952 |

Lalo, Édouard   *Composer*
(*Full name*: Victor Antoine Édouard)
b. Lille, 1823: d. Paris, 1892
Lalo wrote music in all forms, but is best known for his *Symphonie espagnole*.

| Le Roi d'Ys | Opéra-Comique | 1888 |

Lamoureux, Charles   *Conductor*
b. Bordeaux, 1834: d. Paris, 1899
An advocate of Wagner, conductor of the Paris Opéra from 1877 to 1879, Lamoureux was the founder of the concert series which bears his name.

Langendorff, Frieda   *Contralto*
b. Breslau, 1868: d. New York, 1947
She made her debut in Strasbourg in 1901 and at the Metropolitan in 1907:
Amneris, Azucena, Dalila, Fricka, Ortrud.

Laparra, Raoul   *Composer*
b. Bordeaux, 1876: d. near Paris, 1943

A pupil of Fauré and Massenet, and a composer of music for piano and for orchestra. He was killed in an air raid during World War II.

Peau d'âne	Bordeaux	1899
La Habanera	Comique	1908
La Jota	„	1911
Le Joueur de Viole	Paris	1925
Las Toreras	Lille	1929
L'Illustre Fregona	Paris	1931

Larsén-Todsen, Nanny   *Soprano*
b. Kalmar län, Sweden, 1884:
She made her debut in Stockholm as Agathe in 1906, and at the Metropolitan in 1925 as Brünnhilde.
Agathe, Brünnhilde, Fricka, Isolde, Leonore (*Fidelio*).

Larsson, Lars Erik   *Composer*
b. Akarp, Sweden, 1908:
Prinsessan av Cypern
                Stockholm 1937

Lassalle, Jean Louis   *Baritone*
b. Lyons, 1847: d. Paris, 1909
He made his debut at the Opéra in 1872 and at the Metropolitan, singing Nelusko, twenty years later. He was the first to sing Scindia (*Le Roi de Lahore*), and the first High Priest (*Samson et Dalila*).
Ashton (*Lucia di Lammermoor*), Escamillo, Don Giovanni, Hans Sachs, High Priest (*Samson et Dalila*), Nelusko, De Nevers, Rigoletto, Scindia, St. Bris, Guillaume Tell, Telramund.

Lassen, Eduard   *Composer*
b. Copenhagen, 1830: d. Weimar, 1904
It was Lassen who conducted the première of *Samson et Dalila*. He also made a living writing music for stage plays.

Landgraf Ludwigs Brautfahrt	Weimar	1857
Frauenlob	„	1860
Le Captif	Brussels	1865

Lattuada, Felice *Composer*
b. near Milan, 1882:

La Tempestà	Milan	1922
Sandha	Genoa	1924
Le Preziose Ridicole	Milan	1929
Don Giovanni	Naples	1929
La Caverna di Salamanca		
	Genoa	1938

Launis, Armas Emanuel *Composer*
(*Really* Lindberg)
b. Hämeenlinna, Finland, 1884:
A pupil of Jan Sibelius.

Seitsemän Veljestä (*The Seven Brothers*)	Helsingfors	1913
Kullervo	„	1917
Aslak-Hetta	Nice	1938

Lauri-Volpi, Giacomo *Tenor*
b. near Rome, 1892:
He made his debut in Rome in 1920 and at the Metropolitan, singing the Duke (*Rigoletto*), in 1923.
Andrea Chénier, Calaf, Duke, Johnson, Manrico, Nerone, Otello, Radames, Raoul, Rodolfo.

Lawrence, Marjorie *Soprano*
b. near Melbourne, 1909:
This famous singer became paralyzed at the height of her career. Nevertheless she endeavored to keep singing, and appeared as Venus, in *Tannhäuser*, being able in that role to remain seated upon a couch.
Alceste, Brünnhilde, Salome, Venus.

Lazarus, Daniel *Composer*
b. Paris, 1898:

Trumpeldor	Paris (concert)	1946

Lazzari, Sylvio *Composer*
b. Bozen, 1857: d. Paris, 1944

Armor	Prague	1898
La Lépreuse	Paris	1912
Le Sautériot	Chicago	1918
Melaenis	Mulhouse	1927
La Tour de Feu	Paris	1928

Leblanc, Georgette *Soprano*
b. c. 1880: d. Cannes, 1941
The first Ariane (*Ariane et Barbe-Bleue*). She was to have been the first Mélisande, or so her lover Maeterlinck thought, but to his mortification Mary Garden got the part.

Lecocq, Alexandre Charles *Composer*
b. Paris, 1832: d. there, 1918
Lecocq shared the Offenbach prize with Bizet in 1857 when both wrote acceptable operas to the libretto of *Le Docteur Miracle*.

Le Docteur Miracle	Paris	1857
Fleur de Thé	„	1868
La Fille de Mme. Angot	Brussels	1872
Giroflé-Girofla	„	1874

Lee, Dai-Keong *Composer*
b. Honolulu, 1915:
A pupil of Roger Sessions and of Aaron Copland.

The Poet's Dilemma		1940

Lefebvre, Charles Édouard *Composer*
b. Paris, 1843: d. Aix-les-Bains, 1917

Zaïre	Lille	1887
Djelma	Paris	1894
Le Trésor	Angers	1883

Leffler-Burckard, Martha *Soprano*
b. Berlin, 1865: d. Wiesbaden, 1954
She made her debut at Strasbourg in 1890, and at the Metropolitan in 1908.
Brünnhilde, Elisabeth, Elsa, Eva, Isolde, Leonora (*Fidelio*).

Leginska, Ethel *Composer*
(*Really* Liggins)
b. Hull, England, 1886:

Gale	Chicago	1935
The Rose and the Ring	Los Angeles	1957

Legros, Joseph *Tenor*
b. Laon, 1730: d. La Rochelle, 1793
The first French Orfeo (*Orfeo ed Euridice*), the first Achilles (*Iphigénie en*

Aulide), and the first Pylade (*Iphigénie en Tauride*). He also composed a little.

Lehár, Franz   *Composer*
b. Komorn, Hungary, 1870: d. Bad Ischl, 1948

Kukuschka (*or* Tatjana)	Leipzig	1896
Die Lustige Witwe		
(*The Merry Widow*)	Vienna	1905
Der Graf von		
Luxembourg	„	1909
Zigeunerliebe	„	1910

Lehmann, Lilli   *Soprano*
b. Würzburg, 1848: d. Berlin, 1929

Stories about Lilli Lehmann's frugality and modesty would fill a small book. One of the best describes how, when singing as prima donna at the Metropolitan, she rode a horse car to work instead of taking a more ostentatious vehicle. She made her debut in Prague in 1865, and sang for the first time at the Metropolitan in 1885 as Carmen. She was the teacher of Farrar and Fremstad. It is said she knew one hundred and seventy roles. In 1888 she married Paul Kalisch. Her recording of *Casta Diva*, made when she was in her late fifties, is perhaps unequaled.

Aida, Amelia, Donna Anna, Bertha (*Le Prophète*), Brünnhilde, Carmen, Desdemona, Euryanthe, Irene (*Rienzi*), Isolde, Leonore (*Fidelio*), Margherita (*Mefistofele*), Norma, Ortrud, Philine, Queen of Sheba, Rachel, Sieglinde, Sulamith, Woglinde (*coached by Wagner*), Violetta.

Lehmann, Lotte   *Soprano*
b. Perleberg, Germany, 1888:

The first Empress (*Die Frau ohne Schatten*), the first Christine (*Intermezzo*), and the first Composer (*Ariadne auf Naxos*). She made her United States debut at Chicago in 1930, and at the Metropolitan in 1934.

Christine, Composer (*Ariadne auf Naxos*), Empress (*Die Frau ohne Schatten*), Leonore

(*Fidelio*), Marschallin, Octavian, Sieglinde, Tatyana, Tosca.

Leider, Frida   *Soprano*
b. Berlin, 1888:

Like Lotte Lehman, Frida Leider made her first United States appearance in Chicago, in 1928, singing Brünnhilde. She made her Metropolitan debut as Isolde, in 1933.

Brünnhilde, Isolde, Kundry, Marschallin, Senta.

Leigh, Walter   *Composer*
b. Wimbledon, England, 1905: d. Tobruk, Libya, 1942

He was a composer of film, stage and chamber music. He died in action during the African campaign against Rommel in the Second World War.

The Jolly Roger	London	1933
The Pride of the		
Regiment	„	1932

Leinsdorf, Erich   *Conductor*
b. Vienna, 1912:

Assistant conductor at Salzburg in 1934, he went to the Metropolitan in 1938. In 1947 he became conductor of the Rochester Philharmonic.

Lemnitz, Tiana   *Soprano*
b. Metz, 1897:

She made her debut at Frankfurt in 1922.

Eva, Jenufa, Marschallin, Milada (*Dalibor*), Pamina, Sieglinde, Tatyana.

Leo, Leonardo   *Composer*
b. near Brindisi, Italy, 1694: d. Naples, 1744

Pisistrato	Naples	1714
L'Imbroglio Scoperto		1723
Demofoonte		1735
Amor Vuol Sofferenze		1739

Leoncavallo, Ruggiero   *Composer*
b. Naples, 1858: d. Montecatini, 1919

I Pagliacci	Milan	1892
Tommaso Chatterton		1896

La Bohème	Venice	1897
Zaza	Milan	1900
Maia	Rome	1910
Malbruk (*within four days of Maia*)	,,	1910
La Reginetta delle Rose	Rome and Naples	1912
Gli Zingari	London	1912

Leonova, Darya *Contralto*
b. Tver, Russia, 1829: d. St. Petersburg, 1896
A friend of Mussorgsky.

Lesueur, Jean François *Composer*
b. near Abbeville, France, 1760: d. Paris, 1837

La Caverne	Paris	1793
Paul et Virginie	,,	1794
Télémaque	,,	1796
Les Bardes	,,	1804
La Mort d'Adam	,,	1809

Levasseur, Marie Claude Josèphe
(*Called* Rosalie) *Soprano*
b. Valenciennes, France, 1749: d. Neuwied am Rhein, Germany, 1826
The first Armide, the first Alceste in Paris, the first Iphigénie (*Iphigénie en Tauride*), and one of the first to sing that role in the *Iphigénie en Aulide*.

Levasseur, Nicholas Prosper *Bass*
b. Bresles, France, 1791: d. Paris, 1871
The first Bertram (*Robert le Diable*), the first Cardinal (*La Juive*). He made his debut at the Opéra in 1813.
Bertram, Cardinal (*La Juive*), St. Bris, Figaro (*Il Barbiere di Siviglia*), Mosè (by Rossini).

Levi, Hermann *Conductor*
b. Giessen, Germany, 1839: d. Munich, 1900
Although Wagner was afflicted with some degree of anti-Semitism, Levi was the only conductor he would trust with the premiere of *Parsifal*.

Lewis, Brenda *Soprano*
b.
Donna Elvira, Giorgetta (*Il Tabarro*), Lion Tamer (*He Who Gets Slapped*), Marschallin, Musetta, Regina.

Lewis, Richard *Tenor*
b.
Bacchus (*Ariadne auf Naxos*), Ferrando, Idomeneo, Tom Rakewell.

Lhotka, Fran *Composer*
b. Czechoslovakia, 1883:
Lhotka studied with Dvořák, Janáček, and Klička.

Minka	Zagreb	1918
The Sea	,,	1920

Lhotka-Kalinski, Ivo *Composer*
b. Zagreb, 1913:
The son of Fran Lhotka.

Pomet	1944
Matija Gubec	1948

Liatoshinsky, Boris *Composer*
b. Zhitomir, Russia, 1895:
A pupil of Glière.

The Golden Hoop		1931
Shehors	Kiev	1938

Liebermann, Rolf *Composer*
b. Zürich, 1910:

Leonore 40/45	Basel	1952
The School for Wives	Louisville, Ky.	1955
Penelope	Salzburg	1954

Liebling, Estelle *Soprano*
b. New York, 1884:
Best known in New York as a teacher of singing.

Liljefors, Ingemar *Composer*
b. Göteborg, Sweden, 1906:

Hyrkusken	1951

Lind, Jenny *Soprano*
b. Stockholm, 1820: d. Malvern Wells, England, 1887
The Swedish Nightingale. She studied with Manuel García and made her debut

at Stockholm in 1838 as Agathe. Her London debut, as Alice in *Robert le Diable*, occurred in 1847. She was brought to the United States by P. T. Barnum and exhibited as a kind of supernatural being to awe-struck multitudes. She was the first Amalia (*I Masnadieri*, by Verdi).

Adina (*L'Elisir d'Amore*), Agathe, Alice, Amalia (*I Masnadieri*), Amina, Donna Anna, Euryanthe, Giulia (*La Vestale*), Lucia, Marie (*La Figlia del Reggimento*), Susanna (*Le Nozze di Figaro*), Valentine (*Les Huguenots*).

Lindberg, Oskar Fredrik   *Composer*
b. Gagnef, Sweden, 1887: d. Stockholm, 1955
Fredlos   Stockholm   1943

Linley, George   *Composer*
b. Leeds, 1798: d. London, 1865
Francesca Doria   1849
La Poupée de Nurenberg   1861

Linstead, George Frederick   *Composer*
b. Melrose, Massachusetts, 1908:
Eastward of Eden   1935

Lipovska, Lydia Yakolevna   *Soprano*
b. Bessarabia, 1884: d. Beirut, 1955
She made her debut at St. Petersburg in 1909, and sang Lakmé in Boston and Violetta at the Metropolitan that same year.

Gilda, Juliette, Lakmé, Manon Lescaut, Mimi, Susanna (*Il Segreto di Susanna*), Tatyana, Violetta.

Lipton, Martha   *Mezzo-soprano*
b.
Annina (*Der Rosenkavalier*), Brangäne, Frasquita (*Der Corregidor*), Innkeeper (*Boris Gudonov*), Maddalena (*Rigoletto*), Mother Goose (*The Rake's Progress*).

List, Emanuel   *Bass*
b. Vienna, 1891:
He made his debut at Vienna in 1922 singing Méphistophélès in *Faust*. The following year he sang the Landgraf

(*Tannhäuser*) in his first appearance at the Metropolitan.

Fafner, Landgraf (*Tannhäuser*), Méphistophélès (*Faust*), Baron Ochs.

Liszt, Franz   *Composer*
b. Raiding, Hungary, 1811: d. Bayreuth, 1886
Famous as pianist, composer and teacher, he was also a conductor. When *Lohengrin* was prohibited in Germany, Liszt, with all the prestige his name carried, produced and conducted its première at Dresden in 1850. His activity at Weimar made that city a center of opera. His daughter Cosima became the wife first of von Bülow, then of Richard Wagner.

Litvinne, Félia   *Soprano*
b. St. Petersburg, 1861: d. Paris, 1936
She made her debut at Paris in 1885.
Aida, Donna Anna, Brünnhilde, La Gioconda, Isolde, Leonora (*Il Trovatore*).

Ljungberg, Göta   *Soprano*
b. Sundsval, Sweden, 1893: d. near Stockholm, 1955
The first Lady Marigold (*Merry Mount*). She made her Metropolitan debut in 1932. Her first professional appearance occurred in Stockholm, in 1920, as Elsa.
Elsa, Judith (*by Goossens*), Lady Marigold (*Merry Mount*).

Lloyd, David   *Tenor*
b.
Gonsalve (*L'Heure Espagnole*), Pedrillo, Pinkerton, Prince of Tartaglia (*The Love for Three Oranges*), Prince Ramiro (*Cenerentola*).

Lloyd, George   *Composer*
b. St. Ives, England, 1913:
Iernin   Penzance   1934
The Serf   London   1938
John Socman   1951

Locke, Matthew   *Composer*
b. Exeter, England, 1630: d. London, 1677

THE PEOPLE IN OPERA

He wrote part of the first English opera, *The Siege of Rhodes* (1656). He also sang in the production.

Lockwood, Normand *Composer*
b. New York, 1906:
Scarecrow   New York   1945

Locle, Camille de *Librettist*
b. Vaucluse, 1832: d. Capri, 1903
Du Locle wrote the scenario for *Aida*, and with Méry the libretto for *Don Carlos*. He was at one time director of the Opéra-Comique.

London, George *Baritone*
(*Really* Burnstein)
b. Montreal, 1920:
George London began his singing career in Los Angeles, singing in the chorus of the local opera. He first sang in New York as a member of the cast of the show *Desert Song*. This led to a concert series. He went to Europe on his own in order to find acceptance as an opera singer, then returned to make his debut as Amonasro at the Metropolitan in 1951. In 1960 he became the first American to sing Boris at the Bolshoi Theater in Moscow, for which he received a tremendous ovation.
Amfortas, Amonasro, Boris Godunov, Coppelius, Dapertutto, Escamillo, Eugene Onegin, Don Giovanni, Lindorf, Mandryka, Méphistophélès (*Faust*), Docteur Miracle, Parsifal, Scarpia, Graf Waldner (*Arabella*), Wolfram.

Loomis, Clarence *Composer*
b. Sioux Falls, S.D, 1889:
A Night in Avignon
Castle of Gold
Yolande of Cyprus
              London, Ontario   1929
David
The Fall of the House of Usher

Loomis, Harvey Worthington *Composer*
b. Brooklyn, N.Y., 1865: d. Boston, 1930
A pupil of Dvořák.

The Traitor Mandolin
The Maid of Athens
Going Up?

Lorenz, Max *Tenor*
b. Düsseldorf, 1901:
He made his Metropolitan debut in 1931 as Walther.
Aegisth (*Elektra*), Cola Rienzi, Herod (*Salome*), Siegfried, Siegmund, Tristan, Walther.

Lortzing, Gustav Albert *Composer*
b. Berlin, 1801: d. there, 1851
For his first two operas, Lortzing wrote his own libretti.
Zar und Zimmerman   Leipzig   1837
Die Beiden Schützen   „   1837
Der Wildschütz   1842
Undine   Magdeburg   1845
Der Waffenschmied   Vienna   1846

Lotti, Antonio *Composer*
b. Venice, 1667: d. there, 1740
Giove in Argo   Dresden   1717
Ascanio   1718
Teofane   Dresden   1719

Løveberg, Aase *Soprano*
(*Née* Nordmo)
b. Målselv, Norway, 1923:
She made her debut in Oslo in 1948 and at the Metropolitan in 1959.

Lualdi, Adriano *Composer*
b. Larino, Italy, 1885:
A pupil of Wolf-Ferrari.
Guerrin Meschino   Rome   1920
La Figlia del Re   Turin   1922
Le Furie d'Arlecchino
                    Buenos Aires   1924
Il Diavolo ne Campanile
                        La Scala   1925
La Granceola   Venice   1932
Lumavig e la Saetta   Rome   1937

Lubin, Germaine *Soprano*
b. Paris, 1890:

She made her debut at the Opéra-Comique in 1912.
Alceste, Isolde, Kundry.

Luca, Giuseppe de   *Baritone*
b. Rome, 1876: d. New York, 1950
The first Prince (*Adriana Lecouvreur*), the first Sharpless, the first Gianni Schicchi, and the first Paquiro (*Goyescas*). He made his debut as Valentin (*Faust*) in Piacenza in 1897. He first appeared at the Metropolitan as Figaro (*Il Barbiere di Siviglia*), in 1915.
Don Carlo (*La Forza del Destino*), Eugene Onegin, Figaro (*Il Barbiere di Siviglia*), Gianni Schicchi, Hoël (*Dinorah*), Don Pasquale, Paquiro (*Goyescas*), Plunkett (*Martha*), Prince (*Adriana Lecouvreur*), Rigoletto, Rodrigo (*Don Carlos*), Sancho Panza, Sharpless, Zurga (*Les Pêcheurs de Perles*), Valentin (*Faust*).

Lucca, Pauline   *Soprano*
b. Vienna, 1841: d. there, 1908
She made her debut at Olmütz in 1859, singing Elvira (*Ernani*).
Carmen, Cherubino, Elisabetta (*Don Carlos*), Elvira (*Ernani*), Leonora (*La Favorita*), Lucia, Marguérite (*Faust*), Marie (*La Figlia del Reggimento*), Norma, Selika, Valentine (*Les Huguenots*), Zerlina (*Fra Diavolo*).

Lucia, Fernando de   *Tenor*
b. Naples, 1860: d. there, 1925
Canio, Mario Cavaradossi, Don Ottavio.

Ludikar, Pavel   *Bass*
b. Prague, 1882:
He made his debut at Prague, 1904, in Boston, 1913, and at the Metropolitan in 1926. He sang the first Karl (*Karl V*).
Figaro (*Il Barbiere di Siviglia*), Karl V.

Ludwig, William   *Baritone*
(*Really* Ledwidge)
b. Dublin, 1847: d. London, 1923
Hans Sachs, Telramund, Vanderdecken

(*Der Fliegende Holländer*), Wolfram, Wotan.

Luening, Otto   *Composer*
b. Milwaukee, Wisc., 1900:
In association with Vladimir Ussachevsky, Luening is experimenting with electronic music.
Evangeline   New York   1948

Lully, Jean Baptiste   *Composer*
b. Florence, 1632: d. Paris, 1687
At first a dancer in ballets, Lully became in 1672 the producer at the Académie Royale de Musique (Opéra), replacing Perrin and Cambert, and gaining thereby the monopoly for opera production in the nation. He was not known for his friendliness and goodwill. The cause of his death was occupational: he died of gangrene caused by a bruise on his foot which happened when the cane with which he beat time struck it during a performance.
Les Fêtes de L'Amour
   et de Bacchus   Opéra   1672
Alceste   „   1674
Thesée   „   1675

Lussan, Zélie de   *Soprano*
b. Brooklyn, 1863: d. London, 1949
She made her debut in Boston in 1885.
Anne (*Falstaff*), Arline (*The Bohemian Girl*), Carmen, Desdemona, Juliette, Mignon, Musetta, Nedda, Zerlina (*Don Giovanni*).

Lyford, Ralph   *Composer*
b. Worcester, Mass., 1882: d. Cincinnati, 1927
Castle Agrazant   Cincinnati   1926

Lyne, Felice   *Soprano*
b. Slater, Missouri, 1887: d. Allentown, Pa., 1935
She made her debut in London in 1911, singing Gilda.

Maas, Joseph   *Tenor*
b. Dartford, England, 1847: d. London, 1886

Don César de Bazan, des Grieux (*Manon*), Faust (*Faust*), Lohengrin, Radames, Raoul, Cola Rienzi, Thaddeus (*The Bohemian Girl*).

Macbeth, Florence *Soprano*
b. Mankato, Minn., 1891:
Called, perhaps in imitation of Jenny Lind, "The Minnesota Nightingale," she made her debut at Chicago as Rosina (*Il Barbiere di Siviglia*), 1914, and stayed with that company until 1935. For one year she toured the United States with her own company.

Maccunn, Hamish *Composer*
b. Greenock, Scotland, 1868: d. London, 1916
Not only a composer, he was conductor of the Carl Rosa company from 1898 to 1900, and assistant conductor at Covent Garden from 1910.

Jeanie Deans	Edinburgh	1894
Diarmid	London	1897
The Masque of War and Peace	„	1900

Mackenzie, Alexander Campbell
 Composer
b. Edinburgh, 1847: d. London, 1935
A composer, conductor, violinist. He wrote for his own instrument and for chorus, orchestra and chamber groups.

Colomba	London	1883
The Troubador	„	1886
His Majesty	„	1897
The Knight of the Road	„	1905
The Cricket on the Hearth	„	1914

Mackerras, Charles *Conductor*
b. Schenectady, N.Y., 1925:

Maclean, Alexander Morvaren
 Composer
b. Eton, England, 1872: d. London, 1936
Quentin Durward (*Composed 1892*)
 Newcastle on Tyne 1920

Petruccio	London	1895
The King's Price	„	1904
Maître Seiler	„	1909

Maclennan, Francis *Tenor*
b. Bay City, Mich., 1879: d. Port Jefferson, N.Y., 1935
After his debut as Faust at Covent Garden in 1902 he became the first foreigner to sing Tristan in Germany. In 1904 he married Florence Easton.
Faust, Parsifal, Tristan.

Madetoja, Leevi *Composer*
b. Uleaborg, Finland, 1887: d. Helsinki, 1947

| Pohjalaisia | Helsinki | 1924 |
| Juha | „ | 1935 |

Madeira, Jean *Contralto*
b.
Amneris, Baba the Turk (*The Rake's Progress*), Berta (*Il Barbiere di Siviglia*), Carmen, La Cieca, Maddalena, Mother Goose (*The Rake's Progress*), Nurse (*Boris Godunov*), Schwertleite, Ulrica.

Manganini, Quinto *Composer*
b. Fairfield, Conn., 1897:
Tennessee's Partner
 New York (radio) 1942

Magnard, Albéric *Composer*
b. Paris, 1865: d. Oise, 1914
Magnard was more successful as a composer for instruments than as an opera composer. He was killed while defending his home from the Germans during the First World War.

Yolande	Brussels	1892
Guercoeur (*partly lost*)		1910
Bérénice	Opéra-Comique	1911

Mahler, Gustav *Conductor*
b. Kalischt, Poland, 1860: d. Vienna, 1911
He was music director of the Budapest opera from 1888, then at Hamburg, 1891 to 1897, then Vienna. In 1908–1909 he conducted a season at the Metropolitan. He is famous as a symphonist. But in opera his only original work remains unfinished. For a production of *Oberon* he

made an extensive addition of musical accompaniment for the spoken scenes.

Der Herzog von Schwabe   (Unfinished)

Maillart, Louis (or **Aimé**)   Composer
b. Montpellier, France, 1817: d. Moulins, 1871

Gastibelza	Paris	1847
Le Moulin des Tilleuls	„	1849
La Croix de Marie	„	1852
Les Dragons de Villars	„	1856
Les Pêcheurs de Catane	„	1860
Lara	„	1864

Maison, René   Tenor
b. Frameries, Belgium, 1895:
He made his debut at Monte Carlo in 1921, then at Chicago in 1927 where he stayed five years. In 1936 he first appeared at the Metropolitan as Walther.
Admetus, Herod, Don José, Julien, Walther.

Makarova, Nina Vladimirovna
Composer
b. Yurin, Russia, 1908:
The wife of Aram Khatchaturian.

Courage	1942

Malherbe, Edmund Paul Henri
Composer
b. Paris, 1870:
A pupil of Fauré and Massenet.

Madame Pierre	Paris	1912
L'Émeute	„	1912

Malibran   Contralto
(Née Marietta Felicita García)
b. Paris, 1808: d. Manchester, England, 1836
The celebrated daughter of Manuel del Popolo Vicente García, and her father's most famous pupil. In 1826 she married the elderly Malibran, a businessman in New York. Later she married the violinist Bériot. She made her debut as Rosina (Il Barbiere di Siviglia) in London, 1825. She was the first Felicia (Il Crociato in Egitto by Meyerbeer).

Amina, Angelina (Cenerentola), Desdemona, Felicia (Il Crociato in Egitto), Juliette, Leonora (Fidelio), Rosina (Il Barbiere di Siviglia), Zerlina (Don Giovanni).

Malipiero, Gian Francesco   Composer
b. Venice, 1882:
A great modern contributor to the revival of ancient opera, and a composer of some twenty-five operas of his own. He made one of the two standard arrangements of La Favola d'Orfeo.

Canossa	Rome	1914
Sogno d'Un Tramonto d'Autunno		1914
L'Orfeide (trilogy)	Düsseldorf	1925
La Morte delle Maschere		
Sette Canzone		
Orfeo		
(All of these are in revolutionary form, using pantomime, film, multiple stages, etc.)		
Il Mistero di Venezia (trilogy)	Coburg	1932
Le Aquile di Aquileia		
Il Finto Arlecchino		
I Corvi di San Marco		
Il Figliuol Prodigo	Florence	1957
Venere Prigioniera	„	1957

Malipiero, Riccardo   Composer
b. Milan, 1914:
Nephew of Gian Francesco Malipiero.

Minnie La Candida	Parma	1942
La Donna è Mobile		1954

Maliszewski, Witold   Composer
b. Poland, 1873: d. Warsaw, 1939

The Mermaid	Warsaw	1939
Boruta		1930

Mallinger, Mathilde   Soprano
(Née Lichtenegger)
b. Croatia, 1847: d. Berlin, 1920
The first Eva. She made her debut as Norma at Munich, 1866.
Elsa, Eva, Norma.

Malten, Thérèse — Soprano
(*Really* Müller)
b. Prussia, 1855: d. near Dresden, 1930
The third to sing Kundry, there being three who shared in the opening performances of Parsifal. She made her debut in Dresden, 1873.
Agatha, Armida, Brünnhilde, Elisabeth, Genovéva, Iphigénie (*Iphigénie en Tauride*), Isolde, Jessonda, Kundry, Leonore (*Fidelio*), Leonora (*Il Trovatore*), Marguérite (*Faust*), Pamina, Queen of Sheba.

Mancinelli, Luigi — Composer
b. Orvieto, Italy, 1848: d. Rome, 1921
A conductor and a cellist. He led performances at Buenos Aires, Covent Garden and the Metropolitan.

Isora di Provenza	Bologna	1884
Tizianello	Rome	1895
Ero e Leandro	Madrid	1897
Sogno di una Notte d'Estate		
Paolo e Francesca	Bologna	1907

Manén, Joan — Composer
b. Barcelona, 1883:

Giovanna di Napoli	Barcelona	1902
Der Fackeltanz	Frankfurt	1909
Nero und Akté	Karlsruhe	1928
Soledad	Barcelona	1952

Manners, Charles — Bass
b. London, 1857: d. Dublin, 1935
Founder of the Moody-Manners Opera Company. He made his debut with the d'Oyly Carte company in 1882, and married Fanny Moody in 1890.

Manning, Kathleen Lockhart — Composer
b. near Hollywood, 1890: d. Los Angeles, 1951
She was also a singer, and a member of the Hammerstein Opera Company in London.
Mr. Wu
For the Soul of Rafael

Manski, Dorothée — Soprano
b. New York, 1895:

As an actress she had appeared in productions of Max Reinhardt's before she made her debut in opera singing the Witch (*Hänsel und Gretel*), at the Metropolitan in 1927.

Mapleson, James Henry — Manager
b. London, 1830: d. there, 1901
Under the name Enrico Mariani he sang opera in Italy before becoming a manager at Her Majesty's in London, 1862. He subsequently held the same position at Drury Lane, Covent Garden and the New York Academy of Music.

Mapleson, Lionel S. — Librarian
b. London, 1865: d. New York, 1937
The nephew of James Henry Mapleson. He was librarian of the Metropolitan for forty-five years. In that position he was able to make the first recordings of actual performances of the de Reszkes, Calvé, etc.

Marcel, Lucille — Soprano
(*Really* Wassell)
b. New York, 1887: d. Vienna, 1921
She made her debut at Vienna in 1908 singing Elektra, and at Boston singing Tosca in 1912. She married Felix Weingartner in 1911.

Marchesi, Blanche — Soprano
b. Paris, 1863: d. London, 1940
She made her debut in Berlin, 1895, and in London the following year.
Brünnhilde, Elisabeth, Elsa, Eva, Isolde, Kundry, Senta, Sieglinde.

Marcoux, Vanni — Baritone
(*Full name* Jean Émile Diogène Marcoux).
b. Turin, 1877:
The first Colonna (*Monna Vanna*). He made his debut as Friar Laurence in Bayonne, 1900. He claimed a repertory of two hundred forty roles.
Boris, Colonna, Friar Laurence, Méphistophélès (*Faust*).

Marinuzzi, Gino (Giuseppe) *Composer*
b. Palermo, 1882: d. (*murdered*) Milan,
1945
He was director of the Chicago Opera
in 1920–1921, at Rome 1928–1934, and at
La Scala from 1934 to 1945.

Barberina	Palermo	1903
Jacquerie	Buenos Aires	1918
Palla de' Mozzi	La Scala	1932

Marinuzzi, Gino *Conductor*
b. New York, 1920:
Son of Gino Marinuzzi (above), and a
conductor at Rome since 1946.

Mario *Tenor*
(*Really* Giovanni Matteo Mario Cavaliere
di Candia)
b. Cagliari, 1810: d. Rome, 1883
To avoid family embarrassment (for it
was improper for members of the nobility
to act on the stage), he used the plain
"Mario" for his stage name. In 1836 he
quit the army and eloped with a ballerina,
but later he made a more serious marriage
with Grisi. He made his debut at the Paris
Opéra as Robert le Diable in 1838, and
was the first Ernesto (*Don Pasquale*).
Alfredo (*La Traviata*), Count Almaviva
(*Il Barbiere di Siviglia*), Duke, Ernesto
(*Don Pasquale*), Gennaro, Lionel (*Martha*),
Don Ottavio, Raoul, Robert le Diable.

Mario, Queena *Soprano*
(*Really* Tillotson)
b. Akron, Ohio, 1896: d. New York, 1951
She made her Metropolitan debut as
Micaela in 1922. From 1931 she was a
teacher at the Curtis Institute in Phila-
delphia. From 1925 to 1936 she was
Wilfred Pelletier's wife.

Mariz, Vasco *Baritone*
b. Rio de Janeiro, 1921:
He was a Doctor of Jurisprudence at
Rio de Janeiro before making his debut at
Porto Allegre in 1945 as Doctor Bartolo
in *Le Nozze di Figaro*. Then he devoted
himself to music criticism.

Marschner, Heinrich August *Composer*
b. Saxony, 1795: d. Hanover, 1861
He wrote fourteen operas in all.

Der Vampyr	Leipzig	1828
Der Templar und Die		
Judin (*from Ivanhoe*)	„	1829
Hans Heiling	Berlin	1833

Marsick, Armand *Composer*
b. Liège, 1877: d. Brussels, 1959

Lara		1913
L'Anneau Nuptial		1920
La Jane	Liège	1921

Marteau, Henri *Composer*
b. Reims, 1874: d. Lichtenberg, 1934

Meister Schwalbe	Plauen	1921

Martelli, Henri *Composer*
b. Corsica, 1895:

La Chanson de Roland	1923

Martin, Frank *Composer*
b. Geneva, 1890:
Well known in Europe for his music for
plays, orchestral and chamber works.

The Tempest	Vienna	1956

Martin, Riccardo *Tenor*
(*Really* Hugh Whitfield Martin)
b. Hopkinsville, Ky., 1881: d. New York,
1952
He made his debut as Faust in Nantes,
1904. In 1906 he appeared as Canio in his
United States debut at New Orleans. A
year later he came out at the Metropolitan.
Avito, Canio, Enzo, Faust. Hagenbach
(*La Wally*), Mario Cavaradossi, Manrico,
Pinkerton, Rodolfo.

Martin, Vincente *Composer*
(*Really* Martin y Soler)
b. Valencia, 1754: d. St. Petersburg, 1806
Although it receives performances now
and then, his best known opera, *Una Cosa
Rara*, owes its fame to a quotation in Don
Giovanni. Perhaps this happened partly
because the librettist was da Ponte in each
case.

Una Cosa Rara	Vienna	1786

Martinelli, Giovanni   *Tenor*
b. Montagnana, Italy, 1885:
He sang his operatic debut in *Ernani* at
Milan, 1911. Martinelli was a member
of the company of the Metropolitan from
1913 to 1946. His debut there was as
Rodolfo. He sang the first Paolo (*Paolo e
Francesca*), and the first Fernando (*Goy-
escas*).
Calaf, Canio, Don Carlos, Eléazar,
Enzo, Fernando (*Goyescas*), Gennaro,
Gérald, John (*Le Prophète*), Johnson, Don
José, Lensky, Loris (*Fedora*), Manrico,
Oberon, Otello, Paolo (*Paolo e Francesca*),
Radames, Raoul, Riccardo (*Un Ballo in
Maschera*), Rodolfo, Samson, Tristan,
Vasco de Gama.

Martini, Nino   *Tenor*
b. Verona, Italy, 1905:
He made his debut in Philadelphia in
1931 before appearing for the first time at
the Metropolitan two years later as the
Duke in *Rigoletto*.

Martinon, Jean   *Composer*
b. Lyons, 1910:
Hécube   1954

Martinu, Bohuslav   *Composer*
b. Czechoslovakia, 1890: d. Liestal, Swit-
zerland, 1959
The Soldier and the
Ballerina   Brno   1928
Les Lames du Couteau   Paris   1928
Hry o Marii   Brno   1934
Juliette   Prague   1938
The Marriage   NBC/TV   1953

Marty, Eugène Georges   *Composer*
b. Paris, 1860: d. there, 1908
Le Duc de Ferrare   Paris   1899
Daria   ,,   1905

Mascagni, Pietro   *Composer*
b. Leghorn, Italy, 1863: d. Rome, 1945
The protagonist of the Italian "Verismo," producing realistic music drama.
His short opera *Cavalleria Rusticana* which

won the prize of the publisher Sonzogno,
created a sensation and established a trend.
Pinotta
(*composed* 1880)   San Remo   1932
Cavalleria Rusticana   Rome   1890
L'Amico Fritz   ,,   1891
Guglielmo Ratcliff   Milan   1895
Iris   Rome   1898
Le Maschera   ,,   1901
(*Simultaneously produced in six cities.*)
Nerone   Milan   1935

Massa, Juan Bautista   *Composer*
b. Buenos Aires, 1865: d. Rosario, 1938
Zoraide   Buenos Aires   1909
L'Eraso   Rosario   1922
La Magdalena   Buenos Aires   1929

Massé, Victor   *Composer*
b. Lorient, France, 1822: d. Paris, 1884
Les Noces de Jeannette   Paris   1853

Massenet, Jules Émile Fréderic
Composer
b. near St. Étienne, 1842: d. Paris, 1912
A pupil of Ambroise Thomas and him-
self a teacher of many opera composers.
Don César de Bazan   Paris   1872
Le Roi de Lahore   ,,   1877
Hérodiade (Salomé)   Brussels   1881
Manon   Paris   1884
Le Cid   ,,   1885
Werther   Vienna   1892
Thaïs   Paris   1894
Le Portrait de Manon   ,,   1894
La Navarraise   London   1894
Sapho   Paris   1897
Le Jongleur de
Notre Dame   Monte Carlo   1902
Don Quichotte   ,,   1910

Materna, Amalie   *Soprano*
b. Styria, 1845: d. Vienna, 1918
She was the very first among the three
sopranos who shared the role of Kundry
at the opening of *Parsifal*. She was also
the first Brünnhilde in *Siegfried*. Her debut
was in 1864, and her first appearance at the
Metropolitan, as Elisabeth, in 1885.

Brünnhilde, Elisabeth, Kundry, Rachel, Selika, Valentine (*Les Huguenots*).

Matzenauer, Margarete
Soprano and Mezzo-soprano
b. Hungary, 1881:
She made her debut in Strasbourg in 1901 and at the Metropolitan, as Amneris, in 1911. The following year she married the singer Ferrari-Fontana.

Aida, Amelia, Amneris, Donna Anna, Azucena, Brünnhilde, Carmen, Dalila, Donna Elvira, Erde, Fatima (*Oberon*), Gioconda, Kostelnika (*Její Pastorkyňa*), Kundry, Leonore (*Fidelio*), Mignon, Norma, Ortrud, Santuzza, Selika, Ulrica, Venus.

Maurel, Victor *Baritone*
b. Marseilles, 1848: d. New York, 1923
The first Iago, the first Tonio, and the first Falstaff. He made his debut at the Opéra in 1868 singing de Nevers.

Count Almaviva (*Le Nozze di Figaro*), Amonasro, Cacique (*Il Guarany*), Domingo (*Paul et Virginie*, by Massé), Dutchman, Falstaff, Don Giovanni, Guillaume Tell, Hamlet, Hoël, Iago, Conte di Luna, de Nevers, Peter the Great, Renato, Telramund, Tonio, Valentin (*Faust*), Wolfram.

Mayr, Richard *Bass*
b. near Salzburg, 1877: d. Vienna, 1935
He made his debut as Hagen at Bayreuth in 1902, and as Pogner at the Metropolitan in 1927.

Gurnemanz, Don Gomez (*Ernani*), Hagen, Idomeneo, King Marke, Baron Ochs, Pogner, Wotan.

McArthur, Edwin *Conductor*
b. Denver, Colo., 1907:
He began his operatic career as pianist for Flagstad, Jeritza and Pinza. He subsequently conducted at Chicago, San Francisco and St. Louis.

McCormack, John *Tenor*
b. Athlone, Ireland, 1884: d. near Dublin, 1945

The story goes that the novelist James Joyce once contemplated singing as a career, but decided against it when he heard John McCormack singing opposing him in a contest. McCormack made his debut in Covent Garden as Turiddu in 1907, and at New York as Alfredo Germont in 1909.

Alfredo Germont, Duke, Faust (*Faust*), Faust (*Mefistofele*), Gérald, Gritzko (*The Fair at Sorotchinsk*), Mario Cavaradossi, Pinkerton, Don Ottavio, Rodolfo, Tonio, Turiddu.

McCoy, William J. *Composer*
b. Crestline, Ohio, 1848: d. Oakland, Calif. 1920

Egypt	Berkeley, Calif.	1921

McCracken, James *Tenor*
b.
Alvaro, Bacchus, Otello.

Mediņš, Janis *Composer*
b. Riga, Lithuania, 1890:

Uguns un Nakts		
(*Fire and Night*)	Riga	1921
Deevi un Cilveki	„	1922

Méhul, Étienne Nicolas *Composer*
b. Givet, France, 1763: d. Paris, 1867

Ariodant	Opéra-Comique	1799
Joseph	„	1807
Les Amazones	Opéra	1811

Meisle, Kathryn *Contralto*
b. Philadelphia, 1899:
She made her debut as Erda at Chicago and as Amneris at the Metropolitan, 1935.

Melba, Nellie *Soprano*
(*Really* Helen Porter Armstrong, *née* Mitchell)
b. near Melbourne, 1861: d. Sydney, Australia, 1931
A famous Lucia, the first Hélène (*Saint-Saëns*), she made her stage name from the name of her home town. She first sang at Brussels as Gilda in 1887 and at the Metropolitan as Lucia in 1893. Melba toast is named for her.

Brünnhilde, Elsa, Gilda, Juliette, Lucia, Margherite (*La Damnation de Faust*), Marguérite (*Faust*), Maguerite de Valois, Micaela, Mimi, Nedda, Ophélie, Rosina (*Il Barbiere di Siviglia*), Violetta.

Melchior, Lauritz   *Tenor*
b. Copenhagen, 1890:
This famous heroic tenor made his debut at his birthplace as Canio in 1913, then at the Metropolitan in 1926 as Tannhäuser.
Canio, Otello, Parsifal, Siegfried, Siegmund, Tannhäuser, Tristan.

Melis, Carmen   *Soprano*
b. Cagliari, Sardinia, 1885:
A pupil of Jean de Reszke and herself the teacher of Renata Tebaldi. She made her debut at Naples in 1906 and at the Metropolitan as Tosca in 1909.

Mellers, Wilfrid Howard *Composer*
b. Leamington, England, 1914:
The Tragical History of
 Christopher Marlowe   1952

Melnikov, Ivan Alexandrovitch *Bass*
b. St. Petersburg, 1832: d. there, 1906
The first to sing Boris Godunov in a complete performance.

Melton, James   *Tenor*
b. Moultrie, Ga., 1904:
A pupil of Giuseppe de Luca. He made his debut at Cincinnati in 1938 and sang at the Metropolitan from 1942 to 1950. He is fairly well known outside opera as a collector of antique automobiles.

Mendelssohn-Bartholdy, Felix *Composer*
(*Full name* Jakob Ludwig Felix Mendelssohn-Bartholdy)
b. Hamburg, 1809: d. Leipzig, 1847
Famous as a symphonist and for his delicious music to the *Midsummer Night's Dream* of Shakespeare, Mendelssohn is also notable for having brought out in 1829 the *St. Matthew Passion* of Bach

which had lain unheard since its composer's death.
Loreley (*unfinished*)
Die Hochzeit des
 Camacho   Berlin 1827

Menotti, Gian-Carlo   *Composer*
b. Cadegliano, Italy, 1911:
Menotti is celebrated for his excellent staging—he frequently directs productions of his own works. He is a pioneer in the field of television opera. Besides libretto's for his own works, Menotti wrote the libretto for and staged Barber's *Vanessa*.
Amelia Goes to the
 Ball   Philadelphia 1937
The Old Maid and the
 Thief   NBC 1939
The Island God Metropolitan 1942
The Medium New York 1946
The Consul   ,, 1950
Amahl and the Night
 Visitors   NBC/TV 1951
The Saint of
 Bleecker Street New York 1954
Maria Golovin Brussels 1958

Mercadante, Giuseppe Saverio Raffaele
         Composer
b. Altamura, 1795: d. Naples, 1870
L'Apoteosi d'Ercole Naples 1819
Elisa e Claudio   La Scala 1821
Il Giuramento   Milan 1837

Merikanto, Oskar   *Composer*
b. Helsinki, 1868: d. Hausjarvi-Oiti, 1924
Pohjan Neiti   Viborg 1908
Elinan Surma   Helsinki 1910
Regina von Emmeritz ,, 1920

Merrill, Robert   *Baritone*
b. Brooklyn, N.Y., 1917:
He made his debut at the Metropolitan in 1945 as Germont.
Escamillo, Count di Luna, Figaro (*Il Barbiere di Siviglia*), Germont, Renato (*Un Ballo in Maschera*), Rigoletto, Rodrigo, Tonio.

Messager, André Charles Prosper
Composer
b. Montlucon, France, 1853: d. Paris, 1929
A conductor too, he led the first performance of *Pelléas et Mélisande*.

La Basoche	Paris	1890
Madame Chrysanthème	„	1893
Mirette	London	1894
Véronique	Paris	1898
Monsieur Beaucaire	Birmingham	1919

Messner, Joseph
Composer
b. Tyrol, 1893:

Hadassa	Aachen	1925
Das Letzte Recht		1932
Ines		1933
Agnes Bernauer		1935

Metastasio, Abbé
Librettist
(*Really* Pietro Trapassi)
b. Rome, 1698: d. Vienna, 1782
He made his stage name by an anagram of his original name plus the Greek word for change—*meta*, "beyond." He composed music, played the harpsichord and sang. He wrote twenty-nine dramas, eight oratorios, and many other works. Among his dramas are *Semiramide* (used by Gluck, Meyerbeer and others), *Artaserse* (by the same, forty-one times), *La Clemenza di Tito* (used by Gluck, Mozart, etc.), *Il Re Pastore* (Gluck, Mozart, etc.).

Meyerbeer, Giacomo
Composer
(*Really* Jakob Liebmann Beer)
b. Berlin, 1791: d. Paris, 1864
Meyerbeer's operas are the prototypes of that style called "grand opera." They are distinguished not so much for size of cast or production, but for a formality and richness of style plus, usually, a choice of subject of grand proportions.

Robert le Diable	Opéra	1831
Les Huguenots	„	1836
Le Prophète	„	1849
L'Étoile du Nord	Opéra-Comique	1854
Dinorah	„	1859
L'Africaine	Opéra	1865

Meyerowitz, Jan
Composer
b. Breslau, 1913:

Simoon	Tanglewood, Mass.	1949
The Barrier	New York	1950
Eastward in Eden	Detroit	1951
Bad Boys in School	Tanglewood	1953
Esther	Urbana, Ill.	1957

Michaelides, Solon
Composer
b. Nicosia, Cyprus, 1905:
Ulysses (*Libretto by the composer.*)

Mignone, Francisco
Composer
b. São Paulo, Brazil, 1897:

O Contractador dos Diamantes	Rio de Janeiro	1924
L'Innocente	„	1928

Mihalovici, Marcel
Composer
b. Bucharest, 1898:
L'Intransigeant Pluton

Phèdre		1948
Die Heimkehr	Frankfurt Radio	1954

Milanov, Zinka
Soprano
b. Zagreb, 1906:
A pupil of Ternina, she made her debut in Zagreb in 1927 as Leonora (*Il Trovatore*), and at the Metropolitan in 1937 in the same role. She is famous for her high pianissimi.

Aida, Amelia, Donna Anna, Desdemona, Elvira (*Ernani*), Gioconda, Leonora (*La Forza del Destino*), Leonora (*Il Trovatore*), Maddalena, Maria (*Simon Boccanegra*), Norma, Reiza, Santuzza, Tosca.

Milde, Hans Feodor von
Baritone
b. near Vienna, 1821: d. Weimar, 1899
The first Telramund, the first High Priest (*Samson et Dalila*). He was a pupil of Manuel García the younger, and the husband of Rosa Agthé.

Mildenburg, Anna von *Soprano*
b. Vienna, 1872: d. there 1947
Amneris, Brünnhilde, Iphigénie (*Iphig-énie en Aulide*), Isolde, Klytemnestra, Kundry.

Milder, Anna *Soprano*
(*Really* Pauline Anne Milder-Hauptmann)
b. Constantinople, 1785: d. Berlin, 1838
The first Leonore (*Fidelio*). When Haydn heard her sing, as a child, he said "My dear, you have a voice like a house." She made her debut in Vienna in 1803.
Alcestis, Armida (*Gluck*), Donna Elvira, Iphigénie (*Iphigénie en Tauride*), Leonore (*Fidelio*), Susanna (*Le Nozze di Figaro*).

Miles, Philip Napier *Composer*
b. Gloucestershire, England, 1865: d. Bristol, 1935

Westward Ho!	London	1913
Markheim		1926
Queen Rosamund		

Milhaud, Darius *Composer*
b. Aix-en-Provence, 1892:
A very prolific composer of music in all forms; one of "Les Six." His three *Minute Operas* are little gems.

Les Choëphores	Paris	1919
La Brebis Égarée	„	1923
Les Malheurs d'Orphée	Brussels	1926
Agamemnon	Paris	1927
Le Pauvre Matelot	„	1927
Les Euménides	Antwerp	1927
Christophe Colomb	Berlin	1930
Maximilien	Paris	1932
Esther de Carpentras	„	1938
Medée	Antwerp	1939
Bolivar	„	1950
David	Jerusalem	1954

Miller, Mildred *Mezzo-Soprano*
b. Cleveland, Ohio, 1924:
She had her debut at Stuttgart in 1949. In 1951 she sang for the first time at the Metropolitan as Cherubino.

Carmen, Cherubino, Dorabella, Fyodor (*Boris Godunov*), Octavian, Orlovsky, Preziosilla (*La Forza del Destino*), Suzuki.

Millöcker, Karl *Composer*
b. Vienna, 1842: d. there, 1899

| Der Bettelstudent | Vienna | 1882 |

Mitropoulos, Dmitri *Conductor*
b. Athens, 1896: d. Milan, 1960
A famous symphony conductor who also conducted opera at the Metropolitan and elsewhere.

Mitterwurzer, Anton *Baritone*
b. Sterzing, Germany, 1818: d. near Vienna, 1876
The first Wolfram, the first Kurnewal.

Mödl, Martha *Soprano*
b. Nürnberg, 1912:
She made her debut as Dorabella in Düsseldorf in 1944.
Brünnhilde, Carmen, Composer (*Ariadne auf Naxos*), Dorabella, Princess Eboli, Isolde, Klytemnestra, Jocasta, Kundry, Lady Macbeth, Leonore (*Fidelio*), Magda (*The Consul*), Marie (*Wozzeck*), Octavian, Ortrud.

Mohaupt, Richard *Composer*
b. Breslau, 1904: d. Reichenau, Austria, 1957

Die Wirtin von Pinsk	Dresden	1938
Die Bremer Stadtmusikanten	Bremen	1949
Double Trouble	Louisville, Ky.	1954

Monaco, Mario Del *Tenor*
b. Florence, 1915:
He made his debut as Pinkerton in Milan in 1941, and as des Grieux at the Metropolitan in 1950.
Don Alvaro, Andrea Chénier, Canio, Dick Johnson, Enzo, Faust (*Mefistofele*), des Grieux, Don José, Luigi (*Il Tabarro*), Manrico, Mario Cavaradossi, Otello, Pinkerton, Radames, Samson.

Mondonville, Jean Joseph Cassanea de
                    Composer
b. Narbonne, France, 1711: d. Paris, 1772

Isbé	Paris	1742
Le Carnaval du Parnasse	,,	1749

Moniusko, Stanislaus   *Composer*
b. Minsk, 1820: d. Warsaw, 1872
Moniuszko wrote twenty operas.

Halka	Vilna	1848
Flis	Warsaw	1858
Der Paria	,,	1869

Monsigny, Pierre Alexandre   *Composer*
b. near St. Omer, France, 1729: d. Paris, 1817

Le Déserteur	Paris	1769
Rose et Colas	,,	1764
Le Faucon	,,	1772
La Belle Arsène	,,	1775

Montéclair, Michel Pinolet de
                    Composer
b. Andelot, France, circa 1666: d. near
Paris, 1737
A composer and a very early double-bass player.

Jephté	Opéra	1732

Monti, Toti dal   *Soprano*
(*Really* Antonietta Meneghal)
b. Treviso, Italy, 1893:
Cio-cio San, Gilda.

Montemezzi, Italo   *Composer*
b. near Verona, 1875: d. 1952

Giovanni Gallurese	Turin	1905
Hellera	,,	1909
L'Amore dei Tre Re	La Scala	1913
La Nave	Milan	1918
La Notte di Zoraima	,,	1931
L'Incantesimo	NBC	1943

Monteux, Pierre   *Conductor*
b. Paris, 1875:
Celebrated conductor of symphony and opera; continued an active career in his eighties.

Monteverdi, Claudio   *Composer*
b. Cremona, 1567: d. Venice, 1643

One of the greatest of opera composers. He spent the most productive part of his career in Venice. He is credited, with the invention of the pizzicato and the tremolo (not the vibrato) as orchestral techniques. Of his *Arianna*, only one *Lamento* remains, and it is one of the most beautiful melodies in all opera.

La Favola d'Orfeo	Mantua	1607
Arianna	,,	1608
Il Ballo delle Ingrate	,,	1608
Il Combattimento di		
Tancredi e Clorinda	Venice	1624
Proserpina Rapita	,,	1630
Il Ritorno d'Ulisse		
in Patria	,,	1641
Le Nozze di Enea		
con Lavinia	,,	1641
L'Incoronazione di Poppea	,,	1642

Moody, Fanny   *Soprano*
b. Redruth, Cornwall, 1866: d. near Dublin, 1945
Co-founder with her husband of the Moody-Manners Opera Company. She had married him in 1890.
    Elisabeth, Elsa, Eva, Irene (*Rienzi*), Isolde, Kundry, Senta, Sieglinde.

Moor, Emanuel   *Composer*
b. Hungary, 1862: d. 1931

Die Pompadour	Cologne	1902
Andreas Hofer	,,	1902
Hochzeitsglocken	Kassel	1908

Moore, Douglas   *Composer*
b. Cutchogue, N.Y., 1893:

The Headless Horseman		1936
The Devil and		
Daniel Webster	New York	1939
The Emperor's		
New Clothes	,,	1949
Giants in the Earth	,,	1951
The Ballad of Baby Doe		
Central City, Colo.		1956

Moore, Frank Ledlie   *Composer*
b. Cambridge, Mass., 1923:

A composer of dramas in music to his own libretti, and of music in all forms.

The Anarchists	1955
John Brown	1957
Ryan	1958
Mine Host	1960

Moore, Grace   *Soprano*
b. Jellico, Tenn., 1901: d. Copenhagen, 1947
She made her debut at the Metropolitan as Mimi in 1928. She sang in many films.
Fiora, Louise, Manon, Mimi.

Morel, Jean   *Conductor*
b. Abbeville, France, 1903:
He has been with the Metropolitan since 1956.

Morelli, Carlo   *Baritone*
(*Really* Zanelli)
b. Valparaiso, Chile, 1897:
He sang at the Metropolitan from 1935 to 1940.
Barnaba, Manfredo (*L'Amore dei Tre Re*), Wolfram.

Morena, Berta   *Soprano*
(*Really* Meyer)
b. Mannheim, 1878: d. Rottach Eggern, 1952
She made her debut as Agathe in Munich, 1898, and as Sieglinde at the Metropolitan in 1908.
Agathe, Brünnhilde, Elisabeth, Elsa, Eva, Isolde, Sieglinde.

Mortari, Virgilio   *Composer*
b. near Milan, 1902:
He completed the unfinished opera L'Oca del Cairo, by Mozart, for performance in Salzburg, 1936.

Secchi e Sberlecchi	Udine	1927
La Scuola delle Moglie		1930
La Figlia del Diavolo	Milan	1954

Moscona, Nicola   *Bass*
b. Athens, 1907:
He made his debut at the Metropolitan in 1937 singing Ramfis.

Alvise, Arkel, Colline, Ferrando (*Il Trovatore*), Old Hebrew (*Samson et Dalila*), Oroveso, Ramfis, Sparafucile, Il Talpa (*Il Tabarro*).

Moszkowski, Moritz   *Composer*
b. Breslau, 1854: d. Paris, 1925
He was famous as a pianist and a composer for the piano.

| Boabdil | Berlin | 1892 |

Mottl, Felix   *Composer*
b. near Vienna, 1856: d. Munich, 1911
He put *Der Barbier von Bagdad* into its present form, and conducted the premiere of the first complete production of *Les Troyens*.

| Agnes Bernauer | Weimar | 1880 |
| Fürst und Sänger | Karlsruhe | 1893 |

Mouret, Jean Joseph   *Composer*
b. Avignon, France, 1682: d. Charenton, 1738

| Ariane | Paris | 1717 |

Moussorgsky
See Mussorgsky

Mozart, Wolfgang Amadeus
     Composer
b. Salzburg, Austria, 1756: d. Vienna, 1791
One of the most famous composers in every form of music in use in Europe, Mozart made changes in the technique of opera that are still basic today, and which infuse his own work with an excitement throughout every scene. Although he continued the practice of dry recitative, his sense of dramatic flow maintains our interest on a high level even in these passages. His arias almost always carry on the action of the play, rather than stopping it for the sake of the voice, and their musical character is always closely in tune with their dramatic purpose. He had studied with Haydn, and had himself given Beethoven a few lessons. In composing *Don Giovanni* Mozart worked very closely

THE PEOPLE IN OPERA

with his librettist, and even spent a few days at cafes working out dramatic ideas with the famous Casanova. This, however, could hardly have been as instructive to Mozart, who was himself an experienced enchanter of court ladies, as it must have been pleasurable.

Although he was remarkably successful in opera and in concerts, Mozart died, at the age of thirty-five, penniless.

La Finta Semplice	Salzburg	1769
Bastien et Bastienne	Vienna	1768
L'Oca del Cairo	(Unfinished)	
Lo Sposo Deluso	"	
Mitridate	Milan	1770
Ascanio in Alba	"	1771
Il Sogno di Scipione	Salzburg	1772
Lucio Silla	Milan	1772
La Finta Giardiniera	Munich	1775
Il Re Pastore	Salzburg	1775
Zaïda	(Unfinished)	
Idomeneo	Munich	1781
Die Entführung aus dem Serail	Vienna	1782
Der Schauspieldirektor	Schönbrunn	1786
Le Nozze di Figaro	Vienna	1786
Don Giovanni	Prague	1787
Così fan Tutte	Vienna	1790
La Clemenza di Tito	Prague	1791
Die Zauberflöte	Vienna	1791

Muck, Karl   *Conductor*
b. Darmstadt, 1859: d. Stuttgart, 1940
Conductor of the Boston Symphony and of the Berlin Opera.

Mugnone, Leopoldo   *Conductor*
b. Naples, 1858: d. there, 1941
He conducted the first performance of *Cavalleria Rusticana.*

Müller, Maria   *Soprano*
b. Leitmoritz, Austria, 1898: d. Bayreuth, 1958
She made her Metropolitan debut as Sieglinde in 1925.
Helena (*Die Aegyptische Helena*),

Iphigénie (*Iphigénie en Tauride*), Jenufa, Marenka (*Prodaná Nevĕsta*), Rezia, Senta, Sieglinde.

Mullings, Frank   *Tenor*
b. Walsall, England, 1881:
The first Apollo (*Alkestis* by Boughton).
Apollo (*Alkestis*), Otello, Parsifal, Radames, Siegfried, Tannhäuser, Tristan.

Munsel, Patrice   *Soprano*
b. Spokane, Wash., 1925:
She made her debut at the Metropolitan in 1943, the youngest debutante the Metropolitan ever had.
Adele (*Die Fledermaus*), Gilda, Juliette, Lakmé, Lucia, Musetta, Rosina (*Il Barbiere di Siviglia*), Violetta, Zerlina (*Don Giovanni*).

Muratore, Lucien   *Tenor*
b. Marseilles, 1876: d. Paris, 1954
He made his debut at the Opéra-Comique, in 1902, and at the Metropolitan in 1913.
Faust (*Faust*), Don José, Rinaldo (*Armide*), Romeo.

Murska, Ilma di   *Soprano*
b. Croatia, 1836: d. Munich (*suicide*), 1889
She made her debut at Florence in 1862.
Amina, Astrifiamante, Constanze, Dinorah, Inez, Linda, Lucia, Martha, Senta.

Mussorgsky, Modest   *Composer*
b. near Pskov, 1839: d. St. Petersburg, 1881
The greatest of the Russian composers of opera, one of the "Mighty Five." He is well known also in concerts for his piano piece, *Pictures at an Exhibition.*

Boris Godunov	St. Petersburg	1874
Khovantchina	"	1885
The Fair at Sorotchinsk		1911
Zhenitba	"	1917

Muzio, Claudia   *Soprano*
b. Pavia, Italy, 1889: d. Rome, 1936

She had her debut at Arezzo in 1912 as Manon, and at the Metropolitan in 1916 as Tosca. She was the first Giorgetta (*Il Tabarro*).

Aida, Bertha (*Le Prophète*), Fiora, Giorgetta, Leonora (*La Forza del Destino*), Maddalena, Manon, Marguerite (*Mefistofele*), Norma, Tatyana, Tosca, Turandot, Violetta.

Nabokov, Nicolas   *Composer*
b. near Minsk, R., 1903:
The Holy Devil   Louisville, Ky.   1958

Nachbaur, Franz   *Tenor*
b. Giessen, Germany, 1830: d. Munich, 1902
The first Walther.
Adolar, Lohengrin, Mime, Walther.

Napoli, Jacopo   *Composer*
b. Naples, 1911:
Il Malato Immaginario   Naples   1939
Miseria e Nobilità   "   1945
Un Curioso
Accidente   Bergamo   1950
Masaniello   La Scala   1951

Napravnik, Eduard F.   *Composer*
b. Bohemia, 1839: d. St. Petersburg, 1916
In St. Petersburg he became the chief conductor of the Imperial Opera where he led over three thousand performances.
Nizhegorotzy   St. Petersburg   1869
Harold   "   1886
Dubrovsky   "   1895
Francesca da Rimini   "   1902

Nardini, Emilio   *Tenor*
b. Parma, 1823: d. Boulogne sur Mer, 1890
The first Vasco da Gama.

Naumann, Johann Gottlieb   *Composer*
b. near Dresden, 1741: d. Dresden, 1801
He wrote twenty-four operas.
La Clemenza di Tito   1769
Armida   1773
Amphion (*in Swedish*)   1776
Cora   1780

Nessler, Victor E.   *Composer*
b. Baldenheim, Alsace, 1841: d. Strasbourg, 1890   •
Der Rattenfänger
von Hameln   Leipzig   1879
Der Trompeter
von Säkkingen   "   1884
Die Rose von Strassburg   Munich   1890

Neumann, František   *Composer*
b. Moravia, 1874: d. Brno, 1929
He not only wrote his own operas, but conducted most of the first performances of those by Janáček. From 1925 to 1929 he was director of the Czech National Opera.
Leyer und Schwert   1901
Die Brautwerbung   Linz   1901
Liebelei   Frankfurt   1910
Herbststurm   Berlin   1919
Beatrice Caracci   Brno   1922

Nevada, Emma   *Soprano*
(*Née* Wixom)
b. Alpha, Calif., 1859: d. Liverpool, 1940
She made her debut as Amina in London in 1880.
Amina, Lucia, Mireille, Zora (*La Perle du Brésil*).

Nevada, Mignon Marie   *Soprano*
b. Paris, 1886:
Daughter of Emma Nevada. She made her debut as Rosina in *Il Barbiere di Siviglia* in 1907.

Nevin, Arthur Finley   *Composer*
b. Edgeworth, Pa., 1871: d. Sewickley, Pa., 1943
Nevin's best known work, *Poia*, survived only four performances.
Poia   Berlin   1910
A Daughter of
the Forest   Chicago   1918

Neway, Patricia   *Soprano*
b.
The first Magda (*The Consul*). Always an organizer, in 1960 she formed her own opera company in New York.

Magda (*The Consul*), Marie (*Wozzeck*), Mother (*Amahl and the Night Visitors*), Mother (*Maria Golovin*), Nelly (*Wuthering Heights*), Santuzza.

Nicholls, Agnes *Soprano*
b. Cheltenham, England, 1877:
She made her debut in London as Dido (*Dido and Aeneas*), in 1895.

Nicolai, Karl Otto Ehrenfried
Composer
b. Königsberg, 1810: d. Berlin, 1849
The founder of the Berlin Philharmonic. He was organist of the Prussian Embassy at Rome, Kapellmeister in Vienna, and head of the Berlin Opera.

Rosmonda d'Inghilterra	Turin	1838
Il Templario	„	1840
Odoardo e Gildippe	„	1841
Il Proscrito	Milan	1841
Die Lustigen Weiber von Windsor	Berlin	1849

Nicolini *Tenor*
(*Originally* Ernest Nicolas)
b. Saint-Malo, France, 1834: d. Pau, 1898
He made his debut at the Opéra-Comique in 1857. In 1886 he married Patti.
Edgardo, Faust (*Faust*), Lohengrin, Raoul.

Nielsen, Carl August *Composer*
b. Funen, Denmark, 1865: d. Copenhagen, 1931
The most celebrated composer of Denmark, his symphonies are popular.

Saul and David	Copenhagen	1902
Maskarade	„	1906

Nielsen, Ludolf *Composer*
b. Nørre-Tvede, Denmark, 1876: d. Copenhagen, 1939

Isabella	Copenhagen	1915
Uhret (*The Clock*)	„	1920
Lola	„	1920

Niemann, Albert *Tenor*
b. near Magdeburg, Germany, 1831: d. Berlin, 1917

He made his debut at Hanover in 1860 and at the Metropolitan, singing Siegmund, in 1886.
Florestan, John of Leyden, Joseph, Lohengrin, Parsifal, Raoul, Siegfried, Siegmund, Tannhäuser, Walther.

Nikolaidi, Elena *Contralto*
b. Smyrna, Greece, 1914:
She made her debut in Vienna in 1936.

Nilsson, Birgit *Soprano*
b. Västra Karup, Sweden, 1921:
Brünhilde, Elektra, Elisabeth (*Tannhäuser*), Salome, Turandot (Puccini).

Nilsson, Christine *Soprano*
b. near Vexiö, Sweden, 1843: d. Stockholm, 1921
She made her debut as Violetta in Paris, 1864. Her first appearance at the Metropolitan was the night that theater opened; she sang Marguérite. She sang the first Myrrha (*Sardanapale*).
Astrifiamante, Cherubino, Countess Almaviva (*Le Nozze di Figaro*), Desdemona, Elsa, Donna Elvira, Gioconda, Helen (*Mefistofele*), Lucia, Marguérite (*Faust*), Mignon, Myrrha (*Sardanapale*), Ophélie, Violetta.

Nissen, Hans Hermann *Baritone*
b. near Danzig, 1896:
Father (*Le Pauvre Matelot*), Hans Sachs, Orest (*Elektra*), Wotan.

Nordica, Lillian *Soprano*
(*Née* Norton-Gower)
b. Farmington, Maine, 1857: d. Java, 1914
She came out first in Milan as Donna Elvira, 1879. She first sang in New York in 1883 as Marguérite. Her Metropolitan debut was in 1890.
Aida, Amelia, Donna Anna, Brünnhilde, Elsa, Donna Elvira, Gilda, Gioconda, Isolde, Lucia, Marguérite (*Faust*), Ophélie, Philine, Selika, Susanna (*Le Nozze di Figaro*), Valentine (*Les Huguenots*), Violetta.

Norena, Eide *Soprano*
(*Really* Kaja Hansen Eide)
b. Horten, Norway, 1884:
She made her debut at the Metropolitan in 1933 as Mimi.
Desdemona, Gilda, Liù, Mimi.

Noskowsky, Sigismund *Composer*
b. Warsaw, 1846: d. Wiesbaden, 1909

Livia Quintilla	Lemberg	1898
Wyrok	Warsaw	1907

Nouguès, Jean *Composer*
b. Bordeaux, 1875: d. Auteil, 1932
His opera *Quo Vadis* had a spectacular success.

Quo Vadis	Nice	1909

Nourrit, Adolphe *Tenor*
b. Paris, 1802: d. Naples (*suicide*), 1839
After a debut as Pylade (*Iphigénie en Tauride*) at the Opéra in 1821, Nourrit sang the following roles for their first performances:
Arnold (*Guillaume Tell*), Douglas (*Macbeth*), Eléazar, Masaniello, Raoul, Robert le Diable, Stradella (by Niedermayer).

Nourrit, Louis *Tenor*
b. Montpellier, 1780: d. Brunoy, 1831
The father of Adolphe Nourrit, and famous as a singer himself. But he never gave up his trade as a diamond merchant.

Novák, Vitezslav *Composer*
b. Bohemia, 1870: d. Slovakia, 1949

Burgkobold	Prague	1915
A Night at Karlstein	,,	1916
Lucerna	,,	1923
Deduv Odkaz (*The Grandfather's Heritage*)	Brno	1926

Novello, Clara *Soprano*
b. London, 1818: d. Rome, 1908
A famous singer in concert and opera. She made her debut in Padua in 1841, but spent the greater part of her professional career in England.

Novotna, Jarmila *Soprano*
b. Prague, 1903:

A pupil of Destinn. She made her debut in *La Traviata* at Prague, 1926. Her first appearance in this country was at San Francisco, 1939, when she sang Suzuki.
Cherubino, Euridice, Frasquita (*Der Corregidor*), Freia, Marenka, Octavian, Orlovsky, Pamina, Suzuki, Wife (*Le Pauvre Matelot*).

Ober, Margarete
Soprano and Mezzo-soprano
b. Berlin, 1885:
She made her debut at Frankfurt in 1906 singing Azucena, and at the Metropolitan in 1913 as Ortrud.
Amneris, Azucena, Brangäne, Dalila, Eglantine, Erda, Fidès, Fricka, Klytemnestra (*Iphigénie en Aulide*), Laura, Marina Mnishek, Octavian, Ortrud, Waltraute, Witch (*Hänsel and Gretel*).

Oboussier, Robert *Composer*
b. Antwerp, 1900: d. Zürich (*murdered*), 1957

Amphitryon	Berlin	1951

Offenbach, Jacques *Composer*
(*Really* Jacob Eberst)
b. Cologne, 1819: d. Paris, 1880
From 1855 to 1866 Offenbach was manager of his own theater *Les Bouffes Parisiens*. Things did not go well until he brought out his hilarious *Orphée aux Enfers* and became a success for life. His most famous, but not his best, work, *Les Contes d'Hoffmann*, was completed by Bizet's friend Guiraud.

Orphée aux Enfers	Paris	1858
Geneviève de Brabant	,,	1859
La Belle Hélène	,,	1864
La Vie parisienne	,,	1866
La Grande Duchesse de Gérolstein	,,	1867
La Périchole	,,	1868
Les Contes d'Hoffmann	Opéra-Comique	1881

Olczewska, Maria *Contralto*
b. near Augsburg, Germany, 1892:

She made her debut in Leipzig in 1920 and at the Metropolitan, singing Brangäne, thirteen years later.
Brangäne, Carmen, Herodias (*Salome*), Octavian.

Ollone, Max d'   *Composer*
b. Besançon, France, 1875: d. Paris, 1959
A pupil of Massenet.

Le Retour	Angers	1913
Les Uns et les Autres	Paris	1922
L'Arlequin	„	1924
Georges Dandin	„	1930
La Samaritaine	„	1937

Olsen, Ole   *Composer*
b. Hammerfest, Norway, 1850: d. Oslo, 1927
He wrote his own libretti.

Stig Hvide		1876
Stallo		1902
Klippeøerne		1905
Lajla	Oslo	1908

Onégin, Sigrid   *Contralto*
b. Stockholm, 1889: d. Magliaso, Switzerland, 1943
She made her debut as Carmen in Stuttgart in 1912, and as Amneris at the Metropolitan ten years later.
Amneris, Carmen, Dalila, Lady Macbeth.

Orefice, Giacomo   *Composer*
b. Vicenza, 1865: d. Milan, 1922
Besides his original works, he arranged *La Favola d'Orfeo* for a production in Milan, 1909.

Mariska	Turin	1889
Consuelo	Bologna	1895
Il Gladiatore	Madrid	1898
Chopin	Milan	1901
Cecilia	Vicenza	1902
Mosè	Genoa	1905
Il Pane d'Altrui	Venice	1907
Radda	Milan	1912

Orff, Carl   *Composer*
b. Munich, 1895:

Orff has startled a good many audiences with his primitive-sounding music. He prefers harmonic simplicity to contrapuntal complexity. He is best known for his cycle of choral songs, *Carmina Burana*, to medieval texts.

Der Mond	Munich	1939
Die Kluge	Frankfurt	1943
Antigonae	Salzburg	1949
Oedipus Tyrannus	Stuttgart	1959

Osborn, Jane   *Soprano*
(*Really* Osborn-Hannah)
b. Wilmington, Ohio, 1873: d. New York, 1943
She made her debut at Leipzig in 1904 and sang Elisabeth in her Metropolitan debut in 1910.
Brünnhilde, Elisabeth, Elsa, Eva, Irene, Isolde, Senta.

Ostrčil, Ottokar   *Composer*
b. near Prague, 1879: d. there, 1935

Vlasty Skon (*Vlasta's death*)	Prague	1904
Kunálovy Oči (*Kunala's eyes*)	„	1908
Poupě (*The Bud*)	„	1911
Legenda z Erinu (*Legend of Erin*)	Brno	1921
Honzovo Králòvstvi (*Johnny's Kingdom*)	„	1934

Pacini, Giovanni   *Composer*
b. Catania, Italy, 1796: d. Pescia, 1867
He wrote nearly ninety operas. (*See* Piccini). *Saffo* was composed in twenty-eight days.

Saffo	Naples	1840
Medea	Palermo	1843
La Regina di Cipro	Turin	1846

Pacini, Leonardo   *Composer*
b. near Pistoia, Italy, 1885: d. Viareggio, 1937

Alla Muda	Viareggio	1925
Mirta		

Pacius, Fredrik   *Composer*
b. Hamburg, 1809: d. Helsinki, 1891

He wrote the first Finnish opera.

| Kung Karlsjakt | Helsinki | 1852 |
| Lorelei | ,, | 1887 |

Paderewski, Ignacy Jan *Composer*
b. Podolia, Poland, 1860: d. New York, 1941
A very famous pianist, and also a very famous Polish patriot. He became the first prime minister of the Polish Republic after World War I.

| Manru | Dresden | 1901 |

Paër, Ferdinand *Composer*
b. Parma, 1771: d. Paris, 1839
He wrote over forty operas. His Leonora is on the same subject as Beethoven's *Fidelio*

Camilla	Vienna	1799
Leonora	Dresden	1804
Le Maître de chapelle	Paris	1821

Pahissa, Jaime *Composer*
b. Barcelona, 1880:

La Presó de Lleida	Barcelona	1906
Gala Plácida	,,	1913
Marianella	,,	1925

Paisiello, Giovanni *Composer*
b. Taranto, 1740: d. Naples, 1816
His operas were the mainstays of the Italian tradition until Rossini came along. His *Barbiere* is beginning to find a public again.

Il Barbiere di Siviglia	St. Petersburg	1782
Il Re Teodoro	Vienna	1784
Nina, o La Pazza per . Amore	Naples	1788

Palester, Roman *Composer*
b. Poland, 1907:

| The Living Stones | | 1944 |

Palma, Athos *Composer*
b. Buenos Aires, 1891: d. Miramar, Argentina, 1951

| Nazdah | Buenos Aires | 1924 |
| Los Hijos del Sol | ,, | 1928 |

Palmgren, Selim *Composer*
b. Björneborg, Finland, 1878: d. Helsinki, 1951
Best known for his piano pieces, Palmgren was also a conductor.

| Daniel Hjort | Åbo | 1910 |

Panizza, Ettore *Composer*
b. Buenos Aires, 1875:
Famous as a conductor, he began at Covent Garden in 1907 and led performances there, at La Scala, at the Metropolitan and in Berlin.

Il Fidanzato del Mare	Buenos Aires	1897
Medio evo Latino	Genoa	1900
Aurora	Buenos Aires	1908
Bisanzio	,,	1939

Paolis, Alessio de *Tenor*
b.
The first to play the Philistine in *Samson et Dalila*.
Don Basilio (*Le Nozze di Figaro*), Borsa, Emperor Altoum, Figaro (*Il Barbiere di Siviglia*), Fool (*Wozzeck*), Gastone, Gherardo, Goro, Isèpo, Philistine (*Samson et Dalila*), Remondado, Schuisky, Spoletta, Valzacchi, Zorn.

Papandopulo, Boris *Composer*
b. Honef am Rhein, Germany, 1906:

| Amphytrion | | 1940 |
| Sunflower | | 1942 |

Parepa-Rosa, Euphrosyne *Soprano*
b. Edinburgh, 1836: d. London, 1874
She made her debut as Amina at Malta, 1853. In 1867 she married Carl Rosa.
Amina, Donna Anna, Camilla, Elsa, Elvira (*I Puritani*), Norma, Zerlina (*Fra Diavolo*), Zerlina (*Don Giovanni*).

Parker, Horatio William *Composer*
b. Auburndale, Mass., 1863: d. Cedarhurst, N.Y., 1919
Parker won ten thousand dollars for each of his two operas, both of which are now nearly forgotten. The Metropolitan awarded him a prize for *Mona*;

the National Federation of Women's Clubs one for *Fairyland*.

| Mona | Metropolitan | 1912 |
| Fairyland | Los Angeles | 1915 |

Parry, Joseph *Composer*
b. Wales, 1841: d. Penarth, 1903

Blodwen	Aberdare	1878
Virginia	„	1883
Arianwen	Cardiff	1890
Sylvia	„	1895
King Arthur		1897

Pasquini, Bernardo *Composer*
b. Tuscany, 1637: d. Rome, 1710
La Forza d'Amore

| Dov' è Amore e Pietà | | 1679 |

Pasta, Giuditta *Soprano*
b. near Milan, 1798: d. Blavio, near Como, 1865
The first Amina, the first Norma, Anna Bolena, and Niobe.

Paton, Mary Anne *Soprano*
b. Edinburgh, 1802: d. Chapelthorpe, 1864
The first Rezia. She was a harpist, pianist, and a violinist. In addition she also composed religious music. She made her operatic debut in London as Susanna (*Le Nozze di Figaro*), in 1822.

Agathe, Alice (*Robert le Diable*), Rezia, Susanna (*Le Nozze di Figaro*).

Patti, Adelina *Soprano*
b. Madrid, 1843: d. Brecknock, Wales, 1919
A most celebrated soprano. She made her debut as Amina in London, 1861, and as Lucia in New York, 1859. By 1882 she commonly received five thousand dollars (minimum) per performance.

Aida, Amina, Carmen, Dinorah, Gilda, Juliette, Lakmé, Lucia, Marguérite (*Faust*), Marie (*La Figlia del Reggimento*), Martha, Mireille, Ophélie, Rosina (*Il Barbiere di Siviglia*), Violetta, Zerlina (*Fra Diavolo*), Zerlina (*Don Giovanni*).

Patzak, Julius *Tenor*
b. Vienna, 1898:
He made his debut in Reichenberg, 1927, and in the United States at Cincinnati in 1954. He was the first Burgomeister in *Friedenstag*.

Burgomeister (*Friedenstag*), Florestan, Herod (*Salomé*), Midas (*Die Liebe der Danae*), Palestrina, Titus (*La Clemenza di Tito*).

Pauly, Rosa *Soprano*
b. Eperjes, Hungary, 1895:
She made her debut in Hamburg as Aida.

Aida, Elektra, Empress (*Die Frau ohne Schatten*), Káta Kabanová, Leonore (*Fidelio*), Marie (*Wozzeck*).

Paumgartner, Bernhard *Composer*
b. Vienna, 1887:
For the Salzburg performance in 1949 he arranged *La Clemenza di Tito*.

| Rossini in Neapel | Zürich | 1936 |

Paur, Emil *Conductor*
b. Bukovina, 1855: d. Mistek, Czechoslovakia, 1932
A conductor at the Metropolitan from 1900 to 1904.

Pears, Peter *Tenor*
b. Farnham, England, 1910:
He is generally associated with the operas of Benjamin Britten, having created the following roles: Peter Grimes, Male Chorus (*Rape of Lucretia*), Vere (*Billy Budd*), and Essex (*Gloriana*).

Male Chorus (*Rape of Lucretia*), Essex (*Gloriana*), Ferrando (*Così fan tutte*), Jenik (*Prodaná Nevěsta*), MacHeath (*The Beggar's Opera*), Oedipus, Peter Grimes, Vere (*Billy Budd*).

Pederzini, Gianna *Mezzo-Soprano*
b. Avio, 1908
Baba (*The Medium*), Carmen, Charlotte, Dido, Fedora, Kostelnicka (*Její Pastorkyňa*) Lady Macbeth (by Bloch), Mignon,

Princess (*Adriana Lecouvreur*), Rezia, Rosa (*L'Arlesiana*).

Pedrell, Carlos   *Composer*
b. Minas, Uruguay, 1878: d. near Paris, 1941
The nephew of Felipe Pedrell.

Ardid de Amor	Buenos Aires	1917
Cuento de Abril	Madrid	1924
La Guitare	„	1924

Pedrell, Felipe   *Composer*
b. Tortosa, Spain, 1841: d. Barcelona, 1922

El último Abencerrage	Barcelona	1874
Quasimodo	„	1875
Los Pirineos (*trilogy*)	„	1902
La Celestina		1903

Pedrollo, Arrigo   *Composer*
b. Near Vicenza, Italy, 1878:

Terra Promessa	Cremona	1908
Juana		1914
La Veglia	Milan	1920
L'Uomo che Ride	Rome	1920
L'Amante in Trappola	Verona	1936

Peerce, Jan   *Tenor*
(*Really* Jacob Perelmuth)
b. New York, 1904:
He made his debut as the Duke in *Rigoletto*, Philadelphia, 1938. He first appeared at the Metropolitan as Alfredo in 1941.
Alfredo, Duke, Edgardo, Faust (*Mefistofele*), Mario Cavaradossi, Don Ottavio, Riccardo (*Un Ballo in Maschera*), Rodolfo, Turiddu.

Pelemans, Willem   *Composer*
b. Antwerp, 1901:

Le Juif Errant (*choral*)	1932
Flores et Blanchefleur (*choral*)	1939
Le Petit Soldat de Plomb	1945

Pelissier, Victor   *Composer*
b. (unknown)

Pelissier was a virtuoso of the horn and a composer for the theater.

Edwin and Angelina	New York	1796
Ariadne Abandoned by Theseus on the Isle of Naxos	„	1797
The Vintage		1799

Pelletier, Wilfred   *Conductor*
b. Montreal, 1896:
Conductor at the Metropolitan since 1932, and conductor at San Francisco from 1921 to 1931. In 1925 he married Queena Mario, but divorced her in 1936 and married Rose Bampton a year later.

Pepusch, Doctor John Christopher
       Composer
b. Berlin, 1667: d. London, 1752
It was he who collected and (partly) composed the music for the perdurable *Beggar's Opera* in 1728, *The Wedding* (1729), and *Polly* (1729). He also founded, in those ancient times, an Academy of Ancient Music. He was a thorn in the side of his fellow German, Handel, whose operas had to compete against *The Beggar's Opera*.

Peragallo, Mario   *Composer*
b. Rome, 1910:

Ginevra degli Almieri	Rome	1937
Lo Stendardo di S. Giorgio		1941
La Gita in Campagna	Milan	1954

Pergolesi, Giovanni Battista   *Composer*
b. near Ancona, Italy, 1710: d. Pozzuoli, 1736
At least one opera commonly attributed to Pergolesi, *Il Maestro di Musica*, is now considered to be the work of someone else. His most famous work is the *Stabat Mater*.

Lo Frate innamorato	Naples	1732
Il Prigioniero Superbo	„	1733
La Serva Padrona (*intermezzo to the above*)	„	1733
Adriano in Siria	„	1734

Livietta e Tracollo
(*intermezzo to the above,
also called* La Finta
Polacca)   Naples   1734
L'Olimpiade   Rome   1735

Peri, Jacopo   *Composer*
b. Florence, 1561: d. there, 1633
    A member of the Florentine Camerata
(*see* Bardi and Corsi). It was his *Dafne*
which was chosen for performance as its
first opera. His *Euridice* was performed
for the marriage of Maria de' Medici to
Henri IV of France. Peri also composed
the recitatives for Monteverdi's lost
Arianna.

Dafne	Florence	1597
Euridice	,,	1600
Adone		1620
La Precedenza delle		
Dame	Florence	1625
La Flora (*with*		
Gagliano)	,,	1628

Périer, Jean   *Tenor*
b. Paris, 1869: d. there, 1954
    The first Pelléas.

Perini, Flora   *Contralto*
b. Rome, 1887:
    The first Princess (*Suor Angelica*), the
first Pepa (*Goyescas*). She made her debut
at La Scala in 1908 and at the Metropolitan in 1915.

Perlea, Jonel   *Conductor*
b. Ograda, Rumania, 1900:
    Conductor of the Bucharest Opera
from 1934 to 1944, of the Metropolitan
from 1949, and of the Connecticut
Symphony Orchestra since 1955.

Perrin, Pierre   *Librettist*
(*Called* L'Abbé Perrin.)
b. Lyons, 1616: d. Paris, 1675
    With Cambert he won the first patent
to establish the Académie Royale de
Musique (Opéra) in 1668, but lost it to
Lully in 1672. Perrin wrote the libretto to

the first French Opera, *La Pastorale*, and to
Pomone and *Ariane* (all by Cambert).

Perron, Karl   *Baritone*
b. Palatinate, 1858: d. Dresden, 1928
    A famous Amfortas, he sang the first
Jokanaan, the first Orest (*Elektra*), and the
first Baron Ochs.

Pertile, Aureliano   *Tenor*
b. Montagnana, 1885: d. 1952
    The first Nerone (*by Mascagni*).
    Fra Diavolo, Faust (*Mefistofele*), des
Grieux (*Manon*), Julien, Lionel, Loris,
Mario Cavaradossi, Maurizio, Nerone (*by
Mascagni*), Osaka (*Iris*), Otello, Paolo,
Pinkerton, Radames, Rodolfo.

Peschka-Leutner, Minna   *Soprano*
(*Née* Leutner)
b. Vienna, 1839: d. Wiesbaden, 1890
    Agathe, Aida, Alice (*Robert le Diable*),
Almira (*Almira*, by Handel), Eglantine,
Isabel, Marguerite of Valois.

Peters, Roberta   *Soprano*
b. New York, 1930:
    On very short notice she made her
debut at the Metropolitan in 1950 as
Zerlina in *Don Giovanni*. She married
Robert Merrill in 1952 but was later
divorced.
    Adele (*Die Fledermaus*), Arline, Despina,
Gilda, Queen of the Night, Rosina (*Il
Barbiere di Siviglia*), Shepherd (*Tannhäuser*), Sophie (*Der Rosenkavalier*), Susanna (*Le Nozze di Figaro*), Zerlina (*Don
Giovanni*).

Petersen, Wilhelm   *Composer*
b. Athens, 1890: d. Darmstadt, 1957
    Der Goldne Topf   Darmstadt   1941

Petrassi, Goffredo   *Composer*
b. near Rome, 1904:

Il Cordovano	La Scala	1949
La Morte dell' Aria	Rome	1950

Petrella, Enrico   *Compose*
b. Palermo, 1813: d. Genoa, 1877

Marco Visconti	Naples	1854
Ione (*after* The Last Days		
of Pompeii)	Milan	1858
La Contessa d'Amalfi	Turin	1864
Giovanni II di Napoli	Naples	1869
I Promessi Sposi	Lecco	1869

Petrelli, Eleanora   *Soprano*
(*Née* Wigström)
b. Simtuna, Sweden, 1835: d. Chicago, 1904
A pupil of Viardot-Garcia.

Petrov, Ossip Afanassievitch   *Bass*
b. Elizavetgrad, Russia, 1807: d. St. Petersburg, 1878
He was the first to sing Varlaam in a concert performance of the Inn scene from *Boris Godunov* before the opera had been accepted by the officials. He was the first Ivan Susanin, the first Russlan, and the first Miller in Dargomyzhsky's *Russalka*. He made his debut as Sarastro at St. Petersburg in 1830.

Pfitzner, Hans   *Composer*
b. Moscow, 1869: d. Salzburg, 1949

| Palestrina | Munich | 1917 |
| Der Arme Heinrich | Mainz | 1895 |

Philidor, François André   *Composer*
b. Dreux, France, 1726: d. London, 1795
The composer made his living as a professional chess-player.

Le Maréchal Ferrant	Comique	1761
Sancho Pança dans		
son Isle	„	1762
Tom Jones	„	1765
Ernelinde (*Sandomir*)	„	1767

Phillipps, Adelaide   *Contralto*
b. Stratford on Avon, 1833: d. Karlsbad, 1882
She was a protégée of Jenny Lind. She made her debut as Rosina (*Il Barbiere di Siviglia*) at Milan in 1854 and as Azucena in New York, 1856.

Piccini, Niccolò   *Composer*
b. Bari, 1728: d. Passy, 1800

This unfortunate composer was made the unwilling battle banner of the warriors against the Gluckists. When they prevailed upon him to write an *Iphigénie en Tauride* to contest Gluck's position (which failed miserably), the war fizzled. Piccini wrote one hundred thirty-nine operas, ten of them during the single year 1761.

La Cecchina		1760
La Buona Figliuola	Rome	1760
Roland	Paris	1778
Iphigénie en Tauride	„	1781
Didon	„	1783

Pickhardt, Ione   *Composer*
b. New York, 1900:

| Moira | | 1931 |

Pick-Mangiagalli, Riccardo   *Composer*
b. Bohemia, 1882: d. Milan, 1949
The first opera to be broadcast by radio anywhere was his *L'Ospite Inatteso*.

Basi e Bote	Rome	1927
Casanova a Venezia	La Scala	1929
L'Ospite Inatteso	Milan Radio	1931
Il Notturno Romantico	Rome	1936

Pierné, Henri Constant Gabriel
     Composer
b. Metz, 1863: d. Ploujean, 1937
A pupil of Massenet and Franck.

La Coupe Enchantée	Royan	1895
Vendée	Lyons	1897
La Fille de Tabarin	Opéra-	
	Comique	1901
On ne Badine pas		
avec l'Amour	„	1910
Sophie Arnould	„	1927

Pierson, Henry Hugo   *Composer*
(*Originally* Pearson)
b. Oxford. 1815: d. Leipzig, 1873

| Leila | Hamburg | 1848 |
| Contarini | „ | 1872 |

Pijper, Willem   *Composer*
b. Zeist, Holland, 1894: d. Leidschendam, 1947

| Halewijn | Amsterdam | 1933 |
| Merlijn (*unfinished*) | | 1946 |

272

Pinza, Ezio   *Bass*
b. Rome, 1892: d. Stamford, Conn., 1957
Widely known not only for opera, but for his part in the Broadway show *South Pacific*. He made his operatic debut in Rome, 1920, as King Marke and his Metropolitan debut in 1926 as Pontifex Maximus (*La Vestale*). He sang the first Nerone (by Boito).

Archibaldo, Don Basilio (*Il Barbiere di Siviglia*), Boris Godunov, King Marke, Don Giovanni, Mefistofele (*Mefistofele*), Méphistophélès (*Faust*), Nerone (*Boite*), Nilakantha, Pontifex Maximus (*La Vestale*), Tcherevik (*The Fair at Sorotchinsk*).

Pipkov, Lubomir   *Composer*
b. Lovetch, Bulgaria, 1904:
Nine Brothers of Yanina	Sofia	1937
Momtchil	,,	1948

Pizzeti, Ildebrando   *Composer*
b. Parma, 1880:
Fedra	Milan	1915
Débora e Jaéle	,,	1922
Fra Gherardo	,,	1928
Lo Straniero	Rome	1930
Orsèolo	Florence	1935
L'Oro	Milan	1947
Vanna Lupa	Florence	1949
Ifigenia	,,	1951
Cagliostro	Milan	1953
La Figlia di Jorio	Naples	1954
L'Assassinio nel Cattedrale	Milan	1958

Plançon, Pol Henri   *Bass*
b. Ardennes, 1854: d. Paris, 1914
He made his debut at Lyons in 1877, at the Opéra, as Méphistophélès (*Faust*), in 1883, and at the Metropolitan in the same role ten years later.

Alvise, Balthasar (*La Favorita*), St. Bris, Capulet, Escamillo, Friar Laurence, Henry the Fowler, High Priest (*Aida*), Hermann (*Tannhäuser*), King (*Aida*), Méphistophélès (*La Damnation de Faust*), Méphistophélès (*Faust*), Oroveso, Phanuel (*Hérodiade*), Plunkett, Pogner.

Planquette, Robert   *Composer*
b. Paris, 1848: d. there, 1903
Les Cloches de Corneville	Paris	1877
Rip van Winkle		1882

Polacco, Giorgio   *Conductor*
b. Venice, 1875:
Conductor at San Francisco, at the Metropolitan and at Chicago.

Poleri, David   *Tenor*
b.
Alfredo, Mario Cavaradossi, Don José, Rodolfo, Turiddu.

Polignac, Armande de   *Composer*
b. Paris, 1876:
A pupil of Fauré and D'Indy.
Morgane
L'Hypocrite Sanctifié

Ponchielli, Amilcare   *Composer*
b. near Cremona, 1834: d. Milan, 1886
I Promessi Sposi	Cremona	1856
La Gioconda	Milan	1876
Il Figliuolo Prodigo	,,	1880
Marion Delorme	,,	1885

Poniatowski, Joseph   *Composer*
(*Fully* Prince Joseph Michael Xavier Francis John Poniatowski)
b. Rome, 1816: d. Chiselhurst, 1873
Ruy Blas	Lucca	1842
La Contessina	Paris	1868

Pons, Lily   *Soprano*
b. Draguignon, France, 1904:
She made her debut in Mulhouse, singing Lakmé, and at the Metropolitan in 1931 as Lucia.

Gilda, Lakmé, Linda di Chamounix, Lucia, Marie (*La Figlia del Reggimento*), Rosina (*Il Barbiere di Siviglia*), Violetta.

Ponselle, Carmela   *Soprano*
b. Schenectady, N.Y., 1892:
She made her debut at the Metropolitan as Amneris in 1925.

Ponselle, Rosa   *Soprano*
(*Carmela Ponselle's sister*)
b. Meriden, Conn., 1897:

She made her debut at the Metropolitan as Leonora (*La Forza del Destino*) in 1918 opposite Caruso.

Aida, Carmen, Elisabetta (*Don Carlos*), Fiora, Gioconda, Leonora (*La Forza del Destino*), Margared (*Le Roi d'Ys*), Rachel, Rezia, Santuzza, Selika, Violetta.

Ponte, Lorenzo da   *Librettist*
b. Ceneda, near Venice 1749: d. New York, 1838

A very colorful poet, responsible for the librettos of some of the most famous operas. He was professor of rhetoric at Treviso until banished for speaking against the government there. He became laureate at Venice until banished in 1779. From 1782 to 1792 he worked in Vienna, where he created librettos for the Imperial Theater and for Mozart. After that he tried Paris and London. Arriving in New York in 1803 he dealt in tea, tobacco and drugs to make a living, but failing in this he took to teaching Italian. Again in Sunbury, Pennsylvania, he tried business as a manufacturer of liquors, but failed again. He taught Italian at Columbia College, now Columbia University. His famous libretti are: *Le Nozze di Figaro*, *Don Giovanni*, and *Così fan Tutte*.

Poot, Marcel   *Composer*
b. near Brussels, 1901:
A pupil of Dukas.
Moretus   1943

Porpora, Nicçolò Antonio   *Composer*
b. Naples, 1686: d. there, 1768.
A famous singing teacher, and Handel's chief rival in London. He wrote 44 operas.
Siface   1726

Porrino, Ennio   *Composer*
b. Sardinia, 1910:
Gli Orazi   Milan   1941

Poulenc, Francis   *Composer*
b. Paris, 1899:
One of "Les Six."

Les Gendarme Incompris		1920
Les Mamelles de	Opéra-	
Tirésias	Comique	1947
Les Dialogues des		
Carmélites	La Scala	1957

Pratella, Francesco Balilla   *Composer*
b. Romagna, 1880: d. Ravenna, 1955

Lilia	Luga	1905
La Sina d'Uargoun		
(*his own libretto*)	Bologna	1909
L'Aviatore Dro		
(*his own libretto*)	Lugo	1920
Fabiano	Bologna	1939

Pratt, Silas Gamaliel   *Composer*
b. Addison, Vt., 1846: d. Pittsburgh, 1916

His niche in the hall of fame is due to what may be an apochryphal story: it is said that when he met Wagner in Germany the following conversation took place: Wagner: "I hear that you are the Richard Wagner of America." Pratt: "Then, Herr Wagner, you must be the Silas G. Pratt of Germany."

Zenobia	Chicago	1883
Triumph of Columbus		1892

Price, Leontyne   *Soprano*
b.

She made her name singing Bess in 1952. She first sang opera in 1955 as Tosca, on television. Her stage debut came in San Francisco as the Mother Superior in *Dialogues des Carmelites*.

Aida, Cio-Cio San, Donna Anna, Bess, Leonora (*Il Travatore*), Liù (Puccini's *Turandot*), Mother Superior, Pamina, Tosca.

Prohaska, Felix   *Conductor*
b. Vienna, 1912:
He conducted at Graz, Duisberg, and Strasbourg before going to Vienna in 1945.

Prokofiev, Sergey   *Composer*
b. near Ekaterinoslav, Russia, 1891: d. Moscow, 1953

He is famous for the musical fairy tale for narrator and orchestra, *Peter and the Wolf*. His best known opera, after a comedy by Carlo Gozzi, is *The Love for Three Oranges*.

Maddalena		1913
The Flaming Angel		1919
The Love for Three Oranges	Chicago	1921
The Gambler	Brussels	1929
War and Peace	Leningrad	1946

Provenzale, Francesco *Composer*
b. Naples, 1627: d. there, 1704
A composer of operas, oratorios and other works. It is sometimes said that he "invented" the da capo aria.

Puccini, Giacomo *Composer*
(*Full Name* Giacomo Antonio Domenico Michele Secondo Maria Puccini)
b. Lucca, 1858: d. Brussels, 1924
One of the greatest opera composers after Verdi, and a very successful exponent of the style *verismo*. He was a pupil of Ponchielli.

Le Villi	Milan	1884
Edgar	La Scala	1889
Manon Lescaut	Turin	1893
La Bohème	,,	1896
Tosca	Rome	1900
Madama Butterfly	La Scala	1904
La Fanciulla del West	Metropolitan	1910
La Rondine	Monte Carlo	1917
Il Trittico	Metropolitan	1918
Il Tabarro		
Suor Angelica		
Gianni Schicchi		
Turandot	La Scala	1928

(*Completed by Franco Alfano*.)

Puente, Giuseppe del *Baritone*
b. Naples, 1841: d. New York, 1900
He sang Valentin in the opening production of the Metropolitan.
Alfio, Barnaba, Escamillo, Figaro (*Il Barbiere di Siviglia*), Lescaut (*Manon*), De Nevers, Valentin (*Faust*).

Purcell, Henry *Composer*
b. London, 1658: d. Westminister, 1695
This greatest of English composers wrote several masques, but only one opera, and that was first produced not in a theater but in a boarding school for girls. He was a pupil of Pelham Humphries, who was, in turn, a pupil of Lully.
Dido and Aeneas　　Chelsea　1689

Pylkkänen, Tauno *Composer*
b. Helsinki, 1918:

Jaakio Ilkka	1937
Bathsheba Saarenmaalla	1940
Mare ja hänen poikansa	1945
Simo Hurtta	1948
Suden Morsian	1950
Varjo	1952

Quagliati, Paolo *Composer*
b. Chioggia, 1555: d. Rome, 1628
Carro di Fedeltà d'Amore　　Rome　1606

Quinault, Phillipe *Librettist*
b. Paris, 1635: d. there, 1688
Librettist for most of the operas of Lully.

Raaff, Anton *Tenor*
b. near Bonn, 1714: d. Munich, 1797
The first Idomeneo.

Raalte, Albert van *Conductor*
b. Amsterdam, 1890: d. there, 1952
Conductor at Leipzig and at the Hague until 1922, then an independent conductor.

Rabaud, Henri *Composer*
b. Paris, 1873: d. there, 1949

La Fille de Roland	Opéra-Comique	1904
Le premier glaive	Beziers	1908
Marouf	Opéra-Comique	1914
Antoine et Cléopâtre		1917
L'Appel de la Mer	Leipzig	1924
Le Miracle des Loups	Comique	1924
Rolande et le Mauvais Garçon	Opéra	1934

Le Jeu de l'amour
et du Hasard   Monte Carlo   1954

Rachmaninov, Sergey   *Composer*
b. near Novgorod, 1873: d. Beverly Hills,
Calif. 1943
Best known as a pianist, he was also
director of the Moscow Opera from 1904
to 1906.

Aleko	Moscow	1893
Francesca da Rimini	,,	1906
The Miserly Knight	,,	1906

Radford, Robert   *Bass*
b. Nottingham, England, 1874: d. London, 1933
A founder of the British National Opera
Company.
Boris Godunov, Commendatore (*Don
Giovanni*), Fasolt, Louise's Father, Hunding, Méphistophélès (*Faust*), Osmin,
Sarastro.

Rains, Leon   *Bass*
b. New York, 1870: d. Los Angeles, 1954
He made his debut at the Metropolitan
in 1908.

Raisa, Rosa   *Soprano*
b. Bialystok, Poland, 1893:
She made her debut at Parma in 1913,
and at Chicago the following year. She sang
the first Asteria (*Nerone*, Boito), and the
first Turandot.
Aida, Asteria (*Nerone*, Boito), Elena,
Francesca, Rachel, Turandot, Valentine
(*Les Huguenots*).

Rameau, Jean Philippe   *Composer*
b. Dijon, 1683: d. Paris, 1764
Rameau is frequently called the father
of harmony, for his treatise which was the
first on that subject.

Hippolyte et Aricie	Opéra	1733
Castor et Pollux	,,	1737
Dardanus	,,	1739

Rangström, Ture   *Composer*
b. Stockholm, 1884: d. there, 1947

Kronbruden	Stuttgart	1919
Middelalderlig	Stockholm	1921
Gilgamesh (*completed*		
by *Fernström*)	,,	1952

Rankin, Nell   *Mezzo-soprano*
b.
Amneris, Marina Mnishek, Carmen.

Rankl, Karl   *Conductor*
b. near Vienna, 1898:
Starting at Graz in 1932, he has conducted at Prague, Covent Garden, and in
Glasgow, among other places.

Rappold, Marie   *Soprano*
b. London, 1873: d. Hollywood, 1957
She sang Sulamith (*Die Königin von
Saba*) in her first appearance at the Metropolitan in 1905.
Aida, Desdemona, Elizabeth, Elsa, Euridice, Inez, Iphigénie (*Iphigénie en Tauride*),
Marguérite (*Faust*), Micaela, Princess
(*Lobetanz*), Sulamith, Venus.

Rathaus, Karol   *Composer*
b. Tarnopol, Poland, 1895: d. New York,
1954
Fremde Erde
(*Strange World*)   Berlin   1930

Rauzzini, Venanzio   *Composer*
b. Rome, 1747: d. Bath, England, 1810

Piramo e Tisbe	1775
Le Ali d'Amore	1776

Ravel, Maurice   *Composer*
b. Ciboure, France, 1875: d. Paris, 1937
Famous everywhere for his orchestral
Bolero.
L'Heure Espagnole   Opéra-
                     Comique   1911
L'Enfant et les
Sortilèges   Monte Carlo   1925

Rebikov, Vladimir   *Composer*
b. Siberia, 1866: d. Crimea, 1920
Rebikov is best known for his little
piano pieces for children.

In the Thunderstorm	Odessa	1894
The Christmas Tree	Moscow	1903

Reed, Herbert Owen *Composer*
b. Odessa, Missouri, 1910:
Michigan Dream   1955

Reeves, Sims *Tenor*
(*Really* John Sims Reeves)
b. Woolwich, England, 1818: d. Worthing, 1900
A famous Captain MacHeath. He made his debut at Newcastle on Tyne as Rodolfo in *La Sonnambula* in 1839, and at La Scala as Edgardo in 1846.

Carlo (*Linda di Chamounix*), Dandini, Edgardo, Florestan, Sir Huon, MacHeath, Ottocar (*Der Freischütz*), Rodolfo (*La Sonnambula*).

Refice, Licinio *Composer*
b. near Rome, 1883: d. Rio de Janeiro, 1954
Cecilia   Rome   1934
Margherita da Cortona   Milan   1938

Reichmann, Theodor *Bass*
b. Rostock, 1849: d. Marbach, 1903
The first Amfortas.

Amfortas, Creon (*Medea*), Dutchman, Hans Sachs, Pizzarro, Trompeter von Säkkingen, Wotan.

Reinecke, Carl Heinrich Carsten
Composer
b. Altona, Germany, 1824: d. Leipzig, 1910
An all-round musician, he was a pianist, a conductor and a famous teacher.
König Manfred   Weisbaden   1867
Auf hohen Befehl   Hamburg   1886

Reiner, Fritz *Conductor*
b. Budapest, 1888:
Beginning at his birthplace in 1911, he subsequently conducted at Dresden, Cincinnati, San Francisco, Covent Garden, Pittsburgh, Chicago and the Metropolitan. In 1953 he became conductor of the Chicago Symphony Orchestra.

Reiner, Karel *Composer*
b. Žatec, Czechoslovakia, 1910:

A pupil of Alois Hába.
Tale of an Enchanted Song   1949

Reiss, Albert *Tenor*
b. Berlin, 1870: d. Nice, 1940
He made his debut at the Metropolitan in 1901 singing both the Sailor and the Shepherd in *Tristan und Isolde*. In the productions of *Der Schauspieldirektor* and *Bastien et Bastienne* in 1916, he both sang and directed.

Bastien (*Bastien et Bastienne*), Jacquino, Mozart (*Der Schauspieldirektor*), Sailor and Shepherd (*Tristen und Isolde*).

Reizenstein, Franz *Composer*
b. Nuremberg, 1911:
A pupil of Paul Hindemith.
Men Against the Sea   1949
Anna Kraus   1952

Renan, Émile *Baritone*
b.
Alcindoro, Dr. Bartolo (*Le Nozze di Figaro*), Benoit, Court Attendant (*Der Prozess*), Dancairo, Doctor (*Wozzeck*), Masetto, Marquis d'Obigny, Oscar (*Regina*), Pantalone (*The Love for Three Oranges*), Remondado, Sacristan, Schaunard, Secret Police Agent (*The Consul*), Sharpless, Willem (*Der Prozess*), Yamadori.

Renaud, Maurice Arnold *Baritone*
b. Bordeaux, 1861: d. Paris, 1933
He made his debut in Brussels in 1883.
Beckmesser, Escamillo, Germont (wearing eighteenth-century costume), Don Giovanni, Hamlet, Karnac (*Le Roi d'Ys*), Méphistophélès (*La Damnation de Faust*), Nelusko, de Nevers, Rigoletto, Valentin (*Faust*), Wolfram.

Resnik, Regina *Soprano*
b. New York, 1922:
After a debut in Mexico City in 1943 she came out at the Metropolitan in *Il Trovatore* the following year. She sang the first Delilah (*The Warrior*), and the first Baroness in *Vanessa*.

Baroness (*Vanessa*), Delilah (*The Warrior*), Ellen (*Peter Grimes*), Donna Elvira, Leonore (*Fidelio*), Magdalene, Marcellina Marina Mnishek, Musetta, Rosalinda, Sieglinde, Venus.

Resphighi, Ottorino　　　*Composer*
b. Bologna, 1879: d. Rome, 1936
One of the principal Italian modernists; he made one of the standard arrangements of *La Favola d'Orfeo*. He is best known for his orchestral pieces *The Pines of Rome* and *The Fountains of Rome*.

Re Enzo	Bologna	1905
Belfagor	Milan	1923
La Campana Sommersa	Hamburg	1927
Lucrezia	Milan	1937

Reszke, Edouard de　　　*Bass*
b. Warsaw, 1853: d. Garnek, Poland, 1917
Brother of Jean de Reszke. He made his debut singing Amonasro under Verdi's direction at Paris, 1876. He first appeared in the United States as Henry the Fowler in Chicago, 1891, and at the Metropolitan as Friar Laurence the same year.

Almaviva (*Le Nozze di Figaro*), Amonasro, Basilio, St. Bris, Count (*La Sonnambula*), Diego (*L'Africana*), Hagen, Hans Sachs, Henry the Fowler, Hunding, Indra (*Le Roi de Lahore*), King of Egypt, Kurnewal, Friar Laurence, Leporello, Marcel, King Marke, Mefistofele (*Mefistofele*), Méphistophélès (*Faust*), Nilakantha, Oberthal, Ramfis.

Reszke, Jean de　　　*Tenor*
b. Warsaw, 1850: d. Nice, 1925
Brother of Edouard de Reszke and a famous teacher. At first a baritone, he made his debut as Alfonso in *La Favorita* at Venice in 1874. As a tenor he first sang in Madrid, 1879, in the title role of Robert le Diable. With his brother he appeared in Chicago as Lohengrin in his first appearance in this country, 1891. He sang the first Cid, and the first stage performance of Faust (*La Damnation de Faust*).

Alfonso (*La Favorita*), Almaviva (*Il Barbiere di Siviglia*), Le Cid, Faust (*La Damnation de Faust*), Faust (*Faust*), Figaro (*Il Barbiere di Siviglia*), Don Giovanni, des Grieux (*Manon*), John of Leyden, St. John (*Hérodiade*), Don José, Lohengrin, Fra Melitone, de Nevers, Otello, Don Ottavio Radames, Raoul, Riccardo, Robert le Diable, Romeo, Tristan, Valentin (*Faust*), Walther, Werther.

Reszke, Josephine de　　　*Soprano*
b. Warsaw, 1855: d. there, 1891
Sister of the two brothers. She made her debut as Ophélie at the Opéra in 1875.
Aida, Marguérite, Ophélie.

Rethberg, Elisabeth　　　*Soprano*
(*Really* Sattler)
b. Saxony, 1894:
The first Helena (*Aegyptische Helene*). She made her debut at the Metropolitan in 1922, singing Aida.
Agathe, Aida, Cio-Cio San, Desdemona, Elisabeth, Fiora, Helene (*Die Aegyptische Helene*), Iris, Marenka, Sieglinde.

Reusse-Belce, Luise　　　*Soprano*
b. Vienna, 1860: d. Aibach, Germany, 1945
She was the first woman stage manager at Nuremberg in 1913. She made her debut as Elsa at Karlsruhe in 1881, and at the Metropolitan in 1902.

Reutter, Hermann　　　*Composer*
b. Stuttgart, 1900:

Saul	Baden-Baden	1928
Der Verlorene Sohn	Stuttgart	1929
Doktor Johannes Faust	Frankfurt	1936
Odysseus	„	1942
Don Juan und Faust	Stuttgart	1950
Ballade der Landstrasse	„	1952
The Bridge of San Luis Rey	Frankfurt Radio	1954
Die Witwe von Ephesus	Cologne	1954

Rey, Cemal Reschid   *Composer*
b. Istanbul, 1904:
Notable Turkish composer, who studied in Paris.

Faire sans Dire	1920
Yann Marek	1922
Sultan Cem	1923
Zeybeck	1926

Reyer, Louis Étienne Ernest   *Composer*
(*Originally* Rey)
b. Marseilles, 1823: d. Hyères, 1909

Sigurd	Brussels	1884
La Statue	Paris	1861
Salammbô	Brussels	1890

Rezniečk, Emil Nicolaus von   *Composer*
b. Vienna, 1860: d. Berlin, 1945

Donna Diana	Prague	1894
Till Eulenspiegel	Karlsruhe	1902
Ritter Blaubart	Darmstadt	1920
Holofernes	Berlin	1923
Spiel oder Ernst	Dresden	1930
Der Gondoliere des Dogen	Stuttgart	1931

Ricci, Luigi   *Composer*
b. Naples, 1805: d. Prague, 1859

Chiara di Rosemberg	Milan	1831
Crispino e la Comare	Venice	1850

Richter, Hans   *Conductor*
b. Raab, Hungary, 1843: d. Bayreuth, 1916
He conducted the first performance of *Siegfried*.

Rieti, Vittorio   *Composer*
b. Alexandria, Egypt, 1898:

Orfeo		1928
Teresa nel Bosco	Venice	1934
Don Perlimplin	Urbana, Ill.	1952
The Pet Shop	New York	1958

Righini, Vincenzo   *Composer*
b. Bologna, 1756: d. there, 1812
Like many of his contemporaries, he not only composed but also conducted and sang.

Selva Incantata		1802
Gerusalemme Liberata		1802
Il Convietato di Pietra (*Don Giovanni*)	Vienna	1777

Rimsky-Korsakov, Nicolai   *Composer*
b. near Novgorod, 1844; d. near St. Petersburg, 1908
Rimsky-Korsakov was one of the most prolific composers of his time in Russia. But he was also a tireless editor and advocate of the works of others. It was he who brought Moussorgsky's masterpiece, *Boris Godunov*, the fame which it now has by reorchestrating and editing it in detail. He performed the same service for *Prince Igor* by Borodin. He is well known for one of his orchestral pieces, the orchestral fairy tale *Scherherazade*.

Pskovityanka (*The Maid of Pskov*)	St. Petersburg	1873
Maiskaya Notch (*May Night*)	„	1880
Snyegurotchka (*Snow Maiden*)	„	1882
Mlada	„	1892
Notch pered Rozhdestrom (*The Night before Christmas*)	„	1895
Sadko	Moscow	1898
Mozart i Salieri	„	1898
Boyarynia Vera Sheloga	„	1898
Tsarskaya Neviesta (*The Tsar's Bride*)	„	1899
Tsar Sultan	„	1900
Servilia	St. Petersburg	1902
Kaschey Bezmertny (*Kaschey the Immortal*)	Moscow	1902
Pan Voyevoda (*The Commander*)	St. Petersburg	1904
Kitezh	„	1907
Le Coq d'Or	Moscow	1909

Rinuccini, Ottavio   *Librettist*
b. Florence, 1562: d. there, 1621
The author of the first operas, *Dafne*, *Euridice* and *Arianna*. He was, of course, a most influential member of the Florentine Camerata (*see* Bardi and Corsi).

Rivier, Jean   *Composer*
b. Villemonble, France, 1896:
Vénitienne   Paris   1937

Rocca, Lodovico   *Composer*
b. Turin, 1895:

In Terra di Leggenda	Milan	1933
Il Dibuk	„	1934
La Morte di Frine	„	1937
Monte Ivnor	Rome	1939
L'Uragano	Milan	1952

Rogatis, Pascual de   *Composer*
b. Teora, Italy, 1881:

Amfion y Zeto	Buenos Aires	1915
Huémac	„	1916
La Novia del ᴴereje	„	1935

Roger, Gustave Hippolyte   *Tenor*
b. near Paris, 1815: d. there, 1879
The first John of Leyden. He made his debut at the Opéra-Comique in 1838, but his operatic career was cut short when he lost his right arm in a hunting accident and was forced to retire from the stage.

Roger-Ducasse, Jean Jules Aimable·   *Composer*
b. Bordeaux, 1873: d. near there, 1954
A pupil of Fauré.
Cantegril   Opéra-Comique   1931

Rogers, Bernard   *Composer*
b. New York, 1893:

The Marriage of Aude	Rochester, N.Y.	1931
The Warrior	Metropolitan	1947
The Veil	Bloomington, Ind.	1950

Rogers, Clara Kathleen   *Soprano*
(*Née* Barnett)
b. Cheltenham, England, 1844: d. Boston, 1931

She made her debut as Isabella in *Robert le Diable*, Turin 1863. She came out in New York ten years later.

Roland-Manuel, Alexis   *Composer*
(*Really* Lévy)
b. Paris, 1891:

Isabelle et Pantalon	Paris	1922
Le Diable Amoureux		1929

Romani, Felice   *Librettist*
b. Genoa, 1788: d. Riviera, 1865
He is said to have written nearly one hundred libretti. Among the best known are: *La Sonnambula, Norma, L'Elisir d'Amore, Lucrezia Borgia, Il Turco in Italia,* and *Il Pirata.*

Ronconi, Giorgio   *Baritone*
b. Milan, 1810: d. Madrid, 1890
Don Basilio (*Il Barbiere di Siviglia*), Belcore, Enrico, Figaro (*Il Barbiere di Siviglia*), Don Giovanni, Riccardo (*I Puritani*), Rigoletto, Tasso.

Rooy, Anton van   *Bass*
b. Rotterdam, 1870: d. Munich, 1932
This famous basso made his debut in Bayreuth in 1897 and at the Metropolitan the following year as Wotan.
Dutchman, Escamillo, Hans Sachs, Jokanaan, Kurnewal, Valentin (*Faust*), Wolfram, Wotan.

Ropartz, Guy   *Composer*
b. Guingamp, France, 1864: d. there, 1955
Le Pays   Nancy   1912

Rorem, Ned   *Composer*
b. Richmond, Ind., 1923:

A Childhood Miracle	New York	1952
The Robberᶠ	„	1958

Rosa, Carl August   *Conductor*
(*Originally* Rose)
b. Hamburg, 1842: d. Paris, 1889
Founder of the Carl Rosa Opera Company. In 1867 he married Euphrosyne Parepa.

Roselius, Ludwig *Composer*
b. Kassel, 1902:

Doge und Dogaressa	Dortmund	1928
Godiva	Nuremberg	1933
Gudrun	Graz	1939

Rosenberg, Hilding *Composer*
b. Bosjökloster, Sweden, 1892:

| Resan till America (*Voyage to America*) | Stockholm | 1932 |
| Marionettes | „ | 1939 |

Rosenstock, Joseph *Conductor*
b. Cracow, 1895:
Beginning in Darmstadt in 1922, he has conducted in Wiesbaden, Mannheim, Tokyo, New York City and Cologne.

Rossi, Giulio *Bass*
b. Rome, 1865: d. Milan, 1931
He made his debut at Parma in 1887 and at the Metropolitan in 1908.

Rossi, Luigi *Composer*
b. Foggia, 1597: d. Rome, 1653
He produced the first Italian opera in Paris.
Le Mariage d'Orphée et Euridice

Rossi-Lemeni, Nicola *Bass*
b. Constantinople, 1922:
The first Tomasso Becket, he first appeared in the United States at San Francisco in 1951, as Boris Godunov.
Abbot (*La Forza del Destino*), Archibaldo, Don Basilio (*Il Barbiere di Siviglia*), Boris Godunov, Sir George (*I Puritani*), Don Giovanni, Guillaume Tell, Macbeth (by Bloch), Mefistofele, Oroveso, Selim, Tomasso Becket, Uberto (*La Serva Padrona*).

Rossini, Gioacchino Antonio *Composer*
b. Pesaro, Italy, 1792: d. Paris, 1868
The son of the town trumpeter. This genius of opera retired as a composer at the age of thirty-seven and did not write

another note for the stage for the rest of his long life.

Tancredi	Venice	1813
L'Italiana in Algeri	„	1813
Aureliano in Palmira	Milan	1813
Il Turco in Italia	„	1814
Elisabetta, Regina d'Inghilterra	Naples	1815
Torvaldo e Dorliska	Rome	1815
Il Barbiere di Siviglia	„	1816
Otello	Naples	1816
La Cenerentola	Rome	1817
La Gazza Ladra	Milan	1817
Armida	Naples	1817
Mosè in Egitto	„	1818
Semiramide	Venice	1823
Le Siège de Corinthe	Paris	1826
Guillaume Tell	Opéra	1829

Roswaenge, Helge *Tenor*
b. Copenhagen, 1897:
Ivan Susanin, Florestan, Oberon, Tamino.

Rota, Nino *Composer*
b. Milan, 1911:

| Ariodante | Parma | 1942 |
| I Due Timidi | | 1950 |

Rothier, Léon *Baritone*
b. Reims, 1874: d. New York, 1951
He made his debut as Jupiter in *Philémon et Baucis* at the Opéra-Comique, then appeared at the Metropolitan for the first time in 1910 as Méphistophélès (*Faust*).
Barbe-Bleue, Comte des Grieux, Jupiter (*Philémon et Baucis*), Méphistophélès (*Faust*), Nilakantha.

Rothmüller, Marko *Baritone*
b. Yugoslavia, 1908:
Jokanaan, Macbeth, Scarpia, Wozzeck.

Rousseau, Jean Jacques *Composer*
b. Geneva, 1712: d. near Paris, 1778
Famous as a philosopher, Rousseau was also a music theorist and composer.

| Les Muses Galantes | | 1745 |
| Le Devin du Village | Fontainebleau | 1752 |

Rousseau, Marcel August *Composer*
(*Professional name* Samuel-Rousseau)
b. Paris, 1882: d. there, 1955

Tarass Boulba	Paris	1919
Le Hulla	„	1923
Le Bon Roi Dagobert	„	1927
Kerkeb	„	1951

Roussel, Albert Charles *Composer*
b. Tourcoing, France, 1869: d. Royan 1937

| Le Testament de la Tante Caroline | Olomouc, Czechoslovakia | 1936 |

Roze, Marie Hippolyte *Soprano*
(*Née* Ponsin)
b. Paris, 1846: d. near there, 1926
She made her debut at the Opéra-Comique as Marie (by Hérold) in 1865.
Carmen, Elsa, Leonore (*Fidelio*), Manon, Marguérite (*Faust*), Marie (by Hérold).

Rubini, Giovanni Battista *Tenor*
b. near Bergamo, 1794: d. there 1854
The first Arturo (*I Puritani*), he made his debut at Pavia in 1814.
Arturo (*I Puritani*), Otello (by Rossini), Don Ottavio.

Rudolf, Max *Conductor*
b. Frankfurt, 1902:
He has conducted in Germany, Prague and at the Metropolitan. In 1958 he was appointed conductor of the Cincinnati Symphony Orchestra.

Ruffo, Titta *Baritone*
(*Really* Ruffo Titta)
b. Pisa, 1877: d. Florence, 1953
One of the great baritones of all time, whom many consider to have possessed the largest voice ever heard on the operatic stage. He made his debut in Rome in 1898 as the Herald in *Lohengrin*, and his American debut in Philadelphia in 1912 as Rigoletto. He first appeared at the Metropolitan in 1922, singing Figaro in the *Il Barbiere di Siviglia*.

Rysanek, Leonie *Soprano*
b. Vienna
She made her debut in Innsbrück, Austria.
Agathe, Aida, Ariadne (*Ariadne auf Naxos*), Brünnhilde, Danae, Elisabeth of Valois, Empress (*Die Frau ohne Schatten*), Gilda, Lady Macbeth.

Sabata, Victor de *Composer*
b. Trieste, 1892:
He is best known as a conductor, at Monte Carlo and La Scala.

| Il Macigno | La Scala | 1917 |

Sack, Erna *Soprano*
b. Berlin, 1906:
Famous for her extraordinary range which included the C above high C. She appeared in concert in New York in 1937 and 1955.

Saint-Saëns, Charles Camille *Composer*
b. Paris, 1835: d. Algiers, 1921
A composer in all forms, not excluding music for films (silent films with an orchestra in the pit). He is best known for his orchestral *Danse Macabre*, and the poetic cello piece, *Le Cygne*, from the orchestral suite *Le Carnaval des Animaux*.

La Princesse Jaune	Paris	1872
Le Timbre d'Argent	„	1877
Samson et Dalila	Weimar	1877
Étienne Marcel	Lyons	1879
Henry VIII	Paris	1883
Proserpine	„	1887
Ascanio	„	1890
Phryné	„	1893
Les Barbares	„	1901
Hélène	Monte Carlo	1904
L'Ancêtre	„	1906
Déjanire	„	1911

Saléza, Albert *Tenor*
b. near Bayonne, 1867: d. Paris, 1916
He made his debut as Mylio (*Le Roi d'Ys*) at the Opéra-Comique, 1888.
Le Cid, Faust (*Faust*), Don José, Mylio (*Le Roi d'Ys*), Otello, Romeo, Siegmund.

THE PEOPLE IN OPERA

Salieri, Antonio *Composer*
b. Legnano, 1750: d. Vienna, 1825
One of Beethoven's teachers, and a teacher of Schubert and Liszt. He wrote thirty-nine operas.

La Grotto di		
Trionfonio	Vienna	1785
Tarare	Opéra	1787

Salmhofer, Franz *Composer*
b. Vienna, 1900:

Die Dame in Traum	Vienna	1935
Iwan Tarassenko	„	1938
Das Werbekleid	„	1946

Saltzmann-Stevens, Minnie *Soprano*
b. Bloomington, Ill., 1878:
A famous Brünnhilde and Kundry.
Brünnhilde, Kundry, Sieglinde.

Saminsky, Lazare *Composer*
b. Odessa, 1882: d. Port Chester, N.Y., 1959
A pupil of Rimsky-Korsakov, and a specialist in Jewish liturgical music.

The Vision of Ariel		1916
Gagliarda of a		
Merry Plague	New York	1925
The Daughter of Jephta		1929
Julian the Apostate Caesar		1938

Sammarco, Mario *Baritone*
b. Palermo, 1873: d. Milan, 1930
The first Gérard (*Andrea Chénier*). He made his debut at Milan, 1894. In 1905 he came out as Scarpia at Covent Garden, and in 1908 as Tonio in his first New York appearance.
Alvise, Falstaff (*Falstaff*), Gérard (*Andrea Chénier*), Gil (*Il Segreto di Susanna*), Don Giovanni, Iago, Orfeo (*La Favola d'Orfeo*), Rafaele, Rigoletto, Scarpia, Tonio.

Sanderson, Sybil *Soprano*
b. Sacramento, Calif., 1865: d. Paris, 1903
The first Thaïs, and the first Phryné (by Saint-Saëns). She made her Metropolitan debut in 1895 as Manon.

Sandi, Luis *Composer*
b. Mexico City, 1905:

Carlota	Mexico City	1948

Santley, Charles *Baritone*
b. Liverpool, 1834: d. near London, 1922
A pupil of Manuel García. Gounod wrote two of his most famous airs, *Avant de quitter ces lieux* and *Dio Possente*, for Santley.
Almaviva (*Le Nozze di Figaro*), Caspar, Fra Diavolo, Doctor Grenvil (*La Traviata*), Dutchman, Herr Fluth, Hoël, de Nevers, Peter the Great, Valentin (*Faust*).

Sargent, Harold Malcolm Watts
Conductor
b. London, 1895:
He conducted the first performance of *Hugh the Drover*.

Sarti, Giuseppe *Composer*
b. Faenza, 1729: d. Berlin, 1802
Sarti remains audible on the opera stage principally because of Mozart's quotation of an aria from his *I Due Litiganti* in *Don Giovanni*.

Il Re Pastore	Venice	1753
I Due Litiganti	Milan	1782
Armida e Rinaldo		
	St. Petersburg	1786

Sass, Marie *Soprano*
(*Really* Marie Saxe)
b. Ghent, 1838: d. St. Perine, 1907
The first Elisabeth (*Don Carlos*), and the first Selika.
Elisabeth (*Don Carlos*), Elisabeth (*Tannhäuser*), Donna Anna, Selika.

Sauguet, Henri *Composer*
b. Bordeaux, 1901:

Le Plumet du Colonel	Paris	1924
La Contrebasse	„	1932
La Chartreuse de Parme	′„	1939
La Gageuse Imprévue	„	1944
Les Caprices de		
Marianne	Aix-en-Provence	1954

283

Saville, Frances   *Soprano*
b. San Francisco, 1862: d. Burlingame,
Calif., 1935
She made her debut at Brussels in 1892.
Three years later she appeared at the
Metropolitan for the first time, singing
Juliette.

Sayao, Bidu   *Soprano*
b. Rio de Janeiro, 1902:
A pupil of Jean de Reszke. She made
her debut at the Metropolitan in 1937 as
Manon.
Gilda, Juliette, Manon, Marguérite
(*Faust*), Mélisande, Mimi, Nedda, Norina
(*Don Pasquale*), Serpina, Susanna (*Le
Nozze di Figaro*).

Saygun, Ahmed Adnam   *Composer*
b. Izmir, Turkey, 1907:
A pupil of Vincent d'Indy; he com-
posed operas on Turkish subjects.
Tas Babek   Ankara   1934
Keren   „   1953

Scalchi, Sofia   *Contralto*
b. Turin, 1850: d. Rome, 1922
One of the company in the Metropolitan's opening season, 1883. She made her
debut at Mantua in 1866, singing Ulrica.
In 1868 she came out at Covent Garden
as Azucena.
Azucena, La Cieca, Frédéric (*Mignon*),
Martha (*Faust*), Pierotte (*Linda di Chamounix*), Semiramide, Siebel, Ulrica, Vania
(*Ivan Susanin*).

Scaria, Emil   *Bass*
b. Graz, Austria, 1838: d. Blasewitz, 1886
The very first to sing Gurnemanz, there
having been two singers for the role in
opening performances of *Parsifal*.
Bertram, St. Bris, Escamillo, Gurnemanz, Hans Sachs, Marcel, Wotan.

Scarlatti, Alessandro   *Composer*
b. Palermo, Sicily, 1660: d. Naples, 1725
The founder of the Neapolitan school
of opera. He is said to have made the

first use of accompanied recitatives in 1693
in his opera *Teodora Augusta*. In all he
turned out one hundred fifteen operas.
Olimpia Vendicata   Naples   1685
Teodora Augusta   Rome   1693
Il Tigrane   Naples   1715
Il Trionfo dell'Onore   „   1718

Schack, Benedict   *Tenor*
(*Original spelling* Žak)
b. Bohemia, 1758: d. Munich, 1826
The first Tamino. He not only sang
but also composed some operas himself.
Count Almaviva (*Le Nozze di Figaro*),
Don Ottavio, Tamino.

Schalk, Franz   *Conductor*
b. Vienna, 1863: d. Edlach, 1931
He conducted at the Metropolitan
from 1898 to 1899, then went to Berlin,
and later to Vienna.

Scharwenka, Xaver   *Composer*
b. Samter, Germany, 1850: d. Berlin,
1924
Famous as a composer for piano and
for orchestra.
Mataswintha   Weimar   1896

Scheidemantel, Karl   *Baritone*
b. Weimar, 1859: d. there, 1923
He wrote a new text for *Così fan Tutte*,
after Calderón, produced in Dresden in
1909 as *Die Dame Kobold*.
Amfortas, Dutchman, Don Fernando
(*Fidelio*), Hans Heiling, Hans Sachs,
Herald (*Lohengrin*), Klingsor, Kothner,
Kurnewal, Wolfram.

Scherman, Thomas   *Conductor*
b. New York, 1917:
In 1947 he organized the Little Orchestra
Society of New York, and has performed
many otherwise forgotten operatic works
in concert form with that group.

Schibler, Armin   *Composer*
b. Kreuzlingen, Switzerland, 1920:
Der Spanische
Rosenstock   Bern   1950

Der Teufel im Winterpalais 1953
Das Bergwerk von Falun 1953
Die Füsse im Feuer   Zürich 1955

Schick, George   *Conductor*
b. Prague, 1908:
He made his debut at the Metropolitan
conducting *Rigoletto*.

Schick, Margarete Luise   *Soprano*
(*Née* Hanel)
b. Mainz, 1773: d. Berlin, 1809
Susanna (*Le Nozze di Figaro*), Zerlina
(*Don Giovanni*).

Schikaneder, Emanuel Johann
                               Librettist
b. Straubing, Austria, 1751: d. Vienna,
1812
The subject of Mozart's *Der Schauspieldirektor*. With the help of Gieseke, he
completed the libretto for *Die Zauberflöte*.
He had been an actor, and had even
played Hamlet. A lover of comic parts,
he was the first Papageno. It was Schikaneder, as a manager, who commissioned
Beethoven's *Fidelio*.

Schillings, Max von   *Composer*
b. Düren, Germany, 1868: d. Berlin, 1933
Chiefly known for his opera *Mona Lisa*,
he also was active as conductor and opera
director.
Mona Lisa   Stuttgart 1915

Schipa, Tito   *Tenor*
b. Lecce, 1889:
The first Ruggero (*La Rondine*). He
made his debut in Chicago in 1920.
Twelve years later he first appeared at the
Metropolitan as Nemerino, a part for
which he was famous.
Fra Diavolo, Duke, Ernesto (*Don
Pasquale*), Federico (*L'Arlesiana*), Fritz, des
Grieux(*Manon*), Nemerino, Don Ottavio,
Ruggero, Werther, Wilhelm.

Schippers, Thomas   *Conductor*
b. Kalamazoo, Mich., 1930:
He has conducted opera at the New York

City Center, beginning in 1951, and at
the Metropolitan since 1955.

Schiuma, Alfredo   *Composer*
b. Buenos Aires, 1885:
Amy Robsart   Buenos Aires 1920
La Sirocchia   „   1922
Tabaré   „   1925
Las Virgenes del Sol „   1939
La Infanta   „   1941

Schlusnus, Heinrich   *Baritone*
b. Braubach, Germany, 1888: d. Frankfurt, 1952
Famous as Amfortas and as Montforte
(*I Vespri Siciliani*).

Schmedes, Erik   *Tenor*
b. near Copenhagen, 1868: d. Vienna,
1931
He made his debut at Wiesbaden in 1891
singing the Herald in *Lohengrin*. In 1908
he came out at the Metropolitan as
Siegmund.
Herald (*Lohengrin*), Palestrina, Parsifal,
Pedro (*Tiefland*), Siegmund, Tannhäuser,
Tristan.

Schmidt, Franz   *Composer*
b. Pressburg, 1874: d. near Vienna, 1939
Notre Dame   Vienna 1914
Fredigundis   Berlin 1922

Schnorr von Carolsfeld, Ludwig *Tenor*
b. Munich, 1836: d. Dresden, 1865
The first Tristan, playing opposite his
wife. Forty-one days after the première
he died. He was also a pianist, a poet and
a painter.
Lohengrin, Naphtali, Robert le Diable,
Tristan.

Schnorr von Carolsfeld, Malwina
                               Soprano
b. Copenhagen, 1832: d. Karlsruhe, 1904
In 1865 she sang the first Isolde, opposite
her husband. Later she became a famous
teacher of singers.

Schoeck, Othmar   *Composer*
b. Brunnen, Switzerland, 1886: d. Zürich,
1957

Don Ranudo de
Colibrados Zürich 1919
Das Wandbild Halle 1921
Venus Zürich 1922
Penthesilea Dresden 1927
Massimilla Doni „ 1937
Das Schloss Dürande Berlin 1943

Schoemaker, Maurice *Composer*
b. near Brussels, 1890:
Swane 1933

Schoenberg, Arnold *Composer*
b. Vienna, 1874: d. Los Angeles, 1951
One of the most influential musical minds of the twentieth century, creator of the twelve-tone method of composition (known also as the dodecaphonic system), in which all principal themes are constructed on a basic series of twelve different notes. One of his best known works is *Verklärte Nacht* (*Transfigured Night*).
Von Heute auf
Morgen Frankfurt 1930

Schöffler, Paul *Baritone*
b. Dresden, 1897:
This famous Hans Sachs made his New York debut as Jokanaan at the Metropolitan in 1949.
Hans Sachs, High Priest (*Alceste*), Jokanaan, Jupiter (*Die Liebe der Danae*), Orest (*Elektra*).

Schorr, Friedrich *Bass*
b. Nagyvárad, Hungary, 1888: d. Farmington, Conn., 1953
He made his debut at Chicago in 1911, but it was thirteen years before he made his first appearance at the Metropolitan as Wolfram.
Altair, Amfortas, Dutchman, Hanns Sachs, Jokanaan, Orest (*Elektra*), Wolfram, Wotan.

Schott, Anton *Tenor*
b. Swabia, 1846: d. Stuttgart, 1913
He made his debut as Max in *Der Freischütz*. In 1884 he appeared for the first

time at the Metropolitan, singing Tannhäuser.
Benvenuto Cellini, Florestan, Max (*Der Freischütz*), Rienzi, Siegmund, Tannhäuser.

Schreker, Franz *Composer*
b. Monaco, 1878: d. Berlin, 1934
Der Ferne Klang (*The
Distant Sound*) Frankfurt 1912
Die Gezeichneten
(*The Stigmatized*) „ 1918
Der Schatzgräber (*The
Treasure Hunter*) „ 1920

Schröder-Devrient, Wilhelmine
Soprano
b. Hamburg, 1804: d. Coburg, 1860
The first Adriano (*Rienzi*), the first Senta, and the first Venus. She made her debut as Pamina in Vienna, 1822.
Adriano (*Rienzi*), Agathe, Amina, Desdemona, Iphigénie (*Iphigénie en Aulide*), Leonore (*Fidelio*), Marie (*Barbe-Bleue* by Grétry), Norma, Pamina, Senta, Venus.

Schubert, Franz Peter *Composer*
b. Vienna, 1797: d. there, 1828
The great composer of German *Lieder*.
Alfonso und Estrella Weimar 1854
Der Häusliche Krieg Frankfurt 1861
Fierrebras Karlsruhe 1897

Schuch, Ernst von *Conductor*
b. Graz, 1846: d. Dresden, 1914
The first to conduct *Feuersnot*, *Salome*, *Elektra* and *Der Rosenkavalier*.

Schumann, Elisabeth *Soprano*
b. Merseburg, Germany, 1885: d. New York, 1952
She made her debut at Hamburg in 1910, and at the Metropolitan, singing Sophie, in 1914. She was especially known for her singing of the works of Bach and Richard Strauss.
Donna Anna, Constance, Ilia (*Idomeneo*), Marzelline, Sophie (*Der Rosenkavalier*).

Schumann, Robert Alexander
Composer
b. Zwickau, Saxony, 1810: d. near Bonn, 1856

The celebrated composer, creator of the romantic style in piano compositions, songs and symphonies. He died insane.

Genoveva   Leipzig   1850

Schumann-Heink, Ernestine   *Contralto*
(*Née* Rössler)
b. Lieben, Czeckoslovakia, 1861: d. Hollywood, 1936

The first Klytemnestra (*Elektra*); and therein lies a story: she came away after that first night completely annoyed and disgusted with what she thought was a harsh, unmusical and unrewarding role.

She made her debut as Azucena at Dresden in 1878, as Erda at Covent Garden in 1892 and as Ortrud at Chicago in 1898 and at the Metropolitan the following year. For years after she had retired she made a ritual of singing the hymn *Silent Night* over the air on Christmas Eve.

Azucena, Brangäne, Carmen, The Countess (*Der Trompeter von Säkkingen*), Erda, Fides, Fricka, Klytemnestra, Ortrud, Waltraute.

Schütz, Heinrich   *Composer*
b. Köstritz, Germany, 1585: d. Dresden, 1672

The great predecessor of Bach, best known for his organ works and his numerous *Sacred Concerts*. His *Dafne* was the first German opera. It had a text by Opitz after Rinuccini, but the music is lost.

Dafne   Torgau   1627

Schützendorf, Gustav   *Baritone*
b. Cologne, 1883: d. Berlin, 1937

He made his debut at the Metropolitan in 1922 singing von Faninal.

Schwarzkopf, Elisabeth   *Soprano*
b. near Poznan, 1915:

She made her debut in Berlin in 1938. She was the first Anne Trulove.

Anne Trulove, Blondchen, Cio-Cio San, Constanze, Countess (*Capriccio*), Elsa, Donna Elvira, Esmeralda (*Prodaná Nevesta*), Eva, Gilda, Lauretta (*Gianni Schicchi*), Liù, Manon, Margherita (*Mefistofele*), Marzellina, Mimi, Musetta, Pamina, Rosina (*Il Barbiere di Siviglia*), Sophie (*Der Rosenkavalier*), Violetta, Waldvogel (*Siegfried*), Zerbinetta.

Scontrino, Antonio   *Composer*
b. Trapani, Sicily, 1850: d. Florence, 1922

Matelda	Milan	1879
Sortilegio	Turin	1882

Scott, Cyril   *Composer*
b. Oxton, England, 1879:

The Alchemist   Essen   1925

Scott, Tom   *Composer*
b. Campbellsburg, Ky., 1912:
American folk singer.

The Fisherman   1956

Scotti, Antonio   *Baritone*
b. Naples, 1866: d. there, 1936

He made his debut at Malta in 1889 as Amonasro. In 1899, as Don Giovanni, he came out at the Metropolitan and at Covent Garden. He sang with the Metropolitan for thirty-four years.

Almaviva (*Le Nozze di Figaro*), Amonasro, Ashton, Belcore, Escamillo, Falstaff (*Falstaff*), Germont, Gil, Don Giovanni, Iago, Lescaut (*Manon Lescaut*), Marcel, de Nevers, Rigoletto, Scarpia, Sharpless, Tonio, Valentin (*Faust*).

Scribe, Augustin Eugène   *Librettist*
b. Paris, 1791: d. there, 1861

Scribe was one of the most prolific of successful librettists, numbering the following among his works:

Fra Diavolo, La Juive, Les Huguenots, Le Prophète, L'Africaine, L'Etoile du Nord, Gustave III, I Vespri Siciliani (with Duveyier), *Masaniello* and *Robert le Diable* (with Delavigne).

Sebastian, George   *Conductor*
b. Budapest, 1903:
He has conducted at Hamburg, Leipzig, and the Metropolitan.

Seefried, Irmgard   *Soprano*
b. Köngetried, Bavaria, 1919:
She made her debut at Vienna as Eva in 1943 and at the Metropolitan as Susanna (*Le Nozze di Figaro*) ten years later.
Agathe, Antonia, Cio-Cio San, Composer (*Ariadne auf Naxos*), Eva, Fiordiligi, Giulietta, Marenka, Marzelline, Nanetta (*Falstaff*), Nedda, Nuri (*Tiefland*), Olympia, Pamina, Stella, Susanna (*Le Nozze di Figaro*).

Seidl, Anton   *Conductor*
b. Budapest, 1850: d. New York, 1898
From 1873 to 1879 he conducted at Bayreuth. After a short time in Bremen, he conducted at the Metropolitan from 1885 until his death. He married Auguste Krauss in 1885.

Seidl-Krauss, Auguste   *Soprano*
b. Vienna, 1853: d. Kingston, N.Y., 1939
The wife of the conductor Anton Seidl.
Agathe, Annchen (*Der Freischütz*), Brünnhilde, Elisabeth, Elsa, Eva, Irene, Isolde, Leonore (*Fidelio*), Rezia, Senta, Sieglinde.

Sekles, Bernhardt   *Composer*
b. Frankfurt, 1872: d. there, 1934
Scheherazade   Mannheim   1917
Die Zehn Küsse   Frankfurt 1926

Sembrich, Marcella   *Soprano*
b. Galicia, 1858: d. New York, 1935
One of the most accomplished musicians who ever sang in opera. On 21 April 1884 she took part in a benefit at the Metropolitan, playing the *Violin Concerto* by Bériot, a Chopin *Mazurka* on the piano, and singing. She made her debut in Athens in 1877 as Elvira (*I Puritani*), and in London, 1880, as Lucia. In 1883 she appeared for the first time at the Metropolitan in the same role.

Amina, Elvira (*Ernani*), Elvira (*I Puritani*), Eva, Frau Fluth, Gilda, Harriett (*Martha*), Lucia, Marie (*La Figlia del Reggimento*), Norina, Rosina (*Il Barbiere di Siviglia*), Susanna (*Le Nozze di Figaro*), Valentine (*Les Huguenots*), Violetta, Zerlina (*Don Giovanni*).

Serafin, Tullio   *Conductor*
b. near Venice, 1878:
Conductor at the Metropolitan from 1924 to 1935.

Serov, Alexander   *Composer*
b. St. Petersburg, 1820: d. there, 1871
➤ Judith   St. Petersburg   1863
  Rogneda   „   1865
  Vrazhya Sila (*The Power
  of Evil*) (*Finished by
  Soloviev*)   „   1871

Sessions, Roger   *Composer*
b. Brooklyn, N.Y., 1896:
One of the most important American composers of the modern school; also a distinguished teacher.
The Trial of
  Lucullus   Berkeley, Calif. 1947
  Montezuma   1947

Seymour, John Laurence   *Composer*
b. Los Angeles, 1893:
A pupil of Vincent d'Indy.
In the Pasha's
  Garden   Metropolitan   1935

Shacklock, Constance   *Soprano*
b.
Carmen, Octavian, Salome.

Shaporin, Yuri   *Composer*
b. Ukraine, 1889:
The Decembrists   Moscow   1953

Sheridan, Margaret   *Soprano*
b. County Mayo, Ireland, 1889: d. near Dublin, 1958
Cio-cio San, Desdemona, Iris, Maddalena (*Andrea Chénier*), Manon Lescaut, Wally.

Shostakovitch, Dmitri   *Composer*
b. St. Petersburg, 1906:
Celebrated Soviet symphonist, who ceased to write operas after the official condemnation he received for his *Lady Macbeth of Minsk*. In 1959 he produced a light opera.

The Nose	Leningrad	1930
Lady Macbeth of Minsk	,,	1934
Moskva Tchernomushki	Moscow	1959

Shuard, Amy   *Soprano*
b. London, 1924:
Aida, Amelia (*Simon Boccanegra*), Carmen, Cio-Cio San, Princess Eboli, Freia, Gerhilde, Giorgetta (*Il Tabarro*), Giulietta (*Les Contes d'Hoffmann*), Káta Kabanová, Magda Sorel, Marguérite (*Faust*), Musetta, Nedda, Santuzza, Venus.

Sibelius, Jean   *Composer*
b. Tavastehus, Finland, 1865: d. Järvenpää, 1957
Finland's most illustrious composer

Jungfruburen	Helsinki	1896

Siems, Margarete   *Soprano*
b.
The first Chrysothemis (*Elektra*), the first Marschallin, and the first Zerbinetta (*Ariadne auf Naxos*).

Siepi, Cesare   *Bass*
b. Milan, 1923:
He made his debut in Rigoletto in Venice, 1941.
Alvise, Don Basilio (*Il Barbiere di Siviglia*), Don Giovanni, Boris Godunov, Colline, Figaro (*Le Nozze di Figaro*), Mefistofele (*Mefistofele*), Oreveso, Padre Guardiano, Philip II, Sparafucile.

Simionato, Giulietta   *Mezzo-soprano*
b. Forli, Italy, 1916:
Azucena, Charlotte, Isabella (*L'Italiana in Algeri*), Marina Mnishck, Mignon, Preziosilla (*La Forza del Destino*), Rosina

(*Il Barbiere di Siviglia*), Sorceress (*Dido and Aeneas*).

Singher, Martial   *Baritone*
b. Oloron, Ste. Marie, France, 1904:
He made his debut at the Metropolitan in 1943.
Coppelius, Dapertutto, Golaud, High Priest (*Alceste*), Lindorf, Marouf, Dr. Miracle, Pelléas.

Skilton, Charles Sanford   *Composer*
b. Northampton, Mass., 1868: d. Lawrence, Kans., 1941

The Sun Bride	1930

Slezak, Leo   *Tenor*
b. Moravia, 1875: d. Bavaria, 1946
A pupil of Jean de Reszke. He made his London debut and his Metropolitan debut both in 1909, singing Otello. His first appearance in opera was in Brünn, 1896, singing Lohengrin. He is the father of the actor Walter Slezak.
Hermann (*Pique-Dame*), Julien, Lohengrin, Manrico, Otello, Radames, Tannhäuser, Walther.

Smallens, Alexander   *Conductor*
b. St. Petersburg, 1889:
He is usually the conductor of productions of *Porgy and Bess*, of which he conducted the première. He has conducted at Boston, Chicago and Philadelphia.

Smetana, Bedřich   *Composer*
b. Litomysl, Bohemia, 1824: d. Prague, 1884
National Bohemian composer, best known for his orchestral music, especially *The Moldau*.

Braniboři v Čechách (*The Brandenburgers in Bohemia*)	Prague	1866
Prodaná Nevěsta (*The Bartered Bride*)	,,	1866
Dalibor	,,	1868
Dvě vdovy (*The Two Widows*)	,,	1874

Hubička (*The Kiss*)   Prague   1876
Tajemství (*The Secret*)   „   1878
Libuše   „   1881
Čertova stěna
(*The Devil's Wall*)   „   1882

Smyth, Ethel Mary   *Composer*
b. Kent, England, 1858: d. Surrey, 1944
England's most famous woman composer and a fervid believer in the rights of women; fervid enough to have been arrested and jailed in 1911 for her agitations in favor of woman's suffrage.

Der Wald (*The Forest*)   Dresden   1901
Fantasio   Weimar   1902
The Wreckers   Leipzig   1906
The Boatswain's Mate   London   1916
Fête Galante   Birmingham   1923
Entente Cordiale   Bristol   1926

Sodero, Cesare   *Conductor*
b. Naples, 1886: d. New York, 1947
Music Director of NBC and the Mutual Network Conductor of the San Carlo Opera and the Philadelphia Opera.

Solti, Georg   *Conductor*
b. Budapest, 1912:
Conductor at Munich, Frankfurt and San Francisco.

Sontag, Henriette   *Soprano*
(Countess Rossi)
b. Coblenz, 1806: d. Mexico City, 1854
The first Euryanthe.
Amina, Donna Anna, Desdemona, Elvira (*I Puritani*), Euryanthe, Isabella (*L'Italiana in Algeri*), Lucrezia Borgia, Marie (*La Figlia del Reggimento*), Norina, Rosina (*Il Barbiere di Siviglia*), Semiramide, Susanna (*Le Nozze di Figaro*), Zerlina (*Don Giovanni*).

Spelman, Timothy   *Composer*
b. Brooklyn, N.Y., 1891:
La Magnifica   1920
The Sunken City   1930
The Courtship of Miles Standish   1943

Spohr, Ludwig   *Composer*
b. Brunswick, 1784: d. Kassel, 1859
Famous as a violinist and composer of instrumental music. He wrote eleven operas. As a conductor he brought out *Der Fliegende Holländer* and *Tannhäuser*, but was officially restrained from bringing out *Lohengrin*.

Faust   Prague   1816
Jessonda   Kassel   1823
Zemire und Azor   Frankfurt   1819

Spontini, Gasparo   *Composer*
b. near Ancona, Italy, 1774: d. there, 1851
A prolific composer of operas and other works. He met his greatest successes in France where *La Vestale*, which took him fifteen years to compose, was finally performed. There he was director of the Italian Opera, and later became court composer. He also held the latter post in Berlin for a few years.

La Vestale   Opéra   1807
Fernand Cortez   „   1809
Olympie   „   1819

Stabile, Mariano   *Baritone*
b. Palermo, 1888:
Alfonso (*Così fan Tutte*), Falstaff (*Falstaff*), Giovanni (*Francesca da Rimini*), Don Giovanni, Iago, Lescaut (*Manon Lescaut*), Plunkett, Poet (*Il Turco in Italia*), Rigoletto, Scarpia.

Stagno, Roberto   *Tenor*
b. Palermo, 1836: d. Genoa, 1897
The first Turiddu. He was among the company in the Metropolitan's opening season, 1883.
Grimaldo, Lionel, Manrico, Don Ottavio, Turiddu.

Stanford, Charles Villiers   *Composer*
b. Dublin, 1852: d. London, 1924
Savonarola   Hamburg   1884
The Canterbury
Pilgrims   London   1884

Starer, Robert   *Composer*
b. Vienna, 1924
The Intruder   New York   1956

Staudigl, Josef   *Bass*
b. Wöllersdorf, Austria, 1807: d. near
Vienna, 1861
King Marke, Pietro (*Masaniello*), Pizarro, Pogner, Sarastro, Wotan.

Staudigl, Josef, Jr.   *Baritone*
b. Vienna, 1850: d. Karlsruhe, 1910
Pogner, Rocco, King Marke.

Steber, Eleanor   *Soprano*
b. Wheeling, W.Va., 1916:
The first Vanessa. She made her debut
at the Metropolitan in 1940 as Sophie.
Alice Ford, Countess Almaviva, Donna
Anna, Antonia, Arabella, Constanze, Desdemona, Elizabeth de Valois, Elsa, Eva,
Donna Elvira, Fiordiligi, Giulietta, Marguérite (*Faust*), Marie (*Wozzeck*), Marschallin, Micaela, Minnie, Sophie, Tosca,
Vanessa, Violetta, Barak's Wife (*Die Frau
ohne Schatten*).

Stefano, Giuseppe di   *Tenor*
b. Catania, 1921:
Alfredo, Arthur (*I Puritani*), Canio,
Duke, Edgar, Manrico, Mario Cavara-
dossi, Riccardo (*Un Ballo in Maschera*),
Rodolfo, Turiddu, Wilhelm.

Stehle, Sophie   *Soprano*
b. Hohenzollern-Sigmaringen, Germany,
1838: d. near Hanover, 1921
The first Fricka, Brünnhilde (*Walküre*),
Alice Ford, Nedda, and Walter (*La
Wally*).
Agathe, Alice Ford, Brünnhilde, Elisa-
beth, Elsa, Eva, Fricka, Nedda, Senta,
Walter (*La Wally*).

Steinberg, William   *Conductor*
b. Cologne, 1899:
Conductor at Cologne, Prague and
elsewhere. In 1952 he was engaged as
conductor of the Pittsburgh Symphony
Orchestra.

Stephens, Catherine   *Soprano*
b. London, 1794: d. there, 1882
Polly Peachum, Susanna (*Le Nozze di
Figaro*), Rosetta (*Love in a Village*).

Stevens, Risë   *Mezzo-soprano*
b. New York, 1913:
She made her debut in Prague in 1938
as Mignon, and at the Metropolitan the
same year in the same role.
Carmen, Dalila, Mignon, Octavian.

Stiedry, Fritz   *Conductor*
b. Vienna, 1883:
Has conducted at Berlin, Vienna, and
the Metropolitan.

Stignani, Ebe   *Mezzo-soprano*
b. Italy, 1905:
Adalgisa, Amneris, Dalila, Princess
Eboli, Fidalma, Laura, Leonora (*La
Favorita*), Martha (*Khovantchina*), Rosa
(*L'Arlesiana*), Rubria (*Nerone* by Boito),
Ulrica.

Still, William Grant   *Composer*
b. Woodville, Miss., 1895:
Blue Steel	1935
Troubled Island	1938
A Bayou Legend	1940
Miss Sally's Party	1940
A Southern Interlude	1942
Castasio	1949

Stokowski, Leopold   *Conductor*
b. London, 1882:
Celebrated conductor, especially noted
for his zeal in bringing new works and
new composers to public notice.

Stoltz, Rosina   *Mezzo-soprano*
(*Really* Victoire Noël)
b. Paris, 1815: d. there, 1903
The first Leonora (*La Favorita*), the first
Agathe, Desdemona (Rossini's *Otello*), and
Zayda (*Dom Sébastien*).
Agathe, Desdemona (by Rossini), Fides,
Leonora (*La Favorita*), Rachel, Zayda
(*Dom Sébastien*).

Stolz, Teresa *Soprano*
b. Bohemia, 1834: d. Milan, 1902
Aida, Leonora (*La Forza del Destino*).

Storace, Ann Selina *Soprano*
b. London, 1766: d. Dulwich, 1817
A sister of Stephen Storace. The first
Susanna in *Le Nozze di Figaro*.

Storace, Stephen *Composer*
b. London, 1763: d. there, 1796
Brother of Ann Storace.

The Haunted Tower	London	1789
No Song, No Supper	„	1790
Cherokee	„	1794
Mahmoud (*completed by*		
Kelly and Ann Storace)	„	1796

Stradella, Alessandro *Composer*
b. Montefestino, Italy, 1642: d. (*murdered*)
Genoa, 1682
A composer of opera, but most famous
because of the opera made about him by
Flotow in which speculations about his
murder are greatly romanticized.

Strakosch, Maurice *Manager*
b. Moravia, 1825: d. Paris, 1887
He presented Italian opera in New York
in 1857, and in Chicago in 1859.

Strauss, Johann, Jr. *Composer*
b. Vienna, 1825: d. there, 1899
The Waltz King.

Indigo	Vienna	1871
Der Karneval in Rome	„	1873
Die Fledermaus (*The Bat*)	„	1874
Cagliostro in Wien	„	1875
Zigeunerbaron		
(*The Gypsy Baron*)	„	1885

Strauss, Richard Georg *Composer*
b. Munich, 1864: d. Garmisch-Parten-
kirchen, 1949
The celebrated composer of operas and
symphonic poems, among which *Don
Juan, Till Eulenspiegel, Death and Trans-
figuration* are famous. He also arranged
Iphigénie en Tauride for the Metropolitan
in 1916, and *Idomeneo* for Vienna in 1931.

Guntram	Weimar	1894
Feuersnot	Dresden	1901
Salome	„	1905
Elektra	„	1909
Der Rosenkavalier	„	1911
Ariadne auf Naxos	Stuttgart	1912
Die Frau ohne Schatten	Vienna	1919
Intermezzo	Dresden	1924
Die Aegyptische		
Helene	„	1928
Arabella	„	1933
Die Schweigsame Frau	„	1935
Friedenstag	Munich	1938
Daphne	Dresden	1938
Capriccio	Munich	1942
Die Liebe der Danae	Salzburg	1952

Stravinsky, Feodor *Bass*
b. Tchernigov, Russia, 1843: d. Wildun-
gen, Germany, 1902
Father of Igor Stravinsky. His most
famous role was Méphistophélès in *Faust*.

Stravinsky, Igor *Composer*
b. Orianienbaum, Russia, 1882:
One of the great composers of the
twentieth century, and a tremendous
influence on the music of the generations
that followed him. Stravinsky began in a
style somewhat like that of Rimsky-
Korsakov, with whom he had taken a few
lessons. Some of his most popular ballets
date from that period. But he effectively
demolished that reputation with the
astonishingly primitive orchestral work
Le Sacre du Printemps, which became a
landmark in the change of direction of
musical composition. His later works
have shown no diminution of originality
but have tended to be more of a religious
and poetic nature than the ballets which
made him famous. Like the last quartets
of Beethoven, Stravinsky's latest works
are of a new style, somewhat neoclassic
but harmonically very complex. After
many years in Paris he settled in California. His *Oedipus Rex* was performed in
New York with magnificent, sticklike

marionettes by Bufano, twice the size of human beings. These acted out the story over the heads of the chorus, which was only dimly visible below.

Rossignol		
(*The Nightingale*)	Paris	1914
Mavra	„	1922
Renard (*The Fox*)	„	1922
Oedipus Rex	„	1927
The Rake's Progress	Venice	1951

Strepponi, Giuseppina *Soprano*
b. Lodi, Italy, 1815: d. Busseto, 1897
The first Abigaille in *Nabucco*. In 1859 she married Verdi.

Stückgold, Grete *Soprano*
b. London, 1895:
She made her Metropolitan debut as Eva in 1927.

Sucher, Rosa *Soprano*
(*Née* Hasselbeck)
b. Velburg, Germany, 1849: d. Berlin, 1927
As Isolde she made her Covent Garden debut in 1892 and her Metropolitan three years later.
Brünnhilde, Elsa, Euryanthe, Eva, Isolde, Kundry, Senta.

Sullivan, Arthur Seymour *Composer*
b. London, 1842: d. Westminster, 1900
In association with W. S. Gilbert, he wrote the music of some of the most famous English light operas, which have a style of their own. All those listed below were with Gilbert. His other works, of which there were many, do not survive on the stage. His "grand opera," *Ivanhoe*, produced in London in 1891, had only a transitory success.

Trial by Jury	London	1875
The Sorcerer	„	1877
HMS Pinafore	„	1878
The Pirates of		
Penzance	New York	1878
Patience	London	1881
Iolanthe		1882

Princess Ida	1884
The Mikado	1885
Ruddigore	1887
Yeomen of the Guard	1888
The Gondoliers	1889

Sullivan, Brian *Tenor*
b.
He made his Vienna debut as Erik (*Der Fliegende Holländer*) in 1959.
Alfred (*Die Fledermaus*), Avito, Erik (*Der Fliegende Holländer*), Ferrando, Grigori, Don José, Lohengrin, Pinkerton, Rodolfo, Walther.

Sundelius, Marie *Soprano*
b. Karlsbad, Sweden, 1884: d. Boston, 1958
She made her debut at the Metropolitan in 1916. Subsequently, she became a singing teacher.

Supervia, Conchita *Mezzo-soprano*
b. Barcelona, 1899: d. London, 1936
Her records reveal that this was a great voice.
Carmen, Concepcion (*L'Heure Espagnole*).

Suppé, Franz von *Composer*
(*Really* Francesco Ezechiele Ermenegildo)
b. Dalmatia, 1819: d. Vienna, 1895
Only the overtures to his operas remain popular today.

The Poet and Peasant	Vienna	1846
Boccaccio	„	1879
Light Cavalry	„	1866

Sutherland, Joan *Soprano*
b. Sydney, Australia, 1926:
Gifted with a remarkable capacity for study and control of a fine voice, she made her English opera debut at Covent Garden in 1952, and appeared at the Metropolitan in 1961. She ranks with Tebaldi and Callas as one of the most important singers of her time.
Amina, Desdemona, Dido, Elvira, Judith.

Svanholm, Set   *Tenor*
b. Västeras, Sweden, 1904:
He made his debut at Stockholm as
Silvio in *Pagliacci*. In 1957 he became
General Manager of the Stockholm opera.
Aegisth, Figaro (*Il Barbiere di Siviglia*),
Parsifal, Siegfried, Siegmund, Silvio,
Tristan, Walther.

Swarthout, Gladys   *Contralto*
b. Deepwater, Missouri, 1904:
She made her debut at the Metropolitan
as La Cieca in 1929, five years after her
first appearance in opera in Chicago.
Carmen, La Cieca, Stéphano (*Roméo et
Juliette*).

Szell, George   *Conductor*
b. Budapest, 1897:
He has conducted at Strasbourg, Prague,
Darmstadt, Düsseldorf, Berlin and at the
Metropolitan in New York (1942–1945).
In 1946 he became conductor of the
Cleveland Orchestra.

Tagliavini, Ferruccio   *Tenor*
b. Reggio, Italy, 1913:
In Florence, 1939, he made his debut
singing Rodolfo. He came out at the
Metropolitan in the same role in 1947.
Duke, Faust (*Mefistofele*), Fritz, des
Grieux (*Manon*), Mario Cavaradossi,
Rodolfo, Werther.

Tajo, Italo   *Bass*
b. Pinerolo, 1915:
Don Basilio (*Il Barbiere di Siviglia*),
Colline, Gianni Schicchi, Leporello, Ramfis, Timur (*Turandot*).

Talley, Marion   *Soprano*
b. Nevada, Missouri, 1907:
She made her debut as Gilda at the
Metropolitan in 1926. She was one of the
few American singers to be engaged there.
Her career was, however, soon ended.

Tamagno, Francesco   *Tenor*
b. Turin, 1850: d. Varese, 1905

The first Otello (Verdi's opera), he made
his debut as Riccardo in *Un Ballo in
Maschera* at Palermo, 1874. His first
appearance at the Metropolitan took place
in 1894 when he sang Arnold in *Guillaume
Tell*.
Arnold (*Guillaume Tell*), Otello, Radames, Riccardo (*Un Ballo in Maschera*),
Samson.

Tamberlik, Enrico   *Tenor*
b. Rome, 1820: d. Paris, 1889
The first Don Alvaro (*La Forza del
Destino*). He made his debut at Covent
Garden in 1850 singing Masaniello.

Tamburini, Antonio   *Baritone*
b. Faenza, Italy, 1800: d. Nice, 1876
The first Riccardo (*I Puritani*), and the
first Doctor Malatesta (*Don Pasquale*).

Taneyev, Sergey Ivanovich   *Composer*
b. Vladimir, Russia, 1856: d. Moscow,
1915
Orestes
    (*trilogy*)   St. Petersburg 1895

Tansman, Alexander   *Composer*
b. Lodz, 1897:
La Nuit Kurde   1927
Le Serment   Brussels 1955

Taskin, Émile Alexandre   *Bass*
b. Paris, 1853: d. there, 1897
Taskin received a medal for his success
in calming the audience at the Opéra-
Comique when a fire broke out during a
performance of *Mignon* in 1887 and destroyed the theater. He was singing
Lotario at the time.

Tauber, Richard   *Tenor*
(*Really* Ernest Seiffert)
b. Linz, Austria, 1892: d. London, 1948
He made his debut as Tamino at Frankfurt in 1913. He also, however, wrote and
produced his own opera:
Old Chelsea   London 1943

Taylor, Deems   *Composer*
b. New York, 1885:

THE PEOPLE IN OPERA

Well known as a critic and as a broadcast commentator on music. His suite *Through the Looking Glass* is still popular.

| The King's Henchman | Metropolitan | 1927 |
| Peter Ibbetson | „ | 1931 |

Tchaikovsky, Modest *Librettist*
b. St. Petersburg, 1850: d. Moscow, 1916
Brother of the symphonist Piotr Ilyich Tchaikovsky, and librettist for two operas by him: *Pique-Dame* and *Iolanthe*.

Tchaikovsky, Piotr Ilyitch *Composer*
b. near Viatka, Russia, 1840: d. St. Petersburg, 1893
Famous everywhere for his romantic music, which is well exemplified in his last three symphonies, and his *Romeo and Juliet* Overture. Equally celebrated are his ballets (*The Swan Lake, The Sleeping Beauty, The Nutcracker*).

Voyevode	Moscow	1869
Undine		1869
Opritchnik	St. Petersburg	1874
Vakula the Smith	„	1876
Eugene Onegin	Moscow	1879
The Maid of Orleans	St. Petersburg	1881
Mazeppa	Moscow	1884
Tcherevichki (*a revision of* Vakula the Smith)	„	1887
The Sorceress	St. Petersburg	1887
Pique-Dame	„	1890
Iolanthe	„	1892

Tcherepnin, Alexandre *Composer*
b. St. Petersburg, 1899:
He completed Mussorgsky's *Zhenitba* for the performance in Essen, 1937. His father had done the same for the same composer's *Fair at Sorochintsky* in performance at Monte Carlo, 1923.

Ol-ol	Weimar	1928
Die Hochzeit der Sobeide	Vienna	1933
The Farmer and the Fairy	Aspen, Colo.,	1952

Tebaldi, Renata *Soprano*
b. Pesaro, Italy, 1922:
This great artist of the voice made her debut at Trieste in 1946 as Desdemona, then at Covent Garden in 1950 and the Metropolitan, 1955, in the same role. She is remarkable among prima donnas for her calm approach and her intense study of the emotional and musical fabric of each role.

Aida, Amelia (*Simon Boccanegra*), Cio-Cio San, Desdemona, Elsa, Helen of Troy (*Mefistofele*), Leonora (*La Forza del Destino*), Leonora (*Il Trovatore*), Maddalena (*Andrea Chénier*), Manon Lescaut, Margherite (*Mefistofele*), Mathilde (*Guillaume Tell*), Mimi, Olimpia (Spontini's opera), Tosca, Violetta, Wally.

Telemann, Georg Philip *Composer*
b. Magdeburg, 1681: d. Hamburg, 1767
Best known for his chamber works, especially those including flute, strings, and harpsichord. He wrote forty operas.

| Der Gedultige Socrates | Hamburg | 1721 |
| Der Neu-Modische Liebhaber Damon | „ | 1724 |

Ternina, Milka *Soprano*
b. near Zagreb, 1863: d. there, 1941
She made her debut at her birthplace in 1882, and at the Metropolitan as Elsa in 1896.

Aida, Amelia (*Un Ballo in Maschera*), Brünnhilde, Elisabeth, Elsa, Gretchen (*Der Wildschütz*), Isolde, Kundry, Leonore (*Fidelio*), Selika, Tosca.

Tetrazzini, Eva *Soprano*
b. Milan, 1862: d. Salsomaggiore, 1938
Sister of Luisa Tetrazzini. She made her debut as Marguérite (*Faust*) in Florence, 1882. Five years later she married Cleofonte Campanini.

Tetrazzini, Luisa *Soprano*
b. Florence, 1871: d. Milan, 1940
Sister of Eva Tetrazzini, and a very

famous singer. As Melba toast was named for Nellie Melba, so Chicken Tetrazzini preserves this soprano's name for people who know nothing of opera. She made her debut as Inez in Florence, 1895. In London, 1907 and at the Manhattan opera 1908, she made debuts as Violetta.

Amina, Desdemona, Dinorah, Elvira (*I Puritani*), Gilda, Inez, Lakmé, Leila, Lucia, Marie (*La Figlia del Reggimento*), Rosina (*Il Barbiere di Siviglia*), Violetta.

Teyte, Maggie   *Soprano*
(*Née* Tate)
b. Wolverhampton, England, 1888:
A pupil of Jean de Reske. She changed the spelling of her name in order to avoid popular mispronunciations in France. She is usually associated with the role of Mélisande. It was in Monte Carlo that she made her debut in 1907 as Zerlina (*Don Giovanni*).

Antonia, Cherubino, Cio-cio San, Giulietta, Mélisande, Mimi, Olympia (*Les Contes d'Hoffmann*), Stella, Zerlina (*Don Giovanni*).

Thebom, Blanche   *Mezzo-soprano*
b. Monessen, Pa., 1918:
She made her debut as Fricka at the Metropolitan in 1944.

Adalgisa, Amneris, Azucena, Baba the Turk, Brangäne, Carmen, Dalila, Dorabella, Princess Eboli, Fricka, Laura Adorno, Marina Mnishek, Orlovsky, Ortrud, Venus.

Thiriet, Maurice   *Composer*
b. Meulan, France, 1906:

Le Bourgeois de Falaise	Paris	1937
La Véridique Histoire du Docteur		1937

Thoma, Therese   *Soprano*
b. Tutzing, Germany, 1845: d. Munich, 1921

The first Sieglinde. She married Heinrich Vogl in 1868.
Brünnhilde, Isolde, Sieglinde.

Thomas, Charles Louis Ambroise   *Composer*
b. Metz, 1811: d. Paris, 1896
A French composer of romantic operas. He taught at the Paris Conservatory for many years, and in 1871 became its director.

Le Caïd	Paris	1849
Le Songe d'une Nuit d'Éte	„	1850
Raymond	„	1851
Mignon	„	1866
Hamlet	„	1868

Thomas, John Charles   *Baritone*
b. Meyersdale, Pa., 1891: d. Los Angeles, 1960
This famous singer of concert and radio made his operatic debut in Brussels in 1925. He came out as Valentin (*Faust*) in Covent Garden, 1928, and as Giorgio Germont at the Metropolitan in 1934.

Amonasro, Athanaël, Figaro (*Il Barbiere di Siviglia*), Giorgio Germont, Valentin (*Faust*).

Thompson, Randall   *Composer*
b. New York, 1899:

Solomon and Balkis	New York (radio)	1942

Thomson, Virgil   *Composer*
b. Kansas City, Missouri, 1896:
His scores have a certain brash simplicity that wins them popularity. He has been an influential critic in New York.

Four Saints in Three Acts	Ann Arbor, Mich.	1933

(*First stage performance, Hartford, Conn.,* 1934)

The Mother of us All	New York	1947

Thorborg, Kerstin   *Contralto*
b. Venjan, Sweden, 1896:

296

Eleven years after her debut in Stockholm, 1925, she came out as Fricka at the Metropolitan.

Eglantine, Fricka, Herodias (*Salome*), Klytemnestra (*Elektra*), Kundry, Marina Mnishek, Doña Mercedes (*Der Corregidor*), Orfeo, Ulrica.

Thuille, Ludwig Wilhelm Andreas Maria   *Composer*
b. Bolzano, 1861: d. Munich, 1907
He is best known for his treatise on harmony.

Theuerdank	Munich	1894
Lobetanz	Karlsruhe	1898
Gugeline	Bremen	1901

Tibbett, Lawrence   *Baritone*
b. Bakersfield, Calif., 1896: d. New York, 15 July 1960
A famous radio singer in the United States. He made his debut at the Metropolitan in 1923.

Don Carlo (*La Forza del Destino*), Ford (*Falstaff*), Iago, Michele (*Il Tabarro*), Rance, Scarpia, Simon Boccanegra, Valentin (*Faust*), Wolfram.

Tichatschek, Joseph Aloys   *Tenor*
b. Bohemia, 1807: d. Dresden, 1886
The first Cola Rienzi, the first Tannhäuser.

Tietjens, Therese   *Soprano*
b. Hamburg, 1831: d. London, 1877
She made her debut at Hamburg in 1849 and at London in 1858.

Alice Ford (*Falstaff*), Countess Almaviva, Amelia (*Un Ballo in Maschera*), Donna Anna, Elvira (*Ernani*), Fidès, Frau Fluth (*Die Lustigen Weiber von Windsor*), Iphigénie (*Iphigénie en Tauride*), Leonore (*Fidelio*), Leonora (*La Forza del Destino*), Leonora (*Il Trovatore.*) Lucrezia Borgia, Marguérite (*Faust*), Martha, Medea, Mireille, Norma, Ortrud, Pamina, Rezia, Semiramide, Valentine (*Les Huguenots*).

Tippett, Michael   *Composer*
b. London, 1905:

The Midsummer Marriage	London	1955

Toch, Ernst   *Composer*
b. Vienna, 1887:

Wegwende		1925
Die Prinzessin auf der Erbse (*The Princess on the Pea*)	Baden Baden	1927
Egon und Emilie	Mannheim	1928
Der Fächer (*The Fan*)	Königsberg	1930

Tokatyan, Armand   *Tenor*
b. Bulgaria, 1899:
He made his operatic debut at Milan in 1921, and came out as Lucio (*Anima Allegra* by Vittadini) at the Metropolitan two years later.

Avito, Lucio (*Anima Allegra* by Vittadini), Paco (*La Vide Breve*).

Tomasi, Henri   *Composer*
b. Marseille, 1901:

Atlantide	Mulhouse	1954
Don Juan de Mañara	Munich	1956
Sampiero Corso	Bordeaux	1956

Tosatti, Vieri   *Composer*
b. Rome, 1920:

Dionisio		1947
Il Sistema della Dolcezza (*The System of Sweetness*)		1949
La Partita a Pugni (*Prize Fight*)	Venice	1953

Toscanini, Arturo   *Conductor*
b. Parma, 1867: d. New York, 1957
So famous a conductor as to be a legend in his own time even among people who never heard a concert. His career began in Rio de Janeiro where he stepped up from the orchestra to conduct Aida, taking the place of a conductor who had been hissed out of the house by the hostile audience. He conducted the first *Pagliacci*,

the first *La Bohème*, and the first United States performances of *Armide, Ariane et Barbe-Bleue, Boris Godunov, L'Amore dei Tre Re*, and many more. He became more widely known through his regular broadcasts with the NBC symphony orchestra which became the Symphony of the Air after his retirement. Because of his near blindness, he habitually committed each work to his fabulous memory and conducted without score.

Tourel, Jennie   *Mezzo-soprano*
b. Montreal, 1910:
The first to sing Baba the Turk in *The Rake's Progress*. She made her debut at the Opéra-Comique in 1933 as Carmen.

Tovey, Donald Francis   *Composer*
b. Eton, 1875: d. Edinburgh, 1940
Tovey is primarily known to students of music as the author of a series of critical analyses of music, with particular study of Beethoven.
The Bride of
Dionysius   Edinburgh   1932

Tozzi, Giorgio   *Bass*
b. Chicago:
Tozzi began as a baritone but became a bass in 1950. He came to the Metropolitan in 1955 as Alvise (*La Gioconda*).
Ashby, Amonasro, Commendatore (*Don Giovanni*), Count di Luna, Germont (*La Traviata*), Phillip the Second, Pimen, Pogner, Prince Gremin (*Eugene Onegin*), Count Rodolfo (*La Sonnambula*), Samuele (*Un Ballo in Maschera*), Sarastro, Tarquinius (*The Rape of Lucretia*), Tonio.

Traetta, Tommaso   *Composer*
b. Naples, 1727: d. Venice, 1779
He wrote nearly forty operas.
Ippolito ed Aricie   Parma   1759
Ifigenia in Aulide   Vienna   1759
Armida   ,,   1761

Tranchell, Peter   *Composer*
b. Cuddalore, India, 1922:

The Mayor of
Casterbridge   Cambridge,
              England   1951

Traubel, Helen   *Soprano*
b. St. Louis, 1899:
Famous as Isolde and as Brünnhilde, she made her debut at the Metropolitan as Sieglinde in 1939.

Trebelli, Zelia   *Mezzo-soprano*
(*Really* Gilbert)
b. Paris, 1838: d. Étretat, 1892
She made her debut at Madrid, 1859, singing Rosina in *Il Barbiere di Siviglia*.
Amneris, Arsace, Azucena, Carmen, Elena (*Mefistofele*), Fatima (*Oberon*), Frédéric (*Mignon*), Nancy (*Martha*), Maffeo Orsini, Rosina (*Il Barbiere di Siviglia*), Urbain.

Tréville, Yvonne de   *Soprano*
(*Really* Edyth la Gierse)
b. Galveston, Tex., 1881: d. New York, 1954
She made her debut as Marguérite in New York, 1898.

Tucker, Richard   *Tenor*
b. New York, 1914:
He made his debut at the Metropolitan in 1945, singing Enzo.
Don Alvaro, Don Carlos, Enzo, Ferrando, Des Grieux (*Manon Lescaut*), Don José, Lensky, Mario Cavaradossi, Radames, Rodolfo, Turiddu.

Turina, Joaquín   *Composer*
b. Seville, 1882: d. Madrid, 1949
Margot   Madrid   1914
Jardín de Oriente   ,,   1923

Turner, Claramae   *Mezzo-soprano*
b. Dinuba, Calif., 1920:
The first Madame Flora (*The Medium*).
Azucena, Carmen, Madame Flora, La Frugola (*Il Tabarro*), La Vecchia (*Gianni Schicchi*), Madame de Croissy (*Les Dialogues des Carmélites*), Marquise de

298

Berkenfield, Princess (*Suor Angelica*), Witch (*Hänsel und Gretel*).

Ugalde, Delphine *Soprano*
(*Née* Beaucé)
b. Paris, 1829: d. there, 1910
This capable woman was manager of the Bouffes-Parisiens from 1866 to 1871, and the composer of an opera. She made her debut as a soprano in Auber's *Domino Noir* in 1848, singing Angèle.
Angèle (*Domino Noir*), Blonde, Euridice (*Orphée aux Enfers*), Leonora (*Il Trovatore*), Papagena, Rezia, Susanna (*Le Nozze di Figaro*), Taven (*Mireille*),
She composed:
La Halte au Moulin   Paris 1867

Uhde, Hermann *Baritone*
A member of the Metropolitan Opera Company in 1960 noted for his interpretation of the role of Scarpia. He was also a magnificent Wozzeck.

Ullmann, Viktor *Composer*
b. Teschen, Austria, 1898:
Peer Gynt
Der Sturz des Anti-Christ

Unger, Georg *Tenor*
b. Leipzig, 1837: d. there, 1887
A famous Siegfried.

Unger, Hermann *Composer*
b. Kamenz, Germany, 1886: d. Cologne, 1958
Der Zauberhandschuh
(*The Magic Glove*)   1927
Richmodis von Aducht   1928

Uppman, Theodor *Baritone*
b.
The first Billy Budd.
Billy Budd, Masetto, Papageno, Paquillo (*La Périchole*), Pelléas.

Urlus, Jacques *Tenor*
b. near Aachen, 1867: d. Noordwijk, 1935

In 1894 in Amsterdam he made his debut as Beppo. As Tristan he came out in Boston in 1912 and at the Metropolitan the following year.
Beppo, Florestan, Lohengrin, Parsifal, Siegmund, Tristan.

Ursuleac, Viorica *Soprano*
b. Cernauti, Romania, 1899:
The first Arabella, Maria (*Friedenstag*), Danae, and Countess (*Capriccio*). To her and to Clemens Krauss, whom she married, Strauss dedicated *Friedenstag*. Her debut came at Berlin, in 1933.
Arabella, Countess (*Capriccio*), Danae, Helena (*Die Aegyptische Helena*), Maria (*Friedenstag*).

Usandizaga, José-María *Composer*
b. San Sebastien, Spain, 1887: d. Yanti, 1915
A pupil of d'Indy.
Mendy-Mendiyan   Bilbao 1910
Las Golondrinas
(*The Swallows*)   Madrid 1914
La Llama (*The Flame*)   „   1915

Valleria, Alvina *Soprano*
(*Really* Schoening)
b. Baltimore, Md., 1848: d. Nice, 1925
She made her debut in London in 1871, then at the Metropolitan as Marguérite (*Faust*), in 1879.
Aida, Elisabeth, Leonore (*Fidelio*), Linda di Chamounix, Marguérite (*Faust*), Margherite (*Mefistofele*), Martha, Micaela.

Valleti, Cesare *Tenor*
b.
Alfredo Germont, Almaviva (*Il Barbiere di Siviglia*), Lindoro (*Il Turco in Italia*), Don Ottavio, Werther.

Vanesi, Felice *Baritone*
b. Calais
The first Giorgio Germont, the first Rigoletto, and the first Macbeth. His place in history is not so much due to his singing the first Giorgio Germont, but to

the fact that his annoyance at that part, for some reason or another, caused him to make a fool of himself and nearly of Verdi by sauntering throughout the evening, thus destroying any sense of stage timing.

Vanni, Helen   *Soprano*
b.
Cherubino, Inez (*Il Travatore*).

Varnay, Astrid   *Soprano*
b. Stockholm, 1918:
The first Telea (*The Island God*), she made her debut at the Metropolitan in 1941 by singing, without rehearsal, the part of Sieglinde.

Aida, Brünnhilde, Elektra, Elisabeth, Elsa, Isolde, Kundry, Lady Macbeth, Leonore (*Fidelio*), Leonora (*Il Trovatore*), Marschallin, Ortrud, Salome, Santuzza, Senta, Sieglinde, Telea (*The Island God*), Tosca, Venus.

Vaughan Williams, Ralph   *Composer*
b. Gloucestershire, England, 1872: d. London, 1958
His characteristically English style is well illustrated in his remarkable work for string orchestra, the *Fantasy on a Theme by Thomas Tallis*, and in his choral and operatic music.

Hugh the Drover	London	1924
Sir John in Love	,,	1929
The Poisoned Kiss		
(*composed* 1928)	Cambridge	1936
Riders to the Sea	London	1937
The Pilgrim's Progress		
(*Incorporating*		
The Shepherds of the		
Delectable Mountains)		
	London	1951

Vecchi, Orazio   *Composer*
b. Modena, 1550: d. there, 1605
A canon of the Cathedral of Modena, he wrote a series of madrigals based upon Commedia dell'Arte technique, which was the immediate precursor of real opera.

L'Amfiparnaso	Modena	1594

Venth, Karl   *Composer*
b. Cologne, 1860: d. San Antonio, Tex., 1938

The Rebel	Fort Worth	1926

Verdi, Giuseppe Francesco   *Composer*
b. Le Roncole, Italy, 1813: d. Milan, 1901
Verdi was one of the most famous and most prolific of opera composers of all time. One of his masterpieces, *Falstaff*, was completed in his eightieth year. During most of his life he was involved somewhat in the political turmoil of the unification of Italy. Many of his works bear evidence of this, for instance in the choice of subjects of a highly patriotic nature. He himself may not have taken an active role in that revolution, but his choruses were frequently used as signals for great demonstrations of patriotism among the people. He also found turmoil outside national politics, however. He tried twice to cope with the strict requirements of the formal French Opéra and was twice depressed by the results. But in other directions his fame helped him greatly by bringing in magnificent commissions such as that of the Khedive of Egypt who wished to have an opera to mark the opening of the Suez Canal. *Aida* was that work.

Oberto	La Scala	1839
Un Giorno di Regno	,,	1840
Nabucco	,,	1842
I Lombardi	,,	1843
Ernani	Venice	1844
Macbeth	Florence	1847
Luisa Miller	Naples	1849
Rigoletto	Venice	1851
Il Trovatore	Rome	1853
La Traviata	Venice	1853
I Vespri Siciliani	Opéra	1855
Simon Boccanegra	Venice	1857
Un Ballo in Maschera	Rome	1859
La Forza del		
Destino	St. Petersburg	1862
Don Carlos	Opéra	1867

Aida	Cairo	1871
Otello	La Scala	1887
Falstaff	,,	1893

Vere, Clementine de *Soprano*
b. Paris, 1864: d. Mt. Vernon, N.Y., 1954
She made her debut as Marguerite de Valois in Florence, 1880. She came out at the Metropolitan in 1896 as Marguerite in *La Damnation de Faust*.

Aida, Dinorah, Gilda, Infanta (*Le Cid*), Lucia, Marguerite (*La Damnation de Faust*), Marguérite (*Faust*), Marguerite de Valois, Micaela, Ophélie, Rachel, Violetta.

Verrall, John *Composer*
b. Britt, Iowa, 1908:
A pupil of Zoltán Kodály, and Aaron Copland.

The Cowherd and the Sky Maiden	Seattle	1952
The Wedding Knell	,,	1952
Three Blind Mice	,,	1955

Vestris, Lucia Elizabeth *Mezzo-soprano*
b. London, 1797: d. Fulham, 1856
The first Fatima in Oberon.
Blonde, Fatima, Pippo (*La Gazza Ladra*), Susanna (*Le Nozze di Figaro*).

Vianesi, Auguste *Conductor*
b. Livorno, 1837: d. New York, 1908
He conducted the opening performance of the Metropolitan Opera, in 1883, the opera that night being *Faust*.

Viardot-Garcia, Pauline *Mezzo-soprano*
b. Paris, 1821: d. there, 1910
Famous daughter of the tenor Garcia, she studied piano with Liszt and composition with Reicha. She was an accomplished pianist, composer and singer. She sang the first Sapho and the first Fidès. Her debut was in London, 1839, as Desdemona in Rossini's *Otello*.

Alceste, Alice Ford, Amina, Donna Anna, Arsace, Desdemona (*Otello* by Rossini), Fidès, Iphigénie (*Iphigénie en Tauride*), Isabelle, Lady Macbeth, Leonora (*La Favorita*), Lucia, Norma, Orfeo, Rachel, Romeo (*I Capuletti ed I Montecchi*), Rosina, Sapho, Valentine (*Les Huguenots*), Zerlina (*Don Giovanni*).

Vieuille, Félix *Bass*
b. Saugeon, France, 1872: d. there, 1953
The first Father-in-law (*Le Pauvre Matelot*), the first Barbe-Bleue, and the first Arkel.

Villa-Lobos, Heitor *Composer*
b. Rio de Janeiro, 1887: d. there 1959
Villa-Lobos is very well known for his series called Chôros, especially the Chôros for an orchestra of cellos, of which instrument he is very fond, being a cellist himself.

Izaht (*composed 1914, revised 1932*)	Rio de Janeiro (Concert)	1940
Zoé		1919
Malazarte		1921
Magdalena	Los Angeles	1948

Vinay, Ramon *Tenor*
b. Chile
Canio, Don José, Otello, Parsifal, Radames, Samson, Tannhäuser, Tristan.

Violette, Wesley La *Composer*
b. St. James, Minn., 1894:

Shylock	Chicago (in part)	1930
The Enlightened One		1955

Vitalis, George *Composer*
b. Athens, 1895:
Perseus and Andromeda
The Return of the Gods

Golfo	New York (Concert)	1949

Vittadini, Franco *Composer*
b. Pavia, 1884: d. there, 1948

Anima Allegra	Rome	1921
Nazareth	Pavia	1928
La Sagredo	La Scala	1930
Caracciolo	Rome	1938

Vivaldi, Antonio *Composer*
b. Venice, circa 1669: d. Vienna, 1741

Vivaldi, so famous for his pieces for string orchestra, such as *The Seasons*, may have written as many as forty operas.

| Ipermestra | Florence | 1727 |
| L'Olimpiade | Venice | 1734 |

Vix, Geneviève *Soprano*
b. Nantes, 1879: d. Paris, 1939
She made her debut at Chicago in 1917 as Manon.

Vogl, Heinrich *Tenor*
b. near Munich, 1845: d. Munich, 1900
The first Loge, the first Siegmund. He made his debut as Max in *Der Freischütz* at Munich, 1865. In 1868 he married Therese Thoma. He also composed an opera:

| Der Fremdling | Munich | 1899 |

Völker, Franz *Tenor*
b. Neu-Isenburg, 1899:
A famous Lohengrin.
Dalibor, Fra Diavolo, Florestan, Lohengrin, Menelaus, Pedro (*Tiefland*), Siegmund.

Votipka, Thelma *Soprano*
b.
La Ciesca (*Gianni Schicchi*), Curra (*La Forza del Destino*), Gerhilde, Inez (*Il Trovatore*), Giovanna (*Rigoletto*), Lucia (*Cavalleria Rusticana*), Marianne, Marta (*Mefistofele*), A Woman (*Boris Godunov*).

Voyer, Giovanni *Tenor*
b. Benicarlo, Spain, 1901:
Faust (*La Damnation de Faust*), Hagenbach, Maurizio, Nerone (*Boito*).

Vroons, Franz *Tenor*
b.
Don Basilio (*Il Barbiere di Siviglia*), Oberon, Oedipus, Paco (*La Vida Breve*), Riccardo (*Un Ballo in Maschera*).

Wachtel, Theodor *Tenor*
b. Hamburg, 1823: d. there, 1893
He made his debut in Berlin in 1865.
Chappelou (*Le Postillion de Longjumeau*), Raoul, Stradella, Vasco da Gama.

Wagenaar, Bernard *Composer*
b. Arnhem, Netherlands, 1894:

| Pieces of Eight | New York | 1944 |

Waghalter, Ignatz *Composer*
b. Warsaw, 1882: d. New York, 1949

Der Teufelsweg	Berlin	1911
Mandragola	„	1914
Jugend	„	1917
Der Späte Gast	„	1922
Sataniel	„	1923

Wagner, Cosima *Manager*
b. Bellaggio, near Lake Como, 1837: d. Bayreuth, 1930
Daughter of Liszt, she first married the conductor and pianist von Bülow, then left him for Richard Wagner in 1870. After Wagner's death she managed the Festspielhaus at Bayreuth and established many of the forms of education and production which it follows today.

Wagner, Johanna *Soprano*
b. Hanover, 1826: d. Wurzberg, 1894
Richard Wagner's niece. She was a pupil of Viardot-García, and was the first to sing Elisabeth in *Tannhäuser*. Her debut was in *Der Freischütz* at Dresden in 1843, when she sang Agathe.
Adriano (*Rienzi*), Agathe, Donna Anna, Elisabeth, Euryanthe, Fidès, Leonore (*Fidelio*), Leonora (*La Favorita*), Lucrezia, Norma, Rezia, Romeo, Susanna (*Le Nozze di Figaro*), Tancredi, Valentine (*Les Huguenots*).

Wagner, Richard *Composer*
b. Leipzig, 1813: d. Venice, 1883
Wagner attempted to create a German myth in opera, upon libretti of his own. He accomplished his aim, producing an incalculable effect on the writing of opera for the next generations. In the nineteenth century, any progress in the art was therefore usually hooted down as "Wagnerism," whether the composer, thus vilified, admired Wagner or not.

Die Feen		
(composed 1833)	Munich	1888
Das Liebesverbot	Magdeburg	1836
Rienzi	Dresden	1842
Der Fliegende		
Holländer	„	1843
Tannhäuser	„	1845
Lohengrin	Weimar	1850
Tristan und Isolde	Munich	1865
Die Meistersinger	„	1868
Das Ring des Nibelungen		
(Prologue and Trilogy):		
Das Rheingold	„	1869
Die Walküre	„	1870
Siegfried	Bayreuth	1876
Götterdammerung	„	1876
Parsifal	„	1882

Wagner, Siegfried *Composer*
b. Triebchen, 1869: d. Bayreuth, 1930
He was director of his father's operas at Bayreuth from 1894 until his death.

Der Bärenhäuter	Munich	1899
Der Kobold	Hamburg	1904

Wagner, Wieland *Manager*
b. Bayreuth, 1917
Grandson of Richard Wagner. As stage director in Bayreuth, he proved a most radical innovator, particularly in his simplified manner of staging Wagner's operas.

Walker, Edyth *Mezzo-soprano*
b. Hopewell, N.Y., 1867: d. New York, 1950
She made her debut at Berlin as Fidès in 1894, and at the Metropolitan as Amneris in 1903.
Amneris, Elektra, Fidès, Kundry, Leonora (La Favorita), Nancy (Martha).

Wallace, William Vincent *Composer*
b. Waterford, Iowa, 1812: d. Pyrenees, 1865

Maritana	Drury Lane	1845
Lurline	Covent Garden	1860

Walter, Bruno *Conductor*
(Really B. W. Schlesinger)
b. Berlin, 1876:
Conductor at the Vienna Opera from 1901, at Munich from 1914, and at the Metropolitan from 1941. He was renowned also for his conducting of symphonic works, especially those of Mahler.

Walton, William *Composer*
b. Lancashire, England, 1902:
Troilus and Cressida   London   1954

Ward, Robert *Composer*
b. Cleveland, 1917:
A pupil of Bernard Rogers and Howard Hanson.
He Who Gets
Slapped   New York   1956

Warren, Leonard *Baritone*
b. New York, 1911: d. there, 1960
He made his debut at the Metropolitan as Paolo in 1939, and became one of the leading singers of the company. He died as he began his exit after his last aria in the second act of La Forza del Destino.
Amonasro, Barnaba, Don Carlo (La Forza del Destino), High Priest (Alceste), Iago, Ilo (The Island God), Macbeth, Paolo, Rigoletto, Scarpia, Tonio.

Weber, Carl Maria von *Composer*
(Full name Carl Maria Friedrich Ernst von Weber)
b. near Oldenberg, Germany, 1786: d. London, 1826
His first successful opera, but not his first work in the form, was Das Waldmädchen, which he wrote at the age of fourteen. His innovations in harmony and in the romantic continuity of his operas had a very deep influence on other composers, particularly Wagner.

Das Waldmädchen	Freiberg	1800
Der Freischütz	Berlin	1821
Euryanthe	Vienna	1823
Oberon	London	1826

Weede, Robert *Baritone*
b. Baltimore, 1903:
He made his debut at the Metropolitan in 1937.
Giorgio Germont, Manfredo (*L'Amore dei Tre Re*), Michele (*Il Tabarro*), Rance, Scarpia.

Weigel, Eugene *Composer*
b. Cleveland, 1910:
A pupil of Hindemith.

The Lion Makers		1953
The Mountain Child	Missoula, Montana	1958

Weil, Hermann *Baritone*
b. Karlsruhe, 1877: d. Blue Mountain, N.Y., 1949
The first in the United States to sing Orfeo (*La Favola d'Orfeo*), in a concert at the Metropolitan in 1912. He made his debut at Freiberg in 1901 as Wolfram.
Amfortas, Hans Sachs, Kurnewal, Orfeo (*La Favola d'Orfeo*), Pylade (*Iphigénie en Tauride*), Wolfram.

Weill, Kurt *Composer*
b. Dessau, 1900: d. New York, 1950
A composer in the more or less popular style of whatever country he happened to be working in, he is very well known in the United States for his high-school operetta *Down in the Valley*, and for his highly sophisticated *The Threepenny Opera*, *Street Scene*, and *Lost in the Stars*.

Der Protagonist	Dresden	1926
The Royal Palace	Berlin	1927
Mahagonny	Baden-Baden	1927
Die Dreigroschenoper (*The Threepenny Opera*)		
	Berlin	1928
Die Bürgschaft	„	1932
Der Silbersee		1933
Marie Galante		1933
Street Scene	New York	1947
Lost in the Stars	„	1949

Weinberg, Jacob *Composer*
b. Odessa, 1879: d. New York, 1956

Hechalutz (*The Pioneers of Israel*)	New York	1934

Weinberger, Jaromir *Composer*
b. Prague, 1896:
The Polka and Fugue from *Schwanda* are very popular in the United States.

Švanda Dudák (*Schwanda the Bagpiper*)	Prague	1927
Die Geliebte Stimme	Munich	1930
Lidé z Pokerflatu (*The Outcasts of Poker Flat*)	Brno	1932
A Bed of Roses	Prague	1934
Wallenstein	Vienna	1937

Weingartner, Felix *Composer*
b. Dalmatia, 1863: d. Winterthur, Switzerland, 1942
Not only a composer, he conducted opera at Berlin, Vienna, and Boston.

Sakuntala	Weimar	1884
Die Dame Kobold		1916
Orestes (*trilogy*)		1925

Weisgall, Hugo *Composer*
b. Czechoslovakia, 1912:
A pupil of Roger Sessions.

Night		1932
Lilith		1934
The Tenor	Baltimore	1952
The Stronger	Westport, Conn.	1952
Six Characters in Search of an Author		1956

Weldon, John *Composer*
b. Chichester, England, 1676: d. London, 1736

She Would and She Would Not	1703
The Agreeable Disappointment	1715

Welitsch, Ljuba *Soprano*
b. near Varna, Bulgaria, 1913:
She made her debut as Nedda at Graz in 1936, as Donna Anna at London in 1947, and as Salome at the Metropolitan in 1949.

Aida, Amelia (*Un Ballo in Maschera*), Donna Anna, Barbarina, Cherubino, Cio-cio San, Composer (*Ariadne auf Naxos*), Fiordiligi, Hansel, Jenufa, Leonora (*Il Trovatore*), Lisa, Manon Lescaut, Mimi, Minnie, Musetta, Nedda, Rosalinda, Salome, Tatyana, Tosca.

Wellesz, Egon   *Composer*
b. Vienna, 1885:
A scholar, theorist, and composer. He was an associate in Vienna of Schoenberg. He eventually settled in England.
Die Prinzessin

Girnara	Hanover	1921
Alkestis	Mannheim ·	1924
The Bacchae	Vienna	1931
Incognita	Oxford	1951

Werrenrath, Reinald   *Baritone*
b. Brooklyn, N.Y., 1883: d. Pittsburg, 1953
He made his debut at the Metropolitan in 1919, singing Silvio in *I Pagliacci*.

Wettergren, Gertrud   *Contralto*
(*Née* Palson)
b. Eslov, Sweden, 1897:
She made her debut in Stockholm in 1922 and at the Metropolitan, singing Amneris, in 1935.

White, Carolina   *Soprano*
b. Dorchester, Mass., 1883:
Gutrune, Maliella, Susanna (*Il Segreto di Susanna*).

White, Clarence Cameron   *Composer*
b. Clarksville, Tenn., 1880: d. New York, 1960

Ouanga	Chicago (*in part*)	1932

Whitehill, Clarence Eugene   *Bass*
b. Mareno, Iowa, 1871: d. New York, 1932
The first American male singer to appear at the Opéra-Comique where he made his debut in 1900, the same year that he had come out at the Metropolitan.
Altair, Amfortas, Athanael, Hans Sachs, Jokanaan, Friar Laurence.

Wickham, Florence Pauline   *Contralto*
b. Beaver, Pa., 1882:
She made her American debut as Kundry in 1904.
Adriano (*Rienzi*), Amneris, Brangäne, Emilia (*Otello*), Fricka, Kundry, Laura, Adorno, Maddalena, Orfeo, Ortrud, Waltraute.

Wilder, Alec   *Composer*
b. Rochester, N.Y., 1907:

The Lowland Sea	1951
Sunday Excursion	1953
Kittiwake Island	1955

Wildgans, Friedrich   *Composer*
b. Vienna, 1913:

Der Baum der Erkenntniss	1935

Williams, Camilla   *Soprano*
b. Danville, Virginia:
Aida, Cio-cio San, Mimi.

Williams, Ralph Vaughan
See Vaughan Williams, Ralph

Winkelmann, Hermann   *Tenor*
b. Brunswick, Germany, 1849: d. Vienna, 1912
The very first to sing Parsifal, being the first of the three who shared the opening performances.
Admetus, Lohengrin, Otello, Parsifal, Rinaldo (*Armida*), Tannhäuser, Tristan, Walther.

Winter, Peter   *Composer*
b. Mannheim, 1754: d. Munich, 1825
Winter spent most of his creative life in Munich, although he had successes in other cities, especially Vienna.

Der Bettelstudent	Munich	1785
Das Unterbrochene Opferfest	Vienna	1796
Marie von Montalban	Munich	1800
Colmal	„	1809

Wissmer, Pierre   *Composer*
b. Geneva, 1915:

Marion	Geneva Radio	1947
Capitaine Bruno	Geneva	1952
Léonidas	Paris	1958

Witherspoon, Herbert *Bass*
b. Buffalo, N.Y., 1873: d. New York, 1935
He made his debut at the Metropolitan in 1908 singing Titurel.

Wittich, Marie *Soprano*
b. Giessen, 1868: d. Dresden, 1931
The first Salome. She tried dancing the dance of the veils herself, but Strauss was appalled by the performance and stopped her. Since then a dancer generally has taken the place of the singer in that scene. Isolde, Kundry, Salome, Sieglinde.

Wolf, Hugo *Composer*
b. Windischgraz, 1860: d. Vienna, 1903
Famous as a composer of songs.
Der Corregidor   Mannheim   1896
Manuel Venegas   „ (in part)   1903

Wolf-Ferrari, Ermanno *Composer*
b. Venice, 1876: d. there, 1948
Cenerentola   Venice   1900
Le Donne Curiose   Munich   1903
Il Segreto di Susanna   „   1909
I Quattro Rusteghi   „   1906
I Gioielli della Madonna   Berlin   1911

Wolff, Albert *Composer*
b. Paris, 1884:
He was also conductor at the Opéra-Comique and at the Metropolitan.
L'Oiseau Bleu   Metropolitan   1919

Wolpe, Stefan *Composer*
b. Berlin, 1902:
Schöne Geschichten   1927
Zeus und Elida   1927

Yamada, Kosçak *Composer*
b. Tokyo, 1886:
Alladine et Palomides   1913
The Depraved Heavenly Maiden (composed 1908)   Tokyo   1929
Ayame   „   1935
The Black Ships   „   1940
Yoake   „   1940
Hsiang Fei   1946

Yeend, Frances *Soprano*
b.
She made her Metropolitan debut in 1961 as Chrysothemis (Elektra)
Countess Almaviva, Marguérite (Faust), Micaela, Mimi, Turandot, Violetta.

Young, Alexander *Tenor*
b. London, 1920:

Ysaÿe, Eugène *Composer*
b. Liège, 1858: d. Brussels, 1931
A famous violinist. His only opera, which he wrote in the last years of his life, was to a libretto in the Walloon dialect.
Piér li Hovieu (Peter the Miner)   Liège   1931

Zadek, Hilde *Soprano*
b. Bromberg, 1917:
Aida, Donna Anna, Ariadne (Ariadne auf Naxos), Elsa, Eva, Magda (The Consul), Vitellia (La Clemenza di Tito).

Zádor, Eugene *Composer*
b. Bátaszék, Hungary, 1894:
Zádor now lives in the United States.
Diana   Budapest   1923
A Holtak Szigete (The Island of the Dead)   „   1928
Columbus   New York   1939

Zandonai, Riccardo *Composer*
b. Trentino, 1883: d. Pesaro, 1944
Il Grillo del Focolare (The Cricket on the Hearth)   Turin   1908
Conchita   Milan   1911
Francesca da Rimini   Turin   1914
Giulietta e Romeo   Rome   1922

Zandt, Marie van *Soprano*
b. New York, 1861: d. Cannes, 1919
The first Lakmé. She made her debut at Turin in 1879, and at the Metropolitan in 1891.
Amina, Cherubino, Dinorah, Lakmé, Manon, Mignon, Rosina (Il Barbiere di Siviglia), Zerlina (Don Giovanni).

Zanten, Cornelia van *Soprano*
b. Dordrecht, Netherlands, 1855: d. The Hague, 1946

Zeisl, Eric *Composer*
b. Vienna, 1905: d. Los Angeles, 1959
Leonce und Lena   Prague   1937

Zemlinsky, Alexander von *Composer*
b. Vienna, 1872: d. Larchmont, N.Y., 1942
He was a conductor and a teacher. Arnold Schoenberg was among his pupils.
Es War Einmal   Vienna   1900
Kleider Machen Leute   ,,   1910

Zenatello, Giovanni *Tenor*
b. Verona, 1876: d. New York, 1949
The first Pinkerton. He married Maria Gay in 1913.
Andrea Chenier, Canio, Enzo, Hermann (*Pique-Dame*), Loris, Manrico, Otello, Pinkerton, Radames, Silvio.

Zeno, Apostolo *Librettist*
b. Venice, 1668: d. there, 1750
He was court poet to the Emperor Charles VI. He wrote seventy-one libretti for the Italian opera at Vienna.

Zerr, Anne *Soprano*
b. Baden-Baden, 1822: d. Winterbach, 1881
The first Harriett (*Martha*).
Astrifiammante, Harriett (*Martha*), Lucia, Rosa (*Faust* by Spohr).

Zingarelli, Niccolo Antonio *Composer*
b. Naples, 1752: d. Torre del Greco, 1837
He wrote thirty-seven operas.
Giulietta e Romeo   La Scala   1796
Clitemnestra   ,,   1800

Zolotarev, Vassily *Composer*
b. Taganrog, Russia, 1873:
A pupil of Rimsky-Korsakov.
The Decembrists   Moscow   1925
Ak-gul   1942

THE CHARACTERS IN THE OPERAS

After the name of each important character you will find a list of some of the important singers who have undertaken the role. In some cases the first to perform the role is indicated at the beginning of the list, as: 1st Grisi.

An index to this section, in which the characters are arranged according to voice, will be found at the end of the book.

CHARACTER	ROLE	SINGER	OPERA
Abate di Chazeuil Tenor			*Adriana Lecouvreur*
Abbate Cospicuo Baritone			*Arlecchino*
Abbé Tenor			*Andrea Chénier*
Abbess Silent			*Robert le Diable*
Abbess Mezzo-soprano			*Suor Angelica*
Abdallo Tenor	Nabucco's officer		*Nabucco*
Abdisa Tenor	Patriarch of Assyria		*Palestrina*
Abdullah Speaker	A pirate		*Oberon*
Abigaille Soprano	Slave, supposed daughter of Nabucco	1st Giuseppina Strepponi	*Nabucco*
Abimilech Bass	Philistine Satrap of Gaza	Burke	*Samson et Dalila*
Abraham Speaker	Innkeeper		*Háry János*
Abul Hassan Ali Ebn Bekar Bass	A barber	Gura	*Barbier von Bagdad, Der*
Achilles Tenor	Thessalian warrior	1st Legros; Bentonelli	*Iphigénie en Aulide*
Actors Chorus			*Gloriana, Mignon*
Actresses Chorus			*Mignon*

THE CHARACTERS IN THE OPERAS

CHARACTER	ROLE	SINGER	OPERA
Adalgisa Mezzo-soprano	Temple virgin	1st Grisi; Barbieri, Stignani, Thebom	*Norma*
Adelaide Mezzo-soprano	Arabella's mother	Dunn	*Arabella*
Adele Soprano	Eisenstein's maid	Munsel, Peters	*Die Fledermaus*
Adelma Mezzo-soprano	Turandot's slave		*Turandot* (Busoni)
Adina Soprano	Wealthy young farm owner	Lind	*L'Elisir d'Amore*
Admetus Baritone	Alceste's husband	1st Giuseppe Tibaldi; Maison, Rakewski, Winkelmann	*Alceste*
Admiral Lefort *See* Lefort, Admiral			
Adolar Tenor		Alvary, Nachbauer	*Euryanthe*
Adonisedek Baritone			*Debora*
Adorno *See* Gabriel Adorno			
Adriana Lecouvreur Soprano	Actress, in love with Maurizio	1st Pandolfini; Brema, Caniglia, Cavalieri, Cobelli, Favero, Giachetti, Olivero, Oltra-Bella	*Adriana Lecouvreur*
Adriano Mezzo-soprano	Collonna's son	1st Schröder-Devrient; Wagner, Wickham	*Rienzi*
Aegisth Tenor	Klytemnestra's lover	1st Semback; Lorenz, Svanholm, Wölfl	*Elektra*
Aeneas Tenor	Trojan general	Pears	*Dido and Aeneas*
Aeneas *See also* Eneé			
Aennchen Soprano	Agathe's cousin	Seidl-Krauss	*Freischütz, Der*
Afanasy Viazemsky, Prince Tenor			*Pskovityanka*

309

THE CHARACTERS IN THE OPERAS

CHARACTER		ROLE	SINGER	OPERA
Afra	Tenor	Landlady, in love with Hagenbach	1st Stehle; Bertana	*La Wally*
Afron, Prince	Baritone			*Coq d'Or, Le*
Agamemnon	Baritone	King of Mycenae	1st Larrivée; Baklanov	*Iphigénie en Aulide*
Agata	Contralto		Kobart	*Maria Golovin*
Agathe	Soprano	Cuno's daughter	1st Stoltz; Borkh, Fisher, Gadski, Goltz, Kronold, Larsen-Todsen, Lind, Malten, Morena, Paton, Peschka-Leutner, Rethberg, Rysanek, Schröder-Devrient, Seefried, Seidl-Krauss, Stehle, Wagner	*Der Freischütz*
Agnes	Mezzo-soprano	Micha's wife		*Prodana Nevešta*
Agricultural laborers	Chorus			*The Boatswain's Mate*
Ahmed	Bass	Pastry cook		*Marouf*
Aida	Soprano	Ethiopian princess, slave to Amneris	1st Pozzini; Alda, Arangi-Lombardi, Bampton, Boninsegna, Borkh, Brouwenstijn, Callas, Caniglia, Cigna, Cross, Destinn, Eames, Easton, Flagstad, Fursch-Madi, Gadski, Giannini, Goltz, Hauk, Juch, Kellogg, Krauss, Lilli Lehman, Litvinne, Mantelli, Matzenauer, Milanov, Muzio,	*Aida*

310

THE CHARACTERS IN THE OPERAS

CHARACTER	ROLE	SINGER	OPERA
		Nordica, Patti, Pauly, Ponselle, Price, Raisa, Rappold, Josephine de Reszke, Rethberg, Rysanek, Shuard, Teresa Stoltz, Tebaldi, Ternina, Torriani, Eva Turner, Valleria, Varnay, Vere, Welitsch, Williams, Zadek	
Aithra Soprano	A sorceress	1st Rajdl; Fleischer, Heidersbach	*Die Aegyptische Helene*
Alberich Bass Baritone	Nibelung dwarf, Wotan's enemy	1st Hill; Bispham	*Das Ring des Nibelungen*
Albert Bass	Sergeant		*La Juive*
Albert Baritone	Charlotte's fiancé		*Werther*
Albert Herring Tenor	Greengrocer's assistant		*Albert Herring*
Albert K Bass			*Der Prozess*
Albine Contralto	Abbess		*Thaïs*
Albrecht *See* Alberich			
Albrecht von Brandenburg, Cardinal Tenor	Archbishop of Mainz		*Mathis der Maler*
Alcalde Bass			*Maritana*
Alcalde, The *See* Juan Lopez			
Alceste Soprano	Wife of Admetus	1st Antonia Bernasconi; Cigna, Flagstad, Lawrence, Levasseur, Lubin, Milder, Viardot-Garcia	*Alceste*
Alcindoro Bass	Musetta's latest escort	Baccaloni, Renan	*La Bohème*

CHARACTER		ROLE	SINGER	OPERA
Alcmene Mezzo-soprano		A queen, formerly beloved by Jupiter		*Die Liebe der Danae*
Alessio	Bass	Villager		*La Sonnambula*
Alfio	Baritone	Village teamster	1st Salasso; Bispham, Franci, Panerai, del Puente	*Cavalleria Rusticana*
Alfonso, Don Baritone			1st Benucci; Lorenzo Alvary, Brownlee, Stabile	*Così fan Tutte*
Alfonso, XI Baritone		King of Castile	Ancona, Jean de Reszke	*La Favorita*
Alfonso D'Arcos Tenor		Son of the Viceroy in Naples	Koegel	*Masaniello*
Alfonso D'Este Baritone		Duke of Ferrara	Faure, Novara	*Lucrezia Borgia*
Alfred	Tenor	A singer	Sullivan	*Die Fledermaus*
Alfredo Germont Tenor		Violetta's lover	1st Graziani; Conley, Gigli, Hislop, Mario, McCormack, Peerce, Poleri, di Stefano, Valletti	*La Traviata*
Ali	Baritone	Marouf's friend		*Marouf*
Alice Mezzo-soprano		Lucia's companion		*Lucia di Lammermoor*
Alice	Soprano	Robert's foster sister	1st Derus-Gras; Caron, Falcon, Lind, Paton, Peschka-Leutner, Viardot-Garcia	*Robert le Diable*
Alice Ford	Soprano	Ford's wife	1st Stehle; Curtin, Eames, Steber, Tietjens	*Falstaff*
Alice Ford *See also* Fluth, Frau				
Alidoro	Bass	A philosopher and magician		*La Cenerentola*

CHARACTER	ROLE	SINGER	OPERA
Alisa *See* Alice			
Alladine Pantomine	Former wife of Barbe-Bleue		*Ariane et Barbe-Bleue*
Almanzor Speaker	Emir of Tunis		*Oberon*
Almaviva, Count Tenor		1st Manuel Garcia, Sr; Hackett, Mario, Phillips, Jean de Reszke, Schack, Valleti	*Il Barbiere di Siviglia*
Almaviva, Count Baritone		1st Mandini; Bassi, Beck, Brownlee, Capoul, Cassell, Duprez, Landi, Maurel, T. Phillips, Poell, Edouard de Reszke, Santley, Scotti	*Le Nozze di Figaro*
Almaviva, Countess Soprano		1st Laschi; della Casa, Carvalhe, Cruvelli, Eames, Brouwenstijn, Faull, Hempel, Jurinac, Christine Nilsson, Steber, Tietjens, Yeend	*Le Nozze di Figare*
Almira Soprano		Peschka-Leutner	*Almira* (Handel)
Alms Collector Soprano			*Suor Angelica*
Alwa Tenor	Schon's son, a writer		*Lulu*
Altair Baritone		1st Burg; Hotter, Prohaska, Schorr, Whitehill	*Die Aegyptische* *Helena*
Altichiara Mezzo-soprano	Francesca's woman		*Francesca da Rimini*
Alto, The Contralto	Klymene in Lully's Opera		*Cardillac*
Altoum, Emperor Bass	Turandot's father	de Paolis, Fried	*Turandot* (Busoni)

THE CHARACTERS IN THE OPERAS

CHARACTER	ROLE	SINGER	OPERA
Alvar, Don Tenor	Councillor		*L'Africaine*
Alvaro, Don Tenor	Leonora's lover	1st Tamberlik; Baum, Caruso, Gigli, del Monaco, Tucker	*La Forza del Destino*
Alvise, Badoero Bass	Inquisitor	Moscona, Novara, Pasero, Sammarco, Siepi	*La Gioconda*
Amalia Soprano		1st Lind	*I Masnadieri* (Verdi)
Amantio di Nicolao, Ser Baritone	Lawyer		*Gianni Schicchi*
Amaryllus Tenor	Son of the empress		*The Poisoned Kiss*
Ambassadors Chorus			*Rienzi*
Ambrogio Bass	Bartolo's servant		*Il Barbiere di Siviglia*
Ambroise, Maître Bass	Vincent's father	Gassier	*Mireille*
Amelfa Contralto	Royal housekeeper		*Le Coq d'Or*
Amelia Soprano	Renato's wife, beloved by Riccardo	Brouwenstijn, Callas, Caniglia, Cigna, Cross, Destinn, Goltz, Grob-Prandl, Hempel, Lilli Lehmann, Matzenauer, Milanov, Nordica, Ternina, Tietjens, Eva Turner, Welitsch	*Un Ballo in Maschera*
Amelia Boccanegra Soprano	Simon's daughter brought up as Maria Grimaldi	Milanov, Shuard, Tebaldi	*Simon Boccanegra*
Amfortas Baritone	Ruler of the Kingdom of the Grail	1st Reichmann; Amato, Bender, Burke, Gura, Janssen, London, Perron, Plaschke,	*Parsifal*

314

CHARACTER		ROLE	SINGER	OPERA
			Scheidl, Scheider-mantel, Schlusnus, Scherr, Weil, Whitehill	
Amina	Soprano	The sleepwalker, engaged to Elvine	1st Pasta; Albani, Callas, Charton-Demeur, Cole, Galli-Curci, Gerster, Hauk, Lind, Malibran, Murska, Nevada, Parepa-Rosa, Patti, Schröder-Devrient, Sembrich, Sontag, Luisa Tetrazzini, Viardot-Garcia, van Zandt	*La Sonnambula*
Aminta	Soprano	Wife of Henry Morosus. An actress.	1st Cebotari; Carosio, Carroll	*Die Schweigsame Frau*
Amme, Die *See* Nurse				
Amneris	Contralto	Daughter of the King of Egypt	1st Grossi; Barbieri, Bible, Brandt, Brema, Cary, Castagna, Fornia-Labey, Gulbranson, Harshaw, Homer, Kirkby-Lunn, Langendorf, Madeira, Mantelli, Matzenauer, Meisle, Mildenburg, Minghini-Cattaneo, Nikolaidi, Ober, Onegin, Carmela Ponselle, Rankin, Stignani, Thebom, Trebelli, Walker, Wettergren, Wickham	*Aida*

CHARACTER	ROLE	SINGER	OPERA
Amonasro, Baritone	King of Ethiopia. Aida's father	1st Costa; Ancona, Beck, Formichi, Gobbi, Kaschmann, London, Maurel, Edouard de Reszke, Scolera, Scotti, Thomas, Tibbett, Warren	*Aida*
Amor Soprano	God of love	Gluck, Gueden	*Orfeo ed Euridice*
Anabaptists Chorus			*Le Prophète*
Anaide Contralto	Zaza's mother		*Zaza*
Anatol Tenor	Son of Vanessa's only lover	1st Gedda	*Vanessa*
Anckarström			*Gustave III*
Anckarström See Renato			
Anckarström, Mrs. Soprano		1st Falcon	*Gustave III*
Andrea Chénier Tenor	Revolutionary and poet	1st Borgatti; Beval, Gigli, Lauri-Volpi, del Monaco, Zenatello	*Andrea Chénier*
Andreloux Mezzo-soprano	Shepherd		*Mireille*
Andrès Tenor	Stella's servant		*Les Conte d'Hoffmann*
Andres Tenor			*Wozzeck*
Andrew J. Tenor			*The Mother of Us All*
Andrew Khovansky, Prince Tenor	Ivan's son		*Khovantschina*
Andromaque Pantomine	Hector's widow		*Les Troyens*
Anfinomo Tenor	Penelope's suitor		*Il Ritorno d'Ulisse in Patria*
Angel More Soprano			*The Mother of Us All*

THE CHARACTERS IN THE OPERAS

CHARACTER		ROLE	SINGER	OPERA
Angèle	Soprano		Ugalde	*Domino Noir* (Auber)
Angelic Voices (Three)	Sopranos			*Palestrina*
Angelica	Soprano	Tormentilla's maid		*The Poisoned Kiss*
Angelica, Suor	Soprano	A nun	1st Farrar; dalla Rizza, Mazzolini, Carena, Oltra-Bella	*Suor Angelica*
Angelina	Contralto	Don Magnifico's step-daughter, Cinderella	1st Giorgi-Righetti; Bible, Malibran	*La Cenerentola*
Angelotti *See* Cesare Angelotti				
Angels	Chorus			*Faust, Palestrina, Pilgrim's Progress*
Angels (Two)	Soprano and Mezzo-soprano			*Le Jongleur de Nôtre Dame*
Animal Tamer		(Later Redrig)		*Lulu*
Animal Tamer	Tenor			*Der Rosenkavalier*
Animals	Chorus			*L'Enfant et les Sortilèges*
Anita	Soprano		1st Calvé	*La Navarraise*
Anna	Contralto	Servant of Inez		*L'Africaine*
Anna	Soprano	Gaveston's ward, the White Lady	1st Rigaut; Gadski, Krauss	*La Dame Blanche*
Anna	Soprano	Chambermaid		*Intermezzo*
Anna	Soprano	Zaccaria's sister		*Nabucco*
Anna	Contralto	Didon's sister		*Les Troyens*
Anna Bolena	Soprano	Mother of Elisabeth, and wife of Henry VIII	1st Pasta; Grisi	*Anna Bolena*
Anna, Donna	Soprano	Don Ottavio's fiancée	1st Teresa Saporiti; Camporese, Danco, Destinn, Dickons,	*Don Giovanni*

317

THE CHARACTERS IN THE OPERAS

CHARACTER	ROLE	SINGER	OPERA
		della Casa, Falcon, Faull, Fisher, Fursch-Madi, Harshaw, Krauss, Lilli Lehmann, Lind, Litvinne, Matzenauer, Milanov, Nordica, Parepa-Rosa, Price, Schumann, Sontag, Steber, Tietjens, Viardot-Garcia, Wagner, Welitsch, Zadek	
Anna Gomez Soprano			*The Consul*
Anna Hope Mezzo-soprano			*The Mother of Us All*
Anna Reich Soprano	Ann Page	Flagstad	*Die Lustigen Weiber von Windsor*
Anne Soprano			*The Mother of Us All*
Anne *See* Ninetta *See also* Aennchen			
Anne Page *See* Anna Reich			
Anne Trulove Soprano		1st Schwarzkopf; Gueden, Morison, Berger, Harvey	*The Rake's Progress*
Annina Contralto	Valzacchi's partner	Evans, Glaz, Lipton	*Der Rosenkavalier*
Annina Soprano	Violetta's confidante		*La Traviata*
Annius Mezzo-soprano	Young patrician of Rome		*La Clemenza di Tito*
Annunziata Silent	Matteo's wife		*Arlecchino*
Anthony, Susan B. *See* Susan B. Anthony			
Antigonae Soprano	Daughter of Oedipus	Goltz	*Antigonae (Orff)*

CHARACTER		ROLE	SINGER	OPERA
Antinoo	Bass	Penelope's suitor		*Il Ritorno d'Ulisse in Patria*
Anton Buis von Müglitz	Bass	Archbishop of Prague		*Palestrina*
Antonia	Soprano	Singer	1st Isaac; Amara, della Casa, Fremstad, Hempel, Jurinach, Seefried, Steber, Teyte	*Les Contes d'Hoffmann*
Antonia	Soprano			*Tiefland*
Antonia's Mother's Voice	Mezzo-soprano			*Les Contes d'Hoffmann*
Antonida	Soprano	Ivan's daughter	Albani, Cebotari	*Ivan Susanin*
Antonio	Baritone	Linda's father		*Linda di Chamounix*
Antonio	Bass	Servant		*Mignon*
Antonio	Bass	Susanna's uncle, a gardener	1st Bussani; Pröglhof	*Le Nozze di Figaro*
Apollo	Tenor			*Daphne*
Apollo *See* Bass, The				
Apollon	Bass	A voice	1st Laschi	*Alceste*
Apollon	Baritone			*Eumenides*
Apollyon	Bass			*Pilgrim's Progress*
Apparition of a Youth	Tenor			*Die Frau ohne Schatten*
Apprentice	Baritone			*Louise*
Apprentices	Chorus			*Die Meistersinger*
Arabella	Soprano		1st Ursuleac; della Casa, Steber	*Arabella*
Arbace	Tenor	Idomeneo's confidant	1st Panzacchi	*Idomeneo*
Arcas		Agamemnon's messenger		*Iphigénie en Aulide*

319

CHARACTER	ROLE	SINGER	OPERA
Archbishop *See* Albrecht Von Brandenburg			
Archdale, Mr. Speaker	A white man		*Porgy and Bess*
Archer Tenor			*Francesca da Rimini*
Archer, First Bass			*Khovantschina*
Archer, Second Bass			*Khovantschina*
Archer, Third Tenor			*Khovantschina*
Archers Chorus			*Francesca da Rimini, Khovantschina, Luisa Miller, Pskovityanka*
Archibaldo Bass	King of Altura	1st de Angelis; Autori, Didur, Lazzari, Mardonis, Pasero, Pinza, Rossi-Lemeni	*L'Amore dei Tre Re*
Ariadne Soprano *Also called* Prima Donna		1st Jeritza; Goltz, Jurinac, Rysanek, Zadek	*Ariadne auf Naxos*
Ariane Mezzo-soprano	Bluebeard's sixth wife	1st Leblanc; Farrar	*Ariane et Barbe-Bleue*
Arianna Soprano		1st Virginia Andreini	*Arianna*
Aristée *See* Pluton			
Arithmetic Tenor	A little old man	(*The same singer sings* La Rainette)	*L'Enfant et les Sortilèges*
Arkel Bass	King of Allemonde, Pelléas' grandfather	1st Vieuille; Lorenzo Alvary, Hines, Morena	*Pelléas et Mélisande*
Arlecchino Speaker	Harlequin		*Arlecchino*
Arlecchino *See also* Beppe			
Arline Soprano	The Count's daughter	Kemp, Lussan, Peters	*The Bohemian Girl*

CHARACTER	ROLE	SINGER	OPERA
Armida Soprano		1st Levasseur; Callas, Fremstad, Gluck, Malten	*Armida* (Gluck)
Armored Men *See* Men in Armor (Two)			
Arnheim, Count Bass	Governor		*The Bohemian Girl*
Arnold Tenor	Swiss patrol, Mathilde's suitor	1st Nourrit; Tamagno	*Guillaume Tell*
Arrigo Tenor	Young Sicilian in love with Elena		*I Vespri Siciliani*
Arsace Contralto	General of the Assyrians	Viardot-Garcia, Trebelli	*Semiramide*
Arsena Soprano	Zsupan's daughter		*Zigeunerbaron*
Artaban Tenor	Financier		*Esther de Carpentras*
Artemis *(This part was inserted by Richard Wagner in Act III in his revision of 1846.)*	The goddess		*Iphigénie en Aulide*
Arthur Bucklaw, Lord Tenor			*Lucia di Lammermoor*
Arthur Jones Baritone	Impressed seaman		*Billy Budd*
Arthur Talbot Tenor	Cavalier, Elvira's lover	1st Rubini; Bonci, di Stefano	*I Puritani*
Artilleryman, First and Second Speakers			*Háry János*
Artists Chorus			*La Rondine*
Arturo *See* Arthur Bucklaw *See also* Arthur Talbot			
Arvidson *See* Ulrica			

THE CHARACTERS IN THE OPERAS

CHARACTER	ROLE	SINGER	OPERA
Ascagne Soprano	Aeneas' son		*Les Troyens*
Ascanio Mezzo-soprano	Cellini's apprentice		*Benvenuto Cellini*
Ashby Bass	Wells-Fargo man	Tozzi	*La Fanciulla del West*
Ashton *See* Enrico			
Asmodus Baritone	Spirit voice		*Doktor Faustus*
Aspasia Soprano		Bernasconi	*Mitridate*
Aspirant Sisters Mezzo-sopranos			*Suor Angelica*
Assad Tenor			*Die Königin von Saba*
Assan Baritone	Sorel's friend		*The Consul*
Assur Baritone	Prince, accomplice of Semiramide	Faure, Foli, Gassier, Lablache	*Semiramide*
Astaroth Soprano	Slave of the Queen of Sheba		*Die Königin von Saba*
Asteria Soprano		1st Raisa; Cigna, Arangi-Lombardi, Laszlo, Scacciati	*Nerone*
Astolfo Bass	Lucrezia's servant		*Lucrezia Borgia*
Astrologer Tenor			*Le Coq d'Or*
Astynax Pantomime	Andromaque's son		*Les Troyens*
Athanaël Baritone	Young monk	1st Delmas; Bechi, Thomas, Whitehill	*Thaïs*
Athena's Statue *See* Statue d'Athéna, La			
Attendants Chorus			*L'Africaine, La Favorita, Lohengrin*
Augusta Tabor Mezzo-soprano		Bible	*The Ballad of Baby Doe*
Auguste Tenor			*Zaza*
Augustin Moser Tenor	Mastersinger and tailor		*Die Meistersinger*

322

THE CHARACTERS IN THE OPERAS

CHARACTER	ROLE	SINGER	OPERA
Aunt Contralto			*Její Pastorkyňa* (Jenufa)
Auntie Contralto	Landlady of The Boar	1st Coates	*Peter Grimes*
Avis Soprano	Laurence's daughter, 17		*The Wreckers*
Avito Tenor	Former prince, in love with Fiora	1st Ferrari-Fontana; F. Albanese, Crimi, Gigli, Le Giudice, Jagel, Kullman, Marcato, Martin, Merli, Piccaluga, Sullivan, Tokatyan	*L'Amore dei Tre Re*
Avosmediano Bass-baritone	Bishop of Cadiz		*Palestrina*
Azema Soprano	Princess, beloved by Arsace		*Semiramide*
Azriel Tenor			*Debora e Jaele*
Azucena Mezzo-soprano	Old gypsy woman of Biscay	1st Goggi; Barbieri, Brandt, Cary, Dalis, Fremstad, Gay, Harshaw, Homer, Howard, Langendorf, Matzenauer, Ober, Phillips, Scalchi, Schumann-Heink, Simoniato, Thebom, Trebelli, Claramae Turner, Viardot-Garcia	*Il Trovatore*
Ball Hanan Baritone	Palace overseer		*Die Königin von Saba*
Baba Contralto	Madame Flora, a medium	1st C. Turner; Powers, Pederzini	*The Medium*
Baba Mustapha Tenor	A cadi		*Der Barbier von Bagdad*
Baba the Turk Mezzo-soprano	A bearded lady	1st Tourel; Madeira, Thebom	*The Rake's Progress*
Babekan Speaker	Saracen prince		*Oberon*

THE CHARACTERS IN THE OPERAS

CHARACTER	ROLE	SINGER	OPERA
Babinsky Tenor	Romantic bandit		*Švanda Dudák*
Baby Doe Soprano			*The Ballad of Baby Doe*
Bacchantes Chorus			*Fête Galante, Tannhäuser*
Bacchus Tenor *Also called* The Tenor		McCracken	*Ariadne auf Naxos*
Bacchus Speaker	A god		*Orphée aux Enfers*
Baculus Bass	Schoolmaster		*Der Wildschütz*
Baggott, Miss Contralto	Housekeeper, *called* Gladys Parworthy *in Acts I and II*		*Let's Make an Opera*
Bailli, Le Bass	Charlotte's father, 50	Lorenzo Alvary	*Werther*
Baldassare Baritone	Old shepherd		*L'Arlesiana*
Baldassare *See also* Balthazar			
Balducci Bass	Papal Treasurer and Teresa's father		*Benvenuto Cellini*
Ballad Seller Tenor			*Hugh the Drover*
Ballad Singer Bass	A blind man		*Gloriana*
Ballad Singer *See also* Gioconda			
Balstrode, Captain Baritone	Retired merchant skipper	1st Roderick Jones; Pease	*Peter Grimes*
Balthasar Zorn Tenor	Mastersinger and pewterer	de Paolis	*Die Meistersinger*
Balthazar Bass	Superior of the monastery	Plançon	*La Favorita*
Bandit Chief			*Don Quichotte*
Bandits Chorus			*Don Quichotte, Ernani*
Banquo Bass	A general, Macbeth's rival	Hines	*Macbeth*
Barak Bass	Jewish commander		*Debora e Jaele*

324

THE CHARACTERS IN THE OPERAS

CHARACTER	ROLE	SINGER	OPERA
Barak Bass–baritone	A dyer	.	*Die Frau ohne Schatten*
Barak Baritone	Calaf's servant		*Turandot* (Busoni)
Barak's Wife Soprano		Steber	*Die Frau ohne Schatten*
Barbacan Baritone	Concierge of the synagogue		*Esther de Carpentras*
Barbara Mezzo-soprano	Foster child of the Kabanovs		*Katya Kabanova*
Barbarina Soprano	Antonio's daughter	1st Nanetta Gottlieb; Feldbermayer, Welitsch	*Le Nozze di Figaro*
Barbe-Bleue Bass	Bluebeard	1st Vieuille; Rothier	*Ariane et Barbe-Bleue*
Barber *See* Abul Hassan *See also* Figaro *See also* Schneider-bart			
Barce Soprano	Servant		*Hubička*
Bard Speaker	Narrator		*Duke Bluebeard's Castle*
Bardolph Tenor	Falstaff's friend		*Falstaff*
Barena Soprano	Servant at the mill		*Její Pastorkyňa* (*Jenufa*)
Barinkay *See* Sandor Barinkay			
Barnaba Baritone	Inquisition spy	Bassi, Bonelli, Colzani, Franci, Giraldoni, Inghilleri, Morelli, del Puento, Warren	*La Gioconda*
Baroncelli Tenor	Roman citizen		*Rienzi*
Baroness, The Old Soprano		1st Resnik	*Vanessa*

THE CHARACTERS IN THE OPERAS

CHARACTER	ROLE	SINGER	OPERA
Bartolo, Doctor Bass	Rosina's guardian	d'Angelo, Baccaloni, Corsina	Il Barbiere di Siviglia
Bartolo, Doctor Bass		1st Bussani; Allin, Baccaloni, Corena, Mariz, Renan	Le Nozze di Figaro
Basilio Bass	A singing teacher	Chaliapin, Foli, Formes, Hines, Mirabella, Pinza, Edouard de Reszke, Ronconi, Rossi-Lemeni, Siepi, Tajo, Vroons	Il Barbiere di Siviglia
Basilio, Don Tenor	Organist and music-master	1st Michael Kelly; Murray Dickie, de Paolis	Le Nozze di Figaro
Bass, The Bass	Apollo in Lully's opera		Cardillac
Bayan Tenor	Bard		Russlan and Ludmilla
Bear Silent			Siegfried
Béatrice Mezzo-soprano	Leonato's niece	1st Charton-Demeur	Béatrice et Bénédict
Beauty From Chorus			Iris
Beckmesser, Sixtus Bass	Mastersinger and Town Clerk	1st Hölzel; Bispham, Doench, Griswold, Kunz, Renaud	Die Meistersinger
Beelzebub Tenor	Spirit voice		Doktor Faustus
Beggar Speaker			The Beggar's Opera
Belcore Baritone	Sergeant	Ronconi, Scotti	L'Elisir d'Amore
Belinda Soprano	Dido's lady in waiting		Dido and Aeneas
Bellangère Soprano	Former wife of Barbe-Bleue		Ariane et Barbe-Bleue
Belmonte Tenor	Spanish nobleman	1st Ademberger; Kullmann, Rounseville	Die Entführung aus dem Serail

THE CHARACTERS IN THE OPERAS

CHARACTER	ROLE	SINGER	OPERA
Ben Baritone		1st Kwarton	*The Telephone*
Ben Budge From Chorus	Gentleman of the road	Rogier	*The Beggar's Opera*
Bench, The Child			*L'Enfant et les Sortilèges*
Bénédict Tenor	An officer		*Béatrice et Bénédict*
Benes Bass	Jailer		*Dalibor*
Benn, Harry Tenor	Former boatswain		*The Boatswain's Mate*
Benno Robertson, Sir Tenor	Puritan		*I Puritani*
Benoit Bass	Landlord	Baccaloni, Renan	*La Bohème*
Benton, Mistress Mezzo-soprano	Governess and chaperone		*Lakmé*
Benvenuto Cellini Tenor	Goldsmith and sculptor	1st Duprez; Schott	*Benvenuto Cellini*
Benvolio Tenor	A Montague retainer		*Roméo et Juliette*
Beppe Mezzo-soprano	A gypsy		*L'Amico Fritz*
Beppe Tenor	Harlequin	Urlus	*I Pagliacci*
Beppo Tenor	Bandit		*Fra Diavolo*
Bergère, La Soprano	The Louis XV Chair		*L'Enfant et les Sortilèges*
Bermate Bass			*Snyegurotchka*
Bernardino Bass	Artisan for Cellini		*Benvenuto Cellini*
Bernardo Novagerio Tenor	Papal legate		*Palestrina*
Bersi Mezzo-soprano	Madeleine's maid		*Andrea Chénier*
Berta Soprano	Marcellina, Rosina's governess	Madeira, Petina	*Il Barbiere di Siviglia*
Bertha Soprano	John's bride	Alvarez, Lilli Lehmann, Muzio	*Le Prophète*
Bertram Bass	The Devil disguised	Foli, Formes, Scaria	*Robert le Diable*

CHARACTER	ROLE	SINGER	OPERA
Bess Soprano	Crown's girl	1st Anne Brown; Leontyne Price	*Porgy and Bess*
Beth Soprano	A child	1st Newton	*The Tender Land*
Béthune, Di Bass	French officer		*I Vespri Siciliani*
Betto di Signa Bass	Dead Buoso's brother-in-law	Cehanovsky	*Gianni Schicchi*
Betty Doxy From Chorus	Lady of the town		*The Beggar's Opera*
Bianca Contralto	Lucretia's nurse		*The Rape of Lucretia*
Bianca Soprano	Magda's friend		*La Rondine*
Biancofiore Soprano	Francesca's woman		*Francesca de Rimini*
Biaso Tenor	Scribe		*I Gioielli della Madonna*
Bijou Baritone	Chappelou's friend		*Le Postillion de Longjumeau*
Billows, Lady Soprano	Elderly autocrat	1st Cross	*Albert Herring*
Billy Budd Baritone	Seaman, stammerer	1st Uppman	*Billy Budd*
Billy Jackrabbit Bass	An (American) Indian		*La Fanciulla del West*
Bird See Waldvogel			
Birdie Soprano		Faull	*Regina*
Bishop Baritone			*Friedenstag*
Bishop See Cardinal See also Ercole Severolus			
Bishop of Budoja Tenor	Italian bishop		*Palestrina*
Bishop of Thelesia Silent			*Palestrina*
Biterolf Bass	Knight and minnesinger		*Tannhäuser*

CHARACTER		ROLE	SINGER	OPERA
Black Bob	Bass	Sweepmaster, *called* Norman Chaffinch in *Acts I and II. Also plays* The Coachman.		*Let's Make an Opera*
Blanche	Soprano		Duval, Kirsten	*Les Dialogues des Carmélites*
Blanche	Soprano			*Louise*
Blind, Doctor	Tenor	Eisenstein's attorney	Franke	*Die Fledermaus*
Blondchen *See* Blonde				
Blonde	Soprano	Constanze's maid	1st Therese Teyber; Haskins, Schwarzkopf, Ugalde, Vestris	*Die Entführung aus dem Serail*
General Blood and Thunder	Speaker			*Háry János*
Bluebeard, Duke	Bass			*Duke Bluebeard's Castle*
Bluebeard *See also* Barbe-bleue				
Blunt *See* Henry Morosus Blunt *See also* Morusus Blunt, Sir				
Bob Boles	Tenor	Fisherman and Methodist	1st M. Jones	*Peter Grimes*
Bobil	Tenor			*Snyegurotchka*
Bobilicka	Mezzo soprano			*Snyegurotchka*
Bodyguards	Chorus			*Khovantschina, Pskovityanka*
Bohemian, Old	Baritone			*Louise*
Bois-Rosé	Tenor	Huguenot soldier	·	*Huguenots, Les*

CHARACTER	ROLE	SINGER	OPERA
Boleslav Lazinski Pantomime	Pianist		*Fedora*
Bombasto, Doctor Bass			*Arlecchino*
Bomely Bass			*Pskovityanka*
Boniface Baritone	Monastery cook		*Le Jongleur de Notre Dame*
Bonze, The Bass	Cio-cio San's uncle, Priest	Lorenzo Alvary	*Madama Butterfly*
Bonze Bass			*Le Rossignol*
Barella Bass	Fisherman		*Masaniello*
Boris Godunov Baritone	Tsar of Russia	1st Melnikov; Baklanov, Chaliapin, Christoff, Didur, Kipnis, London, Marcoux, Pinza, Radford, Rossi-Lemeni, Siepi, Silveri, Stear	*Boris Godunov*
Boris Grigorievitch Tenor	In love with Katya	Jones	*Kata Kabanova*
Borov Baritone	Doctor		*Fedora*
Borromeo *See* Carlo Borromeo			
Borsa *See* Matteo Borsa			
Bostana Mezzo soprano	Baba Mustapha's servant		*Der Barbier von Bagdad*
Bosun Baritone	Boatswain		*Billy Budd*
Bourdon Bass			*Le Postillon de Longjumeau*
Boy Soprano			*The Warrior*
Boy (John) Silent	Apprentice		*Peter Grimes*
Boyar Chruschtschov *See* Khrushchev			

CHARACTER	ROLE	SINGER	OPERA
Boyar Guard Tenor			*Boris Godunov*
Boyars Chorus			*Boris Godunov, Pskovityanka, Prince Igor*
Boys Chorus			*Carmen, Cavalleria Rusticana, Hugh the Drover, Pskovityanka*
Boy's Voice			*L'Amore dei Tre Re*
Boys and Girls Chorus			*La Bohème, Hänsel und Gretel*
Branda Bass			*Damnation de Faust*
Brangäne Mezzo soprano	Isolde's maid	1st Anne Deinet; Brandt, Branzell, Brema, Cahier, Fremstad, Gay, Homer, Kirkby-Lunn, Klose, Lipton, Ober, Olczewska, Schumann-Heink, Thebom, Wickham	*Tristan und Isolde*
Bretigny, De Baritone	Nobleman		*Manon*
Bridal Couples (Three)			*Guillaume Tell*
Brighella Tenor		Curzi	*Ariadne auf Naxos*
Bronislawa, Countess Soprano	Laura's sister		*Der Bettelstudent*
Brünnhilde Soprano	A Valkyr	1st (In Walküre) Stehle; Brema, Easton, Fischer, Flagstad, Fremstad, Fuchs, Gadski, Grob-Prandl, Gulbranson, Harshaw, Kappel, Klafsky, Larsen-Todsen, Lawrence, Leffler-Burchhard, Lilli Lehmann, Leider, Litvinne, Malten, Marchesi,	*Das Ring des Nibelungen*

THE CHARACTERS IN THE OPERAS

CHARACTER	ROLE	SINGER	OPERA
		Materna, Matzenauer, Melba, Mildenburg, Mödl, Morena, Nordica, Ohms, Osborn, Rysanek, Saltzmann-Stevens, Seidl-Krauss, Sucher, Ternina, Thoma, Traubel, Varnay	
Bubble, Madam Mezzo-soprano			*Pilgrim's Progress*
Buda Soprano	Arline's attendant		*The Bohemian Girl*
Budd, Superintendant Bass			*Albert Herring*
Budivoj Baritone	Captain of the guard		*Dalibor*
Buffoons, Four Two Mezzo-sopranos, Tenor, Bass			*Sadko*
Bugler Bass			*Friedenstag*
Burghers Chorus			*Falstaff*
Burghers Chorus	Guildsmen		*Die Meistersinger*
Burghers' Sons Chorus			*Pskovityanka*
Burgomaster Tenor		Patzak	*Friedenstag*
Bürstner, Fräulein Soprano		1st della Casa; Curtin	*Der Prozess*
Bussy Baritone	Journalist		*Zaza*
Butterfly See Cio-cio San			
By-ends, Madame Contralto			*Pilgrim's Progress*
By-ends, Mister Tenor			*Pilgrim's Progress*
Cabin Boy Speaker			*Billy Budd*
Cacan Baritone	Theater lover		*Esther de Carpentras*

THE CHARACTERS IN THE OPERAS

CHARACTER		ROLE	SINGER	OPERA
Cacique	Baritone		Faure, Maurel	*Il Guarany*
Cadi	Bass			*Marouf*
Caesar de Bazan	Tenor			*Maritana*
See also César de Bazan, Don				
Caius, Doctor	Bass	Unsuccessful suitor to Anne Page		*Die Lustigen Weiber von Windsor*
Cajus, Peter	Tenor	Unsuccessful suitor to Nanetta	Bada	*Falstaff*
Calaf	Tenor	Unknown prince, suitor to Turandot		*Turandot* (Busoni)
Calaf	Tenor	Son of Timur, suitor to Turandot	Gismondo, Lauri-Volpi, Martinelli, Merli, Tobin	*Turandot* (Puccini)
Calchas		High priest		*Iphigénie en Aulide*
Caliph, The	Baritone			*Der Barbier von Bagdad*
Caliph's Entourage	Chorus			*Der Barbier von Bagdad*
Camilla	Soprano		Parepa-Rosa	*Zampa*
Camille	Soprano			*Louise*
Camille Desmoulins	Tenor		1st Patzak	*Dantons Tod*
Canciano	Bass	Wealthy merchant		*I Quattro Rusteghi*
Canio	Tenor	Pagliaccio, chief of the players	1st Giraud; Caruso, Ferrari-Fontana, Gigli, Lucia, Martin, Martinelli, Melchior, del Monaco, di Stefano, Vinay, Zenatello	*I Pagliacci*
Capito, Wolfgang	Tenor	Cardinal's councillor, Lutheran		*Mathis der Maler*
Cappadocian	Bass			*Salome*
Captain	Bass			*Eugene Onegin*

CHARACTER	ROLE	SINGER	OPERA
Captain Tenor			*Simon Boccanegra*
Captain Tenor		Franke	*Wozzeck*
Captain of Hell's Guard Tenor			*Švanda Dudák*
Captain of the Guard Bass			*The Bohemian Girl*
Captain of the Guard Baritone			*Maritana*
Captains, Three Two Tenors, Baritone			*The Warrior*
Captains Chorus			*Aida, Boris Godunov, L'Africaine*
Capuchin Monks Chorus			*Lucrezia Borgia*
Capulet, Count Bass		Plançon	*Roméo et Juliette*
Cardillac Baritone	A famous goldsmith		*Cardillac*
Cardinal From Chorus			*Tosca*
Cardinal *See* Albrecht von Brandenburg *See also* Carlo Borromeo *See also* Christoph Madruscht			
Cardinal, Le Tenor	Bishop of Carpentras		*Esther de Carpentras*
Cardinal de Brogni Bass			*La Juive*
Cardinal of Lorraine Bass			*Palestrina*
Cardinal Salviati *See* Salviati, Cardinal			
Card Players, Three From Chorus			*Arabella*

CHARACTER	ROLE	SINGER	OPERA
Caribiniers Chorus			*Fra Diavolo*
Carlo Borromeo, Cardinal Baritone			*Palestrina*
Carlo di Vargas, Don Baritone	Leonora's brother	de Luca, Tagliabue, Tibbett, Warren	*La Forza del Destino*
Carlos, Don Tenor	Heir to the Spanish throne	Martinelli, Tucker	*Don Carlos*
Carlos, Don Baritone	King of Castile	1st Superchi; Betz, Graziani	*Ernani*
Carlotta Mezzo-soprano	Actress	R. Sarfaty	*Die Schweigsame Frau*
Carmela Mezzo-soprano	Gennaro's mother	Gay	*I Gioielli della Madonna*
Carmele Mezzo-soprano	Young girl who marries Paco		*La Vide Breve*
Carmen (Mezzo) Soprano	Gypsy	1st Galli-Marié; Ambré, Barbieri, Bellincioni, Besanzoni, Bourguignon, Brehms, Bressler-Giandi, Cahier, Calvé, Castagna, Coates, Djanel, Easton, Farrar, Fornia-Labey, Fremstad, Garden, Gay, Giannini, Gilly, Gutheil-Schoder, Hauk, Jeritza, Labia, Lilli Lehmann, Lucca, Lussan, Matzenauer, Miller, Mödl, Olczewska, Onegin, Patti, Pederzini, Ponselle, Rankin, Roze, Schumann-Heink, Shacklock, Shuard, Stevens, Supervia, Swarthout, Thebom, Tourel, Trebelli, Claramae Turner	*Carmen*

CHARACTER	ROLE	SINGER	OPERA
Carnero *See* Conte Carnero			
Carolina　Soprano	Geronimo's younger daughter, secretly married to Paolino		*Il Matrimonio Segreto*
Carthaginians 　　　　Chorus			*Les Troyens*
Cascart　Baritone	Music hall performer		*Zaza*
Caspar　　Bass	Forester	Bohnen, Faure, Foli, Formes, Koegel, O. Krauss, Santley	*Der Freischütz*
Cassandre　Soprano	Trojan prophetess		*Les Troyens*
Cassandre, The Ghost of 　Mezzo-soprano			*Les Troyens*
Cassio　　Tenor	Otello's lieutenant		*Otello*
Cat　Mezzo-soprano			*L'Enfant et les Sortilèges*
Cats (Two)	Behind the scenes		*The Boatswain's Mate*
Catarina　Soprano		Farrar	*Madame Sans-Gêne*
Caterina　Soprano	Fritz's housekeeper		*L'Amico Fritz*
Catherine　Soprano		Curtin	*Wuthering Heights*
Catholic Ladies and Gentlemen 　　　　Chorus			*Les Huguenots*
Cavalier　Tenor			*Cardillac*
Cavaradossi, Mario *See* Mario Cavaradossi			
Cecco del Vecchio 　　　　Bass	Roman citizen		*Rienzi*
Cecil, Sir Robert 　　　　Baritone	Secretary to the council		*Gloriana*
Celestial Messenger 　　　　Tenor			*Pilgrim's Progress*

CHARACTER	ROLE	SINGER	OPERA
Celestial Phalanxes Chorus			*Mefistofele*
Celio Bass	Magician, the King's protector		*The Love for Three Oranges*
Cellini, Benvenuto *See* Benvenuto Cellini			
Cenerentola, La *See* Angelina			
Ceprano, Count Bass			*Rigoletto*
Ceprano, Countess Mezzo Soprano		Amara	*Rigoletto*
Cerinto Contralto			*Nerone*
Certain Persons Cloth'd in Gold Chorus			*Pilgrim's Progress*
César de Bazan, Don Baritone *See also* Caesar de Bazan		1st Bouhy; Maas	*Don César de Bazan*
Cesare Angelotti Bass	Escaped political prisoner	Lorenzo Alvary	*Tosca*
Chamber Maid			*Adriana Lecouvreur*
Chamberlain Bass			*Le Rossignol*
Chappelou Tenor	Postillion with a fine voice	1st Chollet; Wachtel	*Le Postillion de Longjumeau*
Charlemagne Speaker	Emperor of the Franks		*Oberon*
Charles Tenor	Vicomte, in love with Linda		*Linda di Chamounix*
Charles Gérard Baritone	Revolutionary leader	1st Sammarco; Danise, Formichi, Franci, Guelfi, Inghilleri, Silveri	*Andrea Chénier*
Charlotte Mezzo-soprano	Le Bailli's daughter, Albert's wife, in love with Werther	1st Marie Renard; Delna, Eames, Farrar, Gay, Heidt, Lowe, Pederzini, Simoniato	*Werther*

CHARACTER	ROLE	SINGER	OPERA
Chateauneuf *See* Marquis de Chateauneuf			
Chauve-Souris, Le Soprano	The Bat		*L'Enfant et les Sortilèges*
Cheap Jack Baritone			*Hugh the Drover*
Cheap Jewelry Woman Mezzo-soprano			*A Village Romeo and Juliette*
Cherubino Soprano	Page to the Count- ess Almaviva	1st Bussani; Adams, Bible, Carvalho, Cross, Danco, Evans, Farrar, Gueden, Lucca, Miller, Christine Nilsson, Novotna, Teyte, Vanni, Welitsch, van Zandt	*Le Nozze di Figaro*
Cherubs Chorus			*Mefistofele*
Chief Sailor Tenor			*Marouf*
Chiffres, Les Children	Numbers		*L'Enfant et les Sortilèges*
Child Mezzo-soprano			*L'Enfant et les Sortilèges*
Children Chorus	Children of the Boyars		*Boris Godunov*
Children Chorus			*Esther de Carpentras, Pique-Dame, Le Prophète, Les Troyens, Werther, Wozzeck*
Childrens' Voices, Six Sopranos, Contraltos			*Die Frau Ohne Schatten*
Chinese Cup Mezzo-contralto			*L'Enfant et les Sortilèges*
Chloé Soprano	In a masque		*Pique-Dame*

THE CHARACTERS IN THE OPERAS

CHARACTER	ROLE	SINGER	OPERA
Chorèbe Baritone	Cassandra's lover		*Les Troyens*
Chorèbe's Ghost Baritone			*Les Troyens*
Chorus Chorus			*Agamemnon, Choëphores, Gloriana*
Chorus, Female Soprano			*The Rape of Lucretia*
Chorus, Male Tenor		1st Peter Pears;	*The Rape of Lucretia*
Choryphée			*Alceste*
Chouette, La Soprano	The little owl		*L'Enfant et les Sortilèges*
Chris the Citizen Baritone			*The Mother of Us All*
Christians Chorus			*La Juive, Nerone*
Christine Soprano	Storch's wife who nags	1st Lotte Lehmann	*Intermezzo*
Christoph Tenor	Kepler's brother		*Die Harmonie der Welt*
Christoph Madruscht, Cardinal Bass			*Palestrina*
Christopher Columbus (I) Baritone	As an old man		*Christophe Colomb*
Christopher Columbus (II) Baritone	As a young man		*Christophe Colomb*
Chronicler *See* Pimen			
Cho-Cho San *See* Cio-Cio San			
Chruschtschov *See* Khrushchev			
Chrysothemis Soprano	Elektra's sister	1st Siems; Hilde Konetzni, Faull, Yeend	*Elektra*

339

CHARACTER		ROLE	SINGER	OPERA
Church-Goers				*Doktor Faustus*
	Chorus			
Cicillo	Tenor	Cammorist		*I Gioielli della Madonna*
Cieca, La	Contralto	Gioconda's blind mother	Madeira, Schalchi, Swarthout	*La Gioconda*
Cieco, Il	Bass	Blind man, Iris's father		*Iris*
Ciesca, La	Mezzo-soprano	Marco's wife, 38	Votipka	*Gianni Schicchi*
Cigarette Girls	Chorus			*Carmen*
Cinderella *See* Angelina				
Cio-Cio San	Soprano	Pinkerton's Japanese wife	1st Storchio; Adami-Corradetti, Albanese, de los Angeles, Callas, della Casa, Cebotari, Cross, Destinn, Farrar, Faull, Favero, Giannini, Kirsten, Krusceniski, dal Monte, Price, Rethberg, Schwarzkopf, Seefried, Sheridan, Shuard, Tebaldi,Teyte, Welitsch, Williams	*Madama Butterfly*
Cirillo	Baritone	Coachman		*Fedora*
Cis	Soprano	Child		*Albert Herring*
Citizens	Chorus			*Andrea Chénier, La Bohème, Damnation de Faust, Les Huguenots, Iris, Mefistofele, Le Prophète, The Rake's Progress, Roméo et Juliette, La Rondine, Tosca, Les Troyens*

THE CHARACTERS IN THE OPERAS

CHARACTER	ROLE	SINGER	OPERA
City Crier Baritone			*Gloriana*
Claggert Bass	Master at Arms		*Billy Budd*
Claison Contralto	Actress	Christa Ludwig	*Capriccio*
Clara Soprano	Jake's wife	1st Abbie Mitchell	*Porgy and Bess*
Claretta Soprano			*Zaza*
Clarissa, Princess Contralto	The King's niece		*The Love for Three Oranges*
Claudio Baritone	An officer in love with Hero		*Béatrice et Bénédict*
Clem Tenor	Black Bob. *Also plays* Max Westleton *in Acts I and II, and* Alfred the gardener		*Let's Make an Opera*
Clémence Soprano			*Mireille*
Cleopatra Pantomime			*Faust*
Clorinda Soprano	Don Magnifico's daughter		*La Cenerentola*
Clorinda Pantomime	Saracen maiden in man's armor		*Il Combattimento di Tancredi e Clorinda*
Clotilde Soprano	Norma's friend		*Norma*
Clytemnestra Soprano	Agamemnon's wife		*Agamemnon*
Clytemnestra Mezzo-soprano	Agamemnon's wife	1st du Plant; Cyrena von Gordon	*Iphigénie en Aulide*
Clytemnestra See also Klytemnestra			
Clytemnestra's Ghost See Spectre de Clytemnestra, Le			
Coal Gatherer Mezzo-soprano			*Louise*
Coaxer, Mrs. From Chorus	Lady of the town		*The Beggar's Opera*

CHARACTER	ROLE	SINGER	OPERA
Chochenille Tenor	Spalanzani's servant		*Les Contes d'Hoffmann*
Cockburn Lord Tenor	Tourist		*Fra Diavolo*
Cockerel, The Golden Soprano			*Le Coq d'Or*
Coigny, Comtesse de Mezzo-soprano	Madeleine's mother		*Andrea Chénier*
Cola Rienzi Tenor	Roman tribune	1st Tichatschek; Althouse, Max Alvary, Lorenz, Mass, Schott	*Rienzi*
Colas Baritone		Bispham	*Bastien et Bastienne*
Collatinus Bass	Soldier, Lucretia's husband		*The Rape of Lucretia*
Colline Bass	Young, starving philosopher	Moscona, Siepi, Tajo	*La Bohème*
Colonna *See* Steffano Colonna			
Columbine Mezzo-soprano	Arlecchino's wife		*Arlecchino*
Columbine Soprano			*Fête Galante*
Columbine *See* Nedda			
Comedians and Clowns Chorus			*Prodana Neveta*
Commandant Bass			*Christophe Colomb*
Commandant Baritone	of the beseiged town	1st Hotter; Prohaska	*Friedenstag*
Commendatore Bass	Donna Anna's father	1st Giuseppe Lelli; Böhme, Foli, Radford, Tozzi, Wildermann	*Don Giovanni*
Commercial Councillor Baritone	Storch's friend		*Intermezzo*

THE CHARACTERS IN THE OPERAS

CHARACTER	ROLE	SINGER	OPERA
Commère Mezzo-soprano		1st A. Hines	*Four Saints in Three Acts*
Commissioner, Imperial *See* Imperial Commissioner			
Companion Tenor	of Cardillac's daughter		*Cardillac*
Compère Bass		1st Abner Dorsey	*Four Saints in Three Acts*
Composer Soprano		1st Lotte Lehmann; Jurinac, Mödl, Seefried, Welitsch	*Ariadne auf Naxos*
Concepcion Soprano	Torquemada's wife	1st. Vix; Albanese, Bori, Franca Duval, Supervia	*L'Heure Espagnole*
Concetta Soprano			*I Gioielli della Madonna*
Conductor *Also* Mr. Harper *in acts I and II*			*Let's Make an Opera*
Confidante Soprano	to Klytemnestra		*Elektra*
Conrad Nachtigall Bass	Mastersinger and bucklemaker		*Die Meistersinger*
Constable Bass			*Hugh the Drover*
Constable From Chorus			*Il Barbiere di Siviglia*
Constance Fletcher Soprano			*The Mother of Us All*
Constanze Soprano	A Spanish lady		*Die Entführung aus dem Serail*
Conte Carnero Baritone	Commissioner of morals		*Zigeunerbaron*
Conte di Luna Baritone	of Aragon	Maurel, Tozzi, Panerai	*Il Trovatore*
Cook Tenor			*Christophe Colomb*

THE CHARACTERS IN THE OPERAS

CHARACTER	ROLE	SINGER	OPERA
Cook Bass	An evil giant		*The Love for Three Oranges*
Cook Mezzo-soprano	to the Emperor		*Le Rossignol*
Coppelius Baritone	Scientist, Spalanzani's rival	London	*Les Contes d'Hoffmann*
Coq d'Or, Le *See* Cockerel, the Golden			
Corcy, Marquis de Tenor	Head of the Paris Opèra		*Le Postillon de Longjumeau*
Corentini Tenor	Bagpiper		*Dinorah*
Corifeas (Two)			*L'Assassinio nel' Cattedrale*
Coroner Speaker			*Porgy and Bess*
Corporal Bass	of the grenadiers	Cehanovsky	*La Figlia del Reggimento*
Corporal Baritone			*Friedenstag*
Corporal *See also* José, Don			
Corregidor, Der *See* Eugenio di Zuniga, Don			
Cossacks Chorus			*The Fair ot Sorochintsky*
Cossé Tenor			*Les Huguenots*
Councillors			*L'Africaine*
Counsel for the Prosecution Speaker			*Christophe Colomb*
Count Baritone	Brother of the countess	Wächter	*Capriccio*
Count *See under proper name as:* Almaviva, Count *See also* Conte			

344

CHARACTER	ROLE	SINGER	OPERA
Countess Soprano	The Count's sister	1st Ursuleac; Cebotari, della Casa, Schwarzkopf	*Capriccio*
Countess Mezzo-soprano			*Pique-Dame*
Countess Contralto		Schumann-Heink	*Der Trompeter von Säkkingen*
Countess See under proper name, as: Almaviva, Countess			
Country People Chorus			*Doktor Faustus*
Counts Chorus			*Lohengrin*
Coupava See Koupava			
Carrier Tenor			*La Fanciulla del West*
Court Attendant Bass		Renan	*Der Prozess*
Court Officials Chorus			*Nabucco*
Court Servants Chorus			*Háry János*
Courtiers Chorus			*Un Ballo in Maschera, Christophe Colomb, Le Coq d'Or, Dido and Aeneas, Doktor Faustus, La Favorita, Fête Galante, The Love for Three Oranges, Martha, Rigoletto, Le Rossignol, Les Troyens*
Courtois Bass			*Zaza*
Crab Man Tenor			*Porgy and Bess*
Crébillon Bass-baritone	Perichaud's friend		*La Rondine*
Creditors Chorus			*Christophe Colomb*

CHARACTER	ROLE	SINGER	OPERA
Creditors Chorus			*Die Liebe der Danae*
Creon Bass-baritone	Jocasta's brother		*Oedipus Rex*
Crespel Baritone	Antonia's father		*Les Contes d'Hoffmann*
Cretans *See* People of Crete			
Cricket, A Soprano			*Das Heimchen am Herd*
Cristian *See* Silvano			
Crobyle Soprano	A slave		*Thaïs*
Croupiers Chorus			*Manon*
Crowd Chorus			*Ariane et Barbe-Bleue*
Crowds, Mute Silent			*Der Prozess*
Crown Baritone	Stevedore	1st Coleman	*Porgy and Bess*
Crusty *See* Lunardo			
Cuno Bass	Head forester		*Der Freischütz*
Cupidon Soprano	Cupid		*Orphée aux Enfers*
Curra Mezzo-soprano	Leonora's maid	Votipka	*La Forza del Destino*
Don Curzio Tenor	A lawyer	1st Michael Kelly; Meyer-Wolfing	*Le Nozze di Figaro*
Customs Officer Bass			*La Bohème*
Cutbeard	A barber	Ukena	*Die Schweigsame Frau*
Cypriotes Chorus			*Otello*
Czar *See* Tsar			
Czipra Mezzo-soprano	Gypsy woman		*Zigeunerbaron*
Daland Bass	Norwegian sea-captain	Fischer, Foli, Griswold	*Der Fliegende Holländer*

THE CHARACTERS IN THE OPERAS

CHARACTER	ROLE	SINGER	OPERA
Dalibor Tenor	Knight, imprisoned for murder	1st Lukas; Völker	*Dalibor*
Dalila Mezzo-soprano	Philistine seductress	1st Müller; Barbieri, Brema, Gay, Hastreiter, Homer Kirkby-Lunn, Langendorf, Matzenauer, Ober, Onegin, Stevens, Stignani, Thebom, Wettergren	*Samson et Dalila*
Dalila *See also* Delilah			
Dalua Baritone	Lord of shadow	1st Boughton (*The composer*)	*The Immortal Hour*
Danae Soprano	Daughter of Pollux	1st Ursuleac; Dow, Kupper, Rysanek	*Die Liebe der Danae*
Dancairo, El Baritone	A smuggler	Cehanovsky, Renan	*Carmen*
Dancer Dancer			*Capriccio, Louise*
Dancers Dancers		.	*Gloriana, Mefistofele, La Rondine, La Traviata, Turandot (Busoni), I Vespri Siciliani*
Dancers (Six) Dancers			*Four Saints in Three Acts*
Dancing Girl Dancer			*Hugh the Drover*
Dancing Master Tenor		Fried	*Ariadne auf Naxos*
Dandini Bass	The prince's valet	Lablache, Reeves, Tamburini	*La Cenerentola*
Dangeville, Mlle. Mezzo-soprano	of the Comedie Française		*Adriana Lecouvreur*
Daniel Tenor		Capoul	*Le Chalet*
Daniel Hizler Bass	Vicar of Linz, *later* Vicar of Regensburg, *also* Mercury		*Das Harmonie der Welt*

347

CHARACTER	ROLE	SINGER	OPERA
Daniel Webster Baritone			*The Mother of Us All*
Danieli Tenor	Young Sicilian		*I Vespri Siciliani*
Dansker Bass	An old seaman		*Billy Budd*
Danton *See* Georg Danton			
Dapertutto Baritone	A sorcerer	London	*Les Contes d'Hoffmann*
Daphne Soprano		Bampton, Cebotari, Cigna	*Daphne*
Daphnis Contralto	Character in a masque, *played by* Pauline		*Pique-Dame*
Da-Ud Tenor	Altair's son		*Die Aegyptische Helene*
Daughter of Cardillac Soprano			*Cardillac*
David Baritone	A rabbi	Danise	*L'Amico Fritz*
David Tenor	Hans Sachs' apprentice	Franke	*Die Meistersinger*
Dead Composers (Nine) Three Tenors, Three Baritones, Three Basses			*Palestrina*
Death From Chorus			*Iris*
Death Contralto			*Le Rossignol*
Death Bass			*Savitri*
Debora Mezzo-soprano	Prophetess	1st Tess; Spani, Carbone	*Debora*
Delilah (Mezzo) Soprano		1st Resnik	*The Warrior*
Delilah *See also* Dalila			
Demas Baritone			*Pilgrim's Progress*
Demi-Mondaines Chorus			*La Rondine*

CHARACTER	ROLE	SINGER	OPERA
Demons Chorus			*Faust*
Desdemona Mezzo-soprano	Otello's wife	1st Stoltz; Viardot-Garcia	*Otello* (Rossini)
Desdemona Soprano	Otello's wife	1st Pantaleone; Albani, Alda, Caniglia, Caron, Charton-Demeur, Ciani, Cross, Brouwenstijn, Eames, Farrar, Fodor-Mainvielle, Goltz, Ilitsch, Lilli Lehmann, Lussan, Malibran, Milanov, Christine Nilsson, Norena, Pampanini, Rappold, Rethberg, Scacciati, Schröder-Devrient, Sheridan, Sontag, Steber, Tebaldi, Eva Tetrazzini, Luisa Tetrazzini	*Otello* (Verdi)
Desiré Tenor	Valet		*Fedora*
Desmoulins *See* Camille Desmoulins			
Despina Soprano	Fiordiligi's and Dorabella's maid	1st Bussani; Gueden, Peters	*Così fan Tutte*
Detective Speaker			*Porgy and Bess*
Devil, The Bass			*Švanda Dudák*
Devil's Familiar Spirit Tenor			*Švanda Dudák*
Devilshoof Bass	Chief of the gypsies		*The Bohemian Girl*
Dew Fairy Soprano			*Hänsel und Gretel*
Dewman Soprano		Nicholls	*Hänsel und Gretel*
Diana Soprano	Goddess		*Iphigénie en Tauride*
Diane Soprano	Goddess		*Orphée aux Enfers*

CHARACTER		ROLE	SINGER	OPERA
Dickson	Tenor	Tenant of the White Lady		*La Dame Blanche*
Dido	Soprano	Queen of Carthage	Flagstad, Nicholls, Pederzini	*Dido and Aeneas*
Didon Mezzo-soprano		Queen of Carthage	1st Charton-Demeur; Delna, Mandikian	*Les Troyens*
Diego, Don	Bass	Councillor, Vasco's rival	Edouard de Reszke	*L'Africaine*
Diemut	Soprano		Destinn	*Feuersnot*
Dikoy	Bass	Merchant, uncle of Boris		*Katya Kabanova*
Dimitri	Contralto	Groom		*Fedora*
Dimitri *See* Grigorij				
Dinorah	Soprano	A peasant girl	1st Cabel; Barrientos, Carvalho, Galli-Curci, Murska, Patti, Luisa Tetrazzini, Vere, van Zandt	*Dinorah*
Dipsacus	Bass	Magician, Tormentilla's father		*The Poisoned Kiss*
Director-Representative Bass				*Der Prozess*
Disguised Jews Chorus				*Esther de Carpentras*
Djamileh Mezzo-soprano		A slave	1st Prelly	*Djamileh*
Djura		Mandryka's servant		*Arabella*
Dmitri *See* Grigorij				
Doctor				*Arabella*
Doctor	Speaker			*Lulu*
Doctor	Bass			*Macbeth*

CHARACTER	ROLE	SINGER	OPERA
Doctor Bass		Doench, Renan	*Wozzeck*
Doctor, The Old Bass		1st Tozzi	*Vanessa*
Doctor, Jewish *See* Médicin Juif, Le			
Doctor of Natural History Baritone			*Doktor Faustus*
Doctor Thorp Silent			*Peter Grimes*
Doctors (Eight) Tenors, Basses			*Turandot* (Busoni)
Doctors Chorus			*The Love for Three Oranges*
Dodon, King Bass			*Le Coq d'Or*
Dolcina, Suor Mezzo-soprano	A nun		*Suor Angelica*
Doleful Creatures Chorus			*Pilgrim's Progress*
Dolly Trull From Chorus	Lady of the town		*The Beggar's Opera*
Dominik, Graf Baritone	Arabella's suitor		*Arabella*
Don *See proper name, as:* Giovanni, Don			
Doña Mercedes *See* Mercedes, Doña			
Donald Baritone	A seaman		*Billy Budd*
Donald Gallop Tenor			*The Mother of Us All*
Donato Bass-baritone	A young blind man		*Maria Golovin*
Donella Mezzo-soprano	Francesca's woman		*Francesca da Rimini*
Donner Bass Baritone	Norse god	Gura, Hargrave	*Das Ring des Nibelungen*
Dorabella Soprano	Fiordiligi's sister	1st Villeneuve; Jurinac, Miller, Mödl, Thebom	*Così fan Tutte*

CHARACTER		ROLE	SINGER	OPERA
Dorotka	Soprano	Schwanda's wife		*Švanda Dudák*
Dositheus	Bass	Leader of the Old Believers, and enemy of the Tsar	Allin	*Khovantschina*
Dositeo	Baritone	A Roman		*Nerone*
Dot	Soprano	John's wife		*Das Heimchen am Herd*
Douphol, Baron	Baritone	Alfredo's rival for Violetta	Cehanovsky	*La Traviata*
Dragoons	Chorus			*Carmen*
Dressmaker	Soprano			*Der Rosenkavalier*
Dressmakers	Chorus			*The Poisoned Kiss*
Druids	Chorus			*The Immortal Hour*
Drum-Major	Tenor		Baum	*Wozzeck*
Drummers	Chorus			*Billy Budd*
Drunkards	Chorus			*The Love for Three Oranges*
Dryade	Contralto	A nymph		*Ariadne auf Naxos*
Duchess of Parma	Soprano			*Doktor Faustus*
Duchesse de Krakenthorp	Soprano			*La Figlia del Reggimento*
Duclou	Baritone	Stage manager		*Zaza*
Duenna				*Arabella*
Duenna	Mezzo-soprano			*Der Corregidor*
Dufla, General	Speaker			*Háry János*
Dufresne, Mme	Mezzo-soprano	Milio's wife		*Zaza*

CHARACTER	ROLE	SINGER	OPERA
Duke of Mantua Tenor		1st Mirate; Bjoerling, Bonci, Borgioli, Caruso, Conley, Gigli, Hislop, Lauri-Volpi, Mario, Martini, McCormack, Peerce, Piccaver, Schipa, di Stefano, Tagliavini	*Rigoletto*
Duke of Parma Tenor			*Doktor Faustus*
Duke of Verona Bass			*Roméo et Juliette*
Dulcamara Bass	Quack, peddler of aphrodisiacs	Baccaloni	*L'Elisir d'Amore*
Dulcinée, La Belle Contralto		1st Lucy Arbell; Easton, Garden, Lyne	*Don Quichotte*
Dumas Baritone	President of the Tribunal		*Andrea Chénier*
Duncan Silent	King of Scotland		*Macbeth*
Dutchman, The Baritone	A damned soul	1st Wächter; Berglund, Bertram, Bispham, Bockel- mann, Hotter, Janssen, Maurel, Reichmann, Rooy, Santley, Scheider- mantel, Schorr	*Der Fliegende Holländer*
Dwarf *See* Alberich *See also* Mime			
Earth *See* Johannes Kepler			
Ebelasztin, Ritter Von Tenor	Marie's chamberlain		*Háry János*
Eberbach, Count Baritone			*Der Wildschütz*

CHARACTER	ROLE	SINGER	OPERA
Eberbach, Countess Contralto			*Der Wildschütz*
Eboli, Principessa Mezzo-soprano	Lady in waiting, in love with Don Carlos	Barbieri, Mödl, Shuard, Stignani, Thebom	*Don Carlos*
Echo Soprano			*Ariadne auf Naxos*
Ecureuil, L' Mezzo-soprano	The squirrel		*L'Enfant et les Sortilèges*
Edgar See Edgardo			
Edgardo Tenor	Edgar of Ravens-wood	1st Duprez; Campanini, Caruso, Nicolini, Peerce, Reeves, de Stefano	*Lucia di Lammermoor*
Edmondo Tenor	A student		*Manon Lescaut*
Edward Plummer Tenor			*Das Heimchen am Herd*
Eglantine Soprano		Brandt, Borkh, Ober, Peschka-Leutner, Thorborg	*Euryanthe*
Egyptians Chorus			*Aida*
Eisenstein See Gabriel von Eisenstein			
Elder Gleaton Tenor			*Susannah*
Elder Hayes Tenor			*Susannah*
Elder McLean Baritone			*Susannah*
Elder Ott Bass		Hecht	*Susannah*
Elders Chorus			*Friedenstag*
Elders (Two) Tenor, Bass	of Novgorod		*Sadko*
Elders of Thebes Chorus			*Antigonae* (Orff)
Eléazar Tenor	Jewish goldsmith	1st Nourrit; Caruso, Duprez, Koegel, Martinelli	*La Juive*

CHARACTER		ROLE	SINGER	OPERA
Electors	Chorus			*Ernani*
Electra	Soprano	Greek princess	1st Elisabeth Wendling; Birgit Nilsson	*Idomeneo*
Electre	Soprano			*Les Choëphores*
Elektra	Soprano	Agamemnon's daughter	1st Anny Krull; Borkh, Easton, Gutheil-Schoder, Kappel, Anni Konetzni, Kruscenski, Marcel, Pauly, Varnay, Walker	*Elektra*
Elemer, Graf	Tenor	Arabella's suitor		*Arabella*
Elena	Soprano	Helen of Troy	Arangi-Lombardi, Cary, Easton, Fenn, Martinis, Christine Nilsson, Raisa, Rasa, Tebaldi, Trebelli	*Mefistofele*
Elena, Duchess	Soprano		1st Cruvelli; Callas, Anni Konetzni	*I Vespri Siciliani*
Elisabeth	Soprano	Niece of the Land-grave Hermann	1st J. Wagner; Ackté, Albani, Eames, Cross, Brouwenstijn, Farrar, Fisher, Flagstad, Fornia-Labey, Fremstad, Gadski, Goltz, Harshaw, Jeritza, Juch, Kurt, Leffler-Burckhard, Malten, Marchesi, Materna, Moody, Morena, Birgit Nilsson Osborn, Rappold, Rethberg, Sass, Seidl-Krauss, Stehle, Ternina, Valleria, Varnay	*Tannhäuser*

CHARACTER	ROLE	SINGER	OPERA
Elisabeth the First Soprano	Queen of England	1st Cross	*Gloriana*
Elisabetta di Valois Soprano	Queen of Spain, beloved by Don Carlos	1st Sass; Brouwenstijn, Cigna, Caniglia, Grandi, Lucca, Ponselle, Rysanek, Steber	*Don Carlos*
Elise Soprano			*Louise*
Elisetta Soprano	Geronimo's older daughter		*Il Matrimonio Segreto*
Ellen Soprano	An English lady		*Lakmé*
Ellen Orford Soprano	Widow, school-mistress	1st Cross; Danco, Fisher, Manning, Resnik	*Peter Grimes*
Elsa of Brabant Soprano		1st Agthé; Ackté, Albani, Brandt, Destinn, Eames, Easton, Cross, Farrar, Fisher, Flagstad, Fremstad, Gadski, Jeritza, Juch, Krauss, Leffller-Burckhard, Mallinger, Marchesi, Melba, Moody, Morena, Christine Nilsson, Nordica, Osborn, Parepa-Rosa, Rappold, Reuss-Belce, Roze, Malvina Schnorr von Carolsfield, Schwarzkopf, Seidl-Krauss, Steber, Stehle, Sucher, Tebaldi, Ternina, Varnay, Vere, Zadek	*Lohengrin*
Elvino Tenor	Farmer, engaged to Amina		*La Sonnambula*
Elvira Soprano	Spanish princess		*Masaniello*

356

CHARACTER		ROLE	SINGER	OPERA
Elvira	Soprano	Silvano's relative, beloved by Ernani	Lucca, Sembrich, Tietjens	*Ernani*
Elvira	Soprano	The Bey's wife	1st Grisi; Barrientos, Callas, Gerster, Pinkert, Literazzini,	*L'Italiana in Algeri*
Elvira	Soprano	Lord Gaulthier Walton's daughter		*I Puritani*
Elvira, Donna	Soprano	A lady from Burgos, deserted by Don Giovanni	1st Catarina Micelli; Adams, Brandt, Carvalho, Casa, Cross, Farrar, Galli-Curci, Eugenie Garcia, Gerster, Jurinac, Lewis, Matzenauer, Milde, Christine Nilsson, Nordica, Resnik, Schwarzkopf, Steber	*Don Giovanni*
Elves (Three) Sopranos, Contralto				*Die Aegyptische Helene*
Emilia Mezzo-soprano		Iago's wife, Desdemona's lady	Wickham	*Otello* (Verdi)
Emma	Soprano	Young girl	Ziliani	*Khovantschina*
Emma	Soprano		Grisi	*Zelmira* (Handel)
Emmie	Soprano	A child		*Albert Herring*
Emperor	Tenor			*Die Frau ohne Schatten*
Emperor Altoum	Tenor	Turandot's father		*Turandot* (Puccini)
Emperor of China	Baritone			*Le Rossignol*
Empress	Soprano	The woman who had no shadow	1st Lotte Lehmann; Kemp, Hilde Konetzni, Pauly, Rysanek	*Die Frau ohne Schatten*
Empress of Austria	Soprano			*Háry János*

THE CHARACTERS IN THE OPERAS

CHARACTER	ROLE	SINGER	OPERA
Empress Persicaria Contralto	Mother of Amaryllus		*The Poisoned Kiss*
Enan, The Blind Bass			*Debora e Jaele*
Enée Tenor	Aeneas, Trojan hero	1st Monjauze; Kentish	*Les Troyens*
Enrichetta *See* Henrietta			
Enrico Baritone	Lord Henry Ashton of Lammermoor	Galassi, Lassalle, Ronconi, Scotti	*Lucia di Lammermoor*
Enterich Baritone	Prison governor		*Der Bettelstudent*
Entourage, The Caliph's Chorus			*Der Barbier von Bagdad*
Envoy of Japan *See* Japanese Envoy			
Envy Bass			*Pilgrim's Progress*
Enzo Grimaldo Tenor	Genoese nobleman in love with Laura	Baum, Caruso, Gigli, Marconi, Martin, Martinelli, Merli, del Monaco, Tucker, Zenatello	*La Gioconda*
Eochaidh Baritone	King in love with Etain		*The Immortal Hour*
Ercole Severolus, Bishop Bass Baritone			*Palestrina*
Erda Mezzo-soprano	Goddess of Earth	Homer, Matzenauer, Meisle, Ober, Schumann-Heink	*Das Ring des Nibelungen*
Eric Tenor	A huntsman	Althouse, Berger, Sullivan	*Der Fliegende Holländer*
Ericlea Mezzo-soprano	Penelope's nurse		*Il Ritorno d'Ulisse in Patria*
Erika Mezzo-soprano	Vanessa's niece	1st Elias	*Vanessa*

358

THE CHARACTERS IN THE OPERAS

CHARACTER	ROLE	SINGER	OPERA
Ernani Tenor	Really John of Aragon, as a bandit chieftain in love with Elvira	1st Guasio	*Ernani*
Ernesto Tenor	Don Pasquale's nephew	1st Mario; Schipa	*Don Pasquale*
Eroshka Tenor	Gudok player		*Prince Igor*
Errand Girl Soprano			*Louise*
Erinnyes Chorus			*Eumenides*
Erster Bürger Tenor	First citizen		*Die Lustigen Weiber von Windsor*
Escamillo Baritone	Famous toreador	1st Bouhy; Amato, Bispham, Campanari, Cassel, Galassi, Guarrera, Journet, Lassalle, London, Merrill, Plançon, del Puente, Renaud, van Rooy, Scaria, Scotti, Tibbett	*Carmen*
Esmeralda Soprano	A dancer	Schwarzkopf	*Prodana Nevešta*
Esquires Chorus			*Tristan und Isolde*
Esquires (Four) Sopranos, Tenors			*Parsifal*
Essex, Robert Devereux Earl of Tenor	Favorite of Queen Elisabeth	1st Pears	*Gloriana*
Estrella Speaker	Lady in waiting		*Háry János*
Etain Soprano	Manru's daughter		*The Immortal Hour*
Ethiopian Slaves Chorus			*Aida*
Eudoxia, Princess Soprano	The emperor's niece		*La Juive*
Eugene Onegin Baritone		London, de Luca, Sved	*Eugene Onegin*
Eugenio de Zuniga, Don Tenor	The magistrate	1st Breuer; Kelley	*Der Corregidor*

CHARACTER		ROLE	SINGER	OPERA
Eumete	Tenor	Swineherd		*Il Ritorno d'Ulisse in Patria*
Eunuchs	Chorus			*Turandot* (Busoni)
Eunuchs of the Harem	Chorus			*L'Italiana in Algeri*
Euridice	Soprano	Orfeo's wife	Gatti	*La Favola d'Orfeo*
Euridice	Soprano	Orphée's wife		*Les Malheurs d'Orphée*
Euridice	Soprano	Orfeo's wife	Adams, Arnould, Billington, Gadski, Hasteriter, Novotna, Rappold	*Orfeo ed Euridice*
Euridice	Soprano	Orphée's wife	Ugalde	*Orphée aux Enfers*
Eurimacho	Tenor	Melanto's lover		*Il Ritorno d'Ulisse in Patria*
Europa	Soprano	A Queen, formerly loved by Jupiter		*Die Liebe der Danae*
Euryanthe of Savoy	Soprano		1st Sontag; Flagstad, Hempel, Lilli Lehmann, Lind, Sucher, Wagner	*Euryanthe*
Eurydice *See* Euridice				
Eva	Soprano	Pogner's daughter	1st Mathilde Mallinger; Albani, de los Angeles, Brandt, Dux, Eames, Farrar, Gadski, Goltz, Hempel, Jurinac, Leffler-Burckhard, Lemnitz, Marchesi, Moody, Morena, Osborn, Schwarzkopf, Seidle-Krauss, Sembrich, Steber, Stehle, Stückgold, Sucher, Zadek	*Die Meistersinger*
Evander	Tenor			*Alceste*

CHARACTER	ROLE	SINGER	OPERA
Evangelist Bass			*Pilgrim's Progress*
Evil, Choir of Chorus			*The Poisoned Kiss*
Evil Spirits Chorus			*Robert le Diable*
Executioner Tenor			*Švanda Dudak*
Executioners Chorus			*La Juive*
Fafner Bass	Giant, builder of Valhalla	List	*Das Ring des Nibelungen*
Fairies Chorus			*La Damnation de Faust*
Fairy *See* Dew Fairy			
Falcon's Voice, The Soprano			*Die Frau ohne Schatten*
Falke, Doctor Baritone	Eisenstein's friend	Brownlee	*Die Fledermaus*
Falstaff, Sir John Baritone		1st Maurel; Tibbett, Gobbi, Stabile	*Falstaff*
Falstaff, Sir John Bass		1st Zschiesche; Allin, Betz, Bispham, Sammarco, Scotti	*Die Lustigen Wieber von Windsor*
Faninal, Herr von Baritone	Sophie's father	Brownlee, Schützendorf	*Der Rosenkavalier*
Fanuèl Baritone	A Christian	1st Galeffi; Franci	*Nerone*
Farfallo Bass	An actor	Hecht	*Die Schweigsame Frau*
Farfarello Bass	A devil		*The Love for Three Oranges*
Farlaf Bass	Suitor of Ludmilla, a warrior		*Russlan and Ludmilla*
Farmer Bass			*Die Kluge*
Farmers Chorus			*Martha*
Farmer's Daughter Soprano	The wise maiden		*Die Kluge*

THE CHARACTERS IN THE OPERAS

CHARACTER	ROLE	SINGER	OPERA
Fasolt Bass Baritone	Giant, builder of Valhalla	Radford	*Das Rheingold*
Fata Morgana Soprano	A witch, Leandro's protectress	Faull	*The Love for Three Oranges*
Father-in-Law Bass		1st Vieuille; Nissen, Inghilleri	*Le Pauvre Matelot*
Father of Louise Bass		Radford	*Louise*
Fatima Mezzo-soprano	Reiza's companion	1st Vestris; Matzenauer, Trebelli	*Oberon*
Fatimah Soprano	Marouf's shrewish wife		*Marouf*
Fauns Chorus			*Les Troyens*
Faust Tenor	A learned man	1st Jean de Reszke; Alvarez, Binci, Campanini, Dalmorès, Merli, Rousseliere, Voyer	*La Damnation de Faust*
Faust Tenor	A learned doctor	1st Barbot; Alvarez, Ansseau, Bonci, Campanini, Capoul, Caruso, Dalmorès, Hislop, Jadlowker, Kullmann, Maas, MacLennan, R. Martin, McCormack, Muratore, Nicolini, Jean de Reszke, Saléza, Tagliavini	*Faust*
Faust Tenor	A learned doctor	Campanini, Caruso, Gigli, Masini, McCormack, Merli, del Monaco, Peerce, Pertile, Tagliavini	*Mefistofele*
Faust, Doktor Baritone	A learned man		*Doktor Faust*

CHARACTER		ROLE	SINGER	OPERA
Fauteuil, Le	Bass	The armchair		*L'Enfant et les Sortilèges*
Federica	Contralto	Duchess, Walter's niece		*Luisa Miller*
Federico	Tenor	Fritz's friend		*L'Amico Fritz*
Federico	Tenor	Rosa's son, in love with the girl from Arles	1st Caruso; Schipa	*L'Arlesiana*
Fedora Romanov, Princess	Soprano		1st Bellincioni; Caniglia, Cavalieri, Giachetti, Jeritza, Pederzini	*Fedora*
Feklusha	Mezzo-soprano	Servant		*Katya Kabanova*
Felice	Soprano	Canciano's wife		*I Quattro Rusteghi*
Felicia	Contralto		1st Malibran	*Crociato* (Meyerbeer)
Felicia *See* Felice				
Fellah	Tenor			*Marouf*
Femme du Peuple *See* Woman				
Fenella	Pantomime	Masaniello's sister, in love with Alfonso		*Masaniello*
Fenena	Soprano	Nabucco's daughter		*Nabucco*
Fenton	Tenor	Young gentleman in love with Nanetta	Bonci	*Falstaff*
Fenton	Tenor	Anne Page's lover	Dippel	*Die Lustigen Weiber von Windsor*
Feodor	Mezzo-soprano	Son of Boris Godunov	Miller	*Boris Godunov*
Ferdinand	Tenor	Young novice, in love with Leonora	Campanini, Caruso	*La Favorita*
Ferdinand *See* King of Spain				
Ferdinand II, Kaiser *Also* Rudolf, *also* The Sun	Bass			*Die Harmonie der Welt*

CHARACTER		ROLE	SINGER	OPERA
Fernando	Tenor	Rosario's lover	1st Martinelli; Civil	*Goyescas*
Fernando	Baritone		1st Galli; Faure	*La Gazza Ladra*
Fernando, Don	Bass	The King's minister	Gura, Middleton, Scheidermantl	*Fidelio*
Fernando *See also* Ferdinand				
Ferrando	Bass	Captain of the guard of di Luna	Gassier, Moscona	*Il Trovatore*
Ferrando	Tenor	Dorabella's fiancé	1st Calvesi; F. Austin, Lewis, Nash, Pears, Sullivan, Tucker	*Così fan Tutte*
Fiakermilli	Soprano	Singer at the Fiaker Ball		*Arabella*
Fidalma	Mezzo-soprano	Geronimo's sister	Stignani	*Il Matrimonio Segreto*
Fiddler, The Dark	Baritone	Real owner of the disputed land		*A Village Romeo and Juliet*
Fidelio *See* Leonora		Really Leonora, disguised as a man		
Fidès	Mezzo-soprano	Mother of John of Leyden	1st Viardot-Garcia; Alboni, Brandt, Brema, Homer, Ober, Schumann-Heink, Stoltz, Tietjens, Wagner, Walker	*Le Prophète*
Fieramosca	Baritone	Cellini's rival, a papal sculptor		*Benvenuto Cellini*
Fiesco *See* Jacopo Fiesco				
Figaro	Baritone	A barber	1st Zamboni; Ancona, Balfe, Forti, Manuel Garcia II, Gassier, Gobbi, Guarrera, Ludikar, Merrill, del Puente, Jean de Reszke, Ronconi, Ruffo, Svanholm, Thomas	*Il Barbiere di Siviglia*

THE CHARACTERS IN THE OPERAS

CHARACTER		ROLE	SINGER	OPERA
Figaro	Bass	Servant to Count Almaviva	1st Benucci; Carey, Faure, Forti, Gassier, Kindermann, Kunz, Siepi	Le Nozze di Figaro
Filch	Tenor	Pickpocket, employed by Mr. Peachum		The Beggar's Opera
Filina See Philine				
Filipeto	Tenor	Maurizio's son		I Quattro Rusteghi
Filipievna Mezzo-soprano		Tatiana's nurse		Eugene Onegin
Filippo II	Bass	King of Spain	Christoff, Hines, Siepi, Tozzi	Don Carlos
Finn	Tenor	Good wizard		Russlan and Ludmilla
Fiora	Soprano	Manfredo's wife	1st Villani; Bori, Cobelli, Edvina, Jepson, Kirsten, Moore, Muzio, Petrella, Rethberg, Ponselle, dalla Rizza, Scuderi	L'Amore dei Tre Re
Fiordiligi	Soprano	Dorabella's sister	1st Farrarese del Bene; Danco, Goltz, Gueden, Hempel, Jurinac, Seefried, Steber, Welitsch	Così fan Tutte
Fiorello	Bass	Almaviva's servant	Cehanovsky, de Paolis	Il Barbiere di Siviglia
Fiorilla	Soprano		Callas	Il Turco in Italia
Fire Also Princess, also Le Rossignol	Soprano			L'Enfant et les Sortilèges
First Citizen See Erster Bürger				
Fisherfolk	Chorus			Peter Grimes
Fisherman	Tenor			Le Rossignol

THE CHARACTERS IN THE OPERAS

CHARACTER		ROLE	SINGER	OPERA
Fishermen	Chorus			*Les Pêcheurs de Perles, The Wreckers*
Flamand	Tenor	A musician	Gedda	*Capriccio*
Flaminio	Tenor	Castle guard		*L'Amore dei Tre Re*
Flavio	Tenor	A centurion	Franke	*Norma*
Fleance	Silent	Banquo's son, Macbeth's nemesis		*Macbeth*
Fléville	Baritone	Cavalier		*Andrea Chénier*
Flint, Mr.	Baritone	Sailing master		*Billy Budd*
Flora	Soprano		1st Olive Dyer	*The Turn of the Screw*
Flora Bervoix	Mezzo-soprano	Violetta's friend	1st Speranza; Evans	*La Traviata*
Flora, Madame *See* Baba				
Florence Pike	Contralto	Lady Billow's housekeeper		*Albert Herring*
Florestan	Tenor	A Spanish nobleman	1st Demmer; Davies, Niemann, Patzak, Reeves, Schott, Urlus, Völker	*Fidelio*
Florestein	Tenor	Count Arnheim's nephew		*The Bohemian Girl*
Floria Tosca *See* Tosca				
Floriana	Soprano	Music hall singer		*Zaza*
Flosshilde	Mezzo-soprano	A Rhinemaiden		*Das Ring des Nibelungen*
Flower Maidens, Choirs of Sopranos, Contraltos				*Parsifal*
Flower Maidens (Six) Sopranos				*Parsifal*
Flute Player	Silent			*Der Rosenkavalier*

CHARACTER	ROLE	SINGER	OPERA
Fluth, Frau Soprano	Mrs. Ford	Sembrich, Tietjens	*Die Lustigen Weiber von Windsor*
Fluth, Herr Baritone	Mr. Ford	Santley	*Die Lustigen Weiber von Windsor*
Followers of Count di Luna Chorus			*Il Trovatore*
Followers of Danae Chorus			*Die Liebe der Danae*
Followers of Don Carlos Chorus			*Ernani*
Followers of Manrico Chorus			*Il Trovatore*
Followers of Pollux Chorus			*Die Liebe der Danae*
Followers of Silva Chorus			*Ernani*
Foltz *See* Hans Folz			
Fool Bass			*Hugh the Drover*
Fool Tenor		de Paolis	*Wozzeck*
Fool *See also* Simpleton			
Footman		1st Nagy	*Vanessa*
Ford Baritone	A wealthy burgher	Cassell, Tibbett	*Falstaff*
Ford *See also* Fluth, Herr			
Ford, Mrs. *See* Fluth, Frau *See also* Alice Ford			
Foreign Woman Soprano			*The Consul*
Foreman Baritone	At the mill		*Její Pastorkyňa* (Jenufa)
Forest Bird *See* Waldvogel			
Forest Rangers (Two) Tenor, Bass			*Švanda Dudák*

CHARACTER	ROLE	SINGER	OPERA
Forewoman Mezzo-soprano			*Louise*
Former Wives (Three)			*Duke Bluebeard's Castle*
Fortune Teller Soprano			*Arabella*
Fouquier-Tinville Baritone	Attorney General		*Andrea Chénier*
Fra Diavolo Tenor	Bandit chieftain	1st Chollet; Bonci, Cox, Pertile, Santley, Schipa, Völker	*Fra Diavolo*
Frances, Countess of Essex Mezzo-soprano			*Gloriana*
Francesca da Rimini Soprano	Beloved by Paolo	1st Edvina; Alda, Caniglia, Carbone, Cigna, Raisa, dalla Rizza, Somigli	*Francesca da Rimini*
Francesco Tenor	Artisan for Cellini		*Benvenuto Cellini*
Francesco Bass		Bohnen	*Mona Lisa*
Françoise Contralto		Delna	*L'Attaque du Moulin*
Frank Baritone	Prison governor		*Die Fledermaus*
Frantz Tenor	Crespel's servant		*Les Contes d'Hoffmann*
Franz Bass			*Der Prozess*
Frasquita Soprano	A gypsy, friend of Carmen		*Carmen*
Frasquita Mezzo-soprano	Tio Lucas' wife	Cross, Forster-Lauterer, Lipton, Novotna	*Der Corregidor*
Frazier Tenor	Self-styled lawyer for Catfish Row		*Porgy and Bess*
Frédéric Baritone	An English officer		*Lakmé*
Frédéric Tenor/Contralto	Young nobleman	Scalchi, Trebelli (The role has been sung by contraltos since Trebelli first undertook it)	*Mignon*

CHARACTER	ROLE	SINGER	OPERA
Frederick of Telramund Baritone	Count of Brabant	1st Milde; Ancona, Bispham, Lassalle, Ludwig, Maurel	*Lohengrin*
Freia Soprano	Goddess of youth and beauty	1st Haupt; Borkh, Jurinac, Novotna, Shuard	*Das Ring des Nibelungen*
Freimann, Baroness Soprano	Count Eberbach's sister		*Der Wildschütz*
Fricka Mezzo-soprano	Goddess, Wotan's wife	1st Stehle; Branzell, Brema, Cahier, Fremstad, Homer, Klose, Langendorf, Larsen-Todsen, Ober, Schumann-Heink, Thebom, Thorborg, Wickham	*Das Rheingold*
Friend Baritone		1st Musy; Beuf	*Le Pauvre Matelot*
Friends Chorus			*Der Barbier von Bagdad, Don Quichotte, Lucia di Lammermoor, Madama Butterfly, Le Postillion de Longjumeau*
Friends of Esther Chorus			*Esther de Carpentra*
Friends of the Marquise Chorus			*La Figlia del Reggimento*
Fritz Kobus Tenor	A wealthy bachelor	D. Borgioli, Schipa, Tagliavini	*L'Amico Fritz*
Fritz Kothner Bass	Mastersinger and baker	Brownlee, Harrell, Scheidermantel	*Die Meistersinger*
Frogs Chorus			*L'Enfant et les Sortilèges*
Froh Tenor	Norse god	Darcy	*Das Ring des Nibelungen*
Front Line Officer Baritone			*Friedenstag*

THE CHARACTERS IN THE OPERAS

CHARACTER	ROLE	SINGER	OPERA
Frosch Speaker	Jailer		*Die Fledermaus*
Frost, King Bass	The winter		*Snyegurotchka*
Frugola, La Mezzo-soprano	Talpa's wife, 50	Claramae Turner	*Il Tabarro*
Furies Chorus			*Alceste*
Fyodor *See* Feodor			
Gabriel Bass	Employed by Dickson		*La Dame Blanche*
Gabriele Adorno Tenor	A patrician		*Simon Boccanegra*
Gabriel von Eisenstein Tenor		Kullmann	*Die Fledermaus*
Gaea Contralto	Daphne's mother		*Daphne*
Galitzky *See* Vladimir Jaroslavitch			
Gallanthus Baritone	Amaryllus's sister		*The Poisoned Kiss*
Gamblers Chorus			*Manen, Pique-Dame*
Gaoler *See* Jailer			
Garcias Soprano	Admirer of Dulcinée		*Don Quichotte*
Garsenda Soprano	Francesca's woman		*Francesca da Rimini*
Gaspar, Don Tenor	The King's minister		*La Favorita*
Gastone de Letorières Tenor		de Paolis	*La Traviata*
Gauls Chorus			*Norma*
Gaulthiers Walton, Lord Bass	A Puritan		*I Puritani*
Gaveston Bass			*La Dame Blanche*
Gay Brook Treble	Age 13; Bruce *in* Acts I *and* II		*Let's Make an Opera*

CHARACTER	ROLE	SINGER	OPERA
Gazello Bass			*Lucrezia Borgia*
Gedge, Mr. Baritone	Vicar		*Albert Herring*
Geishas Chorus			*Iris*
Gellner Baritone	In love with Wally		*La Wally*
Generals Chorus			*Háry János*
Geneviève Contralto	Mother of Pelléas	1st Gerville-Reache; Gay	*Pelléas et Mélisande*
Genii, Three Sopranos, Mezzo-soprano			*Die Zauberflöte*
Gennaro Tenor	Blacksmith	Bassi, Jagel, Mario, Martinelli, Merli	*I Gioielli della Madonna*
Gennaro Tenor	Nobleman of the Venetian Republic	Campanini	*Lucrezia Borgia*
Genoveva Soprano		Malten	*Genoveva*
Genoveva, Suor Soprano	A nun		*Suor Angelica*
Gentlemen Chorus			*Manon*
Gentlewoman *See* Lady in waiting			
Georg Danton Baritone	French revolutionary	1st Schöffler	*Dantons Tod*
George Walton, Sir Bass	Puritan, brother of Gaulthier	1st Lablache; Rossi-Lemeni	*I Puritani*
Georges Brown Tenor	English officer	1st Ponchard; Naval	*La Dame Blanche*
Gérald Tenor	English officer	1st Talazac; Jagel, Martinelli, McCormack, Thill	*Lakmé*
Gerard *See* Charles Gerard			
Gerhilde Soprano	A valkyr	1st Haupt; Brandt, Shuard, Votipka	*Die Walküre*

CHARACTER	ROLE	SINGER	OPERA
Germont *See* Giorgio Germont *See also* Alfredo Germont (Generally the sur- name serves to designate Giorgio Germont)			
Geronimo Bass	Carolina's father	Lablache	*Il Matrimonio Segreto*
Geronte di Ravoir Bass	Treasurer General	Didur	*Manon Lescaut*
Gertrude Soprano	Mother of Hansel and Gretel		*Hänsel und Gretel*
Gertrude Contralto			*Louise*
Gertrude Mezzo-soprano	Juliette's nurse		*Roméo et Juliette*
Gertrude S. Mezzo-soprano			*The Mother of Us All*
Geschwitz, Gräfin Mezzo-soprano	One of Lulu's later lovers		*Lulu*
Gessler Bass	Tyrannical governor over Switzerland		*Guillaume Tell*
Gherardino Contralto	Gherardo's son, 7		*Gianni Schicchi*
Gherardo Tenor	Dead Buoso's nephew, 40	de Paolis	*Gianni Schicchi*
Ghost of Max's Mother, The			*Der Freischütz*
Ghost of Nino Bass	Semiramide's husband		*Semiramide*
Ghost *See also* Cassandre's Ghost *See also* Chorèbe's Ghost *See also* Commendatore *See also* Quint's Ghost			

THE CHARACTERS IN THE OPERAS

CHARACTER	ROLE	SINGER	OPERA
Ghosts Chorus			*Le Rossignol*
Ghosts, Invisible Chorus			*Les Troyens*
Giacomo Bass	Bandit		*Fra Diavolo*
Gianetta Soprano	Peasant girl		*L'Elisir d'Amore*
Gianni Schicchi Baritone	A sly trickster, age 50	1st de Luca; S. Austin, Baccaloni, Badini, Corena, Galeffi, Stabile, Tajo	*Gianni Schicchi*
Giarno Bass	A gypsy		*Mignon*
Gil, Count Baritone	Susanna's husband, 30	Biasini, Noble, Parvis, Sammarco, Scotti	*Il Segreto di Susanna*
Gilda Soprano	Rigoletto's daughter	1st Brambilla; Ackté, Adams, Albani, Alda, Callas, Dobbs, Farrar, Galli-Curci, Gerster, Gueden, Hempel, Ivogün, Kellogg, Krauss, Kurz, Lipovska, Lyne, Melba, dal Monte, Munsel, Nordica, Norena, Paghliughi, Patti, Peters, Pons, Rysanek, Sayao, Schwarzkopf, Sembrich, Talley, Luisa Tetrazzini, Vere	*Rigoletto*
Gingerbread Woman Soprano			*A Village Romeo and Juliet*
Gioconda, La Soprano	The ballad singer	1st Mariani; Arangi-Lombardi, Bampton, Callas, Cerquetti, Cigna, Destinn, Dow, Durand, Litvinne, Matzenauer, Milanov, Christine Nilsson, Nordica, Ponselle, Roman	*La Gioconda*

373

CHARACTER	ROLE	SINGER	OPERA
Giorgetta Soprano	Michele's wife, 25, in love with Luigi	1st Muzio; Albanese, Carbone, Kennard, Labia, Lewis, Shuard	*Il Tabarro*
Giorgio *See* George Walton, Sir			
Giorgio Germont Baritone	Alfredo's father	1st Vanesi; Amato, Bonelli, Cassell, Gobbi, Renaud, Scotti, Thomas, Tibbett, Weede	*Il Traviata*
Giovanna Soprano	Elvira's servant		*Ernani*
Giovanna Mezzo-soprano	Gilda's duenna	Votipka	*Rigoletto*
Giovanni, Don Baritone	A licentious nobleman	1st Bassi; Beck, Braham, Carey, Cassell, Faure, Forsell, Forti, G. Garcia M., Garcia I, Lablache, Lassalle, London, Maurel, Pinza, Renaud, Jean de Reszke, Ronconi, Rossi-Lemeni, Sammarco, Scotti, Siepi, Stabile	*Don Giovanni*
Giovanni da Prodica Bass	Sicilian revolutionary	Christoff	*I Vespri Siciliani*
Giovanni lo Sciancato Baritone	Lame son of Malatesta	1st Cigada; Amato, Biasini, Danise, Maugeri, Ronconi, Stabile	*Francesca da Rimini*
Giovanni Morone Baritone	Papal legate		*Palestrina*
Giove Tenor	Jove, chief of the gods		*Il Ritorno d'Ulisse in Patria*
Girl with the Hunch-Back Soprano			*Der Prozess*

CHARACTER	ROLE	SINGER	OPERA
Girls Chorus			*L'Arlesiana, Die Meistersinger*
Girls from Sandomir Chorus			*Boris Godunov*
Giulia Soprano		Lind	*La Vestale*
Giulietta Soprano	A Capulet in love with Romeo	1st Grisi	*I Capuletti ed I Montecchi*
Giulietta Soprano	Courtesan	1st Isaac; Elias, Fremstad, Hempel, Jurinac, Seefried, Shuard, Steber, Teyte	*Les Contes d'Hoffmann*
Giuseppe Silent			*Palestrina*
Giuseppe Tenor	Violetta's servant		*La Traviata*
Giuseppe Hagenbach *See* Hagenbach			
Glasha Mezzo-soprano	Servant		*Katya Kabanova*
Gleaton, Mrs. Soprano			*Susanna*
Gloster Heming Mezzo-soprano			*The Mother of Us All*
Gluttons Chorus			*The Love for Three Oranges*
Goatherds (Two) Soprano, Contralto			*Dinorah*
Gob	Evil assistant of Dipsacus		*The Poisoned Kiss*
Gobin Tenor	Perichaud's friend		*La Rondine*
Gobineau, Mr. Baritone	Baba's client		*The Medium*
Gobineau, Mrs. Soprano	Baba's client		*The Medium*
Gobrias Tenor	Follower of Simon Mago		*Nerone*
Godfrey, Duke Silent	Elsa's brother		*Lohengrin*

CHARACTER	ROLE	SINGER	OPERA
Godunov *See* Boris Godunov			
Golaud Baritone	Arkel's grandson, half-brother to Pelléas	1st Dufranne; Amato, Singher, London	*Pelléas et Mélisande*
Gonsalve Tenor	Poet and Concepcion's lover	Kelley, Lloyd	*L'Heure Espagnole*
Good, Choir of Chorus			*The Poisoned Kiss*
Gorislava Soprano	Ratmir's slave		*Russlan and Ludmilla*
Goro Tenor	Marriage broker	Franke, de Paolis	*Madama Butterfly*
Governess Mezzo-soprano			*Pique-Dame*
Government Bass **Director**			*Der Prozess*
Graf von Helfenstein Silent			*Mathis der Maler*
Gräfin von Helfenstein Contralto			*Mathis der Maler*
Grand Inquisitor Bass		Hines	*L'Africaine*
Grand Inquisitor Bass			*Don Carlos*
Grandmother Mezzo-soprano	Salud's grandmother		*La Vida Breve*
Grandmother **Buryja** Contralto	Mill owner		*Její Pastorkyňa* (*Jenufa*)
Gravis Bass	Spirit voice		*Doktor Faustus*
Grazia Dancer			*I Gioielli della Madonna*
Grech Bass	Policeman		*Fedora*
Greek Captain Bass			*Les Troyens*
Greek Chorus Chorus			*Mefistofele*

CHARACTER	ROLE	SINGER	OPERA
Greek Soldiers Chorus			*Les Troyens*
Greeks Chorus			*Iphigénie en Aulide, Iphigénie en Tauride*
Gregory Baritone	Retainer to Capulet		*Roméo et Juliette*
Gregory *See also* Grigorij			
Gremin, Prince Bass	An old general	Didur, Tozzi	*Eugene Onegin*
Grenadiers Chorus			*La Figlia del Reggimento*
Grenvil, Doctor Bass		Santley	*La Traviata*
Gretchen Soprano	Baculus' fiancée	Ternina	*Der Wildschütz*
Gretel Soprano	Hänsel's sister	Gruhn, Mario	*Hänsel und Gretel*
Grieux, Chevalier des Tenor	In love with Manon	1st Talazac; Ansseau, Bentonelli, Bjoerling, Caruso, Clément, Crooks, van Dyke, Gigli, Maas, Jean de Reszke, Schipa, Tagliavini	*Manon*
Grieux, Count des Bass	Father of the Chevalier	Rothier	*Manon*
Grieux, Chevalier des Tenor	In love with Manon Lescaut	Bevel, Bjoerling, Caruso, Gigli, del Monaco, Pertile, Tucker	*Manon Lescaut*
Grigorij Tenor	The false Dimitri, pretender to the throne of Russia	1st Komissarzhevsky; Althouse, Baum, Sullivan	*Boris Godunov*
Grimes *See* Peter Grimes			
Grimgerde Soprano	A valkyr	Elias	*Die Walküre*
Gritzko Tenor	In love with Parassia	McCormack	*The Fair at Sorochintsky*

CHARACTER		ROLE	SINGER	OPERA
Groom				*Arabella*
From Chorus				
Grose, Mrs.			1st Cross	*The Turn of the*
Soprano				*Screw*
Grubach, Frau			Evans	*Der Prozess*
Mezzo-soprano				
Gruff				
English version of				
the name Simon *in*				
I Quattro Rusteghi				
Grüsser, Ulrich				
See Ulrich Grüsser				
Guard	Tenor	of the frontier		*Hubička*
Guard				
See Boyar Guard				
Guardiano, Padre		Franciscan superior	Hines, Rossi-	*La Forza del*
Bass			Lemeni, Siepi	*Destino*
Guards	Chorus			*Un Ballo in Maschera,*
				Boris Godunov, Die
				Entführung aus dem
				Serail, Esther de
				Carpentras, La Favo-
				rita, Fête Galante, La
				Gioconda, Guillaume
				Tell, The Love for
				Three Oranges,
				Manon, Oberon,
				Semiramide
Gubetta	Bass	Serving Lucrezia		*Lucrezia Borgia*
Guccio	Bass	Painter, witness for		*Gianni Schicchi*
		the will		
Guests	Chorus			*Arabella, Ariadne auf*
				Naxos, Fête Galante,
				Eugene Onegin,
				Pique-Dame, La
				Traviata
Guglielmo	Bass	Fiordiligi's fiancé	1st Bussani;	*Così fan Tutte*
			Austin, Didur,	
			Guarrera	

THE CHARACTERS IN THE OPERAS

CHARACTER	ROLE	SINGER	OPERA
Guide Silent			*Carmen*
Guido di Monforte Baritone	Governor of occu-pied Sicily	Schlusnus	*I Vespri Siciliani*
Guidon, Prince Tenor			*Le Coq d'Or*
Guildsmen Chorus			*Die Meistersinger*
Guillaume Tell Baritone	Swiss patriot and hero	Beck, Braham, Faure, Lassalle, Maurel, Rossi-Lemeni	*Guillaume Tell* ·
Guillot de Morfon-taine Tenor	An old roué		*Manon*
Gunther Baritone	Hagen's half-brother	Austin, Gura	*Götterdämmerung*
Gurnemanz Bass	Knight of the Grail	1st Scaria and Siehr; Allin, Andresen, Bohnen, Braun, Delmas, Grengg, Griswold, Hines, Kipnis, F. Kraus, Manowarda, Mayr, Weber	*Parsifal*
Gustave III *See* Riccardo			
Gutrune Soprano	Gunther's sister	Flagstad, Fornia-Labey, White	*Götterdämmerung*
Gypsies Chorus			*Carmen, The Fair at Sorochintsky, Mari-tana, Mignon, Il Trovatore*
Gypsy Bass			*The Fair at Sorochintsky*
Gypsy *See also* Azucena *See also* Carmen *See also* Giarno *See also* Preziosilla			
Gzak Bass	Polovtsian Khan (A Tartar)		*Prince Igor*

THE CHARACTERS IN THE OPERAS

CHARACTER		ROLE	SINGER	OPERA
Hadassa Mezzo-soprano		Esther		*Esther de Carpentras*
Hadji	Tenor	Nilakantha's servant		*Lakmé*
Hagen	Bass	Alberich's descendant, Siegfried's enemy	1st Siehr; Griswold, Hofmann, F. Kraus, Mayr, Edouard de Reszke	*Götterdämmerung*
Hagenbach	Tenor	Of Sölden	Renato Gigli, R. Martin, Merli, Voyer	*La Wally*
Hairdresser	Silent			*Der Rosenkavalier*
Haly	Bass	The Bey's captain of corsairs		*L'Italiana in Algeri*
Hamlet	Baritone	Danish prince	1st Faure; Beck, Maurel, Renaud	*Hamlet*
Hämon	Tenor			*Antigonae* (Orff)
Handmaiden				*L'Amore dei Tre Re*
Handsome	Baritone	A miner		*La Fanciulla del West*
Hanezò	Bass	Fritz's friend		*L'Amico Fritz*
Hangmen (Two) Tenors				*Dantons Tod*
Hans Foltz	Bass	Coppersmith and Mastersinger	Lorenzo Alvary	*Die Meistersinger*
Hans Heiling Baritone			Beck, Scheidermantel	*Hans Heiling*
Hans Sachs	Bass	Mastersinger and cobbler	1st Betz; Ancona, Bender, Berglund, Bockelmann, Delmas, Edelman, Fischer, Griswold, Gura, Hotter, Lassalle, Ludwig, Nissen, Prohaska, Reichmann, Edouard de Reszke, van Rooy, Rode, Scaria, Scheidermantel, Schöffler, Schorr, Soomer, Weil, Whitehill	*Die Meistersinger*

CHARACTER	ROLE	SINGER	OPERA
Hans Schwarz Bass	Mastersinger and stocking weaver		*Die Meistersinger*
Hänsel Mezzo-soprano	Gretel's brother	Bible, Welitsch	*Hänsel und Gretel*
Happy Baritone	A miner		*La Fanciulla del West*
Hardstone			English version for the name Maurizio in *I Quattro Rusteghi*
Harlequin Baritone			*Ariadne auf Naxos*
Harlequin Tenor			*Fête Galante*
Harlequin See also Arlecchino See also Beppe			
Haroun Tenor	A prince	1st Duchesne	*Djamileh*
Haroun al Rashid Speaker	Calif of Bagdad		*Oberon*
Harriet Durham, Lady Soprano	Maid of honour to the Queen, disguised as "Martha"	1st Zerr; Alda, Favero, Mason, Sembrich	*Martha*
Harry Treble	A child		*Albert Herring*
Harry Tenor	A miner		*La Fanciulla del West*
Harry Paddington From Chorus	Gentleman of the road		*The Beggar's Opera*
Harvester Tenor			*Dinorah*
Harvey Bass	Lawrence's brother-in-law		*The Wreckers*
Háry János Baritone	A great liar		*Háry János*
Hate-Good, Lord Bass			*Pilgrim's Progress*
Hayes, Mrs. Soprano			*Susannah*
Heavenly Beings (Two) Soprano, Contralto			*Pilgrim's Progress*

CHARACTER	ROLE	SINGER	OPERA
Hebrew *See* Old Hebrew			
Hebrews Chorus			*Nabucco, Samson et Dalila*
Hector's Ghost Bass			*Les Troyens*
Hécube Mezzo-soprano	Priam's wife		*Les Troyens*
Hedwige Soprano	Tell's wife	Brandt	*Guillaume Tell*
Heinrich der Schreiber Tenor	Knight and Minnesinger		*Tannhäuser*
Helen of Troy Pantomime			*Faust*
Helen of Troy *See* Elena			
Helena Soprano	Wife of Menelaus	1st Rethberg; Jeritza, Müller, Ursuleac	*Die Aegyptische Helena*
Hélène Soprano		1st Melba	*Hélène* (Saint Saëns)
Helenus Tenor	Priam's son		*Les Troyens*
Helmsman Baritone			*Tristan und Isolde*
Helmsman *See also* Steersman			
Helmwige Soprano	A valkyr	Amara, Faull	*Die Walküre*
Henrici	Saxon officer		*Der Bettelstudent*
Henrietta Soprano	Widow of Charles the First of France		*I Puritani*
Henry Ashton *See* Enrico			
Henrietta M Soprano			*The Mother of Us All*
Henry B Tenor			*The Mother of Us All*
Henry Cuffe Baritone	Follower of Essex		*Gloriana*

CHARACTER		ROLE	SINGER	OPERA
Henry Morosus Blunt	Tenor	Actor, nephew to Sir Morosus		*Die Schweigsame Frau*
Henry the Fowler	Bass	King of Germany	Delmas, Fischer, Griswold, Hinckley, Hotter, Plançon, Edouard de Reszke	*Lohengrin*
Herald	Baritone			*Alceste*
Herald	Tenor			*Don Carlos*
Herald	Bass			*The Love for Three Oranges*
Herald	Bass			*Otello*
Herald	Baritone			*Pilgrim's Progress*
Herald *See* King's Herald				
Herault de Sechelles	Tenor		1st P. Klein	*Dantons Tod*
Hercules	Baritone			*Alceste*
Herman Altan	Baritone			*The Mother of Us All*
Hermann	Baritone	Student		*Les Contes d'Hoffman*
Herrmann	Baritone		1st Alsen	*Dantons Tod*
Hermann	Tenor	Gambler, in love with Lisa	1st Figner; Slezak, Zenatello	*Pique-Dame*
Hermann	Bass	Landgrave of Thuringia	1st Dettmer; Griswold, Hines, Journet, List, Plançon	*Tannhäuser*
Hermann Ortel	Bass	Mastersinger and soap boiler		*Die Meistersinger*
Hermione	Soprano	Child of Helena and Melenaus		*Die Aegyptische Helena*
Hermit	Bass		Foli	*Der Freischütz*
Hermit *See* Pimen				
Hero	Baritone	Leonato's daughter in love with Claudio		*Béatrice et Bénédict*

CHARACTER	ROLE	SINGER	OPERA
Herod Antipas Tenor	Governor of Judea	1st Burrian; Borgatti, Dalmorès, Kirchoff, Krauss, Lorenz, Maison, Patzak, Pölzer	*Salome*
Herodias Mezzo-soprano	Herod's wife	1st Chavanne; Olszewska, Shacklock, Thorborg	*Salome*
Herring, Mrs. Mezzo-soprano	Albert's mother		*Albert Herring*
Hester Prynne Soprano		1st Gadski	*The Scarlet Letter* (Damrosch)
Hester Prynne Soprano		1st Giannini	*The Scarlet Letter* (Giannini)
Hever Baritone	A spy		*Debora e Jaele*
High Priest Baritone		1st Laschi; Franci, Schöffler, Singher, Warren	*Alceste*
High Priest Bass			*Die Königin von Saba*
High Priest *See also* Ramfis			
High Priest of Babylon Bass			*Nabucco*
High Priest of Brahma Baritone			*L'Africaine*
High Priest of Dagon Baritone		Bouhy, Lassalle, Milde	*Samson et Dalila*
High Priest of Neptune Tenor			*Idomeneo*
Highbrows Chorus			*The Love for Three Oranges*
Hindu Merchant Tenor			*Sadko*
Hob	Evil servant of Dipsacus		*The Poisoned Kiss*
Hobson Bass	A carrier	1st Vaughan	*Peter Grimes*

THE CHARACTERS IN THE OPERAS

CHARACTER	ROLE	SINGER	OPERA
Hoël Baritone	Goatherd	Faure, de Luca, Maurel, Santley	*Dinorah*
Hoffmann Tenor	Poet, lover of Antonia, Giulietta, Olympia and Stella	Gedda	*Les Contes d'Hoffmann*
Holsteiner Bass	Commander of the besiegers		*Friedenstag*
Homonay *See* Peter Homonay			
Horace Adams, Reverend Tenor		1st Culbert	*Peter Grimes*
Horace Tabor Baritone		Cassell	*The Ballad of Baby Doe*
Horloge Comptoise, L' Baritone	The grandfather clock		*L'Enfant et les Sortilèges*
Horn, Count *See* Tomaso			
Horn-Player, The Poor Tenor			*A Village Romeo and Juliet*
Hortensio Bass	Steward of the Marquise	Lorenzo Alvary	*La Figlia del Reggimento*
Hostess *See* Innkeeper			
Housekeeper Contralto		Kobart	*Die Schweigsame Frau*
Housewife Mezzo-soprano			*Gloriana*
Hugh Crome Treble	Age 8, Ralph *in Acts I and II*		*Let's Make an Opera*
Hugh the Drover Tenor		1st Davies	*Hugh the Drover*
Huguenot Ladies and Gentlemen Chorus			*Les Huguenots*
Hunchback Tenor	Barak's brother		*Die Frau ohne Schatten*
Hunchbacked Bass Fiddler Bass			*A Village Romeo and Juliet*

385

THE CHARACTERS IN THE OPERAS

CHARACTER		ROLE	SINGER	OPERA
Hunding	Bass	Siegmund's enemy	1st Niering; Griswold, Hinckley, Hotter, Koegel, Radford, Edouard de Reszke	*Die Walküre*
Hungarian Sentry Speaker				*Háry János*
Hunters	Chorus			*Doktor Faustus, Der Fliegende Holländer, Guillaume Tell, Lucia di Lammermoor Martha, Les Troyens*
Huntresses	Chorus			*Martha*
Huntsmen	Bass			*Dinorah, Mefistofele, Pskovityanka, Der Wildschütz*
Huon de Bordeaux, Sir	Tenor		1st Braham; Althouse, Kullmann, Reeves	*Oberon*
Hussars (Two) Speakers				*Háry János*
Hylas	Tenor	Trojan sailor		*Les Troyens*
Iago	Baritone	Otello's underling	Faure	*Otello* (Rossini)
Iago	Baritone	Otello's ensign	1st Maurel; Bechi, Biasini, Bispham, Formichi, Galassi, Inghilleri, Rimini, Sammarco, Scotti, Stabile, Tibbett	*Otello*
Idamante	Soprano	Idomeneo's son	1st del Prato; Simoneau	*Idomeneo*
Idiot *See* Simpleton *See also* Fool				
Idomeneo	Tenor	King of Crete	1st Anton Raaf; Lewis	*Idomeneo*
Idreno	Tenor	Indian prince		*Semiramide*
Ighino	Soprano	Palestrina's son	1st Ivogün; Jurinac	*Palestrina*

CHARACTER	ROLE	SINGER	OPERA
Igor Sviatoslavitch Baritone	Prince Igor	Burke	*Prince Igor*
Ilia Soprano	Trojan princess	1st Dorothea Wendling; Gueden, Jurinac, Schumann	*Idomeneo*
Ilka Soprano	Háry's fiancée		*Háry János*
Imperial Commissioner Bass			*Madama Butterfly*
Incredibile Tenor	A Spy		*Andrea Chénier*
Indiana Elliott Mezzo-soprano			*The Mother of Us All*
Indians Chorus	East Indians		*Lakmé*
Indians Chorus			*L'Africaine*
Inez Soprano	Don Diego's daughter	Hauk, Murska, Luisa Tetrazzini	*L'Africaine*
Inez Soprano	Leonora's confidante	Albanese	*La Favorita*
Inez Soprano	Leonora's confidante	1st Quadri; Rappold, Vanni, Votipka	*Il Trovatore*
Infanta Soprano		Vere	*Le Cid*
Innkeeper Mezzo-soprano		Lipton	*Boris Godunov*
Innkeeper Bass			*Hugh the Drover*
Innkeeper From Chorus			*Manon*
Innkeeper Bass			*Manon Lescaut*
Innkeeper Tenor			*Der Rosenkavalier*
Innkeeper See also Lillas Pastia			
Innocente, L' Mezzo-soprano	Rosa's retarded youngest son		*L'Arlesiana*
Inquisitor See Grand Inquisitor			

CHARACTER	ROLE	SINGER	OPERA
Inquisitors Chorus			*L'Africaine*
Inigo Gomez, Don Bass	Banker		*L'Heure Espagnole*
Intendant Tenor			*Linda di Chamounix*
Interpreter Tenor			*Pilgrim's Progress*
Iolanthe Soprano		1st Fremstad	*Der Wald*
Iopas Tenor	Poet of Carthage		*Les Troyens*
Iphigénie Soprano	Daughter of Agamemnon	1st Sophie Arnould; Brouwenstijn, Levasseur, Schröder-Devrient, Tentoni	*Iphigénie en Aulide*
Iphigénie Soprano	Priestess of Diana	1st Levasseur; Bernasconi, Caniglia, Kurt, Malten, Milder, Müller, Neway, Rappold, Tietjens, Viardot-Garcia	*Iphigénie en Tauride*
Irene Soprano	Rienzi's sister	1st Schröder-Devrient; Brandt, Lilli Lehmann, Moody, Osborn, Seidl-Krauss	*Rienzi*
Iris Soprano		1st Darclée; Bori, Eames, Pampanini, Rethberg, Sheridan	*Iris*
Irma Soprano	Louise's fellow worker	Cavan	*Louise*
Iro Tenor	Jester for the suitors		*Il Ritorno d'Ulisse in Patria*
Isabel Wentworth Mezzo-soprano			*The Mother of Us All*
Isabella Soprano	Queen of Spain		*Christophe Colomb*
Isabella Soprano	Princess of Sicily	Juch, Peschka-Leutner, Rogers, Viardot-Garcia	*Robert le Diable*
Isabelle Contralto	Lindoro's beloved	Simionato, Sontag	*L'Italiana in Algeri*

THE CHARACTERS IN THE OPERAS

THE CHARACTERS IN THE OPERAS

CHARACTER		ROLE	SINGER	OPERA
Isabelle	Soprano		Carvalho	*Le Pré aux Clercs*
Isèpo	Tenor	Public scribe	de Paolis	*La Gioconda*
Ismaele	Tenor	Nephew of the king of Jerusalem		*Nabucco*
Ismene		Antigone's sister		*Antigonae* (Orff)
	Mezzo-soprano			
Isolde	Soprano	Irish princess, engaged to King Marke	1st Malvina Schnorr von Carolsfield; Albani, Cobelli, Fisher, Flagstad, Fremstad, Fuchs, Gadski, Grob-Prandl, Harshaw, Kappel, Kurt, Larsen-Todsen, Leffler-Burckhard, Lilli Lehman, Leider, Litvinne, Lubin, Malten, Marchesi, Mildenburg, Mödl, Moody, Morena, Nordica, Osborn, Seidl-Krauss, Sucher, Ternina, Thoma, Traubel, Varnay, Wittich	*Tristan und Isolde*
Isotta	Soprano	An actress	Moody	*Die Schweigsame Frau*
Italian Singer (Soprano)	Soprano			*Capriccio*
Italian Singer (Tenor)	Tenor			*Capriccio*
Ivan Khovansky, Prince	Bass	Leader of the Archers, enemy of the Tsar		*Khovantschina*
Ivan Susanin	Bass	Peasant	1st Petrov; Prohaska, Roswaenge	*Ivan Susanin*
Ivan Vassilievitch, Tsar	Bass	Ivan the Terrible	Chaliapin	*Pskovityanka*

CHARACTER	ROLE	SINGER	OPERA
Ivanov *See* Peter Ivanov			
Jack Mezzo-soprano	Tallan's son, 15		*The Wreckers*
Jacquino Tenor	Rocco's assistant		*Fidelio*
Jacopo Fiesco Bass	Patrician		*Simon Boccanegra*
Jaele Soprano	Hever's wife, Sisera's lover	1st Tess; Spani	*Debora e Jaele*
Jafia Tenor			*Debora e Jaele*
Jago Bass	Silva's squire		*Ernani*
Jahel Baritone			*Le Roi d'Ys*
Jailer Bass			*Die Kluge*
Jailer Bass			*Tosca*
Jailer From Chorus			*Il Trovatore*
Jake Baritone	Fisherman	1st Matthews	*Porgy and Bess*
Jake Wallace Baritone	Minstrel		*La Fanciulla del West*
Jan Janitzky Tenor	Simon's fellow prisoner		*Der Bettelstudent*
Jane, Aunt Contralto	Sister of the constable		*Hugh the Drover*
Janissaries Chorus			*Die Entführung aus dem Serail*
Jankel	Mandryka's servant		*Arabella*
Jano Soprano	Shepherd boy		*Její Pastorkyňa* (Jenufa)
Japanese Envoy I Tenor			*Le Rossignol*
Japanese Envoy II Baritone			*Le Rossignol*
Japanese Envoy III Tenor			*Le Rossignol*
Jaroslavna Soprano	Prince Igor's wife	Brouwenstijn	*Prince Igor*
Javotte Soprano	An Actress		*Manon*
Jean Tenor or Soprano	A tumbler	1st Maréchal; Garden	*Le Jongleur de Notre Dame*

CHARACTER	ROLE	SINGER	OPERA
Jean, Friar Bass			*Roméo et Juliette*
Jemmy Soprano	Tell's son		*Guillaume Tell*
Jemmy Twitcher From Chorus	Gentleman of the road		*The Beggar's Opera*
Jenik Tenor	Micha's son by his first wife	Davies, Kullmann, Pears	*Prodana Nevešta*
Jenny Soprano	Dickson's wife		*La Dame Blanche*
Jenny Diver From Chorus	A lady of the town		*The Beggar's Opera*
Jenny Reefer Soprano			*The Mother of Us All*
Jenufa Soprano	Kostelnika's foster daughter	1st Kabelacova; Brouwenstijn, Caleva, Goltz, Jeritza, Lemnitz, Müller, Welitsch	*Její Pastorkyňa* (Jenufa)
Jessel, Miss Mezzo-soprano			*The Turn of the Screw*
Jesser Baritone			*Debora e Jaele*
Jester Bass			*Francesca da Rimini*
Jester Dancer			*Pilgrim's Progress*
Jesuit See Lowitski See also Rangoni See also Tschernjakovsky			
Jesuits Silent			*Palestrina*
Jewish Doctor See Médicin juif, Un			
Jews (Five) Four Tenors, Bass			*Salome*
Jews Chorus			*Debora e Jaele, The Fair at Sorochintsky, La Juive*
Jews See also Disguised Jews			

CHARACTER		ROLE	SINGER	OPERA
Jim	Baritone	Cotton picker		*Porgy and Bess*
Jitka	Soprano			*Dalibor*
Jo the Loiterer	Tenor			*The Mother of Us All*
Jocasta	Mezzo-soprano	Wife of Oedipus, widow of Laius	Bouvier, Danco, Mödl, Zareska	*Oedipus Rex*
Joe	Tenor	A miner		*La Fanciulla del West*
Johann	Bass	Le Bailli's friend		*Werther*
Johannes Kepler	Baritone	Astronomer, also The Earth		*Die Harmonie der Welt*
John	Baritone			*Das Heimchen am Herd*
John	Silent	Peter's apprentice		*Peter Grimes*
John Adams	Tenor			*The Mother of Us All*
John Bunyan	Bass Baritone	Poet		*Pilgrim's Progress*
John Crome	Treble	Age 15. *Also called* Peter *in Acts I and II*		*Let's Make an Opera*
John of Aragon *See* Ernani				
John of Leyden	Tenor	The Prophet	1st Roger; Alvarez, Caruso, Martinelli, Niemann, Jean de Reszke	*Le Prophète*
John Sorel	Baritone	Member of the underground		*The Consul*
John the Baptist *See* Jokanaan				
John the Butcher	Bass Baritone	Mary's fiancé		*Hugh the Drover*
Johnson, Dick	Tenor	Ramerrez, the bandit	1st Caruso; Lauri-Volpi, Martinelli, Merli, del Monaco	*La Fanciulla del Wes*
Jokanaan	Baritone	John the Baptist, captive	1st Perron; Berger, Berglund, Cassell, Dalmorès, Hotter, Prohaska, van Rooy, Schöffler, Schorr, Whitehill	*Salome*

CHARACTER		ROLE	SINGER	OPERA
Jokers	Chorus			*The Love for Three Oranges*
Jonas	Tenor	Anabaptist		*Le Prophète*
José Castro	Bass	Bandit		*La Fanciulla del West*
José de Santarem, Don	Baritone	Courtier		*Maritana*
José, Don	Tenor	Corporal in the guard	1st Lherie; Alvarez, Max Alvary, Ansseau, Baum, Campanini, Caruso, Clément, Dalmorès, Ferrari-Fontana, Giraldoni, Hamlin, Lestellier, Maison, Martinelli, del Monaco, Muratore, Poleri, Jean de Reszke, Saléza, Sullivan, Thill, Tucker, Vinay	*Carmen*
Josef K	Tenor	The defendant		*Der Prozess*
Monsieur Jourdain		Owner of the house		*Ariadne auf Naxos*
Journeymen	Chorus			*Die Meistersinger*
Jouvenot, Mlle.	Soprano	of the Comédie Française		*Adriana Lecouvreur*
Jove See Giove				
Juan	Tenor	Admirer of Dulcinée		*Don Quichotte*
Juan Lopez	Bass	The Mayor		*Der Corregidor*
Judas Iscariot	Baritone			*Pilgrim's Progress*
Judge	From Chorus			*Un Ballo in Maschera*
Judge	Tenor			*Švanda Dudak*
Judge				*Tosca*
Judge, Examiner	Baritone			*Der Prozess*

CHARACTER		ROLE	SINGER	OPERA
Judges	Chorus			*Pskovityanka*
Judith		Bluebeard's last wife		*Duke Bluebeard's*
	Mezzo-soprano			*Castle*
Juggler	Silent			*Hugh the Drover*
Juggler				
See Jean				
Julie		Danton's wife	1st G. Thury	*Dantons Tod*
	Mezzo-soprano			
Julie	Soprano		Falcon	*La Vestale*
Julien	Tenor	Artist in love with	1st Maréchal;	*Louise*
		Louise	Ansseau, Dalmorès,	
			Maison, Pertile,	
			Slezak, Trantoul,	
			Ziliani	
Juliet				
See Juliette				
See also Giulietta				
Juliet	Soprano	Age 14. *Called* Anne		*Let's Make an Opera*
		Dougall *in Acts I*		
		and II		
Juliette	Soprano	Capulet's daughter	1st Carvalho;	*Roméo et Juliette*
			Ackté, Adams, Alda,	
			Bori, Eames, Farrar,	
			Galli-Curci, Hauk,	
			Lipovska, Lussan,	
			Malibran, Mason,	
			Melba, Munsel,	
			Patti, Perli, Saville,	
			Sayao, Schröder-	
			Devrient	
Junius	Baritone	Roman General		*The Rape of Lucretia*
Junkman	Bass			*Louise*
Junon		Juno, wife of		*Orphée aux Enfers*
	Mezzo-soprano	Jupiter		
Jupiter	Baritone	Chief of the gods	1st Hotter; Poell,	*Die Liebe der Danae*
			Schöffler	
Jupiter	Baritone	King of gods		*Orphée aux Enfers*
Jupiter	Tenor	Also Wallenstein		*Die Harmonie der*
				Welt

CHARACTER	ROLE	SINGER	OPERA
Jupiter *See also* Giove			
Jurist Bass			*Doktor Faustus*
Justizrat Baritone	Storch's friend		*Intermezzo*
Kabanicha *See* Marfa Kabanova			
Kaiser Franz of **Austria** Speaker			*Háry János*
Kaiser *See* Rudolf Kaiser *See also* Ferdinand Kaiser			
Kalman Zsupan Baritone	Pig farmer		*Zigeunerbaron*
Kammersänger Bass	Storch's friend		*Intermezzo*
Karnac Baritone	Enemy general	Renaud	*Le Roi d'Ys*
Karolka Mezzo-soprano	The mayor's daughter		*Její Pastorkyňa* (Jenufa)
Kate Pinkerton Mezzo-soprano	Pinkerton's American wife		*Madama Butterfly*
Katharina Contralto	Kepler's mother, also the Moon		*Die Harmonie der* *Welt*
Katherine Contralto		1st Gerville-Réache	*Le Juif Polonais*
Kathinka Soprano	Marenka's mother		*Prodaná Nevěsta*
Katya (Katerina) **Kabanova** Soprano	Tichon's wife	1st Vesela; Pauly, Shuard	*Katya Kabanova*
Kecal Bass	Marriage broker		*Prodaná Nevěsta*
Keeper of the Mad- **house** Bass		1st Emanuel Menkes	*The Rake's Progress*
Kepler, Johannes *See* Johannes Kepler			
Khivria Mezzo-soprano	Tcherevik's wife		*The Fair at* *Sorochintsky*

CHARACTER		ROLE	SINGER	OPERA
Khrushchev	Tenor	Boyard		*Boris Godunov*
Kilian	Tenor	Rich peasant		*Der Freischütz*
King	Bass Baritone			*Fête Galante*
King	Baritone			*Die Kluge*
King	Bass			*Maritana*
King *See also* Roi				
King Marke	Bass	King of Cornwall,	1st Zottmayer; Bohnen, Fischer, Griswold, Gura, Hotter, Kipnis, Mayr, Pinza, Edouard de Reszke, Staudigl I, Staudigl II, Weber	*Tristan und Isolde*
King of Clubs	Bass	Ruler of the Kingdom		*The Love for Three Oranges*
King of Egypt	Bass		Scolara, Plançon, Edouard de Reszke	*Aida*
King of Fools	Tenor			*Louise*
King of Spain	Bass			*Christophe Colomb*
King of the Ocean	Bass			*Sadko*
King Solomon	Baritone			*Die Königin von Saba*
Kings (Four)	Tenors, Basses	Nephews of Pollux		*Die Liebe der Danae*
King's Herald, The	Bass		Huehn, Ruffo, Scheidermantel, Schmedes	*Lohengrin*
Klingsor	Bass	A magician	1st Hill and Fuchs; Goritz, Scheidermantel	*Parsifal*
Kluge, Die *See* Farmer's daughter				

CHARACTER	ROLE	SINGER	OPERA
Klymene *See* Alto, the			
Klytemnestra Mezzo-soprano	Agamemnon's widow	1st Schumann-Heink; Klose, Mildenburg, Mödl, Thorborg	*Elektra*
Klytemnestra Soprano	Agamemnon's wife	Ober	*Iphigénie en Aulide*
Knight, First Tenor			*Parsifal*
Knight, Second Bass			*Parsifal*
Knights Chorus			*Guillaume Tell, Tannhäuser, Tristan und Isolde*
Knights (Four)			*L'Assassinio nel Cattedrale*
Knights of the Grail Chorus			*Parsifal*
Kofner Bass Baritone			*The Consul*
Kontchak Bass	Polovtsian (Tartar) Khan		*Prince Igor*
Kontchakovna Mezzo-soprano	Kontchak's daughter		*Prince Igor*
Kostelnika, Buryjovka Soprano	Widow, Jenufa's foster mother	Braun, Fisher, Fuchs, Matzenauer, Pederzini	*Její Pastorkyňa* (Jenufa)
Kothner *See* Fritz Kothner			
Koupava Soprano	In love with Misgir		*Snyegurotchka*
Kouzka Baritone	Archer		*Khovantschina*
Kreon Baritone	King, Antigonae's uncle		*Antigonae* (Orff)
Kronthal, Baron Tenor	Brother of the Countess of Eberbach		*Der Wildschütz*
Kruschina Baritone	Peasant, Marenka's father		*Prodana Nevešta*

THE CHARACTERS IN THE OPERAS

CHARACTER		ROLE	SINGER	OPERA
Kuligen	Baritone	Vanja's friend		*Katya Kabanova*
Kundry	Soprano	A bewitched, cursed woman	1st Brandt; Brema, Flagstad, Fuchs, Gulbranson, Harshaw, Kemp, Kirkby-Lunn, Kurt, Leider, Lubin, Malten, Marchesi, Materna, Matze-nauer, Mildenburg, Mödl, Moody, Saltzmann-Stevens, Sucher, Ternina, Thorborg, Varnay, Walker, Wickham, Wittich	*Parsifal*
Kunz Vogelgesang	Tenor	Mastersinger and furrier		*Die Meistersinger*
Kurvenal	Baritone	Tristan's retainer	1st Mitterwurzer; Bispham, Hotter, Edouard de Reszke, van Rooy, Scheidermantel, Weil	*Tristan und Isolde*
Kyoto	Baritone	Japanese pimp		*Iris*
Laborers	Chorus			*Les Troyens*
Laca Klemen	Tenor	Stepbrother of Stewa, in love with Jenufa		*Jeij Pastorkyňa* (*Jenufa*)
Lackey	Bass			*Ariadne auf Naxos*
Ladies	Chorus			*L'Africaine, Ernani, La Favorita, Guillaume Tell, Luisa Miller, Manon, Martha, Roméo et Juliette, Tannhäuser, Tosca*
Ladies (Three)	Sopranos, Mezzo-soprano	Attendants to the Queen of the Night		*Die Zauberflöte*

398

THE CHARACTERS IN THE OPERAS

CHARACTER	ROLE	SINGER	OPERA
Ladies and Gentlemen Chorus			*Adriana Lecouvreur, Andrea Chénier, La Gioconda, Otello, La Rondine, La Traviata*
Ladies in Waiting Chorus			*Lucrezia Borgia*
Ladies of Honor Chorus			*Lohengrin*
Lady Soprano			*Dantons Tod*
Lady Essex *See* Frances, Countess			
Lady in Waiting Soprano			*Gloriana*
Lady in Waiting Soprano	to Lady Macbeth		*Macbeth* (Verdi)
Lady Macbeth Soprano		Pederzini	*Macbeth* (Bloch)
Lady Macbeth Soprano		Borkh, Callas, Dow, Grandi, Mödl, Onegin, Rysanek, Viardot-Garcia, Varnay	*Macbeth* (Verdi)
Laertes Tenor	Actor	Gassier	*Mignon*
Laetitia Soprano		Hurley	*The Old Maid and the Thief*
Laïs Pantomime			*Faust*
Lakmé Soprano	Nilakantha's daughter	1st Van Zandt; Barrientos, Galli-Curci, Lipovska, Munsel, Patti, Pons, Luisa Tetrazzini, Tréville	*Lakmé*
Lamoral, Graf Bass	Arabella's suitor		*Arabella*
Lamplighter Tenor			*Manon Lescaut*
Landgrave *See* Hermann			
Larina Mezzo-soprano	Tatyana's mother		*Eugene Onegin*

THE CHARACTERS IN THE OPERAS

CHARACTER	ROLE	SINGER	OPERA
Larkens Bass	A miner		La Fanciulla del West
Lartigen Bass	Monologuist		Zaza
Laundry Girls Chorus			Iris
Laura Mezzo-soprano	Alvise's wife, in love with Enzo	1st Biancolini-Rodriguez; Barbieri, Castagna, Fursch-Madi, Homer, Kirkby-Lunn, Minghini-Cattaneo, Ober, Stignani, Thebom, Wickham	La Gioconda
Laura Contralto	Peasant girl		Luisa Miller
Laura Soprano		1st Ivogün	Das Ring des Polycrates
Laura, Countess Soprano	Palmatica's daughter		Der Bettelstudent
Laurence, Friar Bass		Marcoux, Plançon, Edouard de Reszke, Whitehill	Roméo and Juliette
Lauretta Soprano	Gianni's daughter, 21	1st Easton; Albanese, Naylor, dalla Rizza, Schwarzkopf	Gianni Schicchi
Laurie Soprano		1st Carlos	The Tender Land
Lawrence Baritone	Lighthousekeeper		The Wreckers
Lawyer			Die Harmonie der Welt
Lawyer Baritone			Der Prozess
Lawyer See also Frazier			
Lazarillo Mezzo-soprano	A poor boy		Maritana
Leaders of the People Soprano, Mezzo-soprano, and Baritone			Alceste

CHARACTER		ROLE	SINGER	OPERA
Leandro	Tenor	Columbine's lover		*Arlecchino*
Leandro	Barítone	Prime minister, King of Spades		*The Love for Three Oranges*
Lechery, Lord				*Pilgrim's Progress*
	Tenor			
Leda	Contralto	A queen, formerly loved by Jupiter		*Die Liebe der Danae*
Lefort, Admiral		Russian ambassador		*Zar und Zimmerman*
	Bass			
Lehl	Contralto	Shepherd		*Snyegurotchka*
Leïla	Soprano	Priestess of Brahma	1st de Maesen; Berger, Calvé, Carosio, Fohström, Galli-Curci, Hempel, Pareto, Luisa Tetrazzini	*Les Pêcheurs de Perles*
Leni	Soprano		1st della Casa; Curtin	*Der Prozess*
Lensky	Tenor	Olga's fiancé	Figner, Jones, Martinelli, Tucker	*Eugene Onegin*
Leonato	Bass	Governor of Messina		*Béatrice et Bénédict*
Leonora	Soprano		1st Falcon	*Alessandro Stradella* (Niedemayer)
Leonora	Soprano	Florestan's wife. When disguised as a man she is called Fidelio	1st Milder; Borkh, Brandt, Brouwen- stijn, Caron, Cruvelli, Fisher, Flagstad, de Gunst, Fornia-Labey, Goltz, Krauss, Larsen-Todsen, Leffler-Burckhard, Lilli Lehman, Lotte Lehmann, Malibran, Malten, Matzenauer, Mödl, Pauly, Resnik, Roze, Schröder-Devrient, Seidl-Krauss, Ternina, Tietjens, Valleria, Varnay, Wagner, Wildbrunn	*Fidelio*

THE CHARACTERS IN THE OPERAS

CHARACTER		ROLE	SINGER	OPERA
Leonora	Soprano	A duchess, beloved of Manrico	1st Penio; Bampton, Brouwenstijn, Callas, Goldini, Krauss, Litvinne, Milanov, Price, Tebaldi, Tietjens, Ugalde, Varnay, Welitsch	*Il Trovatore*
Leonora di Gusman		The King's mistress	1st Stoltz; Borghi-Mamo, Cary, Homer, Lucca, Mantelli, Viardot-Garcia, Wagner, Walker	*La Favorita*
Leonora di Vargas, Donna	Soprano		Callas, Cigna, Milanov, Muzio, Ponselle, Stignani, Teresa Stoltz, Tebaldi, Tietjens	*La Forza del Destino*
Léopold	Tenor	Prince. Working for Eléazar as an apprentice under the name of Samuel	Koegel	*La Juive*
Leporello	Bass	Don Giovanni's servant	1st Felice Ponziani; Baccaloni, Benucci, Chaliapin, Corena, Formes, Manuel García, I, Kunz, Lablache, Mirabella, Edouard de Reszke, Tajo	*Don Giovanni*
Lerma, Count	Tenor		Franke	*Don Carlos*
Lescaut	Baritone	Manon's cousin	del Puente	*Manon*
Lescaut	Baritone	Manon's brother	Guarrera, Scotti, Stabile	*Manon Lescaut*
Leukippos	Tenor	Shepherd in love with Daphne		*Daphne*
Leuthold	Bass	Swiss patriot, shepherd		*Guillaume Tell*

THE CHARACTERS IN THE OPERAS

CHARACTER	ROLE	SINGER	OPERA
Levis Bass	Spirit voice		*Doktor Faustus*
Libellule, La Mezzo-soprano	Dragonfly		*L'Enfant et les Sortilèges*
Lieutenant Tenor			*Doktor Faustus*
Lillas Pastia From Chorus	Innkeeper		*Carmen*
Lillian Russell Soprano			*The Mother of Us All*
Lily Mezzo-soprano	Strawberry woman, Peter's wife		*Porgy and Bess*
Linda Soprano	Beloved of Charles	Barili, Barrientos, Kellogg, Murska, Pons, Valleria	*Linda di Chamounix*
Lindorf Bass	Councillor of Nuremburg	London	*Les Contes d'Hoffmann*
Lindoro Tenor	Italian lover of Isabella	Valletti	*L'Italiana in Algeri*
Linette Contralto	Princess hidden in an orange		*The Love for Three Oranges*
Lion Tamer Soprano		Lewis	*He Who Gets Slapped*
Lionel Tenor	Plunkett's foster brother	Caruso, Gigli, Mario, Pertile, Stagno, Tucker ,	*Martha*
Lisa Soprano	In love with Hermann	Corsi, Destinn, Jurinac, Hilde Konetzni, Welitsch	*Pique-Dame*
Lisa Soprano	Innkeeper, rival for Elvino's love		*La Sonnambula*
Lisette Soprano	Magda's maid, in love with Prunier	1st Ferraris; Fleisher	*La Rondine*
Little Bat McLean Tenor			*Susannah*
Little Devils Chorus			*The Love for Three Oranges*
Little Franz	Storch's 8 year old son		*Intermezzo*

THE CHARACTERS IN THE OPERAS

CHARACTER		ROLE	SINGER	OPERA
Little Suzanne Soprano		Kepler's daughter by his first wife		*Die Harmonie der Welt*
Liù Soprano		Faithful slave girl of Timur	1st Zamboni; Albanese, Favero, Norena, Pampanini, Price, Schwarzkopf, Tebaldi	*Turandot*
Livoretto Tenor		Nobleman of the Venetian Republic		*Lucrezia Borgia*
Lob		Evil assistant of Dipsacus		*The Poisoned Kiss*
Lockit Baritone		Jailer, Lucy's father		*The Beggar's Opera*
Lodoviço Bass		Venetian ambassador		*Otello*
Loge Tenor		Norse god	1st Vogl; Garris	*Das Ring des Nibelungen*
Lohengrin Tenor		Knight of the Grail, son of Parsifal	1st Beck, Althouse, Max Alvary, Berger, Campanini, Caruso, Dalmorès, van Dyke, Gigli, Hensel, Hopf, Maas, Nachbauer, Nicolini, Niemann, Jean de Reszke, Ludwig Schnorr von Carolsfield, Slezak, Sullivan, Urlus, Völker, Winkelmann	*Lohengrin*
Lola Mezzo-soprano		Alfio's wife, having an affair with Turiddu	Bible, Brema, Evans, Homer	*Cavalleria Rusticana*
Lorance Soprano			1st Caron	*Jocelyn*
Lords (Four) Tenor, Baritone and Bass				*The Warrior*
Lorek Baritone		A surgeon		*Fedora*
Lorenz von Pommersfelden Bass		Dean of Mainz		*Mathis der Maler*

CHARACTER	ROLE	SINGER	OPERA
Lorenzo Tenor	Officer of the carabiniers	Matters	*Fra Diavolo*
Lorenzo Tenor	Alfonso's confidant		*Masaniello*
Loris Ipanov, Count Tenor	Accused of murder	1st Caruso; Gigli, Martinelli, Pertile, Zenatello	*Fedora*
Lotario Bass	Deranged minstrel, old man	Faure, Taskin	*Mignon*
Louis the Sixth Bass		Fischer	*Euryanthe*
Louise Soprano	In love with Julien	1st Martha Rioton; Alda, Bori, Destinn, Edvina, Farrar, Favero, Garden, Gutheil-Schoder, Kirsten, dalla Rizza	*Louise*
Lover Tenor			*Fête Galante*
Lowbrows Chorus			*The Love for Three Oranges*
Lowitsky Bass	Jesuit		*Boris Godunov*
Lubava Mezzo-soprano	Sadko's wife		*Sadko*
Lucia Soprano	Lucy of Lammermoor	1st Tacchinardi-Persiani; Albani, Barrientos, Callas, Carvalho, Charton-Demeur, Galli-Curci, Gerster, Hauk, Hempel, Kellogg, Krauss, Liebling, Lind, Lucca, Melba, Moffo, Munsel, Murska, Nevada, Christine Nilsson, Nordica, Pacini, Pareto, Patti, Pons, Sembrich, Luisa Tetrazzini, Vere, Viardot-Garcia, Zerr	*Lucia di Lammermoor*

CHARACTER		ROLE	SINGER	OPERA
Lucia	Soprano	Lucretia's attendant	Gueden	The Rape of Lucretia
Lucia *See also* Mamma Lucia				
Lucieta	Soprano	Lunardo's daughter by his first wife		I Quattro Rusteghi
Lucile	Soprano	Desmoulins' wife	1st Cebotari	Dantons Tod
Lucinda				English.version for the name Lucieta *in* I Quattro Rusteghi
Lucretia	Contralto	Palestrina's dead wife		Palestrina
Lucretia	Contralto	Wife of Collatinus	1st Ferrier	The Rape of Lucretia
Lucrezia Borgia	Soprano		Fursch-Madi, Grisi, Krauss, Sontag, Tietjens, Wagner	Lucrezia Borgia
Lucy *See* Lucia				
Lucy Lockit	Soprano	The Jailer's daughter		The Beggar's Opera
Ludmilla	Soprano	In love with Russlan		Russlan and Ludmilla
Luigi	Tenor	Stevedore, 20	1st Montesanti; Jagel, Johnson, Merli, del Monaco	Il Tabarro
Luisa	Soprano	Rodolfo's beloved	1st Gavazzaniga; Ponselle	Luisa Miller
Lukas	Tenor	Young widower in love with Vendulka		Hubička
Lulu	Soprano		1st Hadzic; Styx, Spletter	Lulu
Lummer, Baron	Tenor			Intermezzo
Luna, Count	Baritone	Envoy from Spain		Palestrina
Luna *See also* Conte di Luna				

CHARACTER		ROLE	SINGER	OPERA
Lunardo	Bass	Merchant, Lucieta's father		*I Quattro Rusteghi*
Luther	Bass	Innkeeper		*Les Contes d'Hoffmann*
Lysiart	Baritone		Gura	*Euryanthe*
Macbeth	Baritone	A general, ambitious for the Scottish throne	1st Vanesi; Chapman, Rothmuller, Taddei, Warren	*Macbeth*
Macduff	Tenor	Scots nobleman, Macbeth's enemy	Bergonzi	*Macbeth*
Macheath, Captain	Tenor	A notorious highwayman	1st John Beard; Incledon, Pears, Reeves, Ranalow	*The Beggar's Opera*
MacIrton	Bass	Justice of the Peace		*La Dame Blanche*
Madame de Croissy Mezzo-soprano			Claramae Turner	*Les Dialogues des Carmélites*
Maddalena Soprano		Linda's mother		*Linda di Chamounix*
Maddalena Contralto		Sparafucile's sister	Gay, Glaz, Lipton, Madeira	*Rigoletto*
Maddalena *See also* Madeleine *See also* Magdalena				
Madeleine Contralto				*Louise*
Madeleine Soprano		Chappelou's wife	1st Roy; de Garmo, Charton-Demeur	*Le Postillion de Longjumeau*
Madeleine de Coigny Soprano		In love with Andrea Chénier	1st Carrera; Caniglia, Milanov, Muzio, Sheridan, Strakosch, Tebaldi	*Andrea Chénier*
Madelon Mezzo-soprano		Old woman		*Andrea Chénier*
Madmen	Chorus			*The Rake's Progress*
Maffio Orsini Contralto		Lucrezia's enemy	Alboni, Trebelli	*Lucrezia Borgia*
Magda Soprano		Rambaldo's mistress	1st dalla Rizza; Bori, Favero	*La Rondine*

THE CHARACTERS IN THE OPERAS

CHARACTER	ROLE	SINGER	OPERA
Magda Sorel Soprano	John's wife	1st Neway; Borkh, Mödl, Petrella, Shuard, Zadek	*The Consul*
Magdalena Mezzo-soprano	Eva's nurse	1st Sophie Dietz; Glaz, Homer, Resnik, Wickham	*Die Meistersinger*
Magi Chorus			*Semiramide*
Magician Bass			*Švanda Dudak*
Magician *See* Nika Magadoff			
Magistrate			*Die Harmonie der Welt*
Magistrate *See also* Eugenio de Zuniga, Don			
Magnates Chorus			*Boris Godunov*
Magnifico, Don Bass	Baron of Montflagon		*La Cenerentola*
Mago *See* Simon Mago			
Mahomet Pantomime	Negro page		*Der Rosenkavalier*
Maid Mezzo-soprano			*Její Pastorkyňa* (Jenufa)
Maid of Honor Mezzo-soprano	to the princess		*Masaniello*
Maid Servants (Three) Sopranos, Mezzo-soprano			*Martha*
Maid Servants Contralto, 2 Mezzo-sopranos, 2 Sopranos			*Elektra*
Maiden Soprano	A Polovtsian (Tartar)		*Prince Igor*
Maiden *See* Farmer's daughter			

THE CHARACTERS IN THE OPERAS

CHARACTER	ROLE	SINGER	OPERA
Maidens Chorus			*Der Fliegende Holländer, Der Prozess*
Maids Chorus			*Pskovityanka, Wozzeck*
Maids (Two) Sopranos			*Daphne*
Maids in Waiting Chorus			*Khovantschina*
Maintop Tenor			*Billy Budd*
Maive Contralto	Etain's mother		*The Immortal Hour*
Majas and Majos Chorus	Ladies and gentlemen		*Goyescas*
Major-Domo Tenor			*Adriana Lecouvreur*
Major-Domo Baritone			*Andrea Chénier*
Major-Domo Speaker		Louw	*Ariadne auf Naxos*
Major-Domo Bass			*Capriccio*
Major-Domo Tenor			*Christophe Colomb*
Major-Domo Tenor	to von Faninal	Franke	*Der Rosenkavalier*
Major-Domo Tenor	to the Marschallin		*Der Rosenkavalier*
Major-Domo Baritone		1st Cehanovsky	*Vanessa*
Malatesta, Doctor Baritone	Don Pasquale's friend	1st Tamburini; de Luca, Gassier	*Don Pasquale*
Malatestino dall' Occhio Tenor	One-eyed son of Malatesta		*Francesca da Rimini*
Malcolm Tenor	Duncan's son		*Macbeth*
Malice Soprano			*Pilgrim's Progress*
Maliella Soprano	Carmela's adopted daughter	Edvina, Giannini, Jeritza, White	*I Gioielli della Madonna*
Mallika Mezzo-soprano	Lakmé's slave		*Lakmé*

CHARACTER	ROLE	SINGER	OPERA
Mama			*The Ballad of Baby Doe*
Mama Lucia Contralto	Turiddu's mother	Votipka	*Cavalleria Rusticana*
Mamalik (Two) Bass			*Marouf*
Man Speaker			*Der Prozess*
Man Servants (Three) Tenor, Basses			*Martha*
Man with the Donkey Tenor			*Die Kluge*
Man with the Mule Baritone			*Die Kluge*
Mancini, Count Tenor		Norman Kelley	*He Who Gets Slapped*
Mandarin Baritone			*Turandot*
Mandryka Baritone	Arabella's suitor	London	*Arabella*
Manfredo Baritone	Archibaldo's son	1st Galeffi; Amato, Bonelli, Cigada, Danise, Guarrera, Inghilleri, Morelli, Tagliabue, Weede	*L'Amore dei Tre Re*
Manfredo Tenor	A Sicilian		*I Vespri Siciliani*
Manon Soprano		1st Marie Heilbronn; Alda, de los Angeles, Bori, Edvina, Farrar, Favero, Garden, Hauk, Jurinac, McWatters, Moore, Muzio, Roze, Schwarzkopf, Sanderson, Vix, van Zandt	*Manon*
Manon Lescaut Soprano		1st Cesira-Ferrani; Alda, Barbato, Bori, Caniglia, Cavalieri, Favero, Kirsten, Lipovska, Oltrabella, Pampanini, Sheridan, Tebaldi, Welitsch	*Manon Lescaut*

CHARACTER		ROLE	SINGER	OPERA
Manrico	Tenor	Troubadour, Leonora's lover. The supposed son of Azucena	1st Boucardé; Bjoerling, Campanini, Caruso, Martin, Martinelli, del Monaco, Slezak, Stagno, di Stefano, Zenatello	*Il Trovatore*
Manuel	Baritone	Carmela's brother		*La Vida Breve*
Manuela Mezzo-soprano		A maid		*Der Corregidor*
Manufacturer Baritone				*Der Prozess*
Manus	Bass	Etain's father		*The Immortal Hour*
Manz	Baritone	Rich farmer, Sali's father		*A Village Romeo and Juliet*
Maometto	Bass		1st Galli	*Maometto* (Rossini)
Mara Mezzo-soprano				*Debora e Jaele*
Marcel	Bass	Huguenot soldier	Foli, Formes, Edouard de Reszke, Scaria, Scotti	*Les Huguenots*
Marcellina	Soprano	Rocco's daughter	1st Müller; della Casa, Schumann, Schwarzkopf, Seefried	*Fidelio*
Marcellina	Soprano	Dr. Bartolo's housekeeper	1st Mandini; Rossel-Majdan	*Le Nozze di Figaro*
Marcellina *See also* Berta				
Marcelline Mezzo-soprano				*L'Attaque du Moulin*
Marcello	Baritone	Young starving painter	Franci, Guarrera, Panerai, Pinza, Tagliabue	*La Bohème*
Marchand de Masques, La Soprano		Mask seller		*Esther de Carpentras*
Marchese di Calatrava	Bass	Leonora's father		*La Forza del Destino*

CHARACTER		ROLE	SINGER	OPERA
Marchese d'Obigny Baritone			Renan	*La Traviata*
Marchioness of Montefiore Mezzo-soprano				*Maritana*
Marco	Bass	Rosa's brother		*L'Arlesiana*
Marco	Baritone	Simone's son, 45		*Gianni Schicchi*
Marco	Tenor	Dufresne's butler		*Zaza*
Marenka	Soprano	In love with Jenik	Cross, Destinn, Jurinac, Hilde Konetzni, Müller, Novotna, Oltrabella, Rethberg, Seefried	*Prodana Nevešta*
Marfa Kabanova Contralto		Widow (Kabanicha), Katya's mother in law		*Katya Kabanova*
Margared	Soprano	The king's daughter	1st Deschamps; Ponselle	*Le Roi d'Ys*
Margarethe Soprano			Brandt	*Genoveva*
Margarita Mezzo-soprano		Lunardo's second wife		*I Quattro Rusteghi*
Margery				*English version for the name* Margarita *in *I Quattro Rusteghi*
Margherita Soprano		Beloved of Faust	Alda, Albanese, Borgi-Mamo, Calvé, Canetti, Caniglia, Eames, Farrar, Lilli Lehmann, Muzio, Christine Nilsson, Scacciati, Schwarz- kopf, Spani, Tebaldi, Valleria	*Mefistofele*
Margiana	Soprano	Baba Mustapha's daughter		*Der Barbier von Bagdad*
Margret	Contralto		Evans	*Wozzeck*
Marguerite Soprano			Calvé, Cigna, Farrar, Gatti, Melba, Vere	*La Damnation de Faust*

CHARACTER	ROLE	SINGER	OPERA
Marguerite Soprano	Old servant		*La Dame Blanche*
Marguérite Soprano	Beloved of Faust	1st Miolan-Carvalho; Ackté, Adams, Albani, Alda, de los Angeles, Borghi-Mamo, Calvé, Carvalho, Eames, Edvina, Farrar, Fursch-Madi, Garden, Hauk, Jeritza, Juch, Jurinac, Kellogg, Lucca, Malten, Melba, Christine Nilsson, Nordica, Patti, Rappold, Josephine de Reszke, Roze, Sayao, Shuard, Steber, Eva Tetrazzini, Tietjens, Treville, Valleria, Vere, Yeend	*Faust*
Marguerite Soprano			*Louise*
Marguerite de Valois Soprano	Betrothed to Henri IV	1st Dorus-Gras; Hempel, Juch, Melba, Peschka-Leutner, Luisa Tetrazzini, Vere	*Les Huguenots*
Maria Soprano	The commandant's wife	1st Ursuleac; Grandi, Weber	*Friedenstag*
Maria Contralto	Cookshop keeper		*Porgy and Bess*
Maria *Another name for* Amelia Boccanegra			
Maria *English version of* Marina, *in I Quattro Rusteghi*			
Maria Golovin Soprano		Franca Duval	*Maria Golovin*

THE CHARACTERS IN THE OPERAS

CHARACTER		ROLE	SINGER	OPERA
Marianne	Soprano	Sophie's duenna	Votipka	*Der Rosenkavalier*
Marie	Soprano		Schröder-Devrient	*Barbe-Bleue* (Grétry)
Marie	Soprano	Foster daughter of a regiment	Lind, Lucca, Patti, Pons, Sembrich, Sontag, Luisa Tetrazzini	*La Figlia del Reggimento*
Marie	Soprano		Roze	*Marie* (Hérold)
Marie	Soprano	Prostitute	1st Sigrid Johanson; Borkh, Danco, Dow, Gatti, Goltz, Mödl, Neway, Pauly, Steber	*Wozzeck*
Marie	Soprano	Van Bett's niece		*Zar und Zimmerman*
Marie-Louise	Mezzo-soprano	Napoleon's second wife		*Háry János*
Marie's Child	Treble			*Wozzeck*
Mariette	Soprano		Jeritza	*Die Tote Stadt*
Marina	Soprano	Filipeto's aunt		*I Quattro Rusteghi*
Marina Mnishek	Mezzo-soprano	Daughter of the Voyevode of Sandomir	1st Platonova; Castagna, Elias, Ober, Rankin, Resnik, Simionato, Thebom, Thorborg	*Boris Godunov*
Marines	Chorus			*Billy Budd*
Mario Cavaradossi	Tenor	Painter in love with Tosca	1st de Marchi; Baum, Borgatti, Borgioli, Caruso, Conley, Cremonini, Crooks, Fernandi, Hamlin, Lucia, Martin, McCormack, del Monaco, Peerce, Pertile, Poleri, di Stefano, Tagliavini, Tucker	*Tosca*
Maritana	Soprano	A gypsy		*Maritana*

CHARACTER		ROLE	SINGER	OPERA
Mark	Tenor	A fisherman, Thirza's lover		*The Wreckers*
Mark *See also* King Marke				
Marlardot	Tenor	Music Hall proprietor		*Zaza*
Marouf	Baritone	Henpecked cobbler	Singher	*Marouf*
Marquis	Silent			*Cardillac*
Marquis de Boisfleury Baritone				*Linda di Chamounix*
Marquis de Chateauneuf Tenor		French ambassador		*Zar und Zimmermann*
Marquis of Montefiore Bass				*Maritana*
Marquise de Birkenfeld Soprano			Claramae Turner	*La Figlia del Reggimento*
Mars	Tenor	The planet, also Ulrich Grüsser		*Die Harmonie der Welt*
Mars	Bass	A god		*Orphée aux Enfers*
Marschallin, The Soprano		Princess von Werdenberg	1st Siems; Cross, Easton, della Casa, Fisher, Hempel, Anni Konetzni, Lotte Lehmann, Leider, Lemnitz, Lewis, Steber, Varnay	*Der Rosenkavalier*
Marta	Soprano		Barrientos, Hempel, Juch, Kellogg, Murska, Patti, Tietjens, Valleria	*Marta*
Marta	Soprano	Sebastiano's mistress	Destinn	*Tiefland*
Martha	Contralto		1st Duclos; Scalchi	*Faust*

CHARACTER	ROLE	SINGER	OPERA
Martha Mezzo-soprano	One of the Old Believers	Stignani	*Khovantschina*
Martha Contralto			*Mefistofele*
Martha *See also* Harriett			
Martha Schwerlein Mezzo-soprano	Marguerite's neighbor		*Faust*
Marti Baritone	Rich farmer, Vreli's father		*A Village Romeo and Juliet*
Martinka Contralto	Vendulka's aunt		*Hubička*
Marullo, Cavaliere Baritone	A courtier		*Rigoletto*
Mary Contralto	Senta's nurse		*Der Fliegende Holländer*
Mary Soprano	Constable's daughter	1st Lewis; Cross	*Hugh the Drover*
Mary Soprano		Bori	*Peter Ibbetson*
Mary Ann Speaker	Servant		*The Boatswain's Mate*
Marzci, Old Baritone	Marie's coachman		*Háry János*
Marzelline *See* Marcellina			
Masaniello Tenor	Fisherman, Fenella's brother	1st Nourrit; Braham, Tamberlik	*Masaniello*
Masha Soprano	Lisa's maid		*Pique-Dame*
Masetto Bass	Peasant	1st Giuseppe Lolli; Walter Berry, Lorenzo Alvary, Bispham, Renan, Uppmann	*Don Giovanni*
Mask Seller *See* Marchand de Masques, La			
Masks Chorus			*La Traviata*
Masquers Chorus			*La Gioconda*
Massarelli Silent			*Palestrina*

CHARACTER	ROLE	SINGER	OPERA
Master of Ceremonies Tenor			*Christophe Colomb*
Master of Ceremonies Bass			*Doktor Faustus*
Master of Ceremonies Tenor			*Gloriana*
Master of Ceremonies Tenor			*The Love for Three Oranges*
Master of Ceremonies Tenor			*Pique-Dame*
Mat of the Mint From Chorus	Gentleman of the Road		*The Beggar's Opera*
Mates, First and Second Baritones			*Billy Budd*
Mathieu Baritone	Waiter		*Andrea Chénier*
Mathilde Soprano	Gessler's sister	Carvalho, Krauss, Tebaldi	*Guillaume Tell*
Mathis Baritone	The painter Grünewald		*Mathis der Maler*
Matous Bass	A smuggler		*Hubička*
Matuta, Boyard Nikita Tenor			*Pskovityanka*
Matteo Tenor		Morell	*Arabella*
Matteo Bass	Innkeeper	Autori, Goritz	*Fra Diavolo*
Matteo Borsa Tenor	A courtier	Franke, de Paolis	*Rigoletto*
Matteo del Sarto Baritone	Tailor and cuckold	Morell	*Arlecchino*
Matthisen Bass	Anabaptist		*Le Prophète*
Maurevert Bass	Catholic noble		*Les Huguenots*
Maruizio Tenor	Count of Saxony	1st Caruso; Campora, Pertile, Voyer	*Adriana Lecouvreur*

THE CHARACTERS IN THE OPERAS

CHARACTER	ROLE	SINGER	OPERA
Maurizio Bass Baritone	Merchant, Filipeto's father		*I Quattro Rusteghi*
Max Tenor	Forester	Althouse, Braham, Schott, Udvardy, Vogl	*Der Freischütz*
May Soprano	A pretty young toy-maker		*Das Heimchen am Herd*
Mayor Bass	of the village		*Jéjí Pastorkyňa* (Jenufa)
Mayor of Hornachuelos Bass			*La Forza del Destino*
Mayor's Wife Mezzo-soprano			*Jéjí Pastorkyňa* (Jenufa)
McLean, Mrs. Mezzo-soprano			*Susannah*
Medea Soprano		Callas, Tietjens	*Medea* (Cherubini)
Médecin Juif, Un Baritone	A Jewish doctor		*Esther de Carpentras*
Medium, I	Servant of the empress		*The Poisoned Kiss*
Medium, II	Servant of the empress		*The Poisoned Kiss*
Medium, III	Servant of the empress		*The Poisoned Kiss*
Medium, The *See* Baba			
Mefistofele Bass		de Angelis, Burke, Chaliapin, Didur, Nanetti, Pasera, Pinza, Edouard de Reszke, Rossi-Lemeni, Siepi	*Mefistofele*
Megärus Tenor	A spirit voice		*Doktor Faust*
Melanto Mezzo-soprano	Penelope's servant		*Il Ritorno d'Ulisse in Patria*
Melcthal Bass	Arnold's father, Swiss patriot		*Guillaume Tell*

CHARACTER	ROLE	SINGER	OPERA
Mélisande Soprano	Former wife of Barbe-Bleu		*Ariane et Barbe-Bleue*
Mélisande Soprano	Golaud's wife, beloved of Pelléas	1st Garden; de los Angeles, Bori, Connor, Edvina, Jepson, Perli, Sayao, Teyte	*Pelléas et Mélisande*
Melitone, Fra Baritone	Franciscan	Corena, Gassier, Jean de Reszke	*La Forza del Destino*
Melnik Bass		Chaliapin	*Roussalka*
Melot Baritone	A courtier	Cehanovsky	*Tristan und Isolde*
Melusine, Countess Speaker	Lady in waiting		*Háry János*
Members of the Revolutionary Tribunal Chorus			*Andrea Chénier*
Memucan Tenor	(Aman)		*Esther de Carpentras*
Men (Three) Tenor,	Baritone, Bass		*Der Prozess*
Men Chorus			*Pilgrim's Progress, Tiefland*
Men and Women Chorus			*Dalibor, La Damnation de Faust*
Men at Arms Chorus			*Lucrezia Borgia, Mefistofele, I Puritani, Tristan und Isolde*
Men in Armor (Two) Tenor, Bass			*Zauberflöte*
Menelaus Tenor	Helena's husband	1st Tauche; Laubenthal, Völker	*Die Aegyptische Helena*
Méphistophélès Bass		Formichi, Galeffi, Gobbi, Plançon, Renaud	*La Damnation de Faust*
Mephistopheles Tenor			*Doktor Faustus*

THE CHARACTERS IN THE OPERAS

CHARACTER	ROLE	SINGER	OPERA
Méphistophélès Bass		1st Balanqué; Bouhy, Chaliapin, Christoff, Delmas, Faure, Foli, Gassier, Giraudet, Hinshaw, Journet, Lablache, List, London, Marcoux, Novara, Pinza, Plançon, Radford, Edouard de Reszke, Rothier, F. Stravinski	*Faust*
Mephistopheles *See also* Mefistofele			
Mercedes Mezzo-soprano	A gypsy	Cross, Evans, Glaz	*Carmen*
Mercedes, Doña Contralto		Thorborg	*Der Corregidor*
Merchants Chorus			*The Fair at Sorochintsky*
Merchants (Two) Tenor, Bass			*Marouf*
Merchants and Wives Chorus			*Manon*
Mercure Tenor	The god Mercury		*Orphée aux Enfers*
Mercury Bass	The planet, also Daniel Hizler		*Die Harmonie der Welt*
Mercury Tenor			*Die Liebe der Danae*
Mercury Bass	The god		*Les Troyens*
Mercutio Baritone	Romeo's friend		*Roméo et Juliette*
Merry-go-round Man Baritone			*A Village Romeo and Juliet*
Méru Baritone	Catholic gentleman		*Les Huguenots*
Messagera, La Soprano	The messenger		*La Favola d'Orfeo*
Messenger Tenor		Franke	*Aida*
Messenger Baritone			*Antigonae* (Orff)

CHARACTER	ROLE	SINGER	OPERA
Messenger Baritone			*Christophe Colomb*
Messenger Bass-baritone			*Oedipus Rex*
Messenger From Chorus			*Il Trovatore*
Messenger Tenor			*La Wally*
Messenger of Peace Soprano			*Rienzi*
Messengers Chorus			*Rienzi*
Metifio Baritone	Horse tender		*L'Arlesiana*
Micaela Soprano	Village girl from Navarra	1st Chapuy; Adams, Alda, Amara, de los Angeles, Bori, Conner, Eames, Farrar, Gueden, Hurley, Mario, Melba, Rappold, Steber, Valleria, Vere, Yeend	*Carmen*
Micha Bass	Landlord, Jenik's father		*Prodaná Nevěsta*
Michael Andreievitch Toucha Tenor	In love with Olga		*Pskovityanka*
Michele Baritone	Barge man, 50	1st Didur; Franci, Galeffi, Tibbett, Weede	*Il Tabarro*
Michelin Baritone	A journalist		*Zaza*
Michonnet Baritone	Stage director		*Adriana Lecouvreur*
Midas Tenor	King of Lydia whose touch turns things to gold	1st Taubmann; Patzak	*Die Liebe der Danae*
Midir Tenor			*The Immortal Hour*
Midshipmen (Four) Chorus			*Billy Budd*

THE CHARACTERS IN THE OPERAS

CHARACTER	ROLE	SINGER	OPERA
Mignon Mezzo-soprano	Foundling brought up as a gypsy	1st Galli-Marie; Albani, Barrientos, Bori, Destinn, Farrar, Juch, Lussan, Matzenauer, Morris, Christine Nilsson, Pederzini, Simionato, Stevens, van Zandt	*Mignon*
Milada Soprano	Dalibor's accuser	Hilde Konetzni, Lemnitz	*Dalibor*
Milio Dufresne Tenor	Zaza's lover	Gigli	*Zaza*
Milkwoman Soprano			*Louise*
Miller Baritone	An old soldier, Luisa's father		*Luisa Miller*
Milliners Chorus			*The Poisoned Kiss*
Mime Tenor	A Nibelung	Nachbauer	*Das Ring des Nibelungen*
Mimi Soprano	Embroiderer, consumptive	1st Cesari-Ferrani; Albanese, Alda, Amara, de los Angeles, Bori, Callas, Cavan, Cebotari, Connor, Cross, della Casa, Esty, Farrar, Favero, Flagstad, Gluck, Gueden, Hempel, Jurinac, Kirsten, Labia, Lipovska, Melba, Moffo, Moore, Norena, Perli, Sayao, Schwarzkopf, Tebaldi, Teyte, Welitsch, Williams, Yeend	*La Bohème*
Miners Chorus			*The Wreckers*

THE CHARACTERS IN THE OPERAS

CHARACTER		ROLE	SINGER	OPERA
Minerve	Soprano	Goddess		*Orphée aux Enfers*
Minerva	Soprano			*Il Ritorno d'Ulisse in Patria*
Mingo	Tenor			*Porgy and Bess*
Minister, The King's *See* Fernando, Don				
Ministers	Chorus			*Aida*
Minnesingers *See the opera* Tannhäuser				
Minnie	Soprano	Saloon keeper	1st Destinn; Barbato, Caniglia, Cobelli, Flagstad, Jeritza, Kirk, dalla Rizza, Steber, Tebaldi, Welitsch	*La Fanciulla del West*
Mirabella	Contralto	Carnero's long lost wife		*Zigeunerbaron*
Miracle, Doctor	Baritone		London	*Les Contes d'Hoffmann*
Mireille	Soprano	In love with Vincent	1st Carvalho; Barrientos, Blauvelt, Eames, Nevada, Patti, Tietjens	*Mireille*
Mizgir	Baritone	In love with the Snow Maiden		*Snyegurotchka*
Missail	Tenor	A vagrant		*Boris Godunov*
Mistress of the Novices	Mezzo-soprano			*Suor Angelica*
Mistrust	Baritone	A neighbor		*Pilgrim's Progress*
Mitrane	Tenor	Captain of the guard		*Semiramide*
Mityukh	Bass	One of the people		*Boris Godunov*

CHARACTER	ROLE	SINGER	OPERA
Mityusha *See* Mityukh			
Mnishek, Marina *See* Marina Mnischek			
Molly Brazen From Chorus	A lady of the town		*The Beggar's Opera*
Mona Soprano		Kemp	*Mona Lisa* (Schillings)
Mona Lisa Soprano		Borkh	*Mona Lisa*
Monforte *See* Guido di Monforte			
Monastery **Attendant** From Chorus			*Manon*
Monica Soprano	Baba's daughter	1st Keller	*The Medium*
Monk Bass			*Don Carlos*
Monks Chorus			*La Favorita, La Gioconda, I Gioielli della Madonna, Les Huguenots, Rienzi, Roméo et Juliette, Thaïs*
Monks, Franciscan Chorus			*La Forza del Destino*
Monostatos Tenor	Sarastro's Moorish servant	Perier	*Zauberflöte*
Monsters Chorus			*The Love for Three Oranges*
Montano Bass	Otello's predecessor in Cyprus		*Otello*
Monterone, Count Baritone			*Rigoletto*
Moon, The Contralto	Also Katherina		*Die Harmonie der Welt*
Morales Bass	Officer of the guard		*Carmen*
Morbio Baritone	An actor	Newman	*Die Schweigsame Frau*

THE CHARACTERS IN THE OPERAS

CHARACTER		ROLE	SINGER	OPERA
Morena	Bass	A fisherman		*Masaniello*
Morgiana	Soprano		1st Falcon	*Ali Baba* (Cherubini)
Morosus Blunt	Bass	An old bachelor	1st Plaschke; Beattie	*Die Schweigsame Frau*
Morphée	Tenor	A god		*Orphée aux Enfers*
Moruccio	Baritone	Miller		*Tiefland*
Mosè	Bass	Moses	Christoff	*Mosè* (Rossini)
Moser, Augustin	Tenor	Mastersinger and tailor		*Die Meistersinger*
Mother	Soprano	Amahl's mother	Neway	*Amahl and the Night Visitors*
Mother	Contralto			*The Consul*
Mother	Contralto			*L'Enfant et les Sortilèges*
Mother			Neway	*Maria Golovin*
Mother Goose	Mezzo-soprano		1st Nell Tangeman; Lipton, Madeira	*The Rake's Progress*
Mother of Louise	Contralto		Gay	*Louise*
Mountaineers	Chorus			*Ernani*
Mountjoy, Charles Blount, Lord	Baritone			*Gloriana*
Mister, or Mrs. *See proper name, as:* Day, Mr. *or* Ford, Mrs.				
Muezzin (Two)	Tenors			*Marouf*
Muff	Tenor	A comedian		*Prodaná Nevěsta*
Muleteers	Chorus			*La Forza del Destino*
Muse of Poetry	Soprano			*Les Contes d'Hoffmann*

CHARACTER		ROLE	SINGER	OPERA
Musetta	Soprano	In love with Marcello	1st Pacini; Fenn, Goltz, Gueden, Lewis, Lussan, Munsel, Resnik, Schwarzkopf, Shuard, Welitsch	*La Bohème*
Music Master Baritone			Herbert	*Ariadne auf Naxos*
Music Master Tenor				*Manon Lescaut*
Music Master *See* Basilio, Don				
Musician Mezzo-soprano			Vanni	*Manon Lescaut*
Musician Monk Baritone				*Le Jongleur de Notre Dame*
Musicians			Players of the Violin, Cello and Cembalo	*Capriccio*
Musicians	Chorus			*Il Barbiere di Siviglia, Francesca da Rimini, Gloriana, Její Pastorkyňa (Jenufa)*
Musketeer	Bass			*Friedenstag*
Mustafa	Bass	The Bey of Algiers		*L'Italiana in Algeri*
Mustapha *See* Baba Mustapha				
Mute	Silent			*Die Entführung aus dem Serail*
Mylio	Tenor	Victorious general	Gigli, Saléza	*Le Roi d'Ys*
Myrrha	Soprano		1st Christine Nilsson	*Sardanapale*
Myrtale Mezzo-soprano		A slave		*Thaïs*
Mystic Choir Chorus				*Mefistofele*

THE CHARACTERS IN THE OPERAS

CHARACTER		ROLE	SINGER	OPERA
Nabi	Baritone	Prince of Nephthali		*Debora e Jaele*
Nabucco	Baritone	Nebuchadnezzar, King of Babylon		*Nabucco*
Nabucodonosor *See* Nabucco				
Nadina	Speaker	Member of Almanzor's harem		*Oberon*
Nadir	Tenor	Fisherman	1st Morini; T. Burke, Caruso, Cremonini, Delmas, Garulli, Lugo	*Les Pêcheurs de Perles*
Naiade	Soprano	A nymph		*Ariadne auf Naxos*
Naiads	Chorus			*Mefistofele, Tannhäuser, Les Troyens*
Naina	Mezzo-soprano	An evil witch		*Russlan and Ludmilla*
Namouna	Speaker	Fatima's grand-mother		*Oberon*
Nancy	Mezzo-soprano	The baker's assistant		*Albert Herring*
Nancy	Contralto			*Hugh the Drover*
Nancy	Contralto	Harriett's waiting maid	Elmo, Howard, Pederzini, Trebelli, Walker	*Martha*
Nandro	Tenor	Shepherd		*Tiefland*
Nanetta	Soprano	Ford's daughter, in love with Fenton	Lussan, Seefried	*Falstaff*
Nanette	Soprano	Maid to the Baroness Freimann		*Der Wildschütz*
Napoleon, Emperor	Baritone			*Háry János*
Napoleone	Baritone		Amato	*Madame Sans-Gêne*
Narbal	Bass	Dido's minister		*Les Troyens*
Narciso, Don	Tenor		Gedda	*Il Turco in Italia*

427

THE CHARACTERS IN THE OPERAS

CHARACTER	ROLE	SINGER	OPERA
Narraboth Tenor	Captain of the guard		*Salome*
Narrator Speaker			*Christophe Colomb*
Narumoff Baritone	A gambler		*Pique-Dame*
Natalia Mezzo-soprano	Zaza's maid		*Zaza*
Nathanael Tenor	A student		*Les Contes d'Hoffmann*
Naval Captain Bass			*Manon Lescaut*
Nazarenes (Two) Tenor, Bass			*Salome*
Nebuchadnezzar *See* Nabucco			
Ned Keene Baritone	Apothecary and quack	1st Donlevy	*Peter Grimes*
Nedda Soprano	"Columbine," Canio's wife in love with Silvio	1st Stehle; Ackté, Amara, Callas, Destinn, della Casa, Fenn, Fornia-Labey, Ilitsch, Kronold, Labia, Lussan, Melba, Sayao, Seefried, Shuard, Welitsch	*I Pagliacci*
Neighbor, A Tenor			*Der Corregidor*
Neighbors Chorus			*Arlecchino, Benvenuto Cellini, Werther*
Nejata Mezzo-soprano	Musician from Kiev		*Sadko*
Nella Soprano	Gherardo's wife, 34		*Gianni Schicchi*
Nelly Soprano		Neway	*Wuthering Heights*
Nelson Tenor			*Porgy and Bess*
Nelusko Baritone	Slave, captured by Vasco da Gama	Ancona, Basiola, Beck, Borgioli, Faure, Lassalle, Renaud, Edouard de Reszke	*L'Africaine*

THE CHARACTERS IN THE OPERAS

CHARACTER	ROLE	SINGER	OPERA
Nemorino Tenor	Young peasant	1st Genero; Caruso, Gigli, Schipa	*L'Elisir d'Amore*
Neptune *See* Nettuno *See also* Voice of Neptune			
Nereo Tenor			*Mefistofele*
Nerone Bass	The emperor Nero	Pinza	*Nerone* (Boito)
Nerone Tenor	The emperor Nero	1st Pertile; Lauri-Volpi, Voyer	*Nerone* (Mascagni)
Nettuno Bass	Neptune		*Il Ritorno d'Ulisse in Patria*
Nevers, Count de Baritone	Catholic nobleman	1st Derivis; Ancona, Faure, Lassalle, Maurel, del Puente, Renaud, Jean de Reszke, Santley, Scotti	*Les Huguenots*
Newspaper Girl Soprano			*Louise*
Nibelungs Chorus			*Das Ring des Nibelungen*
Nicias Tenor	An Alexandrian	1st Alvarez	*Thaïs*
Nick Tenor	Bartender		*La Fanciulla del West*
Nick Shadow Baritone		1st Otakar Kraus; Harrell, Hines	*The Rake's Progress*
Nicklausse Mezzo-soprano	Hoffman's friend	Varno	*Les Contes d'Hoffmann*
Nicola Tenor	Footman		*Fedora*
Nicoletta Mezzo-soprano	Princess hidden in an orange		*The Love for Three Oranges*
Nieces (Two) Sopranos	Main attractions of "The Boar"	1st Iacopi, Blanche Turner	*Peter Grimes*
Night Watch Chorus			*Les Huguenots*
Night Watchman Bass			*Die Meistersinger*
Nightingale *See* Rossignol, Le			

CHARACTER	ROLE	SINGER	OPERA
Nightwatchmen's Voices (Three) Basses			*Die Frau ohne Schatten*
Nika Magadoff Tenor	The magician	Kelley	*The Consul*
Nikititsch Bass			*Boris Godunov*
Nilakantha Bass Baritone	Brahmin priest	E. Burke, Pinza, Edouard de Reszke, Rothier	*Lakmé*
Nimming Ned From Chorus	Gentleman of the road		*The Beggar's Opera*
Ninetta Soprano		Grisi	*La Gazza Ladra*
Ninetta Soprano	Princess hidden in an orange	Hurley	*The Love for Three Oranges*
Ninetta Soprano	Elena's attendant		*I Vespri Siciliani*
Nino *See* Ghost of Nino			
Noble Pages (Four) Sopranos, Contraltos			*Tannhäuser*
Nobles Chorus			*Dalibor, Lohengrin, Le Prophète, Rienzi, Rigoletto, Le Roi d'Ys Roméo et Juliette, Tannhäuser, Tosca*
Nobles of the Venetian Republic Chorus			*Lucrezia Borgia*
Noctambulist Tenor			*Louise*
Noctambulist *See also* Amina			
Nolan, Mrs. Mezzo-soprano	Baba's client	Bible, Evans	*The Medium*
Norina Soprano	Young widow	1st Grisi; Bori, Gueden, Mildmay, Noni, Pareto, Sayao, Sembrich, Sontag	*Don Pasquale*

CHARACTER		ROLE	SINGER	OPERA
Norma	Soprano	Druid High Priestess	1st Pasta; Bampton, Callas, Hauk, Krauss, Lilli Lehmann, Lucca, Mallinger, Matzenauer, Milanov, Muzio, Parepa-Rosa, Ponselle, Schröder-Devrient, Tietjens, Viardot-Garcia, Wagner	*Norma*
Norman	Tenor	Follower of Ashton		*Lucia di Lammermoor*
Normando *See* Norman				
Norma's Children				*Norma*
Norn, First	Contralto	One of the Fates		*Götterdämmerung*
Norn, Second	Mezzo-soprano	One of the Fates		*Götterdämmerung*
Norn, Third	Soprano	One of the Fates		*Götterdämmerung*
Notary				*Il Barbiere di Siviglia*
Notary	Baritone			*Intermezzo*
Notary	Baritone			*Don Pasquale*
Notary	Bass			*Der Rosenkavalier*
Notary	Silent			*La Sonnambula*
Notary's Wife	Soprano			*Intermezzo*
Nourabad	Bass	High Priest of Brahma	1st Guyot; Baronti, E. Burke, Miranda	*Les Pêcheurs de Perles*
Nourrice	Contralto	Nurse		*Ariane et Barbe-Bleue*
Novice	Tenor			*Billy Budd*
Novice's Friend	Baritone			*Billy Budd*
Novices	Chorus			*Suor Angelica*

THE CHARACTERS IN THE OPERAS

CHARACTER	ROLE	SINGER	OPERA
Nowalska, Countess See Palmatica			
Nuns Chorus			Robert le Diable, Il Trovatore
Nuns See also the opera Suor Angelica			
Nureddin Tenor			Il Barbier von Bagdad
Nuri Soprano		Flagstad, Seefried	Tiefland
Nurse Mezzo-soprano	Xenia's nurse	Madeira	Boris Godunov
Nurse Mezzo-soprano		1st Jeritza	Die Frau ohne Schatten
Nurse Soprano	to Jaroslavna		Prince Igor
Nursing Sister Soprano			Suor Angelica
Nymphs Chorus			Russlan and Ludmilla, Tannhäuser, Les Troyens
Nymphs and Shepherds Chorus			La Favola d'Orfeo
Oberon Tenor	King of the fairies	1st Bland; Martinelli, Vrooms	Oberon
Oberthal, Count Baritone		Didur, Edouard de Reszke	Le Prophète
Obigny, Marchese d' See Marchese d'Obigny			
Obstinate Bass	A neighbor		Pilgrim's Progress
Ochs von Lerchenau, Baron Bass	Sophie's would-be suitor	1st Perron; Lorenzo Alvary, Bender, Kipnis, List, Mayr, Stear	Der Rosenkavalier

THE CHARACTERS IN THE OPERAS

CHARACTER	ROLE	SINGER	OPERA
Octavian Mezzo-soprano	Bearer of the Rose	Bible, della Casa, Evans, Goltz, Gutheil-Schoder, Hadrabova, Jurinac, Lotte Lehmann, Miller, Mödl, Novotna, Ober, Olczewska, Shacklock, Stevens, Thebom	*Der Rosenkavalier*
Oedipus Tenor	King of Thebes	Malipiero, Pears, Simoneau, Vrooms	*Oedipus*
Officer Tenor			*Ariadne auf Naxos*
Officer Tenor			*The Bohemian Girl*
Officer Bass			*Cardillac*
Officer From Chorus			*Christophe Colomb*
Officer Baritone			*Friedenstag*
Officer From Chorus			*Tosca*
Officer Baritone			*The Warrior*
Officers Chorus			*Billy Budd, Carmen, Lucrezia Borgia, Pskovityanka*
Official Registrar Baritone			*Madama Butterfly*
Officials Chorus			*Aida*
Old Bard Bass			*The Immortal Hour*
Old Believers Chorus			*Khovantschina*
Old-Clothes Man Tenor			*Louise*
Old Gypsy Baritone			*Il Trovatore*
Old Hebrew Bass		Allin, Moscona	*Samson et Dalila*
Old Men Chorus			*Prince Igor*
Old Men of Thebes Chorus			*Oedipus Rex*

CHARACTER	ROLE	SINGER	OPERA
Old Servant Bass			*Elektra*
Old Woman From Chorus			*L'Amore dei Tre Re*
Olga Contralto	Tatiana's sister	Elias	*Eugene Onegin*
Olga Sukarev, Countess Soprano			*Fedora*
Olga Yourievna Tokmakov, Princess Soprano	In love with Michael		*Pskovityanka*
Olimpia Soprano		Tebaldi	*Olympia* (Spontini)
Olin Blitch Bass-baritone	Evangelist		*Susannah*
Olivier Baritone	Poet	Fischer-Dieskau	*Capriccio*
Ollendorf, Colonel Bass	Governor of Cracow		*Der Bettelstudent*
Olympia Soprano	A mechanical doll	1st Isaac; Dobbs, Fremstad, Hempel, Seefried, Teyte	*Les Contes d'Hoffmann*
Omniscient Mussel, The Contralto			*Die Aegyptische Helena*
One-Arm Bass	Barak's brother		*Die Frau ohne Schatten*
One-Eye Bass	Barak's brother		*Die Frau ohne Schatten*
Opera Singers Chorus			*Le Postillion de Longjumeau*
Ophélie Soprano	Hamlet's beloved	1st Christine Nilsson; Ackté, Albani, Barrientos, Calvé, Gerster, Melba, Mignon Nevada, Nordica, Patti, Josephine de Reszke, Vere	*Hamlet*
Opinion Publique, L' Mezzo-soprano	Public Opinion		*Orphée aux Enfers*
Oracle			*Alceste*
Orator Bass			*Die Zauberflöte*

THE CHARACTERS IN THE OPERAS

CHARACTER		ROLE	SINGER	OPERA
Orest	Baritone	Agamemnon's son, Elektra's brother	1st Perron; Janssen, Nissen, Schorr, Schöffler	*Elektra*
Oreste	Baritone			*Les Choëphores*
Oreste	Baritone			*Eumenides*
Oreste	Baritone	Iphigénie's brother	1st Larrivée; Beck	*Iphigénie en Tauride*
Orfeo	Baritone		1st Giovanni Gualberto; Franci, Galeffi, Kullmann, Sammarco, Weil	*La Favola d'Orfeo*
Orfeo	Contralto		1st Guadagni; Ansseau (*Tenor*), Barbieri, Brema, Butt, Delna, Ferrier, Gay, Gerville-Réache, Hastreiter, Homer, Legros (*Tenor*), Thorborg, Viardot-Garcia, Wickham	*Orfeo ed Euridice*
Orford, Ellen *See* Ellen Orford				
Orlovsky Mezzo-soprano		Rich Russian	Miller, Novotna, Thebom	*Die Fledermaus*
Oroe	Bass	High Priest of the Magi	Foli	*Semiramide*
Oroveso	Bass	Norma's father, Archdruid	Lablache, Moscona, Plançon, Rossi-Lemeni, Siepi, Weiss	*Norma*
Orphans (Three) Soprano, Mezzo-soprano, Contralto				*Der Rosenkavalier*
Orphée	Baritone			*Les Malheurs d'Orphée*
Orphée	Tenor	A superb violinist		*Orphée aux Enfers*
Orsini *See* Paolo Orsini *See also* Maffio Orsini				

THE CHARACTERS IN THE OPERAS

CHARACTER	ROLE	SINGER	OPERA
Ortlinde Soprano or Mezzo-soprano	A Valkyr	Flagstad	*Die Walküre*
Ortrud Mezzo-soprano	Wife of Frederick of Telramund	1st Fasztlinger; Brema, Cahier, Carey, Fisher, Fornia-Labey, Fursch-Madi, Harshaw, Hastreiter, Homer, Kirkby-Lunn, Langendorf, Lilli Lehmann, Matzenauer, Mödl, Ober, Schumann-Heink, Thebom, Tietjens, Varnay, Wickham	*Lohengrin*
Osaka Tenor	Rich young man in love with Iris	Caruso, Gigli, Pertile	*Iris*
Oscar Soprano	A page	Carvalho, Grandi, Kurz, Thorborg, Schwarzkopf	*Un Ballo in Maschera*
Osmin Bass	Overseer of the harem	1st Ludwig Fischer; Ernster, Radford	*Die Entführung aus dem Serail*
Osmina, Suor Soprano	A nun		*Suor Angelica*
Ostasio Baritone	Francesca's brother		*Francesca da Rimini*
Otello Tenor	A moor, Venetian governor of Cyprus	1st Tamagno; Alvarez, Campanini, Lauri-Volpi, Marconi, Martinelli, McCracken, Melchior, Merli, del Monaco, Mullings, Pertile, Jean de Reszke, Rubini, Saléza, Slezak, Trantoul, Vinay, Winkelmann, Zanello, Zenatello	*Otello* (Verdi)

CHARACTER		ROLE	SINGER	OPERA
Ott, Mrs. Contralto				*Susannah*
Ottakar, Prince			Reeves, Robinson	*Der Freischütz*
Ottavio, Don	Tenor	Betrothed to Donna Anna	1st Antonio Baglioni; Bjoerling, Conley, Dermota, Lucia, Mario, McCormack, Peerce, Jean de Reszke, Rubini, Schack, Schipa, Stagno, Valletti	*Don Giovanni*
Ottokar	Tenor	Arsena's lover		*Zigeunerbaron*
Ottoman	Child	Le Pouf		*L'Enfant et les Sortilèges*
Ourrias	Baritone	Bulltender, rival for Mireille's love		*Mireille*
Overseer	Soprano			*Elektra*
Overseer	Baritone			*Der Prozess*
Ovlour	Tenor	Polovtsian traitor		*Prince Igor*
Paco	Tenor		1st Devries; Masini, Tokatyan, Vroons	*La Vida Breve*
Page	Contralto	Of Hérodias	Bible	*Salome*
Page	Mezzo-soprano			*Snyegurotchka*
Page, Mr. See Reich, Herr				
Page, Mistress	Mezzo-soprano			*Falstaff*
Page, Mrs. See Reich, Frau				
Pages	Chorus			*Ernani, Guillaume Tell, Les Huguenots, Lohengrin, Luisa Miller, Martha, Pskovityanka, I Puritani, Rigoletto, Roméo et Juliette*

CHARACTER		ROLE	SINGER	OPERA
Pages *See* Noble Pages (Four)				
Painter	Bass			*Louise*
Painter	Tenor			*Lulu*
Painter-Monk	Baritone			*Le Jongleur de Notre Dame*
Pagliaccio *See* Canio				
Palémon	Bass	An old Cenobite monk		*Thaïs*
Palestrina, Giovanni Pierluigi	Tenor	The composer	1st Karl Erb; Patzak, Schmedes	*Palestrina*
Pali	Bass	A gypsy		*Zigeunerbaron*
Palmatica	Mezzo-soprano	The Countess Nowalska		*Der Bettelstudent*
Paloucky	Bass Baritone	Peasant		*Hubička*
Pamela	Mezzo-soprano	Cockburn's wife, a tourist	1st Boulanger; Matters	*Fra Diavolo*
Pamina	Soprano	Daughter of the queen of the night	1st Nanetta Gottlieb; Carvalho, Davy, Dux, Eames, Cross, della Casa, Hempel, Jurinac, Lemnitz, Malten, Novotna, Schröder-Devrient, Schwarzkpof, Seefried, Siems, Tietjens	*Die Zauberflöte*
Pancratius	Speaker	The Count's major-domo		*Der Wildschütz*
Pang	Tenor	Supreme lord of provisions		*Turandot*
Pantalis	Contralto			*Mefistofele*
Pantalone	Bass	Minister		*Turandot* (Busoni)
Pantaloon				*Fête Galante*

CHARACTER		ROLE	SINGER	OPERA
Pantaloon	Baritone	The king's friend	Renan	*The Love for Three Oranges*
Panthée	Bass	Priest of Troy		*Les Troyens*
Paolino	Tenor	Carolina's secret husband		*Il Matrimonio Segreto*
Paolo Albiani	Baritone	A plebian		*Simon Boccanegra*
Paolo il Bello	Tenor	Handsome son of Malatesta	1st Martinelli; Crimi, Parmeggiani, Pertile, Prandelli, Ziliani	*Francesca da Rimini*
Paolo Orsini	Bass	Roman patrician	Griswold	*Rienzi*
Papagena	Soprano	Destined to be Papageno's wife	1st Gerl; Ugalde	*Die Zauberflöte*
Papageno	Baritone	A bird catcher	1st Schikaneder; Balfe, Carey, Kunz, Uppmann	*Die Zauberflöte*
Papal Nuncios (Two)	Silent			*Palestrina*
Paquiro	Baritone	Toreador	1st de Luca; Poli	*Goyescas*
Parassia	Soprano	In love with Gritzko		*The Fair at Sorochintsky*
Paris, Count	Baritone			*Roméo et Juliette*
Parpignol	Tenor	Toy peddler	Franke	*La Bohème*
Parsifal	Tenor	An innocent and pure youth	1st Winkelmann, Gudehus and Jäger; Althouse, Max Alvary, Berger, Burgstaller, Burrian, Dalmorès, Dippel, van Dyke, Hensel, Hutt, Hyde, Laubenthal, MacLennan, Melchior, Mullings, Niemann, Schmedes, Svanholm, Urlus, Vinay, Winkelmann, Wölfl, Sembach	*Parsifal*

CHARACTER	ROLE	SINGER	OPERA
Pascoe Baritone	Headman and preacher		*The Wreckers*
Pasha *See* Selim Pasha			
Pasquale, Don Bass	An old bachelor	1st Leblache; Baccaloni, Corena, de Luca	*Don Pasquale*
Passer-By Baritone			*Der Prozess*
Pastourelle, Une Soprano	Shepherd girl		*L'Enfant et les Sortilèges*
Pâtre, Un Contralto	Shepherd		*L'Enfant et les Sortilèges*
Patricians Chorus			*Simon Boccanegra*
Patroclus	Friend of Achilles		*Iphigénie en Aulide*
Pauline Contralto	Lisa's friend		*Pique-Dame*
Peachum, Mr. Bass	A fence, an organizer of thieves	Austin	*The Beggar's Opera*
Peachum, Mrs. Mezzo-soprano	Peachum's wife, Polly's mother		*The Beggar's Opera*
Peasant Tenor			*La Figlia del Reggimento*
Peasant, First Bass			*Ariane et Barbe-Bleue*
Peasant, Second Tenor			*Ariane et Barbe-Bleue*
Peasant, Third Bass			*Ariane et Barbe-Bleue*
Peasants Chorus			*Andrea Chénier, Ariane et Barbe-Bleue, Cavalleria Rusticana, L'Elisir d'Amore, La Figlia del Reggimento, Guillaume Tell, Háry János, Ivan Susanin, Linda di Chamounix, Mathis der Maler, Le Prophète, Der Wildschütz*

THE CHARACTERS IN THE OPERAS

CHARACTER	ROLE	SINGER	OPERA
Peasants (Two) Speakers			*Háry János*
Peasants (Two) Baritones			*A Village Romeo and Juliet*
Pedlars Chorus			*La Bohème, Louise*
Pedrillo Tenor	Belmonte's servant		*Die Entführung aus dem Serail*
Pedro, Don Bass	A general		*Béatrice et Bénédict*
Pedro Tenor	The mayor's secretary		*Der Corregidor*
Pedro Tenor		Dalmorès	*La Habanera*
Pedro Soprano	Dulcinée's admirer		*Don Quichotte*
Pedro Tenor	Shepherd	Schmedes, Völker	*Tiefland*
Pedro, Don Bass	The king's councillor		*L'Africaine*
Pelléas Tenor	Arkel's grandson, Golaud's half brother	1st Perier; Singher, Uppmann	*Pelléas et Mélisande*
Peneios Bass	Fisherman, Daphne's father		*Daphne*
Penelope Soprano		1st Goltz	*Penelope (Liebermann)*
Penelope Contralto	Wife of Ulisse		*Il Ritorno d'Ulisse in Patria*
Penitents Chorus			*Mefistofele*
People Chorus			*L'Amore dei Tre Re, Cardillac, Le Coq d'Or, Dido and Aeneas, Eumenides, Fidelio, I Gioielli della Madonna, Die Harmonie der Welt, Háry János, Le Jongleur de Notre Dame, Khovantschina, Manon, Prince Igor, Pskovityanka, Le Roi d'Ys, Die Zauberflöte*

THE CHARACTERS IN THE OPERAS

CHARACTER	ROLE	SINGER	OPERA
People of Bagdad Chorus			*Der Barbier von Bagdad*
People of Crete Chorus			*Idomeneo*
People of Naples Chorus			*Masaniello*
People of New Hope Valley Chorus			*Susannah*
Pepa Mezzo-soprano	Paquiro's sweetheart	1st Perini; Elmo	*Goyescas*
Pepa Soprano			*Tiefland*
Perfilievna Mezzo-soprano	Nurse		*Pskovityanka*
Perichaud Bass-baritone			*La Rondine*
Perside Soprano	A Christian		*Nerone*
Peter Baritone	Father of Hansel and Gretel		*Hänsel und Gretel*
Peter Tenor	The honey-man		*Porgy and Bess*
Peter *English version of the name* Filipeto *in I Quattro Rusteghi*			
Peter I Baritone	Young Tsar of Russia	Santley, Faure, Maurel	*Zar und Zimmermann*
Peter Grimes Tenor	A fisherman	1st Pears; Horne	*Peter Grimes*
Peter Homonay, Graf Baritone	Recruiting officer		*Zigeunerbaron*
Peter Ibbetson Tenor		Johnson	*Peter Ibbetson*
Peter Ivanov Tenor	Russian deserter		*Zar und Zimmermann*
Peter the Great *See* Peter I			

THE CHARACTERS IN THE OPERAS

CHARACTER	ROLE	SINGER	OPERA
Phaecian Sailors Chorus			*Il Ritorno d'Ulisse in Patria*
Phaeton *See* Tenor, The			
Philine Soprano	An actress, in love with Wilhelm	Garrison, Kellogg, Lilli Lehmann, Nordica, Talley	*Mignon*
Philip the Second *See* Filipso II			
Philistine Messenger Tenor		1st de Paolis	*Samson et Dalila*
Philistines Chorus			*Samson et Dalila*
Philosophers (Two) Tenor, Bass			*Louise*
Phryné Pantomime			*Faust*
Phryné Soprano		1st Sanderson	*Phryné (by Saint-Saëns)*
Physician Bass			*Pelléas et Mélisande*
Pianist *See* Boleslav Lazuiski			
Pickthank Contralto			*Pilgrim's Progress*
Piedmontese, A Tenor			*Friedenstag*
Pierrot Baritone			*Fête Galante*
Pierrotto Contralto		Scalchi	*Linda di Chamounix*
Pietists Chorus			*The Wreckers*
Pietro Baritone	Masaniello's friend	Faure, Staudigl	*Masaniello*
Pietro Bass	Plebeian		*Simon Boccanegra*
Pilgrim Tenor	A traveller through life	1st Matters	*Pilgrim's Progress*
Pilgrims Chorus			*Boris Godunov, Faust, La Forza del Destino, Mireille, Tannhäuser*

443

CHARACTER		ROLE	SINGER	OPERA
Pilot	Bass			*La Gioconda*
Pimen	Bass	Hermit and chronicler	Lorenzo Alvary, Gobbi, Hines, Tozzi	*Boris Godunov*
Pinchbeck, Sir James *English version of the name* Canciano *in* I Quattro Rusteghi				
Pinellino	Bass	Cobbler, witness for the will		*Gianni Schicchi*
Ping	Baritone	Grand Chancellor of China		*Turandot*
Pinkerton, Lieutenant B.F.	Tenor	Of the United States Navy	1st Zenatello; Caruso, Conley, Gedda, Hyde, Kullmann, Lloyd, Lugo, R. Martin, McCormack, del Monaco, Pertile, Sullivan	*Madama Butterfly*
Pinkerton, Miss (Two)	Soprano		Faull	*The Old Maid and the Thief*
Pinkerton, Kate *See* Kate Pinkerton				
Pippo	Mezzo-soprano		Vestris	*La Gazza Ladra*
Piram	Baritone			*Debora e Jaele*
Pirates	Chorus			*Oberon*
Pirro	Baritone		Gassier	*I Lombardi*
Pisandro	Tenor	One of Penelope's suitors		*Il Ritorno d'Ulisse in Patria*
Pistol	Bass	Falstaff's friend		*Falstaff*
Pittichinaccio	Tenor	Giulietta's admirer		*Les Contes d'Hoffmann*
Pizarro, Don	Bass	Prison governor	1st Meier; Bender, Bispham, Forti, Goritz, Reichmann, Staudigl	*Fidelio*

CHARACTER		ROLE	SINGER	OPERA
Plainclothes Men (Two)	Silent	Detectives		*The Consul*
Players	Chorus			*Iris*
Plebeians	Chorus			*Simon Boccanegra*
Pliable	Tenor	A neighbor		*Pilgrim's Progress*
Plunkett	Bass	Young farmer	de Luca, Maugeri, Stabile	*Martha*
Pluto		God of the underworld		*La Favola d'Orfeo*
Pluton	Tenor	God of the underworld, on earth called Aristée		*Orphée aux Enfers*
Plutus	Baritone	A role in a masque played by Tomsky		*Pique-Dame*
Poet	Baritone			*Louise*
Poet Monk	Tenor			*Le Jongleur de Notre Dame*
Pogner, Veit	Bass	Mastersinger, goldsmith, Eva's father.	1st Bausewein; Burke, Griswold, Hotter, Kipnis, Mayr, Plançon, Staudigl I, Staudigl II, Tozzi	*Die Meistersinger*
Poisson	Tenor	of the Comedie Française		*Adriana Lecouvreur*
Police	Chorus			*Le Postillion de Longjumeau, Tosca*
Police Commissioner	Bass			*Der Rosenkavalier*
Policeman	Bass			*The Boatswain's Mate*
Policeman	Speaker			*Porgy and Bess*
Policemen (Two)	Baritones			*Louise*
Polish Commander	Baritone			*Ivan Susanin*

445

THE CHARACTERS IN THE OPERAS

CHARACTER	ROLE	SINGER	OPERA
Polish Ladies Chorus			*Boris Godunov*
Polkan, General Bass			*Le Coq d'Or*
Pollione Tenor	Proconsul of Rome in Gaul		*Norma*
Pollux Tenor	King of Eos, Danea's father		*Die Liebe der Danae*
Polly Peachum Soprano		1st Lavinia Fenton; Cibber, Dickons, Stephens	*The Beggar's Opera*
Polovtsian Chiefs Chorus			*Prince Igor*
Polyxène Soprano	Priam's daughter		*Les Troyens*
Pompeo Baritone			*Benvenuto Cellini*
Pong Tenor	Supreme lord of the imperial kitchen	Curzi	*Turandot* (Puccini)
Pontius Pilate Bass			*Pilgrim's Progress*
Pope Pius IV Bass			*Palestrina*
Populace Chorus			*Un Ballo in Maschera, La Gioconda, Les Huguenots, Maritana*
Porgy Bass Baritone	A crippled poor man	1st Todd Duncan; Warfield	*Porgy and Bess*
Porter From Chorus			*Manon*
Pousette Soprano	An actress		*Manon*
Powder Monkeys Chorus			*Billy Budd*
Preacher			*The Wreckers*
Prefect Bass			*Linda di Chamounix*
Prelates Chorus			*Esther de Carpentras*
Preziosilla Mezzo-soprano	A gypsy	Miller, Simionato	*La Forza del Destino*

CHARACTER	ROLE	SINGER	OPERA
Priam Bass	King of Troy		*Les Troyens*
Priam's Ghost Bass			*Les Troyens*
Priest			*Turandot* (Busoni)
Priest *See also* High Priest			
Priestesses of Diana Chorus			*Iphigénie en Tauride*
Priests Chorus			*L'Africaine, Rienzi, Tiefland, Die Zauberflöte*
Priests (Two) Tenor, Bass			*Die Zauberflöte*
Priests (Three)			*L'Assassinio nel Cattedrale*
Priests and Priestesses Chorus			*Aida, Norma*
Priests of Neptune Chorus			*Idomeneo*
Priest's Son, The Tenor	Khivria's lover		*The Fair at Sorochintsky*
Prima Donna Soprano	Who plays Ariadne		*Ariadne auf Naxos*
Primrose Seiler Contralto			*Hugh the Drover*
Prince Tenor	Hypochondriac	Lloyd	*The Love for Three Oranges*
Prince Tenor	A traveller in Africa		*Lulu*
Prince de Bouillon Bass		1st de Luca; Sammarco	*Adriana Lecouvreur*
Prince Ottakar *See* Ottakar, Prince			
Princes and Princesses Chorus			*Prince Igor*

447

CHARACTER		ROLE	SINGER	OPERA
Princess	Soprano	Also Fire, also Le Rossignol		*L'Enfant et Les Sortilèges*
Princess	Soprano		Rappold	*Lobetanz*
Princess	Soprano		Alda, Favero	*Marouf*
Princess	Contralto	Angelica's aunt	1st Perini; Palombini, Claramae Turner	*Suor Angelica*
Princess von Werdenberg *See* Marschallin, The				
Princess de Bouillon Mezzo-soprano		In love with Maurizio	Elmo, Pederzini	*Adriana Lecouvreur*
Prior, The	Bass			*Le Jongleur de Notre Dame*
Prisoner				*Maria Golovin*
Prisoners	Chorus			*Andrea Chénier, Fidelio, Prince Igor, Le Prophète*
Private Soldier	Tenor			*Friedenstag*
Prodica *See* Giovanni da Prodica				
Prophète, Le *See* John of Leyden				
Proserpina				*La Favola d'Orfeo*
Prunier	Tenor	A poet	1st Dominici	*La Rondine*
Public Opinion *See* Opinion Publique				
Publius	Bass	Captain of the Praetorian guard	Edelmann	*La Clemenza di Tito*
Puck	Soprano	Oberon's runner		*Oberon*
Puppets (Four) Soprano, Contralto, Tenor, Bass				*Fête Galante*

THE CHARACTERS IN THE OPERAS

CHARACTER	ROLE	SINGER	OPERA
Puritans Chorus			*I Puritani*
Pylade Tenor	Oreste's friend	1st Legros; Nourrit, Weil	*Iphigénie en Tauride*
Pythie, La Soprano			*Eumenides*
Queen Mezzo-soprano			*Fête Galante*
Queen Iceheart Mezzo-soprano			*Švanda Dudák*
Queen Mother of Samarkand Soprano	A negress		*Turandot* (Busoni)
Queen of Sheba, The Mezzo-soprano		Lilli Lehmann, Malten	*Die Königin von Saba*
Queen of Shemakha Soprano		Dobbs	*Le Coq d'Or*
Queen of the Gypsies Contralto			*The Bohemian Girl*
Queen of the Night Soprano		1st Josefa Hofer; Juch, Peters	*Die Zauberflöte*
Quichotte, Don Bass	Don Quixote	1st Chaliapin; Vanni-Marcoux	*Don Quichotte*
Quickly, Dame (or Mistress) Contralto		Homer	*Falstaff*
Quinault Bass	Of the Comédie Française		*Adriana Lecouvreur*
Quint's Ghost Tenor		1st Pears	*The Turn of the Screw*
Quixote *See* Quichotte			
Rachel Soprano	Eleazar's daughter	1st Falcon; Brandt, Easton, Krauss, Lilli Lehmann, Materna, Ponselle, Raisa, Stoltz, Viardot-Garcia, Vere	*La Juive*

CHARACTER		ROLE	SINGER	OPERA
Radames	Tenor	Captain of the guard	1st Mongini; Baum, Campanini, Caruso, Graziani, Jagel, Lauri-Vòlpi, Maás, Martinelli, Merli, del Monaco, Mullings, Pertile, Jean de Reszke, Slezak, Tamagno, Tucker, Vinay, Zenatello	*Aida*
Rafaele	Baritone	Camorrist leader	Danise, Sammarco, Czaplicki	*I Gioielli della Madonna*
Ragman	Bass		Allin	*Louise*
Ragpicker Mezzo-soprano				*Louise*
Ragpickers	Chorus			*Iris*
Raimbaut	Tenor	Minstrel		*Robert le Diable*
Raimondo	Bass	Papal legate		*Rienzi*
Raimondo *See* Raymond				
Rainette, La	Tenor	The frog		*L'Enfant et les Sortilèges*
Rakewell *See* Tom Rakewell				
Raleigh, Sir Walter	Bass	Captain of the guard		*Gloriana*
Rambaldo Baritone		Wealthy Parisian		*La Rondine*
Ramfis	Bass	High priest	1st Medini; Didur, Moscona, Nanetti, Plançon, Edouard de Reszke, Tajo	*Aida*
Ramiro	Baritone	Muleteer	Cassell, Vieuille	*L'Heure Espagnole*
Ramiro, Don Tenor		Prince of Salerno	Lloyd	*La Cenerentola*
Ramon, Maître Bass		Mireille's father		*Mireille*

THE CHARACTERS IN THE OPERAS

CHARACTER	ROLE	SINGER	OPERA
Ramphis *See* Ramfis			
Rance, Jack Baritone	Sheriff	1st Amato; Borgioli, Franci, Galeffi, Tibbett, Weede	*La Fanciulla del West*
Rangoni Bass	A Jesuit		*Boris Godunov*
Raoul de Nangis Tenor	Huguenot nobleman	1st Nourrit; Campanini, Caruso, Dippel, Lauri- Volpi, Maas, Mario, Martinelli, Nicolini, Niemann, Jean de Reszke, Wachtel	*Les Huguenots*
Ratcliffe, Lt. Bass			*Billy Budd*
Ratmir Contralto	Oriental prince, suitor to Ludmilla		*Russlan and Ludmilla*
Raymond Baritone	Chaplain of Lammermoor		*Lucia di Lammermoor*
Reapers Chorus			*Eugene Onegin*
Recorder of Norwich Bass			*Gloriana*
Recruits Chorus			*Její Pastorkyňa (Jenufa)*
Rector *See* Horace Adams			
Red Whiskers Tenor	An impressed sea- man		*Billy Budd*
Redburn, Mr. Baritone	First lieutenant		*Billy Budd*
Registrar *See* Official Registrar			
Regnard, Baron Baritone		Renan	*He Who Gets Slapped*
Regina Soprano	Schwalb's daughter		*Mathis der Maler*
Regina Giddens Soprano		Lewis	*Regina*
Reich, Frau Mezzo-soprano	Mrs. Page		*Die Lustigen Weiber von Windsor*

CHARACTER		ROLE	SINGER	OPERA
Reich, Herr	Bass	Mr. Page	Gassier	*Die Lustigen Weiber von Windsor*
Reinmar von Zweter	Bass	Knight and Minnesinger		*Tannhäuser*
Reiza *See* Rezia				
Relatives	Chorus			*Madama Butterfly, Lucia di Lammermoor*
Remondado, El	Tenor	A smuggler	de Paolis, Renan	*Carmen*
Renato	Baritone	The governor's secretary, Amelia's husband (Anckarström)	Bechi, Gobbi, Sved	*Un Ballo in Maschera*
Repela	Bass	Valet to the Magistrate	Hesch	*Der Corregidor*
Representative of the Sailors	Speaker			*Christophe Colomb*
Retainers	Chorus			*Lucia di Lammermoor*
Retz, De	Baritone			*Les Huguenots*
Rezia	Soprano	Daughter of Haroun el Rashid	1st Paton; Brouwenstijn, Flagstad, Goltz, Anni Konetzni, Milanov, Müller, Pederzini, Ponselle, Seidl-Krauss, Tietjens, Ugalde, Wagner	*Oberon*
Rhadames *See* Radames				
Ribbing, Count *See* Samuele				
Riccardo	Tenor	Count of Warwick (Gustavus III)	Bjoerling, Bonci, Borgioli, Caruso, Gigli, Martinelli, Peerce, Jean de Reszke, di Stefano, Tamagno, Vroons	*Un Ballo in Maschera*

THE CHARACTERS IN THE OPERAS

CHARACTER	ROLE	SINGER	OPERA
Riccardo, Don Tenor	The King's squire		*Ernani*
Riccardo *See* Richard Forth, Sir			
Riccardo Accolai, Count Tenor	Visitor		*I Quattro Rusteghi*
Rich, Lady Penelope Soprano	Sister of Essex		*Gloriana*
Richard Forth, Sir Baritone	Puritan	1st Tamburini; Beck, Galassi, Gerster, Ronconi, Panerai	*I Puritani*
Richtofen	Saxon officer		*Der Bettelstudent*
Riedinger Bass	Rich Lutheran		*Mathis der Maler*
Rienzi *See* Cola Rienzi			
Rigoletto Baritone	The Duke's jester, Gilda's father	1st Vanesi; Baklanov, Basiola, Brownlee, Formichi, Franci, Galassi, Gobbi, Lassalle, de Luca, Merrill, Renaud, Ronconi, Ruffo, Sammarco, Scotti, Schwarz, Stabile, Warren, Weede	*Rigoletto*
Rinuccio Tenor	Zita's nephew, 24, in love with Lauretta	Conley, Crimi, Davies, Johnson, T. Burke	*Gianni Schicchi*
Roaring Boys and Whores Chorus			*The Rake's Progress*
Robbins Tenor			*Porgy and Bess*
Robert Bass			*Hugh the Drover*
Robert Tenor	Son of the Devil, Duke of Normandy	1st Nourrit; Mario, Jean de Reszke, Schnorr von Carolsfield	*Robert le Diable*

CHARACTER		ROLE	SINGER	OPERA
Roberti From Chorus		Executioner		*Tosca*
Roberto	Bass	French Soldier		*I Vespri Siciliani*
Robespierre	Tenor		1st Witt	*Dantons Tod*
Robinson, Count	Bass	An English lord		*Il Matrimonio Segreto*
Rocco	Bass	Chief jailer	1st Rothe; Braun, Formes, Kipnis, Staudigl II	*Fidelio*
Rocco	Bass	Camorrist		*I Gioielli della Madonna*
Roche, La	Bass	Theater director	Hotter	*Capriccio*
Roderigo	Tenor	Venetian gentleman		*Otello*
Rodolfo	Tenor	Starving young poet	Bonci, Borgioli, Caruso, Conley, Cunningham, Gigli, Hislop, Jagel, Kiepura, Lauri-Volpi, Martin, Martinelli, McCormack, Peerce, Pertile, Poleri, di Stefano, Sullivan, Tagliavini, Tucker	*La Bohème*
Rodolfo	Tenor	In love with Luisa, son of Count Walter		*Luisa Miller*
Rodolpho, Count	Bass	Lord of the castle	Faure, Foli, Gassier, Reeves, Edouard de Reszke	*La Sonnambula*
Rodrig	Bass	Athlete (also plays Animal Tamer)		*Lulu*
Rodrigo	Baritone	Marquis of Posa	1st Faure; de Luca, Merrill	*Don Carlos*
Rodriguez	Tenor	Admirer of Dulcinée		*Don Quichotte*
Roi d'Ys, Le	Bass	King of Ys		*Le Roi d'Ys*
Romans	Chorus			*Nerone, Rienzi*
Romantics	Chorus			*The Love for Three Oranges*
Romeo	Contralto	A Montague in love with Giulietta	1st Giuditta Grisi; Viardot-Garcia, Wagner	*I Capuleti ed I Montecchi*

CHARACTER		ROLE	SINGER	OPERA
Roméo	Tenor	A Montague, enemy to the Capulets	1st Michot; Alvarez, Ansseau, Capoul, Crooks, Gigli, Hislop, Mario Muratore, Jean de Reszke, Saléza	*Roméo et Juliette*
Rosa	Soprano		Zerr	*Faust* (Spohr)
Rosa Mamai	Mezzo-soprano	Federico's mother	1st Fraces; Stignani, Pederzini	*L'Arlesiana*
Rosalia	Contralto			*Tiefland*
Rosalinda	Soprano	Eisenstein's wife	Gueden, Hurley, Resnik, Welitsch	*Die Fledermaus*
Rosario	Soprano	A lady in love with Fernando	1st Fitziu; Carbone	*Goyescas*
Roschana	Speaker	Almanzor's wife		*Oberon*
Rose	Soprano	An English lady		*Lakmé*
Rose	Soprano			*Le Postillion de Longjumeau*
Rossetta	Soprano		Billington, Stephens	*Love in a Village*
Rosette	Soprano	An actress		*Manon*
Rosina	Mezzo-soprano	Dr. Bartolo's ward	1st Giorgi-Righetti; Alboni, de los Angeles, Callas, Carvalho, Dickons, Fodor-Mainvielle, Fornia-Labey, Galli-Curci, Hempel, Holman, Lessugg, Macbeth, Malibran, Melba, Munsel, Mignon, Nevada, Patti, Peters, Phillips, Pons, Schwarzkopf, Sembrich, Simionato, Sontag, Luisa Tetrazzini, Trebelli, Tuminia, Viardot-Garcia, van Zandt	*Il Barbiere di Siviglia*
Rossignol, Le	Soprano	*Also plays* Fire *and* The Princess		*L'Enfant et les Sortilèges*

CHARACTER	ROLE	SINGER	OPERA
Rossignol, Le Soprano	The Nightingale		*Le Rossignol*
Rossweisse Soprano *or* Mezzo-soprano	A Valkyr		*Die Walküre*
Roucher Bass	Andrea's friend		*Andrea Chénier*
Rouvel, Baron Tenor			*Fedora*
Rowan Soprano	Nurse (*Called* Pamela Wilton *in Acts I and II*)		*Let's Make an Opera*
Rozenn Soprano	The king's daughter	Alda	*Le Roi d'Ys*
Rubria Mezzo-soprano	Vestal virgin, secretly a Christian	1st Bertana; Stignani	*Nerone*
Rudolf II, Kaiser Bass *Also* Ferdinand, *also* The Sun			*Die Harmonie der Welt*
Rudolph Tenor	Captain of the guard		*Guillaume Tell*
Rudolph *See also* Rodolfo			
Ruedi Tenor	Fisherman		*Guillaume Tell*
Ruggero Tenor	Young man	1st Schipa; Gigli	*La Rondine*
Ruggiero Baritone	Provost		*La Juive*
Ruiz Tenor	Manrico's soldier	Grazzi	*Il Trovatore*
Rusalka Soprano		Brouwenstijn	*Rusalka*
Russian Sentry Speaker			*Háry János*
Russlan Bass		1st Petrov	*Russlan and Ludmilla*
Rustighello Tenor	Serving Alfonso d'Este		*Lucrezia Borgia*
Ruy Gomez di Silva, Don Bass	Spanish grandee	Mayr	*Ernani*
Saamcheddine, Princess Soprano		1st Davelli; Favero, Alda	*Marouf*
Sachs *See* Hans Sachs			

CHARACTER		ROLE	SINGER	OPERA
Sacristan	Baritone		Baccaloni, Corena, Renan	*Tosca*
Sadko	Tenor	Singer		*Sadko*
Saffi	Soprano	Czipra's foster daughter		*Zigeunerbaron*
Sailor	Tenor			*Dido and Aeneas*
Sailor	Tenor	Returned after fifteen years	1st Legrand; Kreuger, Malipiero, Ostertag, Schiffler	*Le Pauvre Matelot*
Sailor	Tenor		Reiss	*Tristan und Isolde*
Sailors	Chorus			*L'Africaine, Billy Budd, Dido and Aeneas, Der Fliegende Holländer, La Gioconda, Idomeneo, Lakmé, Marouf, Otello, Tristan und Isolde, Les Troyens*
Saints	Double Chorus			*Four Saints in Three Acts*
St. Bris	Baritone	Catholic nobleman	1st Serda; Delmas, Faure, Foli, Kaschmann, Lassalle, Plançon, Edouard de Reszke, Scaria	*Les Huguenots*
St. Chavez	Tenor		1st Embry Bonner	*Four Saints in Three Acts*
St. Corentin	Bass	Patron of Ys		*Le Roi d'Ys*
St. Ignatius Loyola	Baritone		1st Edward Matthews	*Four Saints in Three Acts*
St. Just	Bass		1st L. Weber	*Dantons Tod*
St. Settlement	Soprano		1st Bertha Baker	*Four Saints in Three Acts*
St. Therese I	Soprano		1st Beatrice Wayne	*Four Saints in Three Acts*
St. Therese II	Contralto		1st B. Howard	*Four Saints in Three Acts*
Sali	Soprano	Manz's son, as a child		*A Village Romeo and Juliet*

THE CHARACTERS IN THE OPERAS

CHARACTER		ROLE	SINGER	OPERA
Sali	Tenor	Manz's son, in love with Vreli		*A Village Romeo and Juliet*
Salome (The part requires both a Soprano and a Dancer)	Soprano	Herod's step-daughter	1st Wittich; Ackté, Borkh, Cebotari, Curtin, Destinn, Djanel, Easton, Fremstad, Garden, Goltz, Gutheil-Schoder, Jeritza, Krusceniski, Lawrence, Birgit Nilsson, Shacklock, Varnay, Welitsch	*Salome*
Salud	Soprano	Gypsy in love with Paco	1st Lillian Grenville; de los Angeles, Bori, Carré, dalla Rizza	*La Vida Breve*
Salviati, Cardinal	Bass			*Benvenuto Cellini*
Sam	Treble	Sweepboy, 8 (*called* John *in Acts I and II*)		*Let's Make an Opera*
Sam Polk	Tenor	Susannah's brother		*Susannah*
Samaritana	Soprano	Francesca's sister		*Francesca da Rimini*
Samiel	Speaker	The wild huntsman (the Devil)		*Der Freischütz*
Samson	Tenor	Hebrew hero	Caruso, Merli, del Monaco, Tamagno, Vinay	*Samson and Dalila*
Samson	Baritone		1st Harrell	*The Warrior*
Samuel See Léopold				
Samuele	Bass	The governor's enemy (Count Ribbing)	Lorenzo Alvary	*Un Ballo un Maschera*
Samurai	Chorus			*Iris*
Sancho	Baritone	Don Quixote's squire	1st Gresse; de Luca	*Don Quichotte*
Sandman	Soprano	Bringer of sleep to little children		*Hänsel und Gretel*

THE CHARACTERS IN THE OPERAS

CHARACTER	ROLE	SINGER	OPERA
Sandor Barinkay Tenor			*Zigeunerbaron*
Sante Silent	Count Gil's servant		*Il Segreto di Susanna*
Santuzza Soprano	Village girl in love with Turiddu	1st Bellincioni; Barbieri, Brouwenstijn, Callas, Calvé, Destinn, Eames, Easton, Fremstad, Gay, Goltz, Jeritza, Kronold, Labia, Masiani, Matzenauer, Milanov, Neway, Ponselle, Shuard, Varnay	*Cavalleria Rusticana*
Sapho Soprano		1st Viardot-Garcia; Krauss	*Sapho* (Gounod)
Sapho Soprano		Bellincioni, Calvé, Garden	*Sapho* (Massenet)
Sarastro Bass	High priest of Isis and Osiris	1st Gerl; Bender, Foli, Formes, Kipnis, Petrov, Radford, Staudigl, Tozzi	*Die Zauberflöte*
Sarvaor, Uncle Bass		1st Cotreuil; d'Angelo	*La Vida Breve*
Satraps Chorus			*Semiramide*
Saturn Bass *Also plays* Tansur			*Die Harmonie der Welt*
Satyavan Tenor	Woodman		*Savitri*
Satyrs Chorus			*Fête Galante, Les Troyens*
Savitri Soprano	Satyavan's wife		*Savitri*
Savoyard Mezzo-soprano			*Fedora*
Savoyards Chorus			*Linda di Chamounix*
Scaramuccio Tenor		Manton	*Ariadne auf Naxos*

CHARACTER	ROLE	SINGER	OPERA
Scarpia, Baron Baritone	Chief of police	1st Giraldoni; Baklanov, Cassell, Formichi, Franci, Galeffi, Gobbi, London, Rothmuller, Sammarco, Scotti, Stabile, Taddei, Tibbett, Uhde, Warren, Weede	*Tosca*
Schaunard Baritone	Starving young musician	Cehanovsky, Renan	*La Bohème*
Schigolch Bass	Old man		*Lulu*
Schikaneder Baritone	Opera manager	Bispham	*Der Schauspieldirektor*
Schlemil Bass	Giulietta's lover		*Les Contes d'Hoffmann*
Schmidt Baritone	Jailer		*Andrea Chénier*
Schmidt Tenor	Le Bailli's friend		*Werther*
Schneidebart Baritone	Barber		*Die Schweigsame Frau*
Scholar Silent			*Der Rosenkavalier*
Schön, Doctor Baritone	An editor	Stig	*Lulu*
Schoolboy Contralto	Gymnasiast, *also plays* Wardrobe Mistress		*Lulu*
Schoolboys Chorus			*Der Wildschütz*
Schouisky *See* Schuisky			
Schtschelkalov *See* Shchelkalov			
Schuisky, Wassili Ivanovitsh Tenor	Boyard, ambitious to become Tsar	Bada, Franke, Kullmann, de Paolis	*Boris Godunov*
Schwalb, Hans Tenor	Peasant leader		*Mathis der Maler*
Schwanda the Bagpiper Baritone	Svanda Dudák		*Svanda Dudák*

CHARACTER	ROLE	SINGER	OPERA
Schwertleite Soprano or Mezzo-soprano	A Valkyr	Madeira	*Die Walküre*
Sciarrone Bass	Gendarme	Cehanovsky	*Tosca*
Scindia Baritone		1st Lassalle; Ancona	*Le Roi de Lahore*
Scipio Speaker	A small boy		*Porgy and Bess*
Scribe From Chorus			*Tosca*
Scrivener Tenor			*Khovantschina*
Sculptor Baritone			*Louise*
Sculptor Monk Bass			*Le Jongleur de Notre Dame*
Scythians Chorus			*Iphigénie en Tauride*
Sea Nymph Soprano			*Oberon*
Sebastiano Baritone	Rich land owner		*Tiefland*
Secret Police Agent Bass		Renan	*The Consul*
Secretary *See* Shchelkalov			
Secretary Mezzo-soprano		1st Powers	*The Consul*
Secretary Silent			*Palestrina*
Sedley, Mrs. Mezzo-soprano	Rentier, widow of an East India Company's factor	1st Valetta Jacopi	*Peter Grimes*
Selika Soprano	Captured African queen	1st Sass; Barrientos, Brandt, Caniglia, Fremstad, Anni Konetzni, Lucca, Materna, Matzenauer, Nordica, Ponselle, Rasa, Ternina	*L'Africaine*
Selim Speaker	The pasha		*Die Entführung aus dem Serail*
Sellem Tenor	Auctioneer	1st Hugues Cuenod; Franke	*The Rake's Progress*

THE CHARACTERS IN THE OPERAS

CHARACTER	ROLE	SINGER	OPERA
Selva Bass	Officer of the guard		*Masaniello*
Sélysette Mezzo-soprano	Former wife of Barbe-bleu		*Ariane et Barbe-Bleue*
Semele Soprano	A queen, formerly loved by Jupiter		*Die Liebe der Danae*
Semiramide Soprano	Queen of Babylon	Alboni, Fodor-Mainvielle, Grisi, Krauss, Scalchi, Sontag, Tietjens	*Semiramide*
Senators Chorus			*La Gioconda*
Senta Soprano	Daland's daughter	1st Schröder-Devrient; Borkh, Corsi, Destinn, Flagstad, Hastreiter, Juch, Leider, Marchesi, Moody, Murska, Osborn, Seidl-Krauss, Stehle, Sucher, Varnay	*Der Fliegende Holländer*
Sentry Tenor			*Pskovityanka*
Serena Contralto			*I Gioielli della Madonna*
Serena Soprano	Robbins' wife		*Porgy and Bess*
Sergeant Bass			*Friedenstag*
Sergeant Baritone			*Hugh the Drover*
Sergeant From Chorus			*Manon*
Sergeant From Chorus			*Tosca*
Sergeant of Archers Bass			*Manon Lescaut*
Sergio Baritone	Footman		*Fedora*
Serpina Soprano	Uberto's servant	1st Laura-Monti; Easton, Fleisher, Galli-Marie, Sayao	*La Serva Padrona*
Servant From Chorus			*Arabella*
Servant From Chorus			*Un Ballo in Maschera*

THE CHARACTERS IN THE OPERAS

CHARACTER	ROLE	SINGER	OPERA
Servant From Chorus			*Christophe Colomb*
Servant			*Maria Golovin*
Servant	Silent		*Palestrina*
Servant	Baritone	of Nicias	*Thaïs*
Servants	Chorus		*Adriana Lecouvreur, Andrea Chénier, Der Barbier von Bagdad, Le Coq d'Or, Falstaff, La Forza del Destino, Die Frau ohne Schatten, Die Liebe der Danae, The Love for Three Oranges, Luisa Miller, Martha, Mignon, Madama Butterfly, Pique-Dame, The Rake's Progress, Rigoletto, La Traviata, Der Wildschütz, Wozzeck*
Servants (Two) Baritones			*Don Quichotte*
Servants (Four) Tenors, Basses	of the Marschallin		*Der Rosenkavalier*
Servants (Eight) Four Tenors, Four Basses			*Capriccio*
Servants of Aithra (Two) Soprano, Mezzo-soprano			*Die Aegyptische Helena*
Servilia	Soprano	Wife of Sextus	*La Clemenza di Tito*
Sesto *See* Sextus			
Sextus	Contralto	Young patrician of Rome	*La Clemenza di Tito*
Shades of Trojans Chorus			*Die Aegyptische Helena*

CHARACTER	ROLE	SINGER	OPERA
Shadow, Nick See Nick Shadow			
Shaklovity, Boyard Baritone			*Khovantschina*
Sharpers Chorus			*Manon*
Sharpless Baritone	United States Consul at Nagasaki	1st de Luca; Brownlee, Paci, Renan, Scotti	*Madama Butterfly*
Shchelkalov Baritone	Clerk of the Douma (the parliament)	Cehanovsky	*Boris Godunov*
Shellfish Seller Bass			*Hugh the Drover*
Shepherd Tenor			*Oedipus Rex*
Shepherd Tenor		Franke, Reiss	*Tristan und Isolde*
Shepherd See also Young Shepherd			
Shepherd Boy Contralto		Evans, Glaz	*Tosca*
Shepherds (Three) Tenor, Baritone and Bass			*Pilgrim's Progress*
Shepherds (Four) Tenor, Baritone, Two Basses			*Daphne*
Shepherds Chorus			*L'Enfant et les Sortilèges, Les Troyens, The Wreckers*
Sherasmin Baritone	Sir Huon's squire		*Oberon*
Sheriff Bass			*Martha*
Shillem Tenor			*Debora e Jaele*
Shining Ones (Three) Soprano, Mezzo-soprano, Contralto			*Pilgrim's Progress*
Shopkeepers Chorus			*La Bohème, Iris*

THE CHARACTERS IN THE OPERAS

CHARACTER		ROLE	SINGER	OPERA
Showman	Baritone			*Hugh the Drover*
Showman	Tenor			*The Village Romeo and Juliet*
Shuisky See Schuisky				
Sicilians	Chorus			*I Vespri Siciliani*
Sid	Baritone	Butcher's assistant		*Albert Herring*
Sid	Baritone			*La Fanciulla del West*
Siebel	Mezzo-soprano	Youth in love with Marguerite	1st Faivre; Bible, Scalchi	*Faust*
Siegfried	Tenor	Posthumous son of Siegmund and Sieglinde	1st Betz; Althouse, Max Alvary, Berger, Burgstaller, Hartmann, Lorenz, Melchior, Mullings, Niemann, Svanholm, Unger	*Das Ring des Nibelungen*
Sieglinde	Soprano	Hunding's wife, Siegfried's sister	1st Thoma; Ackté, Bampton, Borkh, Caron, Eames, Easton, Fisher, Flagstad, Fornia-Labey, Fremstad, Gadski, Jeritza, Juch, Klafsky, Lilli Lehmann, Lotte Lehmann, Lemnitz, Marchesi, Moody. Morena, Müller, Resnik, Rethberg, Saltzmann-Stevens, Seidl-Krauss, Traubel, Varnay, Wittich	*Die Walküre*
Siegmund	Tenor	Mortal son of the god Wotan	1st Vogl; Althouse, Max Alvary, Berger, van Dyke, Hyde, Lorenz, Melchior, Niemann, Saléza, Schmedes, Schott, Svanholm, Urlus, Völker	*Die Walküre*

THE CHARACTERS IN THE OPERAS

CHARACTER	ROLE	SINGER	OPERA
Siegrune Soprano or Mezzo-soprano	A Valkyr	Glaz	*Die Walküre*
Silberklang, Madame Soprano		Cavalieri	*Der Schauspieldirektor*
Silla Mezzo-soprano	Palestrina's pupil		*Palestrina*
Silva *See* Ruy Gomez di Silva, Don			
Silvano Baritone	A sailor (Cristian)	Cehanovsky	*Un Ballo in Maschera*
Silvio Baritone	A villager in love with Nedda	Ancona, Cehanovsky, Svanholm, Panerai, Werrenrath, Zenatello	*I Pagliacci*
Simon Tenor	Polish beggar student		*Der Bettelstudent*
Simon Bass		1st G. Hamm	*Dantons Tod*
Simon Bass-baritone	Marina's husband		*I Quattro Rusteghi*
Simon Boccanegra Baritone	Plebeian, elected Doge	Colzani, Gobbi, Tibbett, Warren	*Simon Boccanegra*
Simon Mago Baritone	Sorcerer	1st Journet; Maugeri	*Nerone*
Simon Magus Baritone			*Pilgrim's Progress*
Simona Soprano			*Zaza*
Simone Bass	Dead Buoso's cousin, 70	Lorenzo Alvary	*Gianni Schicchi*
Simpleton, The Tenor		Franke	*Boris Godunov*
Singer Soprano	The first singer of the opera		*Cardillac*
Singer Tenor		Baum	*Der Rosenkavalier*
Singer Mezzo-soprano			*Turandot* (Busoni)
Singer Baritone			*La Vida Breve*
Singers Chorus	of the Papal Chapel		*Palestrina*

CHARACTER	ROLE	SINGER	OPERA
Singers (Five) Two Tenors, Three Basses	from the Chapel of St. Maria Maggiore		*Palestrina*
Sirens Chorus			*Mefistofele, Russlan and Ludmilla, Tannhäuser*
Sirieux, De Baritone	French diplomat		*Fedora*
Sisera Tenor	Enemy of the Jews	1st Sample; Folco, Parmeggiani	*Debora e Jaele*
Sister See the opera Suor Angelica			
Sisters Chorus			*Suor Angelica*
Sixtus Beckmesser See Beckmesser, Sixtus			
Skula Bass	Gudok player		*Prince Igor*
Slammekin, Mrs. From Chorus	A lady of the town		*The Beggar's Opera*
Slave Contralto	of Francesca		*Francesca da Rimini*
Slave Merchant Pantomime			*Djamileh*
Slaves Chorus			*Die Aegyptische Helena, Le Coq d'Or, Die Entführung aus dem Serail, Khovantschina, Oberon, Prince Igor Semiramide, Turandot* (Busoni), *Die Zauberflöte*
Slender See Spärlich			
Slim Girl Soprano			*A Village Romeo and Juliet*
Smeraldina Mezzo-soprano	Fata Morgana's servant	Bible, Evans	*The Love for Three Oranges*
Smugglers Chorus			*Carmen, Hubička*
Snyegurotchka Soprano	The Snow-Maiden, daughter of Winter and Spring	Bori	*Snyegurotchka*

CHARACTER		ROLE	SINGER	OPERA
Sobinjin	Tenor	Soldier, Antonida's bridegroom		*Ivan Susanin*
Sofa	Child	Le Canapé		*L'Enfant et Les Sortilèges*
Soldier	Baritone	Brother of the girl Faust betrayed		*Doktor Faustus*
Soldier, First	Baritone			*Les Troyens*
Soldier, Second	Bass			*Les Troyens*
Soldiers	Chorus			*L'Africaine Aida, Andrea Chénier, Il Barbiere di Siviglia, La Bohème, Carmen, Dalibor, La Damnation de Faust, Debora, Doktor Faustus, L'Elisir d'Amore, Faust, Fidelio, La Figlia del Reggimento, La Forza de Destino, Friedenstag, Guillaume Tell, Die Harmonie der Welt, Háry János, Hugh the Drover, Les Huguenots, Idomeneo, Ivan Susanin, La Juive, Lakmé, The Love for Three Oranges, Manon, Maritana, Marouf, Masaniello, Mathis der Maler, Otello (Verdi), Prince Igor, Le Prophète, Der Prozess, Rienzi, Le Roi d'Ys, Roméo et Juliette, Tosca, Turandot (Busoni), Il Trovatore, I Vespri Siciliani, Wozzeck*

THE CHARACTERS IN THE OPERAS

CHARACTER	ROLE	SINGER	OPERA
Soldiers (Two) Basses			*Salomé*
Soldiers of Babylon Chorus			*Nabucco*
Soldiers of the Commonwealth Chorus			*I Puritani*
Solo Contralto From Chorus			*Les Choëphores*
Solo Soprano From Chorus			*Les Choëphores*
Solomon *See* King Solomon			
Somarona Bass	Orchestra conductor		*Béatrice et Bénédict*
Song Writer Baritone			*Louise*
Sonora Baritone	A miner		*La Fanciulla del West*
Sophie Soprano	Daughter of von Faninal	1st Minnie Nast; Berger, Conner, Dux, della Casa, Gueden, Peters, Schumann, Schwarzkopf, Steber	*Der Rosenkavalier*
Sophie Soprano	Charlotte's sister	1st Forster; Gluck	*Werther*
Sophie Brook Soprano	Age 10, *called* Monica *in Acts I and II*		*Let's Make an Opera*
Sorceress Mezzo-soprano		Simionato	*Dido and Aeneas*
Sourin Bass	Officer		*Pique-Dame*
Spalanzani Tenor	Inventor of a mechanical doll		*Les Contes d'Hoffmann*
Sparafucile Bass	A professional assassin	Foli, Hines, Moscona, Siepi	*Rigoletto*
Spärlich, Junker Tenor	Slender, unsuccessful suitor to Ann Page		*Die Lustigen Weiber von Windsor*

469

THE CHARACTERS IN THE OPERAS

CHARACTER	ROLE	SINGER	OPERA
Spectators, Ten Reasonable Five Tenors, Five Basses			*The Love for Three Oranges*
Spectre de Clytemnestra, Le Mezzo-soprano			*Eumenides*
Spinellocchio, Maestro Bass	Doctor		*Gianni Schicchi*
Spirit Soprano			*Dido and Aeneas*
Spirit Messenger Baritone			*Die Frau ohne Schatten*
Spirit of the Forest Tenor			*Snyegurotchka*
Spirit of the Masque Tenor			*Gloriana*
Spirits of Trees Chorus			*The Immortal Hour*
Spirit Voice Mezzo-soprano			*The Immortal Hour*
Spirits Chorus			*Die Frau ohne Schatten*
Splendiano Tenor	Secretary to the prince	Potel	*Djamileh*
Spoletta Tenor	Police agent	de Paolis	*Tosca*
Sportin' Life Tenor	Dope peddler	1st Bubbles; Long, Calloway (*written for* Calloway)	*Porgy and Bess*
Spring Mezzo-soprano			*Snyegorochka*
Springer Tenor	Manager of a theatrical troupe		*Prodaná Nevesta*
Squeak Tenor	Ship's corporal		*Billy Budd*
Stallkeeper From Chorus			*Hugh the Drover*
Starbemberg, Baron Baritone			*Die Harmonie der Welt*

CHARACTER	ROLE	SINGER	OPERA
Stars, The Chorus			*Die Harmonie der Welt*
Statue d'Athena, La Soprano, Mezzo-soprano and Contralto	A triple-voice role		*Eumenides*
Steersman Tenor		Dippel	*Der Fliegende Holländer*
Steffano Colonna Bass	Roman Patrician	Fischer	*Rienzi*
Stella Soprano	Opera singer	1st Isaac; Fremstad, Hempel, Seefried, Teyte	*Les Contes d'Hoffman*
Stella Soprano			*I Gioielli della Madonna*
Stefanida Matuta, Boyardin Soprano	Olga's friend		*Pskovityanka*
Stephano Soprano	Romeo's page	Swarthout	*Roméo et Juliette*
Steurman *See* Steersman			
Stewa Buryja Tenor	Step brother of Laca		*Její Pastorkyňa* (Jenufa)
Steward Bass			*La Rondine*
Storch, Hofkapell- meister Robert Baritone	Christine's husband		*Intermezzo*
Strange Children Chorus			*Die Frau ohne Schatten*
Street Arab Soprano			*Louise*
Street Folk Chorus			*Falstaff*
Street Sweeper Mezzo-soprano			*Louise*
Streltzy Chorus	Archers		*Boris Godunov, Khovantschina*
Streshniev Tenor			*Khovantschina*

CHARACTER		ROLE	SINGER	OPERA
Stroh, Kapell-meister	Tenor	Storch's friend		*Intermezzo*
Stromminger	Bass	Wally's father		*La Wally*
Student	Speaker			*Háry János*
Student	Tenor			*Louise*
Student	Tenor			*Der Prozess*
Students	Chorus			*La Bohème, La Damnation de Faust, Doktor. Faustus, Faust, Les Huguenots, Manon, Mefistofele, La Rondine*
Students (Three) from Krakov	Tenor, Two Basses			*Doktor Faustus*
Students (Four) from Wittemberg	Tenors			*Doktor Faustus*
Styx, John	Baritone	A fool		*Orphée aux Enfers*
Suky Tawdry	From Chorus	A lady of the town		*The Beggar's Opera*
Sulamith	Soprano	High priests' daughter	Lilli Lehmann, Rappold	*Die Königin von Saba*
Sulpice	Bass	Sergeant of grenadiers	Baccaloni	*La Figlia del Reggimento*
Sultan Miramoulin	Tenor			*Christophe Colomb*
Sultan of Khaitan	Bass			*Marouf*
Sun, The Also Rudolf II, and Ferdinand II	Bass			*Die Harmonie der Welt*
Suor See proper name, as Angelica, Suor				
Superstition	Tenor			*Pilgrim's Progress*
Surgeon	Tenor		Cehanovsky	*La Forza del Destino*
Susan	Soprano			*Hugh the Drover*

THE CHARACTERS IN THE OPERAS

CHARACTER		ROLE	SINGER	OPERA
Susan B. Anthony Soprano		Leader in the cause for woman's suffrage		*The Mother of Us All*
Susanna	Soprano	Later Kepler's wife, also Venus		*Die Harmonie der Welt*
Susanna	Soprano	An old believer		*Khovantschina*
Susanna	Soprano	Maid to Countess Almaviva, Figaro's bride	1st Storace; Camporese, Catalani, Farrar, Gueden, Hurley, Lind, Milder, Moffo, Nordica, Paton, Peters, Sayao, Schick, Seefried, Sembrich, Sontag, Ugalde, Vestris, Wagner, Welitsch White	*Le Nozze di Figaro*
Susanna, Countess Soprano		Gil's wife, 20	Erminia Borghi, Bori, Olive Dyer, Farrar, Lipovska, Oltrabella, Vallin, White	*Il Segreto di Susanna*
Susannah Polk Soprano			Curtin	*Susanna*
Suzanne	Contralto			*Louise*
Suzel	Soprano	Farmer's daughter	1st Calvé; Bori, Favero, Marengo, Magnoni	*L'Amico Fritz*
Suzuki Mezzo-soprano		Cio-cio San's servant	1st Giaconia; Bible, Evans, Gay, Homer, Lejeune, Miller, Novotna	*Madama Butterfly*
Suzy Mezzo-soprano		Magda's friend		*La Rondine*
Svietozar	Bass	Prince of Kiev, Ludmilla's father		*Russlan and Ludmilla*
Swallow	Bass	A lawyer	1st Brannigan	*Peter Grimes*
Sylvester von Schaumberg Tenor		Army officer		*Mathis der Maler*

THE CHARACTERS IN THE OPERAS

CHARACTER		ROLE	SINGER	OPERA
Syndham, Lord Bass		British ambassador		*Zar und Zimmermann*
Tackleton	Bass	Dot's employer, a toymaker		*Das Heimchen am Herd*
Taddeo	Baritone	An old Italian		*L'Italiana in Algeri*
Taddeo *See also* Tonio				
Tallan	Tenor			*The Wreckers*
Talpa	Bass	Stevedore, 55	Moscona	*Il Tabarro*
Tamino	Tenor	An Egyptian prince	1st Schack; Gedda, Gudehus, Kraus, Tauber	*Die Zauberflöte*
Tanato	Baritone	Thanatos, God of death		*Alceste*
Tancredi	Pantomine	A Christian knight		*Il Combattimento di Tancredi e Clorinda*
Tannhäuser	Tenor	Knight and minne-singer, enthralled by Venus	1st Tichatschek; Althouse, Alvarez, Max Alvary, Berger, Burrian, Dippel, van Dyke, Hartmann, Hoose, Kullmann, Melchior, Mullings, Niemann, Schmedes, Slezak, Vinay, Winkelmann	*Tannhäuser*
Tansur Also Saturn	Bass			*Die Harmonie der Welt*
Tarquinius Baritone		Tyrant of Rome		*The Rape of Lucretia*
Tartaglia	Bass	Minister		*Turandot* (Busoni)
Tartars	Chorus			*Prince Igor*
Tatyana	Soprano	In love with Eugene	Amara, Brouwenstijn, Cross, Destinn, Lotte Lehmann, Lipovska, Lemnitz, Miller, Muzio, Welitsch	*Eugene Onegin*

474

CHARACTER	ROLE	SINGER	OPERA
Taupe, Monsieur Tenor			*Capriccio*
Tavannes Tenor	Catholic gentleman		*Les Huguenots*
Taven Mezzo-soprano	Old woman	Ugalde	*Mireille*
Tchaplitsky Tenor	Gambler		*Pique-Dame*
Tchekalinsky Tenor	Officer		*Pique-Dame*
Tchelkalov *See* Shchelkalov			
Tcherevik Bass	Parassia's father	Pinza	*The Fair at Sorochintsky*
Tcherevik's Friend Bass			*The Fair at Sorochintsky*
Tchernikovsky Bass	Jesuit		*Boris Godunov*
Tchernomor	Evil dwarf		*Russlan and Ludmilla*
Tebaldo Soprano	Elisabeth's page		*Don Carlos*
Tebaldo Tenor	French soldier		*I Vespri Siciliani*
Telea Soprano		1st Varnay	*The Island God*
Telemaco Mezzo-soprano	Son of Ulisse		*Il Ritorno d'Ulisse in Patria*
Telramund *See* Frederick of Telramund			
Temple Gate-Keeper Soprano or Tenor			*Die Frau ohne Schatten*
Temple Virgins Chorus			*Norma*
Tempters (Four)			*L'Assassinio nel Cattedrale*
Tenebrun From Chorus			*Don Quichotte*
Tenor Tenor Also Bacchus			*Ariadne auf Naxos*

THE CHARACTERS IN THE OPERAS

CHARACTER		ROLE	SINGER	OPERA
Tenor, The	Tenor	Phaeton in Lully's opera		*Cardillac*
Teresa	Soprano	Cellini's love, Balducci's daughter	1st Dorus-Gras	*Benvenuto Cellini*
Teresa	Soprano	Miller, Amina's foster mother		*La Sonnambula*
Testo	Narrator			*Il Combattimento di Tancredi e Clorinda*
Thaddeus	Tenor		Maas	*The Bohemian Girl*
Thaddeus Stevens Tenor				*The Mother of Us All*
Thaïs	Soprano	A courtesan	1st Sanderson; Edvina, Farrar, Favero, Garden, Jepson, Jeritza	*Thaïs*
Thanatos *See* Tanato				
Theater Director Bass				*Lulu*
Theater Personnel Chorus				*Cardillac*
Theière, La	Tenor	The tea pot		*L'Enfant et les Sortilèges*
Theologian	Bass			*Doktor Faustus*
Theophilus of Imola Tenor		Italian bishop		*Palestrina*
Thessalians	Chorus			*Iphigénie en Aulide*
Thirza Mezzo-soprano		Pascoe's wife, 22, in love with Mark		*The Wreckers*
Thisbe Mezzo-soprano		Don Magnifico's daughter		*La Cenerentola*
Thoas	Bass	The king of Scythia	Braun, Gassier	*Iphigénie en Tauride*
Thomas à Becket *See* Tommaso Becket				
Thoré	Baritone	Catholic gentleman		*Les Huguenots*
Thrasher, The	Bass			*Der Prozess*

THE CHARACTERS IN THE OPERAS

CHARACTER	ROLE	SINGER	OPERA
Tikhon Ivanovitch Kabanov Tenor	Katya's husband		*Kata Kabanova*
Tigellino Bass			*Nerone*
Timorous Tenor	A neighbor		*Pilgrim's Progress*
Timur Bass	Blind, exiled Tartar king	Tajo	*Turandot* (Puccini)
Tina Crome Soprano	Age 8, *called* Mavis *in Acts I and II*		*Let's Make an Opera*
Tinca Tenor	Stevedore, 35	1st Crimi	*Il Tabarro*
Tio Lucas Baritone	A miller	1st Demuth	*Der Corregidor*
Tiresias Tenor	Blind seer		*Antigonae* (Orff)
Tiresias Bass	Blind soothsayer		*Oedipus Rex*
Tisbe Mezzo-soprano		Evans	*La Cenerentola*
Titania Speaker	Oberon's wife		*Oberon*
Titurel Bass	Father of Amfortas, former king	Kindermann, Witherspoon	*Parsifal*
Titurelli Tenor			*Der Prozess*
Titus Tenor	Emperor of Rome, 79–81 A.D.	Patzak	*La Clemenza di Tito*
Toby Dancer	A mute		*The Medium*
Tokmakov, Prince Youry Ivanovitch Bass	Mayor of Pskov		*Pskovityanka*
Toldo Berardengo, Ser Tenor	Lawyer		*Francesca da Rimini*
Tom Cat Baritone			*L'Enfant et les Sortilèges*
Tom Rakewell Tenor	The rake	1st Rounseville; Conley, Lewis, Young	*The Rake's Progress*
Tomaso Bass	The governor's enemy (Count Horn)		*Un Ballo in Maschera*
Tommaso Bass	Village elder		*Tiefland*
Tomasso Becket Bass	Archbishop of Canterbury	1st Rossi-Lemeni	*L'Assassinio nel Cattedrale*

CHARACTER		ROLE	SINGER	OPERA
Tomes	Baritone	Lucas' brother in law		*Hubička*
Tomsky, Count	Baritone			*Pique-Dame*
Tonio	Tenor	Tyrolean peasant, Marie's lover		*La Figlia del Reggimento*
Tonio	Baritone	A clown called Taddeo	1st Maurel; Ancona, Bonelli, Campanari, Delmas, Formichi, Gobbi, Guarrera, McCormack, Merrill, Sammarco, Scotti, Warren	*I Pagliacci*
Tonuelo	Bass	Court messenger		*Der Corregidor*
Torchbearer	Baritone			*Francesca da Rimini*
Torchbearers	Chorus			*Francesca da Rimini*
Tormentilla	Soprano	Daughter of Dipsacus, brought up on a diet of poisons		*The Poisoned Kiss*
Torquemada	Tenor	Clock maker, husband of Concepcion		*L'Heure Espagnole*
Tosca, Floria	Soprano	Celebrated singer in love with Mario	1st Darclée; Albanese, Brouwenstijn, Borkh, Callas, Caniglia, Cavalieri, Cigna, Cobelli, Destinn, Eames, Edvina, Farrar, Fremstad, Goltz, Grandi, Jeritza, Kirsten, Labia, Lotte Lehmann, Marcel, Melis, Milanov, Muzio, Pacetti, Price, Scacciati, Steber, Tebaldi, Ternina, Varnay, Welitsch	*Tosca*

THE CHARACTERS IN THE OPERAS

CHARACTER		ROLE	SINGER	OPERA
Toto	Soprano	Dufresne's child		*Zaza*
Tourists	Chorus			*Lakmé*
Townspeople	Chorus			*Carmen, Friedenstag, Hugh the Drover, Mignon, Peter Grimes*
Toysellers	Chorus			*Hugh the Drover*
Trabucco	Tenor	Muleteer		*La Forza del Destino*
Traders	Chorus			*Pilgrim's Progress*
Trainbearer	Soprano	to Clytemnestra		*Elektra*
Tramps (Three)	Tenor, Baritone and Bass			*Die Kluge*
Trapes, Mrs.	Mezzo-soprano	The tally woman		*The Beggar's Opera*
Travellers	Chorus			*Manon*
Travers, Ned	Baritone	Former soldier		*The Boatswain's Mate*
Tree	Bass			*L'Enfant et les Sortilèges*
Trees	Chorus			*L'Enfant et les Sortilèges*
Trim	Tenor	A miner		*La Fanciulla del West*
Triquet, Monsieur	Tenor			*Eugene Onegin*
Tristan	Tenor	Cornish knight in love with Isolde	1st Ludwig Schnorr von Carolsfield; Althouse, Max Alvary, Berger, Borgatti, Dalmorès, Gudehus, Hartmann, Kalisch, Lorenz, MacLennan, Melchior, Mullings, Niemann, Jean de Reszke, Schmedes, Svanholm, Urlus, Vinay, Vogl, Winkelmann	*Tristan und Isolde*

479

CHARACTER	ROLE	SINGER	OPERA
Tristan de Mickleford, Lord Bass	Harriett's cousin		*Martha*
Trojan Captains Chorus			*Les Troyens*
Trojan Captains (Two) Baritone, Bass			*Les Troyens*
Trojan Prisoners Chorus			*Idomeneo*
Trojan Soldier Baritone			*Les Troyens*
Trojan Soldiers Chorus			*Les Troyens*
Trottolo Boy soprano			*Maria Golovin*
Trouble Silent	Cio-cio San's child		*Madama Butterfly*
Truchsess von Waldburg Bass	Leader of the army		*Mathis der Maler*
Truffaldino Bass		Lorenzo Alvary	*Ariadne auf Naxos*
Truffaldino Tenor	Jester		*The Love for Three Oranges*
Truffaldino Tenor	Chief eunuch		*Turandot* (Busoni)
Trulove Bass	Anne's father	1st Raffaele Arié	*The Rake's Progress*
Trumpeter From Chorus			*Hugh the Drover*
Trumpeter Bass Trombone			*The Love for Three Oranges*
Tsar Berendey Tenor			*Snyegurotchka*
Turandot Soprano	Daughter of Altoum		*Turandot* (Busoni)
Turandot, Princess Soprano	Daughter of Altoum	1st Raisa; Borkh, Callas, Cigna, Easton, Grob-Prandl, Jeritza, Muzio, Nemeth, Rysanek, Salvatini, Scacciati, Yeend	*Turandot* (Puccini)

THE CHARACTERS IN THE OPERAS

CHARACTER		ROLE	SINGER	OPERA
Turiddu	Tenor	Young soldier	1st Stagno; Baum, Bjoerling, Conley, Lucia, McCormack, Masini, Peerce, Poleri, di Stefano, Tucker	*Cavalleria Rusticana*
Turk, Baba The See Baba the Turk				
Turkish Soldiers	Chorus			*Die Entführung aus dem Serail*
Turkish Women	Chorus			*Die Entführung aus dem Serail*
Turnkey	Tenor			*Hugh the Drover*
Tutor	Bass	To Orest		*Elektra*
Tybalt	Tenor	Capulet's nephew		*Roméo et Juliette*
Tyroleans	Chorus			*La Wally*
Uberto	Bass		1st Gioacchino Corrado; d'Angelo, Baccaloni, Rossi-Lemeni	*La Serva Padrona*
Ulisse	Tenor	Ulysses, Greek hero		*Il Ritorno d'Ulisse in Patria*
Ulysses S. Grant	Baritone			*The Mother of Us All*
Ulrica	Contralto	Fortune teller (Arvidson)	Anderson, Klose, Madeira, Matzenauer, Schalchi, Stignani, Thorborg	*Un Ballo in Maschera*
Ulrich Grüsser	Tenor	Kepler's assistant, later a soldier, also Mars		*Die Harmonie der Welt*
Ulrich Eisslinger	Tenor	Mastersinger and grocer		*Die Meistersinger*
Undertaker	Baritone			*Porgy and Bess*
Undine	Soprano		Gadski	*Undine* (Lortzing)
Upfold, Mr.	Tenor	The mayor		*Albert Herring*

THE CHARACTERS IN THE OPERAS

CHARACTER		ROLE	SINGER	OPERA
Urbain Mezzo-soprano		Marguerite's page		*Les Huguenots*
Ursula	Contralto	Hero's friend		*Béatrice et Bénédict*
Ursula	Soprano	Riedinger's daughter, loved by Mathis		*Mathis der Maler*
Usher	Tenor			*Pilgrim's Progress*
Valentin	Baritone	Marguerite's brother	1st Reynald; Bonelli, Dufranne, de Luca, Maurel, del Puente, Renaud, Jean de Reszke, van Rooy, Santley, Thomas, Tibbett	*Faust*
Valentine	Soprano	In love with Raoul, betrothed to de Nevers	1st Falcon; Borini, Cruvelli, Destinn, Juch, Krauss, Lind, Lucca, Materna, Christine Nilsson, Nordica, Raisa, Scacciati, Sembrich, Tietjens, Viardot- Garcia, Wagner	*Les Huguenots*
Valkyr *See the opera* Die Walküre				
Valzacchi	Tenor	Scandalmonger	de Paolis	*Der Rosenkavalier*
Vampire From Chorus				*Iris*
Van Bett	Bass	Burgomaster of Sardam		*Zar und Zimmermann*
Vanessa	Soprano	Spinster	1st Steber	*Vanessa*
Vanja	Contralto	Orphan adopted by Ivan	Leonova, Scalchi	*Ivan Susanin*
Vanya Kudras	Tenor	Dikoy's clerk, in love with Barbara		*Katá Kabanová*
Vanuzzi	Bass	An actor	Voketaitis	*Die Schweigsame Frau*
Varlaam	Bass	Vagrant	1st Petrov; Baccaloni, Flagello	*Boris Godunov*

CHARACTER	ROLE	SINGER	OPERA
Varsonofiev Baritone	Vassily's attendant		*Khovantschina*
Vasco da Gama Tenor	Portuguese explorer	˙1st Naudin; Gigli, Martinelli, Piccaver, Jean de Reszke, Wachtel	*L'Africaine*
Vasek Tenor	Micha's second son, quite timid		*Prodaná Nevěsta*
Vassals Chorus			*Die Götterdämmerung*
Vassily Galitsin, Prince Tenor			*Khovantschina*
Vaucluse Tenor	The bishop's valet		*Esther de Carpentras*
Vaudemont, Count Bass	French officer		*I Vespri Siciliani*
Vecchia, La *See Zita*			
Veit Pogner *See Pogner, Veit*			
Vendors Chorus			*I Gioielli della Madonna*
Vendulka Soprano	Paloucky's daughter		*Hubička*
Venetian Merchant Baritone			*Sadko*
Venus Contralto	Goddess		*Orphée aux Enfers*
Venus Soprano	Supernatural seductress	1st Schröder-Dévrient; Fornia-Labey, Fremstad, Lawrence, Matzenauer, Rappold, Resnik, Shuard, Thebom,	*Tannhäuser*
Venus *See also Susanna*			
Vera Boronel Contralto		Evans	*The Consul*
Vere, Captain Tenor	In command of the ship	1st Pears	*Billy Budd*
Vespone Silent	A servant		*La Serva Padrona*

CHARACTER		ROLE	SINGER	OPERA
Viking Merchant	Baritone			Sadko
Village Elder	Speaker			Háry János
Villagers	Chorus			L'Arlesiana, Cavalleria Rusticana, La Dame Blanche, Faust, La Forza del Destino, Hubička, Její Pastorkyňa (Jenufa), Luisa Miller, Le Nozze di Figaro, I Pagliacci, Prodaná Nevěsta, La Sonnambula
Vincent	Tenor	In love with Mireille	1st Michot	Mireille
Vincenzo Gellner See Gellner				
Violetta Valery	Soprano	A courtesan	1st Salvini-Donatelli; Albanese, Alda, Bellincioni, Bevy, Callas, Cross, Farrar, Fenn, Galli-Curci, Hempel, Jeritza, Juch, Kellogg, Kirsten, Kurz, Labia, Lilli Lehmann, Lipovska, Melba, Munsel, Muzio, Christine Nilsson, Nordica, Novotna, Patti, Pons, Ponselle, Schwarzkopf, Sembrich, Steber, Tebaldi, Luisa Tetrazzini, Vere, Yeend	La Traviata
Virgil T.	Baritone			The Mother of Us All
Vitek	Tenor	Dalibor's squire		Dalibor

THE CHARACTERS IN THE OPERAS

CHARACTER		ROLE	SINGER	OPERA
Vitellia	Soprano	Daughter of the deposed emperor of Rome	Zadek	*La Clemenza di Tito*
Vitellozzo	Bass	Nobleman of the Venetian Republic		*Lucrezia Borgia*
Vivetta	Soprano	Rosa's god-daughter, in love with Federico		*L'Arlesiana*
Vixen, Miss From Chorus		A lady of the town		*The Beggar's Opera*
Vizier	Baritone	The Sultan's adviser		*Marouf*
Vladimir Igorevitch Tenor		Igor's son		*Prince Igor*
Vladimir Yaro-slavovitch Bass		Yaroslavna's brother		*Prince Igor*
Vladislav	Baritone	King of Bohemia		*Dalibor*
Vlassievna Contralto		Nurse		*Pskovityanka*
Vogelgesang *See* Kunz Vogelgesang				
Voice From Chorus				*L'Amore dei tre Re*
Voice	Tenor	In the forge, later of a street seller, later from a distance		*La Vida Breve*
Voice from Above Contralto				*Die Frau ohne Schatten*
Voice from Heaven Soprano			Amara	*Don Carlos*
Voice of a Bird Soprano				*Pilgrim's Progress*
Voice of Neptune Bass				*Idomeneo*
Voice of the Temple Watchman Bass				*Die Königin von Saba*
Voice on a Record Soprano				*The Consul*
Volkhova	Soprano	Princess of the ocean		*Sadko*

CHARACTER	ROLE	SINGER	OPERA
Vreli Soprano	Marti's daughter, in love with Sali		*A Village Romeo and Juliet*
Wagner Baritone	Faust's attendant		*Doktor Faustus*
Wagner Baritone	A student		*Faust*
Wagner Tenor		Ferrari-Fontana	*Mefistofele*
Wailing Women Chorus			*Der Barbier von Bagdad*
Waiters Chorus			*La Bohème*
Waiters (Four) Tenor, Three Basses			*Der Rosenkavalier*
Waldner, Graf Bass	Arabella's father, a gambler	London	*Arabella*
Waldvogel Soprano	A forest bird	Schwarzkopf	*Siegfried*
Wallenstein Tenor	Commander-in-chief, also Jupiter		*Die Harmonie der Welt*
Wally Soprano	In love with Hagenbach	1st Darclée; Caniglia, Cigna, Destinn, Guerrini I, Guerrini II, Sheridan, Tebaldi	*La Wally*
Walter Soprano	Strolling minstrel	1st Stehle	*La Wally*
Walter, Count Bass	Rodolfo's father		*Luisa Miller*
Walter Furst Bass	Swiss patriot		*Guillaume Tell*
Walther von der Vogelweide Tenor	Knight and minnesinger		*Tannhäuser*
Walther von Stolzing Tenor	Franconian knight	1st Betz; Althouse, Alvarez, Max Alvary, Berger, Dippel, Gudehus, Hopf, Hyde, Lorenz, Maison, Nachbauer, Niemann, Jean de Reszke, Slezak, Sullivan, Svanholm, Winkelmann	*Die Meistersinger*

THE CHARACTERS IN THE OPERAS

CHARACTER	ROLE	SINGER	OPERA
Waltraute Soprano or Mezzo-soprano	A valkyr	Homer, Ober, Schumann-Heink, Wickham	*Das Ring des Nibelungen*
Wangenheim	Saxon officer		*Der Bettelstudent*
Wanton, Madam Soprano			*Pilgrim's Progress*
Wardrobe Mistress Contralto	Also plays the schoolboy		*Lulu*
Warlaam *See* Varlaam			
Warrior *See* Samson			
Warriors Chorus			*The Immortal Hour, Prince Igor, Le Roi d'Ys*
Wat Dreary From Chorus	A gentleman of the road		*The Beggar's Opera*
Watch, The Chorus			*Cardillac*
Watchful Baritone	Porter		*Pilgrim's Progress*
Watchman Tenor			*Antigonae* (Orff)
Watchmen (Four) Basses			*Die Liebe der Danae*
Waters, Mrs. Soprano	Landlady		*The Boatswain's Mate*
Wayfarers Chorus			*Mefistofele*
Weeping Women Chorus			*Turandot* (Busoni)
Welko From Chorus	Mandryka's servant		*Arabella*
Wellgunde Soprano	A Rhine maiden		*Das Ring des Nibelungen*
Werther Tenor	Poet, 23	1st van Dyke; Clément, Conley, Jones, Jean de Reszke, Schipa, Tagliavini, Valletti	*Werther*

CHARACTER	ROLE	SINGER	OPERA
Wheel of Fortune Woman Soprano			*A Village Romeo and Juliet*
Whores and Roaring Boys Chorus			*The Rake's Progress*
Wicker Chair, The Child			*L'Enfant et les Sortilèges*
Widow Silent			*Der Rosenkavalier*
Widow Browe *See* Witwe Browe			
Wife Contralto			*Dantons Tod*
Wife Soprano	Faithful to her sailor husband	1st Madeleine Sibille; Enk, Favero, Leskaya, Novotna, Teschemacher	*Le Pauvre Matelot*
Wife of the Court Attendant Soprano			*Der Prozess*
Wigmaker Baritone			*Ariadne auf Naxos*
Wigmaker Silent			*Manon Lescaut*
Wild Girl Mezzo-soprano			*A Village Romeo and Juliet*
Wilhelm Meister Tenor	Student on his travels	1st Achard; Capoul, Davies, Gigli, Maas, Schipa, de Stefano	*Mignon*
Willem Baritone		Renan	*Der Prozess*
William Tenor			*Hugh the Drover*
William Jennings Bryan Bass		Hecht	*The Ballad of Baby Doe*
William Tell *See* Guillaume Tell			
Witch Mezzo-soprano		Homer, Ober, Claramae Turner	*Hänsel und Gretel*
Witches Chorus			*Dido and Aeneas, Macbeth, Mefistofele*

THE CHARACTERS IN THE OPERAS

CHARACTER	ROLE	SINGER	OPERA
Witches (Two) Sopranos			*Dido and Aeneas*
Wits Chorus			*The Love for Three Oranges*
Witwe Browe Contralto			*Zar und Zimmermann*
Wizards Chorus			*Mefistofele*
Woglinde Soprano	A Rhine maiden	Fornia-Labey, Lilli Lehmann	*Das Ring des Nibelungen*
Wolfram von Eschenbach Baritone	Knight and minnesinger	1st Mitterwurzer; Ancona, Bispham, Gura, London, Ludwig, Maurel, Morelli, Renaud, van Rooy, Scheidermantel, Schorr, Tibbett, Weil	*Tannhäuser*
Woman, A Soprano			*Alceste*
Woman, A Soprano			*Friedenstag*
Women Chorus			*Friedenstag, Götterdämmerung, Pilgrim's Progress, Prince Igor, I Puritani, Tiefland, Les Troyens, A Village Romeo and Juliet, The Wreckers*
Women (Two) Soprano and Mezzo-soprano			*Dido and Aeneas*
Women Wailing *See* Wailing Women			
Woodcutter's Boy Soprano			*Pilgrim's Progress*
Wordsworth, Miss Soprano	Church school teacher		*Albert Herring*
Workmen Chorus			*Louise, Les Troyens*

CHARACTER	ROLE	SINGER	OPERA
Workmen (Two) Baritone, Bass			*Wozzeck*
Worldly Glory Baritone			*Pilgrim's Progress*
Wotan Bass Baritone	Norse god	1st Kindermann; Bender, Berglund, Betz, Bispham, Bockelmann, Delmas, Griswold, Hotter, Janssen, Ludwig, Mayr, Nissen, Reichmann, van Rooy, Rode, Scaria, Schorr, Staudigl II	*Das Ring des Nibelungen*
Wowkle Mezzo-soprano	Billy's squaw		*La Fanciulla del West*
Wozzeck Baritone	A soldier	1st Scheele-Müller; Fehr, Gobbi, Hermann, Manowarda, Nillius, Rothmuller, Uhde	*Wozzeck*
Wreckers Chorus			*The Wreckers*
Wurm Bass			*Luisa Miller*
Xanthe Soprano	Danae's servant		*Die Liebe der Danae*
Xenia Soprano	Daughter of Boris Godunov		*Boris Godunov*
Xenia's Nurse *See* Nurse			
Yamadori Baritone	Rich Japanese	Cehanovsky, Renan	*Madama Butterfly*
Yeletsky, Prince Baritone	Lisa's fiancé		*Pique-Dame*
Ygraine Soprano	Former wife of Barbe-Bleue		*Ariane et Barbe-Bleue*
Yniold Soprano	Golaud's son	1st Blondin	*Pélleas et Mélisande*
Young Girl From Chorus			*L'Amore dei Tre Re*
Young Girl From Chorus			*Iris*

THE CHARACTERS IN THE OPERAS

CHARACTER	ROLE	SINGER	OPERA
Young Maid From Chorus			*I Quattro Rusteghi*
Young Men (Two) Tenors			*Dantons Tod*
Young Men and Women Chorus			*The Fair at Sorochintsky*
Young People (Three) Tenor, Baritone, and Bass			*Der Prozess*
Young Servant Tenor			*Elektra*
Young Shepherd Soprano		Peters	*Tannhäuser*
Youshko Velebin Bass	Messenger		*Pskovityanka*
Youth From Chorus			*L'Amore dei Tre Re*
Youth Tenor			*Der Prozess*
Youths and Boys Chorus			*Parsifal*
Yvette Soprano	Magda's friend		*La Rondine*
Zaccaria Bass	High priest of Jerusalem		*Nabucco*
Zacharias Bass	An Anabaptist		*Le Prophète*
Zaretsky Bass			*Eugene Onegin*
Zayda Mezzo-soprano		1st Stoltz	*Dom Sebastiano*
Zaza Soprano	Music-hall singer	1st Storchio; Farrar, Favero	*Zaza*
Zdenek's Ghost			*Dalibor*
Zdenka Soprano	Arabella's sister, brought up as a boy	della Casa Rothenberger	*Arabella*
Zerbinetta Soprano		1st Siems; Gueden, Ivogün, Kurz, Schwarzkopf, Streich	*Ariadne auf Naxos*

CHARACTER		ROLE	SINGER	OPERA
Zerlina	Soprano	Matteo's daughter	1st Alboni; Berger, Carosio, Carvalho, Naylor, Parepa-Rosa, Patti	*Fra Diavolo*
Zerlina	Soprano	Peasant girl engaged to Matteo	1st Teresa Bondini; Adams, Carosio, Carvalho, Connor, della Casa, Farrar, Fleisher, Fodor-Mainvielle, Gueden, Hauk, Hurley, Kellogg, Lucca, Lussan, Malibran, Munsel, Naylor, Parepa-Rosa, Patti, Peters, Schick, Sembrich, Sontag, Teyte, Viardot-Garcia, van Zandt	*Don Giovanni*
Zinida Mezzo-soprano			Sarfaty	*He Who Gets Slapped*
Zita	Contralto	Dead Buoso's cousin, 60	Claramae Turner	*Gianni Schicchi*
Zora	Soprano		Nevada	*La Perle du Brésil*
Zsupan *See* Kalman Zsupan				
Zuane	Bass	A boatman	Cehanovsky	*La Gioconda*
Zuckertanz, Doctor Tenor				*Maria Golovin*
Zulma	Contralto	Elvira's companion		*L'Italiana in Algeri*
Zuniga	Bass	Captain of the guard	Lorenzo Alvary	*Carmen*
Zurga	Baritone	King of the fishermen	1st Ismael; Ancona, Badini, Biasini, Lherie, de Luca, Soulacroix	*Les Pêcheurs de Perles*

FIRST LINES AND TITLES OF FAMOUS MUSICAL NUMBERS

NOTE: In this section the English that appears below first lines in other languages is not necessarily a literal translation since it is an adaptation suited to the music.

FIRST LINE	ROLE	OPERA
A lonely Arab maid	Fatima (Mezzo-soprano)	*Oberon* (Act II)
A red-headed woman	Crown (Baritone)	*Porgy and Bess* (Act II)
A Serpina penserate (Think about me when you're away)	Serpina (Soprano)	*La Serva Padrona* (Part II)
A tanto amor (Thou beautiful flower)	Alfonso (Baritone)	*La Favorita* (Act III)
A te o cara (To thee, my dearest)	Arturo Talbot (Tenor)	*I Puritani* (Act I)
A un dottor della mia sorte* (To a doctor of my luck)	Doctor Bartolo (Bass)	*Il Barbiere di Siviglia* (Act I)
A una fonte aflito e solo (Just by a fountain alone and in sorrow)	Elvira (Soprano)	*I Puritani* (Act III)
A woman is a sometime thing	Jake (Baritone)	*Porgy and Bess* (Act I)
Abends will ich schlafen gehen (When at night I go to sleep) "The Children's Prayer"	Hänsel, Gretel (Soprano, Mezzo-soprano)	*Hänsel und Gretel* (Act II)
Abscheulicher! wo eilst du hin? (Accursed one! where go you now?)	Leonora (Soprano)	*Fidelio* (Act I)

* Note: This aria is sometimes replaced with *Manca un foglio*.

FIRST LINE	ROLE	OPERA
Ach, das Leid hab' ich getragen (Ah, what grief must I now bear)	Nureddin (Tenor)	*Der Barbier von Bagdad* (Act I)
Ach, ich fühl's, es ist verschwunden (Ah, 'tis gone, 'tis gone forever)	Pamina (Soprano)	*Die Zauberflöte* (Act II)
Ach, ich hab' sie ja nur auf die Schulter gekusst (Ah! upon her shoulder have I kissed her)	Colonel Ollendorf (Bass)	*Der Bettelstudent* (Act I)
Ach, ich liebte, war so glücklich (Ah, my love, 'twas so pleasant)	Constanze (Soprano)	*Die Entführung aus dem Serail* (Act I)
Adamastor, re dell' onde profonde (Adamastor, ruler of ocean)	Nelusko (Baritone)	*L'Africaine* (Act III)
Addio alla madre "Turiddu's Farewell"	Turiddu (Tenor)	*Cavalleria Rusticana*
Addio del passato (Farewell to bright visions)	Violetta (Soprano)	*La Traviata* (Act III)
Addio di Mimi See Donde lieta usci		
Addio dolce svegliare (Farewell sweet love)	Mimi, Musetta, Rodolfo, Marcello (Two Sopranos, Tenor, Baritone)	*La Bohème* (Act III)
Adieu, Mignon (Goodbye, Mignon)	Wilhelm (Tenor)	*Mignon* (Act II)
Adieu, notre petite table (Goodbye, our little table)	Manon (Soprano)	*Manon* (Act II)
Agathe's Prayer See Leise, leise, fromme Weise		
Ah, Belinda, I am prest with torment	Dido (Soprano)	*Dido and Aeneas* (Act I)
Ah! che la morte ognora (Ah! pray that peace may attend us) "The Miserere"	Leonora, Manrico (Soprano, Tenor)	*Il Trovatore* (Act III)
Ah! I am suffocating (The Clock Scene)	Boris (Bass)	*Boris Godunov* (Act III)

FIRST LINES AND TITLES OF FAMOUS NUMBERS

FIRST LINE	ROLE	OPERA
Ah! j'ai baisée ta bouche (Ah! I have kissed your mouth)	Salome (Soprano)	*Salome*
Ah, je ris de me voir si belle (Ah! I laugh to see me so beautiful) "The Jewel Song"	Marguérite (Soprano)	*Faust* (Act III)
Ah! lève-toi, soleil (Ah! rise up fair sun!)	Romeo (Tenor)	*Roméo et Juliette* (Act II)
Ah, lo veggio, quell' anima bella (Well I know that a maid so enchanting)	Ferrando (Tenor)	*Così fan Tutte* (Act II)
Ah, malgré moi (Against my will)	Alceste (Soprano)	*Alceste* (Act II)
Ah! mon fils (Ah! my son)	Fidès (Contralto)	*Le Prophète* (Act II)
Ah, non credea mirarti (Ah, I could not believe)	Amina (Soprano)	*La Sonnambula* (Act II)
Ah, non giunge uman pensiero (Ah, the depths of human thought)	Amina (Soprano)	*La Sonnambula* (Act II)
Ah! per sempre io ti perdei (Ah! forever have I lost thee)	Riccardo (Baritone)	*I Puritani* (Act I)
Ah! perchè non posso odiarti? (Ah! why is it I don't hate thee?)	Amina (Soprano)	*La Sonnambula* (Act II)
Ah, chi mi dice mai quel barbaro dov'è (Where shall I find the traitor who stole my heart?)	Donna Elvira (Soprano)	*Don Giovanni* (Act I)
Ah, del Tebro (Ah, thou Roman!)	Oroveso (Bass)	*Norma* (Act III)
Ah! dite alla giovine (Ah! tell it to your daughter)	Violetta (Soprano)	*La Traviata* (Act II)
Ah! fors'è lui (Ah! but for him)	Violetta (Soprano)	*La Traviata* (Act I)
Ah, fuggi il traditore (Ah, the traitor escapes me!)	Donna Elvira (Soprano)	*Don Giovanni* (Act I)
Ah! fuyez, douce image! (Ah! leave me, fairest sight!)	des Grieux (Tenor)	*Manon* (Act III)

495

FIRST LINE	ROLE	OPERA
Ah, pescator, affonda l'esca (Fisherman, now throw in your bait)	Barnaba (Baritone)	*La Gioconda* (Act II)
Ah, pietà! Signori miei (Spare me, spare my life I pray)	Leporello (Bass)	*Don Giovanni* (Act II)
Ah, se l'error t'ingombra (Ah, mid the shadows of error) "The Nun's Chorus"	Count di Luna, Nuns (Baritone, Chorus)	*Il Trovatore* (Act II)
Ah sì ben mio coll'essere (The vows we fondly plighted)	Manrico (Tenor)	*Il Trovatore* (Act III)
Ah sì! che feci (What was I doing?) "The Quintet"	Violetta, Flora Bervoix, Alfredo, Giorgio Germont, Baron Douphol (Two Sopranos, Tenor, two Baritones)	*La Traviata* (Act II)
Ahi! casa acerba (Ah! house of sadness!)	La Messagera (Soprano)	*La Favola d'Orfeo* (Act II)
Ai nostri monti (Back home the mountains)	Azucena, Manrico (Contralto, Tenor)	*Il Trovatore* (Act III)
Alerte! Alerte! (Leave her! Leave her!)	Marguérite, Faust, Méphistophélès, Chorus (Soprano, Tenor, Bass, Chorus)	*Faust* (Act V)
Alles fühlt der Liebe Freuden (All with passion's fever tingle)	Monostatos (Tenor)	*Zauberflöte* (Act II)
Almighty Virgin "Elisabeth's Prayer"	Elisabeth (Soprano)	*Tannhäuser* (Act III)
Als Büblein klein (As little knaves) "The Drinking Song"	Sir John Falstaff (Bass)	*Die Lustigen Weiber von Windsor* (Act II)
Als flotter Geist (As merry a spirit)	Barinkay (Tenor)	*Zigeunerbaron* (Act I)
Am stillen Herd (By silent hearth)	Walther (Tenor)	*Die Meistersinger* (Act I)
Amfortas, die Wunde! (Amfortas, the wound!)	Parsifal (Tenor)	*Parsifal* (Act II)
Amor ti vieta (My love forbids thee)	Count Loris (Tenor)	*Fedora* (Act II)

FIRST LINES AND TITLES OF FAMOUS NUMBERS

FIRST LINE	ROLE	OPERA
Amour, viens aider ma faiblesse (Ah love, come aid my weakness)	Dalila (Mezzo-soprano)	*Samson et Dalila* (Act II)
Andrò ramingo e solo (I go, wandering and alone)	Elektra, Ilia, Idamante, Idomeneo (Three Sopranos, Tenor)	*Idomeneo* (Act III)
Angel's Pantomime	Orchestra	*Hänsel und Gretel* (Act II)
Anvil Chorus	Gypsies (Chorus)	*Il Trovatore* (Act II)
Aprite un po' quegli occhi (Just open your eyes and you'll see them)	Figaro (Baritone)	*Le Nozze di Figaro* (Act IV)
Au fond du temple saint (In the depths of the temple)	Nadir, Zurga (Tenor, Bass)	*Les Pêcheurs de Perles* (Act I)
Avant de quitter ces lieux (Now before I leave my home)	Valentin (Baritone)	*Faust* (Act II)
Ave Maria (Hail Mary)	Desdemona (Soprano)	*Otello* (Act IV)
Avec de la tendresse *See* Durch Zärtlichkeit		
Bacchanale	Ballet	*Samson et Dalila* (Act III)
Bald prangt den Morgen zu verkünden (The rosy dawn that greets us early)	Three Genii (Two sopranos, Mezzo-soprano)	*Die Zauberflöte* (Act II)
Ballabile	Ballet	*Aida* (Act II)
Ballad of the King of Thule *See* Il était un roi de Thulé		
Ballatella *See* Che volo d'augelli		
Bannis la crainte et les alarmes (Banish your fears and your alarms)	Admetus (Baritone)	*Alcestis* (Act II)
Barcarolle *See* Belle nuit ô nuit d'amour		

FIRST LINE	ROLE	OPERA
Batti, batti, o bel Masetto (Chide me, chide me, oh fine Masetto)	Zerlina (Soprano)	*Don Giovanni* (Act I)
Bei Männern, welche Liebe fühlen (The kindly voice of Mother Nature)	Pamina (Soprano)	*Zauberflöte* (Act I)
Bel raggio lusinghier (Bright ray of hopefulness)	Semiramide (Soprano)	*Semiramide* (Act I)
Bell Song, The *See* Où va la jeune hindoue?		
Bella figlia dell' amore (Fairest daughter of the graces)	Gilda, Maddalena, The Duke, Rigoletto (Soprano, Contralto, Tenor, Baritone)	*Rigoletto* (Act IV)
Belle nuit ô nuit d'amour (Fairest night, oh night of love) "The Barcarolle"	Nicklausse, Giulietta (Two Mezzo-sopranos)	*Les Contes d'Hoffmann* (Act II)
Berceuse (Lullaby)	Louise's father (Bass)	*Louise* (Act IV)
Berceuse *See* Cachés dans cet asile		
Bess, you is my woman now	Bess, Porgy (Soprano, Baritone)	*Porgy and Bess* (Act II)
Bevi, bevi	Chorus	*Otello*
Bildnis Aria *See* Dies Bildnis ist bezaubernd schön		
Blick ich umher (Gazing upon you)	Hermann (Baritone)	*Tannhäuser* (Act II)
Brahma! grand dieu! (Brahma, great god!)	Leïla (Soprano)	*Les Pêcheurs de Perles* (Act II)
Brangäne's Warning	Brangäne (Mezzo-soprano)	*Tristan und Isolde* (Act II)
Bridal Chamber Scene *See* Das süsse Lied verhallt		
Bridal Chorus	Chorus, Orchestra	*Lohengrin* (Act III)

FIRST LINES AND TITLES OF FAMOUS NUMBERS

FIRST LINE	ROLE	OPERA
Bridal Procession	Orchestra	*Le Coq d'Or* (Act III)
Brindisi (Drinking Songs) *See* Viva il vino spumeggiante *See* Il segreto per esser felice *See* Libiamo, libiamo *See* O vin, dissipe la tristesse *See* Bevi, bevi		
Brunnhilde's Battle Cry *See* Ho yo to ho		
Buona sera, mio Signore (Then good evening, dear milord)	Rosina, Almaviva, Figaro, Doctor Bartolo, Don Basilio (Mezzo-soprano, Tenor, Baritone, two Basses)	*Il Barbiere di Siviglia* (Act II)
By Wisla's blue waters	Chorus	*Boris Godunov* (Act III)
Cachés dans cet asile (Hidden in this place)	(Tenor)	*Jocelyn*
Calezeva, La*	Soprano	
Calf of Gold *See* Le Veau d'Or		
Canon *See* Mir ist so wunderbar		
Cantiamo, facciam brindisi (Let us sing, let us drink together)	Chorus	*L'Elisir d'Amore* (Act II)
Caro nome (Dearest name)	Gilda (Soprano)	*Rigoletto* (Act II)
Casta diva (Queen of heaven)	Norma (Soprano)	*Norma* (Act I)
Catalog Aria *See* Madamina		
Celeste Aida (Heavenly Aida)	Radames (Tenor)	*Aida* (Act I)
Chanson du Toréador *See* Vôtre toast		

* A Spanish song sometimes used by Adelina Patti in the Music Lesson scene of *Il Barbiere di Siviglia*.

499

FIRST LINES AND TITLES OF FAMOUS NUMBERS

FIRST LINE	ROLE	OPERA
Chaste fille de Latone (Chaste daughter of Latona) "The Hymn to Diana"	Iphigénie (Soprano)	Iphigénie en Tauride
Che farò senza Euridice (I have lost my Euridice)	Orfeo (Contralto)	Orfeo ed Euridice (Act III)
Che fiero momento (What a proud moment)	Orfeo, Euridice (Soprano, Contralto)	Orfeo ed Euridice (Act III)
Che gelida manina (Your tiny hand is frozen) "Rodolfo's Narrative"	Rodolfo (Tenor)	La Bohème (Act I)
Che puro ciel (What heavenly light)	Orfeo (Contralto)	Orfeo ed Euridice (Act II)
Che soave zeffiretto (How soft the breezes)	Susanna, the Countess (Two Sopranos)	Le Nozze di Figaro (Act III)
Che volo d'augelli (Ye birds without number)	Nedda (Soprano)	I Pagliacci (Act I)
Ch'ella mi creda libero (Let her believe they let me go)	Dick Johnson (Tenor)	La Fanciulla del West (Act III)
Chi mai dell' Erebo (Who can return from Hell?)	Furies and Demons (Chorus)	Orfeo ed Euridice (Act II)
Chi mi frena (What restrains me?) "The Sextet"	Lucia, Alisa, Edgardo, Arturo, Enrico, Raimondo (Soprano, Contralto, two Tenors, two Baritones)	Lucia di Lammermoor (Act II)
Chiamo il mio ben così (I call to my happiness)	Orfeo (Contralto)	Orfeo ed Euridice (Act I)
Children's Prayer *See* Abends will ich schlafen gehen		
Chimes in the valley	Euryanthe (Soprano)	Euryanthe (Act I)
Chorus of the Girls of Sandomir *See* By Wisla's blue waters		
Cielo e mar (Heaven and sea)	Enzo Grimaldo (Tenor)	La Gioconda (Act II)
Cinta di fiori (Circled by flowers)	George Walton (Bass)	I Puritani (Act II)

FIRST LINE	ROLE	OPERA
Clapping Game Song	Nurse, Feodor (Soprano, Mezzo-soprano)	*Boris Godunov* (Act II)
Clock Scene *See* Ah! I am suffocating		
Cobbler's Song *See* Schusterlied		
Come un bel dì di Maggio (As one fine day in May)	Andrea (Tenor)	*Andrea Chénier* (Act IV)
Connais-tu le pays? (Knowest thou the land?)	Mignon (Mezzo-soprano)	*Mignon* (Act I)
Conoscete, signor Figaro, questo foglio chi vergò? (Do you recognize, my Figaro, this most shameful little note?)	Almaviva (Baritone)	*Le Nozze di Figaro* (Act II)
Coronation March	Orchestra	*Le Prophète* (Act IV)
Coronation Scene	Boris, the People (Bass, Chorus)	*Boris Godunov* (Prologue)
Cortigiani, vil razza dannata! (Vile race of courtiers!)	Rigoletto (Baritone)	*Rigoletto* (Act III)
Couplets *See* Sittencommissions couplets		
Credeasi misera (Believe me, this miserable one)	Arturo, Elvira (Soprano, Tenor)	*I Puritani* (Act III)
Credo in un Dio crudel (I believe in a cruel god)	Iago (Baritone)	*Otello* (Act II)
Crudel, perchè finora? (O why are you so cruel?)	Susanna, Almaviva (Soprano, Baritone)	*Le Nozze di Figaro* (Act III)
Csardas *See* Klänge der Heimat		
D'amour l'ardente flamme (The ardent flame of love)	Marguerite (Soprano)	*La Damnation de Faust* (Act IV)
Dance in Six	Orchestra	*Guillaume Tell* (Act I)
Dance of the Apprentices	Chorus	*Die Meistersinger* (Acts I and III)

FIRST LINES AND TITLES OF FAMOUS NUMBERS

FIRST LINE	ROLE	OPERA
Dance of the Camorrists	Orchestra	*I Gioielli della Madonna* (Act III)
Dance of the Hours	Ballet	*La Gioconda* (Act III)
Dance of the Seven Veils*	Salome	*Salome*
Das süsse Lied verhallt (That sweetest song is dead) "The Love Duet"	Elsa, Lohengrin (Soprano, Tenor)	*Lohengrin* (Act III)
De' miei bollenti spiriti (Wild was my ardent spirit)	Alfredo (Tenor)	*La Traviata* (Act II)
De noirs pressentiments (The dark presentiments)	Thoas (Bass)	*Iphigénie en Tauride* (Act IV)
Death Scene *See* Hark! the tolling bell *See* Io muojo *See* Sono andate		*Boris Godunov* *La Forza del Destino* *La Bohème*
Death of Don Quixote	Dulcinée, Don Quixote, Sancho Panza (Soprano, two Basses)	*Don Quichotte* (Act V)
Deh non volerli vittimi (They shall not be the victims)	Norma, Pollione, Oroveso (Soprano, Tenor, Bass)	*Norma* (Act II)
Deh per questo istante solo (O this once they grace accord me)	Sextus (Tenor)	*La Clemenza di Tito* (Act II)
Deh vieni alla finestra (Look down now from your window) "Don Giovanni's Serenade"	Don Giovanni (Baritone)	*Don Giovanni* (Act II)
Deh vieni non tardar (Then come to me my love)	Susanna (Soprano)	*Le Nozze di Figaro* (Act IV)
Dell' elisir mirabile (Miraculous, this mixture)	Nemerino (Tenor)	*L'Elisir d'Amore* (Act II)
Depuis le jour (E'er since the day)	Louise (Soprano)	*Louise* (Act III)
Der Arme kann von Strafe sagen ('Tis hard such punishment to suffer)	Three Ladies, Tamino, Papageno (Two Sopranos, Mezzo-soprano, Tenor, Baritone)	*Die Zauberflöte* (Act I)

* Usually performed by a dancer in place of the prima donna.

502

FIRST LINE	ROLE	OPERA
Der Freund ist dein (The friend is yours)	Sulamith (Soprano)	*Die Königen von Saba* (Act III)
Der Gnade Heil *See* Pilgrim's Chorus		
Der Hölle Rache kocht in meinem Herzen (I'll have revenge, no longer can I bear it)	Queen of the Night (Soprano)	*Die Zauberflöte* (Act II)
Der kleine Sandmann bin ich (The little Sandman am I)	Sandman (Soprano)	*Hänsel und Gretel* (Act II)
Der Männer Sippe sass hier im Saal (The host of kinsmen sat in this hall)	Sieglinde (Soprano)	*Die Walküre* (Act I)
Der Vogelfänger bin ich ja (I am the jolly bird catcher)	Papageno (Baritone)	*Die Zauberflöte* (Act I)
Dew Fairy's Song, The	Dew fairy (Soprano)	*Hänsel und Gretel* (Act III)
Di provenza il mar (In the country by the sea)	Giorgio Germont (Baritone)	*La Traviata* (Act II)
Di quella pira (On such a pyre)	Manrico (Tenor)	*Il Trovatore* (Act III)
Di tanti palpiti* (Such palpitations)	Soprano	*Tancredi*
Dich selig Frau (Thou blessed one)	Siegmund (Tenor)	*Die Walküre* (Act I)
Dich, teure Halle (Hail, hall of song)	Elisabeth (Soprano)	*Tannhäuser* (Act II)
Dido's Lament *See* When I am laid in earth		
Die Frist ist um (The time has passed)	Dutchman (Baritone)	*Der Fliegende Holländer* (Act I)
Dies Bildnis ist bezaubernd schön (O loveliness beyond compare) "The Portrait Aria"	Tamino (Tenor)	*Die Zauberflöte* (Act I)

* This is the so-called *Aria dei Rizzi*, having been composed while Rossini was cooking rice. It is sometimes used in the Music Lesson scene of *Il Barbiere di Siviglia*.

FIRST LINE	ROLE	OPERA
Dieu, que me voix tremblante (O God, with my trembling voice)	Eléazar (Tenor)	*La Juive* (Act II)
Dir, Göttin der Liebe soll mein Lied ertönen (Thou, goddess of love shall be my muse of singing) "The Hymn to Venus"	Tannhäuser (Tenor)	*Tannhäuser* (Act II)
Divinités du Styx (Divinities of death)	Alceste (Soprano)	*Alceste* (Act I)
Doch dich rührt kein Flehen (Firm is thy decision)	Constanze (Soprano)	*Die Entführung aus dem Serail* (Act II)
Doll's Song *See* Les oiseaux dans la charmille		
Donde lieta usci (Whence did our happiness come?) "Mimi's farewell"	Mimi (Soprano)	*La Bohème* (Act III)
Donne mie la fate a tanti (Ladies have such variation)	Guglielmo (Bass)	*Così fan Tutte* (Act II)
Donna non vidi mai (Maiden so very fair)	des Grieux (Tenor)	*Manon Lescaut* (Act I)
Dormirò sol nel manto (I shall sleep soundly)	Philip the Second (Bass)	*Don Carlos* (Act IV)
Dove sono (I remember)	Countess Almaviva (Soprano)	*Le Nozze di Figaro* (Act III)
Dream *See* En fermant les yeux		
Dream Pantomime	Orchestra	*Hänsel und Gretel* (Act II)
Drinking Song *See* Als Büblein klein *See* Trinke, Liebchen, trinke schnell *See* Brindisi		
Du bist der Lenz (You are my spring)	Sieglinde (Soprano)	*Die Walküre* (Act I)
Duetto d'Amore *See* Vieni la sera *See* Love Duet		

FIRST LINE	ROLE	OPERA
Duidu	Chorus	*Die Fledermaus* (Act II)
D'un pensiero e d'un accento (But one thought and one accent)	Amina, Elvino (Soprano, Tenor)	*La Sonnambula* (Act I)
Dunque io son, tu non m'inganni (Tell me he loves, say you speak truly)	Rosina, Figaro (Mezzo-soprano, Baritone)	*Il Barbiere di Siviglia* (Act I)
Durch die Wälder, durch die Auen (Through the forest, over meadows)	Max (Tenor)	*Der Freischütz* (Act I)
Durch Zärtlichkeit und Schmeicheln (With tenderness and coaxing)	Constanze (Soprano)	*Die Entführung aus dem Serail* (Act II)
È il sol dell' anima (Love's the sun within my heart)	Gilda, the Duke (Soprano, Tenor)	*Rigoletto* (Act II)
E la fede delle femine (And the faithlessness of women)	Guglielmo, Ferrando, Alfonso (Tenor, Baritone, Bass)	*Così fan Tutte* (Act I)
E lucevan le stelle (The stars were brightly shining)	Mario (Tenor)	*Tosca* (Act III)
E quest' asilo ameno e grato (In this tranquil and lovely abode)	A Happy Spirit (Soprano)	*Orfeo ed Euridice* (Act II)
E scherzo ed è follia ('Tis funny and 'tis madness) "The Quintet"	Amelia, Oscar, Riccardo, Samuele, Tommaso (Two Sopranos, Tenor, two Basses)	*Un Ballo in Maschera* (Act I)
È sogno, o realtà? (A dream or reality?)	Ford (Baritone)	*Falstaff* (Act II)
Ecco ridente in cielo* (O see it smile in the eastern sky)	Count Almaviva (Tenor)	*Il Barbiere di Siviglia* (Act I)
Eccomi a vostri piedi (Behold me at your feet)	Figaro (Baritone)	*Le Nozze di Figaro* (Act IV)
E'er since the day *See* Depuis le jour		
Ein Kobold (A goblin)	Hans Sachs (Bass)	*Die Meistersinger* (Act III)

* This aria was added for the second performance of the opera, after a fiasco in which García sang a Spanish song of his own. This one was originally written for the opera *Aureliano in Palmira*.

FIRST LINE	ROLE	OPERA
Ein Mädchen oder Weibchen (A maiden or a housewife)	Papageno (Baritone)	*Die Zauberflöte* (Act II)
Elisabeth's Prayer *See* Almighty Virgin		
Elle a fui, la tourterelle (The dove has flown)	Antonia (Soprano)	*Les Contes d'Hoffmann* (Act IV)
Elle ne croyait pas (Ah! hardly thinking)	Wilhelm (Tenor)	*Mignon* (Act III)
Elsa's Dream	Elsa (Soprano)	*Lohengrin* (Act I)
Elvira's Mad Scene *See* Qui la voce sua soave		
En fermant les yeux (Now closing my eyes) "The Dream"	des Grieux (Tenor)	*Manon* (Act II)
Entrance of the gods into Valhalla	Orchestra	*Das Rheingold* (Finale)
Enzo Grimaldo, Principe di Santafiore (Enzo Grimaldo, Prince of Santa Fiore)	Enzo, Barnaba (Tenor, Baritone)	*La Gioconda* (Act I)
Er kommt, er kommt, o Wonne meiner Brust (He comes, he comes, o joy within my breast)	Margiana, Bostana, Baba Mustapha (Soprano, Mezzo-soprano, Tenor)	*Der Barbier von Bagdad* (Act II)
Er sterbe (He dies)	Leonora, Florestan, Rocco, Pizzaro (Soprano, Tenor, Baritone, Bass)	*Fidelio* (Act II)
Erda's Warning *See* Weiche, Wotan, Weiche!		
Eri tu che macchiavi (Was it you who stained my name?)	Renato (Baritone)	*Un Ballo in Maschera* (Act V)
Ernani, involami (Ernani, escape with me)	Elvira (Soprano)	*Ernani* (Act I)
Erzählung der Waltraute (Waltraute's Narrative)	Waltraute (Mezzo-soprano)	*Siegfried* (Act I)

FIRST LINE	ROLE	OPERA
Et ta langue elle ne remue plus (And your tongue, it speaks no more)	Salome (Soprano)	*Salome*
Euch lüften, die mein Klagen (You breezes, take my wailings)	Elsa (Soprano)	*Lohengrin* (Act II)
Evening Prayer *See* Abends will ich schlafen gehen		
Evening Star *See* O du mein holder Abendstern		
Fairy's Song, The *See* Dew Fairy's Song, The		
Faites-lui mes aveux (Give her my avowals)	Siebel (Mezzo-soprano)	*Faust* (Act III)
Farewell, O earth *See* O terra addio		
Farewell *See* Addio *See* Adieu		
Femme sensible (O lady bright)	A Bard (Baritone)	*Ariodant* (Act II)
Figlia dei re (Daughter of kings)	Nelusko (Baritone)	*L'Africaine* (Act II)
Figlia, tal nome palpita (Daughter, your name strikes memories)	Simon Boccanegra (Baritone)	*Simon Boccanegra* (Act II)
Finch' han dal vino (While we have wine)	Don Giovanni (Bass)	*Don Giovanni* (Act I)
Fledermaus Waltz, The *See* Duidu		
Flower Song *See* Faites-lui mes aveux *See* Le fleur que tu m'avais jetée		
Forest Murmurs *See* Waldweben		
Forging Scene *See* Nothung! Nothung! *See* Anvil Chorus		

FIRST LINE	ROLE	OPERA
Fredda ed immobile (Coldly and immovable) "The Sextet"	Berta, Rosina, Almaviva, Figaro, Bartolo, Don Basilio (Soprano, Mezzo-soprano, Tenor, Baritone, Two Basses)	*Il Barbiere di Siviglia* (Act I)
Frisch weht der Wind der Heimath zu (Fresh blows the wind unto my home)	Sailor (Tenor)	*Tristan und Isolde* (Act I)
Fuggiam gli ardori inospiti (Let's fly from these hostile skies)	Aida, Radames (Soprano, Tenor)	*Aida* (Act III)
Fünftausend Thaler (Five thousand dollars)	Baculus (Bass)	*Der Wildschütz* (Act II)
Fuor del mar ho un mar in seno* (Away from the sea I have a sea in my heart)	Idomeneo (Tenor)	*Idomeneo* (Act II)
Garden Scene *See* Figlia, tal nome palpita		
Gavotte *See* Me voici dans son boudoir *See* Obeissons quand leur voix appelle		*Mignon* *Manon*
Già i sacerdoti adunanzi (Now have the priests come together)	Amneris (Contralto)	*Aida* (Act IV)
Già mi dicon venal (Enemies call me venal) "Scarpia's Cantabile"	Scarpia (Baritone)	*Tosca* (Act II)
Già nella notta densa (Dark is the night around us) "The Love Duet"	Desdemona, Otello (Soprano, Tenor)	*Otello* (Act I)
Giorno d'orrore (Day of horror)	Semiramide, Arsace (Soprano, Contralto)	*Semiramide*
Giusto cielo rispondete (God of justice hear my prayer)	Edgardo, Enrico (Tenor, Bass)	*Lucia di Lammermoor* (Act III)

* Written as a show piece for Raaff.

FIRST LINE	ROLE	OPERA
Gloire immortelle de nos aïeux (Immortal glory of our forefathers) "The Soldier's Chorus"	Soldiers (Chorus)	*Faust* (Act IV)
Gloria all' Egitto ed ad Iside (Glory unto Egypt and to Isis) "The Grand March"	Chorus	*Aida* (Act II)
Golden Calf, The *See* Le veau d'Or		
Good Friday Spell	Orchestra	*Parsifal* (Act III)
Grand March, The *See* Gloria all' Egitto ed ad Iside		
Grand March	Orchestra	*Tannhäuser* (Act II)
Gypsy Chorus *See* Anvil Chorus		
Ha, seht es winkt? (Ha, see it wink?) "The Treasure Waltz"	Saffi, Czipra, Barinkay (Soprano, Mezzo-soprano, Tenor)	*Zigeunerbaron* (Act II)
Ha! welch' ein Augenblick (Ha! now's the proper time)	Don Pizzaro (Bass)	*Fidelio* (Act I)
Ha, wie will ich triumphieren (Ha, how I shall triumph here)	Osmin (Bass)	*Die Entführung aus dem Serail* (Act III)
Habanera *See* L'amour est un oiseau rebelle		
Hammer Song *See* Ho Ho		
Hark! the tolling bell	Boris (Bass)	*Boris Godunov* (Act III)
Hat man nicht auch Gold bei neben (Life is nothing without money)	Rocce (Bass)	*Fidelio* (Act I)
Hat denn Himmel mich verlassen? (Am I then to be forsaken?)	Max (Tenor)	*Der Freischütz* (Act II)
Heavenly Aida *See* Celeste Aida		

FIRST LINES AND TITLES OF FAMOUS NUMBERS

FIRST LINE	ROLE	OPERA
Heil diesem Hause (Hail to this house!)	Chorus	*Der Barbier von Bagdad* (Act III)
Herz, versage nicht geschwind* (Heart, fail me not too quickly)	The Magistrate (Bass)	*Der Corregidor* (Act II)
Hier soll' ich dich denn sehen, Constanze (Here shall I see you quite soon, Constanze)	Belmonte (Tenor)	*Die Entführung aus dem Serail* (Act I)
Ho capito, signor si (I do understand it, sir)	Masetto (Baritone)	*Don Giovanni* (Act I)
Ho Ho! Schmiede, mein Hammer (Ho Ho! Smith, my hammer!) "The Hammer Song"	Siegfried (Tenor)	*Siegfried* (Act I)
Horch die Lerche singt im Hain (Hark, the skylark sings in the woods)	Fenton (Tenor)	*Die Lustigen Weiber von Windsor* (Act II)
Ho yo to ho (Brunnhilde's Battle Cry)	Brünnhilde (Soprano)	*Die Walküre* (Act II)
Hungarian March *See* Marche Hongroise		
Huntsman's Song *See* Le jour est levé		
Hymn to the Evening Star *See* O du mein holder Abendstern		
Hymn to the Sun *See* Salut a toi soleil de flamme		
Hymn to Venus *See* Dir Göttin der Liebe soll mein Lied ertönen		
I got plenty o' nuttin'	Porgy (Baritone)	*Porgy and Bess* (Act I)
I have attained the highest power	Boris (Bass)	*Boris Godunov* (Act II)
I revel in hope and joy again	Sir Huon (Tenor)	*Oberon* (Act III)

* The words of this song are by Heinrich Heine.

FIRST LINE	ROLE	OPERA
Ich baue ganz auf deine Stärke (I dedicate my all to your power)	Belmonte (Tenor)	*Die Entführung aus dem Serail* (Act III)
Ich hab' kein Geld, bin vogelfrei (I have no gold, I'm free as a bird)	Simon (Tenor)	*Der Bettelstudent* (Act III)
Ich knüpfte manche zarte Bänder (I have tied many delicate bands)	Simon (Tenor)	*Der Bettelstudent* (Act I)
Ich lade gern mir Gäste ein (I like my guest to be most glad)	Prince Orlovsky (Mezzo-soprano)	*Die Fledermaus* (Act II)
Ich sah das Kind (I saw the child)	Kundry (Soprano)	*Parsifal* (Act II)
Ich setz den Fall (I set the trap)	Laura, Simon (Soprano, Tenor)	*Der Bettelstudent* (Act II)
Il cavallo scalpita (Proudly prancing sturdy steed)	Alfio (Baritone)	*Cavalleria Rusticana*
Il core vi dono (This heart that I give you)	Dorabella, Guglielmo (Soprano, Bass)	*Così fan Tutte* (Act II)
Il est doux, il est bon (He is kind, he is good)	Salome (Soprano)	*Hérodiade* (Act I)
Il était un roi de Thulé (It was the king of Thule) "The Ballad of the King of Thule"	Marguérite (Soprano)	*Faust* (Act III)
Il lacerato spirito (A wounded spirit)	Jacopo Fiesco (Bass)	*Simon Boccanegra* (Act I)
Il mio tesoro intanto (Speak, my heart, to my lady)	Don Ottavio (Tenor)	*Don Giovanni* (Act II)
Il nome vostro ditemi (But tell me just your name)	Gilda, the Duke (Soprano, Tenor)	*Rigoletto* (Act II)
Il Padre adorato ritrovo e lo perdo (I've found my beloved father and lost him again)	Idamante (Soprano)	*Idomeneo* (Act I)
Il segreto per esser felice (The secret of living in pleasure)	Maffio Orsini (Contralto)	*Lucrezia Borgia* (Act II)
Im Mohrenland gefangen wir (We found ourselves in Moorish lands)	Pedrillo (Tenor)	*Die Entführung aus dem Serail* (Act III)

FIRST LINE	ROLE	OPERA
Imponete (Now command me)	Violetta, Giorgio Germont (Soprano, Baritone)	*La Traviata* (Act II)
In dem Schatten meiner Locken* (In the shadow of my curls)	Frasquita (Mezzo-soprano)	*Der Corregidor*
In des Lebens Frühlingstagen (In the springtime of my life)	Florestan (Tenor)	*Fidelio* (Act II)
In diesen heil'gen Hallen (In this most holy hall)	Sarastro (Bass)	*Zauberflöte* (Act II)
In fernem Land (In distant lands)	Lohengrin (Tenor)	*Lohengrin* (Act III)
In mia man alfin tu sei (At last you are now in my hands)	Norma, Pollione (Soprano, Tenor)	*Norma* (Act II)
In quelle trine morbide (Between these silken curtains)	Manon Lescaut (Soprano)	*Manon Lescaut* (Act II)
In uomini, in soldati (In men as in soldiers)	Despina (Soprano)	*Così fan Tutte* (Act I)
Infelice, e tu credevi (Thou unfaithful! yet I believed thee)	Don Silva (Bass)	*Ernani* (Act I)
Innkeeper's Song *See* Song of the Drake		
Invano, Alvaro! (In vain, Alvaro!)	Carlo, Alvaro (Tenor, Baritone)	*La Forza del Destino* (Act IV)
Invocation *See* Avant de quitter ces lieux *See* O Isis und Osiris *See* In diesen heil'gen Hallen		
Io muojo (I am dying)	Leonora (Soprano)	*La Forza del Destino* (Act IV)
Io sono ricco e tu sei bella (I'm a rich one, and you are pretty)	Adina, Dulcamara (Soprano, Bass)	*L'Elisir d'Amore* (Act II)
Io sono docile (But I am most docile)	Rosina (Mezzo-soprano)	*Il Barbiere di Siviglia* (Act I)

* A concert song by Hugo Wolf.

FIRST LINE	ROLE	OPERA
Isolde! Tristan! Geliebter! (Isolde! Tristan! Beloved!) "The Love Duet"	Tristan, Isolde (Soprano, Tenor)	*Tristan und Isolde* (Act II)
Isolde's Narrative	Isolde (Soprano)	*Tristan und Isolde* (Act I)
It ain't necessarily so	Sportin' Life (Tenor)	*Porgy and Bess* (Act II)
It takes a long pull to get there	Jake, Chorus (Baritone, Chorus)	*Porgy and Bess* (Act II)
Ja, das Schreiben und das Lesen (Yes, the writing and the reading)	Zsupan (Baritone)	*Zigeunerbaron* (Act I)
Je dis que rien ne m'épouvante (I tell you I'm not weak at heart)	Micaela (Soprano)	*Carmen* (Act III)
Je suis Titania (I am Titania) "The Polonaise"	Philine (Soprano)	*Mignon* (Act II)
Je t'implore et je tremble (I implore you, I tremble)	Iphigénie (Soprano)	*Iphigénie en Tauride* (Act IV)
Je veux vivre dans ce rêve (In this dream I would stay) "Juliette's waltz"	Juliette (Soprano)	*Roméo et Juliette* (Act I)
Je viens célébrer la victoire (I will celebrate the triumph)	Samson (Tenor)	*Samson et Dalila* (Act I)
Jerum! Jerum! *See* Schusterlied		
Jewel Song *See* Ah, je ris de me voir si belle		
Juliette's Waltz *See* Je veux vivre dans ce rêve		
King Marke's Soliloquy	King Marke (Bass)	*Tristan und Isolde* (Act II)
King of Thule, The *See* Il était un roi de Thulé		
Klänge der Heimat (Sounds of Home)	Rosalinda (Soprano)	*Die Fledermaus* (Act II)
Kommt ein schlanker Bursch gegangen (Comes a handsome boy a-wooing)	Aennchen (Soprano)	*Der Freischütz* (Act II)

FIRST LINE	ROLE	OPERA
La biondina in gondolete*	Soprano	
La calunnia (See what calumny)	Don Basilio (Bass)	*Il Barbiere di Siviglia* (Act II)
Là ci darem la mano (Let me adore your hand, love)	Zerlina, Don Giovanni (Soprano, Baritone)	*Don Giovanni* (Act I)
La donna è mobile (Woman is fickle)	The Duke of Mantua (Tenor)	*Rigoletto* (Act IV)
La fatal pietra (The fatal stone)	Aïda, Radames (Soprano, Tenor)	*Aïda* (Act IV)
La fleur que tu m'avais jetée (The flower that you threw to me)	Don José (Tenor)	*Carmen* (Act II)
Le Rêve *See* En fermant les yeux		
La vendetta (Now the vengeance)	Doctor Bartolo (Bass)	*Le Nozze di Figaro* (Act I)
La vergine degli angeli (The Virgin of the angels)	Leonora, Padre Guardiano (Soprano, Bass)	*La Forza del Destino* (Act II)
L'Amour est un oiseau rebelle (Love is a wild bird) "The Habanera"	Carmen (Soprano)	*Carmen* (Act I)
Largo *See* Ombra mai fu		
Largo al factotum della città (Way for the city's factotum)	Figaro (Baritone)	*Il Barbiere di Siviglia* (Act I)
Lasciatemi morire† (O let me die) "The Lament of Arianna"	Arianna (Soprano)	*Arianna*
Last rose of summer, The *See* Qui sola vergin rosa		
Laughing Song *See* Mein Herr Marquis *See* Ah! je ris de me voir si belle *See* L'Ora o Tirsi		

* A barcarolle used by Giorghi-Righetti in the Music Lesson scene of *Il Barbiere di Siviglia*.
† This is all that remains of the opera.

FIRST LINES AND TITLES OF FAMOUS NUMBERS

FIRST LINE	ROLE	OPERA
Lay of Sorrow	Shepherd (Tenor)	*Tristan und Isolde* (Act III)
Le jour est levé (The day is breaking)	Huntsman (Bass)	*Dinorah* (Act III)
Le minaccie (All your threatening)	Carlo, Alvaro (Tenor, Baritone)	*La Forza del Destino* (Act IV)
Le veau d'Or (The Golden Calf)	Faust, Méphistophélès (Tenor, Bass)	*Faust* (Act II)
Lebewohl mein flandrisch Mädchen (Now farewell my Flemish maiden)	Marquis de Chateauneuf (Tenor)	*Zar und Zimmermann* (Act II)
L'Éclat de rire *See* L'Ora o Tirsi		
Leise, leise fromme Weise (Softly, softly, day is ending)	Agathe (Soprano)	*Der Freischütz* (Act II)
Leonora Overture No. III*	Orchestra	
Leporello's Catalog *See* Madamina		
Les Oiseaux dans la charmille (The birds in the bushes) "The Mechanical Doll's Song"	Olympia (Soprano)	*Les Contes d'Hoffmann* (Act I)
Letter Duet *See* Che soave zeffiretto		
Libiamo, libiamo ne' lieti calici (Let's drink, then let's drink from happy glasses) "The Brindisi"	Violetta, Alfredo, Chorus (Soprano, Tenor, Chorus)	*La Traviata* (Act I)
Liebesnacht *See* Isolde! Tristan! Geliebte!		
Liebestod *See* Mild und leise		
Lohengrin's Farewell	Lohengrin (Tenor)	*Lohengrin* (Act III)
L'Ora o Tirsi† (L'Eclat de rire)	Manon Lescaut (Soprano)	*Manon Lescaut* (Act II)

* The most famous of the four overtures to *Fidelio*, now used most often between the scenes of Act II.
† Sometimes used in the Music Lesson scene of *Il Barbiere di Siviglia*.

515

FIRST LINES AND TITLES OF FAMOUS NUMBERS

FIRST LINE	ROLE	OPERA
Love Death *See* Mild und leise		
Love Duet *See* Das süsse Lied verhallt *See* Già nella notte densa *See* Isolde! Tristan! Geliebte! *See* Non la sospiri la nostra casetta *See* Vieni la sera		*Lohengrin* *Otello* *Tristan und Isolde* *Tosca* *Madama Butterfly*
Lullaby *See* Berceuse *See* Summertime		
Ma dall' avido stelo divulsa (Beneath yonder magic flower)	Amelia (Soprano)	*Un Ballo in Maschera* (Act II)
Ma se m'è forza perderti (But if I am forced to lose you)	Riccardo (Tenor)	*Un Ballo in Maschera* (Act III)
Mad Scene *See* Ophélie's Mad Scene *See* Qui la voce sua soave		*Hamlet* *I Puritani*
Mad Scene from Lucia	Lucia (Soprano)	*Lucia di Lammermoor* (Act II)
Mad Scene of Oreste	Oreste (Baritone)	*Iphigénie en Tauride* (Act II)
Madamina (Sweet my lady) "The Catalog"	Leporello (Bass)	*Don Giovanni* (Act I)
Magic Fire Music	Orchestra	*Die Walküre* (Act III)
Magische Töne (Magical music)	Assad (Tenor)	*Die Königen von Saba* (Act II)
Mal reggendo all' aspro assalto (Ill sustaining the vicious assault)	Azucena, Manrico (Contralto, Tenor)	*Il Trovatore* (Act II)
Maledizione (The Malediction) *See* Cortigiani, vil razza dannata *See* Vous qui de Dieu vivant		*Rigoletto* *La Juive*
Manca un foglio (A letter's missing)	Doctor Bartolo (Bass)	*Il Barbiere di Siviglia* (Act I)
March of the Mastersingers	Orchestra	*Die Meistersinger* (Act III)

FIRST LINE	ROLE	OPERA
Marche Hongroise (Hungarian March) "The Rákóczy March"	Orchestra	*La Damnation de Faust* (Act I)
Marsch, Marsch, Marsch (March, March, March)	Pedrillo, Osmin, Belmonte (Two Tenors, Bass)	*Die Entführung aus dem Serail* (Act I)
Martern aller Arten (Tortures unabating)	Constanze (Soprano)	*Die Entführung aus dem Serail* (Act II)
Me voici dans son boudoir (Here am I in her boudoir)	Frédéric (Tenor)	*Mignon* (Act II)
Meco all' altar di Venere (With me at the altar of Venus)	Pollione (Tenor)	*Norma* (Act I)
Meditation	Orchestra	*Thaïs* (Act II)
Mein Aug' bewacht (My eyes on guard)	Saffi, Czipra, Barinkay (Soprano, Mezzo-soprano, Tenor)	*Zigeunerbaron* (Act II)
Mein Freund, in holder Jungendzeit (My friend, in my younger days)	David, Hans Sachs (Tenor, Baritone)	*Die Meistersinger* (Act III)
Mein Herr Marquis (My dear Marquis)	Adele (Soprano)	*Die Fledermaus* (Act II)
Menuet des feux-follets (Minuet of the will-o-the-wisps)	Orchestra	*La Damnation de Faust* (Act III)
Metà di voi quà vadano (Let half of you go down the road)	Don Giovanni (Baritone)	*Don Giovanni* (Act II)
Mi chiamano Mimi (My name is Mimi)	Mimi (Soprano)	*La Bohème* (Act I)
Mi par d'udir ancora (To me as in a dream)	Nadir (Tenor)	*Les Pêcheurs de Perles* (Act I)
Mi tradì quel alma ingrate (All my love was given to him) (This aria was inserted by Mozart for Katharina Cavalieri)	Donna Elvira (Soprano)	*Don Giovanni* (Act II)
Mild und leise (Mild and softly) "The Liebestod"	Isolde (Soprano)	*Tristan und Isolde* (Act III)

FIRST LINE	ROLE	OPERA
Mimi's Farewell *See* Donde lieta usci		
Minuet from Don Giovanni	Orchestra	*Don Giovanni* (Act I)
Minuet *See also* Menuet		
Mir ist so wunderbar* (How wondrous the emotion)	Leonora, Marcellina, Jacquino, Rocco (Two Sopranos, Tenor, Bass)	*Fidelio* (Act I)
Mira, O Norma (Hear me, O Norma)	Norma, Adalgisa (Two sopranos)	*Norma* (Act II)
Miserere *See* Ah! che la morta ognora		
Mit Gewitter und Sturm (With thunder and storm)	Steersman (Tenor)	*Der Fliegende Holländer* (Act I)
Mon coeur s'ouvre à ta voix (My heart at thy sweet voice)	Dalila (Mezzo-soprano)	*Samson et Dalila* (Act II)
Monologue *See* È sogno o realtà *See* I have attained the highest power *See* Nemico della patria *See* O monumento *See* Pari siamo *See* Wie duftet doch der Flieder		*Falstaff* *Boris Godunov* *Andrea Chénier* *La Gioconda* *Rigoletto* *Die Meistersinger*
Monstre affreux! (Fearsome fiend!)	(Bass)	*Dardanus*
Morgenlich leuchtend in rosigem Schein (Morning was gleaming with roseate light) "The Prize Song"	Walther (Tenor)	*Die Meistersinger* (Act III)
Morir! si pura e bella (To die! so pure and lovely)	Radames (Tenor)	*Aida* (Act IV)
Musetta's Waltz *See* Quando me'n vo'soletta		
Music Lesson†	Rosina (Soprano or Mezzo-soprano)	*Il Barbiere di Siviglia* (Act II)

* This is a canon for four voices.

† By tradition, this scene consists of practically any arias and show-pieces the prima donna wishes to display.

FIRST LINE	ROLE	OPERA
My man's gone now	Serena (Soprano)	*Porgy and Bess* (Act I)
My name is Mimi *See* Mi chiamano Mimi		
My native land *See* O patria mia		
Nacqui all' affanno, al pianto (In anxiety and in tears)	Angelina (Contralto)	*La Cenerentola* (Act II)
'Neath almond trees in bloom	Count Adolar (Tenor)	*Euryanthe* (Act I)
Nemico della patria (Enemy of the Fatherland) "The Monologue"	Charles Gérard (Baritone)	*Andrea Chénier* (Act III)
Nessun dorma (None shall sleep)	Calaf (Tenor)	*Turandot* (Act III)
No! Pagliaccio non son! (No! I'm an actor no more!)	Canio (Tenor)	*Pagliacci* (Act II)
Nobles seigneurs, salut (Noble lords, my greeting)	The Page (Contralto)	*Les Huguenots* (Act I)
Nocturne *See* Tornami		
Non, ce n'est point un sacrifice (No, it is hardly a sacrifice)	Alceste (Soprano)	*Alceste* (Act I)
Non imprecare (Cast no more blame)	Leonora, Alvaro, Padre Guardiano (Soprano, Tenor, Bass)	*La Forza del Destino* (Act IV)
Non la sospiri la nostra casetta (Do you not long for our secluded cottage) "The Love Duet"	Tosca, Mario (Soprano, Tenor)	*Tosca* (Act I)
Non mi dir, bell' idol mio (Say no more, my beloved)	Donna Anna (Soprano)	*Don Giovanni* (Act II)
Non più andrai* (No more so slyly)	Figaro (Baritone)	*Le Nozze di Figaro* (Act I)
Non più di fiori vaghe catene (O ne'er shall Hymen spread out his roses)	Vitellia (Soprano)	*La Clemenza di Tito* (Act II)

* Sometimes this aria is played during the second act of *Don Giovanni*.

FIRST LINE	ROLE	OPERA
Non siate ritrosi (O vision so charming)	Guglielmo (Bass)	Così fan Tutte (Act I)
Non so più cosa son, cosa faccio (I don't know what it can be that ails me)	Cherubino (Soprano)	Le Nozze di Figaro (Act I)
Nothung! Nothung! (Nothung is the name of Siegfried's sword) "The Forging Scene"	Siegfried (Tenor)	Siegfried (Act I)
Notte e giorno faticar (Night and day am I weary)	Leporello (Bass)	Don Giovanni (Act I)
Nume, custode e vindici (God, guardian and avenger)	Radames, Ramfis, Chorus (Tenor, Bass, Chorus)	Aida (Act I)
Nun's Chorus See Ah! se l'error t'ingombra		
Nur eine Waffe taugt (Only one weapon serves)	Parsifal (Tenor)	Parsifal (Act III)
Nurse's Song (Once a girl was languishing alone)	Nurse (Contralto)	Boris Godunov (Act II)
Nurse's Song See also Song of the Gnat		
O Araby, dear Araby	Fatima (Mezzo-soprano)	Oberon (Act III)
O Carlo, ascolta! (O Carlos, hear me!)	Rodrigo (Baritone)	Don Carlos (Act IV)
O cieli azzuri See O patria mia		
O diese Sonne (How bright the sunlight)	Max, Cuno, Caspar (Tenor, Two Basses)	Der Freischütz (Act I)
O Dieu, Dieu de nos pères (O God, God of our fathers) "The Passover Scene"	Rachel, Eléazar (Soprano, Tenor)	La Juive (Act II)
O don fatale (O fatal gift)	Princess Eboli (Contralto)	Don Carlos (Act IV)
O du mein holder Abendstern (Thou brightly shining evening star)	Wolfram (Baritone)	Tannhäuser (Act III)

FIRST LINE	ROLE	OPERA
O holdes Bild (O lovely picture)	Nureddin, Margiana (Soprano, Tenor)	Der Barbier von Bagdad (Act II)
O Isis und Osiris (O Isis and Osiris)	Sarastro (Bass)	Zauberflöte (Act II)
O Lola "The Siciliana"	Turiddu (Tenor)	Cavalleria Rusticana
O malheureuse Iphigénie (O unhappy Iphigénie)	Iphigénie (Soprano)	Iphigénie en Tauride
O Mimi, tu più (O Mimi, false one)	Rodolfo, Marcello (Tenor, Baritone)	La Bohème (Act IV)
O mio babbino caro (O my beloved daddy)	Lauretta (Soprano)	Gianni Schicchi
O mio Fernando (O my Ferdinand)	Leonora (Mezzo-soprano)	La Favorita (Act III)
O monumento "Barnaba's Monologue"	Barnaba (Baritone)	La Gioconda (Act I)
O namenlose Freude (O joy inexpressible)	Leonora, Florestan (Soprano, Tenor)	Fidelio (Act II)
O paradiso (O paradise)	Vasco da Gama (Tenor)	L'Africaine (Act III)
O patria mia (O my native land)	Aida (Soprano)	Aida (Act III)
O prêtres de Baal (O priests of Baal) "The Prison Scene"	Fidès (Contralto)	Le Prophète (Act V)
O soave fanciulla (O lovely maiden)	Rodolfo (Tenor)	La Bohème (Act I)
O sommo Carlo (O noble Carlos)	Elvira, Ernani, Don Silva, Chorus (Soprano, Tenor, Baritone, Chorus)	Ernani (Act III)
O statua gentilissima (O statue, most respectfully)	Leporello, Don Giovanni (Baritone, Bass)	Don Giovanni (Act II)
O terra addio (Farewell, Oh earth)	Aida, Radames (Soprano, Tenor)	Aida (Act IV)
O toi qui prolongeas (O thou who prolongest)	Iphigénie (Soprano)	Iphigénie en Tauride

FIRST LINE	ROLE	OPERA
O tu che in seno agli angeli (O thou who in the breast of the angels)	Alvaro (Tenor)	*La Forza del Destino* (Act III)
O vin, dissipe la tristesse (O wine, dismiss our heavy thoughts)	Hamlet (Baritone)	*Hamlet* (Act II)
O wär ich schon mit dir vereint (O were I but with you united)	Leonora (Soprano)	*Fidelio* (Act I)
O welche Lust (O what joy) "The Prisoners' Chorus"	Prisoners (Chorus)	*Fidelio* (Act I)
O wie ängstlich, o wie feurig (O how anxious, o how fiery)	Belmonte (Tenor)	*Die Entführung aus dem Serail* (Act I)
O zittre nicht, mein lieber Sohn (Be not afraid, o noble youth)	Queen of the Night (Soprano)	*Die Zauberflöte* (Act I)
Obbligato, obbligato (Thank you kindly, thank you kindly)	Nemerino, Dulcamara (Tenor, Bass)	*L'Elisir d'amore* (Act I)
Obeissons, quand leur voix appelle (We must obey them when they call) "The Gavotte"	Manon (Soprano)	*Manon* (Act III)
Oh, pourquoi ne m'as-tu regardé? (Oh why did you not look at me?)	Salome (Soprano)	*Salome*
Ombra mai fu (Deeply the shadow) "The Largo"	Xerxes (Contralto)	*Serse*
Ombre légère (Shadows so light) "The Shadow Song"	Dinorah (Soprano)	*Dinorah* (Act II)
Ophélie's Mad Scene	Ophélie (Soprano)	*Hamlet* (Act IV)
Or sai chi l'onore (Now you know for certain)	Donna Anna (Soprano)	*Don Giovanni* (Act I)
Ora e per sempre addio (Now and forever farewell)	Otello (Tenor)	*Otello* (Act II)

FIRST LINES AND TITLES OF FAMOUS NUMBERS

FIRST LINE	ROLE	OPERA
Où va la jeune Hindoue? (Where goes the Hindu maiden?) "The Bell Song"	Lakmé (Soprano)	*Lakmé* (Act II)
Ozean, du Ungeheuer (Ocean, thou mighty monster)	Reiza (Soprano)	*Oberon* (Act II)
Pace, pace mio Dio (Peace, peace, o Lord)	Leonora (Soprano)	*La Forza del Destino* (Act IV)
Padre, germani, addio (Father, my cousins, goodbye)	Ilia (Soprano)	*Idomeneo* (Act I)
Paradiso *See* O Paradiso		
Pari siamo (How like we are) "Rigoletto's monologue"	Rigoletto (Baritone)	*Rigoletto* (Act II)
Parigi, o cara, noi lasceremo (Forever, my dear, must I leave thee)	Violetta, Alfredo (Soprano, Tenor)	*La Traviata* (Act III)
Parmi veder le lagrime (Among the tears that fall)	The Duke of Mantua (Tenor)	*Rigoletto* (Act III)
Passover Scene *See* O Dieu, Dieu de nos pères		
Patria mia *See* O patria mia		
Patter song (Farlaf's Rondo)	Farlaf (Bass)	*Russlan and Ludmilla* (Act II)
Per me ora fatale (Now is the fatal time)	Count di Luna (Baritone)	*Il Trovatore* (Act II)
Per pietà, ben mio, perdona (Ah my love, forgive my madness)	Fiordiligi (Soprano)	*Così fan Tutte* (Act II)
Piangea cantando (With weeping I sing) "The Willow Song"	Desdemona (Soprano)	*Otello* (Act IV)
Piango si voi (I weep for you)	Maria, Gabriele, Simon Boccanegra, Jacopo Fiesco (Soprano, Tenor, Baritone, Bass)	*Simon Boccanegra* (Act III)
Piff! Paff!	Marcel (Baritone)	*Les Huguenots* (Act I)

FIRST LINE	ROLE	OPERA
Pilgrim's Chorus	Chorus	*Tannhäuser* (Acts I, III)
Placido è il mar, andiamo (The sea is quiet now, let's leave here)	Chorus	*Idomeneo* (Act II)
Pogner's Address	Veit Pogner (Bass)	*Die Meistersinger* (Act I)
Polonaise *See* Je suis Titania		
Polonaise from "Boris Godunov"	Orchestra	*Boris Godunov* (Act III)
Polovtsian Dances	Ballet	*Prince Igor* (Act II)
Porgi amor (God of love)	Countess Almaviva (Soprano)	*Le Nozze di Figaro* (Act II)
Portrait Aria *See* Dies Bildnis ist bezaubernd schön		
Pourquoi me reveiller? (O why did you wake me?)	Werther (Tenor)	*Werther* (Act III)
Preislied "Prize song" *See* Morgenlich leuchtend in rosigem Schein		
Près des ramparts de Séville (Under the walls of Seville) "The Seguidilla"	Carmen (Soprano)	*Carmen* (Act II)
Pria di partir (Before we do leave)	Idamante, Elektra, Idomeneo (Two sopranos, Tenor)	*Idomeneo* (Act II)
Printemps qui commence (Spring is beginning)	Dalila (Soprano)	*Samson et Dalila* (Act I)
Prisoner's Chorus *See* O welche Lust		
Prison Scene *See* Alerte! Alerte! *See* O prêtres de Baal		
Prize Song *See* Morgenlich leuchtend in rosigem Schein		

FIRST LINES AND TITLES OF FAMOUS NUMBERS

FIRST LINE	ROLE	OPERA
Procession of the Mastersingers	Orchestra	*Die Meistersinger* (Act III)
Protegga il giusto cielo (May heaven protect us) "The Trio of the Masks"	Donna Anna, Donna Elvira, Don Ottavio (Two Sopranos, Tenor)	*Don Giovanni* (Act I)
Pur ti riveggo mia dolce Aida (I see you again, my sweet Aida)	Radames (Tenor)	*Aida* (Act III)
Qual cor tradisti (The treacherous heart)	Norma, Pollione (Soprano, Tenor)	*Norma* (Act II)
Quado me'n vo'soletta (When I am alone) "Musetta's Waltz"	Musetta (Soprano)	*La Bohème* (Act II)
Quanto amore (What a false love!)	Adina, Dulcamara (Soprano, Baritone)	*L'Elisir d'amore* (Act II)
Quanto e bella (How beautiful)	Nemerino (Tenor)	*L'Elisir d'amore* (Act I)
Quartet from La Bohème *See* Addio dolce svegliare		
Quartet from Rigoletto *See* Bella figlia dell' amore		
Queen of the Night's Aria *See* Der Hölle Rache kocht in meinem Herzen *See also* O zittre nicht mein lieber Sohn		
Questa o quella (This or that one?)	The Duke of Mantua (Tenor)	*Rigoletto* (Act I)
Qui la voce sua soave (How smooth his voice) "Elvira's Mad Scene"	Elvira (Soprano)	*I Puritani* (Act II)
Qui sola vergine rosa ('Tis the last rose of Summer)	Martha (Soprano)	*Martha* (Act II)
Quintet from Un Ballo in Maschera *See* É scherzo ed è follia		
Quintet from Die Meistersinger *See* Selig wie die Sonne		
Quintet from La Traviata *See* Ah si! che feci		

FIRST LINE	ROLE	OPERA
Rachel! quand du seigneur* (Rachel, when from the Lord)	Eléazar (Tenor)	*La Juive* (Act IV)
Rákóczy march See Marche Hongroise		
Recondita armonia (Strange harmony)	Mario (Tenor)	*Tosca* (Act I)
Return victorious! See Ritorna Vincitor!		
Ride of the Valkyries	Orchestra	*Die Walküre* (Act III)
Rienzi's Prayer	Rienzi (Tenor)	*Rienzi* (Act V)
Ritorna vincitor (Return in victory)	Aida (Soprano)	*Aida* (Act I)
Rivolgete a lui lo sguardo†	Bass	
Rodolfo's Narrative See Che gelida manina		
Roi de Thulé, Le See Il était un roi de Thulé		
Rom Erzählung (Rome Narrative)	Tannhäuser (Tenor)	*Tannhäuser* (Act III)
Room for the factotum See Largo al factotum		
Rosa del ciel (Rose of heaven)	Orfeo (Tenor)	*La Favola d'Orfeo* (Act I)
Rudolph's Narrative See Che gelida manina		
Sach's Monologue See Wie duftet doch der Flieder		
Salomé, Salomé, demande (Salome, Salome, but ask)	Herod (Baritone)	*Hérodiade* (Act III)
Salut a toi soleil de flamme (I hail the day's bright light, the sun) "Hymn to the Sun"	Queen (Soprano)	*Le Coq d'Or* (Act II)

* According to Kobbé, Nourrit may have had a hand in the composition of this aria.

† This aria, K.584, was originally planned for Guglielmo in Act I of *Così fan Tutte*, but was not so used.

FIRST LINE	ROLE	OPERA
Salut, demeure chaste et pure (Hail, thou dwelling chaste and pure)	Faust (Tenor)	*Faust* (Act III)
Sandman's Lullaby *See* Der kleine Sandmann bin ich		
Scarpia's Aria *See* Giá mi dicon venal		
Schattentanz *See* Ombre légère		
Schusterlied (*Cobbler's Song*)	Hans Sachs (Baritone)	*Die Meistersinger* (Act II)
Scintille, diamant (Sparkle, diamond)	Dapertutto (Baritone)	*Les Contes d'Hoffmann* (Act III)
Se a caso Madama (If milady should call you)	Figaro (Baritone)	*Le Nozze di Figaro* (Act I)
Se il mio nome saper (Shall I then tell you his name?)	Figaro (Tenor)	*Il Barbiere di Siviglia* (Act I)
Se il padre perdei (If I should lose my father)	Ilia (Soprano)	*Idomeneo* (Act II)
Se vuol ballare (Would you like dancing?)	Figaro (Baritone)	*Le Nozze di Figaro* (Act I)
Secondate aurette amiche (Gentle breezes softly sighing)	Ferrando, Guglielmo (Tenor, Baritone)	*Così fan Tutte* (Act II)
Selig wie die Sonne (Brightly as the sun)	Eva, Magdalena, David, Walther, Hans Sachs (Soprano, Mezzo-soprano, Two Tenors, Bass)	*Die Meistersinger* (Act III)
Sempre libera (Now so freely)	Violetta (Soprano)	*La Traviata* (Act I)
Seguidilla *See* Près des ramparts de Séville		
Sempre in contrasti (Always in contrasts)	Uberto (Bass)	*La Serva Padrona* (Part I)
Sento, O Dio! (Courage fails me) "The Quintet"	Fiordiligi, Dorabella, Ferrando, Guglielmo, Alfonso (Two Sopranos, Tenor, Baritone, Bass)	*Così fan Tutte* (Act I)

FIRST LINE	ROLE	OPERA
Serenade *See* Deh vieni alla finestra *See* Se il mio nome *See* Vous qui faites l'endormie		*Don Giovanni* *Il Barbiere di Siviglia* *Faust*
Sextet from "Lucia" *See* Chi mi frena?		
Shadow Song *See* Ombre légère		
Si la rigueur et la vengeance (If the rigor and the vengeance)	Cardinal de Brogni (Bass)	*La Juive* (Act I)
Si, pel ciel marmoreo giuro (Now, we swear by heaven and earth)	Otello, Iago (Tenor, Baritone)	*Otello* (Act II)
Si può? Signore, Signori (May I, Ladies, Gentlemen?)	Tonio (Tenor)	*I Pagliacci* (Prologue)
Siciliana *See* O Lola		
Siccome un dì caduto (As fugitive one day)	Leïla (Soprano)	*Les Pêcheurs de Perles* (Act II)
Siege of Kazan *See* Varlaam's Song		
Siegfrieds Erzählung (Siegfried's Narrative)	Siegfried (Tenor)	*Siegfried* (Act III)
Siegfried's Rhine Journey	Orchestra	*Siegfried* (Prelude)
Siegmund heiss ich (Siegmund am I)	Siegmund (Tenor)	*Die Walküre* (Act I)
Siegmund's Spring Song *See* Winterstürme wichen		
Simpleton's Lament (Flow, ah! flow my bitter tears)	Simpleton (Tenor)	*Boris Godunov* (Finale)
Sittencommissions couplets	Mirabella, Zsupan, Carnero (Contralto, Two Baritones)	*Zigeunerbaron* (Act II)
Sleepwalking Scene	Lady Macbeth (Soprano)	*Macbeth* (Act IV)

528

FIRST LINE	ROLE	OPERA
Sleepwalking Scene	Amina (Soprano)	*La Sonnambula* (Act III)
Smanie implacabile (Frenzied and implacable)	Dorabella (Soprano)	*Così fan Tutte* (Act I)
So elend und so treu (So miserable and true)	Saffi (Soprano)	*Zigeunerbaron* (Act I)
Soave sia il vento (O may the sea flow calmly)	Fiordiligi, Dorabella, Alfonso (Two Sopranos, Baritone)	*Così fan Tutte* (Act I)
Sogno soave e casto (Dream so fair and chaste)	Ernesto (Tenor)	*Don Pasquale* (Act III)
Soldiers' Chorus *See* Gloire immortelle		
Solenne in quest' ora (Solemnly this hour)	Carlo, Alvaro (Tenor, Baritone)	*La Forza del Destino* (Act III)
Son imbrogliato io già (I'm embroiled in it already)	Uberto (Bass)	*La Serva Padrona* (Part II)
Son vergin vezzosa (I am a blithesome maiden)	Elvira (Soprano)	*I Puritani* (Act I)
Song of Battles *See* Varlaam's Song		
Song of India	The Indian Merchant (Tenor)	*Sadko* (Act II)
Song of the Drake (Once I caught a drake with feathers)	Innkeeper (Mezzo-soprano)	*Boris Godunov* (Act I)
Song of the Gnat	Nurse (Mezzo-soprano)	*Boris Godunov* (Act II)
Song of the Valkyr *See* Ho yo to ho		
Song of the Viking	The Viking Merchant (Bass)	*Sadko* (Act II)
Song to the evening star *See* O du mein holder Abendstern		
Sono andati (Have they all gone now?)	Mimi, Rodolfo (Soprano, Tenor)	*La Bohème* (Act IV)

FIRST LINE	ROLE	OPERA
Sonst spielt ich mit Szepter und Kron (I played with the scepter and crown)	Peter I (Tenor)	*Zar und Zimmermann* (Act III)
Splendon più belle in ciel (The splendor of the sky)	Baldassare (Bass)	*La Favorita* (Act IV)
Standin' in need of prayer	Emperor Jones (Baritone)	*The Emperor Jones* (Act II)
Steuermannslied *See* Mit Gewitter und Sturm		
Stizzoso, mio stizzoso (You vex me, how you vex me!)	Serpina (Soprano)	*La Serva Padrona* (Part I)
Stride la vampa (Let the flames roar)	Azucena (Mezzo-soprano)	*Il Trovatore* (Act II)
Su, e con me vieni, o cara (Come, then, come with me, my dearest)	Euridice, Orfeo (Soprano, Contralto)	*Orfeo ed Euridice* (Act III)
Suicidio! (Suicide!)	La Gioconda (Soprano)	*La Gioconda* (Act IV)
Summertime and the livin' is easy "The Lullaby"	Bess (Soprano)	*Porgy and Bess* (Act I)
Suoni la tromba (O sound the trumpet)	Richard Forth, George Walton (Baritone, Bass)	*I Puritani* (Act II)
Swan Song *See* Lohengrin's Farewell		
Tacea la notte placida (Calmly and gracefully night time)	Leonora (Soprano)	*Il Trovatore* (Act I)
Tannhäuser's Song *See* Göttin der Liebe soll mein Lied ertönen		
Te Deum (Thou, o Lord)	Scarpia, Chorus (Baritone, Chorus)	*Tosca* (Act I)
Te souvient-il du lumineux voyage (Do you remember the luminous voyage)	Athanael, Thaïs (Soprano, Baritone)	*Thaïs* (Act III)

FIRST LINE	ROLE	OPERA
Temple Scene *See* Nume custode		
Terra addio, O *See* O terra addio		
The last rose of summer *See* Qui sola vergine rose		
There's a boat that's leavin' soon for New York	Sportin' Life (Tenor)	*Porgy and Bess* (Act III)
Threatful gather clouds about me	Euryanthe, Eglantine (Soprano, Mezzo-soprano)	*Euryanthe* (Act I)
To you my soul I give	Euryanthe, Count Adolar) (Soprano, Tenor)	*Euryanthe* (Act II)
Toreador's Song *See* Votre toast		
Torna la pace al core* (Now take peace into your heart)	Idomeneo (Tenor)	*Idomeneo* (Act III)
Torna, torna, deh torna, Ulisse (Back, come back, o return, Ulysses)	Penelope (Contralto)	*Il Ritorno d'Ulisse in Patria* (Act I)
Tornami a dir che m'ami (Turn to me and say you love me)	Norina, Ernesto (Soprano, Tenor)	*Don Pasquale* (Act III)
Tortures unabating *See* Martern aller Arten		
Traurigkeit ward mir zum Lose (Sadness was all my destiny)	Constanze (Soprano)	*Die Entführung aus dem Serail* (Act II)
Treasure Waltz *See* Ha, seht es winkt		
Trinke, Liebchen, trinke schnell (Drink, my darling, drink it up)	Rosalinda, Alfred (Soprano, Tenor)	*Die Fledermaus* (Act I)
Trio of the Masks *See* Protegga il giusto cielo		
Tu che a Dio spiegasti l'ali (Thou who to God has spread thy wings)	Edgardo, Raimondo (Tenor, Bass)	*Lucia di Lammermoor* (Act III)

* This aria was not sung in the first performance of the opera.

FIRST LINE	ROLE	OPERA
Ah! du wolltest mich nicht deinen Mund küssen lassen (You would not kiss me)	Salome (Soprano)	*Salome*
Tu sè morta, sè morta mia vita (Thou art dead, my life dies with you)	Orfeo (Tenor)	*La Favola d'Orfeo* (Act II)
Tutte le feste al tempio (On every festal morning)	Gilda (Soprano)	*Rigoletto* (Act III)
Udite, udite, o rustici (O hear me, o hear me, dear villagers)	Dulcamara (Bass)	*L'Elisir d'amore* (Act I)
Un' aura amorosa (Her eyes so alluring)	Ferrando (Tenor)	*Così fan Tutte* (Act II)
Un bel dì vedremo (One fine day I'll see him)	Cio-cio San (Soprano)	*Madama Butterfly* (Act II)
Un dì felice eterea (One day of rapture)	Violetta, Alfredo (Soprano, Tenor)	*La Traviata* (Act I)
Una donna a quindici anni (Once a lady fifteen years old)	Despina (Soprano)	*Così fan Tutte* (Act II)
Una furtiva lagrima (A furtive tear)	Nemerino (Tenor)	*L'Elisir d'amore* (Act II)
Una voce poco fa (Just a while ago I heard)	Rosina (Mezzo-soprano)	*Il Barbiere di Siviglia* (Act I)
Und ob die Wolke (Although a cloud comes)	Agathe (Soprano)	*Der Freischütz* (Act III)
Unis dès la plus tendre enfance (Together since earliest childhood)	Pylade (Tenor)	*Iphigénie en Tauride* (Act III)
Va crudele, al dio spietato (Go, O cruel one, to God the implacable)	Adalgisa, Pollione (Soprano, Tenor)	*Norma* (Act I)
Va, pensiero (Go, my thoughts)	Hebrew captives (Chorus)	*Nabucco* (Act III)
Vallons de l'Helvétie (O valleys of Helvetia)	(Bass)	*Le Chalet*
Varlaam's Song (Long ago at Kazan)	Varlaam (Bass)	*Boris Godunov* (Act I)

FIRST LINE	ROLE	OPERA
Vedrai carino, se sei buonino (O shall I tell you, my dearest)	Zerlina (Soprano)	*Don Giovanni* (Act II)
Vedrò mentr'io sospiro (I'll go while still I have breath)	Almaviva (Baritone)	*Le Nozze di Figaro* (Act III)
Vengeance Aria *See* Or sai che l'onore		
Venite inginocchiatevi (Come here and kneel before me)	Countess Almaviva (Soprano)	*Le Nozze di Figaro* (Act II)
Venusberg Music	Orchestra	*Tannhäuser* (Prelude)
Vesti la giubba (On with the play)	Canio (Tenor)	*Pagliacci* (Act I)
Vi ravviso o luoghi ameni (As I gaze on the scenes of my childhood)	Count Rodolpho (Bass)	*La Sonnambula* (Act I)
Vi ricordo o boschi ombrosi (I recall now the shadowy forest)	Orfeo (Tenor)	*La Favola d'Orfeo* (Act II)
Vien, diletto (Come, beloved)	Elvira (Soprano)	*I Puritani* (Act I)
Vieni fra queste braccia (Come into my arms)	Elvira, Arturo (Soprano, Tenor)	*I Puritani* (Act III)
Vieni la sera (Evening's coming)	Cio-cio San, Pinkerton (Soprano, Tenor)	*Madama Butterfly* (Act I)
Vision fugitive (Fleeting vision)	Herod (Baritone)	*Hérodiade* (Act II)
Vissi d'arte (Thus love and music)	Tosca (Soprano)	*Tosca* (Act II)
Viva il vino spumeggiante (Long live the wine effervescent) "The Brindisi"	Turiddu, Chorus (Tenor, Chorus)	*Cavalleria Rusticana*
Vivat Bacchus (Long live Bacchus)	Pedrillo, Osmin (Tenor, Bass)	*Die Entführung aus dem Serail* (Act II)
Voce di donna o d'angelo (Voice of the lady, or of angels)	La Cieca (Mezzo-soprano)	*La Gioconda* (Act I)
Voi che sapete (Tell me fair ladies)	Cherubino (Soprano)	*Le Nozze di Figaro* (Act II)

FIRST LINES AND TITLES OF FAMOUS NUMBERS

FIRST LINE	ROLE	OPERA
Voi lo sapete (Well do you know it)	Santuzza (Soprano)	*Cavalleria Rusticana*
Votre toast je peux vous le rendre (To your toast I'll give another) "The Toreador's Song"	Escamillo (Baritone)	*Carmen* (Act II)
Vous qui du Dieu vivant (You who of the living God) "Malediction"	Cardinal de Brogni (Bass)	*La Juive* (Act III)
Vous qui faites l'endormie (You pretend to be sleeping)	Méphistophélès (Bass)	*Faust* (Act IV)
Wach! auf! es nahet gen den Tag* (Awake, draws near the break of day)	Chorus	*Die Meistersinger* (Act III)
Wahn! Wahn! Überall Wahn! (Mad, mad, all the world's mad!)	Hans Sachs (Baritone)	*Die Meistersinger* (Act III)
Waldweben (Forest weaving)	Orchestra	*Siegfried* (Act II)
Walpurgis night	Ballet	*Faust* (Act V)
Walther's Prize Song *See* Morgenlich leuchtend in rosigem Schein		
Waltraute's Narrative *See* Erzählung der Waltraute		
Waltz from Eugene Onegin	Orchestra	*Eugene Onegin* (Act I)
Waltz from Faust	Orchestra	*Faust* (Act II)
Waltz from Roméo et Juliette *See* Je veux vivre dans ce rêve		
Waltz from La Bohème *See* Quando me'n vo'soletta		
Waltz from Die Fledermaus	Orchestra	*Die Fledermaus* (Act II)
Waltz from Der Rosenkavalier	Orchestra	*Der Rosenkavalier* (Act II)

* The words to this chorale are by the real Hans Sachs.

FIRST LINE	ROLE	OPERA
Wedding March *See* Bridal Chorus		
Weiche, Wotan, weiche! (Waver, Wotan, waver!)	Erda (Contralto)	*Das Rheingold*
Welch ein Geschick (What dexterity!)	Constanze, Belmonte (Soprano, Tenor)	*Die Entführung aus dem Serail* (Act III)
Welche Wonne, welche Lust (What delight, what freedom)	Blonde (Soprano)	*Die Entführung aus dem Serail* (Act II)
Welcher Kummer herrscht in meiner Seele (What conflicting feelings rule my soul)	Constanze (Soprano)	*Die Entführung aus dem Serail* (Act II)
Wenn der Freuden Thränen fliessen (When the tears of joy are flowing)	Belmonte (Tenor)	*Die Entführung aus dem Serail* (Act II)
Wer ein Liebchen hat gefunden (When a maiden takes your fancy)	Osmin (Bass)	*Die Entführung aus dem Serail* (Act I)
Wer uns getraut? (Who married us?)	Saffi, Barinkay (Soprano, Tenor)	*Zigeunerbaron* (Act II)
When a maiden takes your fancy *See* Wer ein Liebchen hat gefunden		
When I am laid in earth	Dido (Soprano)	*Dido and Aeneas* (Act III)
When zephyrs waft me peace	Count Adolar (Tenor)	*Euryanthe* (Act II)
Where seek to hide	Count Lysiart (Baritone)	*Euryanthe* (Act II)
Wie duftet doch der Flieder (How sweetly smells the elder) "Hans Sach's Narrative"	Hans Sachs (Bass)	*Die Meistersinger* (Act II)
Wie oft in Meers tiefsten Schlund (How often in the ocean's caves)	Dutchman (Baritone)	*Der Fliegende Holländer* (Act I)
Wie stark ist nicht dein Zauberton (O voice of magic melody)	Pamino (Tenor)	*Die Zauberflöte* (Act I)

FIRST LINES AND TITLES OF FAMOUS NUMBERS

FIRST LINE	ROLE	OPERA
Willow Song *See* Piangea cantando		
Winterstürme weichen (Winter's storms are lightening) "Siegmund's spring song"	Siegmund (Tenor)	*Die Walküre* (Act I)
Witch's Song	The Witch (Mezzo-soprano)	*Hänsel und Gretel* (Act III)
Zefiretti lusinghieri (Little breezes, little flatteries)	Ilia (Soprano)	*Idomeneo* (Act III)
Zitti, zitti, piano (Quickly, quickly, softly)	Rosina, Almaviva, Figaro (Mezzo-soprano, Tenor, Baritone)	*Il Barbiere di Siviglia* (Act II)

CHRONOLOGY OF OPERA

YEAR	GENERAL HISTORY	OPERA HISTORY	FIRST PERFORMANCES
1285			Le Jeu de Robin et Marion
1472			Orfeo (Poliziano)
1492	Columbus discovered the West Indies.		
1513	Balboa discovered the Pacific Ocean.		
1540	DIED: Dr. Johann Faust.		
1542	De Soto died on the Mississippi River.		
1546	DIED: Martin Luther.	BORN: Caccini.	
1548	BORN: El Greco (?).		
1550		BORN: Vecchi, Cavalieri.	
1553	DIED: Rabelais.		
1554	England became reconciled to the Papal Court.		
1556	DIED: Charles V of Spain.		
1558	Elizabeth I became Queen of England.		
1560		BORN: Corsi.	
1561	The Huguenots got their name.	BORN: Peri.	
1564	BORN: Shakespeare, Galileo Galilei, DIED: John Calvin.		
1567		BORN: Monteverdi.	
1568	Mary, Queen of Scots defeated at Langside.		

YEAR	GENERAL HISTORY	OPERA HISTORY	FIRST PERFORMANCES
1572	Massacre of St. Bartholomew.		
1576	First theater built in England.		
1581			Circe, a ballad opera at the Louvre
1584	DIED: Ivan the Terrible.		
1585		BORN: Schütz.	
1587	Published: *Historia von D. Johann Fausten.*		
1588	Spanish Armada destroyed. First newspaper in England.		
1590	Written: Marlowe's *Doctor Faustus.*		
1597	Shakespeare's *Romeo and Juliet.*	Published: *L'Amfiparnaso.*	
1598	Boris Godunov became Tsar of Russia.		
1600			Euridice (Peri): La Rappresentazione dell' Anima e del Corpo
1602	First Englishman lands in New England.	DIED: Cavalieri.	
1603	DIED: Elizabeth I. Shakespeare's *Hamlet.*		
1604	French establish colony in Maine.	DIED: Corsi.	
1605	DIED: Boris Godunov. Published: *Don Quixote.*	DIED: Vecchi.	
1607	Jamestown colony founded.		La Favola d'Orfeo
1608	BORN: John Milton.		Dafne (Gagliano); Arianna
1610	Coffee first used in Europe.		

CHRONOLOGY OF OPERA

YEAR	GENERAL HISTORY	OPERA HISTORY	FIRST PERFORMANCES
1613	Pocahontas converted to Christianity.	Monteverdi moved to Venice.	
1614	A colony founded at the mouth of the Hudson.		
1616	DIED: Shakespeare.	BORN: Perrin.	
1617	DIED: Pocahontas.		
1618	Beginning of the Thirty Years' War.	DIED: Caccini.	
1619	Discovery of the circulation of the blood. BORN: Cyrano de Bergerac.		
1620	Colony founded at Plymouth. Invention of the thermometer.		
1622	BORN: Molière.		
1624			Il Combattimento di Tancredi e Clorinda
1625	Nieuw Amsterdam founded. DIED: El Greco.		
1627			Dafne, the first German opera
1628	Bernini began the tomb of Urban.	BORN: Cambert.	
1632	Maryland chartered.	BORN: Lully.	
1633	First schoolmaster arrived in America.	DIED: Peri.	
1634	First hackney coaches in London	BORN: M. A. Charpentier.	
1635	The French Academy founded.	BORN: Quinault.	
1636	Harvard College founded.		
1637	War between settlers and Pequot Indians in Massachusetts.	First public opera house opened at Venice.	

YEAR	GENERAL HISTORY	OPERA HISTORY	FIRST PERFORMANCES
1638	First log cabin in America.	Published: *Il Combattimento di Tancredi e Clorinda.*	
1639	First American post office.		L'Adone
1641	First colonial American patent.		Il Ritorno d'Ulisse in Patria
1642	DIED: Galileo Galilei.		L'Incoronazione di Poppea
1643	Invention of the barometer.	DIED: Monteverdi.	
1644	Cromwell defeated Prince Rupert.		
1645		First Italian opera troupe visits Paris.	
1648	End of the Thirty Years' War.		
1649	Charles I beheaded.		
1653	Cromwell made Lord Protector of England.		
1655	DIED: Cyrano de Bergerac.		Triomphe de l'Amour sur Bergers et Bergères, the first French opera
1656	First Quakers arrive in America.		The Siege of Rhodes, the first English opera
1658	First hospital established at Nieuw Amsterdam.	BORN: Purcell.	
1660	English monarchy restored. Tea introduced to England.	BORN: Campra and A. Scarlatti.	Serse (Cavalli)
1661	Louis XIV established the court of Versailles.		
1662	Connecticut colony chartered.	Covent Garden theatre opened.	
1664	The English establish New York.		
1665	Molière wrote *Le Festin de Pierre* (*Don Juan*). The Great Plague.		

YEAR	GENERAL HISTORY	OPERA HISTORY	FIRST PERFORMANCES
1666	The Great Fire of London.		
1669	BORN: Antonio Vivaldi.		
1670	Charleston, S.C. founded.	BORN: Caldara	
1671		Louis XIV permits the establishment of the Académie Royale de Musique (L'Opéra).	Pomona
1672	First book copyrighted in America.	Lully took over the Opéra. DIED: Schütz.	Les Fêtes de l'Amour et de Bacchus.
1673	DIED: Molière. The first mail carried from New York to Boston.		
1674	DIED: John Milton.		Alceste (Lully)
1675	Indian raid upon Deerfield, Massachusetts.	DIED: Perrin.	
1677	Racine wrote *Phèdre*.	DIED: Cambert.	Isis
1678	First book of poems by Anne Bradstreet, first American poetess.	First opera house built in Germany at Hamburg.	
1679	Great fire at Boston.		Gli Equivoci nel Sembiante (Scarlatti)
1682	First marriage in Pennsylvania.	Stradella murdered.	
1683	The Poles break the Turkish siege of Vienna.	BORN: Rameau.	
1685	BORN: J. S. Bach, Handel and John Gay.		
1686	Charter of Connecticut hidden in an oak tree from Governor Andros.		Acis et Galathée (Lully); Armide (Lully)
1687		DIED: Lully.	
1688	Bacon's *Essays* printed in America.	DIED: Quinault.	
1689	Peter the Great made Tsar of Russia.		Dido and Aeneas

YEAR	GENERAL HISTORY	OPERA HISTORY	FIRST PERFORMANCES
1690	Battle of the Boyne, Ireland		
1691	First ducking stool in New York.		King Arthur
1692	Salem witch hunt began.		The Fairy Queen
1693			Medea (Charpentier)
1694	BORN: Voltaire.		
1695	First streetcleaners in New York.	DIED: Purcell.	
1698		BORN: Metastasio.	
1704	Louis XIV defeated at Blenheim. Massacre at Deerfield, Massachusetts.	DIED: M. A. Charpentier.	Iphigénie en Tauride (Campra)
1705	Newcomen's steam engine.		Almira (Handel)
1706	BORN: Benjamin Franklin.	BORN: Galuppi.	
1707	England and Scotland united.		
1709	First copyright by statute granted in England.		Agrippina
1710	Three thousand refugees from Germany arrive in America.	BORN: Arne, Favart and Pergolesi.	
1712	Carolina divided into North and South parts.	BORN: Rousseau.	Il Pastor Fido—first version
1714	Tea imported to America.	BORN: Gluck.	
1720	New York City had 7000 residents.	Royal Academy of Music established in London.	
1721	First inoculation against smallpox.		
1722		Bach's *Wohltemperiertes Klavier*, celebrating the equal-tempered system of tuning.	
1725	First newspaper in New York.	DIED: A. Scarlatti.	

YEAR	GENERAL HISTORY	OPERA HISTORY	FIRST PERFORMANCES
1726			Alessandro
1728	First organ in Philadelphia.	BORN: Piccini.	The Beggar's Opera
1730	Baltimore settled.		Partenope
1731	First circulating library in America.		Il Maestro di Musica
1732	BORN: G. Washington.	BORN: Beaumarchais, J. Haydn. DIED: John Gay.	Acis and Galatea (Handel)
1733	Savannah, Ga., settled.		La Serva Padrona; Rosamund; Hippolyte et Aricie
1734	The "Great Awakening" religious revival in New England.		Il Pastor Fido—second version
1735	First settlers in Indiana.	BORN: J. C. Bach.	Flora, at Charleston, S.C., the first opera in America
1736	First diagnosis of scarlet fever.	DIED: Pergolesi.	Atalanta
1737			Castor et Pollux
1738	First umbrella in America.	DIED: Caldara.	Serse (Handel)
1739			Dardanus
1740	France and Prussia attack Southern Germany.	BORN: Paisiello, Sophie Arnould.	
1741	First symphony orchestra in America, at Bethlehem, Pa.	BORN: Grétry. DIED: Vivaldi.	
1743	BORN: Thomas Jefferson.	BORN: Adamberger.	
1744	First brewery in Baltimore.	DIED: Campra.	
1746	Defeat of the Scots at Culloden.		
1748			Semiramide Riconosciuta
1749		BORN: Cimarosa, da Ponte and Goethe.	

YEAR	GENERAL HISTORY	OPERA HISTORY	FIRST PERFORMANCES
1750	First human dissection in America. DIED: J. S. Bach.	BORN: Salieri.	The Beggar's Opera, in New York
1752	England adopted the Gregorian Calendar.		Le Devin du Village
1756	Beginning of the Seven Years' War.	BORN: Mozart.	
1757	Clive opened India for England.		
1759	Wolfe defeated Mont-calm at Quebec. BORN: Robert Burns.	DIED: Handel.	
1762	Catherine the Great became ruler of Russia.	BORN: Michael Kelly.	Orfeo ed Euridice Love in a Village
1763	Otis outlined reasons for the American Revolution.	BORN: Incledon, Méhul.	
1764	First spinning mill in Philadelphia.	DIED: Rameau.	Rose et Colas
1767	(Probably) first libretto published in America.	Gluck published his famous preface.	Alceste (Gluck); La Cantarina; The Dis-appointment
1768	New York Chamber of Commerce founded.		Bastien et Bastienne; Iphigénie en Tauride (Galuppi)
1769	Watt patented his steam engine.		La Finta Semplice; Le Déserteur; Le Tableau Parlant
1770	The Boston Massacre.	BORN: Beethoven.	Mitridate
1771	Benjamin Franklin began his autobiography.		Ascanio in Alba; Zémire et Azor
1772	First type foundry in America.	Gluck went to Paris.	Lucio Silla
1773	The Boston Tea Party.		Hippolyte et Aricie; Céphale et Procris
1774	Discovery of oxygen.	BORN: Braham, Spontini.	Iphigénie en Aulide
1775	Battle of Lexington. Beaumarchais' Il Barbiere di Siviglia	BORN: M. García, Sr., Boieldieu.	La Finta Giardiniera

YEAR	GENERAL HISTORY	OPERA HISTORY	FIRST PERFORMANCES
1776	Washington crossed the Delaware. The Declaration of Independence.		
1777	Battle of Saratoga.		Armide (Gluck); Polly
1778	DIED: Voltaire.	DIED: Arne, Rousseau.	
1779	John Paul Jones captured the *Serapis*		Iphigénie en Tauride (Gluck)
1780	Battle of King's Mountain, S.C./N.C.		
1781	English surrender at Yorktown. Spanish capture St. Joseph, Ind. Kant's *Critique of Pure Reason.*		Iphigénie en Tauride (Piccini); Idomeneo; Belmont et Constanze
1782	The American Revolution ends at Charleston.	BORN: Auber. DIED: Metastasio, J. C. Bach.	Die Entführung aus dem Serail; Fra i Due Litiganti; Il Barbiere di Siviglia (Paisiello)
1783	First balloon ascent.		
1784	Slavery abolished in Connecticut and Rhode Island.	BORN: Spohr.	Richard Coeur de Lion
1785	First American turnpike.	BORN: Milder. DIED: Galuppi.	
1786	First *Hamlet* in America.	BORN: Weber.	Der Schauspieldirektor; Le Nozze di Figaro; Doktor und Apotheker; Una Cosa Rara
1787	Slavery prohibited in Northwest territories.	DIED: Gluck.	Don Giovanni
1788	The Constitution of the United States adopted.		
1789	G. Washington made President. The Bastille riot.		
1790	The Constitution ratified.		Così fan Tutte

YEAR	GENERAL HISTORY	OPERA HISTORY	FIRST PERFORMANCES
1791	Congress passed first internal revenue act.	First company of French opera arrived at New Orleans. BORN: Hérold, Scribe, Meyerbeer. DIED: Mozart.	Lodoiska; La Clemenza di Tito; Die Zauberflöte
1792	French Republic victory at Valmy.	BORN: Rossini. DIED: Favart.	Il Matrimonio Segreto
1793	Louis XVI beheaded.		
1794		BORN: Lablache.	Tammany
1795	The French Directoire established.	BORN: Marschner.	
1796	Napoleon defeated the Austrians at Arcola. DIED: Robert Burns.	BORN: Pacini.	The Archers, the first American opera to be performed.
1797		BORN: Donizetti, Schubert.	Anacreon chez Polycrate; Medea (Cherubini); Doktor Faust (Walter)
1798	Napoleon conquers Egypt. First income tax in England.		Falstaff (Salieri)
1799	End of the Directoire. Napoleon made First Consul.	DIED: Beaumarchais.	The Vintage; Ariodant
1800	Spain ceded Louisiana to France.	DIED: Piccini.	Les Deux Journées
1801	Thomas Jefferson inaugurated as President of the United States.	BORN: Bellini, Lortzing. DIED: Cavalieri, Cimarosa. First signs of Beethoven's deafness.	
1802	The first lifeboats.	BORN: Nourrit. DIED: Sophie Arnould.	
1803	The Louisiana Purchase.	BORN: Adam, Berlioz.	La Selva Incantada
1804	Napoleon made Emperor.	BORN: Glinka, Schröder-Devrient. DIED: Adamberger.	

YEAR	GENERAL HISTORY	OPERA HISTORY	FIRST PERFORMANCES
1805	Nelson defeated the Spanish at Trafalgar. Fulton operated the first steamboat.		Fidelio
1806	Webster's Dictionary published.	BORN: Sontag.	
1807	Napoleon defeated the Prussians.	BORN: Staudigl.	Joseph; La Vestale
1808		BORN: Balfe, Malibran.	
1809	BORN: Lincoln.	BORN: Mendelssohn. DIED: J. Haydn.	Fernando Cortez
1810	BORN: Chopin.	BORN: David, Mario, Nicolai, R. Schumann.	Barber of Seville (Paisiello), at New Orleans
1811	First colony in Pacific Northwest.	BORN: Grisi, Liszt, Thomas.	
1812	Napoleon occupied Moscow. United States at war with England.	BORN: Von Flotow.	La Scala di Seta
1813		BORN: Dargomizhsky, Verdi, Wagner, Fry. DIED: Grétry.	L'Italiana in Algeri; Tancredi
1814	Treaty of Ghent. The first gas lights in London.		Il Turco in Italia
1815	Napoleon defeated at Waterloo. The Battle of New Orleans.		
1816	The year in which the northern United States had no summer.	DIED: Paisiello.	Il Barbiere di Siviglia (Rossini); Undine; Faust (Spohr); Otello (Rossini)
1817	"Thanatopsis" by Bryant.	DIED: Méhul.	La Cenerentola; La Gazza Ladra
1818	Executive mansion in Washington painted white to cover scorch marks left by British invaders.	BORN: Gounod.	
1819		BORN: Offenbach.	Olympia
1820	DIED: Daniel Boone.	BORN: Jenny Lind.	

YEAR	GENERAL HISTORY	OPERA HISTORY	FIRST PERFORMANCES
1821	Cherokees adopt the alphabet of Sequoia. BORN: Dostoevsky. DIED: Napoleon.		Der Freischütz
1822		BORN: Arditi, Franck.	
1823	The Monroe Doctrine.	BORN: Lalo.	Semiramide (Rossini); Euryanthe
1824		BORN: Cornelius, Smetana.	
1825	First railroad in England.	BORN: J. Strauss, Jr. DIED: Salieri.	La Dame Blanche; Don Giovanni, in New York
1826	First locomotive in America. DIED: Thomas Jefferson.	DIED: Weber, Kelly, Incledon. García presented opera in New York.	Oberon
1827		BORN: Marie Carvalho. DIED: Beethoven.	Die Hochzeit des Camacho; Il Pirata
1828	BORN: Tolstoi.	DIED: Schubert.	Masaniello; Der Vampyr
1829	First school for the blind in the U.S.	First Italian opera at New York. Rossini retired from opera.	Agnes von Hohenstaufen; Guillaume Tell; Der Templar und die Judin
1830	In a test race, a horse beat a locomotive.	BORN: von Bülow, J. B. Faure, Goldmark.	Fra Diavolo; I Capuleti ed I Montecchi; Anna Bolena.
1831	McCormick invented the reaping machine.	BORN: Tietjens.	La Sonnambula; Zampa; Robert le Diable; Norma
1832	DIED: Goethe.	BORN: L. Damrosch. DIED: M. García, Sr.	L'Elisir d'Amore; Le Pré aux Clercs
1833	BORN: Brahms.	BORN: Borodin. DIED: Hérold.	Hans Heiling; Lucrezie Borgia
1834	Electric motor invented in Vermont.	BORN: Ponchielli, Santley. DIED: Boieldieu.	Le Chalet
1835	Morse invented the telegraph.	BORN: Saint Saëns, Cui. DIED: Bellini.	I Puritani; La Juive; Le Cheval de Bronze; Lucia di Lammermoor
1836	Republic of Texas established.	BORN: Delibes. DIED: Malibran.	Les Huguenots; Le Postillion de Longjumeau; Ivan Susanin

YEAR	GENERAL HISTORY	OPERA HISTORY	FIRST PERFORMANCES
1837	Victoria became Queen of England.		Alessandro Stradella; Zar und Zimmermann
1838	Boston added music to public school curriculum.	BORN: Bizet, Stehle. DIED: da Ponte, Milder.	Maria di Rudenz; Falstaff (Balfe); Benvenuto Cellini
1839	First photographs. BORN: Cézanne.	BORN: Mussorgsky. DIED: Nourrit.	Esmeralda; Oberto— Verdi's first
1840	First U.S. expedition to Antarctica.	BORN: Galli-Marié, Tchaikovsky.	La Figlia del Reggimento; Un Giorno di Regno; La Favorita
1841	First covered wagons arrive in California.	BORN: Chabrier, Dvořák.	
1842	N.Y. Philharmonic Society formed.	BORN: Boito, Brandt, Massenet. DIED: Cherubini.	Nabucco; Linda de Chamounix; Le Roi d'Yvetot (Auber); Rienzi; Russlan and Ludmilla; Der Wildschütz
1843	First soap powder in U.S.	BORN: Patti, Christine Nilsson.	Der Fliegende Holländer; Don Pasquale; I Lombardi; Medea (Pacini); Don Sebastian; The Bohemian Girl
1844	Stephen Foster's first published song.	BORN: Rimsky-Korsakov.	Ernani
1845	Texas annexed to U.S.A.	BORN: G. Fauré, I. Campanini.	Leonora; Tannhäuser; Maritana
1846	United States at war with Mexico.		Attila; The Night Dancers; La Damnation de Faust
1847	DIED: Johnny Appleseed.	BORN: Albani. DIED: Mendelssohn.	Macbeth; Martha
1848	Revolution in Europe. BORN: Gauguin.	BORN: Maurel, Lilli Lehmann. DIED: Donizetti.	Die Lustigen Weiber von Windsor
1849	The California Gold Rush. DIED: Chopin.	BORN: Godard.	Le Caïd: Le Prophète; Luisa Miller
1850	Mormons reached Salt Lake, Utah. First international copyright.	BORN: J. de Reszke, Scalchi.	Le Songe d'Une Nuit d'Été; Lohengrin; Genoveva

YEAR	GENERAL HISTORY	OPERA HISTORY	FIRST PERFORMANCES
1851	*New York Times* founded. *Moby Dick* published.	BORN: d'Indy. DIED: Lortzing, Spontini.	Rigoletto; Sapho (Gounod); Raymond; La Perle du Brésil
1852	*Uncle Tom's Cabin* published.	BORN: Hauk.	
1853	BORN: Van Gogh.	BORN: E. de Reszke.	Il Trovatore; La Traviata
1854	The British light brigade died at Balaklava.	BORN: Chadwick, Janáček, Humperdinck, Plançon. DIED: Sontag.	Halka; L'Étoile du Nord; Alfonso und Estrella
1855	Crimean War ended.		I Vespri Siciliani; L'Ebreo
1856	BORN: Sigmund Freud.	DIED: Adam, Braham, R. Schumann.	Manon Lescaut (Auber); Rusalka; Falstaff (Adam); Les Dragons de Villars
1857	Central Park, N.Y., laid out.	BORN: Nordica. DIED: Glinka.	Simon Boccanegra
1858	First cable across the Atlantic.	Covent Garden rebuilt. BORN: Calvé, Leoncavallo, Puccini, Sembrich. DIED: Lablache.	Orphée aux Enfers; Der Barbier von Bagdad
1859	Italy united. John Brown captured Harpers Ferry, W.Va.	BORN: V. Herbert. DIED: Spohr.	Un Ballo in Maschera; Faust; Dinorah
1860	Lincoln elected to presidency.	BORN: Wolf, Albéniz, Mahler, Alvarez, C. Campanini, G. Charpentier, Paderewski. DIED: Schröder-Devrient.	Philémon et Baucis; Lurline
1861	First great battle of the Civil War at Manassas.	BORN: Melba, Schumann-Heink. DIED: Marschner, Scribe, Staudigl.	La Statue; Der Häusliche Krieg
1862	Battles of Shiloh, Antietam, Vicksburg.	BORN: Debussy, Delius, W. Damrosch.	La Reine de Saba; Lalla Rookh; Béatrice et Bénédict; La Forza del Destino

YEAR	GENERAL HISTORY	OPERA HISTORY	FIRST PERFORMANCES
1863	Battles of Chancellorsville and Gettysburg.	BORN: Juch, Ternina, Mascagni.	Judith (Serov); Notre Dame de Paris; Les Pêcheurs de Perles; Les Troyens—Part II
1864	Battles of the Wilderness and Atlanta.	BORN: d'Albert, R. Strauss. DIED: Fry, Meyerbeer.	Mireille; La Belle Hélène
1865	Booth shot Lincoln.	BORN: Dukas.	L'Africaine; Tristan und Isolde; Die Schöne Galathea; Rognyeda
1866		BORN: Busoni, Cilèa, Scotti, Dippel.	Zaïda (Mozart); Prodana Nevěsta; Mignon
1867	Cigarettes appear in America.	BORN: Eames, Granados, Giordano, Toscanini. DIED: Pacini.	Don Carlos; La Grande Duchesse de Gérolstein; Roméo et Juliette; L'Oca del Cairo (Mozart); König Manfred; La Jolie Fille de Perth
1868	Little Women published.	BORN: Schmedes. DIED: Rossini.	Mefistofele (Boito); Hamlet; Dalibor; Die Meistersinger; La Périchole
1869	First transcontinental railroad completed.	DIED: Berlioz, Grisi, Dargomizhsky.	Das Rheingold
1870	War between France and Germany.	BORN: van Rooy. DIED: Balfe. MARRIED: Wagner to Cosima Liszt von Bülow	Il Guarany; Die Walküre; Der Fliegende Holländer; at Drury Lane, the first Wagner in England
1871	Gilbert and Sullivan commenced their collaboration.	BORN: Converse, Hadley, Dalmorès, Fremstad, Homer, Tetrazzini. DIED: Auber.	Aida
1872		BORN: Vaughan Williams.	Kamenny Gost; Djamileh; Don César de Bazan; La Fille de Mme. Angot
1873	Financial panic in New York.	BORN: Caruso, Chaliapin, Rachmaninov.	Pskovityanka; Le Roi l'à Dit
1874	First public zoo in U.S.	BORN: Didur, Schönberg, DIED: Cornelius.	Boris Godunov; Die Fledermaus; Der Widerspänstigen Zähmung

YEAR	GENERAL HISTORY	OPERA HISTORY	FIRST PERFORMANCES
1875	First American university course in music.	BORN: Hahn, Ravel. DIED: Bizet.	Carmen; Die Königin von Saba; Das Goldene Kreuz
1876	Battle of the Little Big Horn. Custer's last stand.	BORN: Wolf-Ferrari, da Falla.	La Gioconda; Das Ring des Nibelungen (complete); Hubička; Paul et Virginie
1877	Selden invented a horseless carriage.	BORN: Mary Garden. DIED: Tietjens.	Le Roi de Lahore; Samson et Dalila
1878	Edison patented the phonograph.	BORN: Destinn.	
1879	BORN: Einstein, Stalin.	BORN: Beecham.	Eugene Onegin
1880	Sarah Bernhardt appeared in N.Y.	BORN: Bloch. DIED: Offenbach.	
1881	DIED: Dostoevski.	BORN: Bartók, Cadman, Enesco. DIED: Mussorgsky.	Les Contes d'Hoffmann; Libuše; Hérodiade
1882	First streetcars in U.S. (at Appleton, Wisc.)	BORN: Kodály, Farrar, Galli-Curci, Malipiero, Stravinsky.	Snyegurotchka; Françoise de Rimini; Zenobia; Parsifal; Dmitrij; Der Bettelstudent
1883	First vaudeville in U.S. Brooklyn Bridge opened.	BORN: Alda, Zandonai. DIED: Mario, Wagner, von Flotow. Opened: The Metropolitan Opera House.	Henry VIII; Lakmé
1884		BORN: Easton, McCormack. DIED: Smetana.	Sigurd; Manon; Der Trompeter von Säkkingen
1885	Mark Twain published *The Adventures of Huckleberry Finn*	BORN: A. Berg, Hempel, E. Schumann, Martinelli. DIED: L. Damrosch.	Nadeshda; Der Zigeunerbaron
1886	Statue of Liberty unveiled.	DIED: Ponchielli, Liszt.	Khovantschina; Gwendoline
1887		BORN: Villa-Lobos, Jeritza. DIED: Borodin, Jenny Lind.	Le Roi malgré Lui; Otello (Verdi)
1888	The Great Blizzard in New York	BORN: Lotte Lehmann, Teyte, Schorr.	Asrael; Jocelyn; Le Roi d'Ys

CHRONOLOGY OF OPERA

YEAR	GENERAL HISTORY	OPERA HISTORY	FIRST PERFORMANCES
1889	The Johnstown flood.	BORN: Muzio.	Edgar (Puccini)
1890	DIED: Van Gogh.	BORN: Gigli, Melchior, Ibert. DIED: Franck.	Salammbô; Cavalleria Rusticana; La Basoche; Robin Hood; Prince Igor; Pique-Dame; Les Troyens, complete
1891	Zipper patented. Carnegie Hall opened.	BORN: Kipnis, Prokofiev. DIED: Delibes.	Gunlöd; Le Rêve; L'Amico Fritz
1892	Dvořák visited U.S.	BORN: Honegger, Milhaud, Pinza, Rodjinski. DIED: Lalo.	La Wally; Werther; Mala Vita; I Pagliacci; Yolande; Cristoforo Colombo
1893	Financial panic in U.S.	BORN: Hába. DIED: Gounod, Tchaikovsky.	Mme. Chrysanthème; Manon Lescaut (Puccini); Falstaff (Verdi); Aleko; L'Attaque du Moulin; Hänsel und Gretel
1894		BORN: Rethberg. DIED: Chabrier, Von Bülow.	Thaïs; Le Portrait die Manon; La Navarrase; Jeanie Deans
1895	Stephen Crane published *The Red Badge of Courage*	BORN: Hindemith, Orff, Flagstad. DIED: M. Carvalho, Godard.	Kenilworth; Enrico Clifford
1896	Langley's model airplane flew successfully.	BORN: Weinberger, Thorborg, Tibbett, Hanson. DIED: Thomas, I. Campanini	Pepita Jiménez; Sadko; La Bohème (Puccini); The Scarlet Letter (Damrosch); Shamus O'Brien; Andrea Chénier; Der Corregidor; Das Heimchen am Herd
1897	DIED: Brahms.	BORN: Ponselle.	Fierrebras (Schubert); La Bohème (Leoncavallo); L'Arlesiana; Sapho (Massenet); Šarka (Fibich)
1898	War between the United States and Spain.	BORN: Patzak, Gershwin.	Lobetanz; Fedora; Iris; Véronique
1899		BORN: Traubel. DIED: J. Strauss.	Tsarskaya Nyevesta

YEAR	GENERAL HISTORY	OPERA HISTORY	FIRST PERFORMANCES
1900	Casey Jones died in a train wreck.	BORN: Weill, Krenek, Antheil, Copland. DIED: J. Strauss.	Tosca; Louise; Le Juif Polonais; Promethée; Zaza
1901	DIED: Queen Victoria.	BORN: Egk. DIED: Verdi.	Rusalka (Dvořák); Feuersnot
1902		BORN: Walton, Sayao.	Orestes (Weingartner); Le Jongleur de Notre Dame; Merrie England; Der Wald; Pelléas et Mélisande; Adriana Lecouvreur
1903	DIED: Gauguin. First successful airplane.	BORN: Novotna. DIED: Arditi, Wolf.	Ilsebill; The Zaporogues; Tiefland; Siberia
1904	First subway in the world begun in New York.	BORN: Dallapiccola, Peerce, Pons. DIED: Dvorak.	Její Pastorkyňa ("Jenufa"); Madama Butterfly; Koanga; Sakuntala (Coerne); Risurrezione
1905	Japanese defeated the Russians in Manchuria.	DIED: Galli-Marié.	L'Oracolo; Salomé
1906	San Francisco earthquake. DIED: Cézanne.	BORN: Milanov.	The Pipe of Desire; Greysteel; Don Procopio; I Quattro Rusteghi; Aphrodite; The Wreckers
1907		First American performance of Salome. Closed immediately.	Kitezh; A Village Romeo and Juliet; Ariane et Barbe-Bleue; Le Coq d'Or; Zenobia.
1908	Isadora Duncan at height of her dance career.	DIED: Rimsky-Korsakov.	La Habanera
1909		DIED: Albéniz.	Monna Vanna; Elektra; Zhenitba; Safie; Pierrot et Pierrette; Il Segreto di Susanna
1910	DIED: Tolstoi, Mark Twain.	BORN: Pears, Tourel. DIED: Viardot-García. First production of an American opera at the Metropolitan, *The Pipe of Desire.*	Don Quichotte; Poia; Macbeth (Bloch); La Fanciulla del West; Königskinder; Noël

CHRONOLOGY OF OPERA

YEAR	GENERAL HISTORY	OPERA HISTORY	FIRST PERFORMANCES
1911	Charlie Chaplin appeared at New York City.	DIED: Mahler.	Der Rosenkavalier; Natoma; The Sacrifice; The Fair at Sorochintsky; La Jota; L'Heure Espagnole; I Gioielli della Madonna
1912	The steamship *Titanic* sank.	BORN: Ferrier, Mödl. DIED: Massenet.	Mona; Ariadne auf Naxos
1913	Panama Canal completed.	BORN: Britten, Stevens, Tagliavini.	La Forêt Bleue; Cyrano de Bergerac; Madeleine; Penelope; La Vide Breve; L'Amore dei Tre Re; Julien
1914	The First World War began at the Marne.	BORN: Tucker. DIED: J. B. Faure, Nordica, Plançon.	Francesca da Rimini; L'Ombra di Don Giovanni; Marouf; Le Rossignol; The Immortal Hour
1915	Allies defeated at Gallipoli. Poison gas used in war.	BORN: Del Monaco. DIED: Goldmark.	Mme. Sans-Gêne; Fedra
1916	Allies win Verdun and Jutland.	BORN: Steber. DIED: Granados.	Goyescas; The Boatswain's Mate; Savitri
1917	United States entered war. Russian Revolution.	BORN: Kirsten. DIED: E. de Reszke.	The Canterbury Pilgrims; La Rondine; Lodoletta; Arlecchino; Turandot (Busoni); Palestrina; Azora, the Daughter of Montezuma
1918	Second battle of the Marne. Paris bombed. Armistice.	BORN: Thebom. DIED: Debussy, Boito, Cui.	Shanewis; Duke Bluebeard's Castle; Il Trittico
1919	The liquor prohibition amendment (the eighteenth).	DIED: Patti, Leoncavallo, C. Campanini.	Monsieur Beaucaire; Les Choëphores; Die Frau ohne Schatten; Fennimore und Gerda
1920	Air mail service commenced in U.S. First regular radio broadcasting.	At Hammersmith the Beggar's Opera ran 1463 nights.	Rip van Winkle; Ritter Blaubart; Cleopatra's Night; The Tempest; Die Tote Stadt
1921	U.S. initiated quota limitations on immigration.	DIED: Caruso, Brandt, Humperdinck, Christine Nilsson, Saint-Saëns, Stehle.	Antar; Prince Ferelon; Mörder Hoffnung des Fraun; Nusch-Nuschi; Káta Kabanová; The Love for Three Oranges

YEAR	GENERAL HISTORY	OPERA HISTORY	FIRST PERFORMANCES
1922	Mussolini became dictator of Italy.	BORN: Tebaldi. DIED: Santley, Scalchi.	Sancta Susanna; Venus; Sakuntala (Alfano); Mavra; Alkestis
1923		DIED: Maurel.	El Retablo de Maese Pedro; The Perfect Fool; Fête Galante; Debora e Jaele
1924		DIED: G. Fauré, Puccini, Busoni, V. Herbert.	Nerone (Boito); Der Sprung über das Schatten; Hugh the Drover; The Queen of Cornwall; Intermezzo
1925	The Scopes trial, in which Darwin's theory of evolution was at issue.	DIED: J. de Reszke.	L'Enfant et les Sortilèges; Socrate; Doktor Faust; At the Boar's Head; Sarka (Janáček); Wozzeck
1926	The first radio network broadcast.		Judith (Honegger); Der Protagonist; Turandot (Puccini); Les Malheurs d'Orphée; Háry János; Cardillac; Orpheus und Eurydike; A Witch of Salem
1927	Lindberg flew across the ocean alone, non-stop. Sacco and Vanzetti were executed.		Jonny Spielt Auf; La Rosiera; The King's Henchman; Le Poirier de Misère; The Royal Palace; Naïla; Agamemnon; Švanda Dudák; Madonna Imperia; Oedipus Rex (Stravinsky); Hin und Züruck; L'Enlèvement d'Europe; La Campana Sommersa; Eumenides; Le Pauvre Matelot; Antigone (Honegger)
1928	First scheduled television broadcast.	DIED: Janáček.	Die Aegyptische Helena; Fredericka; Die Dreigroschenoper
1929	Collapse in Wall Street brought on the "Great Depression"	DIED: Hauk, Lilli Lehmann.	Sir John in Love; La Femme Nue; Jürg Jenatsch; Neues vom Tage; Judith (Goossens); Engelbrekt; Samuel Pepys

CHRONOLOGY OF OPERA

YEAR	GENERAL HISTORY	OPERA HISTORY	FIRST PERFORMANCES
1930	Four and a half million unemployed in the U.S.A.	DIED: Albani, Destinn.	Le Roi d'Yvetot (Ibert); Z mrtvého Domu; Christophe Colomb; Transatlantic; Wir bauen eine Stadt; Fremde Erde
1931	Many banks closed.	DIED: Melba, d'Indy, Chadwick, Schmedes.	Die Mutter; Peter Ibbetson
1932	Thirteen million unemployed. F. D. Roosevelt elected president.	DIED: d'Albert, Dippel, Van Rooy.	Maximilien
1933	Hitler assumed power in Germany.	DIED: Alvarez.	The Jolly Roger; The Emperor Jones; Arabella
1934		DIED: Delius.	Madrisa; Lady Macbeth of Minsk; Four Saints in Three Acts; Merry Mount; Helen Retires; Lulu
1935	U.S. established its Social Security Administration.	DIED: A. Berg, Dukas, Sembrich.	Nerone (Mascagni); In the Pasha's Garden; Medea (Engel); Die Schweigsame Frau; Porgy and Bess
1936	Edward VIII abdicated.	DIED: Muzio, Scotti, Schumann-Heink.	Oedipus Tyrannus (Enesco); The Poisoned Kiss; Le Testament de la Tante Caroline; Pickwick
1937	Arturo Toscanini became conductor of the N.B.C. Symphony.	DIED: Gershwin, Ravel, Hadley.	Don Juan de Mañera; L'Aiglon; Massimilla Doni; The Man Without a Country; Wallenstein; Riders to the Sea
1938		DIED: Chaliapin.	Esther de Carpentras; Peer Gynt; The Scarlet Letter (Giannini); Mathis der Maler; Karl V; Friedenstag; Daphne (Strauss)
1939	Hitler attacked Poland. DIED: Sigmund Freud.	DIED: Dalmorès, Juch.	The Old Maid and the Thief; Der Mond; Medée (Milhaud)
1940	The British evacuated Europe at Dunkirk.	DIED: Converse, Tetrazzini.	Volo di Notte

YEAR	GENERAL HISTORY	OPERA HISTORY	FIRST PERFORMANCES
1941	Japanese bombed Pearl Harbor.	DIED: Paderewski, Ternina.	Paul Bunyan
1942	Battles of Bataan, The Coral Sea, El Alamein, Guadalcanal, Midway Island.	DIED: Calvé.	Capriccio; Ginevra
1943	Battle of the Gilbert Islands.	DIED: Rachmaninov.	Barbe-Bleue; Die Kluge
1944	The Allied invasion of Europe.	DIED: Zandonai.	
1945	Atomic bomb dropped on Hiroshima, Japan. End of the Second World War.	DIED: Bartók, Mascagni, McCormack.	Peter Grimes; The Scarecrow
1946	U.S. joined UNESCO.	DIED: Didur, Cadman, Falla.	The Medium; The Rape of Lucretia
1947	First scheduled round-the-world commercial flight.	DIED: Hahn, Homer.	Street Scene; The Warrior; The Trial of Lucullus; Albert Herring; Dantons Tod
1948		DIED: Wolf-Ferrari, Giordano.	
1949	Permanent United Nations Headquarters dedicated.	DIED: R. Strauss.	Let's Make an Opera; Till Eulenspiegel(Jeremias); Billy Budd (Ghedini); Regina
1950	The Korean War.	DIED: Weill, Cilèa, de Luca, W. Damrosch.	The Consul; Il Prigioniero; The Triumph of St. Joan; Bolivar
1951	First color-television broadcast.	DIED: Fremstad, Schönberg.	Pilgrim's Progress; The Rake's Progress; Billy Budd (Britten)
1952		DIED: Alda, Eames, E. Schumann.	Leonore 40/45; Die Liebe der Danae
1953	DIED: Stalin.	DIED: Ferrier, Prokofiev, Schorr.	Gloriana; Der Prozess; The Taming of the Shrew
1954	First thermo-nuclear bomb exploded.		The Tender Land; David; The Turn of the Screw; The Mother; Troilus and Cressida; Double Trouble; The Saint of Bleecker Street

YEAR	GENERAL HISTORY	OPERA HISTORY	FIRST PERFORMANCES
1955	DIED: Einstein. Salk vaccine against poliomyelitis developed.	DIED: Hempel, Honegger, Enesco.	Susannah
1956	Segregation in public schools outlawed by Supreme Court.	DIED: G. Charpentier.	He Who Gets Slapped; The Wife of Martin Guerre; The Ballad of Baby Doe
1957	Opening of International Geophysical Year, a cooperative scientific experiment.	DIED: Pinza, Toscanini, Gigli.	Les Dialogues des Carmelites; The Prodigal Son (Malipiero); Die Harmonie der Welt
1958	First U.S. artificial satellite put in orbit.	DIED: Vaughan Williams.	Vanessa; Wuthering Heights; Maria Golovin; L'Assassinio nell' Cattedrale
1959	Rocket to moon fired by Soviet scientists.	DIED: Bloch.	
1960	Unprecedented number of heads of state attend U.N. session.	DIED: Bjoerling, Warren.	

GLOSSARY

a cappella (It.) ah cahPELlah

Without accompaniment, particularly solo or choral music without instrumental accompaniment. The expression in Italian means "in the chapel style."

a demi voix (Fr.) ah d'MEE vwah

At half voice, in a singing whisper, sotto voce.

accompanist

One who accompanies, usually a pianist who substitutes for the orchestra in rehearsals of operatic scenes or in concerts of soloists. Sometimes a regular performance of opera contains passages in which a singer is accompanied by a keyboard instrument, the conductor relinquishing his direction until the passage is done. This is usual in the various kinds of dry recitative.

act

The largest formal unit of opera. Most operas have two, three or four acts which are themselves divided into scenes. The acts are usually separated by intermissions whereas the scenes are not. The separation into acts usually indicates the passage of time in the action, while the changes of scene usually involve less a change of time than one of locale.

adagio (It.) ahDAHzheeo

An indication of tempo; slowly, at a pace slower than a normal walk.

adaptation

An arrangement of the instrumentation, and/or a translation or alteration of the libretto of an opera. An adaptation is usually a fairly free alteration of the sequence and detail of the various scenes and musical pieces, made for the purpose of shortening an opera, or to render it more palatable for a particular audience. It is not to be confused with simple re-orchestration, or with transposition of the music. But many so-called translations of libretti are adaptations.

AGMA

The American Guild of Musical Artists; one of the dominant unions for singers in opera in the United States.

allegretto (It.) ahlegGRETTo

Not as fast as allegro.

allegro (It.) ahLEGgro

A tempo indication; quickly, at a pace faster than a normal walk. The word has a connotation of lightness also, or of happiness, but in music the mood is not always involved.

alto (It.) AHLtoh

High. Formerly used to describe the highest male voice, otherwise sometimes known as the countertenor. Now used for the lowest female voice which sings in that same range, the contralto. For some reason the word *contralto* occurs more often in connection with solo voices, but *alto* with choral.

alzamento (It.) ahltzaMENtoh
Raising the voice, lightening the voice, bringing the tone, as it were, up from the depths of the chest.

anacrusis
From the Greek word which means "a striking-back." Hence an upward movement of the body which by the laws of Newtonian physics must be followed by a downward movement (what goes up must come down). The anacrusis is therefore the feeling of lifting up which prepares a heavy accent. It occurs once in each measure as the upbeat immediately preceding the bar line.

andante (It.) ahnDAHNtay
An indication of tempo; moving, going, at a normal walking pace.

apron
That part of the stage floor which projects toward the audience and beyond the curtain line. The term is usually restricted to the proscenium stage.

arabesque (Fr.) ahrahBESK
Ornament in Arabian style, hence usually a kind of ornamental turning figure on the upbeat, or the unaccented beat.

arena stage
A stage completely surrounded by its audience. This is a very ancient shape for the stage, having its origin perhaps in the threshing-circle at harvest time. It allows a much larger audience to view the action than does a proscenium, but it demands an entirely different concept of staging and acting.

aria (It.) AHree-ah
An air, a song. Usually a formal song within an opera or an oratorio. By nature

it is separated in action from the general flow of the story and the scene around it.

aria concertata (It.) AHree-ah conchayrTAHtah
A concerted air. An aria with an accompaniment closely woven around the voice, as for instance those arias in which the flute accompanies the soprano very closely in duet while both are accompanied by the orchestra.

aria da capo (It.) AHree-ah dah CAHpo
An aria which ends with the same music as that with which it began.

aria parlante (It.) AHree-ah pahrLAHNtay
An aria which is sung in loose rhythm, closely parallel to the rhythm of speech. Not to be confused with *sprechstimme* which is a musical imitation of the tones and rhythms of speech.

arioso (It.) ahreeOHzo
In the manner of an aria. An air. Usually in a freer form than aria, or in closer musical relationship with its context. The arioso is sometimes no more than a melodious moment in music, sometimes an air of larger form and more fullness than an aria.

arrangement
A revision of the music of an opera or of a piece of music. Usually the arrangement involves mainly a change of instrumentation as in the modern arrangements of *La Favola d'Orfeo* which permit performance with modern instruments replacing those which Monteverdi called for but which are no longer available outside museums.

artistic director
The artistic director of an opera company is usually the one person responsible for the overall artistic conception of a particular production. He is

therefore frequently the one who assigns the cast, appoints the conductor, the scene designer and stage director. He does not conduct rehearsals, but tells the others how he wants the rehearsals to be directed.

atonality

Literally without tonality, but usually used to describe a harmonic quality or a system with complex relationships of tonalities between different parts of the piece or different voices. Atonal music has tone, but is intended to sound free of any tonal center. It is not the same as dissonance. *See* dodecaphonism.

avant garde (Fr.) AHvah(n) gard

Those who search ahead. The innovators who attempt new styles and explore their techniques.

backdrop

The curtain, stretched on frames and painted or simply hanging behind the actors, which forms the rear wall of the visible part of the stage. It is to be distinguished from cyclorama in that it is usually painted to represent a definite plane of background, whereas the cyclorama generally represents the sky, or empty space.

backstage

The area behind the visible part of the stage; that which is behind the backdrop and outside the wings, wherever the audience is not permitted to see.

baffleboard

A sound-reflecting construction so placed behind and/or around the orchestra and the singers that their sound may be heard in the outer reaches of the audience. Generally necessary in outdoor productions.

ballabile (It.) bahLAHbeelay

In the style of dancing, a scene in popular dance style, not ballet.

ballad opera

An opera or operetta made for the most part of a series of well known popular songs, with new words arranged and edited to carry along a plot. A fine example of ballad opera is the perennial triumph, *The Beggar's Opera*.

ballata (It.) bahLAHta

A ballad. Also a dance.

ballet (Fr.) bahLAY

A theatrical dance, usually representative of a story or a plot and performed by dancers trained in its special technique. Not to be confused with pantomime, which lacks the fairly abstract form imposed upon ballet, nor with ordinary dancing, which lacks the purpose of story.

Also the group of dancers who perform such works.

Also that part of an opera which is to be performed in dance.

barcarolle (Fr.) bahrcahROHL

A song to be sung in a boat. Frequently associated with Venice, and sung by the gondoliers as they ply their trade along the canals in the quiet of evening.

baritone

The male voice whose range lies below that of the tenor and above that of the bass. Also the singer who has such a voice. Also the name of a deep-voiced brass instrument, not frequently employed in opera.

barocco (It.) bahROHKkoh

Baroque.

baroque (Fr.) bahROHK

The word comes from an obscure root meaning "irregular, bizarre." In music it describes a period and a style which is highly ornamented and in which the ornaments are frequently integrated with the actual structure of the piece. The baroque style crept into opera in the late seventeenth and early eighteenth centuries. Gluck fought against the kind of superficiality it produced.

bass

The lowest male voice, with a range extending below that of the baritone. Also a term designating the lowest of any combination of melodic lines.

basso (It.) BAHso

One who sings in the bass register.

basso cantante (It.) BAHso cahnTAHNtay

A lyric bass voice, a voice of exceptional smoothness in the very low range. The opposite of basso buffo. *See* buffo.

basso continuo (It.) BAHso conTEEnuo

A continuous accompaniment of instruments in which, generally, the harmonization is written not in notes but as a series of numbers indicating notes above the notes of the lowest instrument, to be improvised upon by the player of the keyboard. Frequently employed by the composers of the seventeenth and eighteenth centuries not only to save time in the writing but also to provide the performer a chance to show his abilities.

basso profondo (It.) BAHso proFONdo

A bass voice whose range extends far below the normal bass.

baton (Fr.) bahTO(N)

Literally, *stick*. The little wooden stick used by the conductor to make his hand movements more visible to the players in the pit and on the stage.

beat

The pulse of music. That which the conductor indicates by the regular motion of his baton. Not to be confused with

tempo, which is the frequency of the beats, nor with measure which is their grouping. Nor is beat always audible. When one refers to *the* beat, he frequently means the downbeat. If he means the rhythm, he's wrong.

bel canto (It.) bell CAHNto

"Beautiful song," the lyric style as distinguished from the dramatic or the buffo.

benefit

A performance the proceeds of which are to be donated to a specific charity. It used to be the practice for a composer to organize a benefit to keep himself from starvation. But nowadays the recipient is usually a charitable organization.

berceuse (Fr.) bayrSE(R)Z

A lullaby, a cradle song.

bit

Broadway slang for a very small role. The bit player is usually required to appear on stage and say a line or two, and is thus above the walk-on and the extra.

bocca chiusa (It.) BOCKka keeYUza

With mouth closed while singing; humming. It is worth noting that there are two methods of humming, one of which is employed by choruses who wish to be heard distinctly, and who hum without closed mouths. The directive *bocca chiusa* would prevent that variation.

bouche fermée (Fr.) BOOSH fayrMAY

See bocca chiusa.

brasses

The brass instruments of the orchestra. The trumpets, cornets, trombones, horns and tubas. Such metal instruments as the metal flute, the metal clarinet, and their like are called woodwinds.

GLOSSARY

braut lied (Ger.) BROWT leet
A wedding song.

bravura (It.) brahVOORa
Skill. Usually, in music, great brilliance of execution. The term *bravura* describes brilliance of tone and accuracy of execution at a high level of clarity and is sometimes called heroic.

break
The point at which the tone quality, or timbre of the low register of a voice changes to that of the high register.
Also used to indicate a free moment in an improvisatory piece, especially in jazz.

brindisi (It.) brinnDEEzee
A drinking song.

buffo (f. buffa) (It.) BOOfo (BOOfa)
Comic, in the style of comedy. This refers to the style of delivery of the lines, not to their content. An example of a buffo part would be Dr. Bartolo, in *Il Barbiere di Siviglia.*

cabaletta (It.) cahbahLETtah
A pleasing little song. In Spanish the root is associated with the horse, *caballo*; hence a cabaletta is sometimes a little song one would sing while riding. The cabaletta is the second or third (and usually the more difficult) part of a soprano aria, as in "*Casta diva*," "*Ernani, involami*," and "*Tacea la notte.*"

cadence
Literally fall. The final moment of any melody or a phrase of music; usually the motion implied by the last two or three harmonic movements. It is a harmonic event, which can happen as a temporary stop or a permanent end to a phrase.

cadenza (It.) cahDENza
An ornamented passage in which the flow of the piece has been temporarily

halted while the voice, perhaps accompanied by a solo instrument, indulges in a free improvisation. Sometimes the composer actually writes it out, maintaining the improvisatory quality. Strictly speaking, the cadenza was a florid ornament during the final cadence of a piece.

Camerata, la (It.) cahmayRAHtah, lah
The name applied to a group of Florentine noblemen who met together to discuss the possibility of a revival of the style of the classic drama of Greece. They produced, instead, the first operas. Chief among them were Bardi, Corsi, Peri, Rinuccini, Vincenzo Galilei, Strozzi, Mei, Caccini and Cavalieri.

canon
Literally, "rule". A piece of melodic music, usually sung and usually short, in which the first voice is precisely imitated by the second, then by the third and so forth as each enters the scheme. The simplest canons are rounds such as *Three Blind Mice.* In opera one of the most famous canons is *Mir ist so Wunderbar. See also* fugue.

cantabile (It.) cahnTAHbeelay
Singingly, in an easy flowing style. A direction to the singer to sing most smoothly. Also used to designate an air written to be sung or played in smooth style.

cantando (It.) cahnTAHNdoh
Singing. A directive to the orchestra to play as smoothly as singers should sing.

cantata (It.) cahnTAHta
A piece of vocal music, usually on a religious text but not always. The cantata is a large form, frequently containing arias, interludes and other smaller forms. It is best known as a form for chorus and soloists, differing from opera in that it is not acted and is usually fairly short.

cantilena (It.) cahnteeLAYna
A little song. Sometimes the highest of several singing parts.

canzona (It.) cahnZOHna
A song, but frequently an elaborate song distinguished from an aria by its informality.

capacity house
A full house, an auditorium filled to its capacity.

capo, da
See da capo. See also aria da capo.

cast
Those who appear upon the stage as actors, singers and dancers in a performance. But specifically those who have identity, as distinguished from the chorus and the ballet ensemble.
To cast means to assign people to play the roles required by the opera.

castrato (It.) cahSTRAHto
A male singer who has achieved an abnormally high voice by means of a surgical alteration of his gonadal system during his youth. A eunuch.

cavatina (It.) cahvahTEEna
A little song having only a single strain, and usually simple, expressive and gentle.

chamber opera
Opera intended to be played to a small audience and/or in a small place. Hence frequently an opera without chorus, with a small cast and a piano for accompaniment.

chant
A ritualistic song, a piece for solo or for chorus in ritualistic style. The *Miserere* in *Il Trovatore* is a good example. Another is the choral background for Pimen's monologue in *Boris Godunov*.

chantant (Fr.) shahnTAH(N)
Singing, in a singing style.

chef d'orchestre (Fr.) shay dorKEST
Chief of the orchestra, the conductor.

chest tones
See voce di petto.

chiuso (It.) keeYUzo
Closed. See bocca chiusa.

choral conductor
One who conducts a chorus, the chorus master. In opera the chorus is frequently so placed behind the scenes that the members cannot see the regular conductor. The choral conductor then places himself somewhere where he *can* see the conductor, and the chorus can see him. He then transmits the beat and the cues so that they may be on time. The choral conductor also conducts rehearsals especially for the chorus.

choral opera
An opera in which the chorus is predominant, as in *Boris Godunov*, most of the works of Gluck, *Oedipus Rex* and others. Many composers have sought, in choral opera, an approach to the classic style of Greek drama.

choreography
Dance writing. But in practice it has been such a complex problem to write dance down that the term has come to mean the composition of dance, whether or not any part of it is recorded in writing.

chorus
The group of singers who sing and act always en masse, never as soloists. In some operas, the chorus is not a group but is one singer who comments upon the action. See the opera *The Rape of Lucretia*.

chorus master
The leader of the chorus. Specifically the rehearsal director for the chorus, only infrequently the conductor during performance. *See* choral conductor.

chromatic tones
Tones which have been altered in pitch from the normal tones of any scale. The alteration is a raising by means of sharps, or a lowering by flats. *See* scale.

claque (Fr.) clak
A noisy little knot of people in the audience, or surreptitiously spread among the audience, whose main purpose is to stimulate and to simulate great applause for a certain performer so that that worthy may seem to be more popular than is really the case, and thus more to be respected and salaried for his fame. Most singers, whether they want one or not, have their claques.

classic
Of classic time, standard. In music, generally, the classic period came after the baroque and before the romantic. Some composers, notably Gluck, wrote in a simple but large style, and their works are models of thè genuine form of opera; hence they are classics. But any work which is of long-lasting worth becomes a model in the same way.

clavier
(Fr.) clahveeAY
(Ger.) clahVEER (spelled Klavier)
The keyboard. An instrument which is played by means of a keyboard; hence the harpsichord, the piano, etc.

clef
The symbol which designates the pitch range of the lines and spaces of the staff. The treble clef used to be the letter G, placed upon the line G above middle C.

The bass clef was an F, and points out the F below middle C. Between these is the C clef itself. Soprano and alto voices appear with the treble clef, tenors with the C, and baritones and basses with the F. Nowadays it is quite usual to use the treble clef for tenor, since the C clef is less familiar.

coach
An assistant to the director who helps a singer learn and establish his role during rehearsals. Also an advisor on technical matters to any performer.

coda
The tail end (from the Latin *cauda*, meaning "tail"). An extended embellishment of the ending of a piece of music. Distinguished from cadenza in that the coda involves a written recapitulation of the events of the piece, using the whole orchestra, while the cadenza is a free improvisation for the soloists alone. Frequently the coda is a recapitulation characterized by tremendous acceleration toward the ending—as in the *Viennese Waltz*. In opera many a coda remains buried under the unmusical applause of the audience after the singer has had her high note.

coloratura (*from* It.) coloraTOORah
Colored, that is; colorful. Florid music for the voice; a highly decorated style with many flourishes, trills and complex figures woven about it. Although it can occur in any voice, it appears most often in showpieces for the soprano. The most famous examples are the *Bell Song* from *Lakmé*, Juliette's *Jewel Song*, and the Queen of the Night's aria.

comique (Fr.) coMEEK
Not necessarily comic, but sometimes so. The word describes a style associated with the Opéra-Comique, in Paris. *See*

opéra comique. The correct designation for a comic opera in Italian is *opera buffa,* and in French *opéra bouffe.*

company

The entire personnel of singers, actors, dancers and instrumentalists who perform opera. In practice the term is most usually applied to a more or less stable group such as the company that performs in repertory, or the touring company.

concertmaster

The leading violinist of the orchestra. He sits at the conductor's left and performs certain special duties such as to play the little solos that occur from time to time in the score, or to signal the orchestra to tune up before the conductor himself appears. He also establishes the bowing patterns for the first violins and, in general, acts as the playing leader of the orchestra.

concert performance

A performance of an opera without much staging and action, and usually without costumes. Very frequently a new work, or a work too expensive or experimental to warrant full performance receives a concert performance.

concert pitch

Standard pitch. Defined by the United States Bureau of Standards to be the pitch of 440 vibrations per second for the A above middle C. Many conductors surreptitiously tune their orchestras to a slightly higher pitch in the fond belief that the audience will think the total sound thus produced to be more brilliant than that of other conductors and orchestras.

conductor

He, or she, who leads the orchestra, the singers, the dancers and the chorus in the performance of opera. Not a director in the sense of the stage director.

conservatory

Specifically, a formal school of music.

contralto

The lowest female voice. Sometimes, as in the role of Orfeo, in *Orfeo ed Euridice,* a voice in that range which may be sung by a high male tenor or a female contralto.

contratenor

See countertenor.

counterpoint

Note-against-note. A style of music in which more than one melody may be heard at one time. A canon is a contrapuntal composition. A voice in counterpoint to another is one which serves as a rhythmic and melodic contrast to another, having its own melody.

countertenor

A tenor of exceptionally high range.

crescendo (It.) kraySHENdo

Increasing in volume, growing louder.

czardas (Hungarian) CHARdahsh

A hungarian dance in two movements, slow then fast.

cue

An indication to begin. The conductor gives a cue by signaling with his hand and eye. The score provides a cue by showing the notes or words which immediately preceded an entrance. On a player's part cues are written in very tiny notes.

curtain raiser

A short piece before the curtain rises. In opera generally a comic scene or play preceding the main work of the evening. Not an overture.

cut

A passage which has been deleted. Also that point in the score at which one skips several measures or several pages. Cuts serve to shorten an overlong piece, sometimes to clarify a murky passage, sometimes to relieve an overworked singer.

cyclorama

A backdrop, usually curved, which extends around the sides and rear of a set and which is usually lighted to represent sky or some other indefinite space. It is distinguished from a simple backdrop, which is usually flat and painted to represent a definite scene.

da capo (It.) dah CAHpo

From the top. A directive to the performer to return to the beginning of the piece. *See also* aria da capo.

debut (Fr.) dehBÜ

A coming out. A singer's first appearance on the stage.

décor (Fr.) dehKOR

The set considered as a work of color and design. The design of a setting. The word implies a quality of decoration.

dialogue

The conversation of characters upon the stage. Not their expressive solos, monologues and arias, nor their concerted pieces such as trios and septets, but their responsive talk (whether spoken or sung).

diatonic

Within the natural scale, without altered notes, nonchromatic. Whether or not a piece is based upon the classic major or minor modes, if it is diatonic it makes use of whatever modal system it has without temporary chromatism. In slang terms, diatonic music is "white note" music, as the diatonic function is represented by the white notes of the piano.

diction

Clarity of speech, the quality which makes spoken or sung words understandable. But it is important to keep in mind that for practical purposes diction means clarity of the consonants, since many a singer becomes so involved with the smoothness of his tone that he unconsciously tries to glide over consonants without sounding them. Diction is not to be confused with prosody. Prosody exists in the composition of words and music, while diction can be only in the actual sounding.

diminuendo

Diminishing, growing less in volume, becoming quieter.

director

He who directs. Usually, in opera, the director is primarily the instructor and constructor of stage movement and acting. Sometimes he is also the conductor of the performance. *See also* artistic director.

diva (It.) DEEva

A great lady in opera, a goddess among singers. A prima donna, but in a more complimentary sense.

divisi

Divided. A divisi passage is one in which two performers who have been singing the same line divide to sing different notes, as when the sopranos of the chorus divide to become first and second sopranos.

dodecaphonism

The theory of music based upon the consideration of the twelve equally spaced tones of the tempered system as of equal harmonic value. The composer establishes his thematic thesis as a series of twelve tones, using each of the available tones once. Upon this he builds his piece. This technique was promulgated by Arnold Schoenberg and used by many of his followers. It is the harmonic system of the opera *Lulu*.

donna

Lady, hence a female singer. *See* prima donna.

double bill

A performance consisting of two operas, as the double header in baseball consists of two games. A common double bill contains *Cavalleria Rusticana*, and *I Pagliacci*.

downbeat

The beat indicated by the conductor in moving his baton downward, hence in practice the first beat after the bar line in any measure, the heaviest beat of that measure (though not always).

drama

That which is acted. An acting-out. It is important to remember that drama is not the same as story, tableau, pageant or poem. Drama must be acted to exist, and within it there must be an irreversible transportation of the emotional being of the audience. Drama may not merely portend, it must actually allow that which is portentous to move into its action.

dramma per musica (It.) drahma payr MOOzicka

A play in music. One way to avoid the ambiguity of the word *opera*, which to many composers signifies a series of songs rather than a serious drama in music.

drops

Pieces of scenery which are hung from the flies of the stage, and which therefore can be dropped into place. In practice, drops are cloth hangings rather than constructions. *See also* flats.

dry recitative

See recitativo secco.

duet

A musical piece for two, or for two soloists plus their accompaniment.

duo (It.) DOO-oh

Two. Either a piece for two, or the two who perform it.

durchcomponiert

Through-composed; music written in a continuous, noncyclic form; music that has no "repeats" or simple recapitulations. The composer, having stated his theme once, never states it quite the same way again, but always with new material. The term has come into use to describe a tendency among many modern dramatic composers.

dutchman

A little strip of cloth glued over the joint between two adjacent flats, and painted so that the joint becomes invisible.

dynamics

The world of louds and softs, the crescendos and diminuendos of music. But in opera there is another meaning—the modulations of the tensions and relaxations of emotion that give evidence of the progress of the drama.

eclogue

A song of shepherds, a pastoral.

encore (Fr.) ah(n)KOR

Again. An added song, or other musical piece, to reward an audience for stopping the action of an opera with its tremendous applause. This is entirely pleasing to the performer, sometimes also to the composer and librettist, but hardly ever to the dramatist whose work has been brought to a grinding halt for it.

ensemble (Fr.) ah(n)SOMb

Together. The delicate quality of singing together in tonality and in emotional contact during a performance. It is easier to achieve ensemble in concerted pieces, such as the finale of an opera, but a performance becomes memorable when it has this quality throughout.

entr'acte (Fr.) AH(N)tract

Between the acts. A little piece of music, a ballet or even a little play between the acts of the opera. It may or may not have anything to do with the plot of the opera itself.

entrance

Not only a door or a place to enter upon the stage, but also the point at which a singer or an instrument begins to sing or to play. There is an entrance each time the singer begins, whether for the first time in the piece, or only after a short rest.

epilogue

In Greek, the root means "upon the word," hence it is a final action which comments upon the opera or which informs the audience what happened after the opera ended. In *Boris Godunov*, for instance, the Simpleton's song becomes an epilogue, as he voices the grief for Russia, torn by its czars. An epilogue is not merely a postlude, which can consist only of music.

episode

An event in a drama, not necessarily set apart from other events in form, but a complete event.

extra

Broadway slang for a person who appears as one of a crowd on the stage, a supernumerary, not a member of the company.

fanfare

A musical ovation, an elaborate musical announcement. Fanfares quite generally consist of a flourish or two from the brasses and drums before the entrance of some character of importance, or before the statement of some important idea.

figured bass

A line of music written in the bass clef with numbers inscribed over or under the notes, giving enough information so that a keyboard performer may improvise harmonies upon the bass line; a thorough bass, or basso continuo. The numbers tell the player the intervals of the chord to be built upon the bass note; 6/4 tells him to construct a chord whose tones, if reduced to the least space of one octave, would appear as the sixth and fourth notes above the bass, inclusively.

filar la voce (It.) feelahr la VOchay

To spin out the tone by alternating crescendos and diminuendos.

finale (It.) feeNAHlay

An ending. Usually a grand scene involving some recapitulation of the musical and dramatic events which preceded it, and using as many of the principals of the cast as possible. See the finale in *Don Giovanni*.

Five, The

Nickname for five Russians who collectively revolutionized Russian music. They were: Cui, Rimsky-Korsakov, Borodin, Balakirev and Mussorgsky.

flat

A symbol which lowers a tone the distance of one semitone. A singer who "sings flat" is one who is consistently out of tune downwards, not up to pitch.

flats

Pieces of scenery which are flat. They

usually are made of light canvas, stretched over wooden frames and painted.

flies

The rafters above a stage, the open space above the stage where drops may be hung.

folk opera

An opera made of folk songs and folk material—or what appear to be folk songs and folk material. *Porgy and Bess* has sometimes been called folk opera. The zarzuelas of Spain are more nearly the type.

form

The abstracted structure of a piece of music. The general skeleton into which the composer, ostensibly, fits his ideas. In the classics and romantics, forms seem easier to identify since they have recurring events which help us to reconstruct their skeletons in our minds. But one should not mistake nonrepetitive music for form-less music.

Opera is a form of music, distinguished from symphony, cantata, etc. Within opera, aria is a form distinguishable from scena, recitative, and so forth. Music has been defined as organized sound, hence its form is its being.

forte

Strongly—therefore loudly. The opposite of piano. Marked *f* in music.

fortissimo

Most strongly, as loudly as possible. Marked *ff* on the music.

fugue

A form in music in which a theme, generally first stated in one voice, is successively taken up by another and another voice in imitation and in counter-point to each other. It is a larger form

than canon. Whereas canon is the strictest imitation, fugue is fairly free and may be developed considerably. In opera fugue hardly ever occurs except as a device to imitate increasing excitement, as in the overture to *Il Segreto di Susanna*, and that to *Die Zauberflöte*.

gavotte (Fr.) gahVOTT

A fairly slow dance in duple rhythm characterized by an even balance between its anacrusis and its metacrusis, or its upbeat and its downbeat.

gigue (Fr.) ZHEEG

Derived from the old German word for fiddle; a fast dance in triple time, a jig.

glissando (It.) gliSAHNdo

Sliding. Passing up or down the scale without stopping on the notes.

grace note

A little ornament of one note which introduces another. In vocal technique the grace note has a necessary function as a means of helping the vocal apparatus to commence a trill.

grand opera

Huge opera. That is to say, opera in the grand manner. In France the distinction used to be drawn between opéra comique, which could have spoken dialogue, and the opera, which could not and which had to have a ballet. But nowadays the term is highly emotional, signifying opera which moves by its grandeur, its size in cast, orchestra and sets.

grease paint

Make-up for the stage. Since stage lighting flattens details instead of flattering them, thick make-up is frequently the resort of the actor. It *is* greasy, after exposure to the heat of the lights and of the action.

habanera (Sp.) hahbahnAYRa

A slow Spanish dance in triple time, the most famous operatic example of which is the Habanera in *Carmen*.

harmonics

The overtones, the audible tones which can be distinguished within any tone as it is played or sung. Harmonics exist in an exact relationship to each other, the first harmonic being the basic tone produced, the second being its octave, the third a fifth above that octave, and so on. They are each a multiple of the basic pitch, so that if the basic pitch is 200 vibrations per second, the second harmonic is 400, the third 600, the fourth 800 and so forth. It has been determined that the differences between vowel sounds are caused by different balances of harmonics, and that the different timbres of instruments are similarly created. This is evident on an organ console, where one can mix various harmonic tones to produce imitations of various instruments. Upon the effect of the clash of the harmonics of one note with those of another note sounded simultaneously has been built the science of harmony in music.

harmony

The science of the relationship of tones sounded simultaneously. Harmony considers the tones in their static relationship, while counterpoint deals with the relationship of melodies to each other.

harpsichord

A keyboard instrument played like a piano, which produces its sound by plucking its strings. The keyboard appears as a piano keyboard, but in some instruments the color scheme of the black and white keys is reversed. The plucking is accomplished with little quills actuated by jacks attached to the keys. Frequently there is more than one keyboard, plus a set of stops which connect the keys together to produce different combinations of harmonics. The harpsichord was the standard instrument in the accompaniment of dry recitative. It is presently undergoing a resurgence as a solo instrument.

head voice

See voce di testa.

heldentenor (Ger.)

Heroic tenor. A tenor with a brilliant voice, suited to heroic parts and frequently unsuited for more subtle ones.

heroic

Brilliant, sometimes also dramatic or theatrical. Said of male voices. The opposite of bel canto.

histrionic

Theatrical, dramatic.

house

Where the audience sits. In a figurative sense, the audience itself, as in the expression "a good house," which is an audience that pleases the manager by filling the house, or the actor by being sympathetic to the opera.

hymn

A sacred song, usually in invocation to a deity, as the *Hymn to Venus*.

impresario

One who gathers up performers, finds a place for them to perform and entices the audience to come to see the performance. The impresario is the manager of the opera company rather than one of its directors. His job is the business of contracts and contacts.

imbroglio (It.) imBROlyo
A device which creates a confusion of rhythms, as for instance when a figure strongly suggestive of waltz measure is written out in a measure of four beats. This device occurs throughout opera as an evidence of excitement in any part, and is especially noticeable in the end of the *Leonora Overture No. 3 (Fidelio)*.

incidental music
Music which fills in the empty places in a play. In a good play the incidental music consists of the dances, the songs and perhaps the fanfares called for by the script. But in a bad play it also provides background noise where none should be. Some operas were originally conceived as incidental music to plays, for instance Busoni's *Turandot*.

instrumentation
The assignment of instruments to the orchestra; the use made of them in the score.

interlude
Literally, "between the games." A piece of music or a theatrical episode which comes between important episodes and which generally provides the audience some feeling of rest between activities.

intermezzo (It.) intayrMETzo
An interlude, but of larger proportions. The opera *La Serva Padrona* was conceived and first performed as an intermezzo for another opera. But on the other end of the scale, the little instrumental piece between the parts of *Cavalleria Rusticana* is also an intermezzo.

intonation
Putting into tone. Good intonation is accurately pitched, bad intonation is not. The term has less to do with the quality of tone than its precision.

jeu (Fr.) ZHE(R)
Play. The act of playing, or the play itself, as in *Le Jeu de Robin et Marion*.

jig
See gigue, for which it is the English equivalent.

key
That which one's fingers press to make instruments change their pitch.
Also the tonal system of a musical phrase, demarked by its central or basic note—its tonic, as in "the key of G." Distinguished from mode in that key is restricted to the system of European music, which has only the major and minor modes.

Klavier
See clavier.

largo (It.) LAHRgo
Slowly, slower than adagio.

larynx
The vocal organ, the upper part of the trachea. The seat of the vocal cords.

léger (f. légère) (Fr.) layZHAY (layZHAYR)
Light, lightly. A soprano légère is a soprano with a very light voice.

leitmotiv (Ger.) LIGHTmoteef
A significant phrase or fragment of music used to represent a person or an idea. Wagner made use of the term to describe his concept of the denotative possibilities in music. He gave every important character or object or idea in his operas a leitmotiv, and was thereby able, he claimed, to bring the item to mind via music whenever he wished to refer to it in the drama.

libretto
Literally, "little book." Particularly the book of the words of an opera. The

libretto is usually an adaptation of a play or story, made by a librettist particularly for operatic performance; hence it is not a large book, since music manages to take the place of many descriptive words. The libretto of *Otello*, for an instance, contains slightly more than one fourth the lines of Shakespeare's play.

light opera

Unserious opera, sometimes comic opera. The term describes the lightness with which the subject is treated, not the form of the piece.

line

The line of musical notes on the page which the singer sings or the instrumentalist plays. Therefore, within instrumental music, a line is frequently called a voice. Hence a fugue is spoken of as having three or four voices. But in opera the real vocal line must be distinguished from the instrumental line, and so forth.

lirico basso

See lyric bass.

lullaby

A cradle song; a song, therefore, sung for the purpose of lulling someone to sleep in a pleasant manner. A berceuse.

lute

A stringed instrument slightly similar to the guitar, but with more strings, some of which vibrate in sympathy with others, as resonators. The word is frequently used in a figurative sense; to "take up one's lute" means to sing one's song.

lyre

The harp of the ancient Greeks, usually depicted as a small inverted omega, or the letter U with a bar across the top and six or seven vertical strings which the singer may pluck as a sort of limited

support to his song. It gave its name as an adjective—lyrical.

lyric

From *lyre*, hence singable. Lyrics are words for song. Other words may be intended for scenas and other musical forms, but lyrics are essentially simple and gentle.

lyric bass

A bass voice more suited to smooth singing than to dramatic exclamation.

lyric tenor

As in lyric bass, a tenor voice more suited to smooth song than to heroic declamation.

madrigal

A choral song for the pleasure of singing together. The madrigal was most popular around the sixteenth century, and its subject was usually love. Whereas a motet has a sacred text, a madrigal is always secular. One of the immediate predecessors of opera was *L'Amfiparnaso*, which was a little play made of madrigals. But the polyphonic style did not lend itself to clarity in presentation of a story. It took the re-application of monody, therefore, to make opera possible.

maestro (It.) mahESSstro

The master, the orchestral conductor. One frequently uses the term as a complimentary title. Also, a singing teacher.

major mode

One of the two prevalent modes in modern European music, the other being the minor mode. The major has been roughly characterized as the mode of happiness or brilliance, which is hardly an adequate description of something so applicable to any emotional event. The major mode actually is an entire group of modes in use since centuries before their notation was developed; they all can be reduced to scales in which the first two steps up from the tonic tone are whole tones. This provides a general difference from the minors, which have a half-tone for their second step. The major scale was one of the great joys of Beethoven, but one has only to hear *Orfeo ed Euridice* to realize that the happiness factor is not always there; Orfeo's lament at losing his wife the second time, *Che farò senz' Euridice*, is in a major mode.

make-up

What every actor must paint upon his face and hands to (1) make them visible on the stage, and (2) make them appear to be someone else's face and hands. The term therefore covers more than the cosmetics of day wear; it includes false hair, false eyeglasses, false noses and so forth. But it does not include ornaments for the hair, for instance, which are part of the costume.

mandolin

A stringed instrument with a body shaped like an idealized pear and a neck somewhat like that of a guitar. The mandolin has eight strings, tuned in four pairs with the same notes as the violin. One plays it with a plectrum and sustains a note by continuous plucking.

mask

A false face, or something with which to cover the face or a part of it.

masque (Fr.) mask

A show in which the actors are masked to represent personifications of abstract qualities such as temperance, the devil and what not. Usually performed by amateurs for their own entertainment. *See* the opera *Gloriana*.

masqué (Fr.) masKAY

Masked. Said of a masked ball, which is one at which the participants hide their faces with masks, the better to effect liaisons without being caught at it. *See* the opera *Un Ballo in Maschera*.

measure

A gross unit by which recurrent patterns of rhythm are delineated. A measure is one complete unit in a rhythmic pattern. It contains three motions: the anacrusis which is the lifting up, the crusis which is the main accent or downbeat, and the metacrusis which is the recovery. In the waltz *The Blue Danube*, the first four notes of the theme make the anacrusis, the heavy beat the crusis, and the repeated offbeat figure after it the metacrusis. The measure, therefore, is *not* contained always between the bar lines. Rather, the bar line is a symbol which indicates that the next beat is the crusis. A measure may be very long or very short, it may not have one or the other of the two offbeats, but it always has only one crusis, and that indicated by the bar. Many composers, of course, write with ambiguities for artistic reasons, so that the rule is violated on paper. But the ambiguity they create proves the rule in practice.

melodrama

A drama in song, hence any drama in music. But the word has deteriorated somewhat in the last few decades so that it now represents a kind of play which satirizes the sentimentality of the late nineteenth century. Such plays have a hero, a heroine and a villain and revolve around some impending tragedy such as the foreclosure of the family mortgage. In opera, which should itself be called melodrama, the term serves only to denote passages of extreme sentimentality.

melody

The metaphysical motion of the attention from tone to tone. In practice *melody* is the technical word for any fairly coherent line of music, usually the line that is most prominent in any passage. It is frequently, therefore, the vocal line itself. But in a philosophical sense we should permit ourselves to describe the melody of composite lines. See melos.

melos

Greek for "song," hence used to designate the total emotional line of a musical piece, the musical-emotional line of opera.

messa di voce (It.) MESSa dee VOchay

A gradual swelling and diminishing of the volume of the tone of the voice on a single note, indicated in music by a small crescendo mark followed by an equivalent diminuendo under the same note.

meter

The unheard unit of time measurement in music. Upon the meter the composer builds rhythms. Meter is not to be confused with beat, which is the pulse of time in music. Meter in music is not the same as meter in poetry; in fact what the poet calls the beat is the composer's meter.

metronome

A mechanical device which beats time with an inverted pendulum and a clicking sound. It was invented by Beethoven's contemporary, Maelzel. The pace or tempo of music is usually indicated on the score by a figure which represents the number of beats per minute "m.m.", or on Maelzel's Metronome. Modern metronomes have dispensed with the mechanical pendulum and substituted an electronically actuated blinking light, which since it provides no visible movement does not give the performer quite the same information.

mezza voce (It.) METza VOchay

Half the power of the voice, softly. But not quite as secretly as sotto voce.

mezzo-soprano (It.) METzo soPRAHno

A soprano voice of slightly lower range than the full soprano, but not as low as contralto.

microtone

A very small division of the octave. The normal tuning of the tempered scale of the piano divides the octave into twelve equally spaced tones. This amounts to a practical compromise between the infinite division of the octave in pure intonation and the number of keys that a human hand can reach in playing. In order to notate the pure intonation more closely, many composers have devised systems of smaller intervals. Carrillo in Mexico uses numerals to indicate as many as ninety-six tones to the octave. Others have made more readable systems. Several operas have been written in microtone notation, notably by Alois Hába. Microtones do not constitute a system of harmonic structure as does dodecaphonism, but rather are a means of indicating more accurate variations of pitch on paper.

mime (Fr.) meem

One who pantomimes. An actor who uses no speech but only gesture and movement. Also the act of pantomiming.

minnesinger

A lover of singing and a singer himself. The minnesingers flourished in Germany from the twelfth to the fourteenth centuries. See the opera *Tannhäuser*. See also troubadour.

minstrel

An itinerant singer who accompanies himself on some instrument such as the guitar as he sings little songs. He is distinguished from the bard, who sings of epic events and so forth. In the United States the word became attached to a kind of actor who appeared in blackface. The minstrels toured the early Midwest and presented shows which consisted mostly of jokes and funny songs, sung by a dozen or so minstrels, playing banjos.

minor mode

One of the two modes of modern tonal music, the other being the major mode. Like the major, the minor is really a class of modes, all of which have in common the fact that their second scalewise step upward is a semitone. See major mode.

minuet

A formal dance in triple time, usually somewhat stately and slow.

mise-en-scène (Fr.) MEEZ ah(n) SEN

The putting on the stage, the manner in which a scene is placed upon the stage. By extension, the set and costumes themselves.

modality

The quality of being in a mode. The organization of sound which makes music forces, by definition, some formality onto the structure of a melody. This amounts to the fact that a melody uses a certain group of tones with which it completes its entire design, leaving out other tones which were not useful to it. The effect of whatever relationship the selected tones may produce is the modality of the melody. In practice one may reduce any melody to its notes and put those notes into a single scale (ignoring for the moment the fact that altered notes present some problems of classification). We speak of the tonal effect of that scale as its mode, and hence the mode of the melody. Modes lend themselves to description as

dark, light, sad, happy and so forth. But the adjectives have practically no real meaning.

mode

The tonal structure of the system of any melody. The total tonal framework in which a melody is constructed. Not the same as scale. The mode is the total relationship of its tones. The American blues, for instance, is a mode. See modality.

modulation

Change of key. The word would seem to indicate change of mode, but in practice the transition from A major to B-flat major, though the mode is the same, is a modulation. In early times, however, when scale was an unused concept, the harmonic differences between one major key and another had no meaning; hence the only effective change was one which changed the mode itself. Since the modes were identified with different levels on what we know as the chromatic scale the result *included* a change of key.

Modulation is the great dramatic device of harmony in opera. That sudden change of atmosphere when Florestan is about to be saved was accomplished by a modulation.

monody

Single-voiced song. Theoretically monody should be the unaccompanied song of a single melodic line. But in practice, and in its most important sense, it is melody for solo voice with accompaniment. Monody is the opposite of polyphony. It was necessary for the Camerata (*q.v.*) to put monody to use before opera could be invented. Monody allowed a single person to sing a dramatic song, or to take part verbally in a dramatic event as a personality, whereas with polyphony, which was at that time the general tool of vocal music, no such personalization could occur. Any aria is monody; so is any recitative.

motet

A sacred choral song. The motet was the contemporary of the madrigal, but whereas the madrigal was sung by four or five people for their own pleasure, the motet is frequently sung by a chorus. The motet survives in opera as a choral hymn, but the madrigal which preceded opera does not so remain.

motif

See leitmotiv.

musical

A musical show, particularly the big and brassy kind played on Broadway and as a spectacle on TV. Musicals are a commercial approach to opera. Sometimes there has been a noteworthy bridging of the gap. *Carmen* was adapted as the musical *Carmen Jones*, which was a great hit and a compliment to the original. Bertolt Brecht and Kurt Weill have made several attempts to do likewise on a more bitter level.

musical director

Usually the chief conductor of the company, sometimes the conductor who actually directs the production itself; that is to say, the one who instructs the singers in rehearsal and conducts the performance.

mute

Among the cast of characters, the mute is the silent role.

In the orchestra the mute is the device which a performer attaches to his instrument to alter (i.e., cause mutation in) its tone. It also reduces the volume of its tone, but its primary purpose is the change, not the quietness.

narrator

One who tells the story to the audience. Sometimes, as in *Il Combattimento di Tancredi e Clorinda*, the narrator is a singer. At others it may be a speaker or even a chorus. Narrators are frequently employed in concert performances of operas, to fill in the gaps.

neoclassic

A style in music, not thoroughly associated with any particular era but distinguished by its use of classic forms with modern orchestration. Paul Hindemith, who writes in the most original style, still may be considered to be neoclassic at times in his use of old forms. Likewise Stravinsky evidences a considerable interest in the period of Bellini in his *Rake's Progress*.

nocturne

A night piece, a relatively quiet piece of music meant to be played in the evening or to evoke the atmosphere of night.

notation

The art and science of writing musical ideas on paper. There are many kinds of notation, such as the melodic symbols of the Byzantine church, the horseshoe-and-nail notation of medieval Europe, and the harmonic system of lines, spaces and circular notes which we use today. Several opera composers, realizing the value of accuracy in writing the highly complex intervals of the ordinary vocal melody, have attempted to invent systems which will allow exact reproduction. This has resulted in systems of writing microtones. But in actual practice, when vocal music is written without relationship to tempered instruments (instruments whose tuning is fixed to the twelve equally spaced tones of the tempered octave), the singer sings with microtonic accuracy of pitch and the audience hears it with great clarity.

note

The symbol on the page which indicates which pitch to sound and how long to sound it. Loosely speaking, the tone itself.

notturno (It.) notTOORno

A nocturne

obbligato (It.) obbleeGAHto

Obliged. An indispensable accompaniment, especially a contrapuntal accompaniment to a solo voice as in the case of the flute which plays a duet with the soprano during a coloratura aria, while the orchestra accompanies both of them.

octave

The harmonic distance from one tone to its double; the distance, therefore, of eight scale-notes up or down, counted inclusively. The octave of any tone is its second harmonic. It has the same name as the tone itself. In many harmonic systems it does not occur as the eighth note of a scale; in the pentatonic system of the music of the Scottish Highlands it is the sixth tone. But it is always of twice the frequency of the parent tone, and always has the same name.

octet

A group of eight performers or a piece of music written for such a group. In opera, commonly, an octet consists of eight principals, whether or not their number is augmented by a vast accompaniment. The octet is of infrequent occurrence in modern music. Usually, when eight voices are involved, the grouping is that of two quartets rather than as a single octet. This happens most frequently as four principals join with the chorus, which is also divided into four voices.

open stage

A stage made visible from more than one side. Since the proscenium stage is essentially a three-walled box, it permits a limited variation in style of performance. Forms of open staging are: the arena, visible from all sides; the strip stage, visible from opposite sides; the platform before a backdrop; and (it actually exists) the stage which completely surrounds the audience. Of these the term *open stage* most commonly refers to the platform and backdrop type.

opera

A kind of musical drama, mostly sung, consisting of arias, ensembles, choral scenes and dialogue. Opera is not the only kind of musical drama; the Greeks, for instance, probably presented their classic dramas as musical productions. The term *opera* has become so closely associated with its Italian interpretation that some composers have objected to it as a designation for what they produce. Among these was Wagner, who called his work music-drama or festival-play in order to escape the implication of a string of arias roughly tied together into a story. Even the Italians have objected, Verdi calling many of his works *dramma per musica*, and Monteverdi one of his "a fable." But in any case a good opera is a dramatic event in singing.

opera buffa (It.) opera BOOfa

Comic opera. This term is most useful in order to distinguish comic opera from opéra comique.

opéra comique (Fr.) ohpayrah coMEEK

Not necessarily comic opera, but by tradition an opera with spoken dialogue. Its opposite is grand opera. *Carmen*, as written by Bizet, was opéra comique. Giraud added music to support the dialogue (deleting much of the important dialogue in the process) to make it "grand." The style gets its name from the Opéra-Comique in Paris, which allowed its presentation, while the Académie Royale (the Opéra) did not.

opera seria (It.) opera SAYreeah
Serious opera.

operetta
Light opera.

orchestration
The science of writing music for instruments, or of assigning instruments to music. The orchestration is the arrangement thus made. It is written in the score.

organ point
An instrumental drone bass frequently employed as a dramatic and musical device to represent solidity, gravity. It gets its name from the fact that the pipe organ has a pedal keyboard which is frequently employed to hold a low note for a long time while the hands play fantasias.

ouverture (Fr.) oovayrTÜR
Overture.

ovation
Thunderous applause, great acclaim.

overtones
Those tones which can be heard within any musical tone and which are its harmonics. It is these, the balance of overtones, which create the differences of timbre of instruments.

overture
An opening piece. A rather extensive piece of music for the orchestra to play before the curtain opens. Gluck, in his preface to *Alceste*, says that an overture should prepare the audience for what is about to happen.

pantomime
An act or show without words in which the dramatic event is conveyed to the audience by means of gestures and bodily motion. Not to be confused with ballet and dance, which are formal and fairly abstract movements. Pantomime imitates natural motion in a somewhat conventionalized manner. Pantomime performers are called mimes. Their performances are frequently accompanied by music. In opera there is sometimes a pantomimed moment as when Hamlet presents the dumb show before Claudius in which the mimes mimic the murder Claudius committed.

parlante (It.) pahrLAHNtay
In a manner resembling speech, but particularly in a declamatory manner. Said of musical lines, and not to be confused with *Sprechstimme*, which is the formal imitation of the tones and rhythms of speech.

part
A role, one's part to be played. In the orchestra the part is the instrumental line each player reads. On the stage, the part is the characterization and vocal line each singer (or actor) follows.

pasticcio (It.) pahSTEEcheeo
A little play or story woven together as a sort of pasted-up opera, with music by more than one composer. Frequently the words are written to the music, instead of the reverse.

pastiche (Fr.) pahSTEESH
Pasticcio.

pastoral (*or* pastourelle)
A musical piece or a scene representative of meadows where shepherds and shepherdesses are supposed to frolic. The operas about Orpheus commonly begin with a pastoral. Sometimes complete operas can be called pastoral.

percussion
The group of instruments in the orchestra which produce sound when struck. These include the drums, cymbals, marimbas, timpani, blocks and so forth. The piano is sometimes included, if the composer wishes to use it in that manner.

phonetic
Having to do with sound. The science of phonetics deals with the differences of sounds in various languages and dialects. Not to be confused with that other science of sound, harmonics.

piano
Softly, the opposite of forte. Its symbol on the page is *p*. Because it could be played both softly and loudly without the trouble of pulling out stops as in the harpsichord, allowing the player infinite subtlety of dynamic shading, the pianoforte got its name.

piano score
A score which has been reduced so that a pianist may reproduce its music on his instrument, substituting for the orchestra. Commonly synonymous with *vocal score*.

pianissimo
Most softly.

pit
The place, generally sunken below the line of sight of the audience, where the orchestra sits during a performance of opera.

pitch
Location in the spectrum of tone. Pitch is described in vibrations per second, high pitch being the pitch of higher frequency, and so forth. *See* concert pitch.

pizzicato (It.) pitzzeCAHto
Plucking, especially of the strings of the violin, viola, and other bowed instruments.

plot
The general skeleton of the story of an opera, reduced to simple terms. Not the same as a scenario.

polonaise (Fr.) pollohNEZ
A Polish dance in 3/4 time, containing all kinds of skips and turns, and with much syncopation. One of the most famous in opera runs throughout the Polish scenes of *Boris Godunov*.

polyphony (Greek) pollIFfonee
Music of many lines woven together, in other words, music of many voices, in the sense of melodic lines. The opposite of monody. Until the prevalence of polyphony was broken by the introduction of monody, it was impossible for opera to be invented. But polyphony as a technique abounds in opera now, as in the quintets, the septets and the great ensembles of such masters and Mozart and Gluck. Polyphony is the simultaneous singing of separate voices, not to be confused with chordal music, which is harmonically based.

postlude
An afterpiece. A postlude is short, usually without voices, not to be confused with an epilogue. The postlude is sometimes nothing more than the unheard music after the final curtain which accompanies the audience in its stumblings to the exits.

prelude
An opening piece, an introduction. A short piece of music intended to establish little more than the harmonic context of what is to follow, or briefly to set a mood. Not as big as an overture, and not to be confused with a prologue.

première

A first performance of an opera. A world premiere is the very first performance anywhere, but companies frequently use the word to indicate a first in their repertory, or in the city.

presence

See stage presence.

prima donna (It.) PREEma DONna

The first woman. Logically there can be but one prima donna in a company, and socially there should be but one in order to maintain peace. But the term is used to compliment any of the three or four highest-paid women on the roster. Because of the emotional history of such people, the term *prima donna* is also used to describe a singer who is belligerently defensive about her abilities and her fame.

principal

A leading singer, one of the important singers in the company, or one who sings an important role in the opera.

production

The total putting together and presentation of an opera. The physical equipment, the people in costume and the art of the presentation all make the production. A new production is one which has been newly designed and newly conceived, whether it has new singers and new sets or not. The person who makes the production is not called, as in the film world, a producer, but rather the artistic director.

projection

To a singer, projection is the process by which he makes his voice reach the farthest corner of the hall with clarity. As an actor he must add a psychological integration to his vocal technique so that the character is projected as clearly as the sound.

To the set designer, projection is the process by which he may flash an image on the backdrop to set the scene, thus allowing great speed of changes and less drain on the budget.

prologue

A foreword. A solo which announces the facts they need to know to the audience, as in *I Pagliacci*. But also the prologue may be an extensive scene or two, providing background information for the opera, as in the Coronation Scene and Pimen's monologue, which combine to become the prologue to *Boris Godunov*. The prologue has words, and is thereby distinguished from the prelude and the overture.

prompter

One who whispers or shouts a word or two to remind an actor of his next line. In opera the prompter has a little cabin in the footlights, visible to but hardly noticed by the audience. There he sits with the score before him and barks orders to the singers all the way through performance. Thus a company may maintain a large repertory, or a singer keep many parts at the tip of his tongue.

props

Objects which help the audience identify the scene on the stage, or which are picked up and used by the actors. Books on the table, pistols, candles and so forth are props. But beds are scenery and hats and coats are costume.

proscenium

The arch or frame through which the audience can see the stage. It occurs, of course, only in those theaters which have the boxlike stage. *See* open stage.

prosody

The fitting of words into rhythm.

Good prosody allows words to retain their natural accent and weight in rhythm. Bad prosody does not. Opera abounds in bad prosody, which causes audiences to miss the meanings of the words that are being sung, thereby saving the day for many an impossible libretto.

protagonist
The first to act, therefore the character whose action starts the main dramatic movement of the play. Technically he is opposed to the antagonist, but that term is not so frequently used in opera. Carmen is the protagonist of her opera, the people of Russia sometimes receive that title in *Boris Godunov*.

quartet
A group of four performers or a piece written for four. In opera a quartet usually consists of four principals who are accompanied by the orchestra.

quaver
British term for the eighth-note.

quintet
A group of five performers, or music written for five. As in quartet, the quintet of an opera may consist of five principals plus the orchestra or chorus.

reading
The act of playing through a piece of music or a scene without rehearsal. Also a term used to describe the manner in which a performance was conducted, as "a brilliant reading" or "a sensuous reading."

recapitulation
Restatement in music. A re-use of previous thematic material with or without some variation or development of its harmonic structure.

recitativo (It.) raycheetahTEEvo
A passage of dialogue which, though in the tones of music, is recited more or less like prose speech, and which may be accompanied by anything from a chord or two to a complex web of counterpoint, depending upon the composer's style or intention. Same as *recitative*. See below.

recitativo misurato (It.)
rayseetahTEEvo meezooRAHto
Measured recitative. A recitative supported by measured music instead of the isolated, rhythmless chords of dry recitative. But not yet as musical as a real melody, or an arioso.

recitativo secco (It.)
rayseetahTEEvo SECKo
Dry recitative. One step removed from natural prose speech. The singer intones the words with harmonically determined notes, but not yet with anything that could be called melody. The accompaniment consists of isolated chords and cadences used mostly as punctuation and a means to keep on pitch. This accompaniment, in classic opera, was commonly played on the harpsichord.

recitativo stromentato (It.)
rayseetahTEEvo stromenTAHto
Instrumented recitative. A more musical line than in dry recitative, accompanied by more than a keyboard, and therefore usually the same as recitativo misurato.

reduction
The arrangement of a score for fewer instruments. Operas frequently suffer reduction to fit touring companies or for small theaters where a large orchestra could not be accommodated.

refrain
A stanza which occurs periodically

throughout a ballad or a song. Also, loosely, a memorable tune and thus the ballad or song itself. The word was frequently used as a title for melodies.

régisseur (Fr.) rayzheeSE(R)
The stage director.

repertory
The selection of operas which a company maintains in a state of readiness for production. Also the roles a singer keeps ready to sing with little or no rehearsal. Repertory is much more usual among opera companies than in the speaking theater.

rest
A symbol on the musical page which replaces a note with silence. Also the moment of silence itself.

revival
A new production of an old work, or of a work which has been out of repertory for some time. A revival need not be a really new production, but merely a re-establishment of an old production without significant change.

rhapsody
Literally a sewing together of songs. Hence rhapsody is one of the more remote ancestors of opera. According to some anthropological archaeologists, the ancient Greek rhapsodist was essentially an actor acting a play in music. The fact that he did it all solo only proved his versatility. He narrated his story in song, and embellished it with odes. Unfortunately the Florentines who searched for a way to invent opera did not know about this; they had to go through the process of discovering it as monody all over again.

rhythm
The changes and variations, arranged in patterns in time, which the composer builds upon the pulse of music. Although he uses percussion instruments to emphasize it, rhythm is not effected by drumbeats but by harmonic changes or changes of direction in melody. It is not to be confused with beat or with pulse, both of which are its tools; nor with tempo, which is its pace.

ritornello (It.) reetorNELlo
A little refrain which occurs again and again between stanzas of a ballad or rondo and which serves as a kind of little coda for each section of the piece. There is a ritornello which appears in many places during *La Favola d'Orfeo*.

rococo (It.) roKOko
A variant of *baroque*, usually associated with lighter and more florid music.

role
The part one plays, one's total action on the stage, all the words and singing the performer uses to create a character and to complete that character's life within an opera. A role is not just the image of the character sketched in gesture, but is the entire play of that character against and with the others in an opera.

romance
A song of amorous feeling, or a piece of music intended to stimulate amorous or pleasant imagination.

romantic
Having the quality of wishfulness. But also descriptive of a period in musical history, roughly the nineteenth century, during which many composers became interested in the narrative and descriptive possibilities in music. In concert music they developed the tone poem and its relatives. In opera there came a double result which had the look of extreme realism (verismo) on the one hand and sentimentality on the other. Such works

as *Louise*, *La Bohème*, and *Manon* are prime examples.

rondeau (Fr.) ronDOH
One of the simpler forms of French song.

rondo (It.) RONdoh
A musical piece which has a continually recurring stanza or theme which alternates with other themes or stanzas. The rondo is more usual as a dance piece, hence its recurrent theme is not quite the same thing as a refrain in a ballad.

round
The simplest canon. A canon may be a rather extended piece, even though it is required to be strictly imitative. But a round is a simple song which is sung in canon; i.e., after the first voice has begun, each of the other voices enters in succession until all are singing. Then it comes to an end in reverse fashion or in a tutti, without development.

rubato (It.) rooBAHto
Stolen, robbed. A term to describe the hesitation which is possible within rhythms. In rubato, a little extra time devoted to one beat is made up by hurrying through others within the measure, so that the following measure may occur on time.

run
A melodic passage which travels up or down the scale, either diatonically or chromatically, hitting every note but not dwelling on one more than another. Not to be confused with glissando, which does not sound each note separately, nor with arpeggio, which sounds only the notes of a chord without intermediates. The run is generally an ornamental device.

scale
The systematized reduction of the tones of any mode, gathered up and put into order. Since we have major, minor and other modes we have also major, minor and other scales which are their schematic pictures. The chromatic scale is a scale in the tempered system of tuning, as represented by the twelve tones of the piano's octave. It is common to use the word *scale* when we really mean mode, but it leads to a misunderstanding. Scales are not a natural phenomenon in music, they are orderly arrangements of notes made to help us identify and discuss modes.

scena (It.) SHAYna
A great scene in opera, but more particularly a musical episode wherein the action and dialogue are composed into the musical form as integrally as is an aria. In fact a scena is sometimes an extended aria with dramatic dialogue woven in. Thus the scena is the ultimate accomplishment of dramatic composition in music, being as thoroughly a dramatic event as a musical one. It is identified, when one refers to it, usually by the name of the chief character taking part, as "Lucia's Scena."

scenario
An outline of the sequence of scenes of an opera. The scenario is a working basis for the librettist, the composer and the scene designer. Ideally it is organized in terms of physical action on the stage.

scene
A section of an act of an opera. Nowadays a scene commonly consists of all the music and action which occurs between changes of setting, or important changes of cast. In the old days one scene would end and another begin if and when any member of the cast had an entrance or an exit. But now, since it is recognized that dramatic motion has a rhythm of its own the scene has become defined and bounded by episodes and thus most commonly by changes in setting or time.

Scene is also the setting itself, that which meets the eyes of the audience. This may even include the tableau of actors themselves, and in a psychological sense the emotional background.

scherzo (It.) SKAYRTzo
Literally, "joke." A humorous episode in music, generally one in which the music itself creates the mood, not the words or events.

score
The pages upon which all the vocal and instrumental music of the opera is written out. That which the conductor reads as he conducts. The score does not normally contain all the nonmusical passages of an opera, such as long periods of dialogue, but it does include every detail necessary for the conductor to carry out his job, even notes about the motion of actors on the stage wherever that may be important to the timing. One generally distinguishes the score of an opera from its reductions by calling it the full score. *See also* vocal score *and* piano score.

secco (It.) SECKo
Dry. *See* recitativo secco.

segue (It.) SAYgway
Continue as before, or continue into the next section. Not only a directive, but also the name of the bridge-passage by which different parts of the scene may be strung together.

seguidilla (Sp.) saygeeDEElya
A Spanish dance in 3/4 time. See the excellent example in the opera *Carmen* (*Près des ramparts de Séville*).

semitone
A half step in the diatonic scale, a chromatic step. It is the placement of the semitones in the various scales which

identifies them. The major scale has half steps from its third to its fourth tones and from its seventh to its eighth. The natural minor has them both one step lower in the scale. The symbol for raising a tone one half step is the sharp, to lower it the same amount the flat.

septet
A group of seven performers or the music written for such a group. In opera it does not change their classification if the seven performers are accompanied by the orchestra or the chorus.

serenade
An evening song, therefore commonly associated with a lover's invocation to his beloved.

seria
See opera seria.

set
The entire combination of physical equipment which makes up the visible scene within which the actors play. On a proscenium stage the set consists usually of drops, flats and furniture.

set piece
A musical episode whose form and rhythmic organization within the context of the opera set it apart from the general flow of action, thus bringing that action to a halt. The sextet from *Lucia di Lammermoor* is such a set piece, as is the Toreador's song in *Carmen*.
Also a unit of the set, such as a tree or a papier-maché boulder.

sextet
A group of six performers or the music written for such a group. As in all other ensembles of opera, the fact that they are accompanied by numerous instruments does not affect their classification as a sextet.

signature

The cluster of sharps or flats (or lack of them) which with the clef sign indicate the key of a line of music. Also, loosely, that key itself, expressed in terms of sharps and flats.

Sometimes a signature is a significant passage of music used to remind the audience of the identity of some character on the stage. *See* leitmotiv.

simultaneous set

A stage setting which contains all the elements for all the scenes of the opera, so arranged that changes of scene may be accomplished by no more than the movement of the actors into a new location. In medieval morality plays, the setting was commonly of this type, with the pearly gates of heaven at the one end and the mouth of hell at the other, leaving the characters free to march whichever way their parts led them.

singspiel (Ger.) ZINGshpeel

A play to be sung, a play in which dialogue is spoken between musical numbers. Akin to the ballad opera and the Broadway musical.

solfeggio (It.) solFEDGgio

Training of the ear and the voice so that the one may understand the pitch relationships of the notes it hears, and the other produce notes accurately as they are read from the page. A basic training for any composer or performer.

solo (It.) SOlo

Alone. A singer who sings a part more prominent than other parts which accompany it, or who sings alone. Also, music for one performer with or without accompaniment.

song

A piece to be sung. The song is the most ancient form of free expression in vocal music, and remains the simplest form, complete in itself. The word is inapplicable to extended arias with musical development. The song is essentially emotional and reflective, not dramatic or narrative.

soprano

The highest of the voices, the female voice of highest range. Hence also the highest in any group of melodic lines as the soprano part in a fugue, or the soprano saxophone among other saxophones.

sotto voce (It.) SOTto VOchay

Under the breath, without force in the voice (although still with dramatic intensity), quietly. Not the same, however, as piano or pianissimo. *Sotto voce* implies a quality of secrecy.

soubrette (Fr.) sooBRETT

A theatrical type; the coquettish lady's maid, or the girl of slightly scandalous reputation.

spinto (It.)

A term descriptive of the type of operatic voice that can be stretched to include roles of entirely different character. Most particularly used to describe a soprano voice capable of the whole range of roles from the dramatic, through the lyric to the coloratura. A singer possessing this triple ability would be an asset to any company, but few have it.

Sprechstimme (Ger.) SHPREKstimma

The speaking voice, hence music which is written to be sung in the manner of the speaking voice. *Sprechstimme* designates particularly a technique of imitating the tones and rhythms of speech with music, which permits the composer to direct the dialogue with absolute accuracy and to accompany it with music. It is not to be confused with recitative, which is a sort of chantlike melody with speech rhythm. Sprechstimme, as written on the page, imitates the rise and fall of natural speech as nearly as the composer can.

staccato (It.) staCAHto

Detached, hence notes sung with separation between them; the opposite of legato.

staff

The five-line system upon which one writes musical notes. Actually there have been staves of more or less than five lines.

stage director

The technical supervisor of a production, responsible for the operation of the stage and the set upon it, and the attendance of the actors at rehearsal.

stage presence

An intangible ability by which a performer projects the fact of his existence into the awareness of the audience. It takes a great actor to do this without distracting the audience from the opera itself.

standard opera

Opera which remains constantly in repertory and which rightly or wrongly becomes the measure of other operas.

star system

A system of casting by which the company selects operas to fit the abilities and desires of the famous singers it has available, counting on their names as stars to draw the audience. This can lead to the revival of forgotten works or the premières of new ones, but it also tends to subordinate the drama to the superficiality of the performance. The star system is really the negative of the repertory system, but many companies manage to make use of the advantages of both by having a very large, and very expensive roster of stars.

strings

The instruments of the orchestra which are bowed. Although the piano has strings it is not considered one of them because it is played by keys. Nor is the guitar included, but left in a class of its own.

studio performance

A performance presented in a small place (hardly ever actually in a studio), usually before a select audience of friends and possible patrons of the company. Sometimes equivalent to a reading, but usually put on with more formality and rehearsal in order to make a better impression.

styling

The overall color and effect of a production, its manner as indicated by the kind of detail in its sets, its costumes and so forth, and its musical reading.

succès d'estime (Fr.) sucsay desTEEM

A tremendous success, one which makes the reputation of its composer or performers.

succès de scandale (Fr.) sucsay duh scahnDAHL

A scandalous success, one attributable as much to scandal about its production as to its worth.

sung recitative

Dialogue in music. *See* recitativo secco, recitativo misurato *and* recitativo stromentato.

super

Slang for an extra; a person not a member of the company but hired at the moment to be a member of a crowd upon the stage, or to hold a spear or whatever. A supernumerary.

supporting cast

Those in the cast who are not the principals. The captains of the guard, the notaries, the fathers-in-law and the duennas.

syncopation

The existence of syncopes.

syncope

A rhythmic break, a hesitation where there should have been a beat, or a beat where none should have existed. One can feel the effect of syncope by walking at a normal pace, but thinking of the "beat" as the upward movement of each step.

tableau

A static scene, a scene staged as if it were a picture. Also that quality of any scene which one can retain in the memory as a picture.

tacet

Be silent. A direction to the performer which indicates that he has nothing further to sing or play until the piece has ended, or until the end of the scene.

tempo

Literally, "time." The pace of music, the speed of the meter or the pulse.

tenor

The male voice of highest normal range, higher than the baritone, not as high as the contralto. Also, the person gifted with such a voice.

terzetto (It.) tayrtZETTo

A little piece for three. Terzetto implies a short piece, whereas *trio* does not. Unlike *trio*, *terzetto* may not be used to designate the performers themselves.

tessitura

The average working range of a musical line. The range which is most used throughout the piece, but not including the isolated and infrequent high and low extremes. Tessitura is a measurement of the effective labor the vocal chords must go through to produce the sound of a particular line. Thus an aria may have a high tessitura because most of its notes are in the high range, even though some may be low.

tetralogy

A group of four operas whose stories form a sequence, as does *The Ring of the Nibelungs* — although Wagner himself called the first of them, *Das Rheingold*, a prologue to the others.

theatrical

Quality of fitness for the theater. The word is frequently derisive, being used to describe flamboyant technique.

theme

A significant melody or a significant phrase upon which the composer builds his musical ideas. Also, in opera, the basic idea of the plot.

time

In music, its pace. *See* tempo. Also, the kind of measure, as in 3/4 time.

timbre (Fr.) TAMber

The quality of tone of any instrument or voice. The timbre of the oboe is remarkably different from that of the clarinet. Timbre is the result of the balance of the overtones of any note sounded by the instrument or voice. It has nothing to do with pitch. The vowels sounded by the human voice are strictly differences of timbre, whatever tone they may have.

timpani

Kettledrums, drums of definite pitch which can be altered by mechanical or pneumatic means.

title role

That role which represents the character named in the title, as does the role of Carmen, or Otello, or in *Il Barbiere di Siviglia*, Figaro.

tone

A musical sound of a single, steady pitch. Also the quality of sound, as in pure tone, or high tone, or reedy tone. Also short for whole tone, or scale tone. A tone is symbolized by a note on the staff, which gives rise to the use of the word *note* to designate tone.

tonality

Quality of having tone. In music, tonality is the specific quality of harmonic systems which have a fairly stable structure and which can be reduced to scales. Its opposite is atonality. Tonal relationships may be dissonant or consonant. The word is restricted to the harmonic organization of tones, while *modality* refers to their melodic relationship.

tour

A route of travel, a periplus, through which a company or a performer visits many cities away from its (or his) home base of operation, putting on performances.

transpose

To change the level of pitches of a piece of music. This occurs when an aria lies in a difficult range for a particular singer, or when the performer wishes to establish a different relationship with the context.

trapdoor

A portion of the stage floor which can be opened to permit exits and entrances, or which will permit parts of the set to be raised or lowered through it.

traps

Portions of the stage floor which can be opened. *See* trapdoor. Also, the collection of percussion instruments normally played by one person in a jazz band: the snare drum, cymbals, pedal bass drum, temple blocks, and so forth.

treble

A child's voice, a voice which sings in the range indicated by the treble clef.

Also the name of the clef which indicates the pitch for G above middle C, otherwise known as the G clef.

tremolo

Trembling sound, sound which wavers in volume upon its pitch. The tremolo does not involve a wavering in pitch. For that, *see* vibrato.

trill

A rapid alternation of two notes adjacent to each other. The trill often ends with a little turn, or flourish.

trilogy

A group of three full-length operas with a common thread of story or plot. There are several trilogies based upon the three stories of the life of Orestes.

trio

A group of three performers, or the music written for them. In opera the three may be and usually are accompanied by the orchestra.

troubadour (Fr.)

A wandering singer, a bard. He flourished in the twelfth century in southern France, composing his own words, his own music, and his own peculiar stanza forms. Some of them were the great poets of their age, such as was Bertrand de Born. The opera *Il Trovatore* deals with such a singer. Tannhäuser, the minnesinger, represents the German variation of the type.

troupe

The company or part of one considered as a touring unit. Usually it consists of a nucleus of singers and players which is augmented by local talent wherever it may perform. Many troupes have been organized by singers as vehicles for themselves.

tune

A simple melody. Also, accuracy of pitch. To be in tune signifies the quality of being in unison or harmony with others.

tutti

Everybody. A passage of music in which everybody joins in after a solo or a small ensemble.

twelve-tone system

A melodic and harmonic system of the composition of music based upon the equal temperament of the accurately tuned pianoforte. *See* dodecaphonism.

unison

As one, therefore singing or playing the same notes. The opposite of *divisi*. A canon at the unison is one in which all the entrances occur at the same pitch, although at different times.

unit set

A set which contains all the parts required for all the scenes of the opera. It may be necessary to shift the position of a part here or there to effect changes of scene, hence not necessarily the same as a simultaneous set.

upbeat

The beat which the conductor indicates by a rising motion of his baton, usually an unaccented beat. When one speaks of *the* upbeat, one generally means the anacrusis.

valse (Fr.) vAHLS

Waltz.

vamp

An improvised accompaniment, usually a simple figure more or less filled out for effect, but which can be played over and over until the singer is ready to begin singing.

vaudeville (Fr.) VOHdveel

A short theatrical caprice, usually of comic character, with dialogue and songs.

vehicle

An opera intended as a show piece for a certain singer or perhaps for a new production technique. Hence *Semiramide*, out of the repertory for years, was revived as a vehicle for Tebaldi.

verismo (It.) vayrIZmo

Realism. A style of opera highly developed in the nineteenth century in Italy, and made as imitative of the superficial aspects of real life as possible. Essentially the negative of drama, which is ritualistic. A good example of verismo is the opera *Tosca*; another is *La Fanciulla del West*.

vibrato

Vibrated. Since all musical sound is the result of vibrations, the word really means "wavering in pitch and volume," which produces the feeling of warmth in the human voice. As a matter of fact, it is a natural product of the act of remaining on pitch, the voice constantly moving around the desired pitch, allowing the mind to make constant corrections to keep it in the right place. It is otherwise psychologically impossible for the voice to maintain a pitch the way an instrument can.

vocal score

A score reduced to the vocal parts, and therefore of a size convenient for the singer to hold in his hand during rehearsal. Commonly, the vocal score has a reduction of the orchestral music for the piano written beneath the vocal parts, and is thus essentially a piano score.

vocalise (Fr.) vocahLEEZ
An exercise for voice, especially a repeating melodic exercise which gradually transposes itself to higher and higher ranges.

voce (It.) VOchay
The human voice.

voce di petto (It.) VOchay dee PETto
The chest tones of the voice.

voce di testa (It.) VOchay dee TESTa
The head tones of the voice.

voice
The sound produced by the larynx. Also any line of melody for any instrument, or a line of coherent melody within a context of other such lines, as one voice of a fugue.

volume
Relative loudness of sound. Not to be confused with intensity or projection, which are essentially complexities of voice, diction, rhythm and intonation.

Vorspiel (Ger.) FORshpeel
A prelude, a musical introduction leading directly into a scene.

walk-on
Broadway slang for a bit part without spoken lines, or an extra who appears apart from the crowd.

waltz
A revolving dance in alternating patterns of three steps each. It is therefore really a dance of two triple beats, but is generally written as two equivalent measures in 3/4 time. One of the most famous operatic waltzes runs through *Der Rosenkavalier*.

winds
Those instruments of the orchestra which are blown, both woodwinds and brasses. They do not include the pipe organ.

wings
The flats or drops which conceal the sides of the stage but between which entrances may be effected. Also, therefore, the concealed space to each side of the stage where performers wait before their entrances.

woodwinds
Those instruments which are, or used to be, made of wood and which are blown. Nowadays many of them are made of metal. They include flute, piccolo, clarinet, oboe, bassoon, saxophone and their families. Most of them might better be characterized as reed instruments, since it is the reed in the mouthpiece that vibrates to produce the tone.

workshop
A practical school of opera, or particularly that class in a school which actually mounts performances in order to learn the technique of operatic theater by experience. Most opera in the United States is produced by collegiate opera workshops.

zarzuela (Sp.) zahrzooWAYla
A kind of popular opera in Spain and Spanish-speaking countries. A cousin of the singspiel, the vaudeville and the ballad opera.

THEMES OF THE MOST FAMOUS MUSICAL NUMBERS

While most of the translations which appear after these musical examples are traditional, some have been altered to match the original meanings and music more accurately.

Aida ACT I *Radames*

Celeste Aida, forma divina, mistico serto di luce e fior.

Heavenly Aida, divine form, beauteous mystery of flowers and light.

ACT II *Chorus*

trec- ci,ll lo - to,al lau - ro sul

crin___ dei___ vin - ci - to,- ri.

Gloria all' Egitto ed Iside che il sacro suol protegge! Al re che il delta
regge inni festosi al ziam!
Glory to Egypt and to Isis who wards away disaster! To Egypt's royal master we raise our
festal song!

S'intrecci il loto al lauro sul crin dei vincitori.
Bind the lotus with the laurel to crown the victors.

per dell' ac- cu- sa or- ri- bi- le sco-

par - ti an- cor t'e da- to.

Già i sacerdoti a dunansi Arbitri del tuo fato per dell' accusa orribile
scoparti ancor t'e dato.
Already the priests are meeting to decide your fate after this horribly sweeping
accusation which has been made against you.

ACT IV *Radames*

O ter- ra ad- di- o, ad- di- o, val- le di

pian- ti, sog- no di gau-dio che in do- lor —— sva-

ni. A noi si schiu- de si schiu- de il

ciel. ——

O terra addio, valle di pianti, sogno di gaudio che' in dolor svani. A
noi si schiude il ciel.
Farewell O earth, farewell thou vale of sorrow. Brief dream of joy condemned to end
in woe. To us now opens the sky.

Alceste ACT I *Alceste*

Di- vin- i- tés du Styx, Di- vin- i- tés du Styx, mi- ni- stres de la mort.

Divinités du Styx, ministres de la mort.

O gods of the Styx, ministers of death.

ACT II *Admetus*

O mes en- fants! O mes a- mis!

vous pé- né- trez mon coeur de la plus

douce —— iv- res- se.

O mes enfants! O mes amis! vous pénétrez mon coeur de la plus

douce ivresse.

O my children, O my friends! You wring my heart with the sweetest feelings.

Arianna. LAMENTO D'ARIANNA. *Arianna*

Lasciatemi morire! lasciatemi morire e chi
volete che mi conforte in così dura sorte in così gran martire.
O, let me die, and let me have comfort in this hard fate, this great sacrifice.

Il Barbiere di Siviglia. ACT I. *Almaviva*

puoi   dor - mir   co -   sì ?

Ecco ridente in cielo spunta la bella aurora, e tu non sorgi ancora e
puoi dormir così?
Day comes with all her roses, blushing they redden the distance. Flow'rs wake to new
existence and dost thou slumber yet?

ACT I. *Figaro*

Lar- goal fac- to- tum del-la cit- tà   lar-

go!   la la   la la la la   la la

la !   la !   Pre-   sto a bot-

te- ga che l'al-ba è   già   pre-   sto!

la la   la la   la la b   b   la!   la!

Largo al factotum della città largo! la la la la
la la la! la! Presto a bottega che l'alba è già presto! la la la la la la! la!
Way for the city's factotum here! Make way! Quick to my business, daylight is near,
make way!

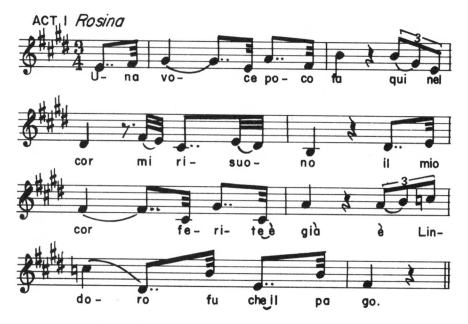

Una voce poco fa qui nel cor mi risuonò il mio cor ferite è già e
Lindoro fu che il pagò.

Just a little while ago a voice within my heart, which already feels a wound, spoke of
Lindoro in words of hope.

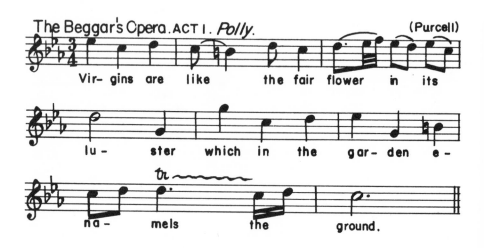

Virgins are like the fair flower in its
luster which in the garden enamels the ground.

ACT I *MacHeath, Polly*

OVER THE HILLS AND FAR AWAY

Were I laid on Green-land's coast, and

in my arms em- braced my lass,

warm a- midst e- ter- nal frosts, too

soon the half- year's night would pass.

Were I laid on Greenland's
coast and in my arms embraced my lass, warm amidst eternal frosts, too soon the half
year's night would pass.

ACT II *Matt*   (Handel)

Let us take the road. Hark! I hear the sound of

coaches = the hour of at- tack ap- proa- ches = t'your

arms   brave   boys   and   load!

Let us take the road. Hark! I hear the sound of coaches—the
hour of attack approaches—t'your arms brave boys and load!

ACT II. *MacHeath*

Man   may   es-   cape   from   rope   and

gun,   nay,   some   have   out-   liv'd   the

doc-   tor's   pill.   Who   takes   a

wo -   man   must   be   un-   done,

Man may escape from rope and gun, nay, some have outliv'd the
doctor's pill. Who takes a woman must be undone,

La Boheme ACT I *Rodolfo*

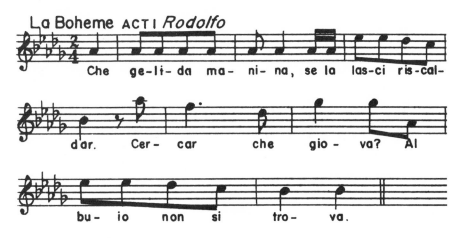

Che gelida manina, se la lasci riscaldar. Cercar che
giova? Al buio non si trova.
Your tiny hand is frozen, let me warm it up in mine. Why search for help there? In
darkness you won't find it.

ACT I *Mimi*

Mi chiamano Mimi ma'il mio nome è Lucia.
They call me Mimi, but my real name is Lucia.

ACT II MUSETTA'S WALTZ. *Musetta*

Quando me'n vo', quando me'n vo' soletta per la

via la gente sosta e mira.

When I'm alone, whenever I'm alone on the street the gentlemen admire me.

Why do you abandon us, O father?

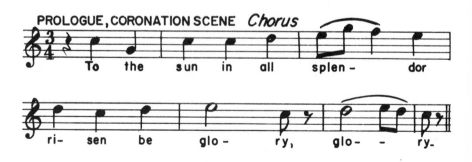

To the sun in all splendor risen be glory.

ACT I *Boris*

ACT I *Innkeeper*

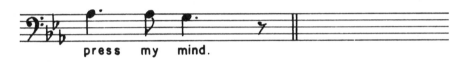

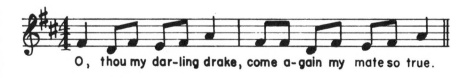

My soul is sad. Against my will strange tremors and evil presentiments
oppress my mind.

Once I caught a drake with feathers green and blue. O, thou my
darling drake, come again, my mate so true.

ACT I *Varlaam*   THE SIEGE OF KAZAN

Long a - go at Ka - zan where I was figh - ting, Tsar I - van sat a - feas-ting with his lea - ders. There the Tar- tar horde he har - ried, spared not man, nor maid, nor mar - ried, then Rus-sia had_____ fine times!

Long ago at Kazan where I was fighting, Tsar
Ivan sat afeasting with his leaders. There the Tartar horde he harried, spared not man
nor maid nor married, then Russia had fine times!

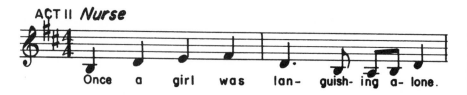

ACT II *Nurse*

Once a girl was lan- guish- ing a- lone.

Once a girl was languishing alone. To her came a boy, so handsome
grown.

ACT II SONG OF THE GNAT *Nurse*

Once a gnat was cutting wood, a flea was kneading
dough. Soon a loaf crisp and good on the gnat she did bestow.

ACT II CLAPPING GAME SONG *Feodor*

pig once laid a large white egg.

I'll tell you a tale and you'll laugh! How once

a hen did hatch a fine calf, how a pig once laid a large white egg.

ACT II *Boris*

I have attained to pow-er. Six years have

passed since first I ruled o'er Rus-sia. But

still no peace re-turns to my re-morse-ful soul.

The hea-vy hand of one a-bove doth press u-

pon my guil-ty soul re-quir-ing jus-tice!

I have attained to power. Six years have passed since first I ruled o'er

Russia. But still no peace returns to my remorseful soul. The heavy hand of one above

doth press upon my guilty soul requiring justice!

ACT III *The Girls from Sandomir*

By Wisla's blue waters beneath an old willow one

flower is blooming with petals all like snowflakes.

FINALE *Simpleton*

Flow, Ah! flow my bitter tears. Weep, lament all ye true believers.

Soon the foe will come, all the world grow dark, dark as blackest night, not a star

shines through.

Carmen ACT I *Boys*

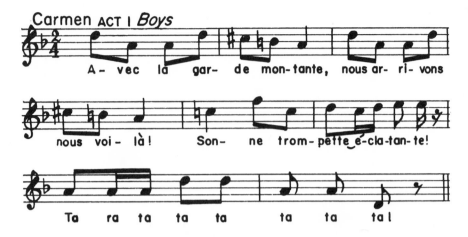

A- vec la gar- de mon-tante, nous ar- ri- vons nous voi- là! Son- ne trom- pette e-cla-tan-te! Ta ra ta ta ta ta ta ta l

Avec la garde montante nous arrivons nous voilà! Sonne
trompette éclatante! Ta ra ta ta ta ra ta ta!
Marching with the changing guard, marching with them here we are. Hear how the
bugles shall sound! Ta ra ta ta.

ACT I HABANERA *Carmen*

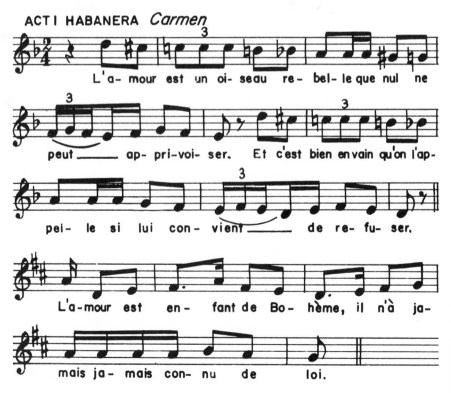

L'a- mour est un oi- seau re- bel- le que nul ne peut____ ap- pri-voi- ser. Et c'est bien en vain qu'on l'ap- pei- le si lui con - vient____ de re- fu- ser. L'a-mour est en - fant de Bo- hème, il n'a ja- mais ja- mais con - nu de loi.

L'Amour est un oiseau rebelle que nul ne peut apprivoiser. Et
c'est bien en vain qu'on l'appelle si lui convient de refuser.
Love's a wild and rebellious bird that flies so free it cannot be tamed. Call in vain, it
will be not heard, for love's reluctant to come by name.

L'Amour est enfant de Bohème, il n'à jamais jamais connu la loi.
For love's a child of gypsy life and love will never never go by law.

Près des ramparts de Séville chez
mon ami Lillas Pastia j'irai danser la Séguidilla et boire du Manzanilla, j'irai chez mon
ami Lillas Pastia.
Under the walls of Sevilla there lives my friend Lillas Pastia. I'll be there to dance
Seguidillas and I'll drink Manzanilla. I'll be waiting there at Lillas Pastia's.

Votre toast je peux vous le rendre, señors, señors,

car avec les soldats, Oui, les toréros peuvent s'entendre pour plaisirs, pour plaisirs, ils
ont les combats!

To your toast I'll give another, señors, señors, to all the soldiers. And to toreros, brave
men among us. For our pleasure, for our fun they fight. How they fight!

Toréador en garde! Toréador, Toréador, Et songe bien, oui, songe en combatant qu'un oeil noir te regarde.

Toreador, be ready, Toreador, and remember as you prepare, dark eyes are upon you.

ACT II *Carmen, Mercédès, Frasquita*

Les tringles des sistres tintaient avec un éclat
métallique. Et sur cette étrange musique les zingarellas se levaient.
The tingling of the little bells surprises with metallic ringing. Upon the sound of such strange singing the gypsy girls dance for the day.

ACT II. *Don José*

Halte là, qui va là? Dragon d'Alcala! Où t'en vas-tu par là, Dragon d'Alcala?

Who goes there? Who goes there? Man of Alcala. Where are you going there, man of Alcala?

ACT III *Micaela*

Je dis — que rien ne m'é-pou-van - te, je dis, Hé-las! que je ré- ponds de moi Mais j'ai beau fai - re la vail- lant- te, au fond du coeur— je meurs d'ef- froi! —

Je dis que rien ne m'épouvante, je dis, Hélas! que je réponds de moi.

Mais j'ai beau faire la vaillante au fond du coeur je meurs d'effroi!

I say I will not be dismayed. I say, alas! but I'm trembling with fear! But my dear, as I answer your heart, at the bottom of mine I'm dying of fright.

Les Contes d'Hoffmann ACT I *Olympia*

Les oi- seaux dans la char -mil - - - - - - - le.

Les oiseaux dans la charmille.

The birds in the grove.

Belle nuit, O nuit d'amour, souris à nos ivresses.

Beauteous night, O night of love, please smile at our excesses.

Ah, Ah! Ah, Belinda, I am prest with torment.

wrongs_____ cre - ate no trou- ble, no

trou - ble in thy breast.

When I am laid in earth, may my wrongs create no trouble, no trouble
in thy breast.

Don Giovanni ACT I *Donna Anna*

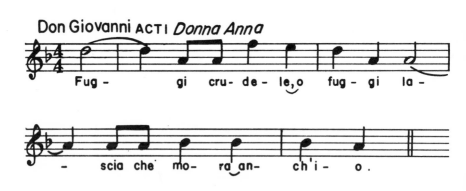

Fug - gi cru- de - le,o fug- gi la -

- scia che mo- ra an- ch'i - o .

Fuggi, crudele, o fuggi, lascia che mora anch'io.
Leave me, my friend, O leave me, please let me bear my sorrow.

ACT I *Donna Elvira*

Ah chi mi di - ce ma - i quel

bar- ba -ro do- v'e. Che per mio scor- no a-

ma - i,   che   mi   man- cò   di   fè.

Ah chi mi dice mai quel barbaro dov'è. Che per mio scorno

amai, che mi mancò di fè.

Where shall I find the traitor who stole my heart away? I gave him all in earnest, he

took it all in play.

ACT I *Leporello*

Ma - da - mi - na,   il ca - to - lo- goe

ques- to   del- le   bel- le che a-moil pa-dron mi- o.

In I-   tal- ia sei cen- toe quar- an- ta,

In Al- ma- gna due cen- toe trent' u- na.

Cen- to in   Fran- cia, Tur- chia no-vant'

u - na, ma,   mai n Is- pa- gna,   main Is -

pa- gna   son   già   mil- lee tre!

617

Madamina, il catalogo è questo delle belle che ama il padron mio.

Dear my lady, let me draw your attention to this long list of names and addresses.

In Italia sei cento e quaranta, in Almagna due cento e trent' una. Cento in Francia, in Turchia novant' una, ma in Ispagna, ma in Ispagna son già mille e tre!

Of Italians six hundred and forty, and in Germany two hundred thirty. Hundred in France and in Turkey 'twas ninety, Ah! but in Spain, ah! but in Spain were a thousand and three!

ACT I *Don Giovanni*

Là ci da-rem la ma-no, là mi di-rai di
sì, ve-di non è lon-ta-no, partiam ben mio da qui.

Là ci darem la mano, là mi dirai di sì; vedi non è lontano
partiam ben mio da qui.

Let me adore your hand, love, then make your answer yes. See, it is not so far, love, to let your heart confess.

ACT I *Donna Elvira*

Ah, fug - gi il tra - di - tor! Non
lo la-sciar più dir. Il lab-bro è men-ti-

618

tor fal- la ————————— ce ci- gli - o.

Ah, fuggi, il traditor! Non lo lasciar più dir. Il labbro è mentidor fallace ciglio.

Be warned of him, my child, and hear his words no more. Do not become beguiled for they'll deceive you.

ACT I QUARTET *D.Elvira,D.Anna,D.Ottavio, D.Giovanni*

Non ———— ti fi- dar, O mi- se-ra, di

quel ri- bal- do cor! Me già tra-di quel

bar- ba- ro te vuol tra - dir an - cor.

Non ti fidar,

O misera, di quel ribaldo cor! Me già tradi quel barbaro te vuol tradir ancor.

Do not confide, unhappy one, in such a trustless heart! Already has he betrayed me. He'll be betraying you!

ACT I *Donna Anna*

Or sai che l'on - o- re ra- pi- re a me

vol - se chi fu il tra - di- to - re che il

pa- dre, che il pa - dre ____ mi tol - se.

Or sai che l'onore rapire a me volse chi fu il traditore che il padre
mi tolse.

You know now for certain the name of the traitor who bartered my honor, who
murdered my father.

ACT I *Don Giovanni*

Fin ch'an del vi - no cal- da la tes- ta

u - na gran fes - ta va pre- pa - rar.

Fin ch' an del vino calda la testa una gran festa va preparar.

Song, wine and women, who'd be without them? I'll have my pleasure both morning
and night.

ACT I *Zerlina*

Bat- ti, bat- ti, O bel Ma - set- to, la tua

po - ve - ra Zer- li - na. Sta- rò qui come a-gnel-

li - na le tue bat- te as- pet- tar.

Batti, batti, O bel Masetto, la tua povera Zerlina. Starò quì come agnellina le tue batte aspettar.

Chide me, chide me, dear Masetto. Chide your little poor Zerlina. I can stand it like a little lamb, your anger I will bear.

ACT II *Don Giovanni*

Deh vieni alla finestra, O mio tesoro. Deh vieni a consolar il pianto mio.

Come near, lean out your window, my prize and my treasure. Come here, console my sorrow, come console my grief.

ACT II *Zerlina*

Vedrai carino se sei buonino che bel rimedio ti voglio dar.

If you will promise me not to betray me I have a remedy to bring you health.

ACT II *Don Ottavio*

Il mio tesoro intanto, andate, andate a consolar.

Speak for me to the lady and tell her, and tell her all I know.

Faust ACT III *Valentin*

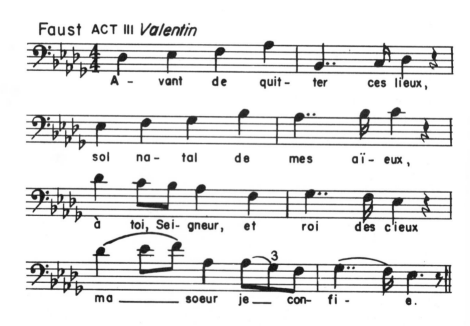

Avant de quitter ces lieux, sol natal de mes aïeux, à toi, Seigneur, et

roi des cieux ma soeur je confie.

Now before I leave this place, the sun of my past, to you Lord, King of Heaven, I

entrust my sister.

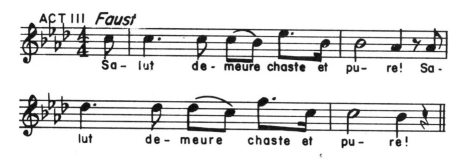

Salut, demeure chaste et pure!

O hail, thou dwelling chaste and pure!

Il était un roi de Thulé qui, jusqu'à la tombe fidèle.

Once there was a great king of Thule who to the last was faithful.

Ah, je ris de me voir si belle en ce miroir.

Ah, I laugh to see myself so pretty in the glass.

Vous qui faites l'endormie n'entendez-vous pas? O Catharine
ma mie, n'entendez vous pas ma voix et mes pas?

While you pretend you are sleeping, don't you hear my steps? O Catherine, my lovely,
don't you hear my song and my steps?

ACT IV SOLDIER'S CHORUS *SOLDIERS*

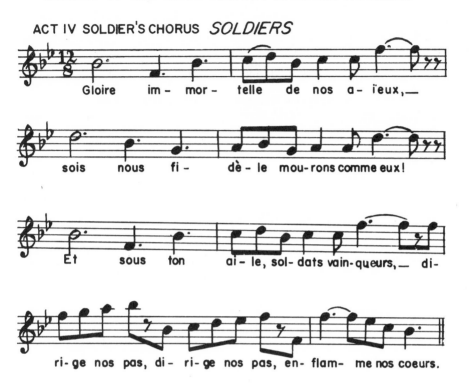

Gloire im – mor – telle de nos a- ïeux,—

sois nous fi – dè – le mou-rons comme eux!

Et sous ton ai – le, sol- dats vain-queurs,— di-

ri- ge nos pas, di- ri- ge nos pas, en- flam- me nos coeurs.

Gloire immortelle de nos aieux, sois nous fidèle,

mourons comme eux! Et sous ton aile, soldats vainqueurs, dirige nos pas, dirige nos

pas, enflamme nos coeurs.

Immortal glory of our ancestors, let us be faithful and die as they did. And under your

wing, soldiers and conquerors, direct our steps and enflame our hearts.

Fidelio ACT I QUARTET – Canon *Marcelline, Leonora, Jacquino, Rocco*

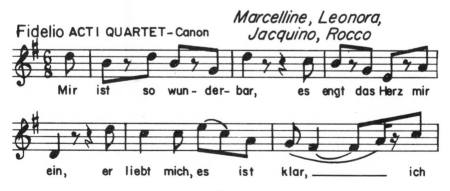

Mir ist so wun- der- bar, es engt das Herz mir

ein, er liebt mich, es ist klar,——— ich

wer - de glück- lich, glück- lich sein.

Mir ist so wunderbar, es engt das Herz mir ein, er liebt mich, es ist klar,
ich werde glücklich sein.
To me he is so dear, it fills my heart with joy. He loves me, that is clear. How happy,
happy I shall be!

Hänsel und Gretel ACT II *Hänsel, Gretel*

A- bends will ich schla- fen gehn, vier-zehn Eng-lein

um mich stehn; zwei zu mei-nen Häup- ten,

zwei zu mei- nen Füs - sen.

Abends will ich schlafen gehn, vierzehn
Englein um mich stehn; zwei zu meinen Häupten, zwei zu meinen Füssen.
When at night I go to sleep, fourteen angels round me keep. Two beside my head stay,
two down at my feet stay.

Iphigénie en Tauride ACT I *Thoas*

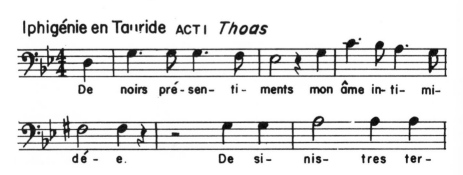

De noirs pré-sen- ti- ments mon âme in-ti- mi-

dé - e. De si- nis- tres ter-

reurs   est   sans   cesse   ob- sé - dé-   e.

De noirs présentiments mon âme intimidée. De

sinistres terreurs est sans cesse obsédée.

O dark, foreboding fears, my soul is quelled in terror. With most ominous fears and

unceasing obsessions.

Lohengrin ACT III *Lohengrin*

In   fer- nem Land   un - nah-bar   eu - ren Schrit-ten

liegt ei-ne Burg   die   Mon-sal- vat   ge-nannt.

Ein lich-ter Tem-pel ste-het dort in   mit-ten   so

kost- bar   als auf Er - den nichts be-   kannt.

In fernem Land unnahbar euren Schritten liegt eine

Burg die Montsalvat genannt. Ein lichter Tempel stehet dort inmitten so kostbar als

auf Erden nichts bekannt.

In distant lands by ways remote and hidden there stands a tower we call Montsalvat. It

holds a shrine to the profane forbidden, more precious there is naught on earth than that.

Lucia di Lammermoor ACT II SEXTET

Chi mi frena in tal momento? Chi troncò dell' ire il corso? Il suo duolo il suo spavento son la prova d'un rimorso!

What from vengeance yet restrains me, words suffice not to upbraid thee. Even terror that thus enchains thee proves that falsely thou betrayed me!

Chi raffrena il mio furore e la man che al brando corse? Della misera in favore nel mio
netto un grido sorse!
What from vengeance now restrains me, will he madly dare upbraid her? Ah, she
dreads me and disdains me. Nevermore will I thus persuade her.

Macbeth ACT I *Banquo*

Come del ciel precipita l'ombra più sempre
oscura! In notte ugual trafissero Duncano il mio signor.
How dark the sky with heavy clouds, darker than any shadow! Such was the night
they killed my lord, when Duncan met his death.

Madama Butterfly ACT I *Cio-cio San*

Un bel dì vedremo le varsi un fil di fumo sull'
estremo confin del mare e poi la nave appare.

He'll return one fine day, I'll see the telltale smoke rise far above the far horizon before
his ship appears.

Manon ACT II *Manon*

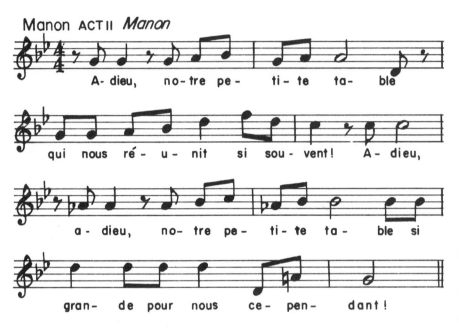

A- dieu, no- tre pe- ti- te ta- ble
qui nous ré - u - nit si sou - vent! A - dieu,
a - dieu, no- tre pe- ti- te ta - ble si
gran- de pour nous ce - pen - dant!

Adieu, notre petite table qui nous reunit si souvent! Adieu,
si grande pour nous cependant!

Goodbye, our little table, which brought us together so often, so large for us all the same.

ACT III *Des Grieux*

Ah, fu- yez douce i- mage,
a mon â- me trop chè- re. Res- pec-tez
un re- pos cru- el- le ment ga- gne.

Ah, fuyez douce image, a mon âme trop chère. Respectez un

repos cruéllement gagné.

Leave me now, image fair, thou to me art too dear. Pay respect to my peace, won by

the cruelest deed.

Martha ACT II *Martha*

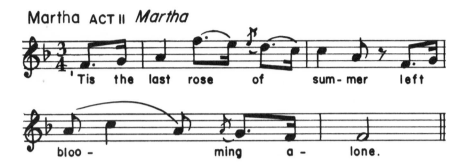

'Tis the last rose of summer left blooming alone.

ACT III *Lionello*

M'appari tutt' amor il mio sguardo l'incontrò.

Everywhere I see love, face to face in every look.

Die Meistersinger – PROCESSION OF THE MASTERSINGERS

ACT I *Walther*

Am stil- len Herd ___ in Win- ter-zeit ___ wann

Burg · und Hof mir ein- ge- scheidt, ____

wie einst der Lenz so lieb - lich lacht!

Am stillen Herd in Winterzeit wann Burg und Hof mir eingescheidt, wie einst der Lenz so lieblich lacht!

By silent hearth in wintertime when town and farm are all cut off, oh how the lovely springtime laughs!

Morgenlich leuchtend im rosigen Schein von Blüth und

Duft geschwellt die Luft, voll aller Wonnen nie ersonnen.

Morning now brightens with roseate light, and sweetest fragrance in the air fills me

with ecstasy in the sunlight.

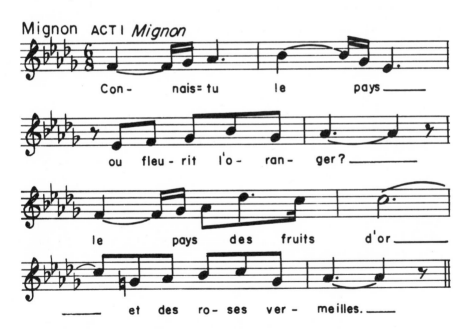

Connais-tu le pays où fleurit l'oranger? Le pays des fruits d'or et des

roses vermeilles.

Do you know the countryside where the orange tree blooms? The country of golden

fruits and of roses.

ACT II *Philine*

Je suis Titania la blonde, je suis Titania fille de l'air.

I am Titania the blond one, I am Titania the daughter of air.

Le Nozze di Figaro ACT I *Figaro*

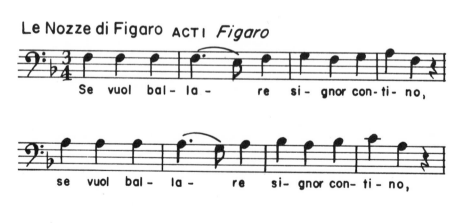

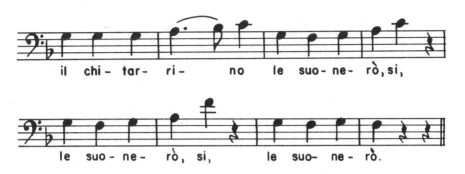

il chi - tar - ri - no le suo - ne - rò, si,

le suo - ne - rò, si, le suo - ne - rò.

Se vuol ballare signor contino, il chitarrino le suonerò, si.

If you would dance, then dance at your pleasure. Let the guitar beat the measure for you. Yes, beat you a measure with the guitar.

ACT I *Cherubino*

Non so più co - sa son, co - sa fac - cio or di

fo - co o,o - ra so - no di ghiac - cio. O - gni

don - na can-giar di co - lo - re, o - gni

don - na mi far pal - pi - tar, o - gni

don - na mi far pal - pi - tar.

Non so più cosa son cosa faccio or di foco ora sono di ghiaccio. Ogni
donna cangiar di colore, ogni donna mi far palpitar.
I don't know what it can be that ails me, either fever or chills; sickness flails me. **Any**
lady can change all my color, any lady can make my heart beat.

ACT I *Figaro*

Non più an-drai far- fa-lo- ne a -mo- ro- so   notte e
gior-   no d'in-tor-   no   gi- ran-   do   del- la
bel-   le   tur-ban-   do il ri -   po-   so   Nar-ci-
set -   to, A-   don- ci -   no   d'a - mor.

Non più andrai farfallone amoroso notte e giorno d'intorno girando
della belle turbando il riposo Narcisetto, Adoncino d'amor.
Now no more escapades as a lover, day and night whispering lies under cover. **Never**
more shall you play as a Paris, as Adonis you'll sigh nevermore.

ACT II *Countess Almaviva*

Por-   gi A- mor,___   qual-che ri -
sto -   ro   al   mio   duo -   lo   a'

miei _____ sos- pir. _____

Porgi Amor, qualche ristoro me al mio duolo a' miei sospir.

God of Love, O do restore me. Hear my sadness and my supplication.

ACT II *Cherubino*

Voi che sa- pe- te che co-sa è a-

mor, don- ne ve- de- te

s'io l'ho nel cor.

Voi che sapete che cosa è amor, donne vedete s'io l'ho nel cor.

You who have seen him tell me about this Love; lady, you know him, say, do I love?

ACT III *Countess Almaviva*

Do- ve so- no i bei mo-

men- ti di dol- cez- za e

di pia - cer? ____

Dove sono i bei momenti di dolcezza e di piacer?

Now where are they, all those fine moments full of pleasure and sweetness and joy?

ACT IV *Susanna*

Deh vie - ni non tar- dar, O gio - ia

bel - la. Vie-ni ove a- mo- re

per go- der t'ap- pel - la.

Deh vieni non tardar, O gioia bella. Vieni ove amore per goder t'appella.

O come and don't be slow, no more delaying. Come where my love is calling you to playing.

Orfeo ed Euridice ACT III *Orfeo*

Che fa - rò sen-za Eu-ri - di - ce, dove an-

drò sen- za il mio ben? Che fa -

rò?__ Do - ve an- drò?__ Che farò sen - za il mio ben?

Che farò senza Euridice, dove andrò senza il mio
ben? Che farò? Dove andrò? Che farò senza il mio ben?
All my joy has now departed, nought but grief and woe I see. Would I ne'er had
known existence! Life alas is dark for me.

Otello ACT I *Otello, Desdemona*

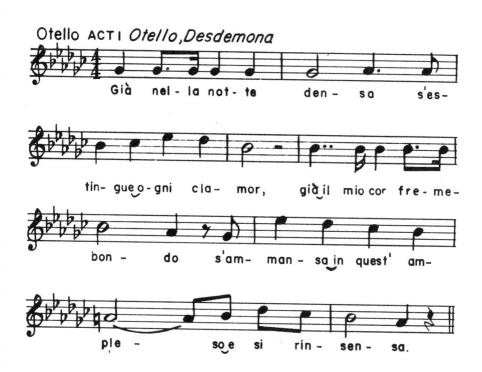

Già nel - la not - te den - sa s'es-
tin- gue o- gni cla- mor, già il mio cor fre - me-
bon - do s'am- man- sa in quest' am-
ple - so e si rin- sen- sa.

Già nella notte densa s'estingue ogni clamor, già il mio cor
fremebondo s'ammansa in quest' amplesso e si rinsensa.
Dark is the night around us. All clamors now have ceased. All the storm of my
passion I quell in your embrace in perfect peace.

ACT II *Otello*

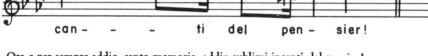

Ora e per sempre addio, santo memorie, addio sublimi incanti del pensier!

Now and forever farewell, sacred remembrance, farewell, sublime music of my thought.

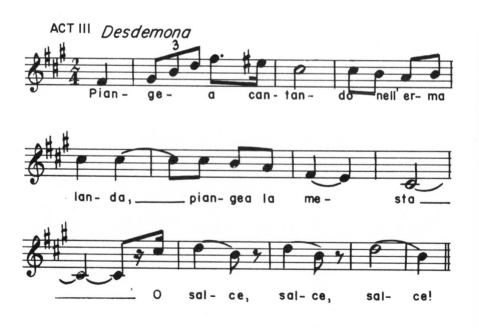

ACT III *Desdemona*

Piangea cantando nell' erma landa, piangea la mesta, O salce, salce!

With weeping I sing alone and lonely upon this lonely strand. O willow, willow!

Pagliacci ACT I *Canio*

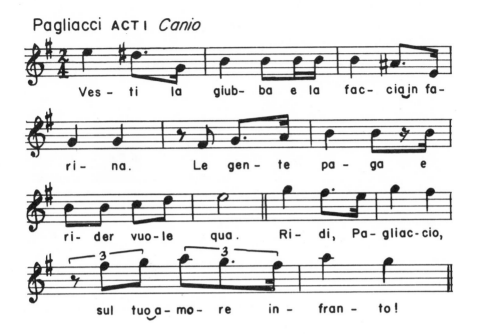

Ves - ti la giub- ba e la fac- cia in fa-ri - na. Le gen - te pa - ga e ri- der vuo-le qua. Ri- di, Pa - gliac-cio, sul tuo a-mo- re in - fran - to!

Vesti la giubba e la faccia infarina. Le gente paga e rider vuole qua.

Ridi, Pagliaccio, sul tuo amore in franto!

Put on your make-up and then smear on the powder! The people pay you and they must have their laugh. Laugh now, Pagliaccio, for the love that is gone now.

Rigoletto ACT I *Gilda*

Ca - ro no- me che il mio cor fes-ti pri - mo pal- pi - tar. Le de- li - zie dell' a-mor mi dei sem- pre ram- men- tar!

Caro nome che il mio cor festi primo palpitar. Le delizie
dell' amor mi dei sempre rammentar!

Dearest name within my heart, name that makes my heartbeat start, O delight of love,
stay with me forever, love.

ACT I Duke of Mantua

Ques-ta o quel- la_____ per me pa - ri
so - no al quant' al - tre d'in-tor - no____
_____d'in- tor- no mi ve - do.

Questa o quella per me pari sono al quant' altre d'intorno mi vedo.

This or that one, O what does it matter to a man of my kind? One is like another.

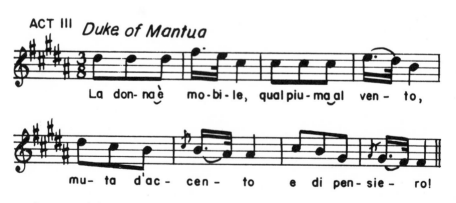

ACT III Duke of Mantua

La don-na è mo-bi-le, qual piu-ma al ven - to,
mu- ta d'ac - cen - to e di pen-sie - ro!

La donna è mobile, qual piuma al vento, muta d'accento e di pensiero!

Woman is changeable, not to be trusted, just like the little breeze that rustles autumn
leaves.

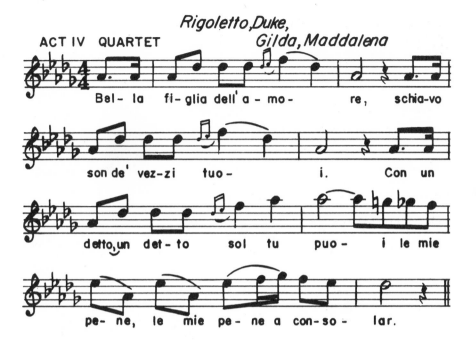

Bella figlia dell' amore,

schiavo son de'vezzi tuoi. Con un detto sol tu puoi le mie pene a consolar.

I'm your slave, dear girl, believe me. Chains like yours cannot be broken. But a word in kindness spoken will my peace of mind restore.

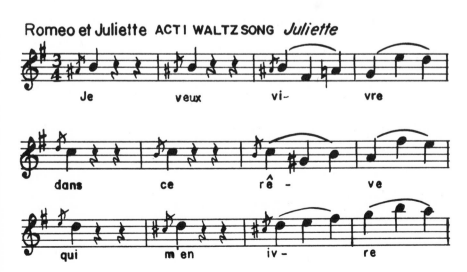

long -   temps   en   cor

Je veux vivre dans ce rêve qui m'en ivre longtemps en cor.
I would go in this dream life that has kept my heart filled with joy.

Der Rosenkavalier   THE WALTZ

Samson et Dalila ACT II *Dalila*

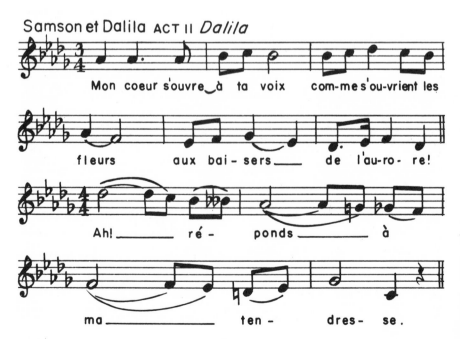

Mon coeur s'ouvre à ta voix   com-me s'ou-vrient les

fleurs   aux bai - sers___   de l'au-ro - re!

Ah!___   ré -   ponds___   à

ma___   ten -   dres - se.

Mon cœur s'ouvre à ta voix comme s'ouvrient les

fleurs aux baisers de l'aurore! Ah! réponds à ma tendresse!

My heart at thy sweet voice doth open like flowers at the dawn. Ah! respond to my

entreaty!

Tannhäuser ACT II HYMN TO VENUS *Tannhäuser*

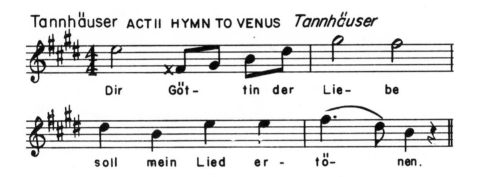

Dir Göttin der Liebe soll mein Lied ertönen.

Thou, Goddess of Love, art all the burden of my song.

ACT III *Wolfram*

O, du mein holder Abendstern, wohl grüsst' ich immer dich so gern.

O thou most holy evening star, how sweet your gaze from heaven far.

ACT III *Pilgrims*

Der Gna- de Heil ward dem Büs- ser be -

schie- den, nun geht er ein in__ der

Se - li- gen Frie - - - den.

Der Gnade Heil ward dem Büsser beschieden, nun geht er ein in der Seligen Frieden!

The grace of God to the sinner is given. His soul shall dwell with the blessed in heaven.

La Tosca ACT II *Tosca*

Vis- si d'ar- te, vis- si d'a-mo- re

non fe-ci mai male ad a - ni-ma vi - va!

Vissi d'arte, vissi d'amore, non feci mai male ad anima viva!

Thus did love and thus did my beauty both give to my art its greatest expression.

La Traviata ACT I *Alfredo*

Libiamo, libiamo ne' lieti calici, che la bellezza in fiora.

Let's drink, let's drink and be merry. Now is the time for the beauties of living.

ACT I *Violetta*

Ah, fors' è lui che l'anima solinga ne tumulti,

Ah, was it him my heart foretold, when in the rush of pleasure,

ACT I *Violetta*

scor- ra il vi - ver mi - o pei sen -

tie - ri del pia - cer.

Sempre libera degg' io follegiare di gioia in gioia, vo' che scorra il

viver mio pei sentieri del piacer.

I'll fulfill the round of pleasure, joying, toying from flow'r to flow'r. I will drain a

brimming measure from the cup of rosy joy.

ACT I *Alfredo*

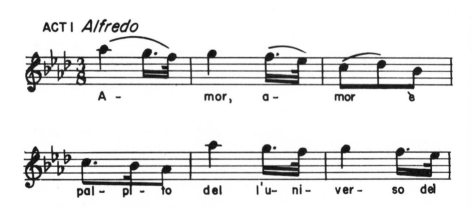

A - mor, a - mor è

pal - pi - to del l'u- ni - ver - so del

u - ni - ver-so- in- te - ro.

Amor, amor è palpito del l'universo intero.

Love is the soul of the universe entire.

ACT II *Giorgio Germont*

Di pro- ven-za il mar il suol chi dal

cor ti can-cel- lò, chi dal cor ti can-cel-lò di pro-

ven-za il mar il suol?

Di provenza il mar il suol chi dal cor ti cancellò?

Have the countryside and sea passed away from memory?

ACT III *Violetta*

Ad- di- o ___ del pas - sa- to ___ bei ___

so- gni ___ ri - den - ti.

Addio del passato bei sogni ridenti.

Forever must I leave thee, thou fair world of sorrows.

ACT I *Alfredo*

Pa- ri- gio ca- ra noi la-sce-

re - mo, la vi· ta u - ni- ti tras- co-re -re-mo.

Parigi o cara noi lasceremo, la vita uniti trascoreremo.

Far from the noisy city I shall take thee, nothing from this hour shall keep you from me.

Il Trovatore ACT II ANVIL CHORUS *Gypsies*

Chi del gi - ta - no i gior - ni ab-

bel - la? bel - la chi? Chi i

gior - ni ab - bel - la, chi?

Chi del gitano i giorni abbella? Chi? Chi i giorni abbella?

Cheer for the happy days when gypsies go a-roving.

ACT III *Manrico*

Ah_____ che la mor- te o - gno - ra

e_____ tar-da nel ve - nir a chi de-
si - a, a chi de-si.- a mo- rir. Ad-di -
o ad- dio Leo- no- ra ad-di - o.

Ah che la morte ognora e tarda nel venir chi desia morir! Addio.

Ah, send thy light, Aurora, carry me soon to death. Tell her I love her, tell her of my desire, addio!

Die Zauberflöte ACT I *Papageno*

Der Vog-el- fän- ger bin ich, ja, stets
lus- tig heis-sa hop-sa- sa! Ich Vo - gel - fän- ger
bin be- kannt bei alt und jung im gan-zen Land.

Der Vogelfänger bin ich, ja, stets lustig heissa

hopsasa! Ich Vogelfänger bin bekannt bei alt und jung im ganzen Land.

O where or when didst ever see as jolly fine a man as me? I am the best bird-catching man, say old and young in every land.

Dies Bildnis ist bezaubernd schön wie noch kein Auge gesehn. Ich
fühl' es wie dies Göttebild mein Herz mit neuer Regung fühllt.

This portrait is beyond compare, as lovely as I've seen. I wonder, I wonder if it's joy
that fills my heart with such a gripping pain?

O Isis und Osiris schenket der Weisheit Geist dem neuen Paar. Die
ihr der Wandrer Schritte lenket.

O Isis and Osiris, hear me pray for these that seek your light. Grant them patience for
their wand'ring.

ACT II *Queen of the Night*

Der Hölle Rache kocht in meinem Herzen; Tod und

Verzweiflung flammen um mich her!

The fires of hell are blazing in my own heart! Death and vengeance fill my heart with joy!

ACT III *Sarastro*

In diesen heil'gen Hallen kennt man die Rache nicht.

In these most holy halls no wrath or sorrow stays.

RECORDINGS OF
COMPLETE OPERAS

Aida
Callas, Tucker, Barbieri, Gobbi, conducted by Serafin
ANGEL 3525–C/L
Tebaldi, del Monaco, Stignani, conducted by Erede
LONDON A–4308
Milanov, Bjoerling, Barbieri, Warren, conducted by Perlea
VICTOR LM–6122
Nelli, Tucker, Gustavson, Valdengo, conducted by Toscanini
VICTOR LM–6132

Alceste
Flagstad, Jobin, Hemsley, conducted by Jones
LONDON A–4411
The same cast, Stereo version
LONDON OSA–1403

Amahl and the Night Visitors
VICTOR LM–1701

Amelia Goes to the Ball
ANGEL D–35140

Andrea Chénier
Tebaldi, del Monaco, Corena, conducted by Gavazzeni
LONDON A–4332
The same cast, stereo version
LONDON OSA–1303

Arabella
Della Casa, Gueden, London, conducted by Solti
LONDON A–4412

The same cast, stereo version
LONDON OSA–1404

Ariadne auf Naxos
Schwarzkopf, Streich, Seefried, conducted by von Karajan
ANGEL 3532–C/L

Arianna
(Since all but the *Lament of Arianna* has been lost, this recording must be considered complete.)
WESTMINSTER XWN–18765

Arlecchino (Busoni)
VICTOR LM–1944

Un Ballo in Maschera
Callas, di Stefano, Barbieri, Gobbi, conducted by Votto
ANGEL 3557–C/L
Nelli, Peerce, Turner, Merrill, conducted by Toscanini
VICTOR LM–6112

Il Barbiere di Siviglia (Rossini)
Callas, Gobbi, Alva, conducted by Galliera
ANGEL 3559–C/L
The same cast, Stereo version
ANGEL S–3559 C/L
de los Angeles, Bechi, Rossi-Lemeni, conducted by Serafin
CAPITOL GCR–7138
VICTOR LM 6104
Simionato, Bastianini, Corena, Siepi, conducted by Erede
LONDON A–4327

654

Der Barbier von Bagdad
ANGEL 3553

Bastien et Bastienne
PERIOD 542

The Beggar's Opera
The Old Vic company, conducted by
Sargent
VICTOR LM–6048
Prietto, Lipton, Noble, conducted by
Austin
WESTMINSTER OPW–1201

Der Bettelstudent
VANGUARD 474–75

La Bohème
Callas, di Stefano, conducted by Votto
ANGEL 3560
Sayao, Tucker, Baccaloni
COLUMBIA 3SL–101
Stella, Poggi, conducted by Molinari
COLUMBIA M2L–401
Tebaldi, Gueden, Inghilleri, conducted by
Erede
LONDON A–4209
Albanese, Peerce, conducted by Toscanini
VICTOR LM–6006
de los Angeles, Bjoerling, Amara, Merrill,
conducted by Beecham
VICTOR LM–6042

Boris Godunov
Belgrade National Opera
LONDON A–4317
Bolshoi Theater
PERIOD 554
Christoff, Borg, Gedda, conducted by
Dobrowen
VICTOR LM–6403

Carmen
Opéra-Comique, conducted by Wolff
LONDON, A–4304
Stevens, Peerce, Albanese, Merrill
VICTOR LM–6102

Cavalleria Rusticana
Callas, Di Stefano, Panerai, conducted by
Serafin

ANGEL 3509–3S/L
ANGEL 3528–C/L*
Harshaw, Tucker, Guarrera, conducted by
Cleva
COLUMBIA SL–123
COLUMBIA SL–124*
del Monaco, Nicolai, conducted by
Ghione
LONDON A–4323*
LONDON A–4216
Zanelli, Visetti, Ferrari, conducted by
Falco
PERIOD 317
Milanov, Bjoerling, Merrill, conducted by
Cellini
VICTOR LM–6046
VICTOR LM–6106*
Tebaldi, Bjoerling, Bastianini, conducted
by Erede
VICTOR LM–6059
The same cast, Stereo version
VICTOR LSC–6059

Les Choëphores
DECCA 9956

**Il Combattimento di Tancredi e
Clorinda**
Conducted by Ephrikian
PERIOD 551
Milan Monteverdiana Ensemble
VOX 8560

The Consul
DECCA DXB–101

Les Contes d'Hoffmann
Dobbs, Simoneau, conducted by Le
Conte
EPIC SC–6028
The same cast, stereo version
EPIC BSC–101
Conducted by Beecham
LONDON A–4302

Der Corregidor
URANIA 208

* Recording of both *Cavalleria Rusticana* and *I Pagliacci*.

La Damnation de Faust
Conducted by Fournet
COLUMBIA 3SL–110
Danco, Poleri, Singher, conducted by Munch
VICTOR LM–6114

Le Devin du Village
ANGEL D 35421
ANGEL T 35421

Don Carlos
VICTOR LM–6124

Don Giovanni
Simoneau, Jurinac, Zadek, London, conducted by Moralt
EPIC 4SC–6010
Danco, Della Casa, Gueden, Siepi, Corena, conducted by Krips
LONDON A–4406
The same cast, stereo version
LONDON OSA–1401

Don Pasquale
Capecchi, Rizzoli, Valdengo, conducted by Molinari-Pradelli
EPIC 4SC–6016
Corena, La Gatta, Poli, Lazzari, conducted by Parodi
URANIA 228

Die Dreigroschenoper
German cast
COLUMBIA O2L–257
The same cast, stereo version
COLUMBIA O2S–201
Lenya, Roswaenge, conducted by Adler
VANGUARD 9002
Original cast
TELEFUNKEN 66053

L'Elisir d'Amore
Gueden, Capecchi, di Stefano, Corena, conducted by Molinari-Pradelli
LONDON A–4321
Carosio, Gobbi, Monti, Luise, conducted by Santini
VICTOR LM–6024

L'Enfant et les Sortilèges
LONDON A–4105

Eugene Onegin
Belgrade National Opera
LONDON A–4324
Russian State Opera
PERIOD 507
Bolshoi Theater
WESTMINSTER OPW–1303

The Fair at Sorochintsky
EPIC 4SC–6017

Falstaff
Gobbi, Schwarzkopf, Barbieri, Panerai, conducted by von Karajan
ANGEL 3552–C/L
The same cast, stereo version
ANGEL S–3552–C/L
Nelli, Merriman, Elmo, Guarrera, conducted by Toscanini
VICTOR LM–6111

La Fanciulla del West
LONDON A–4338

Faust
Steber, Conley, Siepi
COLUMBIA 3SL–112
de los Angeles, Gedda, Christoff, conducted by Cluytens
VICTOR LM–6400

La Favola d'Orfeo
DECCA ARC–3035/36

La Favorita
LONDON A–4322

Fidelio
Rysanek, Seefried, Häflinger, conducted by Fricsay
DECCA DXH–147
Peerce, Bampton, Steber, conducted by Toscanini
VICTOR LM–6025

La Finta Semplice
EPIC 4SC–6021

REDIS OOMPE ORAS

Die Fledermaus
Schwarzkopf, Streich, Gedda, Krebs, conducted by von Karajan
ANGEL 3539–B/L
Pons, Welitsch, Tucker, Kullmann, conducted by Ormandy
COLUMBIA 3SL–108
Gueden, Lipp, Parzak, Dermota, conducted by Krauss
LONDON A–4207

Die Fliegende Holländer
Radio Berlin production, conducted by Fricsay
DECCA–DXC–124
Uhde, Varnay, Weber, conducted by Keilberth
LONDON A–4325

La Forza del Destino
Callas, Tucker, Nicolai, conducted by Serafin
ANGEL 3531–C/L
Tebaldi, del Monaco, Simionato, Siepi, conducted by Molinari-Pradelli
LONDON A–4408
The same cast, stereo version
LONDON OSA–1405
Guerrini, Campora, Corena, conducted by Parodi
URANIA 226

Fra Diavolo
URANIA 204

Die Frau ohne Schatten
LONDON A–4505

Der Freischütz
Cunitz, Loose, Hopf, Poell, conducted by Ackermann
LONDON A–4303
Bohme, Trotschel, Aldenhoff, conducted by Kempe
URANIA 403

La Grande Duchesse de Gérolstein
URANIA UX–115–2
Stereo version
URANIA USD–1015–2

La Gioconda
Cerquetti, del Monaco, Simionato, Siepi, conducted by Gavazzeni
LONDON A–4331
The same cast, stereo version
LONDON OSA–1302
Corridori, Campora, Corena, conducted by Parodi
URANIA 241
Milanov, di Stefano, Elias, Warren, conducted by Previtali
VICTOR LM–2249
The same cast, stereo version
VICTOR LSC–6139

Götterdämmerung
LONDON A–4603

Goyescas
LONDON A–4121
Stereo version
LONDON OSA–1101

Hänsel und Gretel
Schwarzkopf, Grümmer, conducted by von Karajan
ANGEL 3506–B/L
Stevens, Conner, Brownlee, conducted by Rudolf
COLUMBIA SL–102
Berger, Radio Berlin production, conducted by Rothier
URANIA 212

Die Harmonie der Welt
DECCA 9765

L'Heure Espagnole
Duval, Giraudeau, conducted by Cluytens
ANGEL D (or T) 35018
Danco, Hamel, Durenne, conducted by Ansermet
LONDON A–4102

Idomeneo
ANGEL 3574
ANGEL T–35595/97

L'Italiana in Algeri
ANGEL 3529–B/L

657

Ivan Susanin
Belgrade National Opera
LONDON A–4409
Bolshoi Theater
VANGUARD 6010/12

Khovantschina
LONDON A–4405

Kitezh
URANIA 7115

Die Kluge
ANGEL 3551 or
ANGEL T–35389/90
Stereo version
ANGEL S–3551 B/L

Lakmé
LONDON A–4307

Let's Make an Opera
LONDON A–4107

Lohengrin
Bavarian Radio production, conducted by Jochum
DECCA DXB–131
Steber, Varnay, conducted by Kleiber
LONDON A–4502
Schech, Klose, Bohme, conducted by Kempe
URANIA 225

Louise
EPIC 4SC–6018

The Love for Three Oranges
EPIC 4SC–6013

Lucia di Lammermoor
Callas, di Stefano, Gobbi, conducted by Serafin
ANGEL 3503 or T–35038/39
Pons, Tucker, Guarrera, conducted by Cleva
COLUMBIA 3SL–127
Wilson, Poggi, Colzani, conducted by Capuana
URANIA 232

Peters, Peerce, Tozzi, conducted by Leinsdorf
VICTOR LM–6055

Lulu
COLUMBIA 5SL–121

Die Lustigen Weiber von Windsor
URANIA 214

Madama Butterfly
Callas, Gedda, Borriello, conducted by von Karajan
ANGEL 3523 or T–35255/27
de los Angeles, di Stefano, Gobbi, conducted by Gavazzeni
EMI–CAPITOL GCR–7137
VICTOR LM–6121
Steber, Tucker, Valdengo, conducted by Rudolf
COLUMBIA 3SL–104
Tebaldi, Bergonzi, Sordello, conducted by Serafin
LONDON A–4337
The same cast, stereo version
LONDON OSA–1406
Moffo, Valleti, conducted by Leinsdorf
VICTOR LM–6135
The same cast, stereo version
VICTOR LSC–6135

Il Maestro di Musica
WESTMINSTER XWN–18262

Mahagonny
COLUMBIA K3L–243

Les Malheurs d'Orphée
WESTMINSTER OPW–11031

Manon
Micheau, de Luca, conducted by Wolff
LONDON A–4305
de los Angeles, Legay, conducted by Monteux
VICTOR LM–6402

Manon Lescaut
Tebaldi, del Monaco, Corena, conducted by Molinari-Pradelli
LONDON A–4316

Albanese, Bjoerling, Merrill, conducted by Perlea
VICTOR LM–6116

Maria Golovin
VICTOR LM–6142
Stereo version
VICTOR LSC–6142

Matrimonio Segreto, Il
ANGEL 3549 or
ANGEL T–35375/77

Medea (Cherubini)
MERCURY OL–3–104
Stereo version
MERCURY SR–3–9000

The Medium
COLUMBIA OSL–154

Mefistofele
Dall' Argine, Noli, conducted by Capuana
URANIA 230
Christoff, Prandelli, conducted by Gui
VICTOR LM–6049

Die Meistersinger
Franz, Grümmer, Schock, conducted by Kempe
ANGEL 3572 E/L
Gueden, Treptow, Schöffler, conducted by Knappertsbusch
LONDON A–4601
Frantz, Lemnitz, Aldenhoff, conducted by Kempe
URANIA 206

Mireille
ANGEL 3533 or
ANGEL T–35210/12

Der Mond
ANGEL 3567 or
ANGEL T–35389/90

Norma
ANGEL 3517

Le Nozze di Figaro
Jurinac, Streich, Schöffler, conducted by Böhm
EPIC SC–6022

della Casa, Gueden, Danco, Siepi, conducted by Kleiber
LONDON A–4407
The same cast, stereo version
LONDON OSA–1402
Jurinac, Sciutti, Stevens, conducted by Gui
VICTOR LM–6401

Oberon
PERIOD 575

Oedipus Rex
Cocteau (narrating), conducted by Stravinsky
COLUMBIA ML–4644
Pasquier (narrating), conducted by Ansermet
LONDON A–4106

Orfeo ed Euridice
Gedda, Micheau, conducted by Froment
ANGEL 3569 or
ANGEL T–35554/55
Fischer-Dieskau, Streich, conducted by Fricsay
DECCA DXH–143
Simoneau, Danco, conducted by Rosbaud
EPIC 4SC–6019
Klose, Berger, Streich, conducted by Rothier
URANIA 223
Stevens, della Casa, Peters, conducted by Monteux
VICTOR LM–2253

Otello (Verdi)
del Monaco, Tebaldi, conducted by Erede
LONDON A–4312
Sarri, la Pollo, conducted by Peoletti
URANIA 216
Vinay, Nelli, Valdengo, conducted by Toscanini
VICTOR LM–6107

Pagliacci, I
Callas, di Stefano, Gobbi, conducted by Serafin
ANGEL 3527–3S/L
The same cast, together with *Cavalleria Rusticana*
ANGEL 3528 C/L

Amara, Valdengo, Tucker, conducted by Cleva
COLUMBIA SL–113
The same cast, together with *Cavalleria Rusticana*
COLUMBIA SL–124
del Monaco, Petrella, Poli, conducted by Erede
LONDON A–4214
The same cast, together with *Cavalleria Rusticana*
LONDON A–4323
de los Angeles, Bjoerling, Merrill, Warren, conducted by Cellini
VICTOR LM–6405
The same cast, together with *Cavalleria Rusticana*
VICTOR LM–6106

Parsifal
LONDON A–4602

Le Pauvre Matelot
WESTMINSTER OPW–11030

Les Pêcheurs de Perles
Opéra-Comique, conducted by Cluytens
ANGEL 3524 or
ANGEL T–35174/75
Lamoureux concerts, conducted by Fournet
EPIC 4SC–6002

Pelléas et Mélisande
de los Angeles, Janssen, Souzay, conducted by Cluytens
ANGEL 3561 or
ANGEL T–35478/80
Micheau, Maurane, Roux, conducted by Fournet
EPIC 4SC–6003
Danco, Mollet, Rehfuss, conducted by Ansermet
LONDON A–4401

Pique-Dame
LONDON A–4410

Porgy and Bess
Torme, Faye, Duke Ellington Orchestra,

Australian Jazz Quartet,
BETHLEHEM EXLP–1
Conducted by Engel
COLUMBIA OSL–162

Prince Igor
Belgrade National Opera
LONDON A–4503
USSR National Orchestra
PERIOD 552

Prodaná Nevěsta
Slovenian Opera
EPIC 4SC–6020
Richter, Hauser, Peters, Bohme, conducted by Lenzer
URANIA 210
Prague National Theater
URANIA 231

I Puritani
ANGEL 3502

The Rake's Progress
COLUMBIA 5SL–125

El Retablo de Maese Pedro
French Radio production
ANGEL D (or T)–35134
Spanish National Orchestra
LONDON LL–1739
Vienna Philharmonia conducted by Adler
SPA 43

Rigoletto
Callas, di Stefano, Gobbi, conducted by Serafin
ANGEL 3537–5S/L
del Monaco, Gueden, conducted by Erede
LONDON A–4313
Peerce, Warren, Berger, conducted by Cellini
VICTOR LM–6021
Merrill, Peters, Bjoerling, Tozzi, conducted by Perlea
VICTOR LM–6051

Roméo et Juliette
LONDON A–4310

Der Rosenkavalier
Schwarzkopf, Edelmann, Ludwig, conducted by von Karajan
ANGEL 3563–D/L
The same cast, stereo version
ANGEL S 3563–D/L
Reining, Weber, Jurinac, conducted by Kleiber
LONDON A–4404
Baumer, Lemnitz, Bohme, conducted by Kempe
URANIA 201
Munich State Opera, conducted by Krauss
VOX 7774

Le Rossignol
ANGEL D (or T)–35204

Rusalka (Dvořák)
URANIA 219

Russlan und Ludmilla
WESTMINSTER OPW–1401

The Saint of Bleecker Street
VICTOR LM–6032

Salome
LONDON A–4217

Der Schauspieldirektor
PERIOD 532

Die Schöne Galathee
URANIA 7167

Il Segreto di Susanna
DECCA 9770

La Serva Padrona
Carteri, Rossi-Lemeni, conducted by Giulini
ANGEL D (or T)–35279
Mazzoleni, Cortis, conducted by Leitner
DECCA ARC–3039

Simon Boccanegra
EMI–CAPITOL GCR–7126

Snyegurotchka
LONDON A–4504

Socrate
ESOTERIC 510

La Sonnambula
ANGEL 3568

Street Scene
COLUMBIA OL–4139

Suor Angelica
EMI–CAPITOL G–7115

Il Tabarro
VICTOR LM–2057

Tannhäuser
URANIA 211

Thaïs
URANIA 227

Tiefland
EPIC SC–6025

Tosca
Callas, di Stefano, Gobbi, conducted by de Sabata
ANGEL 3508 or
ANGEL T–35060/61
Stella, Poggi, Taddei, conducted by Serafin
COLUMBIA M2L–402
Tebaldi, Campora, Mascherini, conducted by Erede
LONDON A–4213
Milanov, Bjoerling, Warren, conducted by Leinsdorf
VICTOR LM–6052
dall'Argine, Scattolini, Colombo, conducted by Quadri
WESTMINSTER OPW–1288

La Traviata
Stella, di Stefano, Gobbi, conducted by Serafin
ANGEL 3545–B/L
Guerrini, Huder, Silveri
COLUMBIA, 3SL–103
Tebaldi, Poggi, Prottl, conducted by Molinari-Pradelli
LONDON A–4314

Albanese, Peerce, Merrill, conducted by Toscanini
VICTOR LM–6003
Carteri, Valleti, Warren, conducted by Monteux
VICTOR LM–6040

Tristan und Isolde
Flagstad, Suthaus, Thebom, Fischer-Dieskau, conducted by Furtwängler
VICTOR LM–6700
Gewandhaus production, conducted by Konwitschny
URANIA 202

Il Trovatore
Callas, di Stefano, Barbieri, Panerai, conducted by von Karajan
ANGEL 3554–5S/L
Tebaldi, del Monaco, Simionato, Savarese, conducted by Erede
LONDON A–4326
The same cast, stereo version
LONDON OSA–1304
Bjoerling, Milanov, Warren, conducted by Cellini
VICTOR LM–6008

Tsarskaya Nevyesta
WESTMINSTER OPW–1301

Turandot (Puccini)
Callas, Schwarzkopf, Fernandi, conducted by Serafin
ANGEL 3571–C/L
Borkh, Tebaldi, del Monaco, conducted by Erede
LONDON A–4320

Il Turco in Italia
ANGEL 3535–C/L

The Turn of the Screw
LONDON A–4219

Vanessa
VICTOR LM–6138
Stereo version
VICTOR LSC–6138

La Vida Breve
VICTOR LM–6017

Werther
URANIA 233

Wozzeck
COLUMBIA 5SL–118

Z Mrtvého Domu
EPIC–4SC–6005

Zar Und Zimmermann
DECCA DXD–129

Die Zauberflöte
Streich, Stader, Häflinger, Fischer-Dieskau, conducted by Fricsay
DECCA DXJ–134
Gueden, Lipp, Simoneau, Bohme, conducted by Böhm
LONDON A–4319

Zhenitba
WESTMINSTER OPW–1202

Zigeunerbaron
Schwarzkopf, Gedda, Kunz, conducted by Ackermann
ANGEL 3566–B/L
Zadek, Loose, Patzak, Poell, conducted by Krauss
LONDON A–4208
Kunz, Loose, conducted by Paulk
VANGUARD 486/7

SPECIAL INDEXES

Sopranos

Aïno Ackté, Suzanne Adams, Rosa Agthé, Licia Albanese, Emma Albani, Frances Alda, Lucine Amara, Victoria de los Angeles, Sophie Arnould, Rose Bampton, Maria Barrientos, Gemma Bellincioni, Erna Berger, Elizabeth Billington, Lillian Evans Blauvelt, Lucrezia Bori, Inge Borkh, Hélène, Bouvier, Minnie Bower, Marianne Brandt, Gré Brouwenstijn, Maria Callas, Emma Calvé, Violante Camporese, Maria Caniglia, Rose Caron, Joan Carroll, Marie Carvalho, Lisa della Casa, Katharina Cavalieri, Marie Cavan, Maria Cebotari, Susanna Maria Cibber, Gina Cigna, Giuseppina Cobelli, Blanche Cole, Nadine Conner, Joan Cross, Jeanne Cruvelli, Phyllis Curtin, Suzanne Danco, Gloria Davy, Emmy Destinn, Mattiwilda Dobbs, Julie Dorus-Gras, Dorothy Dow, Denise Duval, Franca Duval, Claire Dux, Emma Eames, Florence Easton, Marie Louise Edvina, Eileen Farrell, Geraldine Farrar, Ellen Faull, Mafalda Favero, Jean Fenn, Lavinia Fenton, Sylvia Fisher, Kirsten Flagstad, Editha Fleischer, Josephine Fodor-Mainvielle, Olive Fremstad, Marta Fuchs, Emma Fursch-Madi, Johanna Gadski, Amelita Galli-Curci, Eugenie Garcia, Mary Garden, Mabel Garrison, Gabriele Gatti, Etelka Gerster, Dusolina Giannini, Alma Gluck, Christel Goltz, Margherita Grandi, Giulia Grisi, Gertrude Grob-Prandl, Nora Gruhn, Hilde Gueden, Ellen Gulbranson, Margaret Harshaw, Frieda Hempel, Emilie Herzog, Laurel Hurley, Daniza Ilitsch, Maria Ivogün, Helen Jepson, Maria Jeritza, Emma Juch, Sena Jurinac, Gertrude Kappel, Clara Louise Kellogg, Barbara Kemp, Dorothy Kirsten, Katharina Klafsky, Anny Konetzni, Hilde Konetzni, Marie Krauss, Selma Kronold, Melanie Kurt, Selma Kurz, Maria Labia, Nanny Larsen-Todsen, Marjorie Lawrence, Georgette Leblanc, Martha Leffler-Burckard, Lilli Lehmann, Lotte Lehmann, Frida Leider, Tiana Lemnitz, Rosalie Levasseur, Brenda Lewis, Estelle Liebling, Jenny Lind, Lydia Lipovska, Félia Litvinne, Göta Ljungberg, Aase Løveberg, Germaine Lubin, Pauline Lucca, Zélie de Lussan, Felice Lyne, Florence Macbeth, Mathilde Mallinger, Thérèse Malten, Dorothée Manski, Lucille Marcel, Blanche Marchesi, Queena Mario, Amalie Materna, Margarete Matzenauer, Nellie Melba, Carmen Melis, Zinka Milanov, Anna von Mildenburg, Anna Milder, Mildred Miller, Martha Mödl, Toti dal Monte, Fanny Moody, Grace Moore, Berta Morena, Maria Müller, Patrice Munsel, Ilma di Murska, Claudia Muzio, Emma Nevada, Mignon Nevada, Patricia Neway, Agnes Nicholls, Birgit Nilsson, Christine Nilsson, Lillian Nordica, Eide Norena, Jarmila Novotna, Margarete Ober, Jane Osborn, Euphrosyne Parepa-Rosa, Giuditta Pasta, Mary Anne Paton, Adelina Patti, Rose Pauly, Gianna Pederzini, Minna Peschka-Leutner, Roberta Peters, Eleonora Petrelli, Lily Pons, Carmela Ponselle, Rosa Ponselle, Leontyne

Price, Marie Rappold, Regina Resnik, Josephine de Reszke, Elizabeth Rethberg, Luise Reuss-Belce, Clara Kathleen Rogers, Marie Roze, Leonie Rysanek, Erna Sack, Minnie Saltzmann-Stevens, Sybil Sanderson, Marie Constance Sass, Frances Saville, Bidu Sayao, Margarete Luise Schick, Malvina Schnorr von Carolsfield, Wilhelmine Schröder-Devrient, Elizabeth Schumann, Elizabeth Schwarzkopf, Irmgard Seefried, Auguste Seidl-Kraus, Marcella Sembrich, Constance Shacklock, Margaret Sheridan, Amy Shuard, Margarete Siems, Henriette Sontag, Eleanor Steber, Sophie Stehle, Catherine Stephens, Teresa Stolz, Ann Storace, Giuseppina Strepponi, Joan Sutherland, Rosa Sucher, Marion Talley, Renata Tebaldi, Milka Ternina, Eva Tetrazzini, Luisa Tetrazzini, Maggie Teyte, Therese Thoma, Teresa Tietjens, Helen Traubel, Yvonne de Tréville, Delphine Ugalde, Viorica Ursuleac, Alvina Valleria, Astrid Varnay, Clementine de Vere, Geneviève Vix, Thelma Votipka, Johanna Wagner, Ljuba Welitsch, Carolina White, Camilla Williams, Marie Wittich, Frances Yeend, Hilda Zadek, Marie van Zandt, Cornelia van Zanten, Anna Zerr

Mezzo-sopranos

Frances Bible, Adelaide Borghi-Mamo, Marie Boulanger, Marianne Brandt, Marie Brema, Bruna Castagna, Anne Charton-Demeur, Rosalind Elias, Edith Evans, Rita Fornia-Labey, Olive Fremstad, Marie Galli-Curci, Giuditta Grisi, Marie Gutheil-Schoder, Margaret Harshaw, Minnie Hauk, Louise Homer, Louise Kirkby-Lunn, Margarete Klose, Lorri Lail, Martha Lipton, Margarete Matzenauer, Anna von Mildenberg, Nell Rankin, Giulietta Simionato, Risë Stevens, Eve Stignani, Rosina Stoltz, Marie Sundelius, Conchita Supervia, Blanche Thebom, Jennie Tourel, Zelia Trebelli, Claramae Turner, Lucia Elizabeth Vestris,

Pauline Viardot-Garcia, Edyth Walker

Contraltos

Marietta Alboni, Marian Anderson, Fedora Barbieri, Marianne Brandt, Clara Butt, Sara Jane Cahier, Anna Louise Cary, Edith Coates, Marie Delna, Cloe Elmo, Kathleen Ferrier, Olive Fremstad, Maria Gay, Jeanne Gerville-Réache, Herta Glaz, Margaret Harshaw, Helene Hastreiter, Kathleen Howard, Ruth Kobart, Frieda Langendorf, Darya Leonova, Jean Madeira, Maria Garcia Malibran, Kathryn Meisle, Elena Nikolaidi, Maria Olczewska, Sigrid Onegin, Flora Perini, Adelaide Phillips, Sofia Scalchi, Ernestine Schumann-Heink, Gladys Swarthout, Kerstin Thorborg, Gertrud Wettergren, Florence Pauline Wickham

Male Contralto

Gaetano Guadagni

Tenors

Valentin Adamberger, Paul Althouse, Albert Raymond Alvarez, Max Alvary, Fernand Ansseau, Joseph Barbot, Kurt Baum, John Beard, Joseph Bentonelli, Rudolf Berger, Jussi Bjoerling, Alesandro Bonci, Giuseppe Borgatti, Dino Borgioli, John Braham, Alois Burgstaller, Karel Burian, Italo Campanini, Joseph Capoul, Enrico Caruso, Jean Baptiste Chollet, Eugene Conley, Gaetano Crivelli, Richard Crooks, Hugues Cuenod, Charles Dalmorès, Tudor Davies, Andreas Dippel, Gilbert Duprez, Ernest van Dyke, Nicolay Figner, Paul Franke, Manuel del Popolo Vicente Garcia, Nicolai Gedda, Beniamino Gigli, Lodovico Graziani, Heinrich Gudehus, Charles Hackett, George Hamlin, Carl Hartmann, Heinrich Hensel, Joseph Hislop, Ellison van Hoose, Hans Hopf, Walter Hyde, Charles Benjamin Incledon, Herrmann Jadlowker, Frederick Jagel, Edward Johnson, Rowland Jones, Paul Kalisch, Norman Kelley, Michael Kelly,

Jan Kiepura, Heinrich Knote, Ernst Kraus, Charles Kullman, Giacomo Lauri-Volpi, Joseph Legros, Richard Lewis, David Lloyd, Max Lorenz, Fernando de Lucia, Joseph Maas, Francis MacLennan, René Maison, Giovanni Matteo Mario, Riccardo Martin, Giovanni Martinelli, Nino Martini, John McCormack, Lauritz Melchior, James Melton, Mario del Monaco, Frank Mullings, Lucien Muratore, Franz Nachbauer, Emilio Naudin, Nicolini, Albert Niemann, Adolphe Nourrit, Louis Nourrit, Alessio de Paolis, Julius Patzak, Peter Pears, Jan Peerce, Jean Perier, Aureliano Pertile, David Poleri, Anton Raaff, Sims Reeves, Albert Reiss, Jean de Reszke, Gustave Roger, Helge Roswaenge, Giovanni Battista Rubini, Albert Saléza, Benedict Schack, Tito Schipa, Erik Schmedes, Ludwig Schnorr von Carolsfield, Anton Schott, Leo Slezak, Roberto Stagno, Giuseppe di Stefano, Brian Sullivan, Set Svanholm, Ferrucio Tagliavini, Francesco Tamagno, Enrico Tamberlik, Richard Tauber, Joseph Aloys Tichatschek, Armand Tokatyan, Richard Tucker, Georg Unger, Jacques Urlus, Cesare Valleti, Ramon Vinay, Heinrich Vogl, Franz Völker, Giovanni Voyer, Franz Vroons, Theodor Wachtel, Hermann Winkelmann, Alexander Young, Giovanni Zenatello

Baritones

Pasquale Amato, Mario Ancona, Sumner Austin, George Baklanov, Luigi Bassi, Johann Beck, Rudolf Berger, Franz Betz, David Bispham, Rudolf Bockelmann, Richard Bonelli, Jacques André Bouhy, John Brownlee, Giuseppe Campanari, Francis Carey, Walter Cassell, George Cehanovsky, Karl Doench, Hector Dufranne, Todd Duncan, Jean Baptiste Faure, Edoardo Ferrari-Fontana, Dietrich Fischer-Dieskau, Cesare Formichi, Anton Forti, Benvenuto Franci,

Antonio Galassi, Carlo Galeffi, Gustave García, Édouard Gassier, Eugenio Giraldoni, Tito Gobbi, Igor Gorin, Otto Goritz, Frank Guarrera, Eugén Gura, Mack Harrell, Max Heinrich, Josef Herrmann, William Hinshaw, Ludwig Hofmann, Hans Hotter, Julius Huehn, Giovanni Inghilleri, Herbert Janssen, August Kinderman, Otakar Kraus, Jean Louis Lassalle, Giuseppe de Luca, William Ludwig, Vanni Marcoux, Vasco Mariz, Victor Maurel, Robert Merrill, Hans von Milde, Anton Mitterwurzer, Carlo Morelli, Hans Hermann Nissen, Karl Perron, Giuseppe del Puente, Émile Renan, Maurice Arnold Renaud, Giorgio Ronconi, Leon Rothier, Marko Rothmüller, Titta Ruffo, Mario Sammarco, Charles Santley, Karl Scheidermantel, Heinrich Schlusnus, Paul Schöffler, Gustav Schützendorf, Antonio Scotti, Martial Singher, Mariano Stabile, Josef Staudigl Jr., Antonio Tamburini, John Charles Thomas, Lawrence Tibbett, Herman Uhde, Theodor Uppman, Felice Vanesi, Leonard Warren, Robert Weede, Hermann Weil, Reinald Werrenrath

Basses

Norman Allin, Lorenzo Alvary, Louis d'Angelo, Frederick Austin, Federico Autori, Salvatore Baccaloni, Paul Bender, Michael Bohnen, Karl Braun, Edmund Burke, Feodor Chaliapin, Boris Christoff, Anselmo Colzani, Fernando Corena, Jean François Delmas, Adamo Didur, Emil Fischer, Ludwig Fischer, Allen James Foley, Karl Johann Formes, Filippo Galli, Manuel Patricio García, Alfred Auguste Giraudet, Putnam Griswold, Joshua Hecht, Allen Carter Hinckley, Jerome Hines, Marcel Journet, Alexander Kipnis, Felix von Kraus, Eric Kunz, Luigi Lablache, Nicholas Levasseur, Emanuel List, Pavel Ludikar, Charles Manners, Richard Mayr, Ivan Melnikov, Nicola Moscona, Ossip Petrov, Ezio Pinza, Pol

Henri Plançon, Robert Radford, Leon Rains, Theodor Reichmann, Edouard de Reszke, Anton van Rooy, Giulio Rossi, Nicola Rossi-Lemeni, Emil Scaria, Friedrich Schorr, Cesare Siepi, Josef Staudigl Sr., Feodor Stravinsky, Italo Tajo, Emile Taskin, Giorgio Tozzi, Félix Vieuille, Clarence Whitehill, Herbert Witherspoon

Composers

Adolphe Adam, Adam de la Halle, Isaac Albéniz, Eugene d'Albert, Franco Alfano, George Antheil, Luigi Arditi, Anton Arensky, Attilio Ariosti, Thomas Arne, Daniel François Auber, Louis François Aubert, Edmond Audran, Johann Christian Bach, Michael William Balfe, Granville Bantock, Samuel Barber, Giovanni Bardi, Béla Bartók, Giovanni Battista Bassani, Ludwig van Beethoven, Vincenzo Bellini, Herman Bemberg, Robert Russell Bennett, François Benoist, Peter Benoit, Alban Berg, Natanael Berg, William Bergsma, Lennox Berkeley, Hector Berlioz, Franz Berwald, Henry Bishop, Julius Bittner, Georges Bizet, Boris Blacher, Leo Blech, Marc Blitzstein, Ernest Bloch, Jan Blockx, François Boïeldieu, Arrigo Boïto, Giovanni Bononcini, Alexander Borodin, Giovanni Bottesini, Rutland Boughton, Walter Braunfels, Benjamin Britten, Ignaz Brüll, Bruneau, Ferrucio Busoni, Giulio Caccini, Charles Wakefield Cadman, Antonio Caldara, Robert Cambert, François van Campenhout, André Campra, Henry Carey, Benjamin Carr, Eleazar de Carvalho, Mario Castelnuovo-Tedesco, Alfredo Catalani, Emilio del Cavalieri, Pier Francesco Cavalli, Marcantonio Cesti, Emmanuel Chabrier, George Whitefield Chadwick, Gustave Charpentier, Marc Antoine Charpentier, Ernest Chausson, Luigi Cherubini, Francesco Cilea, Domenico Cimarosa, Albert Coates, Louis Adolphe Coerne, Lawrance Collingwood, Frederick Converse, Aaron Copland, Peter Cornelius, Henry Cowell, César Cui, Luigi Dallapiccola, Leopold Damrosch, Walter Damrosch, Alexander Dargomijsky, Félicien Cesar David, John Davis, Achille Claude Debussy, Marcel Delannoy, Leo Délibes, Frederick Delius, Karl Ditters von Dittersdorf, Gaetano Donizetti, Antonio Draghi, Paul Dukas, Gabriel Dupont, Antonin Dvořák, Werner Egk, Gottfried von Einem, Georges Enesco, Lehman Engel, Camille Erlanger, Frederic d'Erlanger, Oscar Esplà, Manuel de Falla, Gabriel Fauré, Benedetto Ferrari, Henri Fevrier, Zdenek Fibich, Paul le Flem, Friedrich von Flotow, Carlisle Floyd, Josef Foerster, Cecil Forsyth, Lucas Foss, Alberto Franchetti, César Franck, William Henry Fry, Marco da Gagliano, Hans Gal, Vincenzo Galilei, Amintore Galli, Baldassare Galuppi, Nicholas Gatty, Giuseppe Gazzaniga, Franz Richard Genée Edward German, George Gershwin, Ottmar Gerster, François Gevaert, Giorgio Ghedini, Vittorio Giannini, Cecil Armstrong Gibbs, Gilardo Gilardi, Umberto Giordano, Peggy Glanville-Hicks, Alexander Glazounov, Reinhold Glière, Michael Glinka, Christoph Willibald Ritter von Gluck, Vittorio Gnecchi, Benjamin Godard, Alexander Goedicke, Hermann Goetz, Theo Goldberg, Karl Goldmark, Carlos Gomez, Eugene Goossens III, Jakov Gotovac, Charles Gounod, Gabriel Grad, Paul Graener, Enrique Granados, André Grétry, Louis Gruenberg, Michel la Guerre, Guido Guerrini, Ernst Guiraud, Inglis Gundry, Jésus Guridi, Manfred Gurlitt, Adalbert Gyrowetz, Joseph Hass, Alois Hába, Karel Hába, Henry Hadley, Richard Hageman, Reynaldo Hahn, Jacques Halévy, Asger Hamerik, Ebbe Hamerik, Georg Frideric Handel, Howard Hanson, William Harling, Carter Harman, Lou Harrison, Tibor Harsanyi, Frederic Hart,

Librettists

Jules Barbier, Arrigo Boito, Raniero di Calzabigi, Salvatore Cammarano, John Erskine, Charles Favart, John Gay, Antonio Ghislanzoni, William Gilbert, Ludovic Halévy, Zsolt Harsányi, Georges Hartmann, Hugo von Hofmannsthal, Luigi Illica, Johann Friedrich Kind, Camille du Locle, Abbé Metastasio, Pierre Perrin, Lorenzo da Ponte, Phillipe Quinault, Ottavio Rinuccini, Felice Romani, Emanuel Schikeneder, Augustin Eugène Scribe, Modest Tchaikovsky, Apostolo Zeno

Conductors

Kurt Adler, Kurt Herbert Adler, Peter Herman Adler, Victor Alessandro, Emanuel Balaban, Carl Bamberger, Giuseppe Bamboschek, Thomas Beecham, Artur Bodansky, Karl Böhm, Warwick Braithwaite, Hans von Bülow, Fritz Busch, Cleofonte Campanini, Fausto Cleva, Emil Cooper, Walter Ducloux, Alberto Erede, Richard Falk, Ferenc Fricsay, Wilhelm Furtwängler, Giulio Gatti-Casazza, Philippe Gaubert, Gianandrea Gavazzeni, Boris Goldovsky, Carmago Guarnieri, Vittorio Gui, László Halász, Johannes den Hertog, Alfred Hertz, Margaret Hillis, Eugen Jochum, Georg Jochum, Werner Josten, Herbert von Karajan, Joseph Keilberth, Rudolf Kempe, Erich Kleiber, Otto Klemperer, Hans Knappertsbusch, Ernst Knoch, Erich Korngold, Clemens Krauss, Joseph Krips, Karl Krueger, Rafael Kubelik, Charles Lamoureux, Erich Leinsdorf, Hermann Levi, Franz Liszt, Charles Mackerras, Gustav Mahler, Edwin McArthur, Dmitri Mitropoulos, Pierre Monteux, Jean Morel, Felix Mottl, Karl Muck, Leopoldo Mugnone, František Neumann, Sigismund Noskowsky, Ettore Panizza, Bernhard Paumgartner, Emil Paur, Wilfred Pelletier, Jonel Perlea, Giorgio Polacco, Felix Prohaska, Albert van Raalte, Karl Rankl, Carl Reinecke, Fritz Reiner, Hans Richter, Carl Rosa, Joseph Rosenstock, Max Rudolf, Victor de Sabata, Harold Malcom Watts Sargent, Franz Schalk, Thomas Scherman, George Schick, Thomas Schippers, Ernst von Schuch, George Sebastian, Anton Seidl, Tullio Serafin, Alexander Smallens, Cesare Sodero, Georg Solti, William Steinberg, Fritz Stiedry, Maurice Strakosch, George Szell, Arturo Toscanini, Auguste Vianesi, Bruno Walter, Felix Weingartner, Albert Wolff, Eugene Ysaye

Roles for Soprano

Abigaille, Adalgisa, Adele, Adina, Adriana Lecouvreur, Aennchen, Agatha, Aïda, Aithra, Alceste, Alice, Alice Ford, Countess Almaviva, Almira, Alms Collector, Amalia, Amelia, Amelia Boccanegra, Amina, Aminta, Amora, Mrs. Anckarström, Angel More, Angèle, Angelic Voice, Angelica, Suor Angelica, Anita, Anna, Anna Bolena, Donna Anna, Anna Gomez, Anna Reich, Anne, Anne Trulove, Annina, Antigonae, Antonia, Antonida, Arabella, Ariadne, Arianna, Arline, Armida, Arsena, Ascagne, Aspasia, Astaroth, Asteria, Avis, Azema, Barak's wife, Barbarina, Barce, Barena, Baroness, Belinda, Bellangère, La Bergère, Berta, Bertha, Bess, Beth, Bianca, Biancofiore, Lady Billows, Birdie, Blanche, Blonde, Countess Bronislawa, Brünnhilde, Buda, Fraulein Bürstner, Camille, Carolina, Cassandra, Catarina, Caterina, Catherine, La Chauve-Souris, Cherubino, Childrens' Voices, Chloé, Female Chorus, La Chouette, Christine, Chrysothemis, Cio-cio San, Cis, Clara, Claretta, Clémence, Clorinda, Clotilde, Clytemnestra, The Golden Cockerel, Columbine, Composer, Concepcion, Concetta, Confidante, Constance Fletcher, Constanze, Countess, Coupava, A Cricket, Crobyle, Cupidon, Dalilah, Danae, Daphne, Daughter of

Stephano, Street Arab, Sulamith, Susan, Susan B. Anthony, Susanna, Countess Susanna, Suzel, Tatyana, Tebaldo, Telea, Temple Gatekeeper, Teresa, Thaïs, Tina Crome, Tormentilla, Floria Tosca, Toto, Trainbearer, Turandot, Princess Turandot, Undine, Ursula, Valentine, Vanessa, Vendulka, Venus, Violetta Valery, Vitellia, Vivetta, Voice from Heaven, Voice of a Bird, Voice on a Record, Volkhova, Vreli, Waldvogel, Wally, Walter, Waltraute, Madam Wanton, Mrs. Waters, Wellgunde, Wheel of Fortune Woman, Wife, Wife of the Court Attendant, Woglinde, Woman, Woodcutter's Boy, Miss Wordsworth, Xanthe, Xenia, Ygraine, Yniolde, Young Shepherd, Yvette, Zaza, Zdenka, Zelmira, Zerbinetta, Zerlina, Zora

Roles for Mezzo-soprano

Abbess, Adalgisa, Adelaide, Adelma, Adriano, Agnes, Alcmene, Alice, Altichiara, Andrelux, Angel, Anna Hope, Annie, Annius, Antonia's Mother's Voice, Ariane Ascanio, Aspirant Sisters, Augusta Tabor, Azucena, Baba the Turk, Barbara, Béatrice, Mistress Benton, Beppe, Bersi, Bobilicka, Bostana, Boy, Brangäne, Madam Bubble, Buffoon, Carlotta, Carmela, Carmen, Cassandra's Ghost, Cat, Countess Ceprano, Charlotte, Cheap Jewellery Woman, Child, La Ciesca, Coal Gatherer, Comtesse de Coigny, Columbine, Commère, Cook, Countess, Curra, Czipra, Dalila, Mlle. Dangeville, Mrs. Day, Debora, Desdemona, Didon, Djamileh, Suor Dolcina, Donella, Duenna, Mme. Dufresne, Principessa Eboli, L'Ecureuil, Emilia, Erda, Ericlea, Erika, Fatima, Feklusha, Feodor, Fidalma, Fidès, Filipievna, Flora Bervoix, Flosshilde, Forewoman, Countess Frances of Essex, Frasquita, Fricka, Frugola, Genii, Gerhilde, Gertrude, Gertrude S., Gräfin Geschwitz, Giovanna, Glasha, Gloster Heming, Governess, Grandmother, Grimgerde, Frau Grubach, Hadassa, Hänsel, Hécube, Helmwige, Herodias, Mrs. Herring, Housewife, Indiana Elliott, Innkeeper, L'Innocente, Isabel Wentworth, Ismene, Jack, Miss Jessel, Jocasta, Judith, Julie, Junon, Karolka, Kate Pinkerton, Khivria, Klytemnestra, Kontchakovna, Lady, Mme. Larina, Laura, Lazarillo, Leader of the People, La Libellule, Lily, Lola, Lubara, Madame de Croissy, Madelon, Magdalena, Maid, Maid of Honor, Maidservant, Mallika, Manuela, Mara, Marcelline, Marchioness of Montefiore, Margarita, Marie Louise, Marina Mnischek, Martha, Martha Schwerlein, Mayor's Wife, Melanto, Mercedes, Mignon, Mistress of the Novices, Mother Goose, Musician, Myrtale, Naina, Nancy, Natalia, Nejata, Nicklausse, Nicoletta, Mrs. Nolan, Norn, Nurse, Octavian, L'Opinion Publique, Orlovsky, Orphan, Ortlinde, Ortrud, Page, Mistress Page, Palmatica,⁴ Lady Pamela, Mrs. Peachum, Pepa, Perfilievna, Pippo, Preziosilla, Princess de Bouillon, Queen, Queen Iceheart, Queen of Sheba, Ragpicker, Frau Reich, Rosa Mamai, Rosina, Rubria, Savoyard, Schwertleite, Secretary, Mrs. Sedley, Sélysette, Shining One, Siebel, Siegrune, Silla, Singer, Smeraldina, Sorceress, Spectre de Clytemnestre, Spirit Voice, Spring, Statue d'Athena, Streetsweeper, Suzuki, Suzy, Taven, Telemaco, Thirza, Thisbe, Tichon Ivanitsch Kabanov, Tisbe, Mrs. Trapes, Urbain, Waltraute, Wild Girl, Witch, Woman, Wowkle, Zayda, Zinida

Roles for Contralto

Agata, Albine, The Alto, Amelfa, Amneris, Anaide, Angelina, Anna, Annina, Arsace, Aunt, Auntie, Baba, Miss Baggott, Bianca, Madam By-Ends, Cerinto, Children's Voices, Chinese Cup, La Cieca, Clairon, Princess Clarissa, Countess, Daphnis, Death, Dmitri, Dryade, La Belle Dulcinée, Countess of

Eberbach, Elf, Empress Persicaria, Federica, Felicia, Florence Pike, Françoise, Frédéric, Gaea, Geneviève, Gertrude, Gherardino, Goatherd, Gräfin von Helfenstein, Grandmother Buryja, Heavenly Being, Housekeeper, Isabella, Aunt Jane, Katharina, Katherine, Laura, Leda, Shepherd Lehl, Linetta, Lucretia, Maddalena, Mädeleine, Maffio Orsini, Maidservant, Maive, Mamma Lucia, Marfa Kabanova, Margret, Maria, Martha, Martinka, Mary, Doña Mercedes, Mirabella, The Moon, Mother, Mother of Louise, Nancy, Noble Page, Norn, Nourrice, Olga, The Omniscient Mussel, Orfeo, Orphan, Page, Pantalis, Pâtre, Pauline, Penelope, Pickthank, Pierotto, Primrose Seller, Princess, Puppet, Queen of the Gypsies, Dame Quickly, Ratmir, Romeo, Rosalia, St. Theresa II, Schoolboy, Serena, Sextus, Shepherd Boy, Shining One, Slave, Statue D'Athena, Suzanne, Ulrica, Ursula, Vanja, Venus, Vera Boronel, Vlassievna, Voice from Above, Wardrobe Mistress, Wife, Witwe Browe, Zita, Zulma

Roles for Tenor

Abate di Chazeuil, Abbé, Abdallo, Abdisa, Achilles, Adolar, Aegisth, Aeneas, Afanasy Viazemsky, Afra, Albert Herring, Cardinal Albrecht von Brandenburg, Alfonso d'Arcos, Alfred, Alfredo Germont, Count Almaviva, Alwa, Don Alvar, Don Alvaro, Amaryllus, Anatol, Andrea Chenier, Andres, Andrew J., Prince Andrew Khovansky, Anfinomo, Animal Tamer, Apollo, Apparition of a Youth, Arbace, Archer, Arithmetic, Arnold, Arrigo, Artaban, Lord Arthur Bucklaw, Lord Arthur Talbot, Assad, Astrologer, Auguste, Avito, Azriel, Baba Mustapha, Babinsky, Bacchus, Ballad Seller, Balthasar Zorn, Bardolph, Baronelli, Don Basilio, Bayan, Beelzebub, Belmonte, Bénédict, Harry Benn, Sir Benno Robertson, Benvenuto Cellini, Benvolio, Beppe, Beppo, Bernardo

Novagerio, Biasco, Bishop of Budoja, Doctor Blind, Bob Boles, Bobil, Bois-Rosé, Boris Grigorievitch, Boyard Guard, Brighella, Buffoon, Burgomaster, Mr. By-Ends, Don Caeser de Bazan, Doctor Cajus, Calaf, Camille Desmoulins, Canio, Wolfgang Capito, Captain, Captain of Hell's Guard, Cardinal, Don Carlos, Cassio, Cavalier, Celestial Messenger, Chappelou, Charles, Chief Sailor, Male Chorus, Christoph, Cicillo, Clem, Cochenille, Lord Cockburn, Cola Rienzi, Companion, Cook, Marquis de Corcy, Corentino, Cossé, Courier, Crab Man, Don Curzio, Dalibor, Dancing Master, Daniel, Danieli, Da-Ud, David, Dead Composers, Desiré, Devil's Familiar Spirit, Dickson, Doctors, Donald Gallup, Drum-Major, Duke, Duke of Mantua, Duke of Parma, Ritter von Ebelasztin, Mr. Eccles, Edgardo, Edmondo, Edward Plummer, Elder, Eléazar, Graf Elemer, Elvino, Emperor, Emperor Altoum, Enée, Enzo Grimaldo, Eric, Ernani, Ernesto, Eroshka, Erster Bürger, Esquire, Robert Devereux Earl of Essex, Don Eugenio de Zuniga, Eumete, Erimacho, Evander, Executioner, Faust, Federico, Fellah, Fenton, Ferdinand, Fernando, Ferrando, Filch, Filipeto, Finn, Fisherman, Flamand, Flaminio, Flavio, Florestan, Florestein, Fool, Forest Ranger, Fra Diavolo, Francesco, Frantz, Frazier, Fritz Kobus, Froh, Gabriel Adorno, Gabriel von Eisenstein, Don Gaspar, Gastone de Letorières, Gennaro, Georges Brown, Gérald, Gherardo, Giove, Giuseppe, Gobin, Gobrias, Gonsalve, Goro, Chevalier des Grieux, Grigorij, Gritzko, Guard, Prince Guidon, Guillot de Morfontaine, Hadji, Hagenbach, Hämon, Hangman, Harlequin, Haroun, Harry, Harvester, Heinrich der Schreiber, Helenus, Henry B., Henry Morosus Blunt, Herald, Herault de Séchelles, Hermann, Herod Antipas, High Priest of Neptune, Hindu Merchant, Hoffman, Horace Adams, Horn Player,

Hugh the Drover, Hunchback, Sir Huon of Bordeaux, Hylas, Idomeneo, Idreno, Incredibile, Innkeeper, Intendant, Interpreter, Iopas, Iro, Isèpo, Ismaele, Italian Singer, Jacquino, Jafia, Jan Janitzky, Japanese Envoy, Jean, Jenik, Jew, Jo the Loiterer, Joe, John Adams, John of Leyden, Dick Johnson, Jonas, Don José, Josef K., Juan, Judge, Julien, Jupiter, Kilian, King of Fools, King, Knight, Baron Kronthal, Boyar Krutschtschov, Kunz Vogelgesang, Laca Klemen, Laertes, Lamp Lighter, Leandro, Leary, Lord Lechery, Lensky, Léopold, Count Lerma, Leukippos, Lieutenant, Lindoro, Lionel, Livoretto, Loge, Lohengrin, Lord, Lorenzo, Count Loris Ipanov, Lover, Luigi, Lukas, Baron Lummer, Macduff, Captain MacHeath, Maintop, Major-Domo, Malatestino dell'Occhio, Malcolm, Man Servant, Man with the Donkey, Count Mancini, Manfredo, Manrico, Marco, Mario Cavaradossi, Mark, Marlardot, Marouf, Marquis de Chateauneuf, Mars, Masaniello, Master of Ceremonies, Boyar Nikita Matouta, Matteo, Matteo Borsa, Maurizio, Max, Megärus, Memucan, Man in Armor, Menelaus, Méphistophélès, Merchant, Mercure, Mercury, Messenger, Michael Andreievitch Touche, Midas, Midir, Milio Dufresne, Mime, Mingo, Missail, Mitrane, Monostatos, Morphée, Augustin Moser, Muezzin, Muff, Music Master, Mylio, Nadir, Nandro, Don Narciso, Narraboth, Nathanael, Nazarene, Neighbor, Nelson, Nemorino, Nereo, Nerone, Nicias, Nick, Nicola, Nika Magadoff, Noctambulist, Norman, Novice, Nureddin, Oberon, Oedipus, Officer, Old-Clothes Man, Orphée, Osaka, Otello, Don Ottavio, Ottokar, Ovlour, Paco, Painter, Giovanni Pierluigi Palestrina, Pang, Paolino, Paolo il Bello, Parpignol, Parsifal, Peasant, Pedrillo, Pedro, Pélleas, Peter, Peter Grimes, Peter Ibbetson, Peter Ivanov, Phaeton, Philistine Messenger, Philosopher, Piedmontese, Pilgrim, Lt. B. F. Pinkerton, Pisandro, Pittichinaccio, Pliable, Pluton, Poet-Monk, Poisson, Pollione, Pollux, Pong, Priest, Priest's son, Prince, Private Soldier, Prunier, Puppet, Pylade, Quint's Ghost, Radames, Rainbaut, La Rainette, Don Ramiro, Raoul de Nangis, Red Whiskers, El Remondado, Riccardo, Don Riccardo, Count Riccardo Accolai, Rinuccio, Robbins, Robert, Robespierre, Roderigo, Rodolfo, Rodriguez, Roméo, Baron Rouvel, Rudolph, Ruedi, Ruggero, Ruiz, Rustighello, Sacco, Sadko, Sailor, Saint Chavez, Sali, Samson, Sandor Barinkay, Satravan, Scarmuccio, Schmidt, Wassily Ivanovitch Schuisky, Hans Schwalb, Scrivener, Sellem, Sentry, Shepherd, Shillem, Showman, Siegfried, Siegmund, Simon, Simpleton, Singer, King Sisera, Sobinjin, Spalanzani, Junker Spärlich, Reasonable Spectator, Spirit of the Forest, Spirit of the Masque, Splendiano, Spoletta, Sportin' Life, Springer, Squeak, Steersman, Stewa Buryja, Streshner, Kapellmeister Stroh, Student, Student from Krakov, Student from Wittemberg, Sultan Miramoulin, Superstition, Surgeon, Sylvester von Schaumberg, Tallan, Tamino, Tannhäuser, Monsieur Taupe, Tavannes, Tchaplitsky, Tchekalinsky, Tebaldo, Temple Gatekeeper, Tenor, Thaddeus, Thaddeus Stevens, La Théière, Theophilus of Imola, Timorous, Tinca, Tiresias, Titurelli, Titus, Ser Toldo Berandengo, Tom Rakewell, Tonio, Torquemada, Trabucco, Tramp, Trim, Monsieur Triquet, Tristan, Truffaldino, Tsar Berendey, Turiddu, Turnkey, Tybalt, Ulisse, Ulrich Grüsser, Ulrich Eisslinger, Mr. Upfold, Usher, Valzacchi, Vanya Kudrjas, Vasco da Gama, Vasek, Prince Vassily Galatsin, Vaucluse, Captain Vere, Vincent, Vitek, Vladimir Igorevitch, Voice, Wagner, Waiter, Wallenstein, Walter von der Vogelweide, Walther von Stolzing, Watchman, Werther, Wilhelm Meister, William, Young Man, Young Servant, Youth

Roles for Baritone

Abbate Cospicuo, Admetus, Adonisek, Prince Afron, Agamemnon, Alberich, Albert, Alfio, Don Alfonso, Alfonso XI, Alfonso d'Este, Ali, Count Almaviva, Altair, Amantio di Nicolao, Amfortas, Amonasro, Antonio, Apollon, Apprentice, Arthur Jones, Asmodus, Assan, Assur, Athanael, Avosmediano, Baal Hanan, Baldassare, Captain Balstrode, Barak, Barnaba, Belcore, Ben, Bijou, Billy Budd, Bishop, Old Bohemian, Boniface, Boris Godunov, Borov, Bosun, De Bretigny, Budivoj, Bussy, Cacan, Cacique, The Caliph, Captain of the Guard, Captain, Cardillac, Cardinal Carlo Borromeo, Don Carlo di Vargas, Don Carlos, Cascart, Sir Robert Cecil, Don César de Bazan, Charles Gérard, Cheap Jack, Chorèbe, Chorèbe's Ghost, Chris the Citizen, Christopher Columbus, Cirillo, City Crier, Claudio, Colas, Commandant, Commercial Councillor, Conte Carnero, Conte di Luna, Coppelius, Corporal, Count, Crébillon, Creon, Crespel, Crown, Dalua, El Dancairo, Daniel Webster, Dapertutto, David, Dead Composer, Demas, Doctor of Natural History, Graf Dominik, Donald, Donner, Dositeo, Baron Douphol, Duclou, Dumas, The Dutchman, Count of Eberbach, Empress of China, Enrico, Enterich, Eochaidh, Bishop Ercole Severolus, Escamillo, Eugene Onegin, Doctor Falke, Sir John Falstaff, Herr von Faninal, Fanuèl, Fasolt, Doctor Faust, Fernando, The Dark Fiddler, Fieramosca, Figaro, Fléville, Mister Flint, Herr Fluth, Ford, Foreman, Fouquier-Tinville, Frank, Frédéric, Frederick of Telramund, Friend, Front Line Officer, Gallanthus, Mr. Gedge, Gellner, Georg Danton, Gianni Schicchi, Count Gil, Giorgio Germont, Don Giovanni, Giovanni lo Sciancato, Giovanni Morone, Mr. Gobineau, Golaud, Gregory, Guido di Monforte, Guillaume Tell, Gunther, Hamlet, Handsome, Hans Heiling, Happy, Harlequin, Háry János, Helmsman, Henry Cuffe, Herald, Hercules, Herman Atlan, Hermann, Herrmann, Hero, Hever, High Priest, High Priest of Brahma, High Priest of Dagon, Hoël, Horace Tabor, L'Horloge Comptoise, Iago, Igor Sviatoslavitch, Jahel, Jake, Jake Wallace, Japanese Envoy, Jesser, Jewish Doctor, Jim, Johannes Kepler, John, John Bunyan, John Sorel, John the Butcher, Jokanaan, Don José de Santarem, Judas Iscariot, Judge Examiner, Junius, Jupiter, Justizrat, Kalman Zsupan, Karnac, King, King Solomon, Mr. Kofner, Kouzka, Kreon, Kruschina, Kuligen, Kurnewal, Kyoto, Lawrence, Lawyer, Leader of the People, Leandro, Lescaut, Lockit, Lord, Lorek, Count Luna, Lysiart, Macbeth, Major-Domo, Doctor Malatesta, Man with the Mule, Mandarin, Mandryka, Manfredo, Manuel, Manufacturer, Manz, Marcello, Marchese d'Obigny, Marco, Marouf, Marquis de Boisfleury, Marti, Cavaliere Marullo, Old Marzci, Mate, Mathieu, Mathis, Matteo del Sarto, Maurizio, Medecin Juif, Fra Malitone, Melot, Mercutio, Merry-go-Round Man, Méru, Messenger, Metifio, Michele, Michelin, Michonnet, Miller, Doctor Miracle, Misgir, Mistrust, Count Monterone, Morbio, Moruccio, Lord Mountjoy, Music Master, Musician-monk, Nabi, Nabucco, Emperor Napoleon, Napoleone, Narumoff, Ned Keene, Nelusko, Count de Nevers, Newby, Nick Shadow, Nilakantha, Notary, Novice's Friend, Count Oberthal, Officer, Official Registrar, Old Gypsy, Olivier, Orest, Oreste, Orfeo, Orphée, Osgood, Ostasio, Prince Ottokar, Overseer, Painter-monk, Paloucky, Pantaloon, Paolo Albiani, Papageno, Paquiro, Count Paris, Passerby, Peasant Perichaud, Peter, Peter I, Graf Peter Homonay, Pierrot, Pietro, Ping, Piram, Pirro, Plutus, Poet, Policeman, Polish Commander, Pompeo, Porgy, Rafaele, Rambaldo, Ramiro, Jack Rance,

Mr. Redburn, Baron Regnard, Renato, de Retz, Sir Richard Forth, Rigoletto, Rodrigo, Ruggiero, Ryan, Sacristan, Count de St. Bris, St. Ignatius Loyola, Samson, Sancho, Baron Scarpia, Schaunard, Schmidt, Schneidebart, Dr. Schön, Schwanda the Bagpiper, Scindia, Sculptor, Sebastiano, Sergeant, Sergio, Servant, Boyar Shaklovity, Sharpless, Shepherd, Sherasmin, Shikeneder, Showman, Sid, Silvano, Silvio, Simon, Simon Boccanegra, Simon Mago, Singer, de Serieux, Soldier, Song Writer, Sonora, Spirit Messenger, Baron Starbemberg, Hofkapellmeister Robert Storch, John Styx, Taddeo, Tanato, Tarquinius, Taylor, Andrey Tchelkalov, Thoré, Tio Lucas, Tom Cat, Tomes, Count Tomsky, Tonio, Torchbearer, Tramp, Ned Travers, Trojan Captain, Trojan Soldier, Ulysses S. Grant, Undertaker, Valentin, Vanzetti, Varsonoviev, Venetian Merchant, Viking Merchant, Virgil T., Vizier, Vladislav, Wagner, Watchful, Willem, Wolfram von Eschenbach, Workman, Worldly Glory, Wotan, Wozzeck, Prince Yamadori, Prince Yeletsky, Zurga

Roles for Bass

Abimilech, Abul Hassan Alι Ebn Bekar, Ahmad, Albert, Albert K., Alcade, Alcindoro, Alessio, Alidoro, Emperor Altoum, Alvise Badoero, Ambrogio, Maître Ambroise, Antinoo, Anton Buis von Müglitz, Antonio, Apollyon, Archer, Archibaldo, Arkel, Count Arnheim, Ashby, Astolfo, Baculus, Le Bailli, Balducci, Ballad Singer, Balthazar, Banquo, Barak, Barbacan, Barbe-bleue, Doctor Bartolo, Don Basilio, The Bass, Benes, Benoit, Bermate, Bernardino, Bertram, di Béthune, Betto di Signa, Billy Jackrabbit, Biterolf, Black Bob, Duke Bluebeard, Doctor Bombasto, Bomely, The Bonze, Borella, Bourdon, Brander, Supt. Budd, Buffoon, Bugler, Cadi, Dr. Caius, Canciano, Cappadocian,

Captain, Captain of the Guard, Count Capulet, Cardinal de Brogny, Cardinal of Lorraine, Caspar, Cecco del Vecchio, Celio, Count Ceprano, Cesare Angelotti, Chamberlain, Cardinal Christoph Madruscht, Il Cieco, Claggert, Collatinus, Colline, Commandant, Commendatore, Compère, Conrad Nachtigall, Constable, Cook, Corporal, Court Attendant, Courtois, Cuno, Customs Officer, Daland, Dandini, Daniel Hizler, Dansker, Mr. Day, Dead Composer, Death, Devil, Devilshoof, Don Diego, Dikoy, Dipsacus, Director-Representative, Doctor, King Dodon, Dositheus, Duke of Verona, Dulcamara, Elder, Elder Ott, Enan the Blind, Envy, Evangelist, Fafner, Sir John Falstaff, Farfallo, Farfarello, Farlaf, Farmer, Father-in-Law, Father of Louise, Le Fauteuil, Kaiser Ferdinand II, Ferrando, Figaro, Filippo II, Fiorello, Fool, Francesco, Franz, Friend, Fritz Kothner, King Frost, Gabriel, Lord Gaultiers Walton, Gaveston, Gazello, Sir George Walton, Geronimo, Geronte di Ravoir, Gessler, Ghost of Nino, Giacomo, Ciarno, Giovanni da Prodica, Government Director, Grand Inquisitor, Gravis, Grech, Greek Captain, Prince Gremin, Doctor Grenvil, Count des Grieux, Padre Guardiano, Gubetta, Guccio, Guglielmo, Gurnemanz, Gypsy, Gzak, Hagen, Haly, Hanezò, Hans Foltz, Hans Sachs, Hans Schwarz, Harvey, Lord Hate-Good, Hector's Ghost, Henry the Fowler, Herald, Hermann, Hermann Ortel, Hermit, High Priest, High Priest of Babylon, Hobson, Holstein, Hortensio, Hunchbacked Bass Fiddler, Hunding, Huntsman, Imperial Commissioner, Innkeeper, Don Inigo Gomez, Prince Ivan Khovansky, Ivan Susanin, Tsar Ivan Vassilievitch, Jacopo Fiesco, Jago, Jailer, Friar Jean, Jester, Jew, Johann, John Brown, José Castro, Juan Lopez, Junkman, Jurist, Kammer-sänger, Kecal, Keeper of the Madhouse, King, King Marke, King of

Roles for Chorus

Speaking Roles

Silent Roles

Children's Roles

Le Banc, Boy's Voice, Gay Brook, Harry, Hugh Crome, John Crome, Marie's Child, Norma's Children, Ottoman, Sam, Sofa, Trouble, Wicker Chair.

Arias for Soprano

A Serpina penserate
A una fonte aflito e solo
Abscheulicher! wo eilst du hin?
Ach, ich fühl's, es ist verschwunden
Ach, ich liebte, war so glücklich
Addio del passato
Addio di Mimi
Addio notre petite table
Ah, Belinda, I am prest with torment
Ah, chi mi dice mai quel barbaro dov'è
Ah! dite alla giovine
Ah! fors è lui
Ah, fuggi il traditore
Ah! j'ai baisée ta bouche
Ah, je ris de me voir si belle
Ah, malgré moi
Ah, non credea mirarti
Ah, non giunge uman pensiero
Ah! perche non posso odiarti
Ahi, casa acerbo!
Allmächtige Jungfrau
Ave Maria
Batti, batti, o bel Masetto
Bei Männern, welche Liebe fühlen
Bel raggio lusinghier
Brahma! gran Dio
La Caleseva
Caro nome
Casta Diva
Chaste fille de Latone
Che volo d'Augelli
Chimes in the Valley
D'Amour l'ardente flamme
Deh vieni non tardar
Depuis le jour
Der Freund ist dein'
Der Hölle Rache kocht in meinem Herzen
Der Kleine Sandmann bin ich
Der Männer Sippe sass hier im Saal
Dew Fairy's song

Di Tanti Palpiti
Dich, teure Hall
Divinités du Styx
Doch dich rührt kein Flehen
Donde lieta usci
Dove sono
Du bist der Lenz
Durch Zärtlichkeit und Schmeicheln
E amore un ladroncello
E quest' asilo ameno e grato
Elle a ful la tourterelle
Elsa's dream
Ernani, involami
Et ta langue elle ne remue plus
Euch Lüften, die mein Klagen
Hoyoto Ho
Ich Sah' das Kind
Il est doux, il est bon,
Il était un Roi de Thulé
Il padre adorato ritrovo e lo perdo
Imponete!
In quelle trine morbide
In uomini, in soldati
Isolde's Narrative
Je dis que rien ne m'épouvante
Je suis Titania
Je t'implore et je tremble
Je veux vivre dans ce rêve
Klänge der Heimat
Kommt ein schlanker Bursch gegangen
La Biondina in gondoletta
L'Amour est un oiseau rebelle
Lasciatemi morire
Leise, leise, fromme Weise
Les oiseaux dans la charmille
L'Ora o Tirsi
Ma dell' avido stelo divulsa
Mad scene from Lucia
Martern aller Arten
Mein Herr Marquis
Mi chiamano Mimi
Mi tradì quel alma ingrata
Mild und leise
Music Lesson scene
My man's gone now
Non, ce n'est point un sacrifice
Non mi dir, bell' idol mio

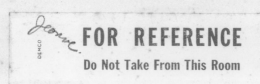